The CIA:
A Forgotten History

US Global Interventions
Since World War 2

William Blum

Zed Books Ltd.
London and New Jersey

The CIA: A Forgotten History was first published by
Zed Books Ltd., 57 Caledonian Road, London N1 9BU, UK,
and 171 First Avenue, Atlantic Highlands, New Jersey 07716,
USA, in 1986.

Copyright © William Blum, 1986.

Cover designed by Ideography.
Typeset by Format Photosetting, Bristol.
Printed in the United Kingdom
by Biddles Ltd., Guildford and King's Lynn.

British Library Cataloguing in Publication Data

Blum, William
   The CIA : a forgotten history : US global
   interventions since World War 2.
   1. United States—Central Intelligence
   Agency—History
   I. Title
   327'1'2' 0973   JK468.I6

   ISBN 0-86232-479-3
   ISBN 0-86232-480-7 Pbk

To:

Adelheid Zöfel

and

Alexander Blum

*Without whose help this book would have been finished
at least one year earlier.*

Contents

Introduction

It was in the early days of the fighting in Vietnam that a Vietcong officer said to his American prisoner: "You were our heroes after the War. We read American books and saw American films, and a common phrase in those days was 'to be as rich and as wise as an American'. What happened?"[1]

An American might have been asked something similar by a Guatemalan, an Indonesian or a Cuban during the ten years previous, or by a Uruguayan, a Chilean or a Greek in the decade subsequent. The remarkable international goodwill and credibility enjoyed by the United States at the close of the Second World War was dissipated country by country, intervention by intervention. The opportunity to build the war-ravaged world anew, to lay the foundations for peace, prosperity and justice, collapsed under the awful weight of anti-communism.

The weight had been accumulating for some time; indeed, since Day One of the Russian Revolution. By the summer of 1918 some 13,000 American troops could be found in the newly-born Union of Soviet Socialist Republics. Two years and thousands of casualties later, the American troops left, having failed in their mission to "strangle at its birth" the Bolshevik state, as Winston Churchill put it.[2]

The young Churchill was Great Britain's Minister for War and Air during this period. Increasingly, it was he who directed the invasion of the Soviet Union by the Allies (Great Britain, the US, France, Japan and several other nations) on the side of the counter-revolutionary "White Army". Years later, Churchill the historian was to record his views of this singular affair for posterity:

> Were they [the Allies] at war with Soviet Russia? Certainly not; but they shot Soviet Russians at sight. They stood as invaders on Russian soil. They armed the enemies of the Soviet Government. They blockaded its ports, and sunk its battleships. They earnestly desired and schemed its downfall. But war — shocking! Interference — shame! It was, they repeated, a matter of indifference to them how Russians settled their own internal affairs. They were impartial — Bang![3]

What was there about this Bolshevik Revolution that so alarmed the most powerful nations in the world? What drove them to invade a land whose soldiers

1

had recently fought alongside them for over three years and suffered more casualties than any other country on either side of the World War?

The Bolsheviks had had the audacity to make a separate peace with Germany in order to take leave of a war they regarded as imperialist and not in any way *their* war, and to try and rebuild a terribly weary and devastated Russia. But the Bolsheviks had displayed the far greater audacity of overthrowing a capitalist-feudal regime and proclaiming the first socialist state in the history of the world. This was uppitiness writ incredibly large. This was the crime the Allies had to punish, the virus which had to be eradicated lest it spread to their own people.

The invasion did not achieve its immediate purpose, but its consequences were nonetheless profound and persist to the present day. Professor D.F. Fleming, the Vanderbilt University historian of the cold war, has noted:

> . . . for the American people the cosmic tragedy of the interventions in Russia does not exist, or it was an unimportant incident long forgotten. But for the Soviet peoples and their leaders the period was a time of endless killing, of looting and rapine, of plague and famine, of measureless suffering for scores of millions — an experience burned into the very soul of a nation, not to be forgotten for many generations, if ever. Also for many years the harsh Soviet regimentations could all be justified by fear that the capitalist powers would be back to finish the job. It is not strange that in his address in New York, September 17, 1959, Premier Khrushchev should remind us of the interventions, 'the time you sent your troops to quell the revolution', as he put it.[4]

History does not tell us what a Soviet Union, allowed to develop in a "normal" way of its own choosing, would look like today. We do know, however, the nature of a Soviet Union attacked in its cradle, raised alone in an extremely hostile world, and, when it managed to survive to adulthood, overrun by the Nazi war machine with the blessings of the Western powers. The resulting insecurities and fears have inevitably led to deformities of character not unlike that found in an individual raised in a similar life-threatening manner.

We in the West are never allowed to forget the political shortcomings (real and alleged) of the Soviet Union; at the same time we are never reminded of the history which lies behind it. The anti-communist propaganda campaign began even earlier than the military intervention. Before the year 1918 was over, expressions like "Red Peril", "the Bolshevik assault on civilization", and "menace to world by Reds is seen" had become commonplace in the pages of the *New York Times*.

During February and March 1919, a US Senate Judiciary Subcommittee held hearings before which many "Bolshevik horror stories" were presented. The character of some of the testimony presented can be gauged by the headline in the *Times* of 12 February 1919.

DESCRIBE HORRORS UNDER RED RULE. R.E. SIMONS AND W.W. WELSH TELL SENATORS OF BRUTALITIES OF BOLSHEVIKI — STRIP WOMEN IN STREETS — PEOPLE OF EVERY CLASS EXCEPT THE SCUM SUBJECTED TO VIOLENCE BY MOBS.

Historian Frederick Lewis Schuman has written: "The net result of these hearings . . . was to picture Soviet Russia as a kind of bedlam inhabited by abject slaves completely at the mercy of an organization of homicidal maniacs whose purpose was to destroy all traces of civilization and carry the nation back to barbarism".[5]

Literally no story about the Bolsheviks was too contrived, too bizarre, too grotesque, or too perverted to be printed and widely believed — from women being nationalized to babies being eaten.* The story about women, wrote Schuman, "was broadcasted over the country through a thousand channels and perhaps did more than anything else to stamp the Russian Communists in the minds of most American citizens as criminal perverts".[6] This tale continued to receive great currency even after the State Department was obliged to announce that it was a fraud. (That the Soviets eat their babies was still being taught by the John Birch Society to its large audience at least as late as 1978.)[7]

By the end of 1919, when the defeat of the Allies and the White Army appeared likely, the *New York Times* treated its readers to headlines and stories such as the following:

30 Dec. 1919: "Reds Seek War With America"

9 Jan. 1920: " 'Official quarters' describe the Bolshevist menace in the Middle East as ominous"

11 Jan. 1920: "Allied officials and diplomats [envisage] a possible invasion of Europe"

13 Jan. 1920: "Allied diplomatic circles" fear an invasion of Persia.

16 Jan. 1920: A page-one headline, eight columns wide: "Britain Facing War With Reds, Calls Council In Paris." "Well-informed diplomats" expect both a military invasion of Europe and a Soviet advance into Eastern and Southern Asia.

The following morning, however, we could read: "No War With Russia, Allies To Trade With Her"

7 Feb. 1920: "Reds Raising Army To Attack India"

11 Feb. 1920: "Fear That Bolsheviki Will Now Invade Japanese Territory"

Readers of the *New York Times* were asked to believe that all these invasions were to come from a nation that was shattered as few nations in history have been; a nation still recovering from a bloody world war; in extreme chaos from a fundamental social revolution that was barely off the ground; engaged in a brutal civil war against forces backed by the major powers of the world; its industries, never advanced to begin with, in a shambles; and the country in the throes of a famine that was to leave many millions dead before it subsided.

---

* As the early pagans believed the Christians guilty of devouring their children; the same was believed of the Jews in the Middle Ages.

If this was reality as presented by the United States' "newspaper of record", one can imagine only with dismay the witch's brew the rest of the nation's newspapers were feeding to their readers.

This, then, was the American people's first experience of a new social phenomenon that had come upon the world, their introductory education on the Soviet Union and this thing called "communism". The students have never recovered from the lesson. Neither has the Soviet Union.

The military intervention came to an end but, with the sole and partial exception of the Second World War period, the propaganda offensive has never let up. In 1943 *Life* magazine devoted an entire issue in honour of the Soviet Union's accomplishments, going far beyond what was demanded by the need for wartime solidarity, going so far as to call Lenin "perhaps the greatest man of modern times".[8] Two years later, however, with Harry Truman sitting in the White House, such fraternity had no chance of surviving. Truman, after all, was the man who, the day after the Nazis invaded the Soviet Union, said: "If we see that Germany is winning, we ought to help Russia, and if Russia is winning, we ought to help Germany, and that way let them kill as many as possible, although I don't want to see Hitler victorious in any circumstances."[9] (Much propaganda mileage has been squeezed out of the Soviet-German treaty of 1939, made possible only by entirely ignoring the fact that the Russians were forced into the pact by the repeated refusal of the Western powers to unite with them in a stand against Hitler.)[10]

From the Red Scare of the 1920s to the McCarthyism of the 1950s to the Reagan Crusade Against the Evil Empire of the 1980s, the American people have been subjected to a relentless anti-communist indoctrination. It is imbibed with their mother's milk, pictured in their comic books, spelled out in their school books; their daily paper offers them headlines that tell them all they need to know; ministers find sermons in it, politicians are elected with it, and *Reader's Digest* becomes rich on it.[11]

The fiercely-held conviction inevitably produced by this insidious assault on the intellect is that a great damnation has been unleashed upon the world, possibly by the devil himself, but in the form of people; people not motivated by the same needs, fears, emotions, and personal morality that govern others of the species, but people engaged in an extremely clever, monolithic, international conspiracy dedicated to taking over the world and enslaving it; the reasons are not always clear perhaps, but evil needs no motivation save evil itself. Moreover, any appearance or claim by these people to be rational human beings seeking a better kind of world or society is a sham, a cover-up, to delude others, and proof only of their cleverness; the repression and cruelties which have taken place in the Soviet Union are forever proof of the bankruptcy of virtue and the evil intentions of these people in whichever country they may be found, under whatever name they may call themselves; and, most important of all, the only choice open to anyone in the United States is between the American Way of Life and the Soviet Way of Life, that nothing lies between or outside these two ways of making the world.

This is how it looks to the simple folk of America. One finds that the sophisticated, when probed slightly beneath the surface of their academic language, see it exactly the same way.

To the mind carefully brought to adulthood in the United States, the truths of anti-communism are self-evident, as self-evident as the flatness of the world once was to an earlier mind; as the Russian people believed that the victims of Stalin's purges were truly guilty of treason.

The foregoing slice of American history must be taken into account if one is to make sense of the vagaries of American foreign policy since the end of World War Two, specifically, the record, as presented in this book, of what the CIA and other branches of the US Government have done to the peoples of the world.

In 1918, the barons of American capital needed no reason for their war against communism other than the threat to their wealth and privilege, although their opposition was expressed in terms of moral indignation.

During the period between the two world wars, US gunboat diplomacy operated in the Caribbean to make "The American Lake" safe for the fortunes of United Fruit and W.R. Grace & Co., at the same time warning of the Bolshevik threat to the hemisphere and to righteousness, from the likes of Augusto Sandino.

By the end of the Second World War, however, every American past the age of 40 had been subjected to some 25 years of anti-communist radiation, the average incubation period needed to produce a malignancy. Anti-communism had developed a life of its own, independent of its capitalist father. Increasingly, in the post-war period, middle-aged Washington policy makers and diplomats saw the world out there as one composed of "communists" and "anti-communists", whether of nations, movements or individuals. This comic-strip vision of the world, with American supermen fighting communist evil everywhere, had graduated from a cynical propaganda exercise to a moral imperative of US foreign policy.

Even the concept of "non-communist", implying some measure of neutrality, has generally been accorded scant legitimacy in this paradigm. John Foster Dulles, one of the major architects of post-war US foreign policy, expressed this succinctly in his typically simple, moralistic way: "For us there are two sorts of people in the world: there are those who are Christians and support free enterprise and there are the others."[12] As several of the case studies in the present book confirm, Dulles put that creed into rigid practice.

It is as true now as ever, that American multinationals derive significant economic advantages from Third World countries due to their being under-industrialized, under-diversified, capitalist-orientated, and relatively powerless.

It is equally true that the consequence of American interventions has frequently been to keep Third World countries in just such an underdeveloped, impotent state.

There is thus at least a prima-facie case to be made for the contention that the engine of US foreign policy is still fuelled predominantly by "imperialism".

But that the consequence illuminates the intent does not necessarily follow. The argument that economic factors have continued to exert an important and direct influence upon United States interventionist policy in modern times does not stand up to close examination. When all the known elements of the interventions are considered, scarcely any cases actually emerge which conform to the economic model, and even in these the stage is shared with other factors. The upshot in the great majority of cases is that tangible economic gain, existing or potential, did not, and could not, play a determining role in the American decision to intervene. The economic model proves woefully inadequate not only as a means of explanation, but even more so as a tool of prediction. In each of the most recent cases, for example — Grenada, El Salvador, and Nicaragua — American intervention was foreseen and warned of well in advance simply, and only, because of the "communist" nature of the targets. But no one seriously suggested that some treasure lay in these impoverished lands luring the American pirates. Indeed, after the conquest and occupation of Grenada, the US business community displayed a marked indifference to setting up shop on the island, despite being implored to do so by Washington for political reasons. In other cases, where the American side failed to win a civil war, such as in China, Vietnam and Angola, Washington put up barriers to American corporations having any commercial dealings with the new regimes which were actually eager to do business with the United States.

Entirely without regard to financial considerations, CIA operations have been triggered by no more than a country receiving aid from the Soviet bloc, or refusing to break diplomatic relations with Cuba, or simply a leader using Marxist rhetoric. In other instances, in the absence of any special "provocation", the CIA still engages in daily, "routine" subversion of local left-wing elements, whether these are in or out of power; this, then, is the Agency's "job", what its officers do for a living.

Although at one level of US foreign policy, anti-communism is pursued for its own sake — a "moral imperative", as discussed above — at another level it is inextricably bound up with a far older seducer of men and nations, the lust for power: the acquisition, maintenance, use and enjoyment of influence and prestige.

In this scheme of things, "communist" is no more than the name ascribed to those people who stand in the way of the realization of such ambitions (as "national security" is the name given for the *reason* for fighting "communists"). It is another twist of the old adage: if communists didn't exist, the United States would have to invent them. And so they have. The word "communist" (as well as "Marxist") has been so overused and so abused by American leaders and the media as to render it virtually meaningless. (The Left has done the same to the word "fascist".) But merely having a name for something — witches or flying saucers — establishes a certain credence to it.

At the same time, the American public, as we have seen, has been soundly conditioned to react Pavlovianly to the term: it means, still, the worst excesses of Stalin, from wholesale purges to Siberian slave-labour camps* . . . it means, as Michael Parenti has observed, that "Classic Marxist-Leninist *predictions* [concerning world revolution] are treated as statements of *intent* directing all present-day communist *actions*."[14] . . . it means "us" against "them".

And "them" can mean a peasant in the Philippines, a mural-painter in Nicaragua, a legally-elected prime minister in British Guiana, or a European intellectual, a Cambodian neutralist, an African nationalist — all, somehow, part of the same monolithic conspiracy; each, in some way, a threat to the American Way of Life; no land too small, too poor, or too far away to pose such a threat, the "communist threat".

The cases presented in this book illustrate that it has been largely irrelevant whether the particular targets of intervention — be they individuals, political parties, movements or governments — called themselves "communist" or not. It has mattered little whether they were scholars of dialectical materialism or had never heard of Karl Marx; whether they were atheists or priests; whether a strong and influential Communist Party was in the picture or not; whether the government had come into being through violent revolution or peaceful elections . . . all have been targets, all "communists".

It has mattered still less that the Soviet KGB was in the picture. The assertion has been frequently voiced that the CIA carries out its dirty tricks largely *in reaction to* operations of the KGB which have been "even dirtier". This is a lie made out of whole cloth. There may be an isolated incident of such in the course of the CIA's 38 years of life, but it has kept itself well hidden. The relationship between the two sinister agencies is marked by fraternization and respect for fellow professionals more than by hand-to-hand combat. Former CIA officer** John Stockwell has written:

---

* In 1982 US Defense Secretary Caspar Weinberger said "the evidence has been mounting that the Soviet Union may be using slave labor" on the trans-European natural gas pipeline. "The evidence is not conclusive", he told a Georgetown University conference, "but the available evidence is profoundly troubling and some have found it persuasive." Two months later, in response to a Congressional request, the CIA said that it could not substantiate such reports, but it could state that about four million Soviet citizens were being compelled to do "forced labor". When one made one's way past the scare headlines and read the text carefully, one discovered that the "forced labor" was nothing more than prison inmates doing socially useful labor while serving their sentences, and other convicted criminals doing the same in lieu of going to prison at all.[13]

** The expressions "CIA officer" or "case officer" are used throughout this book to denote regular, full-time, career employees of the Agency, as opposed to "agent", someone working for the CIA on an ad hoc basis. Other sources which are quoted, it will be seen, tend to use the word "agent" to cover both categories.

Actually, at least in more routine operations, case officers most fear the US ambassador and his staff, then restrictive headquarters cables, then curious, gossipy neighbors in the local community, as potential threats to operations. Next would come the local police, then the press. Last of all is the KGB — in my twelve years of case officering I never saw or heard of a situation in which the KGB attacked or obstructed a CIA operation.[15]

Stockwell later adds that the various intelligence services do not want their world to be "complicated" by murdering each other.

It isn't done. If a CIA case officer has a flat tire in the dark of night on a lonely road, he will not hesitate to accept a ride from a KGB officer — likely the two would detour to some bar for a drink together. In fact CIA and KGB officers entertain each other frequently in their homes. The CIA's files are full of mention of such relationships in almost every African station.[16]

Proponents of "fighting fire with fire" come perilously close at times to arguing that if the KGB, for example, had a hand in the overthrow of the Czechoslovak government in 1968, it is OK for the CIA to have a hand in the overthrow of the Chilean government in 1973. It's as if the destruction of democracy by the KGB deposits funds in a bank account from which the CIA is then justified in making withdrawals.

What then has been the thread common to the diverse targets of American intervention which has brought down upon them the wrath, and often the firepower, of the world's most powerful nation? In virtually every case involving the Third World described in this book, it has been, in one form or another, a policy of "self-determination": the desire, born of perceived need and principle, to pursue a path of development independent of US foreign policy objectives. Most commonly, this has been manifested in a) the ambition to free themselves from political, economic, and often cultural subservience to the United States; b) the refusal to minimize relations with the socialist bloc, or to suppress the left at home, or to welcome an American military installation on their soil; in short, a refusal to be a pawn in the cold war; or c) the attempt to alter or replace a government which held to neither of these aspirations.

It cannot be emphasized too strongly that such a policy of independence has been viewed and expressed by numerous Third World leaders and revolutionaries as one not to be equated by definition to anti-Americanism or pro-communism, but as simply a determination to maintain a position of neutrality and non-alignment vis-à-vis the two superpowers. Time and time again, however, it will be seen that the United States was not prepared to live with this proposition. Arbenz of Guatemala, Mossadegh of Iran, Sukarno of Indonesia, Nkrumah of Ghana, Jagan of British Guiana, Sihanouk of Cambodia . . . all, insisted Uncle Sam, must declare themselves unequivocally on the side of "The Free World" or suffer the consequences. Nkrumah put the case for non-alignment as follows:

The experiment which we tried in Ghana was essentially one of developing the country in co-operation with the world as a whole. Non-alignment meant exactly what it said. We were not hostile to the countries of the socialist world in the way in which the governments of the old colonial territories were. It should be remembered that while Britain pursued at home co-existence with the Soviet Union this was never allowed to extend to British colonial territories. Books on socialism, which were published and circulated freely in Britain, were banned in the British colonial empire, and after Ghana became independent it was assumed abroad that it would continue to follow the same restrictive ideological approach. When we behaved as did the British in their relations with the socialist countries we were accused of being pro-Russian and introducing the most dangerous ideas into Africa.[17]

When Washington officials equate nationalism or self-determination with "communism", there are times when they are "correct". At other times, they are "wrong". It doesn't particularly matter, for in either case they are referring to the same phenomenon. Although, in this book, the Soviet Union, China, various communist parties, etc. are sometimes referred to as "communist", this is primarily a shorthand convenience and a bow to custom, and is not meant to infer a political ideology or practice necessarily different in any way from those governments or parties *not* referred to as communist. Emphasis is placed upon what these bodies have done, not upon reference to what Marx or Lenin wrote.

Perhaps the most deeply ingrained reflex of knee-jerk anti-communism is the belief that the Soviet Union (or Cuba or Vietnam, etc. acting as Moscow's surrogate) is a clandestine force lurking behind the facade of self-determination, stirring up the hydra of revolution, or just plain trouble, here, there and everywhere; yet another incarnation, although on a far grander scale, of the proverbial "outside agitator", he who has made his appearance regularly throughout history . . . King George blamed the French for inciting the American colonies to revolt . . . disillusioned veterans protesting about their circumstances after the revolution (Shays' Rebellion) were branded as British agents out to wreck the republic . . . labour strikes in late 19th-century America were blamed on "anarchists" and "foreigners", during the First World War on "German agents", after the war on "Bolsheviks".

And in the 1960s, said the National Commission on the Causes and Prevention of Violence, J. Edgar Hoover "helped spread the view among the police ranks that any kind of mass protest is due to a conspiracy promulgated by agitators, often Communists, 'who misdirect otherwise contented people'."[18]

The last is the key phrase, one which encapsulates the conspiracy mentality of those in power — the idea that no people, except those living under the enemy, could be so miserable and discontent as to need recourse to revolution or even mass protest; that it is only the agitation of the outsider which misdirects them along this path.

9

Accordingly, if Ronald Reagan were to concede that the masses of El Salvador have every good reason to rise up against their god-awful existence, it would bring into question his accusation, and the rationale for US intervention, that it is principally (only?) the Soviet Union and its Cuban and Nicaraguan allies who instigate the Salvadoreans: that seemingly magical power of communists everywhere who, with a twist of their red wrist, can transform peaceful, happy people into furious guerrillas.*

Moreover, and infinitely more threatening to the American position, it would raise the question: Why does not the United States, if it must intervene, take the side of the rebels? Not only might this better serve the cause of human rights and justice and win the friendship of the new regime, but it would shut out the Russians from their alleged role. What better way to frustrate the International Communist Conspiracy? But this is a question that dares not speak its name in the Oval Office, a question that is relevant to many of the cases in this book.

Instead, the United States remains committed to its all-too-familiar policy of establishing and/or supporting the most vile tyrannies in the world whose outrages against their own people confront us daily in the pages of our newspapers: brutal massacres; systematic, sophisticated torture; public whippings; soldiers and police firing into crowds; hunger, runaway unemployment, the homeless, the refugees, the tens of thousands of disappeared persons . . . a way of life that is virtually a monopoly held by America's allies, from Guatemala, Chile and El Salvador to Turkey, Pakistan and Indonesia, all members in good standing of the Holy War Against Communism, all members of "The Free World", that little known region of which we hear so much and see so little.

Clearly, the restrictions on civil liberties found in the communist bloc, as severe as they are, pale by comparison to the cottage-industry Auschwitzes of "The Free World", and, except in that curious mental landscape inhabited by The Compleat Anti-Communist, can have little or nothing to do with the sundry American interventions supposedly in the cause of a higher good.

It is interesting to note that as commonplace as it is for American leaders to speak of freedom and democracy while supporting dictatorships, so do Russian leaders speak of wars of liberation, anti-imperialism and anti-colonialism while doing extremely little to actually further these causes, American propaganda notwithstanding. The Soviets like to be thought of as champions of the Third World, but they have stood by doing little more than going "tsk, tsk" as progressive movements and governments, even Communist Parties, in Greece, Guatemala, British Guiana, Chile, Indonesia, the Philippines and elsewhere have gone to the wall.

---

* The CIA, as we shall see, tried to spark mass revolt in China, Albania, Cuba, the Soviet Union, and elsewhere in Eastern Europe with a singular lack of success. The Agency's scribes have laid the blame for these failures on the "closed" nature of the societies involved. But in non-communist countries, the CIA has had to resort to military coups or extra-legal chicanery to get its people into power. It has never been able to light the fire of popular revolution.

During the early 1950s, the Central Intelligence Agency instigated several military incursions into Communist China. In 1960, CIA planes, without any provocation, bombed the sovereign nation of Guatemala. In 1973, the Agency encouraged a bloody revolt against the government of Iraq. In the American mass media at the time, and therefore in the American mind, these events did not happen.

"We didn't know what was happening", became a cliché used to ridicule those Germans who claimed ignorance of the events which took place under the Nazis. Yet, was their stock answer as far-fetched as we'd like to think? It is sobering to reflect that in our era of instant world-wide communications, the United States has, on many occasions, been able to mount a large or small scale military operation or undertake another, equally blatant, form of intervention without the American public being aware of it until years later, if ever. Often the only report of the event or of US involvement was a passing reference to the fact that a communist government had made certain charges — just the kind of thing the American public has been well conditioned to dismiss out of hand, and the press not to follow up; as the German people were taught that reports from abroad of Nazi wrong-doings were no more than communist propaganda.

With few exceptions, the interventions never made the headlines or the evening TV news. With some, bits and pieces of the stories have popped up here and there, but rarely brought together to form a cohesive and enlightening whole; the fragments usually appear long after the fact, quietly buried within other stories, just as quietly forgotten, bursting into the foreground only when extraordinary circumstances have compelled it, such as the Iranian hostage crisis which produced a rash of articles on the role played by the United States in the overthrow of the Iranian government in 1953. It was as if editors had been spurred into thinking: "Just what *did* we do in Iran to make all those people hate us so?"

There have been a lot of Irans in America's recent past, but in the absence of the *New York Daily News* or the *Los Angeles Times* conspicuously grabbing the reader by the collar and pressing against his face the full implication of the deed . . . in the absence of NBC putting it all into real pictures of real people on the receiving end . . . in such absence the incidents become *non-events* for the large majority of Americans, and they can honestly say "We didn't know what was happening."

Former Chinese Premier Chou En-lai once observed: "One of the delightful things about Americans is that they have absolutely no historical memory."*

* During the Three Mile Island nuclear power plant accident in Pennsylvania in 1979, a Japanese journalist, Atsuo Kaneko of the Japanese Kyoto News Service, spent several hours interviewing people temporarily housed at a hockey rink — mostly children, pregnant women and young mothers. He discovered that none of them had heard of Hiroshima. Mention of the name drew a blank.[19]

In 1982, a judge in Oakland, California said he was appalled when some 50 prospective jurors for a death-penalty murder trial were questioned and "none of them knew who Hitler was".[20]

To the foreign policy oligarchy in Washington, it is more than delightful. It is *sine qua non*.

So obscured is the comprehensive record of American interventions that when, in 1975, the Congressional Research Service of the Library of Congress was asked to undertake a study of covert activities of the CIA to date, it was able to come up with but a very minor portion of the overseas incidents presented in this book for the same period.[21]

Yet, all the information is there for the reading. I have not had access to the secret archives of the CIA or other government agencies. The details of the interventions have been gathered from books, newspapers, periodicals, and US Government publications freely available in one library or another. But for all that has made its way into popular consciousness, or into school texts, encyclopedias, or other standard reference works, there might as well exist strict censorship in the United States.

The reader is invited to look through the relevant sections of the three principal American encyclopedias, Americana, Britannica, and Colliers, after completing this book. The image of encyclopedias as the final repository of objective knowledge takes a beating. What is tantamount to a non-recognition of American interventions may very well be due to these esteemed works employing a criterion similar to that of Washington officials as reflected in the Pentagon Papers. The *New York Times* summarized this highly interesting phenomenon thus:

> Clandestine warfare against North Vietnam, for example, is not seen . . . as violating the Geneva Accords of 1954, which ended the French Indochina War, or as conflicting with the public policy pronouncements of the various administrations. Clandestine warfare, because it is covert, does not exist as far as treaties and public posture are concerned. Further, secret commitments to other nations are not sensed as infringing on the treaty-making powers of the Senate, because they are not publicly acknowledged.[22]

The *de facto* censorship which leaves so many Americans functionally illiterate about the history of US foreign affairs may be all the more effective precisely because it is not official, heavy-handed or conspiratorial, but woven artlessly into the fabric of education and the media. No conspiracy is needed. The editors of *Reader's Digest* and *U.S. News and World Report* do not need to meet covertly with the man from NBC in an FBI safe-house to plan next month's stories and programmes; for the simple truth is that these men would not have reached the positions they hold if they themselves had not all been guided through the same tunnel of camouflaged history and emerged with the same selective memory.

As extensive as the historical record presented here is, it is by no means meant to be a complete catalogue of every instance and every kind of American intervention since the Second World War. We are, after all, dealing largely with events which were covert when they occurred and which, for the most part, remain officially classified. Moreover, with but a few exceptions, this study does not concern itself with espionage or counter-espionage other than in passing. These areas have been well documented in countless "spy" books. Generally speaking, the study is confined to the more significant or blatant cases of intervention: the use of armed aggression by American and/or native troops acting with the United States; an operation, successful or not, to overthrow a government; an attempt to suppress a popular rebellion or movement; an attempted assassination; gross interference in an election, or other flagrant manipulation of a country's political system.

To serve these ends, the CIA over the years has made use of an extraordinary arsenal of weapons. Because of space considerations and to avoid repetition, only selected examples are given here and there amongst the cases. In actuality, at least one, and usually more, of these tactics was brought to bear in virtually every instance. Principal among them are the following:

1) *CIA schools*: in the United States and Latin America, where many tens of thousands of Third World military and police personnel have been taught modern methods of controlling insurgency and "subversion"; instruction includes techniques of "interrogation" (often a euphemism for torture); members of the labour movement learn the how and why of organizing workers within a framework of free enterprise and anti-communism.

2) *Infiltration and manipulation of selected groups*: political parties, women's organizations, professional, youth and cultural associations, etc. for electoral and propaganda purposes; the creation of unions — local, regional, national and international organizations set up to counterpoise and weaken existing labour groups too closely oriented towards social change or controlled by the left.

3) *News manipulation*: the "hiring" of foreign editors, columnists and journalists . . . "I guess I've bought as much newspaper space as the A & P" (the supermarket chain), chortled a former CIA officer one day;[23] the creation and/or subsidizing of numerous periodicals, news services, radio stations, and book publishers. Considering all assets, the CIA, at least until the late 1970s, has probably run what amounts to the largest news organization in the world; its propaganda/disinformation effect is routinely multiplied by world-wide replay.

4) *Economic means*: in co-operation with other US government agencies, such as AID, private American corporations, and international lending institutions, the methods of manipulating and applying pressure to selected sectors of a country's economy or the economy as a whole are without number.

5) *Dirty tricks department*: bugging, wire-tapping, forged documents, bogus personal letters, planting of evidence, disinformation, blackmail, etc., etc. to create incidents or obtain information to embarrass the left, locally and internationally, particularly to lend credence to charges of a Moscow or Havana conspiracy; to provoke the expulsion of communist-bloc diplomats or the breaking of relations with those countries; to foster distrust and dissension within the left.

Although the cases which follow are presented as more or less discrete stories, fixed in time and with beginnings and ends, this is done mainly to keep the information within manageable bounds and to highlight the more dramatic turns of events, and is not meant to indicate that there was no significant CIA activity in the particular country before or after the years specified. The reader should therefore keep in mind that the above types of operation as well as others are all ongoing programmes, carried out routinely in numerous countries, including many not listed in this book. This is, as mentioned earlier, what CIA officers do for a living.

"The upheaval in China is a revolution which, if we analyze it, we will see is prompted by the same things that prompted the British, French and American revolutions."[24] A cosmopolitan and generous sentiment of Dean Rusk, then Assistant Secretary for Far Eastern Affairs, later Secretary of State. At precisely the same time as Mr Rusk's talk in 1950, others in his government were actively plotting the downfall of the Chinese revolutionary government.

This has been a common phenomenon. For many of the cases described in the following pages, one can find statements of high or middle-level Washington officials which put into question the policy of intervention; which expressed misgivings based either on principle (sometimes the better side of American liberalism) or concern that the intervention would not serve any worthwhile end, might even end in disaster. I have attached little weight to such dissenting statements as, indeed, in the final analysis, did Washington decision-makers who, in controversial world situations, could be relied upon to play the anti-communist card. In presenting the interventions in this manner, I am declaring that American foreign policy *is* what American foreign policy *does*.

It should be rather obvious at this point that I am not neutral on the question of American interventions. I am opposed to them on both political and moral grounds (to the extent that the two can be separated). This bias certainly colours my language, but I have taken pains to keep it from colouring my selection of facts; that is, I have not knowingly omitted any facts which contradict in any significant way the information I have presented, or the implications of that information. Further, I have chosen not to take into account a number of intriguing disclosures concerning American interventions where I felt that the source could not be sufficiently trusted and/or the information was not presented or documented in a manner which made it credible to me. In any event, it is not demanded of the reader that he accept my biases, but that he reflect upon his own.[25]

William Blum
London, March 1986

1. China 1945 to 1960s
Was Mao Tse-tung paranoid?

For four years, numerous Americans, in high positions and obscure, sullenly harboured the conviction that World War II was "the wrong war against the wrong enemies". Communism, they knew, was the only genuine enemy on America's historical agenda. Was that not why Hitler had been ignored/tolerated/appeased? So that the Nazi war machine would turn East and wipe Bolshevism off the face of the earth once and for all? It was just unfortunate that Adolf turned out to be such a megalomaniac and turned West as well.

But that war was over. These Americans were now to have their day in every corner of the world. The ink on the Japanese surrender treaty was hardly dry when the United States began to use the Japanese soldiers still in China alongside American troops in a joint effort against the Chinese communists. (In the Philippines, as we shall see, the US did not even wait for the war to end before subordinating the struggle against Japan to the anti-communist crusade.)

The communists in China had worked closely with the American military during the war, providing important intelligence about the Japanese occupiers, rescuing and caring for downed US airmen.[1] But no matter. Generalissimo Chiang Kai-shek would be Washington's man; he headed what passed for a central government in China. The Office of Strategic Services (OSS, forerunner of the CIA) estimated that the bulk of Chiang's military effort had been directed against the communists rather than the Japanese. He had also done his best to block the co-operation between the Reds and the Americans. Now his army contained Japanese units and his regime was full of officials who had collaborated with the Japanese and served in their puppet government.[2] But no matter. The Generalissimo was as anti-communist as they come. Moreover, he was a born American client. His forces would be properly trained and equipped to do battle with the men of Mao Tse-tung and Chou En-lai.

President Truman was out front about what he described as "using the Japanese to hold off the Communists":

> It was perfectly clear to us that if we told the Japanese to lay down their arms immediately and march to the seaboard, the entire country would be taken over by the Communists. We therefore had to take the unusual step of using the enemy as a garrison until we could airlift Chinese National [Chiang's] troops to South China and send Marines to guard the seaports.[3]

The deployment of American Marines had swift and dramatic results. Two weeks after the end of the war, Peking was surrounded by communist forces. Only the arrival of the Marines in the city prevented the Reds from taking it over.[4] And while Mao's forces were pushing into Shanghai's suburbs, US transport planes dropped Chiang's troops in to seize the city.[5]

In a scramble to get to key centres and ports before the communists, the US transported between 400,000 and 500,000 Nationalist troops by ship and plane all over the vastness of China and Manchuria, places they could never have reached otherwise.

As the civil war heated up, the 50,000 Marines sent by Truman after the close of the war were used to guard railway lines, coal mines, ports, bridges, and other strategic sites. Inevitably, they became involved in the fighting, sustaining dozens, if not hundreds of casualties. US troops, the communists charged, attacked areas controlled by the Reds, directly opened fire on them, arrested military officers, and disarmed soldiers.[6] The Americans found themselves blasting a small Chinese village "unmercifully", wrote a Marine to his congressman, not knowing "how many innocent people were slaughtered".[7]

United States planes regularly made reconnaissance flights over communist territory to scout the position of their forces. The communists claimed that American planes frequently strafed and bombed their troops and in one instance machine-gunned a communist-held town.[8] To what extent, if any, these attacks were carried out by US airmen is not known.

There were, however, American survivors in some of the many crashes of United States aircraft. Surprisingly, the Reds continued to rescue them, tend to their wounds, and return them to US bases. It may be difficult to appreciate now, but at this time the mystique and the myth of "America" still gripped the imagination of peoples all over the world, and Chinese peasants, whether labelled "communist" or not, were no exception. During the war the Reds had helped to rescue scores of American fliers and transported them through Japanese lines to safety. "The Communists", wrote the *New York Times*, "did not lose one airman taken under their protection. They made a point of never accepting rewards for saving American airmen."[9]

When 1946 arrived, about 100,000 American military personnel were still in China, still supporting Chiang. The official United States explanation for the presence of its military was that they were there to disarm and repatriate the Japanese. Though this task was indeed carried out eventually, it was secondary to the military's political function, as Truman's later statement cited above makes abundantly clear.

The American soldiers in China began to protest about not being sent home, a complaint echoed round the world by other GIs kept overseas for political (usually anti-communist) purposes. "They ask me, too, why they're here," said a Marine lieutenant in China at Christmas-time, 1945. "As an officer I am supposed to tell them, but you can't tell a man that he's here to disarm Japanese when he's guarding the same railway with [armed] Japanese."[10]

Strangely enough, the US attempted to mediate in the civil war; this, while being an active, powerful participant on one side. Harry Truman sent General

George Marshall to China to try and arrange a ceasefire and a coalition government. While some temporary success was achieved in an on-and-off truce, the idea of a coalition government was doomed to failure, as unlikely as a marriage between the Czar and the Bolsheviks. As the historian D.F. Fleming has pointed out, "One cannot unite a dying oligarchy with a rising revolution".[11]

What American motivation lay behind this move can only be guessed at; perhaps a public relations exercise to obscure its interventionist role; or a realization that it was either compromise with the communists or see all of China fall under their sway.

Not until early 1947 did the United States begin to withdraw some of its military forces, although aid and support to the Chiang government continued in one form or another long afterward. At about this same time, the Flying Tigers began to operate. The legendary American air squadron under the leadership of General Claire Chennault had fought for the Chinese against the Japanese before and during the world war. Now Chennault, Chiang's former air force adviser, had reactivated the squadron (under the name CAT) and its pilots-of-fortune soon found themselves in the thick of the fray, flying endless supply missions to Nationalist cities under siege, dodging communist shell bursts to airlift food, ammunition, and supplies of all kinds, or to rescue the wounded.[12] Technically, CAT was a private airline hired by the Chiang government, but before the civil war came to an end, the airline had formally interlocked with the CIA to become the first link in the Agency's sprawling air-empire-to-be, best known for the Air America line.

By 1949, United States aid to the Nationalists since the war amounted to almost $2 billion in cash and $1 billion worth of military hardware; 39 Nationalist army divisions had been trained and equipped.[13] Yet the Chiang dynasty was collapsing all around in bits and pieces. It had not been only the onslaught of Chiang's communist foes, but the hostility of the Chinese people at large to his tyranny, his wanton cruelty, and the extraordinary corruption and decadence of his entire bureaucratic and social system. By contrast, the large areas under communist administration were models of honesty, progress and fairness; entire divisions of Chiang's forces defected to the communists. The Nationalist forces, said General David Barr, head of the US Military Mission in China, were under "the world's worst leadership".[14]

The Generalissimo, his cohorts and soldiers fled to the Chinese island of Taiwan. They had prepared their entry two years earlier by terrorizing the islanders into submission — a massacre which took the lives of an estimated 5,000 to 20,000 people.*[15]

---

* Prior to the communist victory, the US Government entertained no doubts that Taiwan (Formosa) was a part of China. Afterward, uncertainty began to creep into the minds of Washington officials. The crisis was resolved in a remarkably simple manner: the US agreed with Chiang that the proper way to view the situation was not that Taiwan belonged to China, but that Taiwan *was* China. And so it was called.

In the wake of the communist success, China scholar Felix Greene has observed, "Americans simply could not bring themselves to believe that the Chinese, however rotten their leadership, could have preferred a communist government".[16] It must have been the handiwork of a conspiracy, an international conspiracy, at the control panel of which sat, not unexpectedly, the Soviet Union.

The evidence for this was thin to the point of transparency. Indeed, ever since Stalin's credo of "socialism in one country" won out over Trotsky's internationalism in the 1920s, the Russians had sided with Chiang more than with Mao, advising the latter more than once to dissolve his army and join Chiang's government.[17] Particularly in the post-World War II years, when the Soviet Union was faced with its own staggering crisis of reconstruction, did it not relish the prospect of having to help lift the world's most populous nation into the modern age. In 1947, General Marshall stated publicly that he knew of no evidence that the Chinese communists were being supported by the USSR.[18]

But in the United States this did not prevent the rise of an entire mythology of how the US had "lost" China: Soviet intervention, State Department communists, White House cowards, military and diplomatic folly, communist dupes and fellow-travellers in the media . . . treachery everywhere . . .

The Truman administration, said Senator Joseph McCarthy with characteristic charm, was composed of "egg-sucking phony liberals" who protected the "Communists and queers" who had "sold China into atheistic slavery".[19]

Yet, short of an all-out invasion of the country by large numbers of American troops, it is difficult to see what more the US Government could have done to prevent Chiang's downfall. Even after Chiang fled to Taiwan, the United States pursued a campaign of relentless assaults against the communist government, despite a request from Chou En-lai for aid and friendship. The Red leader saw no practical or ideological bar to this.*[20]

Many Nationalist soldiers had taken refuge in northern Burma in the great exodus of 1949, much to the displeasure of the Burmese Government. There, the CIA began to regroup this stateless army into a fighting force, and during the early 1950s a number of large- and small-scale incursions into China were carried out.

In one instance, in April 1951, a few thousand troops, accompanied by CIA advisers and supplied by air drops from American C46s and C47s, crossed the border into China's Yunnan province, but they were driven back by the communists in less than a week. The casualties were high and included several CIA advisers who lost their lives. Another raid that summer took the invaders 65 miles into China where they reportedly held a 100-mile long strip of territory.

---

* Instead, the US evidently conspired to assassinate Chou on several occasions. (See Indonesia, 1957-58 chapter and *The Guardian* (London), 24 August 1985).

While the attacks continued intermittently, the CIA proceeded to build up the force's capabilities: American engineers arrived to help construct and expand airstrips in Burma, fresh troops were flown in from Taiwan, other troops were recruited from amongst Burmese hill tribes, CIA air squadrons were brought in for logistical services, and enormous quantities of American heavy arms were ferried in. Much of the supply of men and equipment came in via nearby Thailand.

The army soon stood at more than 10,000 men. By the end of 1952, Taiwan claimed that over 41,000 communists had been killed and more than 3,000 wounded. The figures were most likely exaggerated, but even so, it was clear that the raids would not lead to Chiang's triumphant return to the mainland — although this was not their sole purpose. On the Chinese border two greater battles were raging: in Korea and Vietnam. It was the hope of the United States to force the Chinese to divert troops and military resources away from these areas. The infant People's Republic of China was undergoing a terrible test.

In between raids on China, the "Chinats" (as distinguished from the "Chicoms") found time to clash frequently with Burmese troops, indulge in banditry, and become the opium barons of The Golden Triangle, that slice of land encompassing parts of Burma, Laos and Thailand which was the world's largest source of opium and heroin. CIA pilots flew the stuff all over, to secure the co-operation of those in Thailand who were important to the military operation, as a favour to their Nationalist clients, perhaps even for the money, and, ironically, to serve as cover for their more illicit activities.

The Chinats in Burma kept up their harassment of the Chinese until 1961 and the CIA continued to supply them militarily, but at some point the Agency began to phase itself out of a more direct involvement. When the CIA, in response to repeated protests by the Burmese Government to the United States and the United Nations, put pressure on the Chinats to leave Burma, Chiang responded by threatening to expose the Agency's covert support of his troops there. At an earlier stage, the CIA had entertained the hope that the Chinese would be provoked into attacking Burma, thereby forcing the strictly neutral Burmese to seek salvation in the Western camp.[21] The Chinese did just that, in January 1961, but as part of a combined force with the Burmese to overwhelm the Nationalists' main base and mark finis to their Burmese adventure. Burma subsequently renounced American aid and moved closer to Peking.[22]

For many of the Chinats, unemployment was only short-lived. They soon signed up with the CIA again; this time to fight with the Agency's grand army in Laos.

Burma was not the only jumping-off site for CIA-organized raids into China. The islands of Quemoy and Matsu, about five miles off the Chinese coast, were used as bases for hit-and-run attacks, often in battalion strength; for occasional bombing forays, and to blockade mainland ports. Chiang was "brutally pressured" by the US to build up his troops on the islands beginning around 1953 as a demonstration of Washington's new policy of "unleashing" him.[23]

The Chinese retaliated several times with heavy artillery attacks on Quemoy, on one occasion killing two American military officers. The prospect of an escalated war led the US later to have second thoughts and to ask Chiang to abandon the islands, but he then refused. The suggestion has often been put forward that Chiang's design was to embroil the United States in just such a war as his one means of returning to the mainland.[24]

Many incursions into China were made by smaller, commando-type teams air-dropped in for intelligence and sabotage purposes. In November 1952, two CIA officers, John Downey and Richard Fecteau, who had been engaged in flying these teams in and dropping supplies to them, were shot down and captured by the communists; only two years later did Peking announce their capture and sentencing. The State Department broke its own two-year silence with indignation: the Department claimed that the two men had been civilian employees of the US Department of the Army in Japan who were presumed lost on a flight from Korea to Japan in November 1952. "How they came into the hands of the Chinese Communists is unknown to the United States ... the continued wrongful detention of these American citizens furnishes further proof of the Chinese Communist regime's disregard for accepted practices of international conduct."[25]

Fecteau was released in December 1971, shortly before President Nixon's trip to China; Downey was not freed until March 1973, soon after Nixon publicly acknowledged him to be a CIA officer.

The Peking announcement in 1954 also revealed that eleven American airmen had been shot down over China in January 1953 while on a mission which had as its purpose the "air-drop of special agents into China and the Soviet Union". These men were luckier, being freed after only 2½ years.

All told, said the Chinese, it had killed 106 American and Taiwanese agents who had parachuted into China between 1951 and 1954 and had captured 124 others. Although the CIA had little, if anything, to show for its commando actions, it reportedly maintained the programme until at least 1960.[26]

There were many other CIA flights over China for purely espionage purposes, carried out by high-altitude U-2 planes, pilotless "drones", and other aircraft. These overflights began around the late 1950s and were not discontinued until 1971, to coincide with Henry Kissinger's first trip to Peking. The operation was not without incident. Several U-2 planes were shot down and even more of the drones, 19 of the latter by Chinese count between 1964 and 1969. China registered hundreds of "serious warnings" about violations of its air space, and on at least one occasion American aircraft crossed the Chinese border and shot down a Mig-17.[27]

It would seem that no degree of failure or paucity of result was enough to deter the CIA from seeking new ways to torment the Chinese in the decade following their revolution. Tibet was another case in point. The Peking Government claimed Tibet as part of China, as had previous Chinese governments for more than two centuries, although many Tibetans still regarded themselves as autonomous or independent. The United States made its position clear during the war:

The Government of the United States has borne in mind the fact that the Chinese

Government has long claimed suzerainty over Tibet and that the Chinese constitution lists Tibet among areas constituting the territory of the Republic of China. This Government has at no time raised a question regarding either of these claims.[28]

After the communist revolution, Washington officials tended to be more equivocal about the matter. But US actions against Tibet had nothing to do with the niceties of international law.

Beginning in 1957 or 1958, the CIA began to recruit Tibetan refugees and exiles in neighbouring countries such as India and Nepal. Amongst their number were members of the Dalai Lama's guard, referred to picturesquely as "the fearsome Khamba horsemen", and others who had already engaged in some guerrilla activity against Peking rule and/or the profound social changes being instituted by the revolution. (Serfdom and slavery were, literally, still prevalent in Tibet.) Those selected were flown to the United States, to an unused military base high in the Colorado mountains, an altitude approximating that of their mountainous homeland. There, hidden away as much as possible from the locals, they were trained in the fine points of paramilitary warfare.

After completing training, each group of Tibetans was flown to Taiwan or other friendly Asian countries, thence to be infiltrated back into Tibet, or elsewhere in China, where they occupied themselves in activities such as sabotage, mining roads, cutting communication lines, and ambushing small communist forces. Their actions were supported by CIA aircraft and on occasion led by Agency contract mercenaries.

The operation in Colorado was maintained until some time in the 1960s. How many thousands of Tibetans passed through the course of instruction will probably never be known. Even after the formal training programme came to an end, the CIA continued to finance and supply their exotic clients and nurture their hopeless dream of reconquering their homeland.

In 1961, when the *New York Times* got some wind of the operation, it acceded to a Pentagon request to probe no further. The matter was particularly sensitive because the CIA is expressly forbidden to conduct anything of this sort within the United States.[29]

Above and beyond the bedevilment of China on its own merits, there was the spillover from the Korean war. There were the numerous bombings and strafings by American planes which, the Chinese frequently reported, took civilian lives and destroyed homes. And there was the matter of germ warfare.

The Chinese devoted a great deal of effort to publicizing their claim that the United States, particularly during January to March 1952, had dropped quantities of bacteria and bacteria-laden insects over Korea and north-east China. It presented testimony of about 38 captured American airmen who had purportedly flown the planes with the deadly cargo. Many of the men went into voluminous detail about the entire operation: the kinds of bombs and other containers dropped, the types of insects, the diseases which they carried, etc. At the same time, photographs of the alleged germ bombs and insects were published.

Then, in August, an "International Scientific Committee" was appointed, composed of scientists from Sweden, France, Great Britain, Italy, Brazil and the Soviet Union. After an investigation in China of more than two months, the committee produced a report of some 600 pages, many photos, and the conclusion that:

> The peoples of Korea and China have indeed been the objectives of bacterio-logical weapons. These have been employed by units of the U.S.A. armed forces, using a great variety of different methods for the purpose, some of which seem to be developments of those applied by the Japanese during the second world war.[30]

It should be noted that some of the American airmen's statements contained so much technical biological information and were so full of communist rhetoric — "imperialist, capitalist Wall Street war monger" and the like — that their personal authorship of the statements must be seriously questioned. Moreover, it was later learned that most of the airmen had confessed only after being subjected to physical abuse.[31]

But in view of what we have since learned about American involvement with chemical and biological weapons, the Chinese claims cannot be dismissed out of hand. In 1970, for example, the *New York Times* reported that during the Korean War, when US forces were overwhelmed by "human waves" of Chinese, "the Army dug into captured Nazi chemical warfare documents describing Sarin, a nerve gas so lethal that a few pounds could kill thousands of people in minutes . . . By the mid-nineteen-fifties, the Army was manufacturing thousands of gallons of Sarin".[32]

And during the 1950s and 1960s, the Army and the CIA conducted numerous experiments with biological agents within the United States. To cite just two examples: in 1955, there is compelling evidence that the CIA released whooping-cough bacteria into the open air in Florida; there was an accompanying extremely sharp increase in the incidence of the disease in the state that year.[33] The following year, another toxic substance was disseminated in the streets and tunnels of New York City.[34]

We will also see in the chapter on Cuba how the CIA conducted chemical and biological warfare against Fidel Castro's rule.

In May 1966, Secretary of State Dean Rusk spoke before a Congressional committee about American policy toward China. Mr Rusk, it seems, was perplexed that "At times the Communist Chinese leaders seem to be obsessed with the notion that they are being threatened and encircled". He spoke of China's "imaginary, almost pathological, notion that the United States and other countries around its borders are seeking an opportunity to invade mainland China and destroy the Peiping [Peking] regime". The Secretary then added:

> How much Peiping's 'fear' of the United States is genuine and how much it is artificially induced for domestic political purposes only the Chinese Communist

leaders themselves know. I am convinced, however, that their desire to expel our influence and activity from the western Pacific and Southeast Asia is not motivated by fears that we are threatening them.[35]

2. Italy 1947-1948
Free Elections, Hollywood Style

"Those who do not believe in the ideology of the United States shall not be allowed to stay in the United States," declared the American Attorney-General, Tom Clark, in January 1948.[1]

In March, the Justice Department, over which Clark presided, determined that Italians who did not believe in the ideology of the US would not be allowed to emigrate to, or even enter, the United States.

This was but one tactic in a remarkable American campaign to ensure that Italians who did not believe in the ideology of the United States would not be allowed to form a government of a differing ideology in Italy in their election scheduled for 18 April 1948.

Two years earlier, the Italian Communist Party (PCI), the largest in the world outside the Soviet Union, and the Socialist Party (PSI) had garnered more votes and more seats in the Constituent Assembly election than the Christian Democrats. But the two parties of the left had run separate candidates and thus had to be content with some ministerial posts in a coalition cabinet under a Christian Democrat premier. The results, nonetheless, spoke plainly enough to put the fear of Marx into the Truman administration.

For the 1948 election, the PCI and PSI united to form the Popular Democratic Front (FDP) and in February won municipal elections in Pescara with a 10% increase in their vote over 1946. The Christian Democrats ran a poor second. The prospect of the left winning control of the Italian government loomed larger than ever before. It was at this point that the US began to train its big economic and political guns upon the Italian people. All the good ol' Yankee know-how, all the Madison Avenue savvy in the art of swaying public opinion, all the Hollywood razzmatazz would be brought to bear on the "target market".

Pressing domestic needs in Italy, such as agricultural and economic reform, the absence of which produced abysmal extremes of wealth and poverty, were not to be the issues of the day. The lines of battle would be drawn around the question of "democracy" *vs.* "communism" (the idea of "capitalism" remaining discreetly to one side). The fact that the Communists had been the single most active anti-fascist group in Italy during the war, undergoing ruthless persecution, while the Christian Democrat government of 1948 and other electoral opponents on the right were riddled through with collaborators, monarchists and plain unreconstructed fascists . . . this too would be ignored; indeed, turned around. It was now a matter of Communist "dictatorship" *vs.* their adversaries' love of "freedom"; this was presumed *a priori.* As one example, a group of American congressmen visited Italy in summer 1947 and concluded that "The country is under great pressure from within and without to veer to the left and adopt a totalitarian-collective national organization".[2]

To make any of this at all credible, the whole picture had to be pushed and squeezed into the frame of The American Way of Life *vs.* The Soviet Way of Life, a specious proposition which must have come as somewhat of a shock to leftists who regarded themselves as Italian and neither Russian nor American.

In February, after non-Communist ministers in Czechoslovakia had boycotted cabinet meetings over a dispute concerning police hiring practices, the Communist government dissolved the coalition cabinet and took sole power. The Voice of America pointed to this event repeatedly, as a warning to the Italian people of the fate awaiting them if Italy "went Communist". Yet, by all appearances, the Italian Christian Democrat government and the American government had conspired the previous year in an even more blatant usurpation of power.

In January 1947, when Italian Premier Alcide de Gasperi visited Washington at the United States' invitation, his overriding concern was to plead for crucial financial assistance for his war-torn, impoverished country. American officials may have had a different priority. Three days after returning to Italy, de Gasperi unexpectedly dissolved his cabinet which included several Communists and socialists. The press reported that many people in Italy believed that de Gasperi's action was related to his visit to the United States and was aimed at decreasing leftist, principally Communist influence in the government. After two weeks of tortuous delay, the formation of a centre or centre-right government sought by de Gasperi proved infeasible; the new cabinet still included Communists and socialists although the left had lost key positions, notably the ministries of foreign affairs and finance.

From this point until May, when de Gasperi's Deputy, Ivan Lombardo, led a mission to Washington to renew the request for aid, promised loans were "frozen" by the United States for reasons not very clear. On several occasions during this period the Italian left asserted their belief that the aid was being held up pending the ouster of leftists from the cabinet. The *New York Times*, not going quite as far, noted that, "Some observers here feel that a further Leftward swing in Italy would retard aid." As matters turned out, the day Lombardo arrived in Washington, de Gasperi again dissolved his entire cabinet and suggested that the new cabinet would manage without the benefit of leftist members. This was, indeed, what occurred, and over the ensuing few months, exceedingly generous American financial aid flowed into Italy, in addition to the cancellation of the nation's $1 billion debt to the United States.*[3]

As the last month of the 1948 election campaign began, *Time* magazine pronounced the possible leftist victory to be "the brink of catastrophe".[4]

"It was primarily this fear," William Colby, former Director of the CIA, has written, "that had led to the formation of the Office of Policy Coordination, which gave the CIA the capability to undertake covert political, propaganda, and paramilitary operations in the first place."[5]

But covert operations, as far as is known, played a distinctly minor role. It was the very overtness of the American campaign, without any apparent embarrassment, that stamps the whole endeavour with such uniqueness and arrogance — one might say swagger. The fortunes of the FDP slid downhill with surprising acceleration during the final month in the face of an awesome mobilization of resources such as the following:[6]

● A massive letter writing campaign from Americans of Italian extraction to their relatives and friends in Italy — at first written by individuals in their own words or guided by "sample letters" in newspapers — soon expanded to mass-produced, pre-written, postage-paid form letters, cablegrams, "educational circulars", and posters, needing only an address and signature. And — from a group calling itself The Committee to Aid Democracy in Italy — half a million picture postcards illustrating the gruesome fate awaiting Italy if it voted for "dictatorship" or "foreign dictatorship". In all, an estimated 10 million pieces of mail were written and distributed by newspapers, radio stations, churches, the American Legion, wealthy individuals, etc.; and business advertisements now included offers to send letters airmail to Italy even if you didn't buy the product.

All this with the publicly expressed approval of the Acting Secretary of State and the Post Office which inaugurated special "Freedom Flights" to give greater publicity to the dispatch of the mail to Italy.

The form letters contained messages such as: "A communist victory would ruin Italy. The United States would withdraw aid and a world war would probably result." . . . "We implore you not to throw our beautiful Italy into the arms of that cruel despot communism. America hasn't anything against communism in Russia [sic], but why impose it on other people, other lands, in that way putting out the torch of liberty?" . . . "If the forces of true democracy should lose in the Italian election, the American Government will not send any more money to Italy and we won't send any more money to you, our relatives."

---

* At the very same time, France, which was also heavily dependent upon American financial aid, ousted all its Communist ministers as well. In this case there was an immediate rationale: the refusal of the Communist ministers to support Premier Ramadier in a vote of confidence over a wage freeze. Even so, the ouster was regarded as a "surprise" and considered "bold" in France, and opinion was widespread that American loans were being used, or would be used, to force France to align with the US. Said Ramadier: "A little of our independence is departing from us with each loan we obtain."

These were by no means the least sophisticated. Other themes emphasized were Russian domination of Italy, loss of religion and the church, loss of family life, loss of home and land.

Veteran newsman Howard K. Smith pointed out at the time that "For an Italian peasant a telegram from anywhere is a wondrous thing; and a cable from the terrestial paradise of America is not lightly to be disregarded."

The letters threatening to cut off gifts may have been equally intimidating. "Such letters," wrote a Christian Democrat official in an Italian newspaper, "struck home in southern Italian and Sicilian villages with the force of lightning." A 1949 poll indicated that 16 percent of Italians claimed relatives in the United States with whom they were in touch; this, apparently, was in addition to friends there.

● The State Department backed up the warnings in the letters by announcing that "If the Communists should win . . . there would be no further question of assistance from the United States." The Italian left felt compelled to regularly assure voters that this would not really happen; this, in turn, inspired American officials, including Secretary of State George Marshall, to repeat the threat. (For the aid programme which bore his name, the Marshall Plan, he received the Nobel Peace Prize in 1953.)

● A daily series of direct short-wave broadcasts to Italy backed by the State Department and featuring prominent Americans. (The State Department estimated that there were 1.2 million short-wave receivers in Italy as of 1946.) The Attorney General assured the Italian people that the election was a "choice between democracy and communism, between God and godlessness, between order and chaos." William Donovan, the wartime head of the OSS (forerunner of the CIA) warned that "under a communist dictatorship in Italy," many of the "nation's industrial plants would be dismantled and shipped to Russia and millions of Italy's workers would be deported to Russia for forced labor." If this were not enough to impress the Italian listeners, a parade of unknown but passionate refugees from Eastern Europe went before the microphone to recount horror stories of life behind "The Iron Curtain".

● Several commercial radio stations broadcast to Italy special services held in American Catholic churches to pray for the Pope in "this, his most critical hour". On one station, during an entire week, hundreds of Italian-Americans from all walks of life delivered one-minute messages to Italy which were relayed through the short-wave station. Station WOV in New York invited Italian war brides to transcribe a personal message to their families back home. The station then mailed the recordings to Italy.

● Voice of America daily broadcasts into Italy were sharply increased, highlighting, of course, news of American assistance or gestures of friendship to Italy. A sky-full of show biz stars, including Frank Sinatra and Gary Cooper, recorded a series of radio programmes designed to win friends and influence the vote in Italy. Five broadcasts of Italian-American housewives were aired, and Italian-Americans with some leftist credentials were also enlisted for the cause.

Labour leader Luigi Antonini called upon Italians to "smash the Muscovite fifth column" which "follows the orders of the ferocious Moscow tyranny," or else Italy would become an "enemy totalitarian country".

To counter Communist charges in Italy that negroes in the United States were denied opportunities, the VOA broadcast the story of a negro couple who had made a fortune in the junk business and built a hospital for their people in Oklahoma City. (It should be remembered that in 1948 American negroes had not yet reached the status of second-class citizens.)

●   Italian radio stations carried a one-hour show from Hollywood put on to raise money for the orphans of Italian pilots who died in the war. (It was not reported if the same was done for the orphans of German pilots.)

●   American officials in Italy widely distributed leaflets extolling US economic aid and staged exhibitions among low-income groups. The US Information Service presented an exhibition on "The Worker in America" and made extensive use of documentary and feature films to sell the American way of life. It was estimated that in the period immediately preceding the election more than five million Italians each week saw American documentaries. The 1939 Hollywood film "Ninotchka", which satirized life in Russia, was singled out as a particularly effective feature film. It was shown throughout working-class areas and the Communists made several determined efforts to prevent its presentation. After the election, a pro-Communist worker was reported as saying that "What licked us was 'Ninotchka'."

●   The Justice Department served notice that Italians who joined the Communist Party would be denied that dream of so many Italians, emigration to America. The State Department then ruled that any Italians known to have *voted* for the Communists would not be allowed to even *enter* the terrestial paradise. (A Department telegram to a New York politico read: "Voting Communist appears to constitute affiliation with Communist Party within meaning of Immigration Law and therefore would require exclusion from United States.") It was urged that this information be emphasized in letters to Italy.

●   President Truman accused the Soviet Union of plotting the subjugation of Western Europe and called for universal military training in the United States and a resumption of military conscription to forestall "threatened communist control and police-state rule". During the campaign, American and British warships were frequently found anchored off Italian ports. *Time*, in an edition widely displayed and commented upon in Italy shortly before the election, gave its approval to the sentiment that "The U.S. should make it clear that it will use force, if necessary, to prevent Italy from going Communist."[7]

●   The United States and Italy signed a ten-year treaty of "friendship, commerce and navigation". This was the first treaty of its kind entered into by the US since the war, a point emphasized for Italian consumption.

●   A "Friendship Train" toured the United States gathering gifts and then travelled round Italy distributing them. The train was, naturally, painted red, white and blue, and bore large signs expressing the friendship of American citizens toward the people of Italy.

●   The United States Government stated that it favoured Italian trusteeship over some of its former African colonies, such as Ethiopia and Libya, a wholly unrealistic proposal that could never come to pass in the post-war world. (The Soviet Union made a similar proposal.)

●   The US, Great Britain and France manoeuvred the Soviet Union into vetoing, for the third time, a motion that Italy be admitted to the United Nations. (The first time, the Russians expressed their opposition on the grounds that a peace treaty with Italy had not been signed. After the signing in 1947, they said they would accept the proposal if other World War II enemies, such as Bulgaria, Hungary and Rumania were also made members.)

●   The same three allied nations proposed to the Soviet Union that negotiations take place with a view to returning Trieste to Italy. Formerly the principal Italian port on the Adriatic coast, bordering Yugoslavia, Trieste had been made a "free city" under the terms of the peace treaty. The approval of the Soviet Union was necessary to alter the treaty, and the Western proposal was designed to put the Russians on the spot. The Italian people had an intense sentimental attachment to Trieste, and if the Russians rejected the proposal it could seriously embarrass the Italian Communists. A Soviet acceptance, however, would antagonize their Yugoslav allies. The US prodded the Russians for a response, but none was forthcoming. From the Soviet point of view, the most obvious and safest path to follow would have been to delay their answer until after the election. Yet they chose to announce their rejection of the proposal only five days before the vote, thus hammering another nail into the FDP coffin.

●   A "Manifesto of peace to freedom-loving Italians", calling upon them to reject Communism, was sent to Premier de Gasperi. Its signatories included two former US Secretaries of State, a former Assistant Secretary of State, a former Attorney-General, a former Supreme Court Justice, a former Governor of New York, the former first lady Eleanor Roosevelt, and many other prominent personages. This message was, presumably, suitably publicized throughout Italy, a task easy in the extreme inasmuch as an estimated 82 percent of Italian newspapers were in the hands of those unsympathetic to the leftist bloc.

●   More than 200 American labour leaders of Italian origin held a conference, out of which came a cable sent to 23 daily newspapers throughout Italy similarly urging thumbs down on the Reds. At the same time, the Italian-American Labor Council contributed $50,000 to anti-Communist labour organizations in Italy. The CIA was already secretly subsidizing such trade unions to counteract the influence of leftist unions,[8] but this was, and is, standard Agency practice independent of electoral considerations. (According to a former CIA officer, when, in 1945, the Communists came very near to gaining control of labour unions, first in Sicily, then in all Italy and southern France, co-operation between the OSS and the Mafia successfully stemmed the tide.)[9]

● The CIA, by its own later admission, gave $1 million to Italian "center parties", a king's ransom in Italy 1948.[10]

● An American group featuring noted Italian-American musicians travelled to Rome to present a series of concerts.

● President Truman chose a month before the election as the time to transfer 29 merchant ships to the Italian Government as a "gesture of friendship and confidence in a democratic Italy". (These were Italian vessels seized during the war and others to replace those seized and lost.)

● Four days later, the House Appropriations Committee acted swiftly to approve $18.7 million in additional "interim aid" funds for Italy.

● Two weeks later, the United States gave Italy $4.3 million as the first payment on wages due to 60,000 former Italian war prisoners in the US who had worked "voluntarily" for the Allied cause. This was a revision of the peace treaty which stipulated that the Italian Government was liable for such payments.

● Six days before election day, the State Department made it public that Italy would soon receive $31 million in gold in return for gold looted by the Nazis. (The fact that only a few years earlier Italy had been the "enemy" fighting alongside the Nazis was now but a dim memory.)

● Two days later, the US Government authorized two further large shipments of food to Italy, one for $8 million worth of grains. A number of the aid ships, upon their arrival in Italy during the election campaign, had been unloaded amid ceremony and a speech by the American Ambassador.
A poster prominent in Italy read: "The bread that we eat — 40 per cent Italian flour — 60 per cent American flour sent free of charge." The poster neglected to mention whether the savings were passed on to the consumer or served to line the pockets of the baking companies.

● The American Ambassador, James Clement Dunn, travelled constantly throughout Italy pointing out to the population "on every possible occasion what American aid has meant to them and their country". At the last unloading of food, Dunn declared that the American people were saving Italy from starvation, chaos and possible domination from outside. His speeches usually received wide coverage in the non-left press. By contrast, the Italian Government prohibited several of its own ambassadors abroad from returning home to campaign for the FDP.

● April 15 was designated "Free Italy Day" by the American Sympathizers for a Free Italy with nation-wide observances to be held.

● The American Commission for the Restoration of Italian Monuments, Inc. announced, four days before election day, an additional series of grants to the Italian Ministry of Fine Arts.

In his historic speech of 12 March 1947, which came to be known as "The Truman Doctrine", the president had proclaimed:

I believe it must be the policy of the United States to support free peoples who are resisting attempted subjugation by armed minorities or by outside pressures. I believe that we must assist free peoples to work out their own destinies in their own way.[11]

It scarcely needs to be emphasized how hollow this promise proved to be. But the voices which spoke out in the United States against their government's crusade were few and barely audible above the roar. The Italian-American Committee for Free Elections in Italy held a rally to denounce the propaganda blitz, declaring that "Thousands of Americans of Italian origin feel deeply humiliated by the continuous flow of suggestions, advice and pressure put on the Italians, as though they were unable to decide for themselves whom to elect."[12]

The Progressive Party also went on record, stating: "As Americans we repudiate our Government's threat to cut off food from Italy unless the election results please us. Hungry children must not go unfed because their parents do not vote as ordered from abroad."[13] The party's candidate for president in 1948 was Henry Wallace, the former Vice-President who was an outspoken advocate of genuine detente with the Soviet Union. History did not provide the opportunity to observe what the reaction would have been — amongst those who saw nothing wrong with what the United States was doing in Italy — if a similar campaign had been launched by the Soviet Union in the United States on behalf of Wallace.

Though some Italians must have been convinced at times that Stalin himself was a candidate for the presidency, the actual Soviet intervention in the election hardly merited a single headline. The American press engaged in speculation that the Russians were pouring substantial sums of money into the Communist Party's coffers. However, a survey carried out by the Italian bureau of the United Press revealed that the anti-Communist parties spent 7½ times as much as the FDP on all forms of propaganda, the Christian Democrats alone spending four times as much.[14] As for other Soviet actions, Howard K. Smith's observation is to the point:

> The Russians tried to respond with a few feeble gestures for a while — some Italian war prisoners were released; some newsprint was sent to Italy and offered to all parties for their campaign. But there was no way of resisting what amounted to a tidal wave.
>
> There is evidence that the Russians found the show getting too rough for them and actually became apprehensive of what the American and British reaction to a Communist victory at the polls might be. (Russia's concern about conflict with the West was also expressed within a month of the Italian elections in one of the celebrated Cominform letters to Tito, accusing the Yugoslavs of trying to involve the Soviets with the Western powers when 'it should have been known . . . that the U.S.S.R. after such a heavy war could not start a new one'.)[15]

The evidence Smith was alluding to was the Soviet rejection of the Trieste proposal. By its timing, reported the *New York Times*, "the unexpected procedure caused some observers to conclude that the Russians had thrown the Italian Communist Party overboard."[16] The party's newspaper had a difficult time dealing with the story. Washington did as well, for it undermined the fundamental premise of the Italian campaign: that the Italian Communist Party and the Soviet Union were indistinguishable as to ends and means; that if you buy the one, you get the other as well. Thus the suggestion was put forth that perhaps the Soviet rejection was only a tactic to demonstrate that the US could not keep its promise on Trieste. But the Soviet announcement had not been accompanied by any such propaganda message, and it would not explain why the Russians had waited several weeks until near the crucial end to deliver its body blow to their Italian comrades. In any event, the United States could only come out smelling a lot sweeter than the Russians.

When the Broadway show had ended its engagement in Italy, the Christian Democrats stood as the clear winner with 48 percent of the vote. The leftist coalition had been humiliated with a totally unexpected polling of but 31 percent. It had been a crusade of the kind which Aneurin Bevan had ascribed to the Tories: "The whole art of Conservative politics in the 20th century," the British Labour leader wrote, "is being deployed to enable wealth to persuade poverty to use its political freedom to keep wealth in power."

3. Greece 1947 to Early 1950s
From cradle of democracy to client state

Jorge Semprun is a Spaniard, a Frenchman, a novelist and film-writer, former Communist, former inmate of Buchenwald. He was at the infamous Nazi concentration camp in 1944 with other party members when they heard the news:

> For some days now, we had talked of nothing else . . . At first some of us had thought it was a lie. It had to be. An invention of Nazi propaganda, to raise the morale of the people. We listened to the news bulletins on the German radio, broadcast by all the loudspeakers, and we shook our heads. A trick to raise the morale of the German people, it had to be. But we soon had to face up to the evidence. Some of us listened in secret to the Allied broadcasts, which confirmed the news. There was no doubt about it: British troops really were crushing the Greek Resistance. In Athens, battle was raging, British troops were retaking the city from the ELAS forces, district by district. It was an unequal fight: ELAS had neither tanks nor planes.
>
> But Radio Moscow had said nothing, and this silence was variously interpreted.[1]

The British army had arrived in Greece in October 1944 shortly after the bulk of the Germans had fled, an evacuation due in no small part to ELAS, the People's Liberation Army. Founded during the course of 1941-42 on the initiative of the Greek Communist Party, ELAS and its political wing EAM, cut across the entire left side of the political spectrum, numbering many priests and even a few bishops amongst its followers. The guerrillas had wrested large areas of the country from the Nazi invaders who had routed the British in 1941.

ELAS/EAM partisans could be ruthless and coercive toward those Greeks who did not co-operate with them or who were suspected of collaboration with the Germans. But they also provided another dramatic example of the liberating effects of a world war: the encrusted ways of the Greek old guard were cast aside; in their place arose communities which had at least the semblance of being run by the local residents, inchoate institutions and mechanisms which might have been the precursor of a regenerated Greek society after the war; education, perhaps geared toward propaganda, but for the illiterate education nonetheless; fighting battalions of women, housewives called upon for the first time to act independently of their husbands' control . . . a phenomenon which spread irrepressibly until EAM came to number some one to two million Greeks out of a population of seven million.[2]

This was hardly the kind of social order designed to calm the ulcers of the British old guard (Winston Churchill for one) who had long regarded Greece as their private manor. The Great Man was determined that the Greek king should be restored to his rightful place, with all that that implied, and the British military in Greece lost no time in installing a government dedicated to that end. Monarchists, quislings, and conservatives of all stripes found themselves in positions of political power, predominant in the new Greek army and police; members of EAM/ELAS found themselves dead or in prison.[3]

Fighting broke out in December 1944 between ELAS and the British forces and their Greek comrades-in-arms, many of whom had fought against ELAS during the war and, in the process, collaborated with the Germans; others had simply served with the Germans. (The British Foreign Secretary, Ernest Bevin, acknowledged in August 1946 that there were 228 ex-members of the Nazi Security Battalions, whose main task had been to track down Greek resistance fighters, on active service in the new Greek army.)[4] Further support for the campaign against ELAS came from the US Air Force and Navy which transported more than two British divisions into Greece.[5] All this while the war against Germany still raged in Europe.

In mid-January 1945 ELAS agreed to an armistice, one that had much of the appearance and the effect of a surrender. There is disagreement amongst historians as to whether ELAS had been militarily defeated or whether the Communists in the ELAS and EAM hierarchy had received the word from Stalin to lay down the gun. If the latter were the case, it would have been consistent with the famous agreement between Stalin and Churchill, in October 1944, whereby spheres of influence in Eastern Europe were allocated between the two powers. In this cynical (as Churchill acknowledged) Monopoly game Britain had landed on Greece.[6] Churchill later wrote that Stalin had "adhered strictly and faithfully to our agreement of October, and during all the long weeks of fighting the Communists in the streets of Athens not one word of reproach came from *Pravda* or *Izvestia*".[7]

"It is essential to remember," Professor D.F. Fleming has pointed out in his eminent history of the cold war, "that Greece was the first of the liberated states to be openly and forcibly compelled to accept the political system of the occupying Great Power. It was Churchill who acted first and Stalin who followed his example, in Bulgaria and then in Rumania, though with less bloodshed."[8]

A succession of Greek governments followed, serving by the grace of the British and the United States; thoroughly corrupt governments in the modern Greek tradition, which continued to terrorize the left, tortured them in notorious island prison camps, and did next to nothing to relieve the daily misery of the war-torn Greek people.[9] "There are few modern parallels for government as bad as this," CBS's chief European correspondent Howard K. Smith observed at the time.[10]

In the fall of 1946 the inevitable occurred: leftists took to the hills to launch phase two of the civil war. The Communists had wrenched Stalin's strangulating hand from their throats, for their very survival was at stake and everything that they believed in.

The British were weighed down by their own post-war reconstruction needs, and in February 1947 they informed the United States that they could no longer shoulder the burden of maintaining a large armed force in Greece nor provide sizeable military and economic aid to the country. Thus it was that the historic task of preserving all that is decent and good in Western Civilization passed into the hands of the United States.

Several days later, the State Department summoned the Greek chargé d'affaires in Washington and informed him that his government was to ask the US for aid. This was to be effected by means of a formal letter of request, a document, it turned out, to be written essentially by the State Department. The text of the letter, the chargé d'affaires later reported, "had been drafted with a view to the mentality of Congress . . . It would also serve to protect the U.S. Government against internal and external charges that it was taking the initiative of intervening in a foreign state or that it had been persuaded by the British to take over a bad legacy from them. The note would also serve as a basis for the cultivation of public opinion which was under study."[11]

In July, in a letter to Dwight Griswold, the head of the American Mission to Aid Greece (AMAG), Secretary of State George Marshall said:

It is possible that during your stay in Greece you and the Ambassador will come to the conclusion that the effectiveness of your Mission would be enhanced if a reorganization of the Greek Government could be effected. If such a conclusion is reached, it is hoped that you and the Ambassador will be able to bring about such a reorganization indirectly through discreet suggestion and otherwise in such a manner that even the Greek political leaders will have a feeling that the reorganization has been effected largely by themselves and not by pressure from without.[12]

The Secretary spelled out a further guideline for Griswold, a man the *New York Times* shortly afterwards called the "most powerful man in Greece":[13]

> During the course of your work you and the members of your Mission will from time to time find that certain Greek officials are not, because of incompetence, disagreement with your policies, or for some other reason, extending the type of cooperation which is necessary if the objectives of your Mission are to be achieved. You will find it necessary to effect the removal of these officials.[14]

These contrivances, however, were not the most cynical aspects of the American endeavour. Washington officials well knew that their new client government was so venal and so abusive of human rights that even confirmed American anti-communists were appalled. Stewart Alsop for one. On 23 February 1947 the noted journalist had cabled from Athens that most of the Greek politicians had "no higher ambition than to taste the profitable delights of a free economy at American expense".[15] The same year, an American investigating team found huge supplies of food aid rotting in warehouses at a time when an estimated 75% of Greek children were suffering from malnutrition.[16]

So difficult was it to gloss over this picture, that President Truman, in his address to Congress in March 1947 asking for aid to Greece based on the Greek "request" (the "Truman Doctrine" speech), attempted to pre-empt criticism by admitting that the Greek Government was "not perfect" and that "it has made mistakes". Yet, somehow, by some ideological alchemy best known to the President, the regime in Athens was "democratic", its opponents the familiar "terrorists".[17]

There was no mention of the Soviet Union in this particular speech, but that was to be the relentless refrain of the American rationale over the next 2½ years: the Russians were instigating the Greek leftists so as to kidnap yet another "free" country and drag it kicking and screaming behind the Iron Curtain.

The neighbouring Communist states of Bulgaria, Albania, and particularly Yugoslavia, in part motivated by old territorial claims against Greece, did aid the insurgents by allowing them important sanctuary behind their borders and furnishing them with military supplies (whether substantial or merely token in amount depends on whom you read). The USSR, however, in the person of Joseph Stalin, was adamantly opposed to assisting the Greek "comrades". At a meeting with Yugoslav leaders in early 1948 (a few months before Yugoslavia's break with the Soviet Union), described by Milovan Djilas, second-in-command to Tito, Stalin turned to the foreign minister Edvard Kardelj and asked: "Do you believe in the success of the uprising in Greece?"

> Kardelj replied, 'If foreign intervention does not grow, and if serious political and military errors are not made.'
> Stalin went on, without paying attention to Kardelj's opinion: 'If, if! No, they have no prospect of success at all. What, do you think that Great Britain and the United States — the United States, the most powerful state in the world — will permit you to break their line of communication in the Mediterranean?

Nonsense. And we have no navy. The uprising in Greece must be stopped, and as quickly as possible.'[18]

The first major shiploads of military assistance under the new American operation arrived in the summer of 1947. (Significant quantities had also been shipped to the Greek Government while the British ran the show.) By the end of the year the Greek military was entirely supported by American aid, down to and including its clothing and food. The nation's war-making potential was transformed: continual increases in the size of the Greek armed forces . . . fighter-bombers, transport squadrons, air fields, newly-invented napalm bombs, recoilless rifles, naval patrol vessels, communication networks . . . docks, railways, roads, bridges . . . hundreds of millions of dollars of supplies and equipment, approaching a billion in total since the end of the world war . . . [19]

The US Military Mission took over the development of battle plans for the army from the ineffective Greek generals. The Mission, related British military writer Major Edgar O'Ballance, "took a tough line and insisted that all its recommendations be carried into effect, at once and in full".[20] Eventually, more than 250 American army officers were in the country, many assigned to Greek army divisions to ensure compliance with directives; others operated at the brigade level; another 200 or so US Air Force and Navy personnel were also on active duty in Greece.

All military training methods and programmes were "revised, revitalized and tightened up" under American supervision[21] . . . infantry units made more mobile, with increased firepower; special commando units trained in anti-guerrilla tactics; training in mountain warfare, augmented by some 4,000 mules (sic) shipped to Greece by the United States . . . at American insistence, whole sections of the population uprooted to eliminate the guerrillas' natural base of operation and source of recruits . . .

"Both on the ground and in the air, American support was becoming increasingly active," observed C.M. Woodhouse, the British colonel who served in Greece during the mid-1940s, "and the theoretical line between advice, intelligence and combat was a narrow one."[22]

The Greek leftists held out for three terrible years. Despite losses of many tens of thousands, they were always able to replenish their forces, even increase their number. But by October 1949, foreseeing nothing but more loss of lives to a vastly superior destruction-machine, the guerrillas announced over their radio a "cease fire". It was the end of the civil war.

The extent of American hegemony over Greece from 1947 onwards can scarcely be exaggerated. We have seen Marshall's directives to Griswold, and the American management of the military campaign. There were many other manifestations of the same phenomenon, of which the following are a sample:

In August/September 1947, Prime Minister Tsaldaris agreed to enter a broad coalition and hand over the premiership to someone else. In doing so, said the

New York Times, Tsaldaris had "surrendered to the desires of Dwight P. Griswold . . . of [U.S.] Ambassador MacVeagh, and also of the King".[23] Before Tsaldaris addressed the Greek legislature on the matter, MacVeagh stepped in to make changes to the speech.[24]

Over the next several years, each of the frequent changes of prime minister came about only after considerable American input, if not outright demand.[25] One example of the latter occurred in 1950 when the then American Ambassador Henry Grady sent a letter to Prime Minister Venizelos threatening to cut off US aid if he failed to carry out a government reorganization. Venizelos was compelled to step down.[26]

The American influence was felt in regard to other high positions in Greek society as well. Andreas Papandreou, later to become prime minister himself, has written of this period that "Cabinet members and army generals, political party leaders and members of the Establishment, all made open references to American wishes or views in order to justify or to account for their own actions or positions."[27]

Before undertaking a new crackdown on dissidents in July 1947, Greek authorities first approached Ambassador MacVeagh. The Ambassador informed them that the US government would have no objection to "preventive measures if they were considered necessary". Reassured, the Greeks went ahead and rounded up 4,000 people in one week.[28]

An example of what could land a Greek citizen in prison is the case of the EAM member who received an 18-month sentence for printing remarks deemed insulting to Dwight Griswold. He had referred to the American as "the official representative of a foreign country".[29]

"In the economic sphere," Andreas Papandreou noted, the United States "exercised almost dictatorial control during the early fifties requiring that the signature of the chief of the U.S. Economic Mission appear alongside that of the Greek Minister of Co-ordination on any important documents."[30]

Earlier, American management of the economy may have been even tighter. A memorandum from Athens dated 17 November 1947, from the American Mission to Aid Greece to the State Department in Washington, read in part: "we have established practical control . . . over national budget, taxation, currency issuance, price and wage policies, and state economic planning, as well as over imports and exports, the issuance of foreign exchange and the direction of military reconstruction and relief expenditures . . ."[31]

And then there was the creation of a new internal security agency, named and modelled after the CIA (KYP in Greek). Before long, KYP was carrying out all the endearing practices of secret police everywhere, including systematic torture.

By the early 1950s, Greece had been moulded into a supremely reliable ally-client of the United States. It was staunchly anti-Communist and well integrated into the NATO system. It sent troops to Korea to support the United States' pretence that it was not simply an American war.

It is safe to say that had the left come to power, Greece would have been much more independent of the United States. Greece would likely have been independent as well of the Soviet Union, to whom the Greek left owed nothing. Like Yugoslavia, which is also free of a common border with the USSR, Greece would have been friendly towards the Russians, but independent.

When, in 1964, there came to power in Greece a government which entertained the novel idea that Greece was a sovereign nation, the United States and its Greek cohorts, as we shall see, quickly and effectively stamped out the heresy.

4. The Philippines 1940s and 1950s
America's oldest colony

I walked the floor of the White House night after night until midnight; and I am not ashamed to tell you, gentlemen, that I went down on my knees and prayed [to] Almighty God for light and guidance more than one night. And one night it came to me this way — I don't know how it was, but it came: (1) That we could not give them [the Philippine Islands] back to Spain — that would be cowardly and dishonorable; (2) that we could not turn them over to France or Germany — our commercial rivals in the Orient — that would be bad business and discreditable; (3) that we could not leave them to themselves — they were unfit for self-government — and they would soon have anarchy and misrule over there worse than Spain's was; and (4) that there was nothing left for us to do but to take them all, and to educate the Filipinos, and uplift and civilize and Christianize them, and by God's grace do the very best we could by them, as our fellow-men for whom Christ also died.
William McKinley, President of the United States, 1899[1]

William McKinley's idea of doing the very best by the Filipinos was to employ the United States Army to kill them in the tens of thousands, subject them to torture, burn down their villages, and lay the foundation for an economic exploitation which was proudly referred to at the time as "imperialism" by leading American statesmen and newspapers. After the Spanish had been driven out of the Philippines in 1898 by a combined action of the US and the Filipinos, Spain agreed to "cede" (that is, sell) the islands to the United States for $20 million. But the Filipinos, who had already proclaimed their own independent republic, did not take kindly to being treated like a plot of uninhabited real estate. Accordingly, an American force, numbering at least 50,000, proceeded to instill in the population a proper appreciation of their status.

Thus did America's longest-lasting and most conspicuous colony ever come into being.

Nearly half a century later, the US Army again landed in the Philippines to find a nationalist movement fighting against a common enemy, this time the Japanese. While combatting the Japanese, the American military took many measures aimed at quashing this resistance army, the Huk (a shortening of the Tagalog for "People's Army Against Japan"). Guerrilla forces organized and led by American officers and composed of US and Filipino soldiers (a section of the US Army Forces in the Far East) attacked the Huks, spread disparaging rumours about them to erode their support amongst the peasants, and allowed the Japanese to assault them unmolested. This, while the Huks were engaged in a major effort against the Japanese invaders and Philippine collaborators and frequently came to the aid of American soldiers.

In the closing days of the Second World War, American and Philippine officials arrested leaders of the Huks and the Philippine Communist Party — reportedly on the orders of General MacArthur — forcibly disarmed many Huk soldiers, and removed their followers from local governments which they had set up in areas of Huk popular support.[2] In much of this anti-Huk campaign, the United States made use of Filipinos who were collaborating with the Japanese, such as landlords, large estate owners, many police constables, and other officials. In the post-war period, the US restored to power and position many of those tainted with collaboration, much to the distaste of other Filipinos.[3]

The Huk guerrilla forces had been organized in 1942, largely at the initiative of the Communist Party, in response to the Japanese occupation of the islands. Amongst American policy makers, there were those who came to the routine conclusion that the Huks were thus no more than a tool of the International Communist Conspiracy, to be opposed as all such groups were to be opposed. Others in Washington and Manila, whose reflexes were less knee-jerk, but more cynical, recognized that the Huk movement, if its growing influence was not checked, would lead to sweeping reforms of Philippine society.

The centre-piece of the Huk political programme was land reform, a crying need in this largely agricultural society. (On occasion, US officials would pay lip-service to the concept, but during 50 years of American occupation, nothing had been carried out.) The other side of the Huk coin was industrialization, which the United States had successfully thwarted for so long to provide American industries with a veritable playground in the Philippines. From the Huks' point of view, such changes were but prologue to raising the islanders from their state of backwardness, from illiteracy, grinding poverty, and the diseases of poverty like tuberculosis and beri-beri.[4] "The Communist Hukbalahap rebellion," reported the *New York Times*, "is generally regarded as an outgrowth of the misery and discontent among the peasants of Central Luzon [the main island]."[5] Unmistakably, the Huk movement was a threat to the neo-colonial condition of the Philippines, the American sphere of influence, and those Philippine interests which benefited from the status quo.

The gun-smoke of the war had scarcely cleared when the United States began training and equipping the first force of 50,000 Filipino soldiers.[6] In testimony before a congressional committee, Major General William Arnold of the US Army candidly stated that this programme was "essential for the maintenance of internal order, not for external difficulties at all".[7] None of the congressmen present publicly expressed any reservation about the international propriety of such a foreign policy.

At the same time, American soldiers were kept on in the Philippines, and in at least one infantry division combat training was re-established. This led to vociferous protests and demonstrations by the GI's who wanted only to go home. *Their* war, after all, was over. The inauguration of combat training, the *New York Times* disclosed, was "interpreted by soldiers and certain Filipino newspapers as the preparation for the repression of possible uprisings in the Philippines by disgruntled farm tenant groups . . . The soldiers had a lot to say on the subject of American armed intervention in China and the Netherlands Indies" which was occurring at the time.[8] To what extent American military personnel participated directly in the suppression of dissident groups in the Philippines after the war is unrecorded history.

The Huks, though not trusting Philippine and US authorities enough to voluntarily surrender their arms, did test the good faith of the government by taking part in the April 1946 national elections as part of a "Democratic Alliance" of liberal and socialist peasant political groups. (Philippine Independence was scheduled for three months later — the Fourth of July to be exact.) As matters turned out, the commander-in-chief of the Huks, Luis Taruc, and several other Alliance members and reform-minded candidates who won election to Congress (three to the Senate and seven to the House) were not allowed to take their seats under the transparent fiction that coercion had been used to influence voters; no investigation or review of the cases had even been carried out by the appropriate body, the Electoral Tribunal.[9] (Two years later, Taruc was temporarily allowed to take his seat when he came to Manila to discuss a ceasefire with the government.)

The purpose of denying these men was equally transparent: the less-than-autonomous government was then able to push through Congress the controversial Philippine-US Trade Act — passed by two votes more than required in the House, and by nothing to spare in the Senate — which yielded to the United States bountiful privileges and concessions in the Philippine economy, including "equal rights . . . in the development of the nation's natural resources and the operation of its public utilities".[10] This "parity" provision was eventually extended to every sector of the Philippine economy.[11]

The debasement of the electoral process was followed by a wave of heavy brutality against the peasants carried out by the military, the police, and landlord goon squads. According to Luis Taruc, in the months following the election, peasant villages were destroyed, more than 500 peasants and their leaders killed, and about three times that number jailed, tortured, maimed or missing. The Huks and others felt they had little alternative but to take up arms once again, if only in self-defence.[12]

Certainly, independence was not going to change much of significance. American historian George E. Taylor, of impeccable establishment credentials, in a book which bears the indication of CIA sponsorship, was yet moved to state that independence "was marked by lavish expressions of mutual good will, by partly fulfilled promises, and by a restoration of the old relationship in almost everything except in name . . . Many demands were made of the Filipinos for the commercial advantage of the United States, but none for the social and political advantage of the Philippines."[13]

The American military was meanwhile assuring a home for itself in the Philippines. A 1947 agreement provided sites for 23 US military bases in the country. The agreement was to last for 99 years. It stipulated that American servicemen who committed crimes outside the bases while on duty could be tried only by American military tribunals inside the bases.

By the terms of a companion military assistance pact, the Philippine government was prohibited from purchasing so much as a bullet from any arms source other than the US, except with American approval. Such a state of affairs, necessarily involving training, maintenance and spare parts, made the Philippine military extremely dependent upon their American counterparts. Further, no foreigners other than Americans were permitted to perform any function for or with the Philippine armed forces without the approval of the United States.[14]

By early 1950, the United States had provided the Philippines with over $200 million of military equipment and supplies, a remarkable sum for that time, and was in addition to the construction of various military facilities.[15] The Joint US Military Advisory Group (JUSMAG) reorganized the Philippine defence department, put its chosen man, Ramon Magsaysay, at its head, and formed the Philippine army into battalion combat teams trained for counter-insurgency warfare.[16] The Philippines was to be a laboratory experiment for this unconventional type of combat. The methods and the terminology, such as "search-and-destroy" and "pacification", were later to become infamous in Vietnam.

By September, when Lt. Col. Edward G. Lansdale arrived in the Philippines, the civil war had all the markings of a long, drawn-out affair, with victory not in sight for either side. Ostensibly, Lansdale was just another American military adviser attached to JUSMAG, but in actuality he was the head of CIA clandestine and paramilitary operations in the country. His apparent success was to make him a recognized authority in counter-insurgency.

In his later reminiscences about this period in his life, Lansdale relates his surprise at hearing from informed Filipino civilian friends about how repressive the Quirino government was, that its atrocities matched those of (or attributed to) the Huks, that the government was "rotten with corruption" (down to the policeman in the street, Lansdale observed on his own), that Quirino himself had been elected the previous year through "extensive fraud", and that "the Huks were right", they were the "wave of the future", and violence was the only way for the people to get a government of their own. (The police, wrote a correspondent for the *Saturday Evening Post*, were "bands of uniformed thieves and rapists, more feared than bandits . . . the army was little better.")[17]

Lansdale was undeterred. He had come to do a job. Accordingly, he told himself that if the Huks took over there would only be another form of injustice by another privileged few, backed by even crueller force. By the next chapter, he had convinced himself that he was working on the side of those committed to "defend human liberty in the Philippines".[18]

As a former advertising man, Lansdale was no stranger to the use of market research, motivation techniques, media, and deception. In CIA parlance, such arts fall under the heading of "psychological warfare". To this end, Lansdale fashioned a unit called the Civil Affairs Office. Its activities were based on the premise — one both new and suspect to most American military officers — that a popular guerrilla army cannot be defeated by force alone.

Lansdale's team conducted a careful study of the superstitions of the Filipino peasants: their lore, taboos, and myths in Huk areas were examined for clues to the appropriate appeals that could wean them from supporting the insurgents. In one operation, Lansdale's men flew over these areas in a small plane hidden by a cloud cover and broadcast in Tagalog mysterious curses on any villagers who dared to give the Huks food or shelter. The tactic reportedly succeeded into starving some Huk units into surrender.[19]

Another Lansdale-initiated "psywar" operation played on the superstitious dread in the Philippine countryside of the *asuang*, a mythical vampire. A psywar squad entered a town and planted rumours that an *asuang* lived on in the neighbouring hill where the Huks were based, a location from which government forces were anxious to have them out. Two nights later, after giving the rumours time to circulate among Huk sympathizers in the town and make their way up the hill, the psywar squad laid an ambush for the rebels along a trail used by them. When a Huk patrol passed, the ambushers silently snatched the last man, punctured his neck vampire-fashion with two holes, held his body by the heels until the blood drained out, and put the corpse back on the trail. When the Huks, as superstitious as any other Filipinos, discovered the bloodless comrade, they fled from the region.[20]

Lansdale regularly held "coffee klatsches" with Filipino officials and military personnel in which new ideas were freely tossed back and forth, à la Madison Avenue brain session. Out of this came the Economic Development Corps to lure Huks with a programme of resettlement on their own patch of farm land, with tools, seeds, cash loans, etc. It was an undertaking wholly inadequate to the land problem, and the number that responded was very modest, but like many psywar techniques, a principal goal was to steal from the enemy his most persuasive arguments.[21]

Among other tactics introduced or refined by Lansdale were: production of films and radio broadcasts to explain and justify government actions; infiltration of government agents into the ranks of the Huks to provide information and sow dissension; attempts to modify the behaviour of government soldiers so as to curtail their abuse of people in rural areas (for the Huks had long followed an explicit code of proper conduct towards the peasants, with punishment meted out to violators), but on other occasions, government soldiers were allowed to run amok in villages — disguised as Huks.[22]

This last, revealed L. Fletcher Prouty, was a technique "developed to a high art in the Philippines" in which soldiers were "set upon the unwary village in the grand manner of a Cecil B. De Mille production".[23] Prouty, a retired US Air Force colonel, was for nine years the focal point officer for contacts between the Pentagon and the CIA. He has described another type of scenario by which the Huks were tarred with the terrorist brush, serving to obscure the political nature of their movement and mar their credibility:

> In the Philippines, lumbering interests and major sugar interests have forced tens of thousands of simple, backward villagers to leave areas where they have lived for centuries. When these poor people flee to other areas, it should be quite obvious that they in turn then infringe upon the territorial rights of other villagers or landowners. This creates violent rioting or at least sporadic outbreaks of banditry, that last lowly recourse of dying and terrorized people. Then when the distant government learns of the banditry and rioting, it must offer some safe explanation. The last thing that regional government would want to do would be to say that the huge lumbering or paper interests had driven the people out of their ancestral homeland. In the Philippines it is customary for the local/regional government to get a 10 percent rake-off on all such enterprise and for national politicians to get another 10 percent. So the safe explanation becomes 'Communist-inspired subversive insurgency.' The word for this in the Philippines is *Huk*.[24]

The most insidious part of the CIA operation in the Philippines was the fundamental manipulation of the nation's political life, featuring stage-managed elections and disinformation campaigns. The high-point of this effort was the election to the presidency, in 1953, of Ramon Magsaysay, the co-operative former defence department head.

Lansdale, it was said, "invented" Magsaysay.[25] His CIA front organizations ran the Filipino's campaign with all the license, impunity, and money that one would expect from the Democratic or Republican National Committees operating in the US, or perhaps more to the point, Mayor Daley operating in Chicago. One of these front organizations, the National Movement for Free Elections, was praised in a *New York Times* editorial for its contribution to making the Philippines "the showcase of democracy in Asia".[26]

Once Magsaysay was in office, the CIA wrote his speeches, carefully guided his foreign policy, and used its press "assets" (paid editors and journalists) to provide him with a constant claque of support for his domestic programmes and his involvement in the US-directed anti-communist crusade in south-east Asia, as well as to attack anti-US newspaper columnists. So beholden was Magsaysay to the United States, disclosed presidential assistant Sherman Adams, that he "sent word to Eisenhower that he would do anything the United States wanted him to do — even though his own foreign minister took the opposite view".[27]

One inventive practice of the CIA on behalf of Magsaysay was later picked up by Agency stations in a number of other Third World countries. This particular piece of chicanery consisted of selecting articles written by CIA writer-agents for the provincial press and republishing them in a monthly *Digest of the Provincial Press*. The *Digest* was then sent to congressmen and other opinion makers in Manila to enlighten them as to what "the provinces were thinking".[28]

After Magsaysay died in a plane crash in 1957, various other Filipino politicians and parties were sought out by the CIA as clients, or offered themselves as such. One of the latter was Diosdado Macapagal who was to become president in 1961. Macapagal provided the Agency with political information for several years and eventually asked for, and received, what he felt he deserved: heavy financial support for his campaign. (*Reader's Digest* called his election: "certainly a demonstration of democracy in action".)[29] Ironically, Macapagal had been the bitterest objector to American intervention in the Magsaysay election in 1953, quoting time and again from the Philippine law that "No foreigner shall aid any candidate directly or indirectly or take part in or influence in any manner any election."[30]

Perhaps even more ironic, in 1957 the Philippine government, at American urging, adopted an anti-subversion law which prohibited organizations which have the intent of turning the Philippines over to "the control of a foreign power".[31]

By 1953 the Huks were scattered and demoralized, no longer a serious threat, although their death would be distributed over the next few years. It is difficult to ascertain to what extent their decline was due to traditional military force, or to Lansdale's more unorthodox methods, or to the eventual debilitation of many of the Huks from malnutrition and disease, brought on by the impoverishment of the peasantry; long before the end, many Huks were also lacking weapons, proper military equipment, even sufficient ammunition, bringing into question the oft-repeated charge of Soviet and Chinese aid to them made by Philippine and American authorities.[32]

"Since the destruction of Huk military power," noted George Taylor, "the social and political program that made the accomplishment possible has to a large extent fallen by the wayside."[33]

Fortress America, however, was securely in place in south-east Asia. From the Philippines would be launched American air and sea actions against Korea and China, Vietnam and Indonesia. The Philippine government would send combat forces to fight alongside the United States in Vietnam and Korea. On the islands' bases, the technology and art of counter-insurgency warfare would be imparted to the troops of America's other allies in the Pacific.

5. Korea 1945-1953
Was it all what it appeared to be?

To die for an idea; it is unquestionably noble. But how much nobler it
would be if men died for ideas that were true.
H.L. Mencken, 1919

How is it that the Korean War escaped the protests which surrounded the war in
Vietnam? Everything we've come to love and cherish about Vietnam had its
forerunner in Korea: the support of a corrupt tyranny, the atrocities, the mass
slaughter of civilians, the cities and villages laid to waste, the calculated
management of the news, the sabotaging of peace talks. But the American
people were convinced that the war was an unambiguous case of one country
invading another without provocation. A case of the bad guys attacking the
good guys who were being saved by the even better guys; none of the historical,
political and moral uncertainty that was the dilemma of Vietnam. The Korean
War was seen to have begun in a specific manner: North Korea attacked South
Korea in the early morning of 25 June 1950; while Vietnam . . . no one seemed
to know how it all began, or when, or why.

And there was little in the way of accusations about American "imperialism"
in Korea. The United States, after all, was fighting as part of a United Nations
Army. What was there to protest about? (Another difference was the epidemic
of McCarthyism, then so prevalent, which served to inhibit protest.)

There were, in fact, rather different interpretations to be made of what the
war was all about and how it was being conducted, but these quickly succumbed
to the heat of war fever.

Shortly after the close of the Second World War, the Soviet Union and the
United States occupied Korea in order to expel the defeated Japanese. A
demarcation line between the Russian and American forces was set up along
the 38th Parallel. This line in no way had the explicit or implicit intention of
establishing two separate countries, but the Cold War was soon to intrude. Both
powers insisted that unification of north and south was the principal and desired
goal. However, they also desired to see this carried out in their own ideological
image, and settled thereby into a routine of proposal and counter-proposal,
accusation and counter-accusation, generously intermixed with deviousness,
and produced nothing in the way of an agreement during the ensuing years.
Although both Moscow and Washington and their hand-picked Korean leaders
were not always displeased about the division of the country (on the grounds
that half a loaf was better than none), officials and citizens of both sides

44

continued to genuinely call for unification on a regular basis.[1] That Korea was still one country, with unification still the goal, at the time the war began, was underscored by the chief US delegate to the UN, Warren Austin, in a statement he made shortly afterwards:

> The artificial barrier which has divided North and South Korea has no basis for existence either in law or in reason. Neither the United Nations, its Commission on Korea, nor the Republic of Korea [South Korea] recognizes such a line. Now the North Koreans, by armed attack upon the Republic of Korea, have denied the reality of any such line.[2]

The two sides had been clashing across the Parallel for several years. What happened on that fateful day in June could thus be regarded as no more than the escalation of an ongoing civil war. The North Korean Government has claimed that in 1949 alone, the South Korean army or police perpetrated 2,617 armed incursions into the north to carry out murder, kidnapping, pillage and arson for the purpose of causing social disorder and unrest, as well as to increase the combat capabilities of the invaders. At times, stated the Pyongyang government, thousands of soldiers were involved in a single battle with many casualties resulting.[3]

A State Department official, Ambassador-at-large Philip C. Jessup, speaking in April 1950, put it this way:

> There is constant fighting between the South Korean Army and bands that infiltrate the country from the North. There are very real battles, involving perhaps one or two thousand men. When you go to this boundary, as I did . . . you see troop movements, fortifications, and prisoners of war.[4]

Seen in this context, the question of who fired the first shot on 25 June 1950 takes on a much reduced air of significance. As it is, the North Korean version of events is that their invasion was provoked by two days of bombardment by the South Koreans, on the 23rd and 24th, followed by a surprise South Korean attack across the border on the 25th against the western town of Haeju and other places. Announcement of the southern attack was broadcast over the north's radio later in the morning of the 25th.

Contrary to general belief at the time, no United Nations group — neither the UN Military Observer Group in the field nor the UN Commission on Korea in Seoul — witnessed, or claimed to have witnessed, the outbreak of hostilities. The Observer Group's field trip along the Parallel ended on 23 June. Its statements about what took place afterward are either speculation or based on information received from the South Korean government or the US military.

Moreover, early in the morning of the 26th, the South Korean Office of Public Information announced that southern forces had indeed captured the northern town of Haeju. The announcement stated that the attack had occurred that same morning, but an American military status report as of nightfall on the 25th notes that all southern territory west of the Imjin River had been lost to a depth of at least three miles inside the border *except* in the area of the Haeju "counter attack".

45

In either case, such a military victory is extremely difficult to reconcile with the official Western account, maintained to this day, that has the North Korean army sweeping south in a devastating surprise attack, taking control of everything that lay before it, and forcing South Korean troops to evacuate further south.

Subsequently, the South Korean government denied that its capture of Haeju had actually taken place, blaming the original announcement, apparently, on an exaggerating military officer. One historian has ascribed the allegedly-incorrect announcement to "an error due to poor communications, plus an attempt to stiffen South Korean resistance by claiming a victory". Whatever actually lay behind the announcement, it is evident that no reliance at all can be placed upon anything the South Koreans had to say concerning the start of the war.[5]

There were, in fact, reports in the Western press of the attack on Haeju which make no mention of the South Korean Government's announcement and which appear to be independent confirmations of the event. The London *Daily Herald*, in its issue of 26 June, stated that "American military observers said the Southern forces had made a successful relieving counter-attack near the west coast, penetrated five miles into Northern territory and seized the town of Haeju." This was echoed in *The Guardian* of London the same day: "American officials confirmed that the Southern troops had captured Haeju."

Similarly, the *New York Herald Tribune* reported, also on the 26th, that "South Korean troops drove across the 38th Parallel, which forms the frontier, to capture the manufacturing town of Haeju, just north of the line. The Republican troops captured quantities of equipment." None of the accounts specified just when the attack took place.

On the 25th, American writer John Gunther was in Japan preparing his biography of General Douglas MacArthur. As he recounts in the book, he was playing tourist in the town of Nikko with "two important members" of the American occupation, when "one of these was called unexpectedly to the telephone. He came back and whispered, 'A big story has just broken. The South Koreans have attacked North Korea!' " That evening, Gunther and his party returned to Tokyo where "Several officers met us at the station to tell us correctly and with much amplification what had happened . . . there was no doubt whatever that North Korea was the aggressor."

And the telephone call? Gunther explains: "The message may have been garbled in transmission. [Another error in communication!] Nobody knew anything much at headquarters the first few hours, and probably people were taken in by the blatant, corrosive lies of the North Korean radio."[6]

There is something a little incongruous about the picture of American military and diplomatic personnel, practising anti-Communists each one, being taken in on so important a matter by Communist lies — blatant ones no less.

The head of South Korea, Syngman Rhee, may have had good reason for provoking a full-scale war, apart from his oft-expressed desire and readiness to compel the unification of Korea by force.* On 30 May 1950, elections for the National Assembly were held in the South in which Rhee's party suffered a heavy setback and lost control of the assembly. Like countless statesmen before and after him, Rhee may have decided to play the war card to rally support for his shaky rule. A labour adviser attached to the American aid mission in South Korea, Stanley Earl, resigned in July, expressing the opinion that the South Korean government was "an oppressive regime" which "did very little to help the people" and that "an internal South Korean rebellion against the Rhee Government would have occurred if the forces of North Korea had not invaded".[7]

Nikita Khrushchev, in his reminiscences, makes it plain that the North Koreans had contemplated an invasion of the South for some time and he reports their actual invasion without any mention of provocation on that day. This would seem to put that particular question to rest. However, Khrushchev's chapter on Korea is a wholly superficial account. It is not a serious work of history, nor was it intended to be. As he himself states: "My memories of the Korean War are unavoidably sketchy." His chapter contains no discussion of *any* of the previous fighting across the border, nothing of Rhee's belligerent statements, nothing at all even of the Soviet Union's crucial absence from the UN which, as we shall see, allowed the so-called United Nations Army to be formed and intervene in the conflict. Moreover, his reminiscences as published, are an edited and condensed version of the tapes he made. A study based on a comparison between the Russian-language transcription of the tapes and the published English-language book reveals that some of Khrushchev's memories about Korea were indeed sketchy, but that the book fails to bring this out. For example, North Korean leader Kim Il-sung met with Stalin to discuss Kim's desire "to prod South Korea with the point of a bayonet". The book then states simply: "Kim went home and then returned to Moscow when he had worked everything out." The transcript, however, shows that what Khrushchev said was: "In my opinion, either the date of his return was set, or he was to inform us as soon as he finished preparing all of his ideas. Then, I don't remember in which month or *year*, Kim Il-sung came and related his plan to Stalin." (Emphasis added.)[8]

On 26 June, the United States presented a resolution before the UN Security Council condemning North Korea for its "unprovoked aggression". The resolution was approved, although there were arguments that "this was a fight between Koreans" and should be treated as a civil war, and a suggestion from the

---

* On 26 June the *New York Times* reported that "on a number of occasions, Dr. Rhee has indicated that his army would have taken the offensive if Washington had given the consent." The newspaper noted also that before the war began, "The warlike talk strangely [had] almost all come from South Korean leaders."

Egyptian delegate that the word "unprovoked" should be dropped in view of the longstanding hostilities between the two Koreas.[9] Yugoslavia insisted as well that "there seemed to be lack of precise information that could enable the Council to pin responsibility", and proposed that North Korea be invited to present its side of the story.[10] This was not done. (Three months later, the Soviet foreign minister put forward a motion that the UN hear representatives from both sides. This, too, was voted down, by a margin of 46 to 6, because of North Korea's "aggression", and it was decided to extend an invitation to South Korea alone.)[11]

On the 27th, the Security Council recommended that members of the United Nations furnish assistance to South Korea "as may be necessary to repel the armed attack". President Truman had already ordered the US Navy and Air Force into combat by this time, thus presenting the Council with a *fait accompli*,[12] a tactic the US was to repeat several times before the war came to an end. The Council made its historic decision with the barest of information available to it, and all of it derived from and selected by only one side of the conflict. This was, as journalist I.F. Stone put it, "neither honorable nor wise".

It should be kept in mind that in 1950 the United Nations was in no way a neutral or balanced organization. The great majority of members were nations very dependent upon the United States for economic recovery or development. There was no Third World bloc which today pursues a UN policy largely independent of the United States. And only four countries of the Soviet bloc were members at the time, none on the Security Council.[13]

Neither could Secretary-General Trygve Lie, of Norway, be regarded as neutral in the midst of cold war controversy. In a book he later wrote, Lie makes it only too clear that he was no objective outsider. The language he employs in his chapters on the Korean War is so heavily biased, emotive, and loaded, his charges against Communist countries so unsubstantiated, as to be more appropriate for a US State Department spokesperson than for a Secretary-General of the United Nations. Only a casual reading of Lie's chapters will impart the tenor of his bias and his manoeuvring on the Korean question.[14]

These resolutions were possible only because the Soviet Union was absent from the proceedings due to its boycott of the United Nations over the refusal to seat Communist China in place of Taiwan. If the Russians had been present, they undoubtedly would have vetoed the resolution. Their absence has always posed an awkward problem for those who insist that the Russians were behind the North Korean invasion. One of the most common explanations offered is that the Russians, as a CIA memorandum stated, wanted "to challenge the US specifically and test the firmness of US resistance to Communist expansion."[15] Inasmuch as the same analysis has been put forth by American political pundits for virtually every encounter between the United States and leftists anywhere in the world, before and since Korea, it would appear that the test has been going on for an inordinately long period and one can only wonder why the Soviets have not yet come to a conclusion.

"The finishing touch," wrote I.F. Stone, "was to make the 'United Nations' forces subject to MacArthur without making MacArthur subject to the United

Nations. This came on July 7 in a resolution introduced jointly by Britain and France. This is commonly supposed to have established a United Nations Command. Actually it did nothing of the sort."[16] The resolution recommended "that all members providing military forces and other assistance . . . make such forces and other assistance available to a *unified command under the United States*" (emphasis added). It further requested "the United States to designate the commander of such forces."[17] This would be the redoubtable MacArthur.

It was to be an American show. Military personnel of some 16 other countries took part in one way or another but, with the exception of the South Koreans, there could be little doubt as to their true status or function. Eisenhower later wrote in his memoirs that when he was considering US military intervention in Vietnam in 1954, also as part of a "coalition", he recognized that the burden of the operation would fall on the United States, but "the token forces supplied by these other nations, *as in Korea*, would lend real moral standing to a venture that otherwise could be made to appear as a brutal example of imperialism." (Emphasis added.)[18]

The war, and a brutal one it was indeed, was fought ostensibly in defence of the Syngman Rhee regime. Outside of books published by various South Korean governments, it is rather difficult to find a kind word for the man the United States brought back to Korea in 1945 after decades of exile in America during the Japanese occupation of his country. Flown into Korea in one of MacArthur's airplanes, Rhee was soon manoeuvred into a position of prominence and authority by the US Army Military Government in Korea (USAMGIK). In the process, American officials had to suppress a provisional government, the Korean People's Republic, that was the outgrowth of a number of regional governing committees set up by prominent Koreans and which had already begun to carry out administrative tasks, such as food distribution and keeping order. The KPR's offer of its services to the arriving Americans was dismissed out of hand.

Despite its Communist-sounding name, the KPR included a number of conservatives; indeed, Rhee himself had been given the leading position of chairman. Rhee and the other conservatives, most of whom were still abroad when chosen, perhaps did not welcome the honour because the KPR, on balance, was probably too leftist for their tastes, as it was for the higher echelons of the USAMGIK. But after 35 years under the Japanese, any group or government set up to undo the effects of colonialism had to have a revolutionary tinge to it. It was the conservatives in Korea who had collaborated with the Japanese; leftists and other nationalists who had struggled against them; the make-up of the KPR necessarily reflected this, and it was reportedly more popular than any other political grouping.[19]

Whatever the political leanings or intentions of the KPR, by denying it any "authority, status or form",[20] the USAMGIK was regulating Korean political life as if the country were a defeated enemy and not a friendly state liberated from a common foe and with a right to independence and self-determination.

The significance of shunting aside the KPR went beyond this. John Gunther, hardly a radical, summed up the situation this way: "So the first — and best — chance for building a united Korea was tossed away.[21] And Alfred Crofts, a member of the American military government at the time, has written that "A potential unifying agency became thus one of the fifty-four splinter groups in South Korean political life."[22]

Syngman Rhee would be Washington's man: eminently pro-American, rabidly anti-Communist, sufficiently controllable. His regime was one in which landlords, collaborators, the wealthy, and other conservative elements readily found a home. Crofts has pointed out that, "Before the American landings, a political Right, associated in popular thought with colonial rule, could not exist; but shortly afterward we were to foster at least three conservative factions."[23]

Committed to establishing free enterprise, the USAMGIK sold off vast amounts of confiscated Japanese property, homes, businesses, industrial raw materials and other valuables. Those who could most afford to purchase these assets were collaborators who had grown rich under the Japanese, and other profiteers. "With half the wealth of the nation 'up for grabs', demoralization was rapid."[24] While the Russians did a thorough house-cleaning of Koreans in the north who had collaborated with the Japanese, the American military government in the south allowed many collaborators, and at first even the Japanese themselves, to retain positions of administration and authority, much to the consternation of those Koreans who had fought against the Japanese occupation of their country.[25]

And while the north soon implemented widespread and effective land reform and at least formal equality for women, the Rhee regime remained hostile to these ideals. Two years later, it enacted a land reform measure, but this applied only to former Japanese property. A 1949 law to cover other holdings was not enforced at all, and the abuse of land tenants continued in both old and new forms.[26]

The public resentment against the US/Rhee administration aroused by these policies, as well as by very questionable elections* and the suppression of the KPR, manifested itself in the form of frequent rebellions from 1946 to the beginning of the war, and even during the war. The rebellions were dismissed by the government as "communist-inspired" and repressed accordingly, but, as John Gunther observed, "It can be safely said that in the eyes of Hodge [the commander of US forces in Korea] and Rhee, particularly at the beginning, almost any Korean not an extreme rightist was a communist and potential traitor."[28]

General Hodge evidently permitted US troops to take part in the repression. Mark Gayn, a correspondent in Korea for the *Chicago Sun*, wrote that American soldiers "fired on crowds, conducted mass arrests, combed the hills for suspects, and organized posses of Korean rightists, constabulary and police

* So reluctant was Rhee to allow an honest election, that by 1950 he had become enough of an embarrassment to the United States for Washington officials to threaten to cut off aid if he failed to do so as well as improve the state of civil liberties.[27]

for mass raids."[29] Gayn related that one of Hodge's political advisers assured him (Gayn) that Rhee was not a fascist: "He is two centuries before fascism — a pure Bourbon."[30]

Describing the government's anti-guerrilla campaign in 1948, pro-Western political scientist John Kie-Chiang Oh of Marquette University has written: "In these campaigns, the civil liberties of countless persons were often ignored. Frequently, hapless villagers, suspected of aiding the guerrillas, were summarily executed."[31]

A year later, when a committee of the National Assembly launched an investigation of collaborators, Rhee had his police raid the Assembly: 22 people were arrested, of whom 16 were later found to have suffered either broken ribs, skull injuries or broken eardrums.[32]

At the time of the outbreak of war in June 1950, there were an estimated 14,000 political prisoners in South Korean jails.[33]

Even during the height of the war, in February 1951, reported Professor Oh, there was the "Koch'ang Incident", again involving suspicion of aiding guerrillas, "in which about six hundred men and women, young and old, were herded into a narrow valley and mowed down with machine guns by a South Korean army unit."[34]

Throughout the war, a continuous barrage of accusations was levelled by each side at the other, charging the enemy with engaging in all manner of barbarity and atrocity, against troops, prisoners of war, and civilians alike, in every part of the country (each side occupied the other's territory at times), trying to outdo each other in a verbal war of superlatives almost as heated as the combat. In the United States this produced a body of popular myths, not unlike those emerging from other wars which are widely supported at home. (By contrast, during the Vietnam war the inclination of myths to flourish was regularly countered by numerous educated protestors who carefully researched the origins of the war, monitored its conduct, and publicized studies sharply at variance with the official version(s), eventually influencing the mass media to do the same.)

There was, for example, the consensus that the brutality of the war in Korea must be laid overwhelmingly on the doorstep of the Communists. The Koch'ang Incident mentioned above may be relevant to providing some counterbalance to this belief. Referring to the incident, the British Korea scholar Jon Halliday observed:

> This account not only serves to indicate the level of political violence employed by the UN side, but also confers inherent plausibility on DPRK [North Korea] and Southern opposition accusations of atrocities and mass executions by the UN forces and Rhee officials during the occupation of the DPRK in late 1950. After all, if civilians could be mowed down in the South on *suspicion* of aiding (not even *being*) guerrillas — what about the North, where millions could reasonably be assumed to be Communists, or political militants?[35] (Emphasis in original.)

Oh's account is but one of a number of reports of slaughter carried out by the South Koreans against their own people during the war. The *New York Times* reported a "wave of [South Korean] Government executions in Seoul" in December 1950,[36] René Cutforth, a correspondent for the BBC in Korea, later wrote of "the shooting without trial of civilians, designated by the police as 'communist'. These executions were done, usually at dawn, on any patch of waste ground where you could dig a trench and line up a row of prisoners in front of it."[37] And Gregory Henderson, a US diplomat who served seven years in Korea in the 1940s and 50s, has stated that "probably over 100,000 were killed without any trial whatsoever" by Rhee's forces in the south during the war.[38]

One of the North Korean charges was that following some of the massacres of civilians in the south, the Rhee government turned around and attributed them to northern troops.

One way in which the United States contributed directly to the war's brutality was by introducing a weapon which, although used in the last stage of World War II, and in Greece, was new to almost all observers and participants in Korea. It was called napalm. Here is one description of its effect from the *New York Times*.

A napalm raid hit the village three or four days ago when the Chinese were holding up the advance, and nowhere in the village have they buried the dead because there is nobody left to do so . . . The inhabitants throughout the village and in the fields were caught and killed and kept the exact postures they had held when the napalm struck — a man about to get on his bicycle, fifty boys and girls playing in an orphanage, a housewife strangely unmarked, holding in her hand a page torn from a Sears-Roebuck catalogue crayoned at Mail Order No. 3,811,294 for a $2.98 'bewitching bed jacket — coral'. There must be almost two hundred dead in the tiny hamlet.[39]

The United States may also have waged germ warfare against North Korea and China, as was discussed earlier in the chapter on China.

Another widely-held belief in the United States during the war was that American prisoners in North Korean camps were dying off like flies because of Communist neglect and cruelty. The flames of this very emotional issue were fanned by the tendency of US officials to exaggerate the numbers involved. During November 1951, for example — long before the end of the war — American military announcements put the count of POW deaths at between 5,000 and 8,000.[40] However, an extensive study completed by the US Army two years after the war revealed that the POW death toll for the entire war was 2,730 (out of 7,190 held in camps; an unknown number of other prisoners never made it to the camps, being shot in the field because of the inconvenience of dealing with them in the midst of combat, a practise engaged in by both sides). The study concluded that "there was evidence that the high death rate was not due primarily to Communist maltreatment . . . it could be accounted for largely by the ignorance or the callousness of the prisoners themselves."[41] "Callousness" refers here to the soldiers' lack of morale and collective spirit.* Although not mentioned in the study, the North Koreans, on several occasions, claimed that many American POWs also died in the camps as a result of the heavy US bombing.

The study of course could never begin to catch up with all the scare headlines to which the Western world had been treated for three years. Obscured as well was the fact that several times as many communist prisoners had died in US/ South Korean camps — halfway through the war the official figure stood at 6,600[43] —though these camps did hold many more prisoners than those in the north.

The American public was also convinced, and probably still is, that the North Koreans and Chinese had "brainwashed" US soldiers. This story arose to explain the fact that as much as 30 percent of American POWs had collaborated with the enemy in one way or another, and "one man in every seven, or more than thirteen per cent, was guilty of serious collaboration — writing disloyal tracts . . . or agreeing to spy or organize for the Communists after the war."[44] Another reason the brainwashing theme was promoted by Washington was to increase the likelihood that statements by returning prisoners which questioned the official version of the war would be discounted.

In the words of Yale psychiatrist Robert J. Lifton, brainwashing was popularly held to be an "all-powerful, irresistible, unfathomable, and magical method of achieving total control over the human mind."[45] Although the CIA experimented for a decade or so after the war to develop just such a magic, neither they nor the North Koreans or Chinese before them ever possessed it. Brainwashing, said the Army study, "has become a catch phrase, used for so many things that it no longer has any precise meaning" and "a precise meaning is necessary in this case".[46]

> The prisoners, as far as Army psychiatrists have been able to discover, were not subjected to anything that could properly be called brainwashing. Indeed, the Communist treatment of prisoners, while it came nowhere near fulfilling the requirements of the Geneva Convention, rarely involved outright cruelty, being instead a highly novel blend of leniency and pressure . . . The Communists rarely used physical torture . . . and the Army has not found a single verifiable case in which they used it for the specific purpose of forcing a man to collaborate or to accept their convictions.[47]

According to the study, however, some American airmen, of the 90 or so who were captured, were subjected to physical abuse in an attempt to extract confessions about germ warfare. This could reflect either a greater Communist resentment about the use of such a weapon, or a need to produce some kind of corroboration of a false claim.

* It is to the Army's credit that much of the results of the study were not kept secret; the study, nonetheless, contains some anti-communist statements of the most bizarre sort: lying is often punished in China by death . . . communists live like animals all their lives . . .[42]

American soldiers were instead subjected to political indoctrination by their jailors. Here is how the US Army saw it:

> In the indoctrination lectures, the Communists frequently displayed global charts dotted with our military bases, the names of which were of course known to many of the captives. 'See those bases?' the instructor would say, tapping them on the chart with his pointer. 'They are American — full of war materiel. You *know* they are American. And you can see they are ringing Russia and China. Russia and China do not have *one* base outside their own territory. From this it's clear which side is the warmonger. Would America have these bases and spend millions to maintain them were it not preparing to war on Russia and China?' This argument seemed plausible to many of the prisoners. In general they had no idea that these bases showed not the United States' wish for war, but its wish for peace, that they had been established as part of a series of treaties aimed not at conquest, but at curbing Red aggression.[48]

The Chinese Communists, of course, did not invent this practise. During the American Civil War, prisoners of both the south and the north received indoctrination about the respective merits of the two sides. And in the Second World War, "democratization courses" were held in US and British POW camps for Germans, and reformed Germans were granted privileges. Moreover, the US Army was proud to state that Communist prisoners in American camps during the Korean War were taught "what democracy stands for".[49]

The predicted Chinese aggression manifested itself about four months after the war in Korea began. The Chinese entered the war after American planes had violated their air space on a number of occasions, had bombed and strafed Chinese territory several times (always "in error"), when hydro-electric plants on the Korean side of the border, vital to Chinese industry, stood in great danger, and US or South Korean forces had reached the Chinese border, the Yalu River, or come within a few miles of it in several places.

The question must be asked: How long would the United States refrain from entering a war being waged in Mexico by a Communist power from across the sea, which strafed and bombed Texas border towns, was mobilized along the Rio Grande, and was led by a general who threatened war against the United States itself? Four months? Or four hours?

American airpower in Korea was fearsome to behold. As would be the case in Vietnam, its use was celebrated in the wholesale dropping of napalm, the destruction of villages "suspected of aiding the enemy", bombing cities so as to leave no useful facilities standing, demolishing dams and dikes to cripple the irrigation system, wiping out rice crops . . . and in those moving expressions like "scorched-earth policy", "saturation bombing", and "operation killer".[50]

"You can kiss that group of villages good-bye," exclaimed Captain Everett L. Hundley of Kansas City, Kansas after a bombing raid.[51]

"I would say that the entire, almost the entire Korean Peninsula is just a terrible mess," testified Major General Emmett O'Donnell before the Senate when the war was one year old. "Everything is destroyed. There is nothing standing worthy of the name."[52]

And here, the words of the venerable British military guide, *Brassey's Annual*, in its 1951 yearbook:

> It is no exaggeration to state that South Korea no longer exists as a country. Its towns have been destroyed, much of its means of livelihood eradicated, and its people reduced to a sullen mass dependent upon charity and exposed to subversive influences. When the war ends no gratitude can be expected from the South Koreans, but it is to be hoped that the lesson will have been learned that it is worse than useless to destroy to liberate. Certainly, western Europe would never accept such a 'liberation'.[53]

The worst of the bombing was yet to come. That began in the summer of 1952 and was Washington's way of putting itself in a better bargaining position in the truce discussions with the Communists, which had been going on for a full year while the battles raged. The extended and bitter negotiations gave rise to another pervasive Western belief — that it was predominantly Communist intransigence, duplicity, and lack of peaceful intentions which frustrated the talks and prolonged the war. This is a lengthy and entangled chapter of the Korean War story, but one does not have to probe too deeply to discover the unremarkable fact that the barriers were erected by the anti-Communist side as well. Syngman Rhee, for example, was so opposed to any outcome short of total victory that both the Truman and Eisenhower administrations drew up plans for overthrowing him;[54] which is not to suggest that the American negotiators were not plying the oily arts and voicing the rubbery words; the last thing they wanted to be accused of was having allowed the commies to make suckers of them. So successful were they at this, that in November of 1951 we could read in the *New York Times*:

> The unadorned way that an apparently increasing number of them [American soldiers in Korea] see the situation right now is that the Communists have made important concessions, while the United Nations Command, as they view it, continues to make more and more demands . . . The United Nations truce team has created the impression that it switches its stand whenever the Communists indicate that they might go along with it.[55]

At one point during this same period, when the Communists proposed that a ceasefire and a withdrawal of troops from the combat line should take place while negotiations were going on, the United Nations Command reacted almost as if this were a belligerent and devious act. "Today's stand by the Communists," said the UNC announcement, "was virtually a renunciation of their previously stated position that hostilities should continue during armistice talks."[56]

Once upon a time, the United States fought a great civil war in which the north attempted to reunite the divided country through military force. Did Korea or China or any other foreign power send in an army to slaughter Americans, charging Lincoln with aggression?

Why did the United States choose to wage full-scale war in Korea? Only a year earlier, in 1949, in the Arab-Israeli fighting in Palestine and in the India-Pakistani war over Kashmir, the United Nations, with American support, had intervened to mediate an armistice, not to send in an army to take sides and expand the fighting. And both these conflicts were less in the nature of a civil war than was the case in Korea. If the US/UN response had been the same in these earlier cases, Palestine and Kashmir might have wound up as the scorched-earth desert that was Korea's fate. What saved them, what kept the US armed forces out, was no more than the absence of a communist side to the conflict.

6. Albania 1949-1953
The proper English spy

"To simultaneously plan and sabotage this ill-fated venture must have been a severe test of his energy and ingenuity," wrote one of Kim Philby's biographers.[1] The venture was the attempt, begun in 1949, by the United States and Great Britain to overthrow the pro-Soviet regime of Enver Hoxha through guerrilla-fomented uprisings, or as Philby himself has put it, somewhat more quaintly, "a clandestine operation to detach an East European country from the Socialist bloc".[2]

It ended in disaster, in part because the Russians had apparently been alerted by Philby, the proper Englishman who had gone to all the right schools and penetrated the highest ranks of British and American intelligence, though he had been a Soviet spy since the age of 21.

Philby had moved to Washington the year before to act as the British Secret Intelligence Service (SIS) liaison to the CIA. In that capacity he served as a co-director of the CIA-SIS task force engaged in planning the Albanian operation. The choice had fallen upon Albania because it was regarded as the most vulnerable of the socialist states, the smallest and the weakest, not sharing a border with the Soviet Union, isolated between a US-controlled Greece and a Yugoslavia that was a renegade from the Soviet bloc.

The task force began by recruiting scattered Albanian émigrés who were living in Italy, Greece and elsewhere. They were exposed to basic military training, with a touch of guerrilla warfare thrown in, at sites established on the

British island of Malta in the Mediterranean, in the American occupation zone of West Germany, and, to a lesser extent, in England itself.[3] "Whenever we want to subvert any place," confided Frank Wisner, CIA's head of covert operations, to Philby, "we find that the British own an island within easy reach."[4]

Intermittently, for some three and a half years, the émigrés were sent back into their homeland: slipping up into the mountains of Greece and over the border, parachuting in from planes which had taken off from bases in Western Europe, entering by sea from Italy. American planes and balloons dropped propaganda leaflets and goods as well, such items in scarce supply in Albania as flour, halvah, needles, and razor blades, along with a note announcing that they were a gift from the "Albanian National Liberation Front"[5] — another instance of the subtle "marketing" touch that the CIA, born and raised in America, was to bring to so many of its operations.

In outline, the plan, or the hope, was for the guerrillas to make for their old home regions and try to stir up anti-Soviet and anti-Communist sentiments, eventually leading to uprisings. They were to distribute propaganda, obtain political, economic and military information, engage in sabotage, recruit individuals into cells, and supply them with equipment. Later infusions of men and material would expand these cells into "centers of resistance".[6]

Cold-war conventional wisdom dictated that the masses of Eastern Europe were waiting to be sparked into open rebellion for their freedom. Even if this were the case, the choice of ignition was highly dubious, for the guerrillas included amongst their numbers many who supported a reinstitution of the Albanian monarchy in the person of the exiled King Zog who had been allied to Mussolini, and others who had collaborated with the Italians or Nazis during their wartime occupations of Albania.

To be sure, there were those of republican and democratic leanings in the various émigré committees as well, but State Department papers, declassified some 30 years later, reveal that prominent Albanian collaborators played leading roles in the formation of these committees.* These were individuals the State Department characterized as having "somewhat checkered" political backgrounds who "might sooner or later occasion embarrassment to this government". They were admitted to the United States over the Department's objections because of "intelligence considerations". One of these men was Hasan Dosti, Albania's minister of justice in the Italian occupation, whom the CIA was hoping would take a leading role in the expected future Albanian

---

* We have thus seen that in the postwar world — in China, Italy, Greece, the Philippines, Korea and now Albania — the US worked closely with those who had collaborated with the Germans, the Japanese, and the Italian fascists, worked even with these former enemies themselves, and used them all against many who had supported the US during the war: Communists and others. The adhesive which bound the Americans and their new-found Axis allies together was of course anti-Communism. (See also the chapters on Germany, the Soviet Union and Vietnam.)

Government. Dosti later became the head of the US-sponsored National Committee for a Free Albania.[7]

It was in the name of this same committee that a powerful underground radio station began broadcasting inside Albania, calling for the liberation of the country from the Soviet Union. In early 1951, several reports came out of Albania of open organized resistance and uprisings.[8] To what extent these happenings were a consequence of the Western infiltration and agitation is impossible to determine. Overall, the campaign had little to show for its efforts. It was hounded throughout by logistical foul-ups, and the grim reality that the masses of Albanians greeted the émigrés as something less than liberators, either from fear of the harsh Hoxha regime, or because they supported the social changes taking place. Worst of all, the Albanian authorities usually seemed to know in which area the guerrillas would be arriving, and when.

Kim Philby was not the only potential source of disclosure. The émigré groups were almost certainly infiltrated, and careless talk indulged in by the motley Albanians could have contributed to the fiasco. Philby, referring to the CIA-SIS task force members' habit of poking fun at Albanians, wrote that: "Even in our more serious moments, we Anglo-Saxons never forgot that our agents were just down from the trees."[9]

So lax was security that *New York Times* correspondent Cyrus L. Sulzberger filed several dispatches from the Mediterranean area touching upon the intervention which required virtually no reading between the lines.[10] (The articles carried no attention-grabbing headlines, there was no public comment about them from Washington, no reporters asked government officials any embarrassing questions ... ergo: a "non-event" for Americans — cf. Introduction.)

Despite one failure after another, and without good reason to expect anything different in the future, the operation continued until the spring of 1953, resulting in the death or imprisonment of hundreds of men. It was not simply the obsession with chopping off one of Stalin's fingers. Professional prestige and careers had been invested, a visible success was needed to "recoup past losses" and "justify earlier decisions".[11] And the men who were being lost were, after all, only Albanians, who spoke not a word of the Queen's English and did not yet walk upright properly.

There was, however, the danger of the action escalating into conflict with the Soviet Union. The Soviets did in fact send some new fighter planes to Albania, presumably in the hope that they could shoot down the foreign aircraft making drops.[12] The operation could not fail to remind Stalin, Hoxha, and the entire socialist bloc of another Western intervention 30 years earlier in the Soviet Union. It could only serve to make them yet more "paranoid" about Western intentions and convince them to turn the screw of internal security yet tighter, because "the capitalists may be back to finish the job". Indeed, every now and again over the ensuing years, Hoxha mentioned the American and British "invasion" and used it to justify his policy of isolation.[13]

7. Eastern Europe 1948-1956
Operation Splinter Factor

Jozef Swiatlo surfaced at a press conference in Washington on 28 September 1954. Swiatlo was a Pole, he had been a very important one, high up in the Ministry of Public Security, the secret police. The story went that he had defected in West Berlin the previous December while on a shopping trip, and now the State Department was presenting him to the world to clear up the mystery of the Fields, the American citizens who had disappeared in 1949. Swiatlo revealed that Noel Field and his wife Herta had been arrested in Hungary, and that brother Hermann Field had suffered the same fate in Poland at the hands of Swiatlo himself, all in connection with the trial of a leading Hungarian Communist. The State Department had already dispatched strong letters to the governments of Hungary and Poland.[1]

There is a more expanded and more sinister version of the Jozef Swiatlo story. This story has Swiatlo seeking to defect to the British in Warsaw back in 1948 at a time when he was already in his high security position. The British, for various reasons, turned his case over to the United States and, at the request of Allen Dulles, Swiatlo was told to remain at his post until further notice.

At this time Dulles was not yet Director of the CIA, but was a close consultant to the Agency, had his own men in key positions, and was waiting only until November for Thomas Dewey to win the presidential election and appoint him to the top position. (Harry Truman's surprising re-election postponed this for four years, but Dulles did become Deputy Director in 1951.)

Noel Field, formerly a State Department Foreign Service Officer, was a long-time Communist fellow-traveller, if not a party member in the United States or Europe. During the Second World War, his path converged with Dulles' in intrigue-filled Switzerland. Dulles was an OSS man, Field the representative of the Unitarian Church in Boston helping refugees from Nazi occupation. Field made it a point particularly to help Communist refugees, of which there were many, inasmuch as Communists were second only to Jews on the German persecution list. The OSS aided the operation financially; the Communists in turn were an excellent source of information about happenings in Europe of interest to Washington and its allies.

Toward the end of the war, Field induced Dulles to provide American support for a project which placed agents in various European countries to prepare the way for the advancing Allied troops. The men chosen by Field, unsurprisingly, were all Communists and their placement in certain Eastern

European countries helped them to get their hands on the reins of power long before non-Communist forces were able to regroup and organize themselves.

It could be concluded from this that Allen Dulles had been duped. Added to this was the fact that the OSS, under Dulles' direction and again with Field involved, had financed the publication of a clandestine newspaper inside Germany; anti-fascist and left-wing, the paper was called *Neues Deutschland*, and immediately upon liberation became the official newspaper of the East German Communist Party.

After the war these incidents served as jokes which intelligence services of both East and West could and did appreciate. Before long, the joke fell heavily upon Noel Field.

In 1949 when Field visited Poland he was regarded with grave suspicion. He was seen to have worked during the war in a position which could easily have been a front for Western espionage, a position which brought him into regular contact with senior Communist Party members; and he had, after all, worked closely with Allen Dulles, famous already as a spymaster, and the brother of John Foster Dulles, prominent in Washington official circles and already making his calls for the "liberation" of the Soviet bloc nations.

At the time of Field's arrival in Poland, Jozef Swiatlo was looking to implicate Jakub Berman, a high party and state official of whom Swiatlo was suspicious, and detested. It was his failure to convince the Polish president to act against Berman that reportedly drove Swiatlo to defect the year before. When Noel Field wrote to Berman asking his help in obtaining a job in Eastern Europe, Swiatlo learned of the letter and saw his chance to nail Berman.

But first Noel Field had to be established as an American spy. Given the circumstantial evidence pointing in that direction, that would not be too difficult for a man of Swiatlo's high position and low character. Of course, if Field really *was* working with US intelligence, Swiatlo couldn't very well be exposing him since the Polish security officer was now himself an American agent. Accordingly, he sent his first message to the CIA, describing his plan about Berman and Field and the harm it could do to the Communist Party in Poland. He concluded with: "Any objections?"

Allen Dulles had none. His reaction to Swiatlo's message was one of pleasure and amusement. The time had come to settle accounts with Noel Field. More importantly, Dulles saw that Swiatlo, using Noel Field, "the American spy" as a bludgeon could knock off countless leading Communist officials in the Soviet bloc. It could put the whole of the bloc into a state of acute paranoia and set off a wave of repression and Stalinist tyranny that could eventually lead to uprisings. Dulles called his plan: Operation Splinter Factor.

Thus it was that Jozef Swiatlo was directed to find spies everywhere in Eastern Europe. He would uncover American plots and British plots, "Trotskyist" conspiracies and "Titoist" conspiracies. He would report to Soviet secret-police chief Lavrenti Beria himself that at the centre of the vast network was a man named Noel Haviland Field.

Field was arrested and wound up in a prison in Hungary, as did his wife Herta when she came looking for him. And when his brother Hermann Field sought to track down the two of them, he met the same fate in Poland.

Swialto was in a unique position to carry out Operation Splinter Factor. Not only did he have the authority and command, he had the files on countless Communist Party members in the bloc countries. Any connection they had had with Noel Field, anything that Field had done, could be interpreted to show the hand of American intelligence or an act of real or potential subversion of the socialist states. The Soviets, and Stalin himself, were extremely interested in the "Fieldists". Noel Field had known everyone who was anyone in the Soviet bloc.

Just in case the level of paranoia in the infant, insecure governments of Eastern Europe was not high enough, a CIA double agent would "corroborate" a vital piece of information, or introduce the right rumour at the right time; or the Agency's Radio Free Europe would broadcast certain tantalizing, seemingly-coded messages; or the CIA would direct the writing of letters from "East European expatriates" in the United States to leading Communists in their homelands, containing just the bit of information, or the phrase, carefully designed to lift the eyebrows of a security officer.

Many of the victims of Swiatlo's purges were people who had spent the war years in the West rather than in the Soviet Union and thus had crossed Field's path. These were people who tended to be more nationalist Communists, who wanted to put greater distance between their countries and the Soviet Union, as Tito had done, and who favoured a more liberal regime at home. Dulles brushed aside the argument that these were people to be supported, not eliminated. He felt that they were potentially the more dangerous to the West because if their form of Communism were allowed to gain a foothold in Eastern Europe then Communism might become respectable and accepted; particularly with Italy and France threatening to vote Communists into power, Communism had to be shown at its worst.

There were hundreds of trials all over Eastern Europe — "show trials" and lesser spectacles — in which the name of Noel Field played an important part. What Operation Splinter Factor began soon took on a life of its own: following the arrest of a highly-placed person, others fell under suspicion because they knew him or had been appointed by him; or any other connection to an arrested person might serve to implicate some unlucky soul.

Jozef Swiatlo had his counterpart in Czechoslovakia, a man firmly entrenched in the upper rungs of the Czech security apparatus. The man, whose name is not known, had been recruited by General Reinhard Gehlen, the former Nazi intelligence chief who went to work for the CIA after the war.

Czechoslovakia was the worst case. By 1951 an unbelievable 169,000 card-carrying members of the Czech Communist Party had been arrested — ten percent of the entire membership. There were tens of thousands more in Poland, Hungary, East Germany and Bulgaria. Hundreds were put to death, others died in prison or went insane.[2]

After Swiatlo defected in December 1953, East European intelligence services came to realize that he had been working for the other side all along. Four weeks after Swiatlo held his Washington press conference, the Polish Government announced that it was releasing Hermann Field because investigation had revealed that the charges which had been brought against him by "an American agent and provocateur", Jozef Swiatlo, were "baseless".[3] Field was paid $50,000 for his imprisonment as well as having his convalescence at a sanitorium paid for.[4]

Three weeks later, Noel and Herta Field were released in Hungary. The government in Budapest stated that it could not justify the charges against them.[5] They were also compensated and chose to remain in Hungary.

Once Noel Field had been officially declared innocent, the cases of countless others in East Europe had to be reviewed. First in trickles, then in rushes, the prisoners were released. By 1956 the vast majority stood outside the prison walls.

Throughout the decade following the war, the CIA was fanning the flames of discontent in Eastern Europe in many ways other than Operation Splinter Factor. Radio Free Europe (RFE, cf. Soviet Union chapter), broadcasting from West Germany, never missed a (dirty) trick. In January 1952, for example, after RFE learned that Czechoslovakia was planning to devalue its currency, it warned the population, thus stimulating a nation-wide buying panic.[6] RFE's commentaries about various European Communists were described by Blanche Wiesen Cook in her study of the period, *The Declassified Eisenhower*. She wrote that the broadcasts:

> involved a wide range of personal criticism, tawdry and slanderous attacks ranging from rumors of brutality and torture, to corruption, and to madness, perversion, and vice. Everything was used that could be imagined in order to make communists, whether in England or in Poland, look silly, undignified, and insignificant.[7]

One of the voices heard frequently over RFE on the subject of Communist obnoxiousness was none other than Jozef Swiatlo, who had earned the nickname of "Butcher" for his proclivity to torture. Needless to say, the born-again humanitarian made no mention of Splinter Factor or his double role, although some of his broadcasts reportedly shook up the Polish security system for the better.[8]

Any way the CIA could stir up trouble and nuisance . . . supporting opposition groups in Rumania[9] . . . setting up an underground radio station in Bulgaria[10] . . . dropping propaganda from balloons over Czechoslovakia, Poland and Hungary (on one day in August 1951 alone, 11,000 balloons carrying 13 million leaflets)[11] . . .

In 1955, Eastern Europeans could be found at Fort Bragg, North Carolina training with the Green Berets, learning guerrilla warfare tactics, hopefully to be used in their native lands.[12]

By the following year, hundreds of Hungarians, Rumanians, Poles and others were being trained by CIA paramilitary specialists at a secret installation in West Germany. When, in October 1956, the uprising in Hungary occurred, these men, according to the CIA, were not used because they were not yet ready,[13] but the Agency did send its agents in Budapest into action to join the rebels and help organize them.[14] In the meantime, RFE was exhorting the Hungarian people to continue their resistance, implying that American military assistance was on the way. It never came.

There is no evidence that Operation Splinter Factor contributed to the Hungarian uprising or to the earlier ones in Poland and East Germany. Nonetheless, the CIA could point to all the cold-war, anti-Communist propaganda points it had won because of the witch hunts in the East. A(n) (im)moral victory.

8. Germany 1950s
Everything from juvenile delinquency to terrorism

Within a period of 30 years and two world wars with Germany, the Soviet Union suffered more than 40 million dead and wounded, and enormous devastation to its land; its cities were razed to the ground. At the close of the Second World War, the Russians were not kindly disposed toward the German people. With their own country to rebuild, they placed the reconstruction of Germany far down on their list of priorities.

The United States emerged from the war with relatively minor casualties and its territory completely unscathed. It was ready, willing and able to devote itself to its main priority in Europe: the building of an anti-Communist bulwark in the West, particularly in the strategic location of Germany.

In 1945, official American policy was explicitly "to bring home to the Germans that they could not escape the suffering they had brought upon themselves . . . (and) to control (the) German economy to . . . prevent any higher standard of living than in neighboring nations."[1]

"From the outset," wrote former Secretary of State Dean Acheson, US officials in Germany believed this plan "to be unworkable".[2]

Acheson did not explain what lay behind this prognosis, but its correctness soon became apparent for three distinct reasons: 1) Influential American business and financial leaders, some of them occupying important government positions, had too great a stake in a highly-industrialized Germany (usually dating back to before the war) to allow the country to sink to the depths that some American policy-makers advocated; 2) A revitalized West Germany was seen as an indispensable means of combatting Soviet influence in the Eastern sector of the country, if not in all of Eastern Europe. West Germany was to become "the showcase of Western democracy" — dramatic, living proof of the superiority of capitalism over socialism; 3) In American conservative circles, and some liberal ones as well, wherein a Soviet invasion of Western Europe remained perpetually imminent, the idea of tying West Germany's industrial hands was one which came perilously close to being "soft on communism", if not worse.[3]

Dwight Eisenhower echoed this last sentiment when he later wrote:

> Had certain officials in the Roosevelt administration had their way, Germany would have been far worse off, for there were those who advocated the flooding of the Ruhr mines, the wrecking of German factories, and the reducing of Germany from an industrial to an agricultural nation. Among others, Harry Dexter White, later named by Attorney General Brownell as one who had been heavily involved in a Soviet espionage ring operating within our government . . . proposed exactly that.[4]

Thus it was that the de-industrialization of West Germany met the same fate as de-militarization, as the United States poured in massive economic assistance: $4 billion of Marshall Plan aid and an army of industrial and technical experts.

At the same time, the Soviet Union was pouring massive economic assistance *out* of East Germany. The Soviets dismantled and moved back home entire factories with large amounts of equipment and machinery, and thousands of miles of railroad track. When added to war reparations, the toll reached into the billions of dollars.

By the early 1950s, though social services, employment, and cultural life in East Germany were on a par or superior to that in West Germany, the Western sector had the edge in those areas of prosperity with the most sex appeal: salaries were higher, the eating was better, consumer goods more available, and the neon lights emblazoned the nights along the Kurfürstendamm.

American cold warriors, however, as if discontent with the game score or with leaving so much to chance, instituted a crude campaign of sabotage and subversion against East Germany designed to throw the economic and administrative machinery out of gear. The CIA and other US intelligence and military services in West Germany (with occasional help from the likes of British intelligence and the West German police) recruited, equipped, trained and financed German activist groups and individuals of West and East. Finding recruits for such a crusade was not difficult, for in post-war Germany, anti-communism lived on as the only respectable vestige of Naziism.

The actions carried out by these operatives — most of whom were associated with organizations with names like Fighting Group Against Inhumanity, Association of Political Refugees from the East, and the Investigating Committee of Freedom-minded Jurists of the Soviet Zone — ran the spectrum from juvenile delinquency to terrorism; anything "to make the commies look bad". It added up to the following remarkable record:[5]

- through explosives, arson, short circuiting, and other methods they damaged power stations, shipyards, a dam, canals, docks, public buildings, petrol stations, shops, a radio station, outdoor stands, public transportation.
- derailed freight trains, seriously injuring workers; burned 12 cars of a freight train and destroyed air pressure hoses of others.
- blew up road and railway bridges; placed explosives on a railway bridge of the Berlin-Moscow line but these were discovered in time — hundreds would have been killed.
- used special acids to damage vital factory machinery; put sand in the turbine of a factory, bringing it to a standstill; set fire to a tile-producing factory; promoted work slow-downs in factories; stole blueprints and samples of new technical developments.
- killed 7,000 cows of a co-operative dairy by poisoning the wax coating of the wire used to bale the cows' corn fodder.
- added soap to powdered milk destined for East German schools.
- raided and wrecked left-wing offices in East and West Berlin, stole membership lists; assaulted and kidnapped leftists and, on occasion, murdered them.
- set off stink bombs to disrupt political meetings.
- floated balloons which burst in the air, scattering thousands of propaganda pamphlets down upon unsuspecting East Germans.
- were in possession, when arrested, of a large quantity of the poison cantharidin with which it was planned to produce poisoned cigarettes to kill leading East Germans.
- attempted to disrupt the World Youth Festival in East Berlin by sending out forged invitations, false promises of free bed and board, false notices of cancellations; carrying out attacks on participants with explosives, firebombs, and special tyre-puncturing equipment; setting fire to a wooden bridge on a main motorway leading to the festival.
- forged and distributed large quantities of food ration cards — for example, for 60,000 pounds of meat — to cause confusion, shortages and resentment.
- sent out forged tax notices and other government directives and documents to foster disorganization and inefficiency within industry and unions.
- "gave considerable aid and comfort" to East Germans who staged an uprising on 17 June 1953; during and after the uprising, the US radio station in West Berlin, RIAS (Radio In the American Sector), issued inflammatory broadcasts into East Germany appealing to the populace to resist the government; RIAS also broadcast warnings to witnesses in at least one East German criminal case being monitored by the Investigating Committee of Freedom-minded Jurists of the Soviet Zone that they would be added to the committee's files of "accused persons" if they lied.

Although many hundreds of the American agents were caught and tried by East Germany, the ease with which they could pass back and forth between the two sectors and infiltrate different enterprises without any language barrier provided opportunities for the CIA unmatched anywhere else in Eastern Europe. These circumstances led, in May 1952, to the East Germans instituting the first tightening up of entry into the country from the West.

Throughout the 1950s, the East Germans and the Soviet Union repeatedly lodged complaints with the Soviets' erstwhile allies in the West about specific sabotage and espionage activities and called for the closure of the offices in West Germany they claimed were responsible, and for which they provided names and addresses. In December 1956, East Germany filed a lengthy and detailed formal protest with the United Nations charging the United States with "continually interfering in the internal affairs of the German Democratic Republic, and carrying on subversive activity in breach of the normal rules of international law".[6]

While staging their commando and fifth-column attacks upon East Germany, American authorities and their German agents were apparently convinced that the Soviet Union had belligerent designs upon West Germany. (A text-book case of projection?) On 8 October 1952, the Minister-President of the West German state of Hesse, Georg August Zinn, disclosed that the United States had created a secret civilian army in his state for the purpose of resisting a Russian invasion.

This force of between 1,000 and 2,000 men belonged to the so-called "Technical Service" of the German Youth Federation, the latter described by the *New York Times* as "a Right-wing youth group frequently charged with extremist activities" (a reference to the terrorist tactics described above). The stalwarts of the Technical Service were hardly youths, however, for almost all appeared to be between 35 and 50 and most, said Zinn, were "former officers of the Luftwaffe, the Wehrmacht and the S.S. [Hitler's Black-shirts]". For more than a year they had received American training in infantry weapons and explosives and "political instruction" in small groups at a secluded site in the countryside and at an American military installation.

The intelligence wing of the Technical Service, the state president revealed, had drawn up lists and card indexes of persons who were to be "put out of the way" when the Soviet tanks began to roll. These records, which contained detailed descriptions and intimate biographical information, were of some 200 leading Social Democrats (including Zinn himself), 15 Communists, and various others, all of whom were deemed "politically untrustworthy" and opponents of West German militarization. Apparently, support for peaceful co-existence and detente with the Soviet bloc was sufficient to qualify one for inclusion on the hit-list, for one man was killed at the training site, charged with being an "East-West bridge builder". It was this murder that led to the exposure of the entire operation.

The United States admitted its role in the creation and training of the guerrilla army, but denied any involvement in the "illegal, internal, and political activities" of the organization. But Zinn reported that the Americans had learned of the plotting in May and had not actually dissolved the group until

September, the same month that German Security Police arrested a number of the group's leaders. At some point, the American who directed the training courses, Sterling Garwood, had been "supplied with carbon copies of the card-index entries". It appears that at no time did US authorities communicate anything of this matter to the West German Government.

As the affair turned out, those who had been arrested were quickly released and the United States thwarted any further investigation in this the American Zone of occupied Germany. Commented Herr Zinn: "The only legal explanation for these releases can be that the people in Karlsruhe [the Federal Court] declared that they acted upon American direction."[7]

To add to the furore, the national leader of the Social Democrats accused the United States of financing an opposition group to infiltrate and undermine his party. Erich Ollenhauer, whose name had also appeared on the Technical Service's list, implied that American "clandestine" agencies were behind the plot despite the disapproval of high-ranking US officials.[8]

The revelations about the secret army and its hit-list resulted in a storm of ridicule and denunciation falling upon the United States from many quarters in West Germany. In particular, the delicious irony of the Americans working hand-in-glove with "ex"-Nazis did not escape the much-castigated German people.

9. Iran 1953
Making it safe for the King of Kings

"So this is how we get rid of that madman Mossadegh," announced John Foster Dulles to a group of top Washington policy makers one day in June 1953.[1] The Secretary of State held in his hand a plan of operation to overthrow the prime minister of Iran prepared by Kermit (Kim) Roosevelt of the CIA. There was scarcely any discussion among the high-powered men in the room, no probing questions, no legal or ethical issues raised.

"This was a grave decision to have made," Roosevelt later wrote. "It involved tremendous risk. Surely it deserved thorough examination, the closest consideration, somewhere at the very highest level. It had not received such thought at this meeting. In fact, I was morally certain that almost half of those present, if they had felt free or had the courage to speak, would have opposed the undertaking."[2]

Roosevelt, the grandson of Theodore and distant cousin of Franklin, was expressing surprise more than disappointment at glimpsing American foreign policy-making undressed.

The original initiative to oust Mossadegh had come from the British, for the elderly Iranian leader had spearheaded the parliamentary movement to nationalize the British-owned Anglo-Iranian Oil Company (AIOC), the sole oil company operating in Iran. In March 1951, the bill for nationalization was passed, and at the end of April Mossadegh was elected prime minister by a large majority of parliament. On 1 May, nationalization went into effect. The Iranian people, Mossadegh declared, "were opening a hidden treasure upon which lies a dragon".[3]

As the prime minister had anticipated, the British did not take the nationalization gracefully, although it was supported unanimously by the Iranian parliament and by the overwhelming majority of the Iranian people for reasons of both economic justice and national pride. The Mossadegh government tried to do all the right things to placate the British: it offered to set aside 25% of the net profits of the oil operation as compensation; it guaranteed the safety and the jobs of the British employees; it offered to sell its oil without disturbance to the tidy control system so dear to the hearts of the international oil giants. But the British would have none of it. What they wanted was their oil company back. And they wanted Mossadegh's head. A servant does not affront his lord with impunity.

A military show of force by the British navy was followed by a ruthless international economic blockade and boycott, and a freezing of Iranian assets which brought Iran's oil exports and foreign trade to a virtual standstill, plunged the already impoverished country into near destitution, and made payment of any compensation impossible. Nonetheless, and long after the British had moved to oust Mossadegh, they demanded compensation not only for the physical assets of the AIOC, but for the value of their enterprise in developing the oil fields; a request impossible to meet, and, in the eyes of Iranian nationalists, something which decades of huge British profits had paid for many times over.

The British attempt at economic strangulation of Iran could not have got off the ground without the active co-operation and support of the Truman and Eisenhower administrations and American oil companies. At the same time, the Truman administration argued with the British that Mossadegh's collapse could open the door to the proverbial communist takeover.[4] When the British were later expelled from Iran, however, they had no alternative but to turn to the United States for assistance in toppling Mossadegh. In November 1952, the Churchill government approached Roosevelt, the *de facto* head of the CIA's Middle East division, who told the British that he felt that there was "no chance to win approval from the outgoing administration of Truman and Acheson. The new Republicans, however, might be quite different."[5]

John Foster Dulles was certainly different. The apocalyptic anti-communist saw in Dr Mohammed Mossadegh the epitome of all that he detested in the Third World: unequivocal neutralism in the cold war, tolerance of Communists, and disrespect for free enterprise, as demonstrated by the oil nationalization. (By a curious twist of this morality, the fact that Great Britain in recent years had nationalized several of its own basic industries was apparently not at all disturbing.)

The Iranian leader was indeed an eccentric. And when the Secretary of State considered further that Iran was a nation exceedingly rich in the liquid gold, and that it shared a border with the Soviet Union more than 1,000 miles long, he was not unduly plagued by indecision as to whether Mossadegh should finally retire from public life.

As matters turned out, the overthrow of the Iranian prime minister in August 1953 was an American-only operation. Twenty-six years later, Kermit Roosevelt took the unusual step of writing a book about how he and the CIA carried through the operation. He called his book *Countercoup* to press home the idea that the CIA coup was staged only to prevent a takeover of power by the Iranian Communist Party (The Tudeh) closely backed by the Soviet Union. Roosevelt was thus arguing that Mossadegh had to be removed to prevent a Communist takeover, whereas the Truman administration had felt that Mossadegh had to be kept in power to prevent one.

It would be incorrect to state that Roosevelt offers little evidence to support his thesis of the Communist danger. It would be more precise to say that he offers *no* evidence at all. Instead, the reader is subjected to mere assertions of the thesis which are stated over and over, apparently in the belief that enough repetition will convince even the most sceptical. Thus are we treated to variations on the theme such as the following:

"The Soviet threat (was) indeed genuine, dangerous and imminent" . . . Mossadegh "had formed an alliance" with the Soviet Union to oust the Shah . . . "the obvious threat of Russian takeover" . . . "the alliance between (Mossadegh) and the Russian-dominated Tudeh was taking on a threatening shape" . . . Mossadegh's "increasing dependence on the Soviet Union" . . . "the hand of the Tudeh, and behind them the Russians, is showing more openly every day" . . . "Russian backing of the Tudeh and Tudeh backing of (Mossadegh) became ever more obvious" . . . the Soviet Union was "ever more active in Iran. Their control over Tudeh leadership was growing stronger all the time. It was exercised often and, to our eyes, with deliberate ostentation" . . .[6]

But none of this subversive and threatening activity was, apparently, ever open, obvious, or ostentatious enough to provide Roosevelt with a single example he could impart to a curious reader.

In actuality, although the Tudeh Party more or less faithfully followed the fluctuating Moscow line on Iran, the relation of the party to Mossadegh was much more complex than Roosevelt and other cold-war chroniclers have made it out to be. The Tudeh felt very ambiguous about the wealthy, eccentric, land-owning prime minister who, nonetheless, was standing up to imperialism. On occasion it had supported his policies; more often it had attacked them bitterly, and in one instance, 15 July 1951, a Tudeh-sponsored demonstration was brutally suppressed by Mossadegh, resulting in some 100 deaths and 500 injured.

What, indeed, did Mossadegh have to gain by relinquishing any of his power to the Tudeh and/or the Soviet Union? The idea that the Russians even desired the Tudeh to take power is no more than speculation. There was just as much evidence, or as little, to conclude that the Russians, once again, were more concerned about their relationship with Western governments than with the fate of a local Communist party in a country outside the Soviet domain.[7]

A secret State Department intelligence report, dated 9 January 1953, in the closing days of the Truman administration, stated that Mossadegh had not sought any alliance with the Tudeh, and that "The major opposition to the National Front [Mossadegh's governing coalition] arises from the vested interests, on the one hand, and the Tudeh Party on the other."[8]

The Tudeh Party had been declared illegal in 1949 and Mossadegh had not lifted that ban although he allowed the party to operate openly, at least to some extent because of his democratic convictions, and had appointed some Tudeh sympathizers to government posts.

Many of the Tudeh's objectives paralleled those espoused by the National Front, the State Department report observed, but "An open Tudeh move for power . . . would probably unite independents and non-Communists of all political leanings and would result . . . in energetic efforts to destroy Tudeh by force."[9]

The National Front itself was a coalition of highly diverse political and religious elements including right-wing anti-communists, held together by Mossadegh's personality and by nationalistic sentiments, particularly in regard to the nationalization of oil.

In 1979, when he was asked about this State Department report, Roosevelt replied: "I don't know what to make of that . . . Loy Henderson [US ambassador to Iran in 1953] thought that there was a serious danger that Mossadegh was going to, in effect, place Iran under Soviet domination."[10] Henderson, as we shall see in the Middle East chapter, was a man given to alarmist statements about "communist takeovers".

One can but wonder what Roosevelt, or anyone else, made of a statement by John Foster Dulles before a Senate committee in July 1953, when the operation to oust Mossadegh was already in process. The Secretary of State, the press reported, testified "that there was 'no substantial evidence' to indicate that Iran was cooperating with Russia. On the whole," he added, "Moslem opposition to communism is predominant, although at times the Iranian Government appears to rely for support on the Tudeh party, which is communistic."[11]

The young Shah of Iran had been relegated to little more than a passive role by Mossadegh and the Iranian political process. His power had been whittled away to the point where he was "incapable of independent action", noted the State Department intelligence report. Mossadegh was pressing for control of the armed forces and more say over expenditures of the royal court, and the inexperienced and indecisive Shah — the "King of Kings" — was reluctant to openly oppose the prime minister because of the latter's popularity.

The actual sequence of events instigated by Roosevelt which culminated in the Shah's ascendancy appears rather simple in hindsight, even ingenuous, and owed not a little to luck. The first step was to reassure the Shah that Eisenhower and Churchill were behind him in his struggle for power with Mossadegh and were willing to provide whatever military and political support he needed. Roosevelt did not actually know what Eisenhower felt, or even knew, about the operation, and went so far as to fabricate a message from the president to the Shah expressing his encouragement.[12]

At the same time, the Shah was persuaded to issue royal decrees dismissing Mossadegh as prime minister and replacing him with one Fazlollah Zahedi, a general who had been imprisoned during the war by the British for collaboration with the Nazis. (To what extent his collaboration sprang from sympathy towards the Germans, and to what extent from hostility towards the British and Russian occupation of Iran is not known.)[13]

Late in the night of 14/15 August, the Shah's emissary delivered the royal decree to Mossadegh's home, which was guarded by troops. Not surprisingly, he was received very coolly and did not get in to see the prime minister. Instead, he was obliged to leave the decree with a servant who signed a receipt for the piece of paper dismissing his master from power. Equally unsurprising, Mossadegh did not abdicate. The prime minister, who maintained that only parliament could dismiss him, delivered a radio broadcast the following morning in which he stated that the Shah, encouraged by "foreign elements", had attempted a *coup d'etat*.[14] Mossadegh then declared that he was, therefore, compelled to take full power unto himself. He denounced Zahedi as a traitor and sought to have him arrested, but the general had been hidden by Roosevelt's team.

The Shah, fearing that all was lost, fled with his queen to Rome via Baghdad without so much as packing a suitcase. Undeterred, Roosevelt went ahead and directed the mimeographing of copies of the royal decrees for distribution to the public, and sent two of his Iranian agents to important military commanders to seek their support. It appears that this crucial matter was left to the last minute, almost as an afterthought. Indeed, one of the two Iranians had been recruited for the cause only the same day, and it was only he who succeeded in winning a commitment of military support from an Iranian colonel who had tanks and armoured cars under his command.

Beginning on 16 August, demonstrations supporting Mossadegh and attacking the Shah and the United States broke out in the capital city, Teheran. Roosevelt characterized the demonstrators simply as "the Tudeh, with strong Russian encouragement",[15] once again failing to offer any evidence to support his assertion. The *New York Times* referred to the demonstrators as "Tudeh partisans and Nationalist extremists",[16] the latter term being one which could have applied to individuals comprising a wide range of political leanings.

During the demonstrations, the Tudeh raised their familiar demand for the creation of a democratic republic; they appealed to Mossadegh to form a united front and to provide them with arms to defend against the coup, but the prime minister refused.[17] Instead, on 18 August the prime minister ordered the police and army to put an end to the demonstrations, which they did with considerable force. According to the accounts of Roosevelt and Ambassador Henderson, Mossadegh took this step as a result of a meeting with Henderson in which the ambassador complained of the extreme harrassment being suffered by US citizens at the hands of the Iranians. It is left unclear by both men how much of this harrassment was real and how much manufactured by them for the occasion. In any event, Henderson told Mossadegh that unless it ceased, he would be obliged to order all Americans to leave Iran at once. Mossadegh, says Henderson, begged him not to do this for an American evacuation would make it appear that his government was not able to control the country, although at the same time the prime minister accused the CIA of being behind the issuance of the royal decrees.[18] (The Tudeh newspaper at this time was demanding the expulsion of "interventionist" American diplomats.)[19]

Whatever Mossadegh's motivation, his action was again in sharp contradiction to the idea that he was in alliance with the Tudeh or that the party was in a position to grab the reins of power — it did not take to the streets again.

The following day, 19 August, Roosevelt's Iranian agents staged a parade through Teheran. With a fund of some one million dollars having been established in a safe in the American embassy, the "extremely competent professional organizers", as Roosevelt called them, had no difficulty in buying themselves a mob, probably using but a fraction of the fund. (The various accounts of the CIA role in Iran have the Agency spending from $10,000 to $19 million to overthrow Mossadegh. The larger amounts are based on reports that the CIA engaged in heavy bribery of members of parliament and other influential Iranians to enlist their support against the prime minister.)[20]

Soon a line of people could be seen coming out of the ancient bazaar, led by circus and athletic performers to attract the public. The marchers were waving banners, shouting "Long live the Shah!" Along the edges of the procession, men were passing out Iranian currency adorned with a portrait of the Shah.

The demonstrators gathered followers as they went, people joining and picking up the chants, undoubtedly for a myriad of personal and political reasons. The balance of psychology had swung against Mossadegh.

Along the way, some marchers broke ranks to attack the offices of pro-Mossadegh newspapers and political parties, Tudeh and government offices . . . presently, a voice broke in over the radio in Teheran announcing that "The Shah's instruction that Mossadegh be dismissed has been carried out. The new Prime Minister, Fazlollah Zahedi, is now in office. And His Imperial Majesty is on his way home!"[21]

This was a lie, or a "pre-truth" as Roosevelt suggested. Only then did he go to fetch Zahedi from his hiding place. On the way, he happened to run into the commander of the air force who was among the marching throng. Roosevelt told the officer to get hold of a tank in which to carry Zahedi to Mossadegh's house in proper fashion.

Kermit Roosevelt would have the reader believe that at this point it was all over but the shouting and the champagne he was soon to uncork: Mossadegh had fled, Zahedi had assumed power, the Shah had been notified to return — a dramatic, joyful, and peaceful triumph of popular will. Inexplicably, he neglects to mention at all that in the streets of Teheran and in front of Mossadegh's house that day, a nine-hour battle raged, with soldiers loyal to Mossadegh on one side and those supporting Zahedi and the Shah on the other. Some 300 people were reported killed and hundreds more wounded before Mossadegh's defenders finally succumbed.[22]

The US Military Mission in Iran also played a role in the fighting, as Major General George C. Stewart later testified before Congress:

> Now, when this crisis came on and the thing was about to collapse, we violated our normal criteria and among the other things we did, we provided the army immediately on an emergency basis, blankets, boots, uniforms, electric generators, and medical supplies that permitted and created the atmosphere in which they could support the Shah . . . The guns that they had in their hands, the trucks that they rode in, the armored cars that they drove through the streets, and the radio communications that permitted their control, were all furnished through the military defense assistance program . . .[23]

The latter part of the General's statement would, presumably, apply to the other side as well.

"It is conceivable that the Tudeh could have turned the fortunes of the day against the royalists," wrote Kennett Love, a *New York Times* reporter who was in Teheran during the crucial days of August. "But for some reason they remained aloof from the conflict. My own conjecture is that the Tudeh were restrained by the Soviet Embassy because the Kremlin, in the first post-Stalin year, was not willing to take on such consequences as might have resulted from the establishment of a communist-controlled regime in Teheran."[24]

Love's views, contained in a paper he wrote in 1960, may well have been inspired by information received from the CIA. By his own admission, he was in close contact with the Agency in Teheran and even aided them in their operation.

Earlier in the year, the *New York Times* had noted that "prevailing opinion among detached observers in Teheran" was that "Mossadegh is the most popular politician in the country". During a period of more than 40 years in public life, Mossadegh had "acquired a reputation as an honest patriot".[25]

In July, the State Department Director of Iranian Affairs had testified that "Mossadegh has such tremendous control over the masses of people that it would be very difficult to throw him out."[26] (The gentleman was obviously not privy to his boss's scheme.)

A few days later, "at least 100,000" people filled the streets of Teheran to express strong anti-US and anti-Shah sentiments. Though sponsored by the Tudeh, the turnout far exceeded any estimate of party adherents.[27]

But popularity and masses, of the unarmed kind, counted for little, for in the final analysis what Teheran witnessed was a military showdown carried out on both sides by soldiers obediently following the orders of a handful of officers, some of whom were staking their careers and ambitions on choosing the winning side; others had a more political commitment. The *New York Times* characterized the sudden reversal of Mossadegh's fortunes as "nothing more than a mutiny . . . against pro-Mossadegh officers" by "the lower ranks" who revered the Shah, had brutally quelled the demonstrations the day before, and refused to do the same on 19 August, but instead turned against their officers.[28]

What connection Roosevelt and his agents had with any of these rebellious officers beforehand is not certain. In an interview given at about the same time that he finished his book, Roosevelt stated that a number of pro-Shah officers were given refuge in the CIA compound adjoining the US Embassy at the time the Shah fled to Rome.[29] But inasmuch as Roosevelt mentions not a word of this rather important and interesting development in his book, it must be regarded as yet another of his assertions to be approached with caution.

In any event, it may be that the 19 August demonstration organized by Roosevelt's team was just the encouragement and spark these officers were waiting for. Yet, if so, it further illustrates how much Roosevelt had left to chance.

In light of the questionable, contradictory, and seemingly devious statements which emanated at times from John Foster Dulles, Kermit Roosevelt, Loy Henderson and other American officials, what conclusions can be drawn about American motivation in the toppling of Mossadegh? The consequences of the coup may speak eloquently to this.

For the next 25 years, the Shah of Iran stood fast as the United States' closest ally in the Third World, to a degree that would have shocked the independent and neutral Mossadegh. The Shah literally placed his country at the disposal of US military and intelligence organizations to be used as a cold-war weapon, a window and a door to the Soviet Union: electronic listening and radar posts were set up near the Soviet border; American aircraft used Iran as a base to launch surveillance flights over the Soviet Union; espionage agents were infiltrated across the border; various American military installations dotted the Iranian landscape. Iran, along with South Korea and the Philippines, had become a vital link in the chain being forged by the United States to "contain" the Soviet Union. In a telegram to the British acting Foreign Secretary in September, Dulles said: "I think if we can in coordination move quickly and effectively in Iran we would close the most dangerous gap in the line from Europe to South Asia."[30] In February 1955, Iran became a member of the Baghdad Pact, set up by the United States, in Dulles' words, "to create a solid band of resistance against the Soviet Union".[31]

One year after the coup, the Iranian government completed a contract with an international consortium of oil companies which left Iran as the owner of the oil industry in name only, for obvious public consumption, and the consortium as the *de facto* owners. The sole ownership the British had enjoyed previously was reduced to 40%, another 40% now going to American oil firms, the remainder elsewhere. The British, however, received an extremely generous compensation for their former property.[32]

In 1958, Kermit Roosevelt left the CIA and presently went to work for Gulf Oil Co., one of the American oil firms in the consortium. In this position, Roosevelt was director of Gulf's relations with the US government and foreign governments and had occasion to deal with the Shah. In 1960, Gulf appointed him a vice president.

Subsequently, Roosevelt formed a consulting firm, Downs and Roosevelt, which, between 1967 and 1970, reportedly received $116,000 a year above expenses for its efforts on behalf of the Iranian government. Another client, the Northrop Corporation, a Los Angeles-based aerospace company, paid Roosevelt $75,000 a year to aid in its sales to Iran, Saudi Arabia and other countries.[33] (See the Middle East chapter for Roosevelt's CIA connection with King Saud of Saudi Arabia.)

Another American member of the new consortium was Standard Oil Co. of New Jersey (now Exxon), a client of Sullivan and Cromwell, the New York law firm of which John Foster Dulles had long been the senior member. Brother Allen, Director of the CIA, had also been a member of the firm.[34] Syndicated columnist Jack Anderson reported some years later that the Rockefeller family, who controlled Standard Oil and Chase Manhattan Bank, "helped arrange the CIA coup that brought down Mossadegh". Anderson lists a number of ways in which the Shah demonstrated his gratitude to the Rockefellers, including heavy deposits of his personal fortune in Chase Manhattan, and housing developments in Iran built by a Rockefeller family company.[35]

Despite all the evidence to the contrary, the standard "text-book" account of what took place in Iran in 1953 is that — whatever else one might say for or against the operation — the United States saved Iran from a Soviet/Communist takeover. Yet, during the two years of American and British subversion of a bordering country, the Soviet Union did nothing that would support such a premise. When the British Navy staged the largest concentration of its forces since World War II in Iranian waters,[36] the Soviets took no belligerent steps; nor when Great Britain instituted draconian international sanctions which left Iran in a deep economic crisis and extremely vulnerable, did the oil fields "fall hostage" to the Bolshevik Menace; this, despite "the whole of the Tudeh Party at its disposal" as agents, as Roosevelt put it.[37] Not even in the face of the coup, which clearly showed the imprint of foreign hands, did Moscow make a threatening move; neither did Mossadegh at any point ask for Russian help. One year later, however, the *New York Times* could editorialize that "Moscow . . . counted its chickens before they were hatched and thought that Iran would be the next 'People's Democracy'." At the same time, the newspaper warned, with surprising arrogance, that "underdeveloped countries with rich resources now have an object lesson in the heavy cost that must be paid by one of their number which goes berserk with fanatical nationalism."[38]

A decade afterward, Allen Dulles solemnly stated that Communism had "achieved control of the governmental apparatus" in Iran.[39] And a decade after that, the prestigious *Fortune* magazine, to cite one of many examples, kept the story alive by writing that Mossadegh "plotted with the Communist party of Iran, the Tudeh, to overthrow Shah Mohammed Reza Pahlavi and hook up with the Soviet Union."[40]

And what of the Iranian people? What did being saved from communism do for them? For the preponderence of the population, life under the Shah was a grim tableau of grinding poverty, police terror, and torture. Thousands were executed in the name of fighting communism. Dissent was crushed from the outset of the new regime with American assistance. Kennett Love wrote that he believed that CIA officer George Carroll, whom he knew personally, worked with General Farhat Dadsetan, the new military governor of Teheran, "on preparations for the very efficient smothering of a potential dissident movement emanating from the bazaar area and the Tudeh in the first two weeks of November, 1953".[41]

The notorious Iranian secret police, SAVAK, created under the guidance of the CIA and Israel,[42] spread its tentacles all over the world to punish Iranian dissidents. According to a former CIA analyst on Iran, SAVAK was instructed in torture techniques by the Agency.[43] Amnesty International summed up the situation in 1976 by noting that Iran had the "highest rate of death penalties in the world, no valid system of civilian courts and a history of torture which is beyond belief. No country in the world has a worse record in human rights than Iran".[44]

When to this is added a level of corruption that "startled even the most hardened observers of Middle Eastern thievery",[45] it is understandable that the Shah needed his huge military and police force, maintained by unusually large US aid and training programmes,[46] to keep the lid down for as long as he did. Said Senator Hubert Humphrey, apparently with some surprise:

> Do you know what the head of the Iranian Army told one of our people? He said the Army was in good shape, thanks to U.S. aid — it was now capable of coping with the civilian population. That Army isn't going to fight the Russians. It's planning to fight the Iranian people.[47]

Where force might fail, the CIA turned to its most trusted weapon — money. To insure support for the Shah, the Agency began making payments to Iranian religious leaders, always a capricious bunch. The payments to the ayatollahs and mullahs began in 1953 and continued regularly until 1977 when President Carter abruptly halted them. One "informed intelligence source" estimated that the amount paid reached as much as $400 million a year; others thought that figure too high, which it certainly seems to be. The cut-off of funds to the holy men, it is believed, was one of the things which precipitated the beginning of the end for the King of Kings.[48]

10. Guatemala 1953-1954
While the world watched

Whom do you turn to for help when the police are assaulting you? The old question.

To whom does a poor banana republic turn when a CIA army is advancing upon its territory and CIA planes are bombing the country?

The leaders of Guatemala tried everyone — the United Nations, the Organization of American States, other countries individually, the world press, even the United States itself, in the desperate hope that it was all a big misunderstanding, that reason would prevail in the end.

Nothing helped. Dwight Eisenhower, John Foster Dulles and Allen Dulles had decided that the legally-elected government of Jacobo Arbenz was "communist", therefore must go; and go it did, in June 1954.

In the midst of the American preparation to overthrow the government, the Guatemalan Foreign Minister, Guillermo Toriello, lamented that the United States was categorizing "as 'communism' every manifestation of nationalism or economic independence, any desire for social progress, any intellectual curiosity, and any interest in progressive liberal reforms."[1]

Toriello was close to the truth, but Washington officials retained enough contact with reality and world opinion to be aware of the inappropriateness of coming out against nationalism, independence or reform. Thus it was that Secretary of State Dulles asserted that Guatemalans were living under a "Communist type of terrorism"[2] . . . President Eisenhower warned about "the Communist dictatorship" establishing "an outpost on this continent to the detriment of all the American nations"[3] . . . the US Ambassador to Guatemala, John Puerifoy, declared that "We cannot permit a Soviet Republic to be established between Texas and the Panama Canal"[4] . . . others warned that Guatemala could become a base from which the Soviet Union might actually seize the Canal . . . Senator Margaret Chase Smith hinted, unmistakably, that the "unjustified increases in the price of coffee" imported from Guatemala were due to communist control of the country, and called for an investigation[5] . . . and so it went.

The Soviet Union could be excused if it was somewhat bewildered by all the rhetoric, for the Russians had scant interest in Guatemala, did not provide the country with any kind of military assistance, did not even maintain diplomatic relations with it, thus did not have the normally indispensable embassy from which to conduct such nefarious schemes. (During this period, the height of

McCarthyist "logic", there were undoubtedly those Americans who reasoned: "All the better to deceive us!")

With the exception of one occasion, the countries of Eastern Europe had as little to do with Guatemala as did the Soviet Union. A month before the coup, that is, long after Washington had begun preparation for it, Czechoslovakia made a single arms sale to Guatemala for cash, something the Czechs would no doubt have done for any other country willing to pay the price. (The weapons, it turned out, were, in the words of the *New York Times*, "worthless military junk".*) The American propaganda mill made much of this transaction. Less publicized was the fact that Guatemala had to seek arms from Czechoslovakia because the United States had refused to sell it any since 1948, due to its reformist governments, and had pressured other countries to do the same despite Arbenz's repeated pleas to lift the embargo.[7]

Like the Soviets, Arbenz had reason to wonder about the American charges. The Guatemalan president, who took office in March 1951 after being elected by a wide margin, had no special contact or spiritual/ideological ties with the Soviet Union or the rest of the Communist bloc. Although American policy-makers and the American press, explicitly and implicitly, often labelled Arbenz a communist, there were those in Washington who knew better, at least during their more dispassionate moments. Under Arbenz's administration, Guatemala had voted at the United Nations so closely with the United States on issues of "Soviet imperialism" that a State Department group occupied with planning Arbenz's overthrow concluded that propaganda concerning Guatemala's UN record "would not be particularly helpful in our case".[8] And a State Department analysis paper reported that the Guatemalan president had support "not only from Communist-led labor and the radical fringe of professional and intellectual groups, but also among many anti-Communist nationalists in urban areas".[9]

Nonetheless, Washington repeatedly and adamantly expressed its displeasure about the presence of communists working in the Guatemalan government and their active participation in the nation's political life. Arbenz maintained that this was no more than proper in a democracy, while Washington continued to insist that Arbenz was too tolerant of such people — not because of anything they had done which was intrinsically threatening or offensive to the US or Western civilization, but simply because they were of the species communist, well known for its infinite capacity for treachery. Ambassador Puerifoy — a diplomat whose suit might have been pinstriped, but whose soul was a loud check — warned Arbenz that US-Guatemalan relations would remain strained so long as a single communist remained on the public payroll.[10]

* *Time* magazine pooh-poohed the newspaper's report and cited US military men giving a better appraisal of the weapons. Clearly, neither *Time* nor the military men could conceive that one member of the International Communist Conspiracy could do such a thing to another member.[6]

The centrepiece of Arbenz's programme was land reform. The need for it was clearly expressed in the all-too-familiar underdeveloped-country statistics: in a nation overwhelmingly rural, 2.2 percent of the landowners owned 70 percent of the arable land; the annual per capita income of agricultural workers was $87. Before the revolution of 1944, which overthrew the Ubico dictatorship, "farm laborers had been roped together by the Army for delivery to the low-land farms where they were kept in debt slavery by the landowners."[11]

The expropriation of large tracts of uncultivated acreage which was distributed to approximately 100,000 landless peasants, the improvement in union rights for the workers, and other social reforms, were the reasons Arbenz had won the support of Communists and other leftists, which was no more than to be expected. When Arbenz was criticized for accepting Communist support, he challenged his critics to prove their good faith by backing his reforms themselves. They failed to do so, thus revealing where the basis of their criticism lay.[12]

The party formed by the Communists, the Guatemalan Labor Party, held four seats in Congress, the smallest component of Arbenz's ruling coalition which commanded a total of 51 seats in the 1953-54 legislature.[13] Communists held several important sub-cabinet posts but none was ever appointed to the cabinet. In addition, there were Communists employed in the bureaucracy, particularly in the administration of land reform.[14]

Lacking anything of substance they could accuse the Guatemalan left of, Washington officials were reduced to condemnation by semantics. Thus, Communists, unlike normal human beings, did not take jobs in the government — they "infiltrated" the government. Communists did not support a particular programme — they "exploited" it. Communists did not back Arbenz — they "used" him. Moreover, communists "controlled" the labour movement and land reform — but what type of person is it who devotes himself in an under-developed country to furthering the welfare of workers and peasants? None other than the type that Washington calls "communist".

The basic idea behind the employment of such language was (and still is today) to deny the idea that communists could be people sincerely concerned about social change. American officials denied it to each other as well as to the world. Here, for example, is an excerpt from a CIA report about Guatemala, prepared in 1952 for the edification of the White House and the intelligence community:

> Communist political success derives in general from the ability of individual Communists and fellow travellers to identify themselves with the nationalist and social aspirations of the Revolution of 1944. In this manner, they have been successful in infiltrating the Administration and pro-Administration political parties and have gained control of organized labor . . . [Arbenz] is essentially an opportunist whose politics are largely a matter of historical accident . . . The extension of [communist] influence has been facilitated by the applicability of Marxist 'cliches' to the 'anti-colonial' and social aims of the Guatemalan Revolution.[15]

The first plan to topple Arbenz was a CIA operation approved by President Truman in 1952, but at the eleventh hour, Secretary of State Dean Acheson persuaded Truman to abort it.[16] However, soon after Eisenhower became president, in January 1953, the plan was resurrected.

Both administrations were pressured by executives of United Fruit Company, much of whose vast and uncultivated land in Guatemala had been expropriated by the Arbenz government as part of the land reform programme. The company wanted nearly $16 million for the land, the government was offering $525,000, United Fruit's own declared valuation for tax purposes.[17]

United Fruit functioned in Guatemala as a state within a state. It owned the country's telephone and telegraph facilities, administered its only important Atlantic harbour and monopolized its banana exports. A subsidiary of the company owned nearly every mile of railroad track in the country. The fruit company's influence amongst Washington's power elite was equally impressive. On a business and/or personal level, it had close ties to the Dulles brothers, various State Department officials and congressmen, the American Ambassador to the United Nations, and others. Anne Whitman, the wife of the company's public relations director, was President Eisenhower's personal secretary. Under-secretary of State (and formerly Director of the CIA) Walter Bedell Smith was seeking an executive position with United Fruit at the same time he was helping to plan the coup. He was later named to the company's board of directors.[18]

Under Arbenz, Guatemala constructed an Atlantic port and a highway to compete with United Fruit's holdings, and built a hydro-electric plant to offer cheaper energy than the US-controlled electricity monopoly. Arbenz's strategy was to limit the power of foreign companies through direct competition rather than through nationalization, a policy not feasible of course when it came to the question of land. In his inaugural address, Arbenz stated that,

> Foreign capital will always be welcome as long as it adjusts to local conditions, remains always subordinate to Guatemalan laws, cooperates with the economic development of the country, and strictly abstains from intervening in the nation's social and political life.[19]

This hardly described United Fruit's role in Guatemala. Amongst much else, the company had persistently endeavoured to frustrate Arbenz's reform programmes, discredit him and his government, and induce his downfall.

Arbenz was, accordingly, wary of multinationals and could not be said to welcome them into his country with open arms. This attitude, his expropriation of United Fruit's land, and his "tolerance of communists" were more than enough to make him a marked man in Washington. The United States saw these policies as being inter-related; that is, it was communist influence — not any economic or social exigency of Guatemalan life — which was responsible for the government's treatment of American firms.

In March 1953, the CIA approached disgruntled right-wing officers in the Guatemalan army and arranged to send them arms. United Fruit donated $64,000 in cash. The following month, uprisings broke out in several towns but were quickly put down by loyal troops. The rebels were put on trial and revealed the fruit company's role in the plot, but not the CIA's.[20]

The Eisenhower administration resolved to do the job right the next time around. With cynical glee, almost an entire year was spent in painstaking, step-by-step preparation for the overthrow of Jacobo Arbenz Guzmán. Of the major CIA undertakings, few have been as well documented as has the coup in Guatemala. With the release of many formerly classified government papers, the following story has emerged.[21]

Headquarters for the operation were established in Opa Locka, Florida, on the outskirts of Miami. The Nicaraguan dictator Anastasio Somoza lent/leased his country out as a site for an airstrip and for hundreds of men — Guatemalan exiles and US and Central American mercenaries — to receive training in the use of weapons and radio broadcasting, as well as in the fine arts of sabotage and demolition. Thirty airplanes were assigned for use in the "Liberation", stationed in Nicaragua, Honduras and the Canal Zone, to be flown by American pilots. The Canal Zone was set aside as a weapons depot from which arms were gradually distributed to the rebels who were to assemble in Honduras under the command of Colonel Carlos Castillo Armas before crossing into Guatemala. Soviet-marked weapons were also gathered for the purpose of planting them inside Guatemala before the invasion to reinforce US charges of Russian intervention. And, as important as arms, it turned out, hidden radio transmitters were placed in and around the perimeter of Guatemala, including one in the US Embassy.

An attempt was made to blow up the trains carrying the Czech weapons from portside to Guatemala City; however, a torrential downpour rendered the detonators useless, whereupon the CIA paramilitary squad opened fire on one train, killing a Guatemalan soldier and wounding three others; but the convoy of trains made it safely to its destination.

After the Czech ship had arrived in Guatemala, Eisenhower ordered the stopping of "suspicious foreign-flag vessels on the high seas off Guatemala to examine cargo".[22] The State Department's legal adviser wrote a brief which concluded in no uncertain terms that "Such action would constitute a violation of international law." No matter. At least two foreign vessels were stopped and searched, one French and one Dutch. It was because of such actions by the British, that the United States had fought the War of 1812.

The Guatemalan military came in for special attention. The US ostentatiously signed mutual security treaties with Honduras and Nicaragua, both countries hostile to Arbenz, and dispatched large shipments of arms to them in the hope that this would signal a clear enough threat to the Guatemalan military to persuade it to withdraw its support of Arbenz. Additionally, the US Navy dispatched two submarines from Key West, saying only that they were going "south". Several days later, the Air Force, amid considerable fanfare, sent three B-360 bombers on a "courtesy call" to Nicaragua.

The CIA also made a close study of the records of members of the Guatemalan officer corps and offered bribes to some of them. One of the Agency's clandestine radio stations broadcast appeals aimed at military men, as well as others, to join the liberation movement. The station reported that Arbenz was secretly planning to disband or disarm the armed forces and replace it with a people's militia. CIA planes dropped leaflets over Guatemala carrying the same message.

Eventually, at Ambassador Puerifoy's urging, a group of high-ranking officers called on Arbenz to ask that he dismiss all communists who held posts in his administration. The president assured them that the communists did not represent a danger, that they did not run the government, and that it would be undemocratic to dismiss them. At a second meeting, the officers also demanded that Arbenz reject the creation of the "people's militia".

Arbenz himself was offered a bribe by the CIA, whether to abdicate his office or something less is not clear. A large sum of money was deposited in a Swiss bank for him, but he, or a subordinate, rejected the offer.

On the economic front, contingency plans were made for such things as cutting off Guatemalan credit abroad, disrupting its oil supplies, and causing a run on its foreign reserves.[23] But it was on the propaganda front that American ingenuity shone at its brightest. Inasmuch as the Guatemalan government was being overthrown because it was communist, the fact of its communism would have to be impressed upon the rest of Latin America. Accordingly, the US Information Agency (USIA) began to place unattributed articles in foreign newspapers labelling particular Guatemalan officials as communist and referring to various actions by the Guatemalan government as "communist-inspired". In the few weeks prior to Arbenz's fall alone, more than 200 articles about Guatemala were written and placed in scores of Latin American newspapers.

Employing a method which was to become a standard CIA/USIA feature all over Latin America and elsewhere, as we shall see, articles placed in one country were picked up by newspapers in other countries, either as a result of CIA payment or unwittingly because the story was of interest. Besides the obvious advantage of multiplying the potential audience, the tactic gives the appearance that independent world opinion is taking a certain stand and further obscures the American connection.

The USIA also distributed more than 100,000 copies of a pamphlet entitled "Chronology of Communism in Guatemala" throughout the hemisphere, as well as 27,000 copies of anti-communist cartoons and posters. The American propaganda agency, moreover, produced three films on Guatemala, with predictable content, and newsreels favourable to the United States for showing free in cinemas.

Francis Cardinal Spellman of New York, a prelate possessed of anti-communism, a man who feared social change more than he feared God, was visited by the CIA. Would his Reverence arrange CIA contact with Archbishop Mariano Rossell Arellano of Guatemala? The Cardinal would be delighted. Thus it came to pass that on 9 April 1954, a pastoral letter was read in Guatemalan Catholic churches calling to the attention of the congregations the presence in the country of a devil called communism and demanding that the people "rise as a single man against this enemy of God and country", or at least not rally in Arbenz's defence. To appreciate the value of this, one must remember that Guatemala's peasant class was not only highly religious, but that very few of them were able to read, and so could receive the Lord's Word only in this manner. For those who could read, many thousands of pamphlets carrying the Archbishop's message were air-dropped around the country.

In May, the CIA covertly sponsored a "Congress Against Soviet Intervention in Latin America" in Mexico City. The same month, Somoza called in the diplomatic corps in Nicaragua and told them, his voice shaking with anger, that his police had discovered a secret Soviet shipment of arms (which had been planted by the CIA) near the Pacific Coast, and suggested that the communists wanted to convert Nicaragua into "a new Korean situation". A few weeks later, an unmarked plane parachuted arms with Soviet markings on to Guatemala's coast.

On such fare as that dispensed by the American propaganda campaign have the people of Latin America dined for decades. By such tactics have they been educated about "communism".

In late January 1954 the operation appeared to have suffered a serious setback when photostat copies of Liberation documents found their way into Arbenz's hands. A few days later, Guatemala's newspapers published copies of correspondence signed by Castillo Armas, Somoza and others under banner headlines. The documents revealed the existence of some of the staging, training and invasion plans, involving, amongst others, the "government of the North".[24]

The State Department labelled the accusations of a US role "ridiculous and untrue" and said it would not comment further because it did not wish to give them a dignity they did not deserve. Said a Department spokesperson: "It is the policy of the United States not to interfere in the internal affairs of other nations. This policy has repeatedly been reaffirmed under the present administration."

Time magazine gave no credence whatsoever to the possibility of American involvement in such a plot, concluding that the whole exposé had been "masterminded in Moscow".[25]

The *New York Times* was not so openly cynical, but its story gave no indication that there might be any truth to the matter. "Latin American observers in New York," reported the newspaper, "said the 'plot' charges savored of communist influence." This article was followed immediately on the page by one headed "Red Labor Chiefs Meet, Guatemalan Confederation Opens Its Congress".[26]

And the CIA continued with its preparations as if nothing had happened.

The offensive began in earnest on 18 June with planes dropping leaflets over Guatemala demanding that Arbenz resign immediately or else various sites would be bombed. CIA radio stations broadcast similar messages. That afternoon, the planes returned to machine-gun houses near military barracks, drop fragmentation bombs and strafe the National Palace.

Over the following week, the air attacks continued daily — strafing or bombing ports, fuel tanks, ammunition dumps, military barracks, the international airport, a school, and several cities; nine persons, including a three-year-old girl, were reported wounded, an unknown number of houses were set afire by incendiary explosives. During one night-time raid, a tape recording of a bomb attack was played over loudspeakers set up on the roof of the US Embassy to heighten the anxiety of the capital's residents. When Arbenz went on the air to try and calm the public's fear, the CIA radio team jammed the broadcast.

Meanwhile, the Agency's army had crossed into Guatemala from Honduras and captured a few towns, but its progress in the face of resistance by the Guatemalan army was unspectacular. On the broadcasts of the CIA's "Voice of Liberation" the picture was different: the rebels were everywhere and advancing; they were of large numbers and picking up volunteers as they marched; war and upheaval in all corners; fearsome battles and major defeats for the Guatemalan army. Some of these broadcasts were transmitted over regular public and even military channels, serving to convince some of Arbenz's officers that the reports were genuine. In the same way, the CIA was able to answer real military messages with fake responses. All manner of disinformation was spread and rumours fomented; dummy parachute drops were made in scattered areas to heighten the belief that a major invasion was taking place.

United Fruit Company's publicity office circulated photographs to journalists of mutilated bodies about to be buried in a mass grave as an example of the atrocities committed by the Arbenz regime. The photos received extensive coverage. Thomas McCann of the company's publicity office later revealed that he had no idea what the photos represented: "They could just as easily have been the victims of either side — or of an earthquake. The point is, they were widely accepted for what they were purported to be — victims of communism."[27]

In a similar vein, Washington officials reported on political arrests and censorship in Guatemala without reference to the fact that the government was under siege (let alone who was behind the siege), that suspected plotters and saboteurs were the bulk of those being arrested, or that, overall, the Arbenz administration had a fine record on civil liberties. The performance of the American press in this regard was little better.

The primary purpose of the bombing and the radio broadcasts, as well as other propaganda, was to make it appear that military defences were crumbling, that resistance was futile, thus provoking confusion and division in the Guatemalan armed forces and causing some elements to turn against Arbenz. The psychological warfare conducted over the radio was directed by E. Howard Hunt, later of Watergate fame, and David Atlee Phillips, a newcomer to the

CIA. When Phillips was first approached about the assignment, he asked his superior, Tracy Barnes, in all innocence, "But Arbenz became President in a free election. What right do we have to help someone topple his government and throw him out of office?"

"For a moment," wrote Phillips later, "I detected in his face a flicker of concern, a doubt, the reactions of a sensitive man." But Barnes quickly recovered and repeated the party line about the Soviets establishing "an easily expandable beachhead" in Central America.[28]

Phillips never looked back. When he retired from the CIA over 20 years later, he founded the Association of Retired Intelligence Officers, an organization formed in the mid-1970s to counteract the flood of unfavourable publicity which was sweeping over the Agency at the time.

American journalists reporting on the events in Guatemala continued to exhibit neither an investigative inclination nor a healthy conspiracy mentality. But what was obscure to the US press was patently obvious to large numbers of Latin Americans. Heated protests against the United States broke out during this week in June in at least eleven countries and was echoed by the governments of Ecuador, Argentina, Uruguay, and Chile which condemned American "intervention" and "aggression".

Life magazine noted the events by observing that "world communism was efficiently using the Guatemalan show to strike a blow at the U.S.". It scoffed at the idea that Washington was behind the revolt.[29] *Newsweek* reported that Washington "officials interpreted" the outcry "as an indication of the depth of Red penetration into the Americas".[30] A State Department memo at the time, however, privately acknowledged that much of the protest emanated from non-communist and even pro American moderates.[31]

On 21 and 22 June, Guatemalan Foreign Minister Toriello made impassioned appeals to the United Nations for help in resolving the crisis. American UN Ambassador Henry Cabot Lodge tried to block the Security Council from discussing a resolution to send an investigating team to Guatemala, characterizing Toriello's appeals as communist manoeuvres. But under heavy pressure from UN Secretary-General Dag Hammarskjöld, the Council was convened. Before the vote, while Lodge worked on the smaller nations represented on the Council, Eisenhower and Dulles came down hard on France and Great Britain, both of whom favoured the resolution. Said the President of the United States to his Secretary of State about Britain: "Let's give them a lesson."

As matters turned out, the resolution was defeated by five votes to four, with Britain and France abstaining, although their abstentions were not crucial inasmuch as seven votes were required for passage. Hammarskjöld was so upset with the American machinations, which he believed undercut the strength of the United Nations, that he considered resigning.

During this same period, the CIA put into practice a plan to create an "incident". Agency planes were dispatched to drop several harmless bombs on

Honduran territory. The Honduran government then complained to the UN and the Organization of American States, claiming that the country had been attacked by Guatemalan planes.[32]

Arbenz finally received an ultimatum from certain army officers: resign or they would come to an agreement with the invaders. The CIA and Ambassador Puerifoy had been offering payments to officers to defect, and one army commander reportedly accepted $60,000 to surrender his troops. With his back to the wall, Arbenz made an attempt to arm civilian supporters to fight for the government, but army officers blocked the disbursement of weapons. The Guatemalan president knew that the end was near.

The Voice of Liberation meanwhile was proclaiming that two large and heavily armed columns of invaders were moving towards Guatemala City. As the hours passed, the further advance of the mythical forces was announced, while Castillo Armas and his small band had actually not progressed very far from the Honduran border. The American disinformation and rumour offensive continued in other ways as well, and Arbenz, with no one he could trust to give him accurate information, could no longer be certain that there wasn't at least some truth to the radio bulletins.

Nothing would be allowed to threaten the victory so near at hand: a British freighter docked in Guatemala and suspected of having arrived with fuel for Arbenz's military vehicles, was bombed and sunk by a CIA plane after the crew had been warned to flee. It turned out that the ship had come to Guatemala to pick up a cargo of coffee and cotton.

A desperate Toriello pleaded repeatedly with Ambassador Puerifoy to call off the bombings, offering even to reopen negotiations about United Fruit's compensation. In a long cable to John Foster Dulles, the foreign minister described the aerial attacks on the civilian population, expressed his country's defencelessness against the bombings, and appealed to the United States to use its good offices to put an end to them. In what must have been a deeply humiliating task, Toriello stated all of this without a hint that the United States was, or could be, a party to any of it. The pleas were not simply too late. They had *always* been too late.

The Castillo Armas forces could not have defeated the much larger Guatemalan army, but the air attacks, combined with the belief in the invincibility of the enemy, persuaded Guatemalan military officers to force Arbenz to resign. No Communists, domestic or foreign, came to his aid. He asked the head of the officers, Army Chief of Staff Col. Carlos Diaz, only that he give his word not to negotiate with Castillo Armas, and Diaz, who despised the rebel commander as much as Arbenz did, readily agreed. What Diaz did not realize was that the United States would not be satisfied merely to oust Arbenz. Castillo Armas had been groomed as the new head of government, and that was not negotiable.

A CIA official, Enno Hobbing, who had just arrived in Guatemala to help draft a new constitution (sic) for the incoming regime, told Diaz that he had "made a big mistake" in taking over the government. "Colonel," said Hobbing, "you're just not convenient for the requirements of American foreign policy."

Presently, Puerifoy confronted Diaz with the demand that he deal directly with Castillo Armas. At the same time, the Ambassador showed Diaz a list of Communists he wanted shot within 24 hours.[33] Although the Guatemalan officer was willing to eliminate Communist influence in the country, he refused both requests, and indicated that the struggle against the invaders would continue.[34] Puerifoy left, livid with anger. He then sent a simple cable to CIA headquarters in Florida: "We have been doubled-crossed. BOMB!" Within hours, a CIA plane took off from Honduras, bombed a military base and destroyed the government radio station. Col. Castillo Armas, whose anti-communism the United States could trust, was soon the new leader of Guatemala.

The propaganda show was not yet over. In reaction to scepticism in Latin America and elsewhere, the United States took foreign and American newsmen on a tour of Arbenz's former residence where they could see for themselves rooms filled with school textbooks published in . . . yes, the Soviet Union. The *New York Times* correspondent, Paul Kennedy, considered to be strongly anti-Arbenz, concluded that the "books had been planted" and did not bother to report the story.[35] *Time* made no mention of the books either, but somehow came upon the story that mobs had plundered Arbenz's home and found "stacks of communist propaganda and four bags of earth, one each from Russia, China, Siberia and Mongolia."[36] *Time's* article made it clear enough that it now knew of the American role in Arbenz's downfall (although certainly not the full story), but the magazine had nothing to say about the propriety of overthrowing a democratically elected government by force.

Castillo Armas celebrated the liberation of Guatemala in various ways. In July alone, thousands were arrested on suspicion of communist activity. Many were tortured or killed.[37] Further implementation of the agrarian reform law was stopped and all expropriations of land already carried out were declared invalid.[38] United Fruit Company not only received all its land back, but the government banned the banana workers' unions as well. Moreover, seven employees of the company who had been active labour organizers were found mysteriously murdered in Guatemala City.

The new regime also disenfranchised three-quarters of Guatemala's voters by barring illiterates from the electoral rolls and outlawed all political parties, labour confederations and peasant organizations. To this was added the closing down of opposition newspapers (which Arbenz had not done)[39] and the burning of "subversive" books, including Victor Hugo's *Les Miserables*, Dostoyevsky novels, and the works of Guatemala's Nobel Prize-winning author Miguel Angel Asturias, a biting critic of United Fruit.

Meanwhile, John Foster Dulles, who was accused by Toriello of seeking to establish a "banana curtain" in Central America,[40] was concerned that some Communists might escape retribution. In cables he exchanged with Ambassador

Puerifoy, Dulles insisted that the government arrest those Guatemalans who had taken refuge in foreign embassies and that "criminal charges" be brought against them to prevent them leaving the country, charges such as "having been covert Moscow agents". The Secretary of State argued that Communists should be automatically denied the right of asylum because they were connected with an international conspiracy. The only way they should be allowed to leave, he asserted, was if they agreed to be sent to the Soviet Union. But Castillo Armas refused to accede to Dulles' wishes on this particular issue, influenced perhaps by the fact that he, as well as some of his colleagues, had been granted political asylum in an embassy at one time or another.

One of those who sought asylum in the Argentine Embassy was a 25-year-old Argentine doctor named Ernesto "Che" Guevara. Guevara, who had been living in Guatemala since sometime in 1953, tried to spark armed resistance to the invading forces, but without any success. Guevara's experience in Guatemala had a profound effect upon his political consciousness. His first wife, Hilda Gadea, whom he met there, later wrote:

> Up to that point, he used to say, he was merely a sniper, criticizing from a theoretical point of view the political panorama of our America. From here on he was convinced that the struggle against the oligarchic system and the main enemy, Yankee imperialism, must be an armed one, supported by the people.[41]

On 30 June, while the dust was still settling, Dulles summed up the situation in Guatemala in a speech which was a monument to coldwarspeak:

> [The events in Guatemala] expose the evil purpose of the Kremlin to destroy the inter-American system ... having gained control of what they call the mass organizations, [the communists] moved on to take over the official press and radio of the Guatemalan Government. They dominated the social security organization and ran the agrarian reform program ... dictated to the Congress and to the President ... Arbenz ... was openly manipulated by the leaders of communism ... The Guatemalan regime enjoyed the full support of Soviet Russia ... [the] situation is being cured by the Guatemalans themselves.[42]

When it came to rewriting history, however, Dulles' speech had nothing on these lines from a CIA memo written in August 1954 and only for internal consumption no less: "When the communists were forced by outside pressure to attempt to take over Guatemala completely, they forced Arbenz to resign (deleted). They then proceeded to establish a Communist Junta under Col. Carlos Diaz."[43]

In October, John Puerifoy sat before a Congressional committee and told them: .

> My role in Guatemala prior to the revolution was strictly that of a diplomatic observer ... The revolution that overthrew the Arbenz government was engineered and instigated by those people in Guatemala who rebelled against the policies and ruthless oppression of the Communist-controlled government.[44]

Later, Dwight Eisenhower was to write about Guatemala in his memoirs. The former president chose not to offer the slightest hint that the United States had anything to do with the planning or instigation of the coup, and indicated that his administration had only the most tangential of connections to its execution.*[45]

Thus it was that the educated, urbane men of the State Department, the CIA and the United Fruit Company, the pipe-smoking, comfortable men of Princeton, Harvard and Wall Street, decided that the illiterate peasants of Guatemala did not deserve the land which had been given to them, that the workers did not need their unions, that hunger and torture were a small price to pay for being rid of the scourge of communism.

The terror carried out by Castillo Armas was only the beginning. It was, as we shall see, to get much worse in time. It has continued with hardly a pause for over 30 years.

*   *   *   *   *   *

In 1955, the *New York Times* reported from the United Nations that "The United States has begun a drive to scuttle a section of the proposed Covenant of Human Rights that poses a threat to its business interests abroad." This section dealt with the right of peoples to self-determination and to permanent sovereignty over their natural wealth and resources. Said the newspaper: "It declares in effect that any country has the right to nationalize its resources . . ."[46]

11. Costa Rica mid-1950s
Trying to topple an ally, part 1

If ever the CIA maintained a love-hate relationship, it was with José Figueres, three times the head of state of Costa Rica.

On the one hand, Figueres, by his own admission in 1975, worked for the CIA "in 20,000 ways" . . . "all over Latin America" for 30 years.[1] "I collaborated with the CIA when we were trying to topple Trujillo," he divulged, speaking of the Dominican Republic dictator.[2]

---

* When Soviet leader Nikita Khrushchev's memoirs were published in the West, the publisher saw fit to employ a noted Kreminologist to annotate the work, pointing out errors of omission and commission.

On the other hand, Figueres revealed that the Agency had twice tried to kill him.[3] He did not elaborate, although he stated at the same time that he had tried for two years to get the Bay of Pigs invasion called off. This may have precipitated one or both of the assassination attempts.

The CIA also tried to overthrow the Figueres government. In 1964, the first significant exposé of the Agency, *The Invisible Government*, disclosed that:

> in the mid-1950s CIA agents intruded deeply into the political affairs of Costa Rica, the most stable and democratic republic in Latin America. Knowledgeable Costa Ricans were aware of the CIA's role. The CIA's purpose was to promote the ouster of José (Pepe) Figueres, the moderate socialist who became President in a fair and open election in 1953.[4]

Figueres remained in office until 1958, in this his first term as president; he had headed a liberal junta in the late 1940s.

The Agency's "major grievance", related the exposé, "was that Figueres had scrupulously recognized the right of asylum in Costa Rica — for non-Communists and Communists alike. The large influx of questionable characters complicated the agency's job of surveillance and forced it to increase its staff."[5]

The CIA's problems with Figueres actually went somewhat deeper. Costa Rica was a haven for hundreds of exiles fleeing from various Latin American right-wing dictatorships, such as in the Dominican Republic, Nicaragua, and Venezuela, and Figueres was providing groups of them with material and moral support in their plans to overthrow these regimes.[6] To Figueres, this was entirely in keeping with his anti-totalitarian beliefs, directed against the left as well as the right. The problem was that the targets for overthrow were all members in good standing in the United States' anti-Communist, "Free-World" club. (The American attitude toward Trujillo was later somewhat modified.) Moreover, Figueres had on occasion expressed criticism of the American policy of supporting such dictatorships while neglecting the economic and social problems of the hemisphere.

These considerations could easily outweigh the fact that Figueres had established his anti-Communist credentials, albeit not of the "ultra" variety, and was no more a "socialist" than Hubert Humphrey. Although Figueres spoke out strongly at times against foreign investment, as president he was eminently accommodating to Central America's *bêtes noires*, the multinational fruit companies.[7]

In addition to providing support to Figueres' political opponents,[8] the CIA, reported *The Invisible Government*, tried:

> to stir up embarrassing trouble within the Communist Party in Costa Rica, and to attempt to link Figueres with the Communists. An effort to produce evidence that Figueres had been in contact with leading Communists during a trip to Mexico was unsuccessful. But CIA agents had better luck with the first part of their strategy — stirring up trouble for the Communists. They succeeded in planting a letter in a Communist newspaper. The letter, purportedly from a leading Costa Rican Communist, put him on record in opposition to the Party

line on the [1956] Hungarian revolution.

Unaware that the letter was a CIA plant, the leading officials in the American Embassy held an urgent meeting to ponder its meaning. The political officer then dispatched a long classified report to Washington, alerting top policy makers to the possibility of a startling turn in Latin American Communist politics.[9]

In 1955 the Agency carried out an action against Figueres that was more immediately threatening. A deep personal and political animosity between Figueres and Nicaraguan dictator Anastasio Somoza had escalated into violence: an attempt against Somoza's life, launched from Costa Rica with Figueres' support, was countered by an invasion from Nicaragua by land and air. Figueres' biographer, Charles Ameringer, has related that:

Figueres accused the U.S. Central Intelligence Agency of aiding the Somoza movement against him. He claimed that the CIA felt indebted to Somoza for the help he had given in overthrowing the Arbenz regime. He asserted that the same pilots and planes (the F-47) that had participated in the attack upon Guatemala, 'afterwards came from Nicaragua and machine-gunned eleven defenseless towns in our territory.' According to Figueres, at the same time that the U.S. Department of State arranged the sale of fighter planes for Costa Rica's defense, CIA planes and pilots were flying sorties for the rebels.[10]

It is interesting to note that during this period, when little had yet been revealed about such blatant CIA covert activities, the fact that the Agency had been caught red-handed tapping Figueres' telephone was worthy of condemnatory editorial comment by the *Washington Post* and a like statement by Senator Mike Mansfield on the floor of the Senate.[11]

José Figueres did not regain the presidency of Costa Rica until 1970, at which time a renewed CIA effort to overthrow him was undertaken, for not very different reasons.

12. Syria 1956-1957
Purchasing a new government

"Neutrality," proclaimed John Foster Dulles in 1956, "has increasingly become an obsolete conception, and, except under very exceptional circumstances, it is an immoral and shortsighted conception."[1]

The short-sightedness of the neutralist government lay perhaps in its inability to perceive that its neutralism would lead to John Foster Dulles attempting to overthrow it.

Syria had shied away from US economic and military assistance because it feared the strings which came attached.* When the Syrians tried, in 1955, to purchase American tanks through commercial channels, the United States blocked the transaction. Syria then turned around and purchased Russian tanks from Czechoslovakia. Subsequently, when the Syrians endeavoured to make some military purchases directly from the US government, Dulles refused them, apparently for no other reason than moral indignation.[3]

Syria had not nationalized any American-owned companies, nor did it harbour any potent left-wing party or movement in or outside of parliament threatening to capture the reins of government. But the US Embassy had reports of "leftist tendencies" among some of the younger military officers, truly an incongruous phenomenon to the American mind. What exactly the motivations of these officers were, whether their objectives were more nationalistic than revolutionary, whether they were even anti-Western . . . none of this was terribly clear.[4] What was clear was that the "leftist tendencies" button had been pushed in Washington, and that the Syrian government, although conservative and anti-Communist, could not be relied upon to do anything about the threat posed by these officers, who, in fact, had done nothing themselves.

In the formula-prone minds of the Secretary of State and other State Department officials, the Syrians were now in danger of becoming leftist, Communist, dependent upon the Soviet Union for military equipment, a Soviet satellite, and so on. Nor was this all. A leftist-oriented Syria would threaten American interests in neighbouring Turkey which, in turn, could outflank all the states of the NATO alliance, and so forth and so on.[5] And the Soviet Union itself was not far away.

To this we add the usual Middle-Eastern intrigue: in this case, Iraq plotting with the British to topple the governments in both Syria and Nasser's Egypt; the British pressuring the Americans to join the conspiracy;[6] and the CIA compromising — leave Nasser alone, at least for the time being, and we'll do something about Syria.[7]

An implausible scenario, scandalous, but in the time-honoured tradition of the Middle East. The British were old hands at it. Dulles and the Americans, still exulting in their king-making in Iran, were looking to further remake the oil region in their own image.

Wilbur Crane Eveland was a staff member of the National Security Council, the high-level inter-agency group in Washington which, in theory, monitors and

---

* The acceptance of military aid usually means the presence of American military advisers and technicians. Moreover, the US Mutual Security Act of 1955 specified that the recipient country agree to make a contribution to "the defensive strength of the free world". The Act also declared it US policy "to encourage the efforts of other free nations . . . to foster private initiative and competition . . ."[2]

controls CIA clandestine activities. Because of Eveland's background and experience in the Middle East, the CIA had asked that he be lent to the Agency for a series of assignments there.

Archibald Roosevelt was, like his cousin Kermit Roosevelt, a highly-placed official of the CIA; both were grandsons of Teddy. Kermit had masterminded the overthrow of the Iranian government in 1953. Archie had fond hopes of doing the same in Syria.

Michail Bey Ilyan had once served as Syria's foreign minister. In 1956 he was the leader of the conservative Populist Party.

At a meeting of these three men in Damascus, Syria on 1 July 1956, as described by Eveland in his memoirs, Roosevelt asked Ilyan "what would be needed to give the Syrian conservatives enough control to purge the communists and their leftist sympathizers. Ilyan responded by ticking off names and places: the radio stations in Damascus and Aleppo; a few key senior officers; and enough money to buy newspapers now in Egyptian and Saudi hands."

"Roosevelt probed further. Could these things, he asked Ilyan, be done with U.S. money and assets alone, with no other Western or Near Eastern country involved?"

"Without question, Ilyan replied, nodding gravely."

On 26 July, Egyptian President Gamal Abdul Nasser announced that his government was taking over the operation of the Suez Canal. The reaction of the British and French was swift and inflamed. The United States was less openly hostile, though it was critical and Egyptian government funds in the US were frozen. This unexpected incident put a crimp in the CIA's plans, for — as Ilyan explained to Eveland in despair — Nasser was now the hero of the Arab world, and collaboration with any Western power to overthrow an Arab government was politically indefensible.

Eventually the coup was scheduled for 25 October. The logistics, as outlined by Ilyan, called for senior colonels in the Syrian army to

take control of Damascus, Aleppo, Homs, and Hamah. The frontier posts with Jordan, Iraq, and Lebanon would also be captured in order to seal Syria's borders until the radio stations announced that a new government had taken over under Colonel Kabbani, who would place armored units at key positions throughout Damascus. Once control had been established, Ilyan would inform the civilians he'd selected that they were to form a new government, but in order to avoid leaks none of them would be told until just a week before the coup.

For this operation, money would have to change hands. Ilyan asked for and received half a million Syrian pounds (approximately $167,000). This sum occasioned no problem for the CIA regional finance officer in Beirut. When Eveland put forth his request, the officer "hardly blinked". "Did I need new money, old money, a mixture? Bundled or boxed?" The officer suggested a combination of old and new Syrian bills from various banks in Syria, so that their Lebanese origin could not be traced from the bands on the bundles. "Give me two days," he said, "and I'll have it for you in a nice suitcase purchased in Damascus."

Ilyan further stipulated that to guarantee their participation the Syrian plotters would require assurance from the highest level of the American government that the US would both back the coup and immediately grant recognition to the new government. This, Ilyan explained, could be communicated as follows: in April, President Eisenhower had said that the United States would oppose aggression in the Middle East, but not without congressional approval. Could the president repeat this statement, in light of the Suez crisis, he asked, on a specified date when Ilyan's colleagues would be told to expect it? Eisenhower's words would provide proof of US support and intent to recognize the new government in Syria once it had been formed.

An affirmative reply to Ilyan's plan arrived in Damascus from Washington the next day. A proper occasion for the requested statement would have to be found and Secretary Dulles would be the one to use it. The scheme was for Dulles to make public reference to Eisenhower's statement between 16 and 18 October, thus giving Ilyan the week he needed to assemble his civilian team.

Ilyan accepted this proposal and received a nice suitcase filled with money.

Before long, John Foster Dulles held a press conference. In light of recent Israeli attacks on Jordan, one of the reporters present asked whether the United States might come to Jordan's aid per "our declaration of April 9".

Yes, replied the Secretary of State, repeating the reference to the April statement. The date was 16 October.

But following close on the heels of this was a message from Ilyan in Damascus to Eveland in Beirut postponing the date of the coup for five days to 30 October because Colonel Kabbani had told Ilyan that his people weren't quite ready.

The postponement was crucial. On the morning of the 30th, before dawn, Eveland was roused from his sleep by the persistent ringing of his doorbell. It was Michail Ilyan, his face flushed with anger. "Thanks to God I'm alive to see you," he cried, "and say what a terrible thing you and your government did." Eveland was startled but understood all too soon what had happened. "Last night," Ilyan continued, "the Israelis invaded Egypt and are right now heading for the Suez Canal! How could you have asked us to overthrow our government at the exact moment when Israel started a war with an Arab state?"[8]

By the following spring, however, the CIA officers in Beirut and Damascus had, apparently, nothing better to do than try their hands again at stage-managing a Syrian coup. On this occasion, Kermit Roosevelt, rather than cousin Archibald, was pulling the strings. He arranged for one Howard ("Rocky") Stone to be transferred to Damascus from the Sudan to be sure that the "engineering" was done by a "pro". Stone was, at thirty-two, already a legend in the CIA's clandestine service as the man who'd helped Kim Roosevelt overthrow the Iranian government four years earlier.

The proposed beneficiary of this particular plot was to be Adib Shishakly, former right-wing dictator of Syria, living covertly in Lebanon. Shishakly's former chief of security, Colonel Ibrahim Husseini, now Syrian military attaché in Rome, was secretly slipped into Lebanon under cover of a CIA-fabricated passport. Husseini was then to be smuggled across the Syrian border in the trunk of a US diplomatic car in order to meet with key Syrian CIA agents and provide assurances that Shishakly would come back to rule once Syria's government had been overthrown.

But the coup was exposed before it ever got off the ground. Syrian army officers who had been assigned major roles in the operation walked into the office of Syria's head of intelligence, Colonel Sarraj, turned in their bribe money and named the CIA officers who'd paid them. Lieut. Col. Robert Molloy, the American army attaché, Francis Jeton, a career CIA officer, officially Vice Consul at the US Embassy, and the legendary Howard Stone, with the title of Second Secretary for Political Affairs, were declared *personae non gratae* and expelled from the country in August.

Col. Molloy was determined to leave Syria in style. As his car approached the Lebanese border, he ran his Syrian motorcycle escort off the road and shouted to the fallen rider that "Colonel Sarraj and his commie friends" should be told that Molloy would "beat the shit out of them with one hand tied behind his back if they ever crossed his path again."

The Syrian government announcement which accompanied the expulsion order stated that Stone had first made contact with the outlawed Social Nationalist Party and then with the army officers. When the officers reported the plot, they were told to continue their contacts with the Americans and later met Shishakly and Husseini at the homes of US Embassy staff members. Husseini reportedly told the officers that the United States was prepared to give a new Syrian Government between 300 and 400 million dollars in aid if the government would make peace with Israel.

An amusing aside to the affair occurred when the Syrian Defence Minister and the Syrian Ambassador to Italy disputed the claim that Husseini had anything to do with the plot. The Ambassador pointed out that Husseini had not been in Syria since 20 July and his passport showed no indication that he had been out of Italy since that time.

The State Department categorized the Syrian charge as "complete fabrications" and retaliated by expelling the Syrian Ambassador and a Second Secretary and recalling the American Ambassador from Syria. It marked the first time since 1915 that the United States had expelled a chief of mission of a foreign country.[9]

In the wake of the controversy, the *New York Times* reported that:

There are numerous theories about why the Syrians struck at the United States. One is that they acted at the instigation of the Soviet Union. Another is that the Government manufactured an anti-U.S. spy story to distract public attention from the significance of Syria's negotiations with Moscow.[10]

In the same issue, a *Times* editorial speculated upon other plausible-sounding explanations.[11] Neither in its news report nor in its editorial, did the *New York*

Times seem to consider even the possibility that the Syrian accusation might be true.

President Eisenhower, recalling the incident in his memoirs, offered no denial to the accusation. His sole comment was: "The entire action was shrouded in mystery but the suspicion was strong that the Communists had taken control of the government."[12]

*   *   *   *   *   *

Syria's neutralism continued to obsess the United States; indeed, Washington still worries about it today, though Syria has not yet "gone communist". As an example, in 1962, President Kennedy and British Prime Minister Macmillan agreed, according to a CIA report, on "Penetration and cultivation of disruptive elements in the Syrian armed forces, particularly in the Syrian army, so that Syria can be guided by the West."[13]

13. The Middle East 1957-1958
The Eisenhower Doctrine claims another backyard for America

On 9 March 1957, the United States Congress approved a presidential resolution which came to be known as the Eisenhower Doctrine. This was a piece of paper, like the Truman Doctrine and the Monroe Doctrine before it, whereby the US government conferred upon the US government the remarkable and enviable right to intervene militarily in other countries. With the stroke of a pen, the Middle East was added to Europe and the Western hemisphere as America's field of play.

The resolution stated that "the United States regards as vital to the national interest and world peace the preservation of the independence and integrity of the nations of the Middle East." One month later, as we have seen, the CIA initiated its operation to overthrow the government of Syria.

The business part of the resolution was contained in the succinct declaration that the United States "is prepared to use armed forces to assist" any Middle East country "requesting assistance against armed aggression from any country controlled by international communism". Nothing was set forth about non-communist or anti-communist aggression which might endanger world peace.

Wilbur Crane Eveland, the Middle East specialist working for the CIA at the time, was present at a meeting in the State Department two months earlier called to discuss the resolution. Eveland read the draft which stated that "many, if not all" of the Middle East states "are aware of the danger that stems from international communism". Later he wrote:

> I was shocked. Who, I wondered, had reached this determination of what the Arabs considered a danger? Israel's army had just invaded Egypt and still occupied all of the Sinai Peninsula and the Gaza Strip. And, had it not been for Russia's threat to intervene on behalf of the Egyptians, the British, French, and Israeli forces might now be sitting in Cairo, celebrating Nasser's ignominious fall from power.[1]

The simplistic and polarized view of the world implicit in the Eisenhower Doctrine ignored not only anti-Israeli sentiments but currents of nationalism, pan-Arabism, neutralism and socialism prevalent in many influential quarters of the Middle East. The framers of the resolution saw only a cold-war battlefield and, in doing so, succeeded in creating one.

In April, King Hussein of Jordan dismissed his prime minister, Suleiman Nabulsi, amidst rumours, apparently well-founded, of a coup against the King encouraged by Egypt and Syria and Palestinians living in Jordan. It was the turning point in an ongoing conflict between the pro-West policy of Hussein and the neutralist leanings of the Nabulsi regime. Nabulsi had announced that in line with his policy of neutralism, Jordan would develop closer relations with the Soviet Union and accept Soviet aid if offered. At the same time, he rejected American aid because, he said, the United States had informed him that economic aid would be withheld unless Jordan "severs its ties with Egypt" and "consents to settlement of Palestinian refugees in Jordan", a charge denied by the State Department. Nabulsi added the commentary that "communism is not dangerous to the Arabs".

Hussein, conversely, stated his position as one "to keep Arab land for the Arabs and to stand in the way of new ideas and beliefs that are not required in the Arab world where we have our religion and traditions and history." He accused "international communism and its followers" of direct responsibility for "efforts to destroy my country". When pressed for the specifics of his accusation, he declined to provide any.

When rioting broke out in several Jordanian cities, and civil war could not be ruled out, Hussein showed himself equal to the threat to his continued rule. He declared martial law, purged the government and military of pro-Nasser and leftist tendencies, and abolished all political opposition. Jordan soon returned to a state of relative calm.

The United States, however, seized upon Hussein's use of the expression "international communism" to justify rushing units of the Sixth Fleet to the eastern Mediterranean — a super aircraft carrier, two cruisers, and 15 destroyers, followed shortly by a variety of other naval vessels and a battalion of marines which put ashore in Beirut — to "prepare for possible future intervention in Jordan".[2]

Despite the fact that nothing resembling "armed aggression from any country controlled by international communism" had taken place, the State Department openly invited the King to invoke the Eisenhower Doctrine.[3] But

Hussein, who had not even requested the show of force, refused, knowing that such a move would only add fuel to the fires already raging in Jordanian political life. He survived without it.

Sometime during this year the CIA began making secret annual payments to King Hussein, initially in the millions of dollars per year. The practice was to last for 20 years, with the Agency providing Hussein female companions as well. As justification for the payment, the CIA later claimed that Hussein allowed American intelligence agencies to operate freely in Jordan. Hussein himself provided intelligence to the CIA and distributed part of his payments to other government officials who also furnished information or cooperated with the Agency.[4]

A few months later, it was Syria which occupied the front stage in Washington's melodrama of "International Communism". The Syrians had established relations with the Soviet Union via trade, economic aid, and military purchases and training. The United States chose to see something ominous in this although it was a state of affairs engendered in no small measure by John Foster Dulles, as we saw in the previous chapter. American antipathy toward Syria was heightened in August 1957 following the Syrian government's exposure of the CIA-directed plot to overthrow it.

Washington officials and the American media settled easily into the practice of referring to Syria as a "Soviet satellite" or "quasi-satellite". This was not altogether objective or spontaneous reporting. Kennett Love, a *New York Times* correspondent in close contact to the CIA, later disclosed some of the background:

> The US Embassy in Syria connived at false reports issued in Washington and London through diplomatic and press channels to the effect that Russian arms were pouring into the Syrian port of Latakia, that 'not more than 123 Migs' had arrived in Syria, and that Lieutenant Colonel Abdel Hameed Serraj, head of Syrian intelligence, had taken over control in a Communist-inspired coup. I travelled all over Syria without hinderance in November and December [1956] and found there were indeed 'not more than 123 Migs'. There were none. And no Russian arms had arrived for months. And there had been no coup, although some correspondents in Beirut, just a two-hour drive from Damascus, were dispatching without attribution false reports fed to them by embassy visitors from Damascus and a roving CIA man who worked in the guise of a US Treasury agent. Serraj, who was anti-Communist, had just broken the clumsy British-US-Iraqi-supported plot. Syria was quiet but worried lest the propaganda presage a new *coup d'etat* or a Western-backed invasion.[5]

As if to further convince any remaining sceptics, Eisenhower dispatched a personal emissary, Loy Henderson, on a tour of the Middle East. Henderson, not surprisingly, returned with the conclusion that "there was a fear in all Middle East countries that the Soviets might be able to topple the regimes in each of their countries through exploiting the crisis in Syria".[6] He gave no indication as to whether the Syrians themselves thought they were going through a crisis.

In early September, the day after Henderson returned, the United States announced that the Sixth Fleet was once again being sent to the Mediterranean and that arms and other military equipment were being rushed to Jordan, Lebanon, Iraq and Turkey. A few days later, Saudi Arabia was added to the list. The Soviet Union replied with arms shipments to Syria, Egypt and Yemen.

The Syrian government accused the US of sending warships close to her coast in an "open challenge" and said that unidentified planes had been flying constantly over the Latakia area day and night for four days. Latakia is a Syrian seaport where supplies arrived from the Soviet Union.

Syria further claimed that the US had "incited" Turkey to concentrate an estimated 50,000 soldiers on Syria's border. The Syrians ridiculed the explanation that the Turkish troops were only on manoeuvres. Eisenhower later wrote that the troops were at the border with "a readiness to act" and that the United States had already assured the leaders of Turkey, Iraq and Jordan that if they "felt it necessary to take actions against aggression by the Syrian government, the United States would undertake to expedite shipments of arms already committed to the Middle Eastern countries and, further, would replace losses as quickly as possible." The president had no quarrel with the idea that such action might be taken to repel, in his words, the *anticipated* aggression" of Syria, for it would thus be "basically defensive in nature". (Emphasis added.)[7]

The American role here was apparently more active than Eisenhower suggests. Under-Secretary of State Christian Herter, later to replace an ailing John Foster Dulles as Secretary, "reviewed in rueful detail" to author and administration colleague Emmet John Hughes, "some recent clumsy clandestine American attempts to spur Turkish forces to do some vague kind of battle with Syria".[8]

Dulles gave the impression in public remarks that the United States was anxious to somehow invoke the Eisenhower Doctrine, presumably as a "justification" for taking further action against Syria. But he could not offer any explanation of how this was possible. Certainly Syria was not going to make the necessary request.

The only solution lay in Syria attacking another Arab country which would then request American assistance. This appears to be one rationale behind the flurry of military and diplomatic activity directed at Syria by the US. Indeed, a study carried out for the Pentagon some years later concluded that in "the 1957 Syrian crisis ... Washington seem(ed) to seek the *initial* use of force by target".[9] (Emphasis added; "target" is used for Syria in the socio-political jargon of the study.)

Throughout this period, Washington officials alternated between striving to enlist testimonials from other Arab nations that Syria was indeed a variety of Soviet satellite and a threat to the region, and assuring the world that the United States had received a profusion of just such testimony. But Jordan, Iraq and Saudi Arabia all denied that they felt threatened by Syria. Egypt, Syria's closest ally, of course concurred. At the height of the "crisis", King Hussein of

Jordan left for a vacation in Europe; the Iraqi premier declared that his country and Syria had arrived at a "complete understanding";[10] and King Saud of Saudi Arabia, in a message to Eisenhower, said that US concern over Syria was "exaggerated" and asked the president for "renewed assurances that the United States would refrain from any interference in the internal affairs of Arab states". Saud added that "efforts to overturn the Syrian regime would merely make the Syrians more amenable to Soviet influence", a view shared by several observers on all sides.

At the same time, the *New York Times* reported that "From the beginning of the crisis over Syria's drift to the left, there has been less excitement among her Arab neighbors than in the United States. Foreign diplomats in the area, including many Americans, felt that the stir caused in Washington was out of proportion to the cause."

Eventually, Dulles may have been influenced by this lack of support for the American thesis, for when asked specifically to "characterize what the relation is between Soviet aims in the area and the part that Syria adds to them", he could only reply that "The situation internally in Syria is not entirely clear and fluctuates somewhat". Syria, he implied, was not yet in the grip of international Communism.

The next day, Syria, which had no desire to isolate itself from the West, similarly moderated its tone by declaring that the American warships had been 15 miles offshore and had continued "quietly on their way".[11]

It appears that during this same restless year of 1957, the United States was also engaged in a plot to overthrow Nasser and his troublesome nationalism, although the details are rather sketchy. In January, when King Saud and Iraqi Crown Prince Abdul Illah were in New York at the United Nations, they were approached by CIA Director Allen Dulles and one of his top aides, Kermit Roosevelt, with offers of CIA covert planning and funding to topple the Egyptian leader whose radical rhetoric, nebulous though it was, was seen by the royal visitors as a threat to the very idea of monarchy.*

"Abdul Illah", wrote Eveland, "insisted on British participation in anything covert, but the Saudis had severed relations with Britain and refused. As a result, the CIA dealt separately with each: agreeing to fund King Saud's part in a new area scheme to oppose Nasser and eliminate his influence in Syria; and to the same objective, coordinating in Beirut a covert working group composed of representatives of the British, Iraqi, Jordanian, and Lebanese intelligence services."[13]

---

* Nasser and other army officers had overthrown King Farouk of Egypt in 1952. Ironically, Kim Roosevelt and the CIA have traditionally been given credit for somehow engineering this coup. However, that they did this is by no means certain.[12]

The conspiracy is next picked up in mid-spring at the home of Ghosn Zogby in Beirut. Zogby, of Lebanese ancestry and name, was the chief of the CIA Beirut station. He and Kim Roosevelt, who was staying with him, hosted several conferences of the clandestine planners. "So obvious", Eveland continued, "were their 'covert' gyrations, with British, Iraqi, Jordanian and Lebanese liaison personnel coming and going nightly, that the Egyptian ambassador in Lebanon was reportedly taking bets on when and where the next U.S. coup would take place." At one of these meetings, the man from the British Secret Intelligence Service (SIS) informed the gathering that teams had been fielded to assassinate Nasser.

Shortly afterwards, Eveland learned from a CIA official that John Foster Dulles, as well as his brother Allen, had directed Roosevelt to work with the British to bring down Nasser. Roosevelt now spoke in terms of a "palace revolution" in Egypt.[14]

From this point on we're fishing in murky waters, for the events which followed produced more questions than answers. With the six countries named above, plus Turkey and Israel apparently getting in on the act, and less than complete trust and love existing amongst the various governments, a host of plots, sub-plots and side plots inevitably sprang to life; at times it bordered on low comedy, though some would call it no more than normal Middle East "diplomacy".

Between July 1957 and October 1958, the Egyptian and Syrian governments and media announced the uncovering of what appears to be at least eight separate conspiracies to overthrow one or the other government, to assassinate Nasser, and/or prevent the expected merger of the two countries. Saudi Arabia, Iraq and the United States were most often named as conspirators, but from the entanglement of intrigue which surfaced it is virtually impossible to unravel the particular threads of the US role.[15]

Typical of the farcical going-ons, it seems that at least one of the plots to assassinate Nasser arose from the Dulles brothers taking Eisenhower's remark that he hoped "the Nasser problem could be eliminated" to be an order for assassination, when the president, so the story goes, was merely referring to improved US-Egyptian relations. Upon realizing the error, Secretary Dulles ordered the operation to cease.[16] (Three years later, Allen Dulles was again to "misinterpret" a remark by Eisenhower as an order to assassinate Patrice Lumumba of the Congo.)

Official American pronouncements during this entire period would have had the world believe that the Soviet Union was the *eminence grise* behind the strife in Jordan, the "crisis" in Syria, and unrest generally in the Middle East; that the Soviet aim was to dominate the area, while the sole purpose of US policy was to repel this Soviet thrust and maintain the "independence" of the Arab nations. Yet, on three separate occasions during 1957 — in February, April and September — the Soviet Union called for a four-power (US, USSR, Great Britain and France) declaration renouncing the use of force and interference in the internal affairs of the Middle Eastern countries. The February appeal had additionally called for a four-power embargo on arms shipments to the region, withdrawal of all foreign troops, liquidation of all foreign bases, and a conference to reach a general Middle East settlement.

The Soviet strategy was clearly to neutralize the Middle East, to remove the threat it had long felt from the potentially hostile control of the oil region by, traditionally, France and Great Britain, and now the United States which sought to fill the "power vacuum" left by the decline of the two European nations as Middle East powers.

History does not relate what a Middle East free from big-power manipulation would have been like, for neither France, Great Britain nor the United States was amenable to even calling the Soviet "bluff" if that, indeed, was what it was. The *New York Times* summarized the attitude of the three Western nations to the first two overtures as one that "deprecated the Soviet proposals as efforts to gain recognition of a Soviet right to a direct voice in the affairs of the Middle East. They have told the Russians to take up their complaints through the United Nations."

Following the September proposal, John Foster Dulles, replying to a question at a press conference, said that "the United States is skeptical of these arrangements with the Soviet Union for 'hands-off'. What they are apt to mean is our hands off and their hands under the table." This appears to be the only public comment that the US Government saw fit to make on the matter.[17]

It may be instructive to speculate upon the reaction of the Western nations if the Soviet Union had announced a "Khrushchev Doctrine", ceding to itself the same scope of action in the Middle East as that stipulated in the Eisenhower Doctrine.

In January 1958, Syria and Egypt announced their plans to unite, forming the new nation of the United Arab Republic (UAR). The initiative for the merger had come from Syria who was motivated in no small part by her fear of further American power plays against her. Ironically, under the arrangement the Communist Party, already outlawed in Egypt, was dissolved in Syria, an objective which a year and a half of CIA covert activity had failed to achieve.

Two weeks after the birth of the UAR, and in direct response to it, Iraq and Jordan formed the Arab Union, with the United States acting as midwife. This union was short lived, for in July a bloody coup in Iraq installed a new regime which promptly renounced the pact. The trumpets of Armageddon could once more be heard distinctly in the Oval Office. "We feared the worst", wrote Eisenhower. "This somber turn of events could, without vigorous response on our part, result in a complete elimination of Western influence in the Middle East."[18]

Where Iraq, once the gunsmoke cleared, would land on the international political spectrum could not be predicted with any certainty at that moment. But the United States did not wait to find out.

The time for a mere show of force was over. The very next day, the marines, along with the American navy and air force, were sent in — not to Iraq, but to Lebanon.

Of all the Arab states, Lebanon was easily the United States' closest ally. She alone had supported the Eisenhower Doctrine with any enthusiasm or unequivocally echoed Washington's panic about Syria. To be more precise, it was the president of Lebanon, Camille Chamoun, and the foreign minister Charles Malik, a Harvard Ph.D. in philosophy, who had put all their cold-war eggs into the American basket. Chamoun had ample reason to be beholden to the United States. The CIA apparently played a role in his 1952 election,[19] and in 1957 the Agency, with the approval of the National Security Council, furnished generous sums of money to Chamoun to use in support of candidates in the Chamber of Deputies (Parliament) June elections who would back him and, presumably, US policies. Funds were also provided to specifically oppose, as punishment, those candidates who had resigned in protest over Chamoun's adherence to the Eisenhower Doctrine.

As is customary in such operations, the CIA sent an "election specialist", one Van Deluer, to Beirut to assist in the planning. American officials in Washington and Lebanon proceeded on the assumption, they told each other, that Egypt, Syria and Saudi Arabia would also intervene financially in the elections. The American Ambassador to Lebanon, Donald Heath, argued as well, apparently without ironic intention, that "With both the president and the new chamber of deputies supporting American principles, we'd also have a demonstration that representative democracy could work" in the Middle East.

To what extent the American funding helped, or even how the money was spent, is not known, but the result was a landslide for pro-government deputies; so much so, that it caused considerable protest within Lebanon, including the charge that Chamoun had stacked the parliament in order to amend the constitution to permit him to seek an otherwise prohibited second six-year term of office the following year.[20]

By late April 1958, tensions in Lebanon had reached bursting point. The inordinate pro-American orientation of Chamoun's government and his refusal to dispel rumours that he would seek a second term incensed both Lebanese nationalists and advocates of the Arab nationalism which Nasser was promoting throughout the Middle East. Demands were made that the government return to the strict neutrality provided for in the National Pact of 1943 at the time of Lebanon's independence from France.

A rash of militant demonstrations, bombings and clashes with police took place, and when, in early May, the editor of an anti-government newspaper was murdered, armed rebellion broke out in several parts of the country, and US Information Agency libraries in Tripoli and Beirut were sacked. Lebanon contained all the makings of a civil war.

"Behind everything," wrote Eisenhower, "was our deep-seated conviction that the Communists were principally responsible for the trouble and that President Chamoun was motivated only by a strong feeling of patriotism."

The president did not clarify who or what he meant by "Communists". However, in the next paragraph he refers, without explanation, to the Soviet Union as "stirring up trouble" in the Middle East. On the following page, the old soldier writes that "there was no doubt in our minds" about Chamoun's charge that "Egypt and Syria had been instigating the revolt and arming the rebels".[21]

In the midst of the fighting, John Foster Dulles announced that he perceived "international communism" as the source of the conflict and for the third time in a year the Sixth Fleet was dispatched to the eastern Mediterranean; police supplies to help quell rioters, as well as tanks and other heavy equipment, were airlifted to Lebanon.

At a subsequent news conference, Dulles declared that even if international Communism were not involved, the Eisenhower Doctrine was still applicable because one of its provisions stated that "the independence of these countries is vital to peace and the national interest of the United States. That is certainly a mandate," he said, "to do something if we think that our peace and vital interests are endangered from any quarter."[22] Thus did one of the authors of the doctrine bestow upon himself a mandate.

Egypt and Syria, from all accounts, certainly supported the rebels' cause with arms, men and money, in addition to inflammatory radio broadcasts from Cairo. The extent of the material support is difficult to establish. A UN Observation Group went to Lebanon in June at the request of Foreign Minister Malik, with no objection in the UN from either the UAR or the Soviet Union, and reported that they found no evidence of UAR intervention of any significance. A second UN report in July confirmed this finding. It is open to question, however, what degree of reliance can be placed upon these reports, dealing as they do with so thorny an evaluation and issued by a body in the business of promoting compromise.

In any event, the issue was whether the conflict in Lebanon represented a legitimate, home-grown civil war, or whether it was the doing of the proverbial "outside agitators". On this point, historian Richard Barnet has observed:

> No doubt the Observation Group did minimize the extent of UAR participation. But essentially they were correct. Nasser was trying to exploit the political turmoil in Lebanon, but he did not create it. Lebanon, which had always abounded in clandestine arsenals and arms markets, did not need foreign weapons for its domestic violence. Egyptian intervention was neither the stimulus nor the mainstay of the civil strife. Once again a government that had lost the power to rule effectively was blaming its failure on foreign agents.[23]

Camille Chamoun had sacrificed Lebanon's independence and neutrality on the altar of personal ambition and the extensive American aid that derived from subscribing to the Eisenhower Doctrine. Lebanese Muslims, who comprised most of Chamoun's opposition, were also galled that the Christian president had once again placed the country outside the mainstream of the Arab world, as he had done in 1956 when he refused to break relations with France and Great Britain following their invasion of Egypt.

Chamoun himself had admitted the significance of his pro-American alignment in a revealing comment to Wilbur Crane Eveland. Eveland writes that in late April,

> I'd suggested that he might ease tensions by making a statement renouncing a move for reelection. Chamoun had snorted and suggested that I look at the calendar: March 23 was a month behind us, and no amendment to permit another term could legally be passed after that date. Obviously, as he pointed out, the issue of the presidency was not the real issue; renunciation of the Eisenhower Doctrine was what his opponents wanted.[24]

Instead of renouncing the doctrine, Chamoun invoked it. Although scattered fighting, at times heavy, was continuing in Lebanon, it was the coup in Iraq on 14 July that tipped the scales in favour of Chamoun making the formal request for military assistance and the United States immediately granting it. A CIA report of a plot against King Hussein of Jordan at about the same time heightened even further Washington's seemingly unceasing sense of urgency about the Middle East.

Chamoun had, by this time, already announced his intention to step down from office when his term expired in September. He was now concerned about American forces helping him to stay alive until that date, as well as their taking action against the rebels. For the previous two months, fear of assassination had kept him constantly inside the presidential palace, never so much as approaching a window. The murder of the Iraqi king and prime minister during the coup was not designed to make him feel more secure.

The Eisenhower Doctrine was put into motion not only in the face of widespread opposition to it within Lebanon, but in disregard of the fact that, even by the doctrine's own dubious provisions, the situation in Lebanon did not qualify; it could hardly be claimed that Lebanon had suffered "armed aggression from any country controlled by international communism". If further evidence of this were needed, it was provided by veteran diplomat Robert Murphy who was sent to Lebanon by Eisenhower a few days after the US troops had landed. Murphy concluded, he later wrote, that "communism was playing no direct or substantial part in the insurrection".[25]

Yet, Eisenhower could write that the American Government "was moving in accord with the provisions of the Middle East Resolution, but", he added, "if the conflict expanded into something that the Resolution did not cover, I would, given time, go to the Congress for additional authorization".[26] Apparently, the president did not place too much weight on Dulles having already determined that the Resolution's mandate was open-ended.

Thus it was that American Marines and Army forces were dispatched to Lebanon, totalling over 14,000 at peak strength, more than the entire Lebanese Army and gendarmerie combined. Some 70 American naval vessels and hundreds of aircraft took part in the operation, many remaining as part of the visible American presence.

"In my [radio-TV] address," wrote Eisenhower, "I had been careful to use the term 'stationed in' Lebanon rather than 'invading',"[27] a distinction lost upon many Lebanese, both high and low, supporters of the rebels and supporters of the government, including government tank forces who were prepared to block the entrance into Beirut of US troops; only the last-minute intercession on the spot by the American Ambassador may have averted an armed clash.[28]

At a meeting between Robert Murphy and Lebanese Commander-in-Chief General Faud Chehab, related by Eveland who was briefed by Murphy afterwards, the American diplomat was warned that the Lebanese people were "restless, resentful, and determined that Chamoun should resign and U.S. troops leave at once. Otherwise the general could not be responsible for the consequences. For fifteen years his officers had acted behind his back; now, he feared, they might revolt and attack the American forces."

Murphy had listened patiently, "and then escorted the general to a window overlooking the sea. Pointing to the supercarrier *Saratoga*, swinging at anchor on the horizon, the President's envoy had quietly explained that just one of its aircraft, armed with nuclear weapons, could obliterate Beirut and its environs from the face of the earth. To this, Murphy quickly added that he'd been sent to be sure that it wouldn't be necessary for American troops to fire a shot. Shehab [Chehab], he was certain, would ensure that there were no provocations on the Lebanese side. That, Murphy told me, ended the conversation. It now seemed that the general had 'regained control' of his troops."[29]

Civil warfare in Lebanon increased in intensity during the two weeks following the American intervention. During this period, CIA transmitters in the Middle East were occupied in sending out propaganda broadcasts of disguised origin, a tactic frequently employed by the Agency. In the case of one broadcast which has been reported, the apparent aim was to deflect anti-US feelings on to the Soviet Union and other targets. But the residents of the Middle East were not the only ones who may have been taken in by the spurious broadcast, for it was picked up by the American press and passed on to an unwitting American public; the following appeared in US newspapers:

BEIRUT, July 23 (UPI) — A second mysterious Arab radio station went on the air yesterday calling itself the 'Voice of Justice' and claiming to be broadcasting from Syria.

Its program heard here consisted of bitter criticism against Soviet Russia and Soviet Premier Khrushchev. Earlier the 'Voice of Iraq' went on the air with attacks against the Iraqi revolutionary government.

The 'Voice of Justice' called Khrushchev the 'hangman of Hungary' and warned the people of the Middle East they would suffer the same fate as the Hungarians if the Russians got a foothold in the Middle East.[30]

On 31 July, the Chamber of Deputies easily chose General Chehab to succeed Chamoun as president in September, an event that soon put a damper on the fighting in Lebanon and marked the beginning of the end of the conflict which, in the final analysis, appears to have been more a violent protest than a civil war. Tension was further eased by the US announcement shortly afterwards of its intention to withdraw a Marine battalion as a prelude to a general withdrawal.

The last American troops left Lebanon on 25 October without having fired a shot in anger. What had their presence accomplished?

The authors of the Pentagon study referred to earlier concluded: "A balanced assessment of U.S. behavior in the Lebanon crisis is made difficult by the suspicion that the outcome might have been much the same if the United States had done nothing. Even Eisenhower expressed some doubt on this score."[31]

The case of Iraq, where no intervention took place, can only reinforce such suspicions. Eisenhower, we have seen, "feared the worst" about Iraq. Yet, only a few days after the coup, the president noted that Iraq expressed a "desire to protect commercial and other commitments and to establish good terms" with the United States and Great Britain, and "had been cooperative in protecting United States and British lives and property when we evacuated some of our nationals."[32] Ten days later, the US recognized the new Iraqi regime.

The significance of the Lebanese intervention, as well as the shows of force employed in regard to Jordan and Syria, extended beyond the immediate outcomes. In the period before and after the intervention, Eisenhower, Dulles and other Washington officials offered numerous different justifications for the American military action in Lebanon: protecting American lives; protecting American property; the Eisenhower Doctrine, with various interpretations; Lebanese sovereignty, integrity, independence, etc.; US national interest; world peace; collective self-defence; justice; international law; law and order; fighting "Nasserism" . . . the need to "do something" . . .[33]

In summing up the affair in his memoirs, President Eisenhower seemed to settle upon one rationale in particular, and this is probably the closest to the truth of the matter. This was to put the world — and specifically the Soviet Union and Nasser — on notice that the United States had virtually unlimited power, that this power could be transported to any corner of the world with great speed, that it could and would be used to deal decisively with any situation with which the United States was dissatisfied, for whatever reason.[34]

At the same time, it was a message to the British and the French that there was only one Western superpower in the post-war world, and that their days as commanding powers in the Middle East were over.

14. Indonesia 1957-1958
War and pornography

"I think it's time we held Sukarno's feet to the fire", said Frank Wisner, the CIA's Deputy Director of Plans (covert operations), one day in autumn 1956.[1] Wisner was speaking of the man who had led Indonesia since its struggle for independence from the Dutch following the war. A few months earlier, in May, Sukarno had made an impassioned speech before the US Congress asking for more understanding of the problems and needs of developing nations like his own.[2]

The ensuing American campaign to unseat the flamboyant leader of the fifth most populous nation in the world was to run the gamut from large-scale military manoeuvres to seedy sexual intrigue.

A year earlier, Sukarno had organized the Bandung Conference as an answer to the Southeast Asia Treaty Organization (SEATO), the US-created political- military alliance of area states to "contain communism". At Bandung, the doctrine of neutralism had been proclaimed the faith of the underdeveloped world. To the men of the CIA station in Indonesia the conference was heresy, so much so that their thoughts turned toward assassination as a means of sabotaging it.

In 1975, the Senate committee which was investigating the Agency heard testimony that CIA officers stationed in an East Asian country had suggested that an East Asian leader be assassinated "to disrupt an impending Communist Conference in 1955".[3] (In all likelihood, the leader referred to was either Sukarno or Chou En-lai of China.) But, said the committee, cooler heads prevailed at CIA headquarters in Washington and the suggestion was firmly rejected.*

Elsewhere the committee reported that it had "received some evidence of CIA involvement in plans to assassinate President Sukarno of Indonesia", and that planning had proceeded to the point of identifying an agent whom it was believed might be recruited for the job.[5] Whether the two items referred to the same assassination plan or two separate ones is not clear. (The committee

---

* Nevertheless, a plane carrying eight members of the Chinese delegation, a Vietnamese, and two European journalists to the Bandung Conference crashed under mysterious circumstances. The Chinese government claimed that it was an act of sabotage carried out by the US and Taiwan, a misfired effort to murder Chou-En lai. (See Notes for further discussion.)[4]

noted that at one time, those at the CIA who were concerned with possible assassinations and assassination methods were known internally as the "Health Alteration Committee".)

To add to the concern of American leaders, Sukarno had made trips to the Soviet Union and China (though to the White House as well), he had purchased arms from Eastern European countries (but only after being turned down by the United States),[6] he had nationalized many private holdings of the Dutch, and, perhaps most disturbing of all, the Indonesian Communist Party (PKI) had made impressive gains electorally and in union-organizing, thus earning an important role in the coalition government.

It was a familiar Third World scenario, and the reaction of Washington policy-makers was equally familiar. Once again, they were unable, or unwilling, to distinguish nationalism from pro-communism, neutralism from wickedness. By any definition of the word, Sukarno was no communist. He was an Indonesian nationalist and a "Sukarnoist" who had crushed the PKI forces in 1948 after the independence struggle had been won.[7] He ran what was largely his own show by granting concessions to both the PKI and the Army, balancing one against the other. As to excluding the PKI, with its more than one million members, from the government, Sukarno declared: "I can't and won't ride a three-legged horse."[8]

To the United States, however, Sukarno's balancing act was too precarious to be left to the vagaries of the Indonesian political process. It mattered not to Washington that the Communist Party was walking the legal, peaceful road, or that there was no particular "crisis" or "chaos" in Indonesia, so favoured as an excuse for intervention. Intervention there would be.

It would not be the first. In 1955, during the national election campaign in Indonesia, the CIA had given a million dollars to the Masjumi party, a centrist coalition of Muslim organizations, in a losing bid to thwart Sukarno's Nationalist Party as well as the PKI. According to former CIA officer Joseph Burkholder Smith, the project "provided for complete write-off of the funds, that is, no demand for a detailed accounting of how the funds were spent was required. I could find no clue as to what the Masjumi did with the million dollars."[9]

In 1957, the CIA decided that the situation called for more direct action. It was not difficult to find Indonesian colleagues-in-arms for there already existed a clique of army officers and others who, for personal ambitions and because they disliked the influential position of the PKI, wanted Sukarno out, or at least out of their particular islands. (Indonesia is the world's largest archipelago, consisting of some 3,000 islands.)

The military operation the CIA was opting for was of a scale that necessitated significant assistance from the Pentagon, which could be secured only for a political action mission approved by the National Security Council's "Special Group" (the small group of top NSC officials who acted in the President's name, to protect him and the country by evaluating proposed covert actions and making certain that the CIA did not go off the deep end; known at other times as the 5412 Committee, the 303 Committee, the 40 Committee, or the Operations Advisory Group).

The manner in which the Agency went about obtaining this approval is a text-book example of how the CIA sometimes determines American foreign policy. Joseph Burkholder Smith, who was in charge of the Agency's Indonesian desk in Washington from mid-1956 to early 1958, has described the process in his memoirs: instead of first proposing the plan to Washington for approval, where "premature mention . . . might get it shot down",

> We began to feed the State and Defense departments intelligence that no one could deny was a useful contribution to understanding Indonesia. When they had read enough alarming reports, we planned to spring the suggestion we should support the colonels' plans to reduce Sukarno's power. This was a method of operation which became the basis of many of the political action adventures of the 1960s and 1970s. In other words, the statement is false that CIA undertook to intervene in the affairs of countries like Chile *only after* being ordered to do so by . . . the Special Group . . . In many instances, we made the action programs up ourselves after we had collected enough intelligence to make them appear required by the circumstances. Our activity in Indonesia in 1957-1958 was one such instance.[10] (Emphasis in original.)

When the Communist Party did well again in local elections held in July, the CIA viewed it as "a great help to us in convincing Washington authorities how serious the Indonesian situation was. The only person who did not seem terribly alarmed at the PKI victories was Ambassador Allison. This was all we needed to convince John Foster Dulles finally that he had the wrong man in Indonesia. The wheels began to turn to remove this last stumbling block in the way of our operation."[11] John Allison, wrote Smith, was not a great admirer of the CIA to begin with. In early 1958, after less than a year in the post, he was replaced as ambassador by Howard Jones, whose selection "pleased" the CIA Indonesia staff.[12]

On 30 November 1957, several hand grenades were tossed at Sukarno as he was leaving a school. He escaped injury, but 10 people were killed and 48 children injured. The CIA in Indonesia had no idea who was responsible, but it quickly put out the story that the PKI was behind it "at the suggestion of their Soviet contacts in order to make it appear that Sukarno's opponents were wild and desperate men". As it turned out, the culprits were a Muslim group not associated with the PKI or with the Agency's military plotters.[13]

The theme of Sukarno's supposed hand-in-glove relationship with Communists was pushed at every opportunity. The CIA decided to make capital of reports that a good-looking blonde stewardess had been aboard Sukarno's aircraft everywhere he went during his trip in the Soviet Union and that the same woman had come to Indonesia with Soviet President Kliment Voroshilov and had been seen several times in the company of Sukarno. The idea was that Sukarno's well-known womanizing had trapped him in the spell of a Soviet female agent. He had succumbed to Soviet control, CIA reports implied, as a result of her influence or blackmail, or both.

"This formed the foundation of our flights of fancy," wrote Smith. "We had as a matter of fact, considerable success with this theme. It appeared in the

Indonesia 1957-1958

press around the world, and when *Round Table*, the serious British quarterly of international affairs, came to analyze the Indonesian revolt in its March 1958 issue, it listed Sukarno's being blackmailed by a Soviet female spy as one of the reasons that caused the uprising."

Seemingly, the success of this operation inspired CIA officers in Washington to carry the theme one step further. A substantial effort was made to come up with a pornographic film or at least some still photographs that could pass for Sukarno and his Russian girl friend engaged in "his favourite activity". When scrutiny of available porno films (supplied by the Chief of Police of Los Angeles) failed to turn up a couple who could pass for Sukarno (dark and bald) and a beautiful blonde Russian woman, the CIA undertook to produce its own films, "the very films with which the Soviets were blackmailing Sukarno".[14] One outcome of this effort was a film produced for the Agency by Robert Maheu, former FBI agent and intimate of Howard Hughes. Maheu's film starred an actor who resembled Sukarno. The ultimate fate of the film, which was entitled "Happy Days", has not been reported.[15] The CIA also developed a full-face mask of the Indonesian leader which was sent to Los Angeles where the police were to pay some porno-film actor to wear it during his big scene. This project resulted in some photographs, although they apparently were never used.[16] In other parts of the world, at other times, the CIA has done better in this line of work, having produced sex films of target subjects caught *in flagrante delicto* who had been lured to Agency safe-houses by female agents.*

Sex could be used at home as well to further the goals of American foreign policy. Under the cover of the US foreign aid programme, at that time called the Economic Cooperation Administration, Indonesian policemen were trained and then recruited to provide information on Soviet, Chinese and PKI activities in their country. Some of the men singled out as good prospects for this work were sent to Washington for special training and to be softened up for recruitment. Like Sukarno, reportedly, these police officers invariably had an obsessive desire to sleep with a white woman. Accordingly, during their stay they were taken to Baltimore's shabby sex district to indulge themselves.[18]

The Special Group's approval of the mission was forthcoming in November, 1957.[19] The CIA's paramilitary wheels began to spin. In this undertaking, as in so many others, the Agency enjoyed the advantage of the United States' far-flung military empire. Headquarters for the operation were established in neighbouring Singapore; training bases set up in the Philippines; airstrips laid out in various parts of the Pacific to prepare for bomber and transport missions;

* In 1960, Col. Truman Smith, US Army Ret., writing in *Reader's Digest* about the KGB, declared: "It is difficult for most of us to appreciate its menace, as its methods are so debased as to be all but beyond the comprehension of any normal person with a sense of right and wrong." One of the KGB methods the good colonel found so debased was the making of sex films to be used as blackmail. "People depraved enough to employ such methods," he wrote, "find nothing distasteful in more violent methods . . ."[17]

111

Indonesians, Filipinos, Taiwanese, Americans, and other "soldiers of fortune" were assembled in Okinawa and the Philippines along with vast quantities of arms and equipment.

For this, the CIA's most ambitious military operation to date, tens of thousands of rebels were armed, equipped and trained by the US Army. US Navy submarines, patrolling off the coast of Sumatra, the main island, put over-the-beach parties ashore along with supplies and communications equipment. The US Air Force set up a considerable Air Transport force which air-dropped many thousands of weapons deep into Indonesian territory. And a fleet of fifteen B-26 bombers was made available for the conflict after being "sanitized" to ensure that they were "non-attributable" and that all airborne equipment was "deniable".

In the early months of 1958, rebellion began to break out in one part of the Indonesian island chain, then another. CIA pilots took to the air to carry out bombing and strafing missions in support of the rebels. In Washington, Col. Alex Kawilarung, the Indonesian military attaché, was persuaded by the Agency to "defect". He soon showed up in Indonesia to take charge of the rebel forces. Yet, as the fighting dragged on into spring, the insurgents proved unable to win decisive victories or take the offensive, although the CIA bombing raids were taking their toll.

Sukarno later claimed that on a Sunday morning in April, a plane bombed a ship in the harbour of the island of Ambon — all hands aboard going down — as well as hitting a church, which demolished the building and took the lives of all those inside. He stated that 700 casualties resulted from this single run.

On 15 May, a CIA plane bombed the Ambon marketplace, killing a large number of civilians on their way to church on Ascension Thursday. The Indonesian government had to act to suppress public demonstrations.

Three days later, during another bombing run over Ambon, a CIA pilot, Allen Lawrence Pope, was shot down and captured. Thirty years old, from Perrine, Florida, Pope had flown 55 night missions over Communist lines in Korea for the Air Force. Later he spent two months flying through Communist flak for the CIA to drop supplies to the French at Dienbienphu. Now his luck had run out. He was to spend four years as a prisoner in Indonesia before Sukarno acceded to a request from Robert Kennedy for his release.

Pope was captured carrying a set of incriminating documents, including those which established him as a pilot for the US Air Force and the CIA airline CAT. Like all men flying clandestine missions, Pope had gone through an elaborate procedure before taking off to "sanitize" him, as well as his aircraft. But he had apparently smuggled the papers aboard the plane, for he knew that to be captured as an "anonymous, stateless civilian" meant having virtually no legal rights and ran the risk of being shot as a spy in accordance with custom. A captured US military man, however, becomes a commodity of value for his captors while he remains alive.

The Indonesian government derived immediate material concessions from the United States as a result of the incident. Whether the Indonesians thereby agreed to keep silent about Pope is not known, but on 27 May, the pilot and his documents were presented to the world at a news conference, thus contradicting several recent statements by high American officials.[20] Notable amongst these was President Eisenhower's declaration on 30 April concerning Indonesia: "Our policy is one of careful neutrality and proper deportment all the way through so as not to be taking sides where it is none of our business."[21]

And on 9 May, an editorial in the *New York Times* had stated:

It is unfortunate that high officials of the Indonesian Government have given further circulation to the false report that the United States Government was sanctioning aid to Indonesia's rebels. The position of the United States Government has been made plain, again and again. Our Secretary of State was emphatic in his declaration that this country would not deviate from a correct neutrality . . . the United States is not ready . . . to step in to help overthrow a constituted government. Those are the hard facts. Jakarta does not help its case, here, by ignoring them.

With the exposure of Pope and the lack of rebel success in the field, the CIA decided that the light was no longer worth the candle, and began to curtail its support. By the end of June, Indonesian army troops loyal to Sukarno had effectively crushed the dissident military revolt.

The Indonesian leader continued his adroit balancing act between the Communists and the army until 1965, when the latter, likely with the help of the CIA, finally overthrew his regime.

15. Western Europe 1950s and 1960s
Fronts within fronts within fronts

At the British Labour Party conference in 1960, Michael Foot, the party's future leader and a member of its left-wing, was accused of being a "fellow traveller" by then-leader Hugh Gaitskell. Foot responded with a reference to Gaitskell and others of the party's right wing: "But who," he asked, "are *they* travelling with?"[1]

They, it turned out, had been travelling with the CIA for some years; fellow passengers were Frenchmen, Germans, Dutch, Italians, and a host of other West Europeans; all taking part in a CIA operation to win the hearts and minds of liberals, social democrats, and assorted socialists, to keep them from the clutches of the Russian bear.

It was an undertaking of major proportions. For some 20 years, the Agency used dozens of American foundations, charitable trusts and the like, including a few of its own creation, as conduits for payments to all manner of organizations in the United States and abroad, many of which, in turn, funded other groups. So numerous were the institutions involved, so many were the interconnections and overlaps, that it is unlikely that anyone at the CIA had a grasp of the full picture, let alone exercised broad control over it or proper accounting. (See Appendix I for a partial organizational chart.)

The ultimate beneficiaries of this flow of cash were political parties, magazines, news agencies, journalists' unions, other unions and labour organizations, student and youth groups, lawyers' associations, and any other enterprises already committed to "The Free World" which could be counted upon to spread the gospel further if provided with sufficient funding.

The principal front organization set up by the CIA in this period was the grandly-named Congress for Cultural Freedom (CCF). In June 1950, prominent literati and scientists of the United States and Europe assembled in the Titiana Palace Theatre, in the US Zone of Berlin, before a large audience to launch the organization whose purpose was to "defend freedom and democracy against the new tyranny sweeping the world".[2] The CCF was soon reaching out in all directions with seminars, conferences and a wide programme of political and cultural activities in Western Europe as well as India, Australia, Japan, Africa and elsewhere. It had, moreover, some 20 periodicals under its financial wing, including *Socialist Commentary, Censorship, Survey* (a Soviet affairs quarterly), and *Encounter* in Great Britain (the last appearing also in Spanish and German editions), *Der Monat* in Germany, *Preuves* and *The China Quarterly* in Paris, *Forum* in Vienna, *Tempo Presente* in Rome, and *Vision* in Switzerland, as well as *The New Leader, Africa Report*, and *Atlas* in New York, *Thought* and *Quest* in India, and *El Mundo Nuevo* in Latin America[3] — well-written, political and intellectual magazines which, in the words of former CIA executive Ray Cline, "would not have been able to survive financially without CIA funds".[4]

Amongst the other media-related organizations subsidized by the CIA in Europe at this time were the West German news agency DENA (later known as DPA),[5] the international association of writers PEN, located in Paris, certain French newspapers,[6] the International Federation of Journalists, and Forum World Features, a news feature service in London whose stories were bought by some 140 newspapers around the world, including about 30 in the United States, amongst which were the *Washington Post* and four other major dailies. The Church committee of the US Senate reported that "major U.S. dailies" which took the service were informed that Forum World Features was "CIA-controlled". *The Guardian* and *The Sunday Times* of Great Britain also used the service which earlier had been called Forum Service. By 1967, according to one of Forum's leading writers, the news service had become perhaps "the principal CIA media effort in the world", no small accomplishment when one considers that the CIA, in its heyday, was devoting a reported 29 percent of its budget to media and propaganda.[7]

Another important recipient of CIA beneficence was Axel Springer, the West German press baron who was secretly funnelled about $7 million in the early 1950s to help him build up his vast media empire. Springer, until he died in 1985, was the head of the largest publishing conglomerate in Western Europe, one which still stands as a tower of pro-Western and anti-Communist sentiment. The publisher of the influential weekly *Der Spiegel*, Rudolph Augstein, has observed: "No single man in Germany, before or after Hitler, with the possible exception of Bismarck or the two emperors, has had so much power as Springer." His relationship with the CIA reportedly continued until at least the early 1970s.[8]

The originator of the American programme, the head of the CIA's International Organizations Division, Tom Braden, has said that the Agency placed one agent in the CCF and that another became an editor of *Encounter*;[9] presumably there was at least one CIA agent or officer in each of the funded groups. Braden states that "The agents could . . . propose anti-Communist programs to the official leaders of the organizations." He adds that it was a policy to "protect the integrity of the organization by not requiring it to support every aspect of official American policy."[10]

The Cultural Freedom journals appealed to the non-Marxist left (Forum, by contrast, was conservative), generally eschewing the class struggle and excessive nationalization of industry. They were proponents of Daniel Bell's "the end of ideology", the *raison d'être* of which was that since no one could call for dying for capitalism with a straight face, the idea of dying for socialism had to be discredited. At the same time, the journals advocated a reformed capitalism, a capitalism with a human face.

To the cold warriors in Washington who were paying the bills, however, the idea of reforming capitalism was of minimal interest. What was of consequence was the commitment of the magazines to a strong, well-armed, and united Western Europe, allied to the United States, which would stand as a bulwark against the Soviet bloc; support for the Common Market; advancing the cause of NATO, accompanied by warnings of the growing danger of international communism; scepticism of the disarmament, pacifism, and neutralism espoused by the likes of the Campaign for Nuclear Disarmament (CND) in Great Britain. Criticism of US foreign policy took place within the framework of cold-war assumptions; for example, that a particular American intervention was not the most effective way of combatting communism, not that there was anything wrong with intervention *per se* or that the US was supporting the wrong side.

"Private" publications such as these could champion views which official US government organs like the Voice of America could not, and still be credible. The same was true of the many other private organizations on the CIA payroll at this time.

In 1960, CND and other elements of the Labour Party's left-wing succeeded in winning over the party's conference to a policy of complete, unilateral nuclear disarmament and neutrality in the cold war. In addition, two resolutions supporting NATO were voted down. Although the Labour Party was not in power at the time, the actions carried considerable propaganda and psychological value. Washington viewed the turn of events with not a little anxiety, for such sentiments could easily spread to the major parties of other NATO countries.

The right-wing of the Labour Party, which had close, not to say intimate, connections to the Congress for Cultural Freedom, *Encounter, New Leader*, and other CIA fronts, undertook a campaign to reverse the disarmament resolution. The committee set up for the purpose issued an appeal for funds, and soon could report that many small donations had been received, together with a large sum from a source that wished to remain anonymous. Over the next year, there was sufficient funding for a permanent office, a full-time, paid chairman and paid staff, field workers, travelling expenses, tons of literature sent to a large mailing list within the movement, a regular bulletin sent free, etc.

Their opponents could not come close to matching this propaganda blitz. At the 1961 conference, the unilateralist and neutralist decisions were decisively overturned and the Labour Party returned to the NATO fold.[11]

Supporters of the CIA have invariably defended the Agency's sundry activities in Western Europe on the grounds that the Russians were the first to be so engaged there and had to be countered. Whatever truth there may be in this assertion, the fact remains, as Tom Braden has noted, that the American effort spread to some fields "where they [the Russians] had not even begun to operate".[12] Braden doesn't specify which fields, but it seems that political parties was one: the CIA had working/financial relationships with leading members of the West German Social Democratic Party, two parties in Austria, the Christian Democrats of Italy, the Liberal Party, in addition to the Labour Party, in Britain,[13] and probably at least one party in every other Western European country, all of which purported to be independent of either superpower, something the various Communist parties, whether supported by the Soviet Union or not, could never get away with.

The media provides another case in point. Neither Braden, nor anyone else apparently, has cited examples of publications or news agencies in Western Europe — pro-Communist or anti-Nato, etc. — which, ostensibly independent, were covertly funded by the Soviet Union.

More importantly, it should be borne in mind that all the different types of enterprises and institutions supported by the CIA in Western Europe have been supported by the Agency all over the Third World for decades on a *routine* basis without a Russian counterpart in sight. The growing strength of the left in post-war Europe was motivation enough for the CIA to develop its covert programmes, and this was a circumstance deriving from World War II and the economic facts of life, not from Soviet propaganda and manipulation.

16. British Guiana 1953-1964
The CIA's international labour mafia

For a period of eleven years, two of the oldest democracies in the world, Great Britain and the United States, went to great lengths to prevent a democratically elected leader from occupying his office.

The man was Dr Cheddi Jagan. The grandson of indentured immigrants from India, Jagan had become a dentist in the United States, then returned to his native Guiana. In 1953, at the age of 35, he and the People's Progressive Party (PPP) were elected by a large majority to head the government of the British colony. Jagan's victory was due in part to the fact that Indians comprised about 46 percent of the population; those of African origin made up about 36 percent.

The PPP's programme in office was hardly revolutionary. It encouraged foreign investment in the mining sectors and attempted to institute liberal reforms such as strengthening the rights of unionists and tenant farmers, and removing a ban on the import of "undesirable" publications, films and records. But the British Conservative government was not prepared to live with a man who talked suspiciously like a socialist. The government and the British media subjected the Jagan administration to a campaign of red-scare accusations and plain lies in the fashion of Senator McCarthy whose -ism was then all the rage in the United States.

Four-and-a-half months after Jagan took office, the government of Winston Churchill flung him out. The British sent naval and army forces, suspended the constitution and removed the entire Guianese government. At the same time, they drew up some papers which the Queen signed, so it was all nice and legal.[1]

"Her Majesty's Government," said the British Colonial Secretary during a debate in Parliament, "are not prepared to tolerate the setting up of Communist states in the British Commonwealth."[2]

The American attitude toward this slap in the face of democracy can be surmised by the refusal of the US government to allow Jagan to pass in transit through the United States when he tried to book a flight to London to attend the parliamentary debate. According to Jagan, Pan Am would not even sell him a ticket.[3] (Pan Am has a long history of collaboration with the CIA, a practice initiated by the airline's president, Juan Trippe, the son-in-law of Roosevelt's Secretary of State, Edward R. Stettinius.)

By this time the CIA had already got its foot in the door of the British Guiana labour movement, by means of the marriage of the Agency to the American

Federation of Labor in the United States. One of the early offsprings of this union was the Inter-American Regional Labor Organization (ORIT from the Spanish). In 1953, ORIT was instrumental in the conversion of the leading confederation of unions in Guiana, the Trades Union Council, from a militant labour organization to a vehicle of anti-communism.[4] This was to have serious repercussions for Jagan in later years.

In 1957, Jagan, running on a programme similar to that of four years earlier, won the election again. This time the British deemed it wiser to employ more subtle methods for his removal and the CIA was brought into the picture, one of the rare instances in which the Agency has been officially allowed to operate in a British bailiwick. The CIA has done so, unofficially, on numerous occasions, to the displeasure of British authorities.

The CIA set to work to strengthen those unions which already tended somewhat toward support of Jagan's leading political opponent, Forbes Burnham of the African Party. One of the most important of these was the civil servants' union, dominated by blacks.

Consequently, the CIA turned to Public Services International (PSI) in London, an international trade union secretariat for government employees, one of the international networks which exist to export the union know-how of advanced industrial countries to less-developed countries.

According to a study undertaken by *The Sunday Times* (London), by 1958 the PSI's "finances were low, and its stocks were low with its own parent body, the International Confederation of Free Trade Unions. It needed a success of some kind. The financial crisis was resolved, quite suddenly, by the PSI's main American affiliate union, the American Federation of State, County and Municipal Employees (AFSCME)." Its boss, Dr Arnold Zander, told the PSI executive that he had "been shopping" and had found a donor.

"The spoils were modest at first — only a couple of thousand pounds in 1958. It was, the kind donor had said, for Latin America. The money went towards a PSI 'recruiting drive' in the northern countries of Latin America by one William J. Doherty, Jr., a man with some previous acquaintance of the CIA." (Doherty was later to become the Executive Director of the American Institute of Free Labor Development, the CIA's principal labour organization in Latin America.)

"The donor was presumably pleased, because next year, 1959, Zander was able to tell the PSI that his union was opening a full-time Latin American section in the PSI's behalf. The PSI was charmed."

The PSI's representative, said Zander, would be William Howard McCabe (a CIA labour apprentice).

> McCabe, a stocky, bullet-headed American, appeared to have no previous union history, but the PSI liked him. When he came to its meetings, he distributed cigarette lighters and photographs of himself doling out food parcels to the peasants. The lighters and parcels were both inscribed 'with the compliments of the PSI'.[5]

In 1967, in the wake of numerous revelations about CIA covert financing, the new head of AFSCME admitted that the union had been heavily funded by the Agency until 1964 through a foundation conduit. It was revealed that AFSCME's International Affairs Department, which had been responsible for the British Guiana operation, had actually been run by two CIA "aides".[6]

CIA work within Third World unions typically involves a considerable educational effort, the basic premise of which is that all solutions will come to working people under a system of free enterprise, class co-operation and collective bargaining, and by opposing communism in collaboration with management and government, unless, of course, the government, as in this case, is itself "communist". The most promising students, those perhaps marked as future leaders, are singled out to be sent to CIA schools in the United States for further education.

The CIA, said *The Sunday Times*, also "appears to have had a good deal of success in encouraging politicians to break away from Jagan's party and government. Their technique of financing sympathetic figures was to take out heavy insurance policies for them."[7]

During the 1961 election campaign, the CIA's ongoing programme was augmented by ad hoc operations from other American quarters. The US Information Service took the most unusual step of showing its films, depicting the evils of Castroism and communism, on street corners of British Guiana. And the Christian Anti-Communist Crusade brought its travelling road show down and spent a reported $76,000 on electoral propaganda which lived up to the organization's name.[8] One historian has described this as "a questionable activity for a private organization, which the State Department did nothing to discourage".[9] On the other hand, the activities of US government agencies in British Guiana were no less questionable.

Despite the orchestrated campaign directed against him, Jagan was re-elected by a comfortable majority of legislative seats, though with only a plurality of the popular vote.

A month later, at his request, Jagan was received at the White House in Washington. He had come to talk about assistance for his development programme. President Kennedy and his advisers, however, were interested in determining where Jagan stood on the political spectrum before granting any aid. Oddly, the "interview", as described by Arthur Schlesinger, Jr. who was present, seemed to be conducted as if the Kennedy men were totally unaware of American destabilization activities in British Guiana.

To Jagan's expressed esteem for the politics of British Labour leader Aneurin Bevan, those in the room "all responded agreeably".

To Jagan's professed socialism, Kennedy asserted that "We are not engaged in a crusade to force private enterprise on parts of the world where it is not relevant."

But when Jagan, perhaps naively, mentioned his admiration for the scholarly, leftist journal, *Monthly Review*, he crossed an ideological line which silently and effectively sealed his country's fate.[10]

No economic aid was given to British Guiana while Jagan remained in power, and the Kennedy administration pressured the British to delay granting the country its independence, which had been scheduled to occur within the next year or two.[11] Not until 1966, when Jagan no longer held office, did British Guiana become the independent nation of Guyana.

In February 1962, the CIA helped to organize and finance anti-Jagan protests which used the newly announced budget as a pretext. The resulting strikes, riots and arson were wholly out of proportion to the alleged instigation. A Commonwealth Commission of Enquiry later concluded (perhaps to the discomfort of the British Colonial Office which had appointed it) that:

> There is very little doubt that, despite the loud protestations of the trades union leaders to the contrary, political affinities and aspirations played a large part in shaping their policy and formulating their programme of offering resistance to the budget and making a determined effort to change the government in office.[12]

The CIA arranged, as it has on so many similar occasions, for North American and Latin American labour organizations, with which it had close ties, to support the strikers with messages of solidarity and food, thus enhancing the appearance of a genuine labour struggle.[13]

The centrepiece of the CIA's programme in British Guiana was the general strike (so called, although its support was considerably less than total) which began in April 1963. It lasted for 80 days, the longest general strike in history it is said.[14]

This strike, as in 1962, was called by the Trades Union Council (TUC) which, as we have seen, was a member in good standing of the CIA's international labour mafia. The head of the TUC was one Richard Ishmael who had been trained in the US at the CIA's American Institute of Free Labor Development along with other Guianese labour officials.

The strike period was marked by repeated acts of violence and provocation, including attacks on Jagan's wife and some of his ministers. Ishmael himself was later cited in a secret British police report as having been part of a terrorist group which had carried out bombings and arson attacks against government buildings during the strike.[15]

No action was taken against Ishmael and others in this group by British authorities who missed no opportunity to exacerbate the explosive situation, hoping that it would culminate in Jagan's downfall.

Meanwhile, CIA agents were giving "advice to local union leaders on how to organize and sustain" the strike, the *New York Times* subsequently reported. "They also provided funds and food supplies to keep the strikers going and medical supplies for pro-Burnham workers injured in the turmoil. At one point, one of the agents even served as a member of a bargaining committee from a Guiana dike workers union that was negotiating with Dr. Jagan." This agent was later denounced by Jagan and forbidden to enter the country.[16] This is probably a reference to Gene Meakins, one of the CIA's main labour operatives, who had been serving as public relations advisor and education officer to the TUC. Meakins edited a weekly paper and broadcast a daily radio programme by means of which he was able to generate a great deal of anti-Jagan propaganda.[17]

The Sunday Times study concluded that:

Jagan seems to have thought that the unions could hold out a month. But McCabe was providing the bulk of the strike pay, plus money for distress funds, for the strikers' daily 15 minutes on the radio and their propaganda, and considerable travelling expenses. All over the world, it seemed brother unions were clubbing together.

The mediator sent from London, Robert Willis, the general secretary of the London Typographical Society and a man not noted for his mercy in bargaining with newspaper managements was shocked. 'It was rapidly clear to me that the strike was wholly political', he said. 'Jagan was giving in to everything the strikers wanted, but as soon as he did they erected more demands'.[18]

Financial support for the strike alone, channelled through the PSI and other labour organizations by the CIA, reached the sum of at least one million dollars.

American oil companies provided a further example of the multitude of resources the US can bring to bear upon a given target. The companies co-operated with the strikers by refusing to provide petroleum, forcing Jagan to appeal to Cuba for oil. During Jagan's remaining year in office, in the face of a general US economic embargo, he turned increasingly to the Soviet bloc. This practice of course provided ammunition to those critics of Jagan in British Guiana, the United States and Great Britain who insisted that he was a communist and thus fraught with all the dangers that communists are fraught with.

The strike was maintained primarily by black supporters of Forbes Burnham and by employers who locked out many of Jagan's Indian supporters. This inevitably exacerbated the already-existing racial tensions, although *The Sunday Times* asserted that the "racial split was fairly amicable until the 1963 strike divided the country". Eventually, the tension broke out into bloodshed leaving hundreds dead and wounded and "a legacy of racial bitterness".[19]

Jagan was certainly aware, to some extent at least, of what was transpiring around him during the general strike. After it was over he charged that:

The United States, in spite of protestations to the contrary by some of its leaders, is not prepared to permit a Socialist government or a government committed to drastic and basic reforms to exist in this hemisphere, even when this government has been freely elected . . . It is all too clear that the United States will only support a democratic government if it favors a classic private enterprise system.[20]

In an attempt to surmount the hurdle of US obsession with the Soviet Union and "another Cuba in the western hemisphere", Jagan proposed that British Guiana be "neutralized" by an agreement between the United States and the Soviet Union, as the two powers had done in the case of Austria. Officials in Washington had no comment on the suggestion.[21]

Cheddi Jagan's government managed to survive all the provocations and humiliations. With elections on the agenda for 1964, the British and their American cousins turned once again to the gentlemanly way of the pen.

The British Colonial Secretary, Duncan Sandys, who had been a leading party to the British-CIA agreement, cited the strike and general unrest as proof that Jagan could not run the country or offer the stability that the British government required for British Guiana to be granted its independence. (Sandys was the founder, in 1948, of the European Movement, a CIA-funded cold-war organization.)[22]

This was, of course, a contrived position. Syndicated American columnist Drew Pearson, writing about the meeting between President Kennedy and British Prime Minister Macmillan in the summer of 1963, stated that "the main thing they agreed on was that the British would refuse to grant independence to Guiana because of a general strike against pro-Communist Prime Minister, Cheddi Jagan. That strike was secretly inspired by a combination of U.S. Central Intelligence money and British intelligence. It gave London the excuse it wanted."[23]

The excuse was used further to justify an amendment to the British Guiana constitution providing for a system of proportional representation in the election, a system that appeared certain to convert Jagan's majority of legislative seats into a plurality. Subsequently, the British-appointed Governor of British Guiana announced that he would not be bound to call on the leader of the largest party to form a government if it did not have a majority of seats, a procedure in striking contrast to that followed in Great Britain.

When, in October 1964, the Labour Party succeeded the Conservative Party to power in Great Britain, Jagan had hopes that the conspiracy directed against him would be squashed, for several high-ranking Labour leaders had stated publicly, and to Jagan personally, their opposition to the underhanded and anti-democratic policy of their Conservative Party foes. Within days of taking office, however, the Labour Party dashed these hopes.[24] "Bowing to United States wishes," the *New York Times* disclosed, the Labour Party "ruled out early independence for British Guiana" and was going ahead with the proportional representation elections. Secretary of State Dean Rusk, it was reported, had left the new British Foreign Secretary, Gordon Walker, "in no doubt that the United States would resist a rise of British Guiana as an independent Castro-type state".[25] On a previous occasion, Rusk had urged Walker's Conservative predecessor, Lord Home, to suspend the British Guiana constitution again and "revert to direct colonial government".[26]

The intensive American lobbying effort against British Guiana (the actual campaign of subversion aside), led Conservative MP and former Colonial Secretary, Iain Macleod, to observe in the House of Commons: "There is an irony which we all recognize in the fact of America urging us all over the world towards colonial freedom except when it approaches her own doorstep."[27]

The day before the election of 7 December, a letter appeared in a British Guiana newspaper — a bogus pro-Communist letter, a tactic the CIA has used successfully the world over. The letter was purportedly written by Jagan's wife Janet to Communist Party members, in which she stated: "We can take comfort in the thought that the PNC [Burnham's party] will not be able to stay in power long . . . our communist comrades abroad will continue to help us win eventual total victory."

Ms Jagan quickly retorted that she would not be so stupid as to write a letter like that, but, as in all such cases, the disclaimer trailed weakly and too late behind the accusation.[28]

As expected, Jagan won only a plurality of the legislative seats, 24 of 53. The Governor then called upon Forbes Burnham, who had come in second, to form a new government. Burnham had also been named as a terrorist in the British police report referred to earlier, as had several of his new government ministers.

Jagan refused to resign. British Army troops were put on full alert in the capital city of Georgetown. A week later, Her Majesty's Government waved its hand over a piece of paper, thereby enacting another amendment to the British Guiana constitution and closing a loophole which was allowing Jagan to stall for time. He finally surrendered to the inevitable.[29]

17. Soviet Union late 1940s to 1960s
From spy planes to book publishing

Information . . . hundreds of young Americans and émigré Russians gave their lives so that the United States could amass as much information as possible about the Soviet Union . . . almost any information at all about the land Churchill had described as "a riddle wrapped in a mystery inside an enigma".

There is no evidence, however, that any of the information collected ever *saved* any lives, or served any other useful purpose for the world. Today, tons of files stuffed with reports, volumes of computer printouts, tapes, photographs, etc., lie in filing cabinets, gathering dust in warehouses in the United States and West Germany. Probably a good part of the material has already been burnt. Much of it has never been looked at, and never will be.

Beginning in the late 1940s, the US military, the CIA and the National Security Agency regularly sent aircraft along the borders of the Soviet Union to collect visual, photographic and electronic data of a military or industrial nature, particularly to do with Soviet missile and nuclear capability. The increasingly sophisticated planes and equipment, as well as satellites, submarines, and electronic listening posts in Turkey and Iran, produced vast amounts of computer input. At times, the planes would unintentionally drift over Soviet territory. At other times, they would do so intentionally in order to photograph a particular target, or to activate radar installations so as to capture their signals, or to evaluate the reaction of Soviet ground defences against an attack. It was a dangerous game of aerial "chicken" and on many occasions the planes were met by anti-aircraft fire or Soviet fighter planes.

In 1950 and 1951, two espionage airplanes, each with a crew of 10, were shot down, with no survivors. In 1969, a crew of 31 was lost, this time to North Korean fighters over the Sea of Japan. During the intervening years, there were dozens of air incidents involving American aircraft and Communist firepower, arising from hundreds, if not thousands, of espionage flights. Some of the spy planes made it safely back to base (which might be Turkey, Iran, Greece, Pakistan, Japan or Norway) after being attacked, and even hit; others were downed with loss of life or with crew members captured by the Soviets.[1] To this day, there are at least 20 of these men still held prisoner in the Soviet Union.[2]

The most notable of these incidents was of course the downing of the U-2 piloted by Francis Gary Powers on 1 May 1960. The ultra high-flying U-2 had been developed because of the vulnerability to being shot down of planes flying at normal altitudes. The disappearance of Powers and his U-2 somewhere in the Soviet Union ensnared the United States government publicly in an entanglement of a false cover story, denials, and amendments to denials. Finally, when the Russians presented Powers and his plane to the world, President Eisenhower had no alternative but to admit the truth. He pointedly added, however, that flights such as the U-2's were "distasteful but vital", given the Russian "fetish of secrecy and concealment".[3] One of Eisenhower's advisers, Emmet John Hughes, was later to observe that it thus took the administration only six days "to transform an unthinkable falsehood into a sovereign right".[4]

Over the years, the Soviet Union had lodged numerous complaints about the overflights, both to the United States and the United Nations (as had other East European nations, and even Austria and Switzerland, about flights over their own territories), and many of these had been reported in the US press, but this incident marked the first official American confirmation that the government engaged in air espionage; the first time, it has been said, that the American government had admitted to any kind of spying since the case of Nathan Hale in 1776. The resulting embarrassment led to a discontinuation of U-2 flights over the USSR, but not of other spy planes. Such are the niceties and logic of international politics.

The United States, on the other hand, had protested to the Soviet Union on several occasions about Soviet attacks on American planes which were not actually over Soviet territory, but over the Sea of Japan for example. Though engaged in espionage, such flights, strictly speaking, appear to be acceptable under international law.

The most serious repercussion of the whole U-2 affair was that it doomed to failure the Eisenhower-Khrushchev summit meeting which took place two weeks later in Paris, and upon which so much hope for peace and detente had been placed by people all over the world.

Was the U-2 affair the unfortunate accident of timing that history has made it out to be? Col. L. Fletcher Prouty, US Air Force, Ret. suggests otherwise. From 1955 to 1963, Prouty served as the liaison between the CIA and the Pentagon on matters concerning military support of "special operations". In his book, *The Secret Team*, Prouty suggests that the CIA and certain of the

Agency's colleagues in the Pentagon sabotaged this particular U-2 flight, the last one scheduled before the summit. They did this, presumably, because they did not relish a lessening of cold-war tensions, their *raison d'être*.

The method employed, Prouty surmises, was remarkably simple. The U-2's engine needed infusions of liquid hydrogen to maintain the plane's incredible altitude which placed it outside the range of Soviet firepower and interceptor aircraft. If the hydrogen container were only partly filled upon takeoff from Turkey, it would be simply a matter of time — calculable to coincide with the plane being over Soviet territory — before the U-2 was forced to descend to a lower altitude. At this point, whether the plane was shot down or Powers bailed out, allowing it to crash, is not certain. The Soviet Union claimed that it had shot down the U-2 at its normal high altitude with a rocket, but this was probably a falsehood arising from four years of frustrating failure to shoot a single U-2 from the sky. In any event, the Russians were able to present to the world a partially intact spy plane along with a fully intact spy pilot, complete with all manner of incriminating papers on him, and an unused suicide needle. The presence of identification papers was no oversight, says Prouty: deliberately, "neither pilot nor plane were sanitized on this flight as was required on other flights".[5]

In light of the furore raised by the shooting down of a South Korean commercial airliner by the Soviet Union in 1983, which the Russians claimed was spying, it is interesting to note that Prouty also makes mention of the United States at one time using "a seemingly clean national commercial airline" of an unspecified foreign country "to do some camera spying or other clandestine project".[6]

To the Russians, the spy planes were more than simply a violation of their air space, and they rejected the notion put forth by the US that the flights were just another form of espionage ("intelligence collection activities are practiced by all countries").[7]* The Russians stated that they viewed the flights as particularly provocative because airplanes are a means of conducting warfare, they can be considered as the beginning of hostilities, and may even be carrying bombs. The Russians could not forget that the Nazis had preceded their invasion of the Soviet Union with frequent reconnaissance overflights. Neither could they forget that in April 1958, US planes carrying nuclear bombs had flown over the Arctic in the direction of the USSR due to a false warning signal on American radar. The planes were called back when only two hours flying time separated them from the Soviet Union.[9]

No American plane dropped bombs on the Soviet Union but many of them dropped men assigned to carry out hostile missions. The men who fell from the

---

* At the time of the U-2 affair in 1960, the *New York Times* reported that, according to informed sources, there had been no indication of Soviet flights over the continental United States. Whether any such flights had been made over Alaska was not mentioned.[8]

sky were Russians who had emigrated to the West where they were recruited by the CIA and other Western intelligence organizations.

The leading émigré organization was known as National Alliance of Russian Solidarists, or the National Union of Labor (NTS). It was largely composed of two distinct groups of émigrés: the sons of the Russians who had gone to the West following the revolution, and those Russians who wound up in Western Europe at the close of the Second World War after the Germans had occupied their town or taken them prisoner. Both groups had collaborated with the Nazis during the war. Although NTS was generally classified in the right-wing of the various émigré organizations, the collaboration had been motivated more by anti-Stalinism than by pro-Nazi sentiments.

NTS was based primarily in West Germany where, throughout the 1950s, the CIA was the organization's chief benefactor, often its sole support. At a CIA school set up in Bad Hamburg, under the imposing name of the Institute for the Study of the USSR, as well as at schools in Great Britain and the United States, the Agency provided NTS members with extensive training before airdropping them into Soviet territory; the men landed on their native soil elaborately equipped, with everything from weapons to collapsible bicycles, frogmen suits, and rubber mats for crossing electrically-charged barbed-wire fences.

The Russians were returned to their homeland for a variety of reasons: to gather intelligence about military and technological installations; to commit assassinations; obtain current samples of identification documents; assist Western agents to escape; engage in sabotage, for which they were well-trained (methods of derailing trains and wrecking bridges, actions against arms factories and power plants, etc.); set up spy rings or instigate armed political struggle against Communist rule by linking up with supposed "resistance movements" — a wholly unrealistic goal, but one which some NTS fanatics swore by.

It will never be known just how many men the CIA infiltrated into the Soviet Union, not only by air but by border crossings and by boat as well; many hundreds at least. As to their fate . . . the Soviet Union published a book in 1961 called *Caught in the Act* (= CIA), in which were published the names and other details of about two dozen infiltrators the Soviet Union claimed to have captured, often almost immediately upon landing; some were executed, others received prison sentences. The book asserts that there were many more caught who were not listed. This may have been a self-serving statement, although it was a relatively simple matter for the Russians to infiltrate the émigrés' ranks and learn the entire operation.

The Russians claimed that some of those smuggled in were furnished with special radio beacons to guide planes where to land other agents, and which could also be used to direct US bombers in the event of war; one of the captured émigrés, the book said, was an individual who had taken part in a mass execution of Jews in German-occupied Soviet territory.

Some of the émigrés made it back to Western Europe with their bits and pieces of information, or after attempting to carry out some other assignment;

others, provided with a complete set of necessary documents, were instructed to integrate themselves back into Soviet society and become "agents in place"; still others, caught up in the emotions of being "home", turned themselves in (once again, "the human factor", which no amount of training or indoctrination can get around); the Soviet government made this choice easier by announcing, in January 1960, an amendment to the criminal code which read:

> A citizen of the U.S.S.R. enlisted by a foreign intelligence service to conduct hostile activities against the U.S.S.R. shall not be liable to criminal prosecution if he has committed no acts in pursuance of the criminal assignment given to him and has voluntarily reported to the authorities about his connections with a foreign intelligence service.[10]

No American operation against the Soviet Union would be complete without its propaganda side: bringing the gospel to the heathen, in a myriad of ways that displayed the creativity of the CIA and its team of émigrés.

Novel mechanisms were developed to enable airplanes and balloons to drop anti-Communist literature over the Soviet Union. When the wind was right, countless leaflets and pamphlets were scattered across the land; or quantities of literature were floated downstream in waterproof packages.

Soviet citizens coming to the West were met at every turn by NTS people handing out their newspapers and magazines in Russian and Ukrainian. (To facilitate contact, NTS at times engaged in black market operations and opened small shops which catered to Russians at cheap prices.) From North Africa to Scandinavia, the CIA network confronted Soviet seamen, tourists, officials, athletes, even Soviet soldiers in East Germany, to present them with the Truth as seen by the "Free World", as well as to pry information from them, to induce them to defect, or to recruit them as spies. Hotel rooms were searched, phones tapped, bribes offered, or blackmail threatened in attempts to reach these ends. Actions were also undertaken to entrap or provoke Soviet diplomatic personnel so as to cause their expulsion and/or embarrass the Soviet Union.[11]

The propaganda offensive led the US government into the book publishing business. Under a variety of arrangements with American and foreign publishers, distributors, literary agents and authors, the CIA and the United States Information Agency produced, subsidized or sponsored "well over a thousand books" by 1967 which were deemed to serve a propaganda need.[12] Many of the books were sold in the United States as well as abroad. None bore any indication of US government involvement. Of some, said the USIA, "We control the things from the very idea down to the final edited manuscript."[13] These were books "that would not otherwise be put out, especially those books with a strong anti-communist content."[14]

Other books were published, and at times written, only after the USIA or the CIA agreed to purchase a large number of copies. There is no way of determining what effect this financial incentive had upon a publisher or author concerning a book's tone and direction. In some cases, Washington released classified information to an author to assist him in writing the book.

In 1967, following revelations about CIA domestic activities, this practice purportedly came to an end in the US although it continued abroad. A Senate committee in 1976 stated that during the preceding few years, the CIA was connected with the publication of some 250 books, mostly in foreign languages.[15] Undoubtedly, some of these were later reprinted in the United States.

The actual identity of most of the books, however, is still classified. Among those which have been revealed are: *The Dynamics of Soviet Society* by Walt Rostow, *The New Class* by Milovan Djilas, *Concise History of the Communist Party* by Robert A. Burton, *The Foreign Aid Programs of the Soviet Bloc and Communist China* by Kurt Muller, *In Pursuit of World Order* by Richard N. Gardner, *Peking and People's Wars* by Major General Sam Griffith, a parody of the quotations of Mao, entitled *Quotations from Chairman Liu, The Politics of Struggle: The Communist Front and Political Warfare* by James D. Atkinson, *From Colonialism to Communism* by Hoang Van Chi, *Why Vietnam?* by Frank Trager, and *Terror in Vietnam* by Jay Mallin. In addition, the CIA financed and distributed throughout the world the animated cartoon film of George Orwell's *Animal Farm*.[16]

The most pervasive propaganda penetration of the socialist bloc was by means of the airwaves: numerous transmitters, tremendous wattage, and often round-the-clock programming brought Radio Liberty and Radio Free Russia to the Soviet Union, Radio Free Europe and Radio in the American Sector to Eastern Europe, and the Voice of America to all parts of the world. With the exception of the last, the stations were ostensibly private organizations financed by "gifts" from American corporations, donations from the American public, and other private sources. In actuality, the CIA covertly funded almost all of the costs until 1971; exposure of the Agency's role in 1967 (although it had been widely assumed long before then) led to Congress eventually instituting open governmental financing of the stations.

The stations served the purpose of filling in some of the gaps and correcting the falsehoods of the Communist media, but presented a picture of the world, both East and West, shot through with their own omissions and distortions . . . "emphasizing whatever can make the puppet regimes look bad" is the way Sanche de Gramont, the Pulitzer Prize-winning journalist, described the programming . . . "to many in the CIA," wrote Victor Marchetti, former senior official of the Agency, "the primary value of the radios was to sow discontent in Eastern Europe and, in the process, to weaken the communist governments".[17]

The Russians claimed that Voice of America broadcasts to the Soviet Union were provocative and hostile, and grossly distorted Soviet foreign policy, but that this was not the case with Radio Moscow's broadcasts to the United States. This, said the Russians, constituted a violation of the agreement between the two countries that the broadcasts "were to promote friendly relations between both countries and ease international tension".[18]

Many of the Russians who worked for the various stations, which broadcast at length about freedom, democracy and other humanitarian concerns, were later identified by the US Justice Department as members of Hitler's notorious *Einsatzgruppen* which rounded up and killed numerous Jews in the Soviet Union. One of these worthies was Stanislau Stankevitch, under whose command a mass murder of Jews in Byelorussia was carried out in which babies were buried alive with the dead, presumably to save ammunition. Stankevitch wound up working for Radio Liberty. German war criminals as well were employed by the CIA in a variety of anti-Soviet operations.[19]

By every account, the sundry programmes to collect strategic information about the Soviet Union, particularly via infiltration into the country and encountering Soviet nationals in the West, were a singular flop. The information reported was usually trivial, spotty, garbled, or out-of-date. Worse, it was often embellished, if not out and out fraudulent. Many post-war émigrés in Western Europe made their living in the information business. It was their most saleable commodity. From a real or fictitious meeting with a Soviet citizen they would prepare a report which was often just ordinary facts with a bit of political colour added on. At times, as many as four versions of the report would be produced, differing in style and quantity of "facts"; written by four different people, the reports would then be sold separately to US, British, French and West German intelligence agencies. The CIA's version contained everything in the other three versions, which were eventually transmitted to the Agency by the other countries without their source being revealed. Analysis of all the reports tended to bring the CIA to the conclusion that the NTS was giving them the fullest picture of all, and that the information all tallied. NTS looked good, and the files grew thick.[20]

The CIA's Russian files in Washington, meanwhile, approached mountainous proportions with the data acquired from opening mail between the Soviet Union and the United States, a practice begun in the early 1950s and continued at least into the 1970s.[21] (Said a Post Office counsel in 1979: "If there was no national security mail cover program, the FBI might be inhibited in finding out if a nation was planning war against us.")[22]

Former CIA officer Harry Rositzke, who was closely involved with anti-Soviet operations after the war, later wrote that the primary task of the émigrés infiltrated into the Soviet Union during the early years — and the same could probably be said of the overflights — was to provide "early warning" of a Soviet military offensive against the West, an invasion which, in the minds of cold-warriors in the American government, appeared "imminent". This apprehension was reminiscent of the alarms sounded following the Russian Revolution, and similarly flourished despite the fact of a Russia recently devastated by a major war and hardly in a position to undertake a military operation of any such magnitude. Nevertheless, wrote Rositzke, "It was officially estimated that Soviet forces were capable of reaching the English Channel in a matter of weeks . . . It was an axiom in Washington that Stalin was plotting war. When would it come?"[23] A secret report of the National Security Resources Board of January 1951 warned: "As things are now going, by 1953 if not 1952, the

Soviet aggressors will assume complete control of the world situation."[24]

Rositzke, although a committed anti-Communist, recognized the unreality of such thinking. But, as he explained, his was a minority opinion in official Washington:

> The facts available even at the time suggested the far greater likelihood that Moscow's postwar strategy, including the conversion of Eastern Europe into a western buffer, was basically defensive. I argued this thesis with some of the CIA analysts working on Soviet estimates and with some Pentagon audiences, but it was not a popular view at the time. It is nonetheless a simple fact that no scenario was written then, nor has it been written since, to explain *why* the Russians would want to conquer Western Europe by force or to bomb the United States. Neither action would have contributed in any tangible way to the Soviet national interest and would have hazarded the destruction of the Soviet state. This basic question was never raised, for the Cold War prism created in the minds of the diplomatic and military strategists a clear-cut world of black and white; there were no grays.[25]

Several years were to pass, Rositzke pointed out, before it became clear to Washington that there were no warnings to report. This, however, had no noticeable effect upon the United States' military build-up or cold-war propaganda.

18. Italy 1950s to 1970s
Supporting the Cardinal's orphans and techno-fascism

After the multifarious extravaganza staged by the United States in 1948 to exorcise the spectre of Communism that was haunting Italy, the CIA settled in place for the long haul with a less flamboyant but more insidious operation.

A White House memorandum, prepared after the 1953 election, reported that "Neither the Moscow war stick nor the American economic carrot was being visibly brandished over the voters in this election."[1] Covert funding was the name of the game. Victor Marchetti, former executive assistant to the Deputy Director of the CIA, has revealed that in the 1950s the Agency "spent some $20 to $30 million a year, or maybe more, to finance its programs in Italy." Expenditures in the 1960s, he added, came to about $10 million annually.[2]

The CIA itself admits that between 1948 and 1968, it paid a total of $65,150,000 to the Christian Democrats and other parties, to labour groups, and to a wide variety of other organizations in Italy.[3] It also spent an undisclosed amount in support of magazines and book publishers and other means of news and opinion manipulation, such as planting news items in non-American media around the world which cast unfavourable light upon Communism, then arranging for these stories to be reprinted in friendly Italian publications.[4]

It is not known when, if ever, the CIA ended its practice of funding anti-Communist groups in Italy. Internal Agency documents of 1972 reveal contributions of some $10 million to political parties, affiliated organizations, and 21 individual candidates in the parliamentary elections of that year;[5] and in January 1976 it was disclosed that the CIA had funnelled at least $6 million to political leaders in Italy during the previous month for the coming June elections. Moreover, the largest oil company in the United States, Exxon Corp., admitted that between 1963 and 1972 it had made political contributions to the Christian Democrats and several other Italian political parties totalling $46 million to $49 million. Mobil Oil Corp.'s contribution to the system of free and open elections came to an average of $500,000 a year from 1970 through 1973. There is no report that these corporate payments derived from persuasion by the CIA or the State Department, but it seems rather unlikely that the firms would engage so extravagantly in this unusual sideline with complete spontaneity.[6]

Much of the money given by the CIA to Italian political parties since World War II, said a former high-level US official, ended up "in villas, in vacation homes and in Swiss bank accounts for the politicians themselves".[7]

A more direct American intervention into the 1976 elections was in the form of propaganda. Inasmuch as political advertising is not allowed on Italian television, the US Ambassador to Switzerland, Nathaniel Davis, arranged for the purchase of large blocks of time on Monte Carlo TV to present a daily "news" commentary by the editorial staff of the Milan newspaper *Il Giornale Nuovo* which was closely associated to the CIA.* Davis also arranged for news items which had been placed in other newspapers by the Agency to be read on Monte Carlo TV and Swiss TV, both of which are received in Italy. The programmes were produced in Milan by Franklin J. Tonnini of the US Diplomatic Corps, and Michael Ledeen, a reporter on *Il Giornale Nuovo*.[8] (Ledeen, an American, was later a consultant to the Reagan administration and a senior fellow at the conservative think-tank of Georgetown University in Washington, the Center for Strategic and International Studies.)

The relentless fight against the Italian Communist Party took some novel twists. One, in the 1950s, was the brainchild of American Ambassador Clare Booth Luce. The celebrated Ms. Luce (playwright and wife of *Time*

---

* It was this newspaper that, in May 1981, set in motion that particular piece of international disinformation known as "The KGB Plot to Kill the Pope". The *Daily American* of Rome, for decades the leading English-language newspaper of Italy, has been reported by the leftist press to have (had) equally close ties to the Agency.

magazine publisher Henry Luce) decided to make it known that no US Department of Defense procurement contracts would be awarded to Italian firms whose employees had voted to be represented by the Communist-controlled labour union. In the case of Fiat, this had dramatic results: the Communist union's share of the vote promptly fell from 60 percent to 38 percent.[9]

Then there was the case of Cardinal Giovanni Battista Montini, another beneficiary of CIA largesse. The payments made to him reveal something of the Agency's mechanistic thinking about why people become radicals. It seems that the good Cardinal was promoting orphanages in Italy during the 1950s and 1960s and, says Marchetti, "The thinking was that if such institutions were adequately supported, many young people would be able to live well there and so would not one day fall into Communist hands."[10]

In a 1974 interview, the former CIA executive also spoke of the training provided by the Agency to the Italian security services:

> They are trained, for example, to confront disorders and student demonstrations, to prepare dossiers, to make the best possible use of bank data and tax returns of individual citizens, etc. In other words, to watch over the population of their country with the means offered by technology. This is what I call techno-fascism . . .[11]

William Colby, later Director of the CIA, arrived in Italy in 1953 and devoted the next five years of his life to financing and advising centre/right organizations for the expressed purpose of inducing the Italian people to turn away from the leftist bloc, more specifically the Communist Party, and keep it from taking power in the 1958 elections. In his account of that period he justifies this programme on the grounds of supporting "democracy" or "centre democracy" and preventing Italy from becoming a Soviet satellite.

Colby perceived all virtue and truth to be bunched closely around the centre of the political spectrum, and the Italian Communist Party as an extremist organization committed to abolishing democracy and creating a society modelled after the (worst?) excesses of Stalinist Russia. He offers no evidence to support his conclusion about the Communists, presumably because he regards it as self-evident, as much to the reader as to himself. Neither, for that matter, does he explain what was this thing called "democracy" which he so cherishes and which the Communists were so eager to do away with.[12]

William Colby was a technocrat who carried out the orders of his "side" and mouthed the clichés of the party line without serious examination. When Oriana Fallaci, the Italian journalist, interviewed him in 1976, she remarked at the close of a frustrating conversation, "Had you been born on the other side of the barricade, you would have been a perfect Stalinist." To which, Colby replied: "I reject that statement. But . . . well . . . it might be. No, no. It might not."[13]

American policy makers dealing with Italy since Colby's time there have not suffered any less than he from hardening of the categories. Colby, after all, took pains to point out his *liberal* dealings. Yet, all these years, the Italian

Communist Party was proceeding along a path revisionist enough to make Lenin turn in his grave if he were in one. The path has been marked by billboards proclaiming the "democratic advance to socialism" and the "national road to socialism", the abandonment of "the dictatorship of the proletariat" and denunciation of the Soviet invasion of Czechoslovakia. The party has vaunted its "national" role as responsible opposition, participated in "the drive for productivity", affirmed its support for a multiparty system and for Italy remaining in the Common Market and in NATO, and has been second to none in its condemnation of any form of terrorism. It has been the principal political force in numerous city governments including Rome, Florence and Venice, without any noticeable return to barbarism, and has been a *de facto* participant in the running of the Italian state. (The Socialist Party, a prime target of the United States in the 1948 elections, has been a formal member of the government for much of the 1960s to the present.)

In the files of the State Department and the CIA lie any number of internal reports prepared by anonymous analysts testifying to the reality of the Communist Party's "historic compromise" and the evolution of its estrangement from the Soviet Union known as "eurocommunism".

In the face of this, however — in the face of everything — American policy has remained rooted in place, fixed in a time that is no longer, and probably never was; a policy that has had nothing to do with democracy (by whatever definition) and everything to do with the conviction that a Communist government in Italy would not be the supremely pliant cold-war partner that successive Christian Democrat regimes were for over three decades. It would not be enough for such a government to be independent of Moscow. The problem is that it would probably attempt to adopt the same position towards Washington.

19. Vietnam 1950 to 1973
The Hearts and Minds Circus

Contrary to repeated statements by Washington officials during the 1960s that the United States did not intervene in Vietnam until, and only because, "North Vietnam invaded South Vietnam" — variously designated as having occurred from the late 1950s to the early 1960s — the US was deeply and continually involved in that woeful land from the year 1950 onwards.

The initial, fateful step was the decision to make large-scale shipments of military equipment (tanks, transport planes, etc.) to the French in Vietnam in the spring and summer of 1950. In April, Secretary of State Dean Acheson had told French officials that the United States government was set against France negotiating with their northern-based Vietnamese foes, the Vietminh[1] (also spelled Viet Minh or Viet-Minh; the name was short for League for the Independence of Vietnam, a broadly-based nationalist movement led by Communists). Washington was not particularly sympathetic to France's endeavour to regain control of its colony of 100 years* and had vacillated on the issue, but the rise to power of the Communists in China the previous autumn had tipped the scale in favour of supporting the French. To the Truman administration, the prospect of another Communist government in Asia was intolerable. There was a secondary consideration as well at the time: the need to persuade a reluctant France to support American plans to include Germany in West European defence organizations.

American bombers, military advisers and technicians by the hundreds were to follow, and over the next few years direct American military aid to the French war effort ran to about a billion dollars a year. By 1954, the authorized aid had reached the sum of $1.4 billion and constituted 78% of the French budget for the war.[3]

The extensive written history of the American role in Indochina produced by the Defense Department, later to be known as "The Pentagon Papers", concluded that the decision to provide aid to France "directly involved" the United States in Vietnam and "set" the course for future American policy.[4]

There had been another path open. In 1945 and 1946, Vietminh leader Ho Chi Minh had written at least eight letters to President Truman and the State Department asking for America's help in winning Vietnamese independence from the French. He wrote that world peace was being endangered by French efforts to reconquer Indochina and he requested that the four powers (US, USSR, China and Great Britain) intervene in order to mediate a fair settlement, and bring the Indochinese issue before the United Nations.[5] (This was a remarkable repeat of history. In 1919, following the First World War, Ho Chi Minh had appealed to US Secretary of State Robert Lansing for America's help in achieving basic civil liberties and an improvement in the living conditions for the colonial subjects of French Indochina. This plea, too, was ignored.)[6]

Despite the fact that Ho Chi Minh and his followers had worked closely with the American OSS (the forerunner of the CIA) during the recently-ended world war, while the French authorities in Indochina had collaborated with the Japanese, the United States failed to answer any of the letters, did not reveal that it had received them, and eventually sided with the French. In 1950, part of the publicly stated rationale for the American position was that Ho Chi Minh was not really a "genuine nationalist" but rather a tool of "international

---

* During World War II, the Japanese had displaced the French. Upon the defeat of Japan, the Vietminh took power in the north. The British occupied the south but soon turned it back to the French. Said French General Jean Leclerc in September 1945: "I didn't come back to Indochina to give Indochina back to the Indochinese."[2] Subsequently, the French emphasized that they were fighting for the "free world" against communism, a claim made in no small part to persuade the United States to increase its aid to them.

communism", a conclusion that could be reached only by deliberately ignoring the totality of his life's work. He and the Vietminh had, in fact, been long-time admirers of the United States. Ho was said to have a picture of George Washington and a copy of the American Declaration of Independence on his desk, and according to a former OSS officer Ho sought his advice on framing the Vietminh's own declaration of independence. The actual declaration of 1945 begins with the familiar "All men are created equal. They are endowed by their creator with certain unalienable rights, among these are Life, Liberty and the pursuit of Happiness."[7] But it was the French who were to receive America's blessing. Ho Chi Minh was, after all, some kind of communist.

The United States viewed the French struggle in Vietnam and their own concurrent intervention in Korea as two links in the chain aimed at "containing" China. Washington was adamantly opposed to the French negotiating an end to the war which would leave the Vietminh in power, at least in the northern part of the country, and, at the same time, free the Chinese to concentrate exclusively on their Korean border. In 1952, the US exerted strong pressure upon France not to pursue peace feelers extended by the Vietminh, and a French delegation, scheduled to meet with Vietminh negotiators in Burma, was hastily recalled to Paris.

Bernard Fall, the renowned French scholar on Indochina, believed that the cancelled negotiations "could perhaps have brought about a cease-fire on a far more acceptable basis" for the French "than the one obtained two years later in the shadow of crushing military defeat".[8]

Subsequently, to keep the French from negotiating with the Vietminh, the United States used the threat of a cessation of their substantial economic and military aid.[9] (This prompted a French newspaper to comment that "the Indochina War has become France's number one dollar-earning export".)[10]

In November 1953, the omnipresent CIA airline, CAT, helped the French air force airlift 16,000 men into a fortified base the French had established in a valley in the north called Dien Bien Phu. When the garrison was later surrounded and cut off by the Vietminh, CAT pilots, flying US Air Force C-119's, often through anti-aircraft fire, delivered supplies to the beleaguered French forces, in this their Waterloo.[11]

By 1954, the *New York Times* could report that "The French Air Force is now almost entirely equipped with American planes."[12] The United States had also constructed a number of airfields, ports and highways in Indochina to facilitate the war effort, some of which American forces were to make use of in their later wars in that area.

In April 1954, when a French military defeat was apparent and negotiations at Geneva were scheduled, the National Security Council urged President Eisenhower "to inform Paris that French acquiescence in a Communist take-over of Indochina would bear on its status as one of the Big Three" and that "U.S. aid to France would automatically cease".[13]

A Council paper recommended that "It be U.S. policy to accept nothing short of a military victory in Indo-China" and that the "U.S. actively oppose any negotiatied settlements in Indo-China at Geneva". The Council stated further that, if necessary, the US should consider continuing the war without French participation.[14]

The Eisenhower administration had for some time very seriously considered committing American combat troops to Vietnam. Apparently this move was not made only because of uncertainty about Congressional approval and the refusal of other countries to send even a token force, as they had done in Korea, to remove the appearance of a purely American operation.[15] "We are confronted by an unfortunate fact," lamented Secretary of State John Foster Dulles at a 1954 Cabinet meeting. "Most of the countries of the world do not share our view that Communist control of any government anywhere is in itself a danger and a threat."[16]

In May, the Chairman of the Joint Chiefs of Staff, Admiral Arthur Radford, sent a memorandum to Defense Secretary Charles Wilson on "Studies With Respect to Possible U.S. Actions Regarding Indochina" which stated that "The employment of atomic weapons is contemplated in the event that such course appears militarily advantageous."[17] (General Charles Willoughby, MacArthur's director of intelligence, put it a bit more poetically when he advocated the use of atomic bombs "to create a belt of scorched earth across the avenues of communism to block the Asiatic hordes".)[18]

By this time, two American aircraft carriers equipped with atomic weapons had been ordered into the Gulf of Tonkin, in the north of Vietnam,[19] and Dulles is, in fact, reported to have offered his French counterpart, Georges Bidault, atomic bombs to save Dien Bien Phu. Bidault was obliged to point out to Dulles that the use of atomic bombs in a war of such close armed conflict would destroy the French troops as well as the Vietminh.[20]

Dulles regularly denounced China, in the ultra-sanctimonious manner he was known for, for assisting the Vietminh, as if the Chinese had no cause or right to be alarmed about an anti-Communist military crusade taking place scant miles from their border. As the Geneva conference approached, a CIA propaganda team in Singapore began to disseminate fabricated news items to advance the idea that "the Chinese were giving full armed support to the Viet-Minh" and to "identify" the Viet-Minh "with the world Communist movement". The CIA believed that such stories would strengthen the non-Communist side at the Geneva talks.[21]

Joseph Burkholder Smith was a CIA officer in Singapore. His "press asset" was one Li Huan Li, an experienced local journalist. It is instructive to note the method employed in the creation of one such news report about the Chinese. After Smith and Li had made up their story, Li attended the regular press conference held by the British High Commissioner in Singapore, Malcolm MacDonald. At the conference, Li mentioned the report and asked the Commissioner if he had any comment. As expected, MacDonald had nothing to say about it one way or the other. The result was the following news item:

MORE CHINESE SUPPLIES AND TROOPS SPOTTED EN ROUTE TO HAIPHONG. At the press conference of the British High Commissioner for Southeast Asia today, reports of the sightings of Chinese naval vessels and supply ships in the Tonkin Gulf en route from Hainan to Haiphong were again mentioned.

According to these reports, the most recent of many similar sightings occurred one week ago when a convoy of ten ships were spotted. Among them were two armed Chinese naval vessels indicating that the convoy consisted of troops as well as arms and supplies.

High Commissioner Malcolm MacDonald would not elaborate further about these reports.[22]

The story was put on to a wire service in the morning, and by the evening had gone around the world, coming back to Singapore on the European relay to Asia.

The Geneva conference, on 20 July 1954, put a formal end to the war in Vietnam. The United States was alone in refusing to sign the Final Declaration, purely because it was peeved at the negotiated settlement which precluded any further military effort to defeat the Vietminh. There had been ample indication of American displeasure with the whole process well before the end of the conference. Two weeks earlier, for example, President Eisenhower had declared at a news conference: "I will not be a party to any treaty that makes anybody a slave; now that is all there is to it."[23] But the US did issue a "unilateral declaration" in which it agreed to "refrain from the threat or the use of force to disturb" the accords.[24]

The letter and the spirit of the ceasefire agreement and the Final Declaration looked forward to a Vietnam free from any military presence other than Vietnamese or French, and free from any aggressive operations. While the conference was still in session in June, however, the United States began assembling a paramilitary team inside Vietnam. By August, only days after the close of the conference, the team was in place. Under the direction of CIA leading-light Edward Lansdale*, fresh from his success in the Philippines, a campaign of military and psychological warfare was carried out against the Vietminh. Over the next six months, this clandestine team executed such operations as the following:

●   Encouraged the migration of Vietnamese from the north to the south through "an extremely intensive, well-coordinated, and, in terms of its objective, very successful . . . psychological warfare operation. Propaganda slogans and leaflets appealed to the devout Catholics with such themes as 'Christ has gone to the South' and the 'Virgin Mary has departed from the North'."[25]

●   Distributed other bogus leaflets, supposedly put out by the Vietminh, to instill trepidation in the minds of people in the north about how life would be under Communist rule. The following day, refugee registration to move south

---

* Lansdale's various activities in Vietnam were later enshrined in two semi-fictional works, *The Ugly American* and *The Quiet American*.

tripled. (The exodus of Vietnamese to the south during the "regrouping" period that followed the Geneva Accords was often cited by American officials in the 1960s, as well as earlier, as proof of the fact that the people did not want to live under communism. "They voted with their feet" was the catchphrase.) Still other "Vietminh" leaflets were aimed at discouraging people in the south from returning to the north.

● Infiltrated paramilitary forces into the north under the guise of individuals choosing to live there.

● Contaminated the oil supply of the bus company in Hanoi so as to lead to a gradual wreckage of the bus engines.

● Took "the first actions for delayed sabotage of the railroad (which required teamwork with a CIA special technical team in Japan who performed their part brilliantly) . . ."

● Instigated a rumour campaign to stir up hatred of the Chinese, with the usual stories of rapes.

● Created and distributed an almanac of astrological predictions carefully designed to play on Vietnamese fears and superstitions and undermine life in the north while making the future of the south appear more attractive.

● Published and circulated anti-Communist articles and "news" reports in newspapers and leaflets.

● Attempted, unsuccessfully, to destroy the largest printing establishment in the north because it intended to remain in Hanoi and do business with the Vietminh.

● Laid some of the foundation for the future American war in Vietnam by: sending selected Vietnamese to US Pacific bases for guerrilla training; training the armed forces of the south who had fought with the French; creating various military support facilities in the Philippines; smuggling into Vietnam large quantities of arms and military equipment to be stored in hidden locations; developing plans for the "pacification of Vietminh and dissident areas".[26]

At the same time, the United States began an economic boycott against the North Vietnamese and threatened to blacklist French firms which were doing business with them.[27]

Another development during this period that had even more profound consequences for the coming tragedy was the cancellation of the elections that would have united north and south Vietnam as one nation.

The Geneva Accords specified that elections under international supervision were to be held in July 1956, with "consultations" to prepare for them to be held "from 20 July 1955 onwards". The United States, in its unilateral declaration, had reiterated this pledge: "In the case of nations now divided against their will, we shall continue to seek to achieve unity through free elections supervised by the United Nations to insure that they are conducted fairly."

The elections were never held. On 16 July 1955, four days before the consultations were scheduled to begin, President Ngo Dinh Diem of South Vietnam issued a statement that made it clear that he had no intention of engaging in the consultations, much less the elections.[28] Three days later, North Vietnam sent Diem a formal note calling for the talks, but Diem remained firm in his position. Efforts by France and Great Britain to persuade Diem to begin the talks were to no avail.

The reason for Diem's intransigence is well known. He, like President Eisenhower and John Foster Dulles, knew that Ho Chi Minh would be a certain winner of any national elections. A CIA National Intelligence Estimate in the autumn concluded that the Diem regime (which Lansdale himself called "fascistic")[29] "almost certainly would not be able to defeat the communists in country-wide elections".[30] Later, Eisenhower was to write in his memoirs: "I have never talked or corresponded with a person knowledgeable in Indochinese affairs who did not agree that had elections been held as of the time of the fighting, possibly 80% of the population would have voted for the Communist Ho Chi Minh as their leader rather than Chief of State Bao Dai."[31] (The latter was Diem's predecessor.)

The Pentagon study cited "State Department cables and National Security Council memorandums indicating that the Eisenhower Administration wished to postpone the elections as long as possible and communicated its feelings to Mr. Diem."[32]

This was support that Diem could not have done without, for, as the Pentagon historians point out: "Without the threat of U.S. intervention, South Vietnam could not have refused to even discuss the elections called for in 1956 under the Geneva settlement without being immediately overrun by the Vietminh armies."[33]

The public statements of Diem and Dulles spoke only of their concern that the elections would not be "free" — which served to obscure the fact that Ho Chi Minh did not need to resort to fraud in order to win — as well as ignoring the announcements of both the United Nations and the International Control Commission (set up in Vietnam by the Geneva Accords) that they were ready to supervise the elections.

In any event, Diem's commitment to free elections may be surmised from a referendum he held later in the year in South Vietnam, to invest his regime with a semblance of legality, in which he received 98.2% of the vote. *Life* magazine later reported that Diem's American advisers had told him that a 60% margin would be quite sufficient and would look better, "but Diem insisted on 98%".[34]

With the elections cancelled, the nation still divided, and Diem with his "mandate" free to continue his heavy, tyrannical rule, the turn to violence in South Vietnam became inevitable.

As if in knowledge of and preparation for this, the United States sent 350 additional military men to Saigon in May 1956, an "example of the U.S. ignoring" the Geneva Accords, stated the Pentagon study.[35] Shortly afterwards, Dulles confided to a colleague: "We have a clean base there now, without a taint of colonialism. Dienbienphu was a blessing in disguise."[36]

The Later Phase

"If you grab 'em by the balls, the hearts and minds will follow" . . . "Give us your hearts and minds or we'll burn down your goddam village" . . . the end result of America's anti-communist policy in Vietnam; also its beginning and its middle.

There was little serious effort to win the hearts and minds of the Vietnamese people, even less chance of success, for the price of success was social change, of the kind that Diem was unwilling to accept in Vietnam, the kind the United States has not been willing to accept anywhere in the Third World. If Washington had been willing to accept it, there would have been no need to cancel the elections, no need for intervention in the first place. There was, consequently, no way the United States could avoid being seen by the people of Vietnam as other than the newest imperialist occupiers, following in the footsteps of first the Chinese, then the French, then the Japanese, then the French again.

We will not go into a detailed recounting of all the horror, all the deceptions, the destruction of a society, the panorama of absurdities and ironies; only a selection, a montage . . . lest we forget.

To the men who walked the corridors of power in Washington, to the military men in the field, Indochina — nay, south-east Asia — was a single, large battlefield.

Troops of South Vietnam were used in Laos and Cambodia.

Troops of Thailand were used in Laos, Cambodia and South Vietnam.

Thailand and the Philippines were used as bases from which to bomb the three countries of Indochina.

CIA-supported forces carried out incursions and invasions into China from Laos, Burma and Taiwan.

When there was a (much-publicized) pause in the bombing of North Vietnam, more American planes were thus available to increase the bombing of Laos.

And so it went.

From 1955 to 1959, Michigan State University (MSU), under a US Government contract, conducted a covert police training programme for the South Vietnamese. With the full knowledge of certain MSU officials, five CIA operatives were concealed in the staff of the programme and carried on the university's payroll as its employees. By the terms of a 1957 law, drawn up by the MSU group, every Vietnamese 15 years and older was required to register with the government and carry ID cards. Anyone caught without the proper identification was considered as a National Liberation Front (Vietcong) suspect and subject to imprisonment or worse. At the time of registration, a full set of fingerprints was obtained and information about the person's political beliefs was recorded.[37]

When popular resistance to Ngo Dinh Diem reached the level where he was more of a liability than an asset he was sacrificed. On 1 November 1963, some of Diem's generals overthrew him and then murdered both him and his brother after they had surrendered. The coup, wrote *Time* magazine "was planned with the knowledge of Dean Rusk and Averill Harriman at the State Department, Robert S. McNamara and Roswell Gilpatrick at the Defense Department and the late Edward R. Murrow at the U.S. Information Agency."[38]

Evidently Washington had not planned on assassinations accompanying the coup, but as General Maxwell Taylor, President Kennedy's principal military adviser, has observed: "The execution of a coup is not like organizing a tea party; it's a very dangerous business. So I didn't think we had any right to be surprised when — when Diem and his brother were murdered."[39]

Donald Duncan was a member of the Green Berets in Vietnam. He has written about his training, part of which was called "countermeasures to hostile interrogation", ostensibly how Americans captured by Communists could deal with being tortured; translations of an alleged Soviet interrogation manual were handed out to the class. The manual described in detail such methods as the "Airplane Ride" (hanging by the thumbs), the Cold-Hot Water Treatment, and the lowering of a man's testicles into a jeweller's vise, while the instructor, a Sergeant Lacey, explained some variations of these methods. Then a student had a question:

> "Sergeant Lacey, the name of this class is 'Countermeasures to Hostile Interrogation,' but you have spent most of the period telling us there are no countermeasures. If this is true, then the only reason for teaching them [the torture methods], it seems to me, is so that we'll know how to use them. Are you suggesting we use these methods?"
>
> The class laughs, and Lacey looks down at the floor creating a dramatic pause. When he raises his head, his face is solemn but his deep set eyes are dancing. "We can't tell you that, Sergeant Harrison. The Mothers of America wouldn't approve." The class bursts into laughter at the sarcastic cynicism. "Furthermore," a conspiratorial wink, "we will deny that any such thing is taught or intended."[40]

At the US Navy's schools in San Diego and Maine during the 1960s and 1970s, the course had a different name. There, the students were supposedly learning about methods of "survival, evasion, resistance and escape" which they could use as prisoners of war. There was in the course something of survival in a desert, where students were forced to eat lizards, but the naval officers and cadets were also subjected to beatings, jarring judo flips, "tiger cages" — hooded and placed in a 16-cubic-foot box for 22 hours with a coffee can for their excrement — and a torture device called the "water board": the subject strapped head down on to an inclined board, a towel placed over his face, and cold water poured over the towel; he would choke, gag, retch and gurgle as he experienced the sensation of drowning, just as was done to Vietcong prisoners in Vietnam, along with the tiger cages.

A former student, navy pilot Lt. Wendell Richard Young, claimed that his back was broken during the course and that students were tortured into spitting, urinating and defecating on the American flag, masturbating before guards, and, on one occasion, engaging in sex with an instructor.[41]

Fabrications were required to support the varied State Department claims about the nature of the war and the reasons for the American military actions. A former CIA officer, Philip Liechty, stated in 1982 that in the early 1960s he saw written plans to take large amounts of Communist-bloc arms, load them on a Vietnamese boat, fake a battle in which the boat would be sunk in shallow water, then call in Western reporters to see the captured weapons as proof of outside aid to the Vietcong. This is precisely what occurred in 1965. The State Department's "white paper", "Aggression From the North", which came out at the end of February 1965 relates that a "suspicious vessel" was "sunk in shallow water" off the coast of South Vietnam on 16 February 1965 after an attack by South Vietnamese forces. The boat was reported to contain at least 100 tons of military supplies "almost all of communist origin, largely from Communist China and Czechoslovakia as well as North Vietnam." The white paper noted that "Representatives of the free press visited the sunken North Vietnamese ship and viewed its cargo."

Liechty said that he had also seen documents involving an elaborate operation to print large numbers of postage stamps showing a Vietnamese shooting down a US Army helicopter. The former CIA officer stated that this was a highly professional job and that the very professionalism required to produce the multicolour stamps was meant to indicate that they were produced by the North Vietnamese because the Vietcong would not have had the capabilities. Liechty claimed that letters in Vietnamese were then written and mailed all over the world with the stamp on them "and the CIA made sure journalists would get hold of them". *Life* magazine, in its issue of 26 February 1965, did in fact feature a full colour blow-up of the stamp on its cover, referring to it as a "North Vietnam stamp". This was just two days before the State Department's white paper appeared.

In reporting Liechty's statements, the *Washington Post* noted:

> Publication of the white paper turned out to be a key event in documenting the support of North Vietnam and other communist countries in the fighting in the South and in preparing American public opinion for what was to follow very soon: the large-scale commitment of U.S. forces to the fighting.[42]

Perhaps the most significant fabrication was that of the alleged attack in August 1964 on two US destroyers in the Tonkin Gulf off the coast of North Vietnam. President Johnson used the incident to induce a resolution from Congress to take "all necessary steps, including the use of armed forces" to prevent further North Vietnamese aggression. It was a blanket endorsement for escalation heaped upon escalation. Serious enough doubts were raised at the time about the reality of the attack, but over the years other information has come to light which has left the official story in tatters.[43]

And probably the silliest fabrication: the 1966 US Army training film, "County Fair", in which the sinister Vietcong are shown in a jungle clearing heating gasoline and soap bars in a vicious communist invention called napalm.[44]

The Johnson administration's method of minimizing public concern about escalation of the war, as seen by a psychiatrist:

> First step: Highly alarming rumors about escalation are 'leaked'.
> Second step: The President officially and dramatically sets the anxieties to rest by announcing a much more moderate rate of escalation, and accompanies this announcement with assurances of the Government's peaceful intentions.
> Third step: After the general sigh of relief, the originally rumored escalation is gradually put into effect.
> The succession of 'leaks', denials of leaks, and denials of denials thoroughly confuses the individual. He is left bewildered, helpless, apathetic.
> The end result is that the people find themselves deeply committed to large-scale war, without being able to tell how it came about, when and how it all began.[45]

Senator Stephen Young of Ohio was reported to have said that while he was in Vietnam he was told by the CIA that the Agency disguised people as Vietcong to commit atrocities, including murder and rape, so as to discredit the Communists. After the report caused a flurry in Washington, Young said that he had been misquoted, that the CIA was not the source of the story. Congressman Cornelius Gallagher, who had accompanied Young on the trip, suggested that it "may well be that he [Young] spoke to a Vietcong disguised as a CIA man".[46]

From a speech by Carl Oglesby, President of Students for a Democratic Society (SDS) during the March on Washington, 27 November 1965:

> The original commitment in Vietnam was made by President Truman, a mainstream liberal. It was seconded by President Eisenhower, a moderate liberal. It was intensified by the late President Kennedy, a flaming liberal. Think of the men who now engineer that war — those who study the maps, give the commands, push the buttons, and tally the dead: Bundy, McNamara, Rusk, Lodge, Goldberg, the President himself.
> They are not moral monsters. They are all honorable men. They are all liberals.[47]

During the heat of the fighting in 1966-67, the Soviet Union sold to the United States over $2 million worth of magnesium — a metal vital in military aircraft production — when there was a shortage of it in the United States. This occurred at a time when Washington maintained an embargo on supplying Communist nations with certain alloys of the same metal.[48] At about the same time, China sold several thousand tons of steel to the United States in South Vietnam for use in the construction of new Air and Army bases when no one else could meet the American military's urgent need; this, while Washington maintained a boycott on all Chinese products; even wigs imported into the US from Hong Kong had to be accompanied by a certificate of origin stating that they contained no Chinese hair. The sale of steel may have been only the tip of the iceberg of Chinese sales to the United States at this time.[49]

In 1975, a Senate investigating committee began looking into allegations that the CIA had counterfeited American money during the Vietnam war to finance secret operations.[50]

"Two Vietcong prisoners were interrogated on an airplane flying toward Saigon. The first refused to answer questions and was thrown out of the airplane at 3,000 feet. The second immediately answered all the questions. But he, too, was thrown out." Variations of the water torture were also used to loosen tongues or simply to torment. "Other techniques, usually designed to force onlooking prisoners to talk, involve cutting off the fingers, ears, fingernails or sexual organs of another prisoner."[51]

It is not clear whether these particular Vietnamese were actual prisoners of war, i.e., captured in combat, or whether they were amongst the many thousands of civilians arrested as part of the infamous Phoenix Program. Phoenix was the inevitable consequence of fighting a native population: you never knew who was friend, who was enemy. Anyone was a potential informer, bomb-thrower, or assassin. Safety demanded that, unless proved otherwise, everyone was to be regarded as the enemy, part of what the CIA called the Vietcong infrastructure (VCI).

In 1971, CIA officer William Colby, the director of Phoenix, was asked by a Congressman: "Are you certain that we know a member of the VCI from a loyal member of the South Vietnam citizenry?" "No, Mr. Congressman," replied Colby, "I am not."[52]

Phoenix was a co-ordinated effort of the United States and South Vietnam to wipe out this infrastructure. Under the programme, Vietnamese citizens were rounded up and jailed, often in tiger cages, often tortured, often killed, either in the process of being arrested or subsequently. By Colby's records, during the period between early 1968 and May 1971, 20,587 alleged Vietcong cadres met their death as a result of the Phoenix Program.[53] A similar programme, under different names, had existed since 1965 and been run by the United States alone.[54]

Colby claims that more than 85 percent of the 20,587 figure were actually killed in military combat and only identified afterward as members of the VCI.[55] It strains credulity, however, to think that the tens of thousands of Vietcong killed in combat during this period were picked over, body by body, on the battlefield, for identification and that their connection to the VCI was established.

The South Vietnam government credited Phoenix with 40,994 VCI deaths.[56] The true figure will probably never be known.

A former US military-intelligence officer in Vietnam, K. Barton Osborn, testified before a House Committee that suspects caught by Phoenix were interrogated in helicopters and sometimes pushed out. He also spoke of the use of electric shock torture and the insertion into the ear of a six-inch dowel which was tapped through the brain until the victim died.[57]

Osborn's colleague, Michael J. Uhl, testified that most suspects were captured during sweeping tactical raids and that all persons detained were classified as Vietcong. None of those held for questioning, said Osborn, had ever lived through the process.[58]

Osborn later helped to found an organization of former intelligence officers which stood opposed to Colby's designation as CIA Director, calling his appointment "nothing more than rewards for his having been the CIA's apologist for Phoenix to Congress . . . Mr. Colby's professional qualifications as a mass murderer are not in question here, his appointment to a powerful Government position is."[59]

Arthur Sylvester, Assistant Secretary of Defense for Public Affairs, was the man most responsible for "giving, controlling and managing the war news from Vietnam". One day in July 1965, Sylvester told American journalists that they had a patriotic duty to disseminate only information that made the United States look good. When one of the newsmen exclaimed: "Surely, Arthur, you don't expect the American press to be handmaidens of government," Sylvester replied, "That's exactly what I expect," adding: "Look, if you think any American official is going to tell you the truth, then you're stupid. Did you hear that? — stupid." And when a correspondent for a New York paper began a question, he was interrupted by Sylvester who said: "Aw, come on. What does someone in New York care about the war in Vietnam?"[60]

Meanwhile, hundreds of US servicemen in Asia and Europe were being swindled by phoney American auto dealers who turned up to take down payments on cars which they never delivered. Commented an Illinois Congressman: "We cannot expect our servicemen to fight to protect the free enterprise system if the very system which they fight to protect takes advantage of them."[61]

On 27 January 1973, in Paris, the United States signed the "Agreement on Ending the War and Restoring Peace in Vietnam". Among the principles to which the United States agreed was the one stated in Article 21 of the Agreement:

In pursuance of its traditional policy, the United States will contribute to healing the wounds of war and to postwar reconstruction of the Democratic Republic of Vietnam [North Vietnam] and throughout Indochina.

Five days later, 1 February, President Nixon sent a message to the Prime Minister of North Vietnam reiterating and expanding upon this pledge. The first two principles put forth in the President's message were:

(1) The Government of the United States of America will contribute to postwar reconstruction in North Vietnam without any political conditions.
(2) Preliminary United States studies indicate that the appropriate programs for the United States contribution to postwar reconstruction will fall in the range of $3.25 billion of grant aid over 5 years. Other forms of aid will be agreed upon between the two parties. This estimate is subject to revision and to detailed discussion between the Government of the United States and the Government of the Democratic Republic of Vietnam.[62]

Since that time, the only aid given to any Vietnamese people by the United States has been to those who have left Vietnam and those who have been infiltrated back in to stir up trouble.

Are the victims of the Vietnam war also to be found in generations yet unborn? Tens of millions of pounds of herbicide were unleashed over the country; included in this were quantities of dioxin which has been called the most toxic man-made substance known; three ounces of dioxin, it is claimed, in the New York City water supply could wipe out the entire populace. Studies in Vietnam since the war have pointed to abnormally high rates of cancers, particularly of the liver, chromosomal damage, birth defects, long-lasting neurological disorders, etc. in the heavily-sprayed areas. The evidence collected is not yet conclusive. The statistics that have been kept in the devastated land that is Vietnam are not up to the standards of certain developed nations. But thousands of American veterans of Vietnam have fought for years to receive disability compensation, claiming irreparable damage from simply handling the toxic herbicides. In 1984, several herbicide manufacturers finally agreed to a settlement.

After the Second World War, the International Military Tribunal convened at Nuremburg, Germany. Created by the Allies, the Tribunal sentenced to prison or execution numerous Nazis who pleaded that they had been "only following orders". In an opinion handed down by the Tribunal, it declared that "the very essence of the [Tribunal's] Charter is that individuals have international duties which transcend the national obligations of obedience imposed by the individual state."

During the Vietnam war, a number of young Americans refused military service on the grounds that the United States was committing war crimes in Vietnam and that if they took part in the war they too, under the principles laid down at Nuremberg, would be guilty of war crimes.

One of the most prominent of these cases was that of David Mitchell of Connecticut. At Mitchell's trial in September 1965, Judge William Timbers dismissed his defence as "tommyrot" and "degenerate subversion", and found the Nuremberg principles to be "irrelevant" to the case. Mitchell was sentenced to prison.

Conservative columnist William F. Buckley, Jr., not celebrated as a champion of draft resistance, noted shortly afterward:

> I am glad I didn't have Judge Timbers' job. Oh, I could have scolded Mr. Mitchell along with the best of them. But I'd have had to cough and wheeze and clear my throat during that passage in my catechism at which I explained to Mr. Mitchell wherein the Nuremberg Doctrine was obviously not at his disposal.[63]

In 1971, Telford Taylor, the chief United States prosecutor at Nuremberg, suggested rather strongly that General William Westmoreland and high officials of the Johnson administration such as Robert McNamara and Dean Rusk could be found guilty of war crimes under criteria established at Nuremberg.[64] Yet every American court and judge, when confronted by the Nuremberg defence, had dismissed it without according it any serious consideration whatever.

The West has never been allowed to forget the Nazi holocaust. For 40 years there has been a continuous outpouring of histories, memoirs, novels, feature films, documentaries, television series . . . played and replayed, in every Western language; museums, memorials, remembrances, ceremonies . . . Never Again! But who hears the voice of the Vietnamese peasant? Who can read the language of the Vietnamese intellectual? What was the fate of the Vietnamese Anne Frank? Where, asks the young American, is Vietnam?

20. Cambodia 1955 to 1973
Prince Sihanouk walks the high-wire of neutralism

John Foster Dulles had called on me in his capacity as Secretary of State, and he had exhausted every argument to persuade me to place Cambodia under the protection of the South-East Asia Treaty Organization. I refused . . . I considered SEATO an aggressive military alliance directed against neighbors whose ideology I did not share but with whom Cambodia had no quarrel. I had made all this

> quite clear to John Foster, an acidy, arrogant man, but his brother [CIA Director Allen Dulles] soon turned up with a briefcase full of documents 'proving' that Cambodia was about to fall victim to 'communist aggression' and that the only way to save the country, the monarchy and myself was to accept the protection of SEATO. The 'proofs' did not coincide with my own information, and I replied to Allen Dulles as I had replied to John Foster: Cambodia wanted no part of SEATO. We would look after ourselves as neutrals and Buddhists. There was nothing for the secret service chief to do but pack up his dubious documents and leave.
>
> *Prince Norodom Sihanouk*, in his memoirs, *My War With The CIA*[1]

The visits of the Brothers Dulles in 1955 appear to have been the opening salvos in a campaign of extraordinary measures aimed at pressuring the charismatic Cambodian leader into aligning his nation with the West and joining The Holy War Against Communism. The coercion continued intermittently until 1970 when Sihanouk was finally overthrown in a coup and the United States invaded Cambodia.

In March 1956, after Sihanouk had visited Peking and criticized SEATO, the two countries which sandwich Cambodia — Thailand and South Vietnam, both heavily dependent upon and allied with the United States — suddenly closed their borders. It was a serious move, for the bulk of Cambodia's traffic with the outside world at that time passed either along the Mekong River through South Vietnam or by railway through Thailand.

The danger to the tiny kingdom was heightened by repeated military provocations. Thai troops invaded Cambodian territory and CIA-financed irregulars began to make commando raids from South Vietnam. Deep intrusions were made into Cambodian air space by planes based in the two countries.

To Sihanouk, these actions "looked more and more like preliminary softening-up probes" for his overthrow. He chose to thrust matters out into the open. At a press conference he scolded the US, defended Cambodia's policy of neutrality, and announced that the whole question would be on the agenda of his party's upcoming national congress. There was the implication that Cambodia would turn to the socialist bloc for aid.

The United States appeared to retreat in the face of this unorthodox public diplomacy. The State Department sent a couple of rather conciliatory messages which nullified a threatened cut-off of certain economic aid and included this remarkable piece of altruism: "The only aim of American policy to Cambodia is to help her strengthen and defend her independence." Two days before the national congress convened, Thailand and South Vietnam opened their frontiers. The local disputes which the two countries had cited as the reasons for the blockade had not been resolved at all.[2]

The measures taken against Cambodia were counter-productive. Not only did Sihanouk continue to attack SEATO, but he established relations with the Soviet Union and Poland and accepted aid from China. He praised the latter lavishly for treating Cambodia as an equal and for providing aid without all the strings which, he felt, came attached to American aid.[3]

Such sentiments should not obscure the fact that Sihanouk was as genuine a neutralist as one could be in such a highly polarized region of the world in the midst of the cold war. He did not shy away from denouncing China, North Vietnam or Communism on a number of occasions when he felt that Cambodia's security or neutrality was being threatened. "I foresee perfectly well," he said at one time, "the collapse of an independent and neutral Cambodia after the complete triumph of Communism in Laos and South Vietnam."[4]

In May 1957, a National Security Council (NSC) paper acknowledged that "the United States has been unable to influence Cambodia in the direction of a stable [sic] government and non-involvement in the communist bloc."[5]

The following year, five battalions of Saigon troops, supported by aircraft, crossed the Cambodian border again, penetrated to a depth of almost 10 miles and began putting up new boundary markers. Sihanouk's impulse was to try and repel the invaders but, to his amazement, he was informed by the American Ambassador to Cambodia, Carl Strom, that American military aid was provided exclusively for the purpose of opposing "communist aggression" and in no case could be used against an American ally. The ambassador cautioned that if a single bullet were fired at the South Vietnamese or a single US-supplied truck used to transport Cambodian troops to a military confrontation with them, this would constitute grounds for cancelling aid.[6]

Ambassador Strom was called back to Washington, told that Sihanouk would now have to go and that US aid would be cut off to precipitate his fall. Strom, however, did not think that this was the wisest move to make at that point and was able to convince the State Department to hold off for the time being.[7]

William Shawcross, in his elaborately-researched book, *Sideshow: Kissinger, Nixon and the Destruction of Cambodia*, notes that "NSC papers of the period cited in the Pentagon papers confirm that Washington saw Thai and Vietnamese pressure across the borders as one of the principal weapons to be used in an effort to move Sihanouk toward a more pro-American position."[8]

In addition to Thai and South Vietnamese troops, the CIA had at its disposal two other forces, the Khmer Serei and the Khmer Krom, composed largely of ethnic Cambodians opposed to Sihanouk's rule, who operated out of the two neighbouring countries. The Khmer Serei ("Free Cambodians") were described by Shawcross as the "Cambodian organization with which American officials had had the closest contact".[9] Sihanouk once equated them to the "free" Cubans the United States maintained in Florida.[10]

These forces — recruited, financed, armed and trained by the CIA and the US Special Forces (Green Berets)[11] — began to infiltrate into Cambodia in the latter part of 1958 as part of a complex conspiracy which included, amongst others, a disloyal Cambodian general named Dap Chhuon who was plotting an armed uprising inside the country. At its most optimistic, the conspiracy aimed at overthrowing Sihanouk.

Sihanouk discovered the plan, partly through reports from Chinese and French intelligence. The French were not happy about the American intrusion into what had been their domain for close to a century.

By February 1959 the conspirators had been apprehended or had fled, including Victor Masao Matsui, a member of the CIA station in Cambodia's capital city Phnom Penh, who hurriedly left the country after Sihanouk accused him of being a party to the plot. Matsui, an American of Japanese descent, had been operating under State Department cover as an attaché at the embassy.

The intrigue, according to Sihanouk, began in September 1958 at a SEATO meeting in Thailand and was carried a step further later that month in New York when he visited the United Nations. While Sihanouk was away in Washington for a few days, a member of his delegation, Slat Peou, held several conferences with Americans in his New York hotel room which he did not mention to any of his fellow delegates. Slat Peou, it happened, was a close friend of Victor Matsui and was the brother of General Dap Chhuon. In the aftermath of the aborted conspiracy, Slat Peou was executed for treason.[12] Sihanouk was struck by the bitter irony of the circumstance that while the CIA was plotting against him in New York, he was in Washington being honoured by President Eisenhower with a 21-gun salute.[13]

In a similar vein, several years later, President Kennedy assured Sihanouk "on his honour" that the United States had played no role in the affairs of the Khmer Serei. "I considered President Kennedy to be an honourable man," wrote Sihanouk, "but, in that case, who really represented the American government?"[14]

The Cambodian leader has attested to several other plots he lays at the doorstep of the CIA. Amongst these was a 1959 effort to murder him which was foiled when the police picked a nervous young man, Rat Vat by name, out of a crowd surrounding Sihanouk. He was found to be carrying a hand grenade and a pistol. Investigation showed, writes Sihanouk, that the would-be assassin was instigated by the CIA and the Khmer Serei.[15] Sihanouk also cites three incidents occurring in 1963: an attempt to blow up a car carrying him and the visiting president of China, Liu Shao Chi; an attempt to smuggle arms into Cambodia in a number of crates addressed to the US Embassy; and a partially successful venture aimed at sabotaging the Cambodian economy and subverting key government personnel through the setting up of a bank in Phnom Penh.[16]

On 20 November of the same year, two days before the assassination of John F. Kennedy, the Cambodian National Congress, at Sihanouk's initiative, voted to "end all aid granted by the United States in the military, economic, technical and cultural fields." It was perhaps without precedent that a country receiving American aid voluntarily repudiated it. But Sihanouk held strong feelings on the subject. Over the years he had frequently recited from his register of complaints about American aid to Cambodia: how it subverted and corrupted Cambodian officials and businessmen who wound up "constituting a clientele necessarily obedient to the demands of the lavish bestower of foreign funds"; and how the aid couldn't be used for state institutions, only private enterprise, nor, as mentioned earlier, used against attacks by US allies.[17]

After some American bombings of Cambodian villages near the South Vietnam border in pursuit of North Vietnamese and Vietcong, the Cambodian government, in October 1964, announced that "in case of any new violation of

Cambodian territory by US ground, air, or naval forces, Cambodia will immediately sever diplomatic relations with the United States". The government did just that the following May when American planes bombarded several villages, killing or wounding dozens of peasants.[18] This incident may have been the immediate incitement to breaking relations, but, as we have seen, discontent between the two countries had been simmering for some time.

The pattern over the next few years, as the war in Indochina intensified, was one of repeated forays into Cambodian territory by American, Saigon and Khmer Serei forces in search of Communist supply lines and sanctuaries along the Ho Chi Minh Trail; bombing and strafing, napalming, and placing land mines, with varying numbers of Cambodian civilian casualties; angry accusations by the Cambodian government, followed on occasion by an American apology, promise of an investigation and the taking of "measures to prevent any recurrence of such incidents".[19]

Sihanouk did not at all relish the intrusions into Cambodia by the Vietnamese Communists, nor was he wholly or consistently antagonistic to American pursuit of them, particularly when there was no loss of Cambodian lives. On at least one occasion he disclosed the location of Communist bases which were promptly bombed by the US. However, Sihanouk then went on the radio and proceeded to denounce the bombings.[20] Opportunist that he often revealed himself to be, Sihanouk was nonetheless truly caught between the devil and the deep blue sea, and by the late 1960s his predicament had compelled him to resume American aid and re-establish diplomatic relations with the United States.

Despite all the impulsiveness of his personality and policies, Sihanouk's neutralist high-wire balancing act did successfully shield his country from the worst of the devastation that was sweeping through the land and people of Vietnam and Laos. Cambodia had its own Communist insurgents, the Khmer Rouge, who surely would have unleashed a full-scale civil war if faced with a Cambodian government nestled comfortably in the American camp. This is precisely what later came to pass following the overthrow of Sihanouk and his replacement by the pro-American Lon Nol.

In March 1969, the situation began to change dramatically. Under the new American president, Richard Nixon, and National Security Affairs adviser Henry Kissinger, the isolated and limited attacks across the Cambodian border became sustained, large-scale B-52 bombings — "carpet bombings", in the euphemistic language so dear to the hearts of military men.

Over the next 14 months, no less than 3,630 B-52 bombing raids were flown over Cambodia.[21] To escape the onslaught, the Vietnamese Communists moved their bases further inside the country. The B-52's of course followed, with a concomitant increase in civilian casualties.

The Nixon administration artfully played down the nature and extent of these bombings, going so far as to falsify military records, and was largely successful in keeping it all a secret from the American public, the press and Congress.[22] Not until 1973, in the midst of the Watergate revelations, did a fuller story begin to emerge.

It was frequently argued that the United States had every right to attack Cambodia because of its use as a sanctuary by America's foes in Vietnam. Apropros of this claim, William Shawcross has pointed out that:

> During the Algerian war of independence the United States rejected France's claimed right to attack a Tunisian town inhabited by Algerian guerrillas, and in 1964 Adlai Stevenson, at the U.N., condemned Britain for assaulting a Yemeni town used as a base by insurgents attacking Aden. Even Israel had frequently been criticized by the United States for attacks on enemy bases outside its territory.[23]

On 18 March 1970, Sihanouk, while on a trip abroad, was deposed as Head of State by two of his leading ministers, Lon Nol and Sirik Matak. To what extent, if any, the United States played a direct role in the coup has not been established, but there are circumstances and testimony pointing to American complicity, among which are the following:

● According to Frank Snepp, the CIA's principal political analyst in Vietnam at this time, in early 1970 the Agency was cultivating both Lon Nol and Son Ngoc Thanh, leader of the Khmer Serei, as possible replacements for Sihanouk. The CIA believed, he says, that if Lon Nol came to power, "He would welcome the United States with open arms and we would accomplish everything."[24] (This, presumably, meant *carte blanche* to wipe out Vietnamese Communist forces and sanctuaries in Cambodia, as opposed to Sihanouk's extremely equivocal position on the matter.) Both men, as matters turned out, served as prime minister in the new government, for which diplomatic recognition was immediately forthcoming from Washington.

● The United States could seemingly also rely on Sirik Matak, a committed anti-Communist who had been profiled by the Pentagon's Defense Intelligence Agency as "a friend of the West and . . . co-operative with U.S. officials during the 1950s."[25]

● Investigative journalist Seymour Hersh, in his biographic work on Kissinger, states that Sihanouk's

> immediate overthrow had been for years a high priority of the Green Berets reconnaissance units operating inside Cambodia since the late 1960s. There is also incontrovertible evidence that Lon Nol was approached by agents of American military intelligence in 1969 and asked to overthrow the Sihanouk government. Sihanouk made similar charges in his 1973 memoir, *My War With The CIA*, but they were not taken seriously then.[26]

● Throughout the period surrounding the coup, writes William Shawcross, "various United States agencies were in touch with Lon Nol and Sirik Matak and their associates."[27]

● An opponent of Sihanouk, Prom Thos, who became a minister in the new government, has said that whether Lon Nol had specific promises of

American help before the coup is unimportant: "We all just knew that the United States would help us; there had been many stories of CIA approaches and offers before then."[28]

● The CIA's intimate links to the conspiratorial circle are exemplified by an Agency report prepared six days before the coup, entitled "Indications of Possible Coup in Phnom Penh". It disclosed that anti-Communist demonstrations against the Vietcong and North Vietnamese Embassies in the capital the previous day had been planned by Sirik Matak and Lon Nol as part of a showdown policy against Sihanouk and his followers, and that the two men had put the army on alert "to prepare . . . for a coup against Sihanouk if Sihanouk refused to support" them.[29]

● General William Rosson, deputy to General Creighton Abrams, the Commander of US Forces in Vietnam at the time, has declared that American commanders were informed several days beforehand that a coup was being planned and that United States support was solicited.[30]

● Roger Morris, who was serving under Henry Kissinger on the National Security Council staff when the coup took place, reported that "It was clear in the White House that the CIA station in Phnom Penh knew the plotters well, probably knew their plans, and did nothing to alert Sihanouk. They informed Washington well in advance of the coup . . ."[31]

● William Shawcross asserts that had Sihanouk "returned quickly and calmly to Phnom Penh [following the anti-communist demonstrations] he would most likely have been able to avert disaster." That he did not do so may not have been by chance. Frank Snepp has revealed that the Agency "exacerbated the crisis by throwing up misinformation": it persuaded Sihanouk's mother, the Queen, to send a message to her son abroad reassuring him that the situation was not serious enough to warrant his return; after this, the CIA disseminated worldwide the idea that there was absolutely no chance of Sihanouk returning, although what form this took was not explained.[32]

With Sihanouk and his irritating neutralism no longer an obstacle, American military wheels began to spin. Within hours of the coup, US and South Vietnam forces stationed in border districts were directed to establish communication with Cambodian commanders on the other side and take steps toward military co-operation. The next day, the Cambodian army called in an American spotter plane and South Vietnamese artillery during a sweep of a Vietcong sanctuary by a battalion of Cambodian troops inside Cambodia. The *New York Times* declared that "The battle appeared to be the most determined Cambodian effort yet to drive the Vietcong out of border areas."[33] The Great Cambodian War had begun. It was to persist for five terrible years.

Before long, the enemy confronting the United States and its Saigon and Phnom Penh allies was not simply the North Vietnamese and the Vietcong. The Cambodian Communists, the Khmer Rouge, had entered the conflict, as had sundry Cambodian supporters of Prince Sihanouk. In an effort to enlist peasant support, Lon Nol exploited the Cambodians' traditional fear and hatred of Vietnamese by unleashing a bloodbath against the many ethnic Vietnamese in the country, branding them all as Vietcong.[34]

On 30 April 1970, the first full-scale American invasion of the new war was launched. It produced a vast outcry of protest in the United States, rocking university campuses from coast to coast. Perhaps even more extraordinary were the angry resignations of four men from Henry Kissinger's National Security Council staff, including Roger Morris. (Kissinger labelled the resignations as "the cowardice of the Eastern establishment".)[35]

William Shawcross has vividly captured one aspect of the invasion:

All that day United States and South Vietnamese troops, tanks and planes churned across the earth and the air into the provinces of Ratanakiri, Mondolkiri, Kompong Cham and Svay Rieng. Reporters flying westward by helicopter to cover the invasion noticed that the unmarked border was easily discerned. On the South Vietnamese side the buffalo grazed calmly, well used to the noise of the war above and around them. In Cambodia the animals ran into each other and scattered, terrified.[36]

By the end of May, scores of villages were reduced to rubble and ashes by US air power; hundreds of innocent civilians had been bombed, burned and machine-gunned to death by American and Saigon troops; the long train of Cambodian refugees had begun their march; by autumn, Cambodia's traditional economy had almost vanished.

Three years and a hundred thousand tons of bombs later, 27 January 1973 to be precise, an agreement was signed in Paris putting an end to a decade of American warfare in Vietnam. The bombing of Cambodia, however, continued.

Prior to the Paris agreement, the official position of the Nixon administration, repeatedly asserted, was that the sole purpose of bombing Cambodia was to protect American lives in Vietnam. Yet now, the US not only did not cease the bombing, it increased it, in a last desperate attempt to keep the Khmer Rouge from coming to power. During March, April and May, the tonnage of bombs unloosed over Cambodia was more than double that of the entire previous year. The old Cambodia was being destroyed forever.

It does appear rather ludicrous, in the light of this application of brute force, that the CIA was at the same time carrying out the most subtle of psychological tactics. As an example, to spread dissatisfaction about the exiled Sihanouk amongst the Cambodian peasantry who revered him, a CIA sound engineer, using sophisticated electronics, fashioned an excellent counterfeit of the Prince's distinctive voice and manner of speaking — breathless, high-pitched, and full of giggles. This voice was beamed from a clandestine radio station in Laos with messages artfully designed to offend any good Khmer. In one of the broadcasts, "Sihanouk" exhorted young women to aid the cause by sleeping with the valiant Vietcong.[37]

In a farewell press conference in September, 1973, the American Ambassador to Cambodia, Emory Swank, called what had taken place there "Indochina's most useless war".[38]

Later, Californian Congressman Pete McClosky, following a visit to Cambodia, had harsher words. He was moved to declare that what the United States had "done to the country is greater evil that we have done to any country in the world, and wholly without reason, except for our own benefit to fight against the Vietnamese."[39]

Incredibly, the victorious Khmer Rouge were later to inflict yet more misery upon that unhappy land; although, knowing what we do of the CIA's extraordinary ability to orchestrate world news coverage — what former Agency official Frank Wisner proudly referred to as his "mighty Wurlitzer" — we have to approach the claims of the extent of Khmer Rouge mass executions with caution; to the CIA, the issue was "a natural". Most ironically, the United States later wound up supporting the Khmer Rouge, both at the United Nations and in the field, in their struggle with the Vietnamese.

21. Laos 1957 to 1973
L'Armée Clandestine

For the past two years the US has carried out one of the most sustained bombing campaigns in history against essentially civilian targets in northeastern Laos ... Operating from Thai bases and from aircraft carriers, American jets have destroyed the great majority of villages and towns in the northeast. Severe casualties have been inflicted upon the inhabitants ... Refugees from the Plain of Jars report they were bombed almost daily by American jets last year. They say they spent most of the past two years living in caves or holes.
Far Eastern Economic Review, Hong Kong, 1970[1]

[The Laos operation] is something of which we can be proud as Americans. It has involved virtually no American casualties. What we are getting for our money there ... is, I think, to use the old phrase, very cost effective ...
U. Alexis Johnson, US Under Secretary of State, 1971[2]

The United States undertook the bombing campaign because its ground war against the Pathet Lao had failed.

The ground war had been carried out because the Pathet Lao were led by people whom the State Department categorized as "communist", no more, no less.

The Pathet Lao (re)turned to warfare because of their experiences in "working within the system".

In 1957 the Pathet Lao held two ministerial posts in the coalition "government of national union". This was during John Foster Dulles' era, and if if there was anything the fanatic Secretary of State hated more than neutralism it was a coalition with communists. This government featured both. There could be little other reason for the development of the major American intervention into this impoverished and primitive land of peasants. The American Ambassador to Laos at the time, J. Graham Parsons, was to admit later: "I struggled for sixteen months to prevent a coalition."[3]

In addition to its demand for inclusion in the coalition government, the Pathet Lao had called for diplomatic relations with the countries of the Soviet bloc and the acceptance of aid from them. "Agreement to these conditions," said Washington, "would have given the Communists their most significant gains in Southeast Asia since the partition of Indochina."[4] Others would say that the Pathet Lao's conditions were simply what neutralism is all about.

In May 1958, the Pathet Lao and other leftists, running a campaign based on government corruption and indifference, won 13 of 21 contested seats for the National Assembly and wound up controlling more than one-third of the new legislature.[5] Two months later, however, Prime Minister Souvanna Phouma, a man universally categorized as a neutralist, "resigned" to form a new government which would exclude the Pathet Lao ministers.[6] (He subsequently claimed that he was forced to resign due to continued American opposition to Laotian neutrality; as it happened, one Phoui Sananikone, backed by the US, became premier in the reorganized government.)[7] Then, in January 1959, the non-left majority in the National Assembly voted, in effect, to dissolve the Assembly in order "to counteract communist influence and subversion". The left was now altogether excluded from the government, and the elections scheduled for December were cancelled.[8]

If this wasn't enough to disenchant the Pathet Lao — or anyone else — with the Laotian political process, there was, in the late 1950s and early 1960s, the spectacle of a continuous parade of coups and countercoups, of men overthrown winding up in the new government; regimes headed by men who had sided with the French in their war against Indochinese independence (while the Pathet Lao had fought against the colonialists);[9] government-rigged elections, with the CIA stuffing ballot boxes;[10] different regimes cum warlords governing simultaneously from different "capitals", their armies fighting each other, switching allies and enemies when it suited them; hundreds of millions of US dollars pouring into a tiny kingdom which was 99 percent agricultural, with an economy based more on barter than money, the result being "unimaginable bribery, graft, currency manipulation and waste".[11]

The CIA and the State Department alone could take credit for engineering coups, through force, bribery or other pressures, at least once in each of the years 1958, 1959 and 1960, if not in others.[12] "By merely withholding the monthly payment to the troops," wrote Roger Hilsman (whose career encompassed both agencies, perhaps simultaneously), "the United States could create the conditions for toppling any Lao government whose policies it opposed. As it turned out, in fact, the United States used this weapon twice — to bring down the government of one Lao leader and to break the will of another."[13]

The American wheeling and dealing centred around giving power to the CIA's hand-picked rightist strongman Phoumi Nosavan, ousting Souvanna Phouma and other neutralists, and jailing Pathet Lao leaders, including the movement's head, Souphanouvong (the half-brother of Souvanna Phouma, both being princes of the royal family). Souphanouvong insisted that neither he nor the Pathet Lao were communist, but were rather "ultra-nationalist".[14] Crucial to understanding his statements, of course, is the question of exactly what he meant by the term "communist". This is not clear, but neither is it clear what the State Department meant when it referred to him as such. Semantics aside, the Pathet Lao were the only sizable group in the country serious about social change.

In August 1960, Kong Le, a military officer with his own troop following, staged a coup and set up a neutralist government under Souvanna Phouma, rejecting Pathet Lao help.[15] But when this government became a casualty of a CIA coup in December, Kong Le allied himself with the Pathet Lao; later he turned to the United States for aid and fought against the Pathet Lao; such was the way of the Laotian circus.

No study of Laos of this period appears to have had notable success in untangling the muddle of who exactly replaced whom, and when, and how, and why. After returning from Laos, writer Norman Cousins stated in 1961 that "if you want to get a sense of the universe unraveling, come to Laos. Complexity such as this has to be respected."[16]

One thing that comes through unambiguously, however, is the determination of the CIA and the State Department to save Laos from communism and neutralism. To this end, the CIA set about creating its famous Armée Clandestine, a process begun by the US Army in the mid-1950s when it organized Meo hill-tribesmen (the same ethnic group organized in Vietnam). Over the years, other peoples of Laos were added, reaching as many as 40,000 in the mid-1960s, 15,000 of them more or less full-time soldiers ... 15,000 more from Thailand ... hundreds of other Asians came on board, South Vietnamese, Filipinos, Taiwanese, South Koreans, men who had received expert training from their American mentors in their home countries, now being recycled. An army, said the *New York Times*, "armed, equipped, fed, paid, guided, strategically and tactically, and often transported into and out of action by the United States" ... trained and augmented by the CIA, by men of every branch of the US military with their multiple specialities, the many pilots of the CIA's Air America, altogether some 2,000 Americans in and over Laos, and thousands more Americans in Asia helping with the logistics. A Secret Army, secret, that is, from the American people and Congress — US military personnel were there under various covers, some as civilians in mufti, having "resigned" from the service for the occasion and been hired by a private company created by the CIA; others served as embassy attachés; CIA pilots were officially under contract to the Agency for International Development (AID); Americans who were killed in Laos were reported to have died in Vietnam[17] . . . all this in addition to the "official" government forces, the Royal Laotian Army, greatly expanded and totally paid for by the US government as well . . .[18]

Laos was an American plantation, a CIA playground. During the 1960s, the Agency roamed over much of the land at will, building an airstrip, a hangar, or a base here, a warehouse, barracks, or a radar site there;[19] relocating thousands of people, entire villages, whole tribes, to suit strategic military needs; recruiting warriors "through money and/or the threat or use of force and/or promises of independent kingdoms which it had no intention of fulfilling, and then keeping them fighting long beyond the point when they wished to stop."[20] The "legendary" pilots of Air America roamed far and wide as well, hard drinking, daredevil flying, death defying, great stories to tell the guys back home, if you survived.[21]

At the same time, the hearts and minds of the Laotian people, at least of those who could read, were not overlooked. The US Information Agency was there to put out a magazine with a circulation of 43,000; this, in a country where the circulation of the largest newspaper was 3,300; there were as well USIA wall newspapers, films, leaflet drops, and radio programmes.[22]

In the face of it all, the Pathet Lao more than held their own. The CIA was over-extended, and, unlike the motley band of Asians assembled by the Agency, the soldiers of the Pathet Lao had some idea of what they were fighting for. The Soviet Union, aware of what the United States was doing in Laos, even if Americans were not, acceded to a cold-war knee-reflex by sending military supplies to the Pathet Lao, though nothing on the order of the US commitment.[23]

Beginning in the early 1960s, the North Vietnamese were aiding them as well. Hanoi's overriding interest in Laos was not necessarily the creation of a Communist state, but the prevention of a belligerent government on its border. In January 1961, the *New York Times* reported that "Many Western diplomats in Vientiane [capital of Laos] . . . feel the Communists would have been content to leave Laos alone provided she remained neutral and outside the United States sphere of influence."[24]

Hanoi was concerned not only by the American political and military operations in Laos, but by the actions of US Special Forces teams which were entering North Vietnam to engage in espionage, sabotage, and assassination,[25] and by the bombings of the country being carried out by the US Air Force[26] at a time when the war in South Vietnam was still but a shadow of what was to come. Later, as the wars in Vietnam and Laos became intertwined, Laos formed part of the Ho Chi Minh Trail, the principal route by which Hanoi supplied its comrades in South Vietnam, and the North Vietnamese fought to protect it as well as attacking American radar installations in Laos used to aid US bombing of North Vietnam.

The nature and extent of North Vietnam's aid to the Pathet Lao before this period is difficult to ascertain from Western sources, because such charges typically emanated from the Laotian government or the State Department, and their credibility on the subject is questionable. On a number of occasions, their report of a North Vietnamese military operation in Laos turned out to be a fabrication. William Lederer and Eugene Burdick, in *A Nation of Sheep*, summarized one of these non-events:

> In the summer of 1959 . . . The people of the United States were led to believe that Laos physically had been invaded by foreign Communist troops from across its northern border. Our Secretary of State called the situation grave; our ambassador to the U.N. called for world action; our press carried scare headlines; our senior naval officer implied armed intervention and was seconded by ranking Congressmen . . .
>
> The entire affair was a fraud. No military invasion of Laos had taken place . . . There seemed no doubt that a war embracing thousands of troops, tanks, planes, and mass battles, was raging. Regardless of how the accounts were worded, this was the picture given the nation.[27]

It had all been a ploy to induce Congress not to reduce aid for Laos, something seriously being considered because of the pervasive corruption which had been exposed concerning the aid programme.[28] The Laotian government and the large American establishment in Laos, each for their own reasons, were not about to let the golden goose slip away that easily.

On the last day of 1960, the Laotian government announced to the world that seven battalions of North Vietnamese troops had invaded the country. By all accounts, and by the utter lack of evidence, this claim as well cannot be taken seriously.[29]

And in 1962, reported Bernard Fall, the renowned French scholar on Indochina: after a battle between government forces and the Pathet Lao, in spite of the fact that Col. Edwin Elder, the American commander in the area of the battle, immediately stated that there was

> 'no evidence to show that Chinese or [North] Vietnamese had participated in the attack', the Laotians — and much of the U.S. press, and official Washington with them — immediately claimed that they were again faced with a large-scale 'foreign invasion'.[30]

Shortly after Kennedy became president in January 1961, he had made a sustained diplomatic effort to establish a coalition government in Laos, precisely what the Eisenhower Administration and the CIA had done their best to sabotage. Although he sometimes fell back on conventional cold-war rhetoric when speaking of Laos, one part of John F. Kennedy realized the absurdity of fighting for the backward country, a land he considered not "worthy of engaging the attention of great powers".[31] Soviet Premier Khrushchev, for his part, was reportedly "bored" with the question of Laos, and irritably asked Kennedy's emissary why Washington bothered so much about the country.[32]

Eventually, in July 1962, a multi-nation conference in Geneva signed an agreement for a coalition government in Laos. But in the mountains and plains of the country, this was no longer a viable option. The CIA had too much time, effort, material and emotion invested in its Secret Army; it was the best war the Agency had going anywhere; it was great adventure. And the Pathet Lao were much stronger now than a few years earlier. They were not about to buy such shopworn, suspect goods again, although everyone went through the motions.

Both sides regularly accused each other of violating the agreement, and not without justification. The North Vietnamese, for example, did not withdraw all of their troops from Laos, while the US left behind all manner of military personnel, American and Asian, who remained under AID and other civilian cover, but this was nonetheless a violation of the agreement. Moreover, Christopher Robbins, in his study of Air America, has noted that US "Military advisers and CIA personnel moved across the border into Thailand, where they were flown in every day [to Laos] like commuters by Air America, whose entire helicopter operation was based in Udorn [Thailand]."[33] Air America, by the early 1970s, had no less than 4,000 employees in Thailand.[34]

Thus it was that the fighting dragged on, though only sporadically. In April 1964, the coalition government, such as it was, was overthrown by the right-wing, with the CIA's man Phoumi Nosavan emerging as part of a rightist government headed by the perennial survivor Souvanna Phouma to give it a neutralist fig leaf.[35] The Pathet Lao were once again left out in the cold. For them it was the very last straw. The fighting greatly intensified, the skirmishes were now war; the Pathet Lao offensive soon scored significant advances. Then the American bombing began.

Between 1965 and 1973, more than two million tons of bombs rained down upon the people of Laos,[36] considerably more than the US had dropped on both Germany and Japan during the Second World War, albeit for a shorter period. For the first few years, the bombing was directed primarily at the provinces controlled by the Pathet Lao. Of the bombing, Fred Branfman, a former American community worker in Laos, wrote: "village after village was leveled, countless people burned alive by high explosives, or burnt alive by napalm and white phosphorous, or riddled by anti-personnel bomb pellets"[37] . . . "The United States has undertaken," said a Senate report,". . . a large-scale air war over Laos to destroy the physical and social infrastructure of Pathet Lao held areas and to interdict North Vietnamese infiltration . . . throughout all this there has been a policy of subterfuge and secrecy . . . through such things as saturation bombing and the forced evacuation of population from enemy held or threatened areas — we have helped to create untold agony for hundreds of thousands of villagers."[38]

The American military, however, kept proper records. AID could report to Congress that wounds suffered by civilian war casualties were as follows:

1. Type: Soft tissue, 39 percent. Compound fracture, 30 percent. Amputation, 12 percent. Intra-abdominal, 10 percent. Intra-thoracic, 3 percent. Intra-cranial, 1 percent.
2. Location: Lower extremities, 60 percent. Upper extremities, 15 percent. Trunk, 18 percent. Head, 7 percent.[39]

The fledgling society that the United States was trying to make extinct — the CIA dropped millions of dollars in forged Pathet Lao currency as well, in an attempt to wreck the economy[40] — was one which Fred Branfman described thus:

> The Pathet Lao rule over the Plain of Jars begun in May 1964 brought its people into a post-colonial era. For the first time they were taught pride in their country and people, instead of admiration for a foreign culture; schooling and massive adult literacy campaigns were conducted in Laotian instead of French; and mild but thorough social revolution — ranging from land reform to greater equality for women — was instituted.[41]

Beginning in the late 1960s, the Ho Chi Minh Trail in southern Laos became the principal target of American bombing, though the people of the north were still hurting. In October 1971, for example, one could read in *The Guardian* of London . . .

> although US officials deny it vehemently, ample evidence exists to confirm charges that the Meo villages that do try to find their own way out of the war — even if it is simply by staying neutral and refusing to send their 13-year-olds to fight in the CIA army — are immediately denied American rice and transport, and ultimately bombed by the US Air Force.[42]

Following on the heels of events in Vietnam, a ceasefire was arrived at in Laos in 1973, and yet another attempt at coalition government (this one lasted until 1975, at which time the Pathet Lao took over full control of the country). Laos had become a land of nomads, without villages, without farms; a generation of refugees; hundreds of thousands dead, many more maimed. When the US Air Force closed down its radio station, it signed off with the message: "Good-by and see you next war."[43]

Thus it was that the worst of Washington's fears had come to pass: all of Indochina — Vietnam, Cambodia and Laos — had fallen to the communists. During the initial period of US involvement in Indochina in the 1950s, John Foster Dulles, Dwight Eisenhower and others regularly issued doomsday pronouncements of the type known as the "Domino Theory", warning that if Indochina should fall, other nations in Asia would topple over as well. In one instance, President Eisenhower listed no less than Taiwan, Australia, New Zealand, the Philippines and Indonesia amongst the anticipated "falling dominos".[44]

Such warnings were repeated periodically over the next decade by succeeding administrations and other supporters of US policy in Indochina as a key argument in defence of such policy. The fact that these ominous predictions have turned out to have no basis in reality has not deterred Washington officialdom from promulgating the same dogma to the present day about almost each new world "trouble-spot", testimony to their unshakable faith in the existence and inter-workings of the International Communist Conspiracy.

22. Haiti 1959
The Marines land, again

"Duvalier has performed an economic miracle," remarked a Haitian of his country's dictator. "He has taught us to live without money . . . to eat without food . . . to live without life."[1]

And when Duvalier's voodoo magic wore thin, he could always turn to the US Marines to continue his people's education.

During the night of 12-13 August 1959, a boat landed on the northern coast of Haiti with a reported 30 men, Haitians and Cubans and perhaps others, aboard. The men had set sail from Cuba some 50 miles away. Their purpose was to overthrow the tyrannical Haitian government, a regime whose secret police, it was said, outnumbered its army.

In short order, the raiding party, equipped with heavy weapons, captured a small army post and began to recruit and arm villagers for the cause.[2] The government reported that about 200 persons had joined them.[3] Haitian exiles in Venezuela, in an apparently co-ordinated effort, broadcast appeals to their countrymen to aid the invaders. They set at 120 the number of men who had landed in Haiti, although this appears to be an exaggeration.[4]

The initial reaction of the Duvalier government was one of panic, and the police began rounding up opposition sympathizers.[5] It was at this point that the US military mission, in Haiti to train Duvalier's forces, stepped in. The Americans instituted an air and sea reconnaissance to locate the rebels. Haitian soldiers, accompanied by US Marines, were airlifted to the area and went into the field to do battle with them.[6] Two other US Navy planes and a helicopter arrived from Puerto Rico.[7]

According to their commander, Col. Robert Debs Heinl, Jr., the American Marines took part in the fighting which lasted until 22 August.[8] The outcome was a complete rout of the rebel forces.

Information about the men who came from Cuba derives almost exclusively from the Haitian government and the American mission. These sources claim that the raiding party was composed of about 30 men and that, with the exception of one or two Haitians who led them, they were all Cubans. Another report, referred to in the *New York Times*, stated that there were ten Haitians and two Venezuelans amongst the 30 invaders.[9] The latter ratio is probably closer to the truth, for there was a considerable number of Haitian exiles living in Cuba, many of whom had gained military experience during the revolution; for obvious reasons of international politics and fighting incentive, such men were the most likely candidates to be part of an invasion of their homeland.

The Castro government readily admitted that the raiding party had come from Cuba but denied that the government had known or approved of it. This claim would seem rather hollow were it not for the fact that the Cuban coast guard had thwarted a similar undertaking in April.[10]

The first members of the American military mission had arrived in Haiti in January, largely in response to another invasion attempt the previous July (originating probably in the Dominican Republic). Regardless of all the horror stories about the Haitian regime — such as the one Col. Heinl tells of his twelve-year-old son being arrested when he was overheard expressing sympathy for a group of hungry peasants he saw — Duvalier was Washington's man. After all was said and done, he could be counted upon to keep his black nation, which was usually accorded the honour of being Latin America's poorest, from turning red.

23. Guatemala 1960
One good coup deserves another

In November 1960, as John F. Kennedy was preparing to succeed Dwight Eisenhower, the obsessive priority of American foreign policy — to invade Cuba — proceeded without pause. On the beaches and in the jungles of Guatemala, Nicaragua and Florida, the Bays of Pigs invasion was being rehearsed.

On the 13th of the month, five days after Kennedy's victory, Guatemalan military personnel broke out in armed rebellion against the government of General Miguel Ydigoras Fuentes, seizing two military bases and the port city of Puerto Barrios. Reports of the number of officers involved in the uprising vary from 45 to 120, the latter figure representing almost half the Guatemalan Army's officer corps. The officers commanded as many as 3,000 troops, a significant percentage of the armed forces. Their goals, it later developed, were more nationalistic than ideological. The officers were fed up with the corruption in the Ydigoras regime and in the army, and were particularly incensed about the use of their country by a foreign power as a springboard for an invasion of Cuba; some of them admired Castro for his nationalist policies. One of the dissident officers later characterized the American training base in Guatemala as "a shameful violation of our national sovereignty. And why was it permitted? Because our government is a puppet."[1]

The rebellion was crushed within a matter of days, reportedly by the sole power of the Guatemalan Air Force. Some years later, a truer picture was to emerge.

The rebels were a force to be reckoned with. The ease with which they had taken over the two garrisons and the real possibility of their mutiny spreading to other bases set alarms ringing at the CIA base, a large coffee plantation in a remote corner of south-western Guatemala, where the Agency and the US Air Force were training the army of Cuban exiles who were to launch the attack upon their homeland. The CIA feared, and rightly so, that a new regime would send them, the Cubans, and the whole operation packing.

In Washington, President Eisenhower ordered US naval and air units to patrol the Caribbean coast and "shoot if necessary" to prevent any "communist-led" invasion of Guatemala or Nicaragua.[2] Eisenhower, like Ydigoras, saw the hand of international communism, particularly Cuba, behind the uprising, although no evidence of this was ever presented.[3] It was all most ironic in light of the fact that it was the conspiracy of the two leaders to overthrow Cuba that was one of the reasons for the uprising; and that the US naval fleet ordered into action was deployed from Guantanamo Naval Base in Cuba, an American military installation present in that country against the vociferous objections of the Cuban government.

In Guatemala, meanwhile, the CIA decided upon a solution to the dilemma that was remarkably simple and close at hand: American and Cuban pilots took off from their training ground and bombed and strafed rebel headquarters outside Guatemala City, and bombed the town and airfield of Puerto Barrios. Caught completely by surprise, and defenceless against this superior force, the rebels' insurrection collapsed.[4]

Back at the coffee plantation, the CIA resumed the function which had been so rudely interrupted, the preparation for the overthrow of the Cuban government.

No announcement about the bombings was made in Washington, nor did a report appear in the American press.

The CIA actions were probably not widely known about in Guatemala either, but it became public knowledge that President Ydigoras had asked Washington for the naval and air support, and had even instructed the Guatemalan Ambassador in Washington to "Get in touch immediately with [Assistant Secretary of State for Inter-American Affairs] Thomas Mann to coordinate your action."[5] Thus it was that the Guatemalan president, needing afterward to distance himself a little from so much Yanqui protection, was moved to state that countries like Guatemala are at a disadvantage because "Cuba is a satellite of powerful Russia", but "we are not a satellite of the United States."[6]

The final irony was that some of the dissident officers who went into hiding became more radicalized by their experience. During their revolt they had spurned offers of support from some of the peasants — though this would necessarily have been very limited in any case — because fighting for social change was not at all what the officers had in mind at the time. But as fugitives, they were moved by the peasants' pressing need for land and for a way out of their miserable existence.[7] In 1962, several of the officers were to emerge as leaders of a guerrilla movement which incorporated "November Thirteen" as part of its name. In their opening statement, the guerrillas declared:

> Democracy vanished from our country long ago. No people can live in a country where there is no democracy. That is why the demand for changes is mounting in our country. We can no longer carry on in this way. We must overthrow the Ydigoras government and set up a government which represents human rights, seeks ways and means to save our country from its hardships, and pursues a serious self-respecting foreign policy.[8]

A simple sentiment, stated even simpler, but, as we shall see, a movement fated to come up against the wishes of the United States. For if Washington could casually do away with an elected government in Guatemala, it could be moved by a guerrilla army only as rocks by waves or the moon by howling wolves.

24. France/Algeria 1960s
L'état, c'est la CIA

When John F. Kennedy assumed office in January 1961, he was confronted with a CIA at the zenith of its power and credibility. In the Agency's first 14 years, no formal Congressional investigation of it had taken place, nor had any "watchdog" committee been established; four investigations by independent task forces during this period had ensured that everything relating to things covert remained just that; with the exception of the U-2 incident the year before, no page-one embarrassments, scandals, or known failures; what had received a measure of publicity — the coups in Guatemala and Iran — were widely regarded as CIA success stories.

It is probable that the CIA had more staff officers overseas, under official and unofficial covers, than the State Department, and this in addition to its countless paid agents. Often the CIA Chief of Station had been in a particular country longer than the American Ambassador, had more money at his disposal, and exerted more influence. When it suited their purposes, Agency officers would completely bypass the ambassador and normal protocol to deal directly with the country's head of state and other high officials.

The CIA had its own military capabilities, including its own air force; for all intents and purposes, its own foreign service with, indeed, its own foreign policy, though never at cross-purposes with fundamental US cold-war, anti-communist ideology and goals.

It was all very heady stuff for the officers of the CIA, playing their mens' games with their boys' toys. They recognized scarcely any limitation upon their freedom of action. British colonial governors they were, and all the world was India.

Then, in mid-April, came the disaster at the Bay of Pigs in Cuba. The international repercussions had barely begun to subside, when the CIA was again catapulted into world headlines. On 22 April four French generals in Algeria seized power in an attempt to maintain the country's union with France. The *putsch*, which held out but four days, was a direct confrontation to French President Charles de Gaulle who had dramatically proclaimed a policy leading "not to an Algeria governed from France, but to an Algerian Algeria".

The next day, the leftist Italian newspaper, *Il Paese*, stated that "It is not by chance some people in Paris are accusing the American secret service headed by Allen Dulles of having participated in the plot of the four 'ultra' generals . . ."[1]

Whether *Il Paese* was the original source of this charge remains a mystery. Dulles himself later wrote that the Italian daily was "*one* of the first to launch it". (Emphasis added.) He expressed the opinion that "This particular myth was a Communist plant, pure and simple."[2]

The *New York Times* reported that the rumours apparently began circulating by word of mouth on the day of the *putsch*,[3] a report echoed by the *Washington Star* which added that some of the rumours were launched "by minor officials at the Elysée Palace itself" who gave reporters "to understand that the generals' plot was backed by strongly anti-communist elements in the United States Government and military services."[4]

Whatever its origins, the story spread rapidly around the world, and the French Foreign Office refused to refute the allegation. *Le Monde* asserted in a front-page editorial on 28 April that "the behaviour of the United States during the recent crisis was not particularly skillful. It seems established that American agents more or less encouraged Challe [the leader of the *putsch*] . . . President Kennedy, of course, knew nothing of all this."[5]

Reports from all sources were in agreement that if the CIA had indeed been involved in the *putsch*, it had been so for two reasons: 1) The concern that if Algeria were granted its independence; "communists" would soon come to power, being those in the ranks of the National Liberation Front (NLF) which had been fighting the French Army in Algeria for several years — the legendary Battle of Algiers; it was with the NLF that de Gaulle was expected to negotiate a settlement; 2) The hope that it would precipitate the downfall of de Gaulle, an end desired because the French President was a major stumbling block to US plans to build an integrated military command under NATO: de Gaulle refused to incorporate French troops into the alliance. By all accounts, it appears that the rebel officers had counted on support from important military and civilian quarters in France to extend the rebellion to the home country and overthrow de Gaulle. Fanciful as this may sound, the fact remains that the French government took the possibility seriously — French Premier Michel Debré went on television to warn the nation of an imminent paratroop invasion of the Paris area and to urge mass opposition.[6]

Reaction in the American press to the allegations had an unmistakable motley quality. *Washington Post* columnist Marquis Childs said that the French were so shocked by the generals' coup that they had to find a scapegoat. At the same time he quoted "one of the highest officials of the French government" as saying:

> Of course, your government, neither your State Department nor your President, had anything to do with this. But when you have so many hundreds of agents in every part of the world, it is not to be wondered at that some of them should have got in touch with the generals in Algiers.[7]

Time magazine discounted the story, saying too that the United States was being made a scapegoat and that the CIA had become a "favorite target in recent weeks".[8]

James Reston wrote in the *New York Times* that the CIA:

> was involved in an embarrassing liaison with the anti-Gaullist officers who staged last week's insurrection in Algiers . . . [the Bay of Pigs and Algerian events have] increased the feeling in the White House that the CIA has gone beyond the bounds of an objective intelligence-gathering agency and has become the advocate of men and policies that have embarrassed the Administration.[9]

However, C.L. Sulzberger, who had been the man at the *New York Times* closest to the CIA since its founding, stated flatly that "No American in Algeria had to do with any insurrectional leader . . . No consular employee saw any rebel." (A few days later, Secretary of State Dean Rusk disclosed that an emissary of the rebellious French generals had visited the US Consulate in Algiers to request aid but had been summarily rebuffed.)

The affair, wrote Sulzberger, was "a deliberate effort to poison Franco-American relationships" begun in Moscow but abetted by "anti-American French officials" and "naive persons in Washington". "When one checks, one finds all this began in a Moscow Izvestia article April 25."[10] This last, as we have seen, was incorrect.

Dean of American columnists, Walter Lippmann, who had seen de Gaulle in Paris shortly before the *putsch*, wrote:

> the reason why the French Government has not really exculpated the CIA of encouraging the Algerian rebel generals is that it was already so angry with the CIA for meddling in French internal politics. The French grievance, justified or not, has to do with recent French legislation for the French nuclear weapon, and the alleged effort of CIA agents to interfere with that legislation.[11]

Newsweek repeated the claim that it was "French officials" who had been "the main sources" of the rumours in the first place. When challenged by the American administration the French denied their authorship and tended to soften the charges. Some French officials eventually declared the matter to be closed, though they still failed to explicitly rule out the allegations about American involvement.[12]

In early May 1961, *L'Express*, the widely-read French liberal weekly, published what was perhaps the first detailed account of the mysterious affair.

Their Algerian correspondent, Claude Krief reported:[13]

> Both in Paris and Washington the facts are now known, though they will never be publicly admitted. In private, the highest French personalities make no secret of it. What they say is this: 'The CIA played a direct part in the Algiers coup, and certainly weighed heavily on the decision taken by ex-general Challe to start his *putsch*'.

Not long before, Challe had held the position of NATO Commander-in-Chief, Allied Forces, Central Europe, as a result of which he had been in daily contact with US military officers.[14] Krief wrote that certain American officials in NATO and the Pentagon encouraged Challe, and that the general had had several meetings with CIA officers who told him that "to get rid of de Gaulle would render the Free World a great service". Krief noted that Challe, despite an overweening ambition, was very cautious and serious-minded: "All the people who know him well, are deeply convinced that he had been encouraged by the CIA to go ahead."

At a luncheon in Washington the previous year, Jacques Soustelle, the former Governor-General of Algeria who had made public his disagreement with de Gaulle's Algeria policy, had met with CIA officials, including Richard Bissell, head of covert operations. Soustelle convinced the Agency officials, according to Krief, that Algeria would become, through de Gaulle's blundering, "a Soviet base". This luncheon became something of a *cause célèbre* in the speculation concerning the CIA's possible role. The *New York Times* and others reported that it had been given by the Agency for Soustelle.[15] US officials, however, insisted that the luncheon had been arranged by someone at the French Embassy at Soustelle's request. This French official, they said, had been present throughout the meeting and thus there could have been no dark conspiracy.[16] Why the French Embassy would host a luncheon for a prominent and bitter foe of de Gaulle, a man who only two months earlier had been kicked out of de Gaulle's cabinet for his "ultra" sympathies, was not explained. Nor, for that matter, why in protocol-minded Washington of all places, the CIA would attend. In any event, it seems somewhat fatuous to imply that this was the only chance Soustelle and the CIA had to talk during his stay in the United States which lasted more than a week.

A clandestine meeting in Madrid also received wide currency within the controversy. Krief dates it 12 April 1961, and describes it as a meeting of "various foreign agents, including members of the CIA and the Algiers conspirators, who disclosed their plans to the CIA men". The Americans were reported to have angrily complained that de Gaulle's policy was "paralyzing NATO and rendering the defense of Europe impossible", and assured the generals that if they and their followers succeeded, Washington would recognize the new Algerian Government within 48 hours.

It may well be that the French Government did have evidence of the CIA's involvement. But in the unnatural world of international diplomacy, this would not necessarily lead to an unambiguous public announcement. Such a move could result in an open confrontation between France and the United States, a predicament both sides could be expected to take pains to avoid. Moreover, it would put the French in the position of having to *do* something about it. And what could they do? Breaking relations with the United States was not a realistic option; neither were the French in any position to retaliate economically or militarily. But French leaders were too angry to simply let the matter pass into obscurity. Thus, to complete the hypothetical scenario, they took the backdoor approach with all its shortcomings.

In a similar vein, the Soviet Union knew about the American U-2 flights over its territory for years before making it public. The Soviets were not prepared to admit that they were unable to do anything about the incessant overhead espionage. And the United States knew that the Russians, for at least one year, were intercepting telephone calls in the US of governmental and congressional officials, but said nothing publicly because it was unable to end the practice for technical reasons.[17]

Between 1958 and the middle of the 1960s, there occurred some 30 serious assassination attempts upon the life of Charles de Gaulle, in addition to any number of planned attempts which didn't advance much beyond the planning stage.[18] A world record for a head of state, it is said. In at least one of the attempts, the CIA may have been a co-conspirator.

In 1975, the *Chicago Tribune* featured a story on page one which read in part:

Congressional leaders have been told of Central Intelligence Agency involvement in a plot by French dissidents to assassinate the late French President Charles De Gaulle. Within the last two weeks, a CIA representative disclosed sketchy details of the scheme . . . Sometime in the mid-1960s — probably in 1965 or 1966 — dissidents in the De Gaulle government are said to have made contact with the CIA to seek help in a plot to murder the French leader. Which party instigated the contact was not clear . . . According to the CIA briefing officer, discussions were held on how best to eliminate De Gaulle, who by then had become a thorn in the side of the Johnson administration because of his ouster of American military bases from French soil and his demands that United States forces be withdrawn from the Indochina War. Thus the following plan is said to have evolved after discussions between CIA personnel and the dissident French. There is, however, no evidence the plot got beyond the talking stage.

A hired assassin, armed with a poison ring, was to be slipped into a crowd of old soldiers of France when General De Gaulle was to be the host at a reception for them. The killer would make his appearance late in the day when it could be presumed De Gaulle's hand would be weary and perhaps even numb from shaking hundreds of hands. The assassin would clasp the general's hand in lethal friendship and De Gaule would fail to detect the tiny pin prick of poison as it penetrated his flesh. The executioner would stroll off to become lost in the crowd as the poison began coursing through De Gaulle's veins either to his heart or brain, depending on the deadly poison used. How quickly death would come was not divulged, if that was even discussed at the time . . .

In the outline presented to the congressional leaders, there is no hint of what the CIA's actual role might have been had the plot reached fruition.[19]

The dissidents involved in the alleged plot were embittered French army officers and former Algerian settlers who still bore deep resentment toward de Gaulle for having "sold out French honour" by his retreat from the North African colony.

There was no mention in the reported CIA testimony about any involvement of Lyndon Johnson, although it was well known that there was no love lost between Johnson and de Gaulle. The French leader was firmly convinced that the United States was behind the failure of his trip to South America in 1964. He believed that the CIA had used its network of agents in South America to prevent a big turnout of crowds.[20] There is some evidence to indicate that the General was not just paranoid. In 1970, Dr Alfred Stepan, a professor of political science at Yale, testified before Congress about his experience in South America in 1964 when he was a journalist for *The Economist*:

> When De Gaulle was going to make his trip through Latin America, many of the Latin Americans interviewed [officers of various embassies] said that they were under very real pressure by various American groups not to be very warm towards De Gaulle, because we considered Latin America within the United States area of influence.[21]

After the appearance of the *Chicago Tribune* story, CIA Director William Colby confirmed that "foreigners" had approached the Agency with a plot to kill de Gaulle. The Agency rejected the idea, Colby said, but he did not know if the French government had been advised of the plot.[22] It is not clear whether the incident referred to by Colby was related to the one discussed in the *Tribune*.

In the early evening of Monday, 9 November 1970, Charles de Gaulle died peacefully at the age of 80, sitting in his armchair watching a sentimental television serial called "Nanou".

25. Ecuador 1960 to 1963
A textbook of dirty tricks

If the *Guinness Book of World Records* included a category for "cynicism", one could suggest the CIA's creation of "leftist" organizations which condemned poverty, disease, illiteracy, capitalism, *and* the United States in order to attract committed militants and their money away from legitimate leftist organizations.

The tiny nation of Ecuador in the early 1960s was, as it remains today, a classic of banana-republic underdevelopment; virtually at the bottom of the economic heap in South America; a society in which one percent of the population received an income comparable to United States upper-class standards, while two-thirds of the people had an average family income of about $10 per month — people simply outside the money economy, with little social integration or participation in the national life; a tale told many times in Latin America.

In September 1960, a new government headed by José María Velasco Ibarra came to power. Velasco had won a decisive electoral victory, running on a vaguely liberal, populist, something-for-everyone platform. He was no Fidel Castro, he was not even a socialist, but he earned the wrath of the US State Department and the CIA by his unyielding opposition to the two stated priorities of American policy in Ecuador: breaking relations with Cuba, and clamping down hard on activists of the Communist Party and those to their left.

Over the next three years, in pursuit of those goals, the CIA left as little as possible to chance. A veritable text book on covert subversion techniques unfolded. In its pages could be found the following, based upon the recollections of Philip Agee, the CIA officer who spent this period in Ecuador.[1]

Almost all political organizations of significance, from the far left to the far right, were infiltrated, often at the highest levels. Amongst other reasons, the left was infiltrated to channel young radicals away from support to Cuba and from anti-Americanism; the right, to instigate and co-ordinate activities along the lines of CIA priorities. If, at a point in time, there was no organization that appeared well-suited to serve a particular need, then one would be created.

Or a new group of "concerned citizens" would appear, fronted with noted personalities, which might place a series of notices in leading newspapers denouncing the penetration of the government by the extreme left and demanding a break with Cuba. Or one of the noted personalities would deliver a speech prepared by the CIA, and then a newspaper editor would praise it, or a well-known columnist would do the same, both gentlemen being on the CIA payroll.

Some of these fronts had an actual existence; for others, even their existence was phoney. On one occasion, the CIA Officer who had created the non-existent "Ecuadorean Anti-Communist Front" was surprised to read in his morning paper that a real organization with that name had been founded. He changed the name of his organization to "Ecuadorean Anti-Communist Action".

Wooing the working class came in for special emphasis. An alphabet-soup of labour organizations, sometimes hardly more than names on stationery, were created, altered, combined, liquidated, and new ones created again, in an almost frenzied attempt to find the right combination to compete with existing left-oriented unions and take national leadership away from them. Union leaders were invited to attend various classes conducted by the CIA in Ecuador or in the United States, all expenses paid, in order to impart to them the dangers of communism to the union movement and to select potential agents.

This effort was not without its irony either. CIA agents would sometimes jealously vie with each other for the best positions in these CIA-created labour organizations; and at times Ecuadorean organizations would meet in "international conferences" with CIA labour fronts from other countries, with almost all of the participants blissfully unaware of what was actually going on.

In Ecuador, as throughout most of Latin America, the Agency planted phoney anti-communist news items in co-operating newspapers. These items would then be picked up by other CIA stations in Latin America and disseminated through a CIA-owned news agency, a CIA-owned radio station, or through countless journalists being paid on a piece-work basis, in addition to the item being picked up unwittingly by other media, including those in the United States. Anti-communist propaganda and news distortion (often of the most far-fetched variety) written in CIA offices would also appear in Latin American newspapers as unsigned editorials of the papers themselves.

In virtually every department of the Ecuadorean government could be found men occupying positions, high and low, who collaborated with the CIA, for money as well as, perhaps, their own particular motivation. At one point, the Agency could count amongst this number the men who were second and third in power in the country.

These government agents would receive the benefits of information obtained by the CIA through electronic eavesdropping or other means, enabling them to gain prestige and promotion, or consolidate their current position in the rough-and-tumble of Ecuadorean politics. A high-ranking minister of leftist tendencies, on the other hand, would be the target of a steady stream of propaganda from any or all sources in the CIA arsenal; staged demonstrations against him would further increase the pressure on the president to replace him.

The Postmaster-General, along with other post office employees, all members in good standing of the CIA Payroll Club, regularly sent mail arriving from Cuba and the Soviet bloc to the Agency for its perusal, while the Director of Immigration and customs officials kept the Agency posted on who went to or came from Cuba. When a particularly suitable target returned from Cuba, he would be searched at the airport and documents prepared by the CIA would be "found" on him. These documents, publicized as much as possible, might include instructions on "how to intensify hatred between classes", or some provocative language designed to cause a split in Communist Party ranks; generally, the documents "verified" the worst fears of the public about communist plans to take over Ecuador under the masterminding of Cuba or the Soviet Union; at the same time, perhaps, implicating an important Ecuadorean leftist whose head the Agency was after. Similar revelations, staged by CIA stations elsewhere in Latin America, would be publicized in Ecuador as a warning that Ecuador might be next.

Agency financing of conservative groups in a quasi-religious campaign against Cuba and "atheistic communism" helped to seriously weaken President Velasco's power among the poor, primarily Indians, who had voted overwhelmingly for him, but who were even more deeply committed to their religion. If the CIA wished to know how the president was reacting to this campaign it need only turn to his physician, its agent, Dr Felipe Ovalle, who would report that his patient was feeling considerable strain as a result.

CIA agents would bomb churches or right-wing organizations and make it appear to be the work of leftists. They would march in left-wing parades displaying signs and shouting slogans of a very provocative anti-military nature, designed to antagonize the armed forces and hasten a coup.

During the election campaign, on 19 March 1960, two senior colonels who were the CIA's main liaison agents within the National Police had participated in a riot aimed at disrupting a Velasco demonstration. CIA officer Bob Weatherwax had been in the forefront directing the police during the riot in which five Velasco supporters were killed and many wounded. When Velasco took office, he had the two colonels arrested and Weatherwax was asked to leave the country.

All these CIA-supported activities were carried out without the knowledge of the American Ambassador. When the Cuban Embassy publicly charged the Agency with involvement in various anti-Cuban activities, the American Ambassador issued a statement that "had everyone in the [CIA] station smiling." Stated the Ambassador: "The only agents in Ecuador who are paid by the United States are the technicians invited by the Ecuadorean government to contribute to raising the living standards of the Ecuadorean people."

Finally, in November 1961, the military acted. Velasco was forced to resign and was replaced by Vice-President Carlos Julio Arosemana. There were at this time two prime candidates for the vice-presidency. One was the vice-president of the Senate, a CIA agent. The other was the rector of Central University, a political moderate. The day that Congress convened to make their choice, a notice appeared in a morning paper announcing support for the rector by the Communist Party and a militant leftist youth organization. The notice had been placed by a columnist for the newspaper who was the principal propaganda agent for the CIA's Quito station. The rector was compromised rather badly, the denials came too late, and the CIA man won. His Agency salary was increased from $700 to $1,000 a month.

Arosemana soon proved no more acceptable to the CIA than Velasco. All operations continued, particularly the campaign to break relations with Cuba, which Arosemana steadfastly refused to do. The deadlock was broken in March 1962 when a military garrison, led by Col. Aurelio Naranjo, gave Arosemana 72 hours to send the Cubans packing and fire the leftist Minister of Labour. (There is no need to point out here who Naranjo's financial benefactor was.) Arosemana complied with the ultimatum, booting out the Czech and Polish delegations as well at the behest of the new cabinet which had been forced upon him.

At the CIA station in Quito there was a champagne victory celebration. Elsewhere in Ecuador, angry, desperate people took to arms. But on this occasion, like others, it amounted to naught . . . a small band of people, poorly armed and trained, infiltrated by agents, their every move known in advance — confronted by a battalion of paratroopers, superbly armed and trained by the United States. That was in the field. In press reports, the small band grew to hundreds; armed not only to the teeth, but with weapons from "outside the country" (read Cuba), and the whole operation very carefully planned at the Communist Party Congress the month before.

On 11 July 1963 the Presidential Palace in Quito was surrounded by tanks and troops. Arosemana was out, a junta was in. Their first act was to outlaw communism; "communists" and other "extreme" leftists were rounded up and jailed, the arrests campaign being facilitated by data from the CIA's Subversive Control Watch List (standard at many Agency stations);* civil liberties were suspended; the 1964 elections cancelled; another tale told many times in Latin America.

And during these three years, what were the American people told about this witch's brew of covert actions carried out, supposedly, in their name? Very little, if anything, if the *New York Times* is any index. Not once during the entire period, up to and including the coup, was any indication given in any article or editorial on Ecuador that the CIA or any other arm of the US government had ever played any role whatever in any event which had ever occurred in that country. This is the way the writings read even if one looks back at them with the advantage of hindsight and reads between the lines.

There is a solitary exception. Following the coup, we find a tiny announcement on the very bottom of page 20 that Havana radio had accused the United States of instigating the military takeover.[2] The Cuban government had been making public charges about American activities in Ecuador regularly, but this was the first one to make the *New York Times*. The question must be asked: Why were these charges deemed unworthy of reporting or comment, let alone investigation?

26. The Congo 1960 to 1964
The assassination of Patrice Lumumba

Within days of its independence from Belgium on 30 June 1960, the land long known as the Belgian Congo, and later as Zaire, was engulfed in strife and chaos as multiple individuals, tribes and political groups struggled for dominance. For

---

* This list would include not only the subject's name, but the names and addresses of his relatives and friends and the places he frequented — anything to aid in tracking him down when the time came.

the next several years the world press chronicled the train of Congolese governments, the endless confusion of personalities and conspiracies, exotic place names like Stanleyville and Leopoldville, stories of white mercenaries and European hostages, the brutality and the violence from all quarters with its racist overtones.

Into this disorder the Western powers were "naturally" drawn, principally Belgium to protect its vast mineral investments, and the United States, mindful of the fabulous mineral resources as well, and obsessed, as usual, with fighting "communism".

Successive American administrations of Eisenhower, Kennedy and Johnson, looking through cold-war binoculars perceived an East-West battleground. The CIA station in the Congo cabled Washington in August that "Embassy and station believe Congo experiencing classic communist effort [to] takeover government."[1] And CIA Director Allen Dulles cabled a warning of a ". . . communist takeover of the Congo with disastrous consequences . . . for the interests of the free world . . ."[2] At the same time, Dulles authorized a crash-programme fund of up to $100,000 to replace the existing government of Patrice Lumumba with a "pro-western group".[3]

In actuality the lines were never so sharply drawn, although the Soviet Union at times seemed caught up in the same cold-war "logic".

Patrice Lumumba was the most prominent of the handful of leftist-sounding leaders of the time, the Congo's first prime minister, who called for the nation's economic as well as political liberation and did not shy away from contact with socialist countries. When the United States and the United Nations refused to supply him with transport for his troops to put down the secession in Katanga province, Lumumba turned to the Soviet Union for aid, and received it.[4]

It is entirely inconclusive, however, what radical convictions and perceptions lay behind the rhetoric of the flamboyant Lumumba (a man who "played with Marxist verbiage", wrote a senior State Department official)[5] for he lasted but two months in office before being deposed; a step taken by President Joseph Kasavubu, with the CIA's encouragement,[6] "despite the strong support for Lumumba in the Congolese Parliament."[7]

During the early 1960s, according to a highly-placed CIA officer, the Agency "regularly bought and sold Congolese politicians".[8] It would be surprising if Kasavubu, the only high official to hold power continuously throughout this entire period, was not one of the recipients.

American authorities were apprehensive about even a Lumumba out of office: his "talents and dynamism appear [to be the] overriding factor in reestablishing his position each time it seems half lost" . . . "Lumumba was a spellbinding orator with the ability to stir masses of people to action" . . . "if he . . . started to talk to a battalion of the Congolese Army he probably would have had them in the palm of his hand in five minutes" were their succinct comments.[9]

In September, the CIA sent one of its scientists, Joseph Scheider, to the Congo carrying "lethal biological material" (a virus) specifically intended for use in Lumumba's assassination. The virus, which was supposed to produce a fatal disease indigenous to the Congo area of Africa, was transported via diplomatic pouch.[10]

In 1975, the US Senate committee which investigated intelligence activities ("The Church Committee") went on record with the conclusion that Allen Dulles had ordered Lumumba's assassination as "an urgent and prime objective" (Dulles' words).[11] After hearing the testimony of several officials who believed that the order to kill the African leader had emanated originally from President Eisenhower, the committee decided that there was a "reasonable inference" that this was indeed the case.[12]

As matters evolved in the Congo, the virus was never used. The committee observed, however, that the CIA station in Leopoldville "continued to maintain close contact with Congolese who expressed a desire to assassinate Lumumba. CIA officers encouraged and offered to aid these Congolese in their efforts against Lumumba, although there is no evidence that aid was ever provided for the specific purpose of assassination."[13]

Fearing for his life, Lumumba was on the run until he was taken into custody on 1 December 1960 by troops of Joseph Mobutu, the Army strongman who had taken over the government after Lumumba had been ousted. A 28 November CIA cable indicates that the Agency was involved in tracking down the charismatic Congo leader. The cable spoke of the CIA station working with the Congolese government to get the roads blocked and troops alerted to close a possible escape route of Lumumba's.[14]

Mobutu — whom author and CIA-confidant Andrew Tully describes as having been "discovered" by the CIA[15] — kept Lumumba prisoner until 17 January 1961, the date of his murder as determined by the United Nations Commission of Investigation. On that day, Mobutu transferred Lumumba into the hands of Moise Tshombe of Katanga province, Lumumba's bitter enemy.

In 1978, former CIA Africa specialist John Stockwell related in his book how a ranking Agency officer had told him of driving around with Lumumba's body in the trunk of his car, "trying to decide what to do with it".[16] What he did do with it has not yet been made public.

During the period of Lumumba's imprisonment, US diplomats in the Congo were pursuing a policy of "deploring" his beatings and trying to secure "humane treatment" for him, albeit due to "considerations of international opinion and not from tender feelings toward him".[17] The immediate and the long-term effect of Lumumba's murder was to make him the martyr and symbol all over Africa and elsewhere in the Third World which such American officials had feared.

Less than two weeks after independence, the copper-rich province of Katanga under Moise Tshombe announced that it was seceding from the rest of the Congo. The fighting which quickly erupted as a consequence of this development revealed the perplexity of American policy-makers when treading in terrain that lacked a clearcut "communist" enemy.

On the one hand, the Eisenhower adminstration officially opposed the secession and supported the military steps undertaken by the United Nations to end it. John F. Kennedy, who came into power on 20 January 1961, echoed this policy. On the other hand, Tshombe had outspoken support in the American Congress. Sentiment amongst officials at the State Department and the White House mirrored this division.[18]

Similarly, US Air Force C-130s were flying Congolese troops and supplies against the Katangese rebels; at the same time, however, the CIA and its covert colleagues in the Pentagon put together an air armada of heavy transport aircraft, along with mercenary units, to aid the very same rebels.*[19]

Soviet policy in the Congo reflected a touch of schizophrenia as well. The Soviets supported Lumumba in his drive to end the Katanga secession, but after Lumumba was out of the picture, they condemned the United States and the United Nations for pursuing the same goal. The Russians accused the UN of following a "colonialist" line, and the US for using the UN as a means of getting a military foot-in-the-door of the Congo.

American foreign-policy makers were more in unison when another potential "communist", Antoine Gizenga, achieved a measure of prominence in the continuous, bloody musical-chairs game of Congolese politics. Gizenga, though vice-premier in the central government in Leopoldville, was the leader of a rebel force which had set up a regime in the Stanleyville area which it proclaimed as the legitimate government of the entire Congo. He fancied himself the political and spiritual successor to Lumumba.

The Soviet Union may have believed him, for apparently they were sending him arms and money, using Sudan, which borders the Congo on the north, as a conduit. When the CIA learned that a Czech ship was bound for Sudan with a cargo of guns disguised as Red Cross packages for refugee relief in the Congo, the Agency turned to its most practiced art, bribery, to persuade a crane operator to let one of the crates drop upon arrival. On that day, the dockside was suddenly covered with the new Soviet Kalashnikov rifles, adding to the enlightenment of Sudanese port officials.

Through an equally clever ploy at the Khartoum (Sudan) airport, the CIA managed to separate a Congolese courier from his suitcase of Soviet money destined for Gizenga.[20]

The State Department, meanwhile, was, in its own words,

> urging Adoula [the new prime minister] to . . . dismiss Gizenga and declare him in rebellion against the national government so that police action can now be taken against him. We are also urging the U.N. to take military action to break his rebellion . . . We are making every effort to keep Gizenga isolated from

---

* This marked at least the third instance of the CIA in military opposition to another arm of the US Government: Costa Rica in 1955 (cf. this chapter); and Burma in 1970, if not also earlier, when the US military aided the Burmese air force to mount strikes against Burmese rebels, while the CIA was assisting the rebels from its operation in Laos.

potential domestic and foreign support . . . We have taken care to insure that this [US] aid has been channelled through the central government in order to provide the economic incentive to encourage support for that government.[21]

In January 1962, United Nations forces with strong American backing ousted Gizenga and his followers from Stanleyville, and a year later forced Tshombe to end his secession in Katanga. These actions were carried out in the name of "uniting the Congo", as if this were a matter to be decided by other than Congolese. In any event, the operations served only to temporarily slow down the dreary procession of changing leaders, attempted coups, autonomous armies, shifting alliances, and rebellions.

Shortly after the UN actions, Allen Dulles informed a television audience that the United States had "overrated the danger" of Soviet involvement . . . "it looked as though they were going to make a serious attempt at takeover in the Belgian Congo, well it did not work out that way at all."[22]

Nonetheless, by the middle of 1964, when rebellion was more widespread and furious than ever and the collapse of the central government appeared as a real possibility, the United States was pouring in a prodigious amount of military aid to the Leopoldville regime, reaching, by one estimate, "a million dollars a day for a sustained period".[23]

The government was now headed by none other than Moise Tshombe, a man called "Africa's most unpopular African" for his widely-recognized role in the murder of the popular Lumumba and for his use of white mercenaries, many of them South Africans and Rhodesians, during his secession attempt in Katanga. Tshombe defended the latter action by explaining that his troops would not fight without white officers.[24]

In addition to providing arms and planes, the United States dispatched some 200 military personnel to the Congo to train government troops,[25] while Congolese officers were undergoing training at Fort Knox, Kentucky in what the Defense Department at the time called techniques for protecting "legally constituted governments against subversion and domestic disorder".[26] Yet Lumumba's government had been at least as "legally constituted" as Tshombe's. Lumumba had been chosen prime minister by the newly-elected National Assembly. Tshombe was appointed to his office by President Kasavubu.

Tshombe once again called upon his white mercenary army, numbering 400-500 men, and the CIA called upon its own mercenaries as well, a band which included Americans. Cuban-exile veterans of the Bay of Pigs, Rhodesians, and South Africans, the latter having been recruited with the help of the South African government. "Bringing in our own animals" was the way one CIA operative described the operation. The Agency's pilots carried out regular bombing and strafing missions against the insurgents, although some of the Cubans were reported to be troubled at being ordered to make indiscriminate attacks upon civilians.[27] Looking back at the affair in 1966, the *New York Times* credited the CIA with having created "an instant air force" in the Congo.[28]

When China protested to the United States about the use of American pilots in the Congo, the State Department issued an explicit denial, then publicly reversed itself, but insisted that the Americans were flying "under contract with the Congolese government". The next day, the Department said that the flights would stop, after having obtained assurances from "other arms of the [U.S.] Government", although it still held to the position that the matter was one between the Congolese government and civilian individuals who were not violating American law.[29]

Three weeks later, the Soviet Union lodged an official protest at the United Nations about the air operations being carried out by the United States. By this time, the CIA reportedly was using only Cuban pilots.[30]

The Congolese against whom this array of military might was brought to bear were a coalition of forces. Some of the leading figures had spent time in Eastern Europe, the Soviet Union or China and were receiving token amounts of arms and instruction from those quarters; but they were never in the Communist camp any more than the countless Third Worlders who have gone to university in the United States and have been courted afterwards are necessarily in the Western/capitalist camp. (This does not hold for professional military officers who, unlike students, are a particularly homogeneous group — conservative, authoritarian, and anti-Communist.)

Africa scholar M. Crawford Young has observed that amongst the coalition leadership, "The destruction of the [Leopoldville] regime, a vigorous reassertion of Congolese control over its own destiny, and a vague socialist commitment were recurrent themes. But at bottom it appeared far more a frame of mind and a style of expression, than an interrelated set of ideas."[31] The rebels had no revolutionary programme they could, or did, proclaim.

Co-existing with this element within the coalition were currents of various esoteric churches, messianic sects, witch-finding movements, and other occult inspirations (many believed that the magic of their witch doctors would protect them against bullets), as well as plain opportunists. The insurgents were further divided along tribal lines and were rent by debilitating factionalism. No single group or belief could dominate.[32]

"Rebel success created the image of unified purpose and revolutionary promise," wrote Young. "Only in its subsequent phase of decay and disintegration" did the coalition's "dramatic lack of cohesion" and "disparity in purpose and perception" become fully evident.[33]

In the coalition-controlled area of Stanleyville, between 2,000 and 3,000 white foreigners found themselves trapped by the war. Rebel leader Christopher Gbenye conditioned their safe release upon various military concessions, principally a cessation of American bombing, but negotiations failed to produce an agreement.[34]

Instead, on 24 November 1964, the United States and Belgium staged a dramatic rescue mission in which over 500 Belgian paratroopers were dropped at dawn into Stanleyville from American transport planes. Much chaos followed, and the reports are conflicting, but it appears that more than 2,000 hostages were rescued, in the process of which the fleeing rebels massacred about 100 others and dragged several hundred more into the bush.

American and Belgian officials took great pains to emphasize the purely "humanitarian" purpose of the mission. However, the rescuers simultaneously executed a key military manoeuvre when they "seized the strategic points of the city and coordinated their operation with the advancing columns of Tshombe's mercenary army that was moving swiftly towards the city."[35] Moreover, in the process of the rescue, the rescuers killed dozens of rebels and did nothing to curtail Tshombe's troops when they reached Stanleyville and began an "orgy of looting and killing".[36]

Tshombe may have provided a reminder of the larger-than-humanitarian stake at hand in the Congo when, in the flush of the day's success, he talked openly with a correspondent of *The Times* of London who reported that Tshombe "was confident that the fall of Stanleyville would give a new impetus to the economy and encourage investors. It would reinforce a big development plan announced this morning in collaboration with the United States, Britain and West Germany."[37]

The collapse of the rebels' stronghold in Stanleyville marked the beginning of the end for their cause. By spring 1965 their fortune was in sharp decline, and the arrival of about 100 Cuban revolutionaries, amongst whom was Che Guevara himself, had no known effect upon the course of events. Several months later, Guevara returned to Cuba in disgust at the low level of revolutionary zeal exhibited by the Congolese guerrillas and the local populace.[38]

The concluding tune for the musical chairs was played in November, when Joseph Mobutu overthrew Tshombe and Kasavubu. Mobutu, later to adopt the name Mobutu Sese Seko, has ruled with a heavy dictatorial hand ever since.

In the final analysis, it mattered precious little to the interests of the US government whether the forces it had helped defeat were really "communist" or not, by whatever definition. The working premise was that there was now fixed in power, over a more-or-less unified Congo, a man who would be more co-operative with the CIA in its African adventures and with Western capital, and less accessible to the socialist bloc, than the likes of Lumumba, Gizenga, et al. The CIA has chalked this one up as a victory.

What the people of the Congo (now Zaire) have won is not clear. Under Mobutu, terror and repression are facts of daily life, civil liberties and other human rights are markedly absent. The country remains one of the poorest to be found anywhere despite its vast natural riches. Mobutu, however, is reputed to be one of the richest heads of state in the world. (See Zaire chapter.)

William Atwood, US Ambassador to Kenya in 1964-65, who played a part in the hostage negotiations, also saw the US role in the Congo in a positive light. Bemoaning African suspicions toward American motives there, he wrote: "it was hard to convince people that we had provided the Congo with $420 million in aid since independence just to prevent chaos; they couldn't believe any country could be that altruistic."[39]

Atwood's comment is easier to understand when one realizes that the word "chaos" has long been commonly used by American officials to refer to a situation over which the United States has insufficient control to assure that someone distinctly pro-Western will remain in, or come to, power. When President Eisenhower, for example, decided to send troops into Lebanon in 1958, he saw it as a move, he later wrote, "to stop the trend towards chaos".[40]

27. Brazil 1961 to 1964
Introducing the marvellous new world of death squads

When the leading members of the US diplomatic mission in Brazil held a meeting one day in March 1964, they arrived at the consensus that President João Goulart's support of social and economic reforms was a contrived and thinly veiled vehicle to seize dictatorial power.[1]

The American Ambassador, Lincoln Gordon, informed the State Department that "a desperate lunge [by Goulart] for totalitarian power might be made at any time."[2]

The army chief of staff, General Humberto de Alencar Castelo (or Castello) Branco, provided the American Embassy with a memorandum in which he stated his fear that Goulart was seeking to close down Congress and initiate a dictatorship.[3]

Within a week after the expression of these sentiments, the Brazilian military, with Castelo Branco at its head, overthrew the constitutional government of President Goulart, the culmination of a conspiratorial process in which the American Embassy had been intimately involved. The military then proceeded to install and maintain for two decades one of the most brutal dictatorships in all of South America.

What are we to make of all this? The idea that men of rank and power lie to the public is commonplace, not worthy of debate. But do they as readily lie to each other? Is their need to rationalize their misdeeds so great that they provide each other a moral shoulder to lean on? "Men use thoughts only to justify their wrongdoings," wrote Voltaire, "and speech only to conceal their thoughts."

The actual American motivation in supporting the coup was something rather less heroic than preserving democracy, even mundane as such matters go. American opposition to Goulart, who became president in August 1961, rested upon a familiar catalogue of complaints:

US Defense Secretary Robert McNamara questioned Brazil's neutral stand in foreign policy. The Brazilian Ambassador in Washington, Roberto Campos, responded that "neutralism" was an inadequate term and explained that "what was involved was really a deep urge of the Brazilian people to assert their personality in world affairs."[4]

American officials did not approve of some of the members of Goulart's cabinet, and said so. Ambassador Campos pointed out to them that it was "quite inappropriate" for the United States "to try to influence the composition of the cabinet."[5]

Attorney-General Robert Kennedy met with Goulart and expressed his uneasiness about the Brazilian president allowing communists ("communists") to hold positions in government agencies. (Bobby was presumably acting on the old and very deep-seated American belief that once you welcome one or two communists into your parlour, they take over the whole house and sign the deed over to Moscow.) Goulart did not see this as a danger. He replied that he was in full control of the situation, later remarking to Campos that it was as if he had been told that he had no capacity for judging the men around him.[6]

The American Defense Attaché in Brazil, Col. Vernon Walters, reported that Goulart showed favouritism towards "ultra-nationalist" military officers over "pro-U.S." officers. Goulart saw it as promoting those officers who appeared to be most loyal to his government. He was, as it happens, very concerned about American-encouraged military coups and said so explicitly to President Kennedy.[7]

Goulart considered purchasing helicopters from Poland because Washington was delaying on his request to purchase them from the United States. Ambassador Gordon told him that he "could not expect the United States to like it".[8]

The Goulart administration, moreover, passed a law limiting the amount of profits multinationals could transmit out of the country, and a subsidiary of ITT was nationalized. Compensation for the takeover was slow in coming because of Brazil's precarious financial position, but these were the only actions of significance taken against US corporate interests.

Inextricably woven into all these complaints, yet at the same time standing apart, was Washington's dismay with Brazil's "drift to the left" . . . the communist/leftist influence in the labour movement . . . leftist "infiltration" wherever one looked . . . "anti-Americanism" among students and others (the American Consul General in São Paulo suggested to the State Department that the United States "found competing student organizations") . . . the general erosion of "U.S. influence and the power of people and groups friendly to the United States"[9] . . . one might go so far as to suggest that Washington officials felt unloved, were it not for the fact that the coup, as they well knew from much past experience, could result only in intensified anti-Americanism all over Latin America.

Goulart's predecessor, Jânio da Silva Quadros, had also irritated Washington. "Why should the United States trade with Russia and her satellites but insist that Brazil trade only with the United States?" he asked, and proceeded to negotiate with the Soviet Union and other Communist countries to (re)establish diplomatic and commercial relations. He was, in a word, independent.[10]

Quadros was also more-or-less a conservative who clamped down hard on unions, sent federal troops to the north-east hunger dens to squash protest, and jailed disobedient students.[11] But the American Ambassador at the time, John Moors Cabot, saw fit to question Brazil's taking part in a meeting of "uncommitted" (non-aligned) nations. "Brazil has signed various obligations with the United States and American nations," he said. "I am sure Brazil is not going to forget her obligations . . . It is committed. It is a fact. Brazil can uncommit itself if it wants."[12]

In early 1961, shortly after Quadros took office, he was visited by Adolf Berle, Jr., President Kennedy's adviser on Latin American affairs and formerly ambassador to Brazil. Berle had come as Kennedy's special envoy to solicit Quadros' backing for the impending Bay of Pigs invasion. Ambassador Cabot was present and some years later described the meeting to author Peter Bell. Bell has written:

> Ambassador Cabot remembers a 'stormy conversation' in which Berle stated the United States had $300 million in reserve for Brazil and in effect 'offered it as a bribe' for Brazilian cooperation . . . Quadros became 'visibly irritated' after Berle refused to heed his third 'no'. No Brazilian official was at the airport the next day to see the envoy off.[13]

Quadros, who had been elected by a record margin, was, like Goulart, accused of seeking to set up a dictatorship because he sought to put teeth into measures unpopular with the oligarchy, the military, and/or the United States, as well as pursuing a "pro-communist" foreign policy. After but seven months in office he suddenly resigned, reportedly under military pressure, if not outright threat. In his letter of resignation, he blamed his predicament on "reactionaries" and "the ambitions of groups of individuals, some of whom are foreigners . . . the terrible forces that arose against me."[14] A few months later, Quadros reappeared, to deliver a speech in which he named Berle, Cabot, and US Treasury Secretary Douglas Dillon as being among those who had contributed to his downfall. Dillon, he said, sought to mix foreign policy with Brazil's needs for foreign credits.[15] (Both Berle and Cabot had been advocates of the 1954 overthrow of Guatemalan President Arbenz, whose sins, in Washington's eyes, were much the same as those Goulart was now guilty of.)[16] At the same time, Quadros announced his intention to lead a "people's crusade" against the "reactionaries, the corrupt and the Communists".[17]

As Quadros' vice president, Goulart succeeded to the presidency in August 1961 despite a virtual coup and civil war initiated by segments of the military to block him because he was seen as some sort of dangerous radical. Only the intervention of loyalist military units and other supporters of the constitutional process allowed Goulart to take office.[18] The military opposition to Goulart arose, it should be noted, before he had the opportunity to exhibit his alleged tendencies toward dictatorship. Indeed, as early as 1954, the military had demonstrated its antipathy toward him by forcing President Vargas to fire him from his position as Minister of Labor.[19] The American doubts about Goulart also predated his presidency. In 1960, when Goulart was elected vice president, "concern at the State Department and the Pentagon turned to panic" according to an American official who served in Brazil.[20]

Goulart tried to continue Quadros' independent foreign policy. Speaking before the US Congress in April 1962, he affirmed Brazil's right to take its own stand on some of the cold-war issues. He declared that Brazil identified itself "with the democratic principles which unite the peoples of the West", but was "not part of any politico-military bloc".[21] His government went ahead with resumption of relations with socialist countries, and at a meeting of the Organization of American States in December 1961 Brazil abstained on a vote to hold a special session aimed at discussing "the Cuban problem", and stood strongly opposed to sanctions against the Castro government.[22]

Time magazine, in common with most US media, had (has) a difficult time understanding the concept and practice of independence amongst America's allies. In November 1961, the magazine wrote that Brazil's domestic politics were "confused" and that the country was "also adrift in foreign affairs. Goulart is trying to play the old Quadros game of international 'independence', which means wooing the East while panhandling from the West." *Time* was critical of Goulart in that he had sought an invitation to visit Washington and on the same day he received it he "called in Communist Poland's visiting Foreign Minister, Adam Rapacki, [and] awarded him the Order of the Southern Cross — the same decoration that Quadros hung on Cuba's Marxist mastermind, Che Guevara . . ."[23]

Former *Time* editor and Latin America correspondent, John Gerassi, commented that every visiting foreign dignatory received this medal, the *Cruzeiro do Sul*, as part of protocol. He added:

Apparently *Time* thinks that any President who wants to visit us must necessarily hate our enemies as a consequence, and is "confused" whenever this does not occur. But, of course, *Time* magazine is so unused to the word 'independent' that an independent foreign policy must be confusing indeed. In South America, where everyone would like to follow an independent foreign policy but where only Brazil has, at times, the courage, no one was confused.[24]

Goulart, a millionaire land-owner and a Catholic who wore a medal of the Virgin around his neck,[25] was no more a communist than was Quadros, and he strongly supported the United States during the "Cuban Missile Crisis" of October 1962. He offered Gordon a toast "To the Yankee Victory!",[26] perhaps unaware that only three weeks earlier, during federal and state elections in Brazil, CIA money had been liberally expended in support of anti-Goulart candidates. Former CIA officer Philip Agee states that the Agency spent between 12 and 20 million dollars on behalf of hundreds of candidates.[27] Lincoln Gordon says the funding came to no more than five million.[28] In addition to the direct campaign contributions, the Agency dipped into its bag of dirty tricks to torment the campaigns of leftist candidates,[29] and the Agency for

International Development (AID), at the express request of President Kennedy, allocated monies to projects aimed at benefiting chosen gubernatorial candidates.[30] (While Goulart was president, no new US economic assistance was given to the central government, while regional assistance was provided on a markedly ideological basis. When the military took power, this pattern was sharply altered.)[31]

Agee adds that the CIA carried out a consistent propaganda campaign against Goulart which dated from at least the 1962 election operation and which included the financing of mass urban demonstrations, "proving the old themes of God, country, family and liberty to be as effective as ever" in undermining a government.[32]

CIA money also found its way to a chain of right-wing newspapers, *Diarias Associades*, to promote anti-communism; to the distribution of 50 thousand books of similar politics to high school and college students; to the formation of women's groups with their special Latin mother's emphasis on the godlessness of the communist enemy. The women and other CIA operatives also went into the rumour-mongering business, spreading stories about outrages Goulart and his cronies were supposed to be planning, such as altering the constitution so as to extend his term, and gossip about Goulart being a cuckold and a wife-beater.[33]

The intraservice confrontation which had attended Goulart's accession to power apparently kept a rein on coup-minded officers until 1963. In March of that year the CIA informed Washington, but not Goulart, of a plot by conservative officers.[34] During the course of the following year, the plots thickened. Brazilian military officers could not abide by Goulart's attempts at populist social reforms, though his programme was timid, his rhetoric generally mild, and his actions seldom matched either. (He himself pointed out that General Douglas MacArthur had carried out a more radical distribution of land in Japan after the Second World War than anything planned by the Brazilian Government.) The military men were particularly incensed at Goulart's support of a weakening of military discipline and his attempts to build up a following among non-commissioned officers.[35] This the president was genuinely serious about because of his "paranoia" about a coup.

Goulart's wooing of NCO's and his appeals to the population over the heads of a hostile congress and state governors (something Ronald Reagan has done on several occasions) were the kind of tactics his enemies chose to label as dictatorial.

In early 1964, disclosed *Fortune* magazine after the coup, an emissary was sent by some of the military plotters "to ask U.S. Ambassador Lincoln Gordon what the U.S. position would be if civil war broke out". The emissary "reported back that Gordon was cautious and diplomatic, but he left the impression that if the [plotters] could hold out for forty-eight hours they would get U.S. recognition and help."[36]

The primary American contact with the conspirators was Defense Attaché Vernon Walters who arrived in Brazil after having been apprised that President

Kennedy would not be averse to the overthrow of João Goulart.[37] Walters, who later became Deputy Director of the CIA, had an intimacy with leading Brazilian military officers, particularly General Castelo Branco, going back to World War Two when Walters had served as interpreter for the Brazilian Expeditionary Force then fighting in Italy with the Allies. Brazil was the only Latin American country to send ground combat troops to the war, and it allowed the United States to build huge aircraft staging bases on its territory.[38] The relationship between US and Brazilian officers was continued and enhanced after the war by the creation of the Higher War College (*Escola Superior de Guerra*) in Rio de Janeiro in 1949. Latin America historian Thomas E. Skidmore has observed:

> Under the U.S.-Brazilian military agreements of the early 1950s, the U.S. Army received exclusive rights to render assistance in the organization and operation of the college, which had been modeled on the National War College in Washington. In view of the fact that the Brazilian War College became a rallying point for leading military opponents of civilian populist politicians, it would be worth examining the extent to which the strongly anti-Communist ideology — bordering on an anti-political attitude — [of certain officers] was reinforced (or moderated?) by their frequent contacts with United States officers.[39]

There was, moreover, the ongoing US Military Assistance Program which Ambassador Gordon described as a "major vehicle for establishing close relationships with personnel of the armed forces" and "a highly important factor in influencing [the Brazilian] military to be pro-US."*[40]

A week before the coup, Castelo Branco, who emerged as the leader of the conspirators, gave Walters a copy of a paper he had written which was in effect a justification for a military coup, another variation on the theme of upholding the constitution by preventing Goulart from instituting a dictatorship.[41]

To Lincoln Gordon and other American officials, civil war appeared a real possibility as the result of a coup attempt. As the scheduled day approached, contingency plans were set up.

A large quantity of petroleum would be sent to Brazil and made available to the insurgent officers, an especially vital commodity if Goulart supporters in the state oil union were to blow up or control the refineries.[42]

A US Navy task force would be dispatched to Brazilian coastal waters, the presence of which would deliver an obvious message to opponents of the coup.[43]

Arms and ammunition would be sent to Branco's forces to meet their fighting needs.[44]

Concerned that the coup attempt might be met by a general strike, Washington discussed with Gordon the possible need "for the U.S. to mount a large material program to assure the success of the takeover."[45] The conspirators

---

* From a cable sent by Gordon to Washington. In this and following quotations from cables, I have inserted missing articles and prepositions for the sake of readability.

had already requested economic aid from the United States, in the event of their success, to get the government and economy moving again, and had received a generally favourable response.[46]

At the same time, Gordon sent word to some anti-Goulart state governors emphasizing the necessity, from the American point of view, that the new regime have a claim to legitimacy. The Ambassador also met with former president Juscelino Kubitschek to urge him to take a stronger position against Goulart and to use his considerable influence to "swing a large congressional group and thereby influence the legitimacy issue".[47]

Of the American contingency measures, indications are that it was the naval show of force — which, it turned out, included an aircraft carrier, destroyers, and guided missiles — which most encouraged the Brazilian military plotters or convinced those still wavering in their commitment.[48]

Another actor in the unfolding drama was the American Institute for Free Labor Development. The AIFLD came formally into being in 1961 and was technically under the direction of the American labour movement (AFL–CIO), but was soon being funded almost exclusively by the US government (AID) and serving consistently as a CIA instrument in most countries of Latin America. In May 1963, the AIFLD founded the *Instituto Cultural Trabalho* in Brazil which, over the next few years, gave courses to more than 7,000 union leaders and members.[49] Other Brazilians went to the United States for training. When they returned to Brazil, said AIFLD executive William Doherty, some of them

> became intimately involved in some of the clandestine operations of the revolution before it took place on April 1. What happened in Brazil on April 1 did not just happen — it was planned — and planned months in advance. Many of the trade union leaders — some of whom were actually trained in our institute — were involved in the revolution, and in the overthrow of the Goulart regime.[50]

Doherty did not spell out any details of the AIFLD role in the coup (or revolution as he called it), although *Reader's Digest* later reported that one of the AIFLD-trained labour leaders set up courses for communication workers in combatting communism in the labour movement in Brazil, and "After every class he quietly warned key workers of coming trouble and urged them to keep communications going no matter what happened."[51] Additionally, Richard Martinez, an unwitting CIA contract employee, who was sent to Brazil to work with the Agency's Post, Telegraph and Telephone Workers International (formerly Doherty's domain), has revealed that his field workers in Brazil burned down Communist Party headquarters at the time of the coup.[52]

The coup began on 31 March 1964 with the advance upon Rio of troops and tanks. Officers obtained the support of some units of enlisted men by telling them they were heading for the city to secure it against Goulart's enemies.[53] But at the main air force base pro-Goulart enlisted men, hearing of the move toward Rio, seized the base and put their officers under arrest. Indecision and cold feet intervened however, and what might have reversed the course of events instead came to nought.[54]

Here and there a scattering of workers went out on strike; several short-lived, impotent demonstrations took place, but there was little else. A number of labour leaders and radicals were rounded up on the orders of certain state governors; those who were opposed to what was happening were not prepared for violent resistance; in one incident a group of students staged a protest — some charged up the stairs of an Army organization, but the guard fired into their midst, killing two of them and forcing the others to fall back.[55]

Most people counted on loyal armed forces to do their duty, or waited for the word from Goulart. Goulart, however, was unwilling to give the call for a civil war; he did not want to be responsible, he said, for bloodshed amongst Brazilians, and fled to Uruguay.[56]

Lincoln Gordon cabled Washington the good news, suggesting the "avoidance of a jubilant posture". He described the coup as "a great victory for the free world", adding, in a remark that might have had difficulty getting past the lips of even John Foster Dulles, that without the coup there could have been a "total loss to the West of all South American Republics". Following a victory parade in Rio on 2 April by those pleased with the coup — a March of Family with God for Liberty — Gordon informed the State Department that the "only unfortunate note was the obviously limited participation in the march of the lower classes."[57]

His cable work done, the former Harvard professor turned his attention back to trying to persuade the Brazilian Congress to bestow a seal of "legitimacy" upon the new government.[58]

Two years later, Gordon was to be questioned by a senator during hearings to consider his nomination as Secretary of State for Inter-American Affairs. "I am particularly concerned," said the senator, "with the part you may have played, if any, in encouraging, promoting, or causing that overthrow." Said Lincoln Gordon: "The answer to that, senator, is very simple. The movement which overthrew President Goulart was a purely, 100 percent — not 99.44 — but 100 percent purely Brazilian movement. Neither the American Embassy nor I personally played any part in the process whatsoever."*[59]

Gordon artfully combined fast talk with omission of certain facts of life about Brazilian politics — his summary of Goulart's rise and fall made no mention at all of a key event: the military's move to keep him from taking office in 1961 — to convince the assembled senators that Goulart was indeed seeking to set up a personal dictatorship.[62] Depending on the setting, either "saving Brazil from dictatorship" or "saving Brazil from communism" has been advanced as the rationale for what took place in 1964. (General Andrew O'Meara, head of the US Southern (Latin America) Command, had it both ways. He told a House

---

* Dean Rusk, when asked about Cuban charges that the United States was behind the coup, responded: "Well, there is just not one iota of truth in this. It's just not so in any way, shape, or form."[60] Robert Kennedy's view of the affair, stated to Gordon, was: "Well, Goulart got what was coming to him. Too bad he didn't follow the advice we gave him when I was there."[61]

committee that "The coming to power of the Castelo Branco government in Brazil last April saved that country from an immediate dictatorship which could only have been followed by Communist domination.")[63]

The rescue-from-communism position has been especially difficult to support, the problem being that the communists in Brazil did not, after all, *do* anything which the United States could point to. Moreover, the Soviet Union was scarcely in the picture; early in 1964, reported a Brazilian newspaper, Russian leader Khrushchev told the Brazilian Communist Party that the Soviet government did not wish either to give financial aid to the Goulart regime or to tangle with the United States over the country;[64] in his reminiscences — albeit, as mentioned earlier, not meant to be a serious work of history — in its 1,100 pages, Khrushchev does not so much as mention Brazil. A year after the coup, trade between Brazil and the USSR was running at $120 million per year and a Brazilian mission was planning to go to Moscow to explore Soviet willingness to provide a major industrial plant.[65] The following year, the Russians invited the new Brazilian president-to-be, General Costa e Silva, to visit the Soviet Union.*[66]

Washington is willing to accept this type of independence from a conservative government, even the occasional nationalization of American property, when it knows that the government will keep the left suppressed at home and that it can be relied upon to do its bit in the vital cold-war, anti-communist confrontations abroad. In 1965, Brazil sent 1,100 troops to the Dominican Republic in support of the US invasion, the only country in Latin America to send more than a token force. And in 1971 and 1973, the Brazilian military and intelligence apparatuses contributed to the American efforts in overthrowing the governments of Bolivia and Chile.

The United States did not rest on its laurels. CIA headquarters immediately began to generate hemisphere-wide propaganda, as only the Agency's far-flung press-asset network could, in support of the new Brazilian government and to discredit Goulart.[67] Dean Rusk, concerned that Goulart might be received in Uruguay as if he were still Brazil's president on the grounds that he had not resigned, cabled the American Embassy in Montevideo that "it would be useful if you could quietly bring to the attention of appropriate officials the fact that despite his allegations to the contrary Goulart has abandoned his office."[68]

At the same time, the CIA station in Uruguay undertook a programme of surveillance of Brazilian exiles who had fled from the military takeover, to prevent them from instigating any kind of insurgency movement in their

---

* For an excellent example of what American anti-communist propaganda is, and has been, all about, one must read "The Country That Saved Itself" in the *Reader's Digest* of November 1964. The innumerable lies about what occurred in Brazil, fed without shame to its millions of readers, undoubtedly played no small role in preparing the American public for the great anti-communist crusade in Vietnam just picking up steam at the time.

homeland. It was a simple matter for the Agency to ask their (paid) friend, the head of Uruguayan intelligence, to place his officers at the residences of Goulart and other key Brazilians. The officers would keep logs of visitors while posing as personal security men for the exiles, although it is unlikely that the exiles swallowed the story.[69]

In the first few days following the coup, "several thousand" Brazilians were arrested, "communist and suspected communist" all.[70] AIFLD graduates were promptly appointed by the new government to purge the unions.[71] Though Ambassador Gordon had assured the State Department before the coup that the armed forces "would be quick to restore constitutional institutions and return power to civilian hands,"[72] this was not to be. Within days, General Castelo Branco assumed the presidency and over the next few years his regime initiated all the features of military dictatorship which Latin America has come to know and love: Congress was shut down, political opposition was reduced to virtual extinction, habeas corpus for "political crimes" was suspended, criticism of the president was forbidden by law, labour unions were taken over by government interventors, mounting protests were met by police and military firing into crowds, the use of systematic "disappearance" as a form of repression came upon the stage of Latin America . . . peasants' homes burned down, priests brutalized . . . the government had a name for its programme: the "moral rehabilitation" of Brazil.

Then there was the torture and the death squads, both largely undertakings of the police and the military, both underwritten by the United States.[73] In the chapters on Guatemala and Uruguay, particularly the latter, we shall see how the US Office of Public Safety (OPS), the CIA and AID combined to provide the technical training, the equipment, and the indoctrination which supported the horrors in those countries. It was no less the case in Brazil. Dan Mitrione of the OPS, whom we shall encounter in his full beauty in Uruguay, began his career in Brazil in the 1960s. By 1969, OPS had established a national police force for Brazil and had trained over 100,000 policemen in the country, in addition to 523 receiving more advanced instruction in the United States.[74] About one-third of the students' time at the police academies was devoted to lectures on the communist menace and the need to battle with it;[75] the "bomb school" and techniques of riot control were other important aspects of their education.

Tortures range from simple but brutal blows from a truncheon to electric shocks. Often the torture is more refined: the end of a reed is placed in the anus of a naked man hanging suspended downwards on the *pau de arara* [parrot's perch] and a piece of cotton soaked in petrol is lit at the other end of the reed. Pregnant women have been forced to watch their husbands being tortured. Other wives have been hung naked beside their husbands and given electric shocks on the sexual parts of their body, while subjected to the worst kind of obscenities. Children have been tortured before their parents and vice versa. At least one child, the three month old baby of Virgilio Gomes da Silva was reported to have

died under police torture. The length of sessions depends upon the resistance capacity of the victims and have sometimes continued for days at a time.
Amnesty International[76]

Judge Agamemnon Duarte indicated that the CCC [Commandos to Hunt Communists, a death squad armed and aided by the police] and the CIA are implicated in the murder of Father Henrique Neto. He admitted that . . . the American Secret Service (CIA) was behind the CCC . . .
Jornal do Brazil[77]

In 1970, a US Congress study group visited Brazil. It gave this summary of statements by American military advisers there:

Rather than dwell on the authoritarian aspects of the regime, they emphasize assertions by the Brazilian armed forces that they believe in, and support, representative democracy as an ideal and would return government to civilian control if this could be done without sacrifice to security and development. This withdrawal from the political arena is not seen as occurring in the near future. For that reason they emphasize the continued importance of the military assistance training program as a means of exerting U.S. influence and retaining the current pro-U.S. attitude of the Brazilian armed forces. Possible disadvantages to U.S. interests in being so closely identified with an authoritarian regime are not seen as particularly important.[78]

The CIA never rests . . . A footnote: the *New York Times* reported in 1966 . . .

When the CIA learned last year that a Brazilian youth had been killed in 1963, allegedly in an auto accident, while studying on a scholarship at the Lumumba University in Moscow, it mounted a massive publicity campaign to discourage other South American families from sending their youngsters to the Soviet Union.[79]

28. Peru 1960 to 1965
Fort Bragg moves to the jungle

It was a CIA dream come true. A commando raid by anti-Castro Cubans upon the Cuban Embassy in Lima had uncovered documentary proof that Cuba had paid out "hundreds of thousands" of dollars in Peru for propaganda to foster favourable attitudes toward the Cuban revolution and to promote Communist activities within the country.

This was no standard broad-brush, cold-war accusation, for the papers disclosed all manner of details and names — the culprits who had been on the receiving end of the tainted money; men in unions and universities and in politics; men who had secretly visited Cuba, all expenses paid.[1] To top it all off, these were men the CIA looked upon as enemies.

The only problem — and it wasn't really a problem — was that some of the documents were counterfeit. The raid had certainly taken place, on 8 November 1960 to be exact. And documents had indeed been seized, at gunpoint. But the most incriminating of the documents, presented a month later with the authentic ones, had been produced by the experts of the CIA's Technical Services Division.[2]

It was a propaganda windfall. The story received wide media coverage in Latin America and the United States, accompanied by indignant anti-communist articles and editorials. *The Wall Street Journal* was moved to run an extremely long, slightly hysterical piece, obviously based on Washington handouts, strikingly unquestioned, which warned that "mountainous stacks of intelligence data from the 20 nations stretching from Mexico to Argentina tell of a widening Communist push into the hemisphere".[3]

To be sure, the Cubans insisted that the documents were not genuine, but that was only to be expected. The affair was to cast a shadow over Castro's foreign relations for some time to come.

The most propitious outcome, from the CIA's standpoint, was that within days after the disclosure the Peruvian government broke diplomatic relations with Cuba. This was a major priority of the Agency in Lima, as in most other CIA stations in Latin America, and led further to the Cuban news agency, *Prensa Latina*, being barred from operating in Peru. The news agency's dispatches, declared the Peruvian authorities, were "controlled from Moscow".[4] If true, this did indicate rather flexible deadlines.

A week later, there was further welcome fallout from the incident. The government enacted legislation making it easier to arrest members of the Communist Party, although this was repealed a year later. During its deliberations the Peruvian legislature accepted a sworn statement from one Francisco Ramos Montejo, a recent defector from the Cuban Embassy who had been present during the raid, who "confirmed" that all the documents were genuine. Ramos, who was now living in Miami and working for the CIA, added fresh revelations that there had been detailed plans for the assassination of Peruvian officials and for the overthrow of the government, and that arms had been smuggled into Peru from Bolivia and Ecuador, presumably for these purposes.[5]

Of such stuff is the battle for the hearts and minds of Latin Americans made.

The political history of Peru has been of the classic South American mould — an oligarchy overthrown by a military coup replaced by another oligarchy . . . periodically punctuated by an uprising, sporadic violence from the forgotten below to remind those above that they are still alive, albeit barely. Veteran Latin America newsman John Gerassi described the state of those below in the Peru of the early 1960s:

In Lima, the capital, whose colonial mansions enveloped by ornate wooden balconies help make it one of the most beautiful cities in the world, half of the 1.3 million ihabitants live in rat-infested slums. One, called El Montón, is built around, over, and in the city dump. There, when I visited it, naked children, some too young to know how to walk, competed with pigs for a few bits of food scraps accidentally discarded by the garbage men . . . [The peasants] chew cocaine-producing coca leaves to still hunger pains, and average 500 calories a day. Where there is grass, the Peruvian Andes Indian eats it — and also the sheep he kills when it gets so hungry that it begins tearing another sheep's wool off for its food. The peons who work the land of the whites average one sol (4 cents) a day, and . . . labor from sunup to sundown . . .[6]

During this period, a movement led by Hugo Blanco organized peasants into unions, staged strikes and seized land. The movement engaged in little which could be termed guerrilla warfare, using its meagre arms to defend the squatters, and was easily and brutally put down by the police and army, apparently without significant American assistance other than the "routine" arming and training of such forces.

By 1965, however, several guerrilla groups had evolved in the eastern slopes of the Andes, cognizant of the bare truth that organizing peasants was, by itself, painfully inadequate; some would say suicidal. Inspired by the Cuban revolution, impressed with the social gains which had followed, and, in some cases, trained by the Cubans, these sons of the middle class met in May to plan a common strategy. Guerrilla warfare began in earnest the following month. By the end of the year, however, a joint Peruvian-American counter-insurgency operation had broken the back of three rebel groups, two of them in less than two months. Those guerrillas who remained alive and active were reduced to futile and impotent skirmishes over the next year or so.[7]

The role of the CIA in this definitive military mop-up has been concisely depicted by the former high official of the Agency, Victor Marchetti:

Green Berets participated . . . in what was the CIA's single large-scale Latin American intervention of the post-Bay of Pigs era. This occurred in the mid-1960s, when the agency secretly came to the aid of the Peruvian government, then plagued by guerrilla troubles in its remote eastern regions. Unable to cope adequately with the insurgent movement, Lima had turned to the U.S. government for aid, which was immediately and covertly forthcoming.

The agency financed the construction of what one experienced observer described as 'a miniature Fort Bragg' in the troubled Peruvian jungle region, complete with mess halls, classrooms, barracks, administrative buildings, parachute jump towers, amphibious landing facilities, and all the other accoutrements of paramilitary operations. Helicopters were furnished under cover of official military aid programs, and the CIA flew in arms and other combat equipment. Training was provided by the agency's Special Operations Division personnel and by Green Beret instructors on loan from the Army.[8]

Typically, and ironically, such training would have included instilling in the Peruvian officers the motivation for doing battle with the insurgents in the first place. As US-military-affairs scholar Michael Klare has pointed out:

> Many Latin American military officers would rather command elite units like jet fighter squadrons, naval flotillas, or armored brigades than slug it out with the guerrillas in long, unspectacular jungle campaigns. U.S. training programs are designed, therefore, to emphasize the importance of counterguerrilla operations (and to suggest, thereby, that the United States will reward those officers who make a good showing at this kind of warfare).[9]

The extent to which American military personnel engaged directly in combat is not known. They did, however, set up their headquartes in the centre of an area of heavy fighting, in the village of Mazanari, and in September 1965 the *New York Times* reported that when the Peruvian army opened a major drive against the guerrillas, "At least one United States Army counter-insurgency expert was said to have helped plan and direct the attack."[10]

In the urban areas a concurrent round-up of guerrilla supporters was carried out, based materially on CIA intelligence: the list of "subversives" regularly compiled by Agency stations throughout the world for just such occasions.[11] The CIA is usually in a much better position to collect this information than the host government, due to its superior experience in the field, funds available for hiring informants, technical equipment for eavesdropping, and greater motivation.

While this was taking place the war in Vietnam and the militant protest against it had already captured the front pages of American newspapers, and the isolated dispatch referred to above easily passed into oblivion. Yet, the American objective in Peru — to crush a movement aimed at genuine land reform and the social and political changes inevitably "threatening" thereby — was identical to its objective in Vietnam, and the methods employed were very similar: burning down peasants' huts and villages to punish support for the guerrillas, defoliating the countryside to eliminate guerrilla sanctuaries, saturation bombing with napalm and high explosives, even throwing prisoners out of helicopters.[12] The essential difference, one which spelled disaster for the Peruvian insurgents, was that their ranks were not augmented in any appreciable number by the Indian peasants, a group with little revolutionary consciousness and even less daring; four centuries of dehumanization had robbed them of virtually all hope and the sense of a right to revolt; and when this sense stirred even faintly, such as under Hugo Blanco, it was met head-on by the brick wall of official violence.

As common in the Third World as it is ludicrous, the bulk of the armed forces employed to keep the peasants pacified were soldiers of peasant stock themselves. It is a measure of the ultimate cynicism of the Peruvian and American military authorities that soldiers were stationed outside their home areas to lessen their resistance when the order was given to shoot.[13]

But it all worked. It worked so well that more than a decade was to pass before desperate men took to arms again in Peru.

29. Dominican Republic 1960 to 1966
Saving democracy from communism by getting rid of democracy

On the night of 30 May 1961, Generalissimo Rafael Trujillo, mass murderer, torturer par excellence, absolute dictator, was shot to death on a highway in the outskirts of the capital city, Ciudad Trujillo.

The assassination set off a chain of events over the next five years which featured remarkably gross and sustained intervention into the internal affairs of the Dominican Republic by the United States, the likes of which had not been seen in Latin America since the heyday of American gunboat diplomacy.

The United States had been an accomplice in the assassination itself of the man it had helped to climb to power and endure for some 30 years. This marks one of the rare occasions that the US government has acted to overthrow a right-wing despot, albeit anti-communism was still the motivating force.

Whatever repugnance individual Washington policy makers may have felt toward Trujillo's incredible violations of human rights over the years, his fervent adherence to American policies, his repression of the left, and, as a consequence, the vigorous support he enjoyed in Congress and in other influential American circles, were enough to keep successive United States administrations looking the other way.

When, in January 1959, Fulgencio Batista fell before the forces of Fidel Castro in nearby Cuba, a reconsideration of this policy was thrust upon Washington's agenda. This historic event seemed to suggest that support of right-wing governments might no longer be the best way of checking the rise of revolutionary movements in Latin America, but rather might be fostering them. Indeed, in June a force of Dominican exiles launched an invasion of their homeland from Cuba. Although it was as much a disaster as the Bay of Pigs was to be two years later, it could only serve to heighten Washington's concern.

'Batista is to Castro as Trujillo is to _____' was the implicit assumption, and Washington wanted to ensure that it could help fill in the blank," is the way one analyst has formulated the problem. "As a result, the United States began to cast about for a way to get rid of Trujillo and at the same time to ensure a responsible successor."[1] Ironically, it was to Trujillo's Dominican Republic that Batista had fled.

The decision to topple Trujillo was reinforced in early 1960 when the United States sought to organize hemispheric opposition to the Castro regime. This

195

policy ran head-on into the familiar accusation that the United States opposed only leftist governments, never those of the right, no matter how tyrannical. The close association with Trujillo, widely regarded as Washington's "protégé", was proving increasingly to be an embarrassment. The circumstances were such that President Eisenhower was led to observe that "It's certain that American public opinion won't condemn Castro until we have moved against Trujillo."[2] (The president's apparent belief in the independence of the American mind may have been overly generous, for the American public knew nothing definite of any American move against Trujillo until 1975, yet fell readily into line in condemning Castro even before Trujillo's assassination.)

As early as 1958, the then-CIA chief of station in the Dominican Republic, Lear Reed, along with several Dominicans, had plotted an assassination of Trujillo, one which never got off the ground.[3] What the Agency's motivation was, and whether it was acting on its own or at the behest of higher echelons in Washington, is not known. However, in February 1960 the National Security Council's Special Group in Washington gave consideration to a programme of covert aid to anti-Trujillo Dominicans.[4] Two months later, Eisenhower approved a contingency plan which provided, in part, that if the situation deteriorated still further: ". . . the United States would immediately take political action to remove Trujillo from the Dominican Republic as soon as a suitable successor regime can be induced to take over with the assurance of U.S. political, economic, and — if necessary — military support."[5]

Seemingly unaware of the currents swirling about him, Trujillo continued to live up to his gangster reputation. In June, his henchmen blew up a car carrying Venezuelan President Romulo Betancourt, an outspoken critic of the Dominican dictator. As a result, Washington came under renewed pressure from several of the more democratic Caribbean countries for action against Trujillo. Betancourt, who had survived the blast, told US Secretary of State Christian Herter: "If you don't eliminate him, we will invade."[6]

For a full year, the dissidents and various American officials played cloak-and-dagger games: there were meetings in New York and Washington, in Ciudad Trujillo and Venezuela; Americans living in the Dominican Republic were enlisted for the cause by the CIA; schemes to overthrow Trujillo were drawn up at different times by the State Department, the CIA, and the dissidents, some approved by the Special Group. A training camp was set up in Venezuela for Dominican exiles flown there from the United States and Puerto Rico by the CIA; the dissidents made numerous requests for weapons, from sniper rifles to remote-control detonating devices, for the understood purpose of assassinating Trujillo and other key members of his regime. Several of the requests were approved by the State Department or the CIA; support for the dissidents was regularly reiterated at high levels of the US government . . . yet, after all was said and done, none of the ambitious plans was even attempted (the actual assassination was essentially a spur of the moment, improvised affair), only three pistols and three carbines were ever passed to the anti-Trujillistas, and it is not certain that any of these arms were used in the assassination.[7]

In the final analysis, the most significant aid received by the dissidents from the United States was the assurance that the "Colossus to the North" would not intervene militarily to prevent the assassination and would support them afterwards if they set up a "suitable" government. In Latin America this is virtually a *sine qua non* for such undertakings, notably in the Dominican Republic where American marines have landed on four separate occasions in this century, the last intervention having created a centralized Dominican National Guard which the US placed under the control of a young officer it had trained named Rafael Trujillo.

The gap between the word and the deed of the American government concerning the assassination appears to have been the consequence of a growing uncertainty in Washington about what would actually take place in the wake of Trujillo's demise — would a pro-Castro regime emerge from the chaos? A secondary consideration, perhaps, was a reluctance to engage in political assassination, both as a matter of policy and as a desire to avoid, as one State Department official put it, "further tarnishing in the eyes of the world" of the "U.S. moral posture".[8] This was particularly the expressed feeling of President John Kennedy and others in his administration who had assumed office in January 1961, although they were later to undertake several assassination attempts against Castro.

The dismal failure of the Bay of Pigs invasion in April further dampened the enthusiasm of Washington officials for any Caribbean adventure (except against Cuba in revenge) and induced them to request a postponement of the assassination. The plotters, however, were well past the point of no return.

The Dominicans who pulled the trigger and their fellow conspirators were in no way revolutionaries. They came from the ranks of the conservative, privileged sectors of Dominican society and were bound together primarily by an intense loathing of Trujillo, a personal vendetta — each of them, or someone close to them, had suffered a deep humiliation at the hands of the diabolical dictator, if not torture or murder.

Their plan as to what would follow the elimination of Trujillo was only half-baked, and even this fell apart completely. As matters turned out, the day after the assassination, Rafael ("Ramfis") Trujillo, Jr. rushed home from his playboy's life in Paris to take over the reins of government. Little had been resolved, either in the Dominican Republic or in Washington. The Kennedy administration was confronted with the same ideological questions which had caused it so much indecision before the assassination, as they had the Eisenhower administration. To wit: What is the best way of preventing the establishment of left-wing governments intent upon radical social change? The traditional iron fist of right-wing dictatorship, or a more democratic society capable of meeting many of the legitimate demands of the populace? How much democracy? Would too much open the door for even greater, and unacceptable, demands and provide the left with a legal platform from which to sway ("dupe", Washington would call it) the public? And if it is a dictatorship that is to be supported, how are liberal American leaders to explain this to the world and to their own citizens?

John F. Kennedy and his men from Harvard tended to treat such policy questions in a manner more contemplative than American political figures are usually inclined to do; on occasion, it might be said, they even *agonized* over such questions. But in the end, their Latin American policy was scarcely distinguishable from that of conservative American administrations. A leader who imposed "order" with at least the facade of democracy, who kept the left submerged without being notoriously brutal about it; in short, the anti-communist liberal, still appeared to be the safest ally for the United States; if such an ally were not available, said Kennedy, then a Trujillo would do in preference to a Castro.[9]

Rafael Trujillo, Jr. was clearly not ideal. Besides bearing the inescapable stigma of his name and family, he carried out a bloodbath of revenge over the next six months.[10] But, unlike his father in his last years, Ramfis could be prodded by Washington into making a few token reforms, and both parties might have been content to continue in this fashion indefinitely had not many people of the Dominican Republic felt terribly cheated by the turn of events. Their elation over the assassination had soured in the face of business-as-usual.

Resentment spilled over into the streets. By October, the protests were occurring daily and were being put down by tanks; students were shot dead by government troops. The following month, when Ramfis elected to return to the pleasure temples of Europe and his two uncles made their move to continue the Trujillo oligarchy, the United States decided to take the intiative. The situation in the streets and high places of the government was anarchic enough, Washington feared, to provide an opening for the proverbial "communist takeover", although, in fact, the left in the Dominican Republic was manifestly insignificant from years of repression.

American diplomats met in the capital city with the Trujillos and Dominican military leaders and bluntly told them that US military power would, if necessary, be used to compel the formation of a provisional government headed by Joachim Balaguer until elections could be held. Balaguer had been closely tied to the Trujillo family for decades, was serving as president under Trujillo at the time of the assassination, and had remained in the same capacity under Ramfis, but he was not regarded as a threat to continue the tyranny. As Kennedy put it: "Balaguer is our only tool. The anticommunist liberals aren't strong enough. We must use our influence to take Balaguer along the road to democracy."[11] Just how committed John F. Kennedy was to democracy in the Dominican Republic we shall presently see.

To make certain that the Dominicans got the message, a US naval task force of eight ships with 1,800 Marines aboard appeared off the Dominican coast on 19 November, just outside the three-mile limit but in plain sight of Ciudad Trujillo. Spanish-language broadcasts from the offshore ships warned that the Marines were prepared to come ashore; while overhead, American jet fighters streaked along the coastline. Brigadier General Pedro Rodriguez Echevarria, a key military figure, was persuaded by the United States presence to put aside any plans for a coup he may have been harbouring and to support the American action. Rodriguez proceeded to order the bombing of the air base outside the capital where Trujillistas had been massing troops. Over the next two days, "the wicked uncles" and many other Trujillistas left for the good life in Florida.[12]

However, when Balaguer proved to be a major obstacle to beginning the process of democratization and indicated that he did not regard his regime as temporary, the United States added its own special pressure to that of Balaguer's domestic opposition to force him to resign after only two months in office. Washington then turned around and issued a stern warning to Rodriguez and mounted another naval show-of-force to help other military officers overturn the general's attempt to seize power.[13]

While a seven-man "Council of State" then administered the affairs of government, the US continued to treat the Dominican Republic as its private experiment in the prevention of communism. The American Ambassador, John Bartlow Martin, pressed the Council to curb left-wing activity. By his own admission, Martin urged the use of "methods once used by the police in Chicago": harassment of suspects by repeated arrests, midnight raids on their homes, beatings, etc.[14]

When street disturbances erupted, US Attorney General Robert Kennedy arranged for riot-control equipment to be sent to Santo Domingo (the original name of the capital, now restored). The equipment came complete with two Spanish-speaking Los Angeles detectives to impart to their Dominican counterparts the fine art of quelling such uprisings that they had acquired in the Mexican barrios of east Los Angeles. In a few weeks, Ambassador Martin could report that the Council had "rewon the streets, thanks almost entirely to those two detectives".[15]

This riot-control unit remained as a permanent part of the Santo Domingo police force. Known as the *Cascos Blancos* (white helmets), they came to be much hated by the populace. Shortly afterwards, the US military undertook a long-range programme to transform the country's armed forces into what was hoped would be an efficient anti-guerrilla organization, although guerrillas were as rare on the Caribbean island as members of the Trujillo family.[16]

Finally, in December 1962, elections were held, under terms dictated in large part by Ambassador Martin to the two major candidates. His purpose was to introduce into the Dominican Republic some of the features that Americans regard as necessary to a viable and democratic electoral system, but Martin's fiat was inescapably a highly condescending intrusion into the affairs of a supposedly sovereign nation. His instructions extended down to the level of what the loser should say in his concession speech.

Further, under an "Emergency Law", the United States and the Council arranged for the deportation of some 125 Trujillistas and "Castro communists" to the United States, from where they were not allowed to leave until after the election in order "to help maintain stability so elections could be held".[17]

The winner, and first more-or-less democratically elected president of the Dominican Republic since 1924, was Juan Bosch, a writer who had spent many years in exile while Trujillo reigned. Here at last was Kennedy's liberal anti-communist, non-military and legally elected by a comfortable majority as well.

Bosch's government was to be the long-sought-after "showcase of democracy" that would put the lie to Fidel Castro. Bosch was given the grand treatment in Washington shortly before he took office in February 1963.

He was true to his beliefs. He called for land reform, including transferring some private land to the public sector as required; low-rent housing; modest nationalization of business; an ambitious project of public works, serving mass needs more than vested interests; a reduction in the import of luxury items; at the same time, he favoured incentives to private enterprise and was open to foreign investment provided it was not excessively exploitive of the country — all in all, standard elements in the programme of any liberal, Third World leader serious about social change. He was likewise serious about the thing called civil liberties: Communists or those labelled as such, or anyone else, were not to be persecuted unless they actually violated the law.

A number of American officials and congressmen expressed their discomfort with Bosch's plans, as well as his stance of independence from the United States. Land reform and nationalization are always touchy issues in Washington, the stuff that "creeping socialism" is made of. In several quarters of the US press Bosch was red-baited and compared with Castro, and the Dominican Republic with Cuba. (Castro, for his part, branded Bosch a "Yankee puppet".) Some of the press criticism was clearly orchestrated, in the manner of many CIA campaigns.[18]

In both the United States and the Dominican Republic, the accusation most frequently cast at Bosch was the one typically used against Latin American leaders who do not vigorously suppress the left (cf. Arbenz and Goulart): Bosch was allowing "communists" to "infiltrate" into the country and into the government, and he was not countering "communist subversion", the latter referring to no more than instances of people standing up for their long-denied rights. Wrote a reporter for the *Miami News*: "Communist penetration of the Dominican Republic is progressing with incredible speed and efficiency." He did not, however, name a single communist in the Bosch government.[19]

The CIA made a contribution to this atmosphere. Ambassador Martin has reported that the Agency "gave rumors [about communists] a credibility far higher than I would have . . . In reporting a Castro/Communist plot, however wildly implausible, it is obviously safer to evaluate it as 'could be true' than as nonsense."[20]

John F. Kennedy also soured on Bosch, particularly for his refusal to crack down on radicals. Said the president to Ambassador Martin one day: "I'm wondering if the day might not come when he'd [Bosch] like to get rid of some of the left. Tell him we respect his judgment, we're all for him, but the time may come when he'll want to deport 30 or 50 people, when it'd be better to deport them than to let them go. I suppose he'd have to catch them in something . . ."[21]

When the United States failed to commit any new economic assistance to the Dominican Republic and generally gave the indication that Juan Bosch was a doomed venture, right-wing Dominican military officers could only be encouraged in their craving to be rid of the president and his policies. Sam Halper, former Caribbean Bureau Chief of *Time* magazine, later reported that the military coup ousting Bosch went into action "as soon as they got a wink from the U.S. Pentagon".[22]

In July, a group of officers formally presented Bosch with an ultimatum: their loyalty to his regime was conditioned upon his adoption of a policy of rigorous anti-communism. Bosch reacted by going on television and delivering a lecture about the apolitical role required of the military in a democratic society, surely an occult subject to these products of 31 years of Trujilloism.

The beleaguered president could see that a premature demise lay ahead for his government. His speech on television sounded very much like a farewell. The failure of Washington to intervene on his behalf could only enlarge the writing on the wall. Indeed, Bosch and some of his aides strongly suspected that the US military and the CIA were already conspiring with the Dominican officers. Several American military officers had disregarded diplomatic niceties by expressing their reservations about Bosch's politics loud enough to reach his ears.[23]

A week before the inevitable coup, the CIA-created union federation in the Dominican Republic, CONATRAL, which had been set up to counter and erode Bosch's support in the labour movement, placed an ad in a leading newspaper urging the people to put their faith in the army to defend them against communism.[24]

The end came in September, a scant seven months after Bosch had taken office. He had not had the time to accomplish much that was worthwhile in this hopelessly corrupt society before the military boots marched, as they have always marched in Latin America.

The United States did nothing to stand in the way of the coup. There would be no display of military might this time — although Bosch asked for it — "unless a Communist takeover were threatened," said the State Department.[25]

"Democracy", said *Newsweek* magazine, "was being saved from Communism by getting rid of democracy."[26]

There were the customary expressions of regret in Washington about the death of democracy, and there was the *de rigueur* withholding of recognition of the new regime. But two months later, when opposition to the repressive dictatorship began to manifest itself noticeably, the junta yelled "communist" and was quickly embraced by the United States with recognition and the other perquisites which attach to being a member in good standing of the "Free World".[27]

Nineteen months later, a revolution broke out in the Dominican Republic which promised to put the exiled Bosch back in power at the hands of a military-civilian force that would be loyal to his programme. But for the fifth time in the century, the American Marines landed and put an abrupt end to such hopes.

In the early morning of Saturday, 24 April 1965, a group of young army officers of middle rank, acting in concert with civilian Bosch partisans, declared themselves in revolt against the government. The "constitutionalists", as they called themselves, were soon joined by other officers and their units. Spurred by ecstatic radio proclamations, thousands of Dominicans poured into the streets shouting "Viva Bosch" and grabbed up the arms handed out by the rebel military forces.

The television station was taken over and for two days a "potpourri of politicians, soldiers, women, children, adventurers, hoodlums and anyone who wished to, shouted against the status quo."[28]

The participants in the uprising were a mixed bag, not all of them sympathetic to Bosch or to social reform; there were others, to the right, with their own varied motivations. But the impetus clearly lay with the constitutionalists and the uprising was thus viewed with alarm by the rest of the military, and the US Embassy, as a movement to restore Bosch to power with all that that implied.

Philip Geyelin of the *Wall Street Journal* (and formerly with the CIA) who had access to the official embassy cables and the key actors in the drama has written:

> What the record reveals, in fact, is that from the very outset of the upheaval, there was a concerted U.S. Government effort, if not actually a formal decision, to checkmate the rebel movement by whatever means and at whatever cost.
>
> By Sunday, April 25 . . . the Santo Domingo embassy had clearly cast its lot with the 'loyalist' military cabal and against the rebellion's original aim: the return of Juan Bosch . . . Restoration of the Bosch regime would be 'against U.S. interests,' the embassy counseled. Blocking Bosch could mean further bloodshed, the embassy conceded. Nonetheless, Washington was advised, the embassy military attaches had given 'loyalist' leaders a go-ahead to do 'everything possible' to prevent what was described as the danger of a 'Communist take-over'.[29]

The attachés as well as the US Consul made emergency visits to several still-uncommitted Dominican military commanders to persuade them, apparently with notable success, to support the government.[30]

A bloody civil war had broken out in the streets of Santo Domingo. During the first few days, the momentum of battle swung to one side, then the other. By the night of 28 April, however, the military and police inside Santo Domingo had collapsed, and the constitutionalists were preparing to attack the military's last bastion, San Isidro, their main base about 10 miles away.[31]

"The Generals at San Isidro were dejected, several were weeping, and one was hysterically urging 'retreat'," read the cable sent by the American Ambassador W. Tapley Bennett to Washington in the early evening of the 28th. (Bennett, as we shall see, was given to hyperbole of the worst sort, but the Dominican military certainly were isolated and demoralized.) Bennett added, whether in the same cable or another one is not clear, that if US troops did not immediately land, American lives would be lost and "Castro-type elements" would be victorious.[32]

Within hours, the first 500 US Marines were brought in by helicopter from ships stationed a few miles off the coast. Two days later, American forces numbered over 4,000. At the peak, some 23,000 troops, marine and army, were to take up positions in the beleaguered little Caribbean country, with thousands more standing by on a 35-ship task force offshore.

The American action was in clear violation of several international agreements, including the Charter of the Organization of American States (OAS) which prohibited intervention "directly or indirectly, for any reason whatever, in the internal or external affairs of any other state".

During the entire course of the US military occupation, American pronouncements would have had the world believe that its forces were in the Dominican Republic in a "neutral" capacity: to protect the lives of Americans and other foreigners, establish a ceasefire, ensure free elections, etc. As we have seen, however, the United States had committed itself to one side from the start of hostilities. This continued to be the case. The morning after the landing of the first Marines, Ambassador Bennett was instructed by the State Department that US military officers should be used "to help San Isidro develop operational plans to take the rebel stronghold downtown".[33]

Within a few days, American troops were deployed in an armed corridor through the centre of Santo Domingo so as to divide the constitutionalist's zone and cut off their main body from access to the rest of the country, bottling them up in a small downtown area with their backs to the sea. Other American forces were stationed throughout the countryside. The rebel offensive against San Isidro had been prevented. It was the end of their revolution.

The American forces came to the aid of the Dominican military in a number of ways, supplying them with equipment, food and even their salaries, but it was the direct military involvement that was most telling. On one striking occasion, the sea of American troops parted to allow the Dominican military to pass through and brutally attack and mop up the northern section of the rebel zone while the main rebel force in the south remained helplessly blocked behind the American line. This "smashing victory" the *New York Times* reported, was "visibly aided by United States troops". Other American journalists also reported that US troops took part in the fighting, although Washington officials angrily denied it.[34]

The rebels were reduced to little more than sniping attacks on American soldiers, for which they paid a heavy price. US forces blasted apart a building in downtown Santo Domingo from which sniper fire was coming; advancing into a constitutionalist zone, again after sniper fire, they killed some 67 rebels and bystanders; American paratroops were seen firing at rebels who were retreating, and the constitutionalists' Minister of Justice and Police was "reported to have been killed by United States machine-gun fire as he attempted to capture the empty Presidential Palace in midtown with a squad of his troops."[35]

When the Johnson administration was not denying such actions outright, it was claiming that they were either contrary to orders, "individual indiscretions", or "isolated incidents".

A covert team of Green Berets arrived at one point to help assure the safety of American civilians. But when they discovered that some of the Americans were assisting rebel forces, "their main objective shifted from protecting their fellow countrymen to spying on them".[36]

The Green Berets also found the time to lay the groundwork for the assassination of one of the leading constitutionalist leaders, Col. Francisco Caamaño. The plot was cancelled at the last moment due to the excessive risk involved.[37]

Another group of American visitors was that of some leaders of the National Student Association, ostensibly come to the Dominican Republic to talk with their counterparts about educational matters, but actually there at the behest of the CIA to gather information on local students. This was still two years before the exposé of the long-lasting relationship between the CIA and the prominent student organization.[38]

Throughout this period, the communication guns of the US government were aimed at the people of the United States, the Dominican Republic and the world to convince them that "communists" were a dominant element amongst the constitutionalists, that they represented a threat to take over the movement, or that they had already taken it over, with frightening consequences for all concerned.

At various times the Johnson administration released lists of "communists and Castroites" in the ranks of the rebels. These lists totalled 53 or 58 or 77 names and became a *cause célèbre* as well as an object of media ridicule. Besides the laughably small numbers involved (in a rebellion of tens of thousands with numerous leaders), several of those on the lists, it turned out, were in prison while others were out of the country.

The American Embassy in Santo Domingo assured reporters that if they went to rebel headquarters, they would see the named communist agents in the flesh. The newspeople went and looked but could find no identifiable communists (however one identifies a communist). Subsequently, administration officials explained that the reason that newspeople had seen such little evidence of communist activity was that the American landings had scared the reds into hiding.

Eventually, officials admitted their doubt that they could prove that communists had gained control of the constitutionalists, although President Johnson had pressed the CIA and FBI into an intensive search for evidence.*[39]

Former CIA officer Philip Agee, stationed in Uruguay at the time, wrote later that the new password at his station became "Fifty-eight trained communists". The proper reply was "Ten thousand marines".[40]

The embassy, and Ambassador Bennett in particular, poured forth "a rising stream of hysterical rumors, atrocity stories, and alarmist reports"[41] about the rebels, reminiscent of the Bolshevik horror stories which had filled the pages of the American press following the Russian revolution: embassies being ransacked ... "Castroite-style mass executions" ... rebels parading in the streets with the heads of their victims on poles ...

---

* A CIA cable to Washington on 25 April 1965 reported that the Communist Party (Partido Socialista Dominicano) had been "unaware of the coup attempt".

President Johnson made reference to the "atrocities" in public statements, but none of the stories were ever proven, for none were true; no one ever located any of the many headless Dominicans; and American officials, in a monument to *chutzpah*, later denounced the press for reporting such unverified rumours.[42]

Meanwhile, the CIA, the Defense Intelligence Agency and the US Information Agency were conducting their own intensive propaganda campaign in the Dominican Republic to give credence to the American position and discredit Dominican groups opposed to it. Experts on psychological warfare arrived to ply their trade, radio stations and newspapers were covertly set up, rebel radio stations jammed, leaflets airdropped in the countryside. The USIA also secretly subsidized the publication of pro-administration material aimed for distribution in the United States.[43]

From all the wild charges and the frequent contradictory statements made by American officials, the expression "credibility gap" entered the American popular language and soon came to haunt the Johnson presidency.[44]

Historian Richard Barnet has noted another interesting side to the American propaganda effort:

> To justify the intervention, which had aroused violent opposition from traditional friends of the United States because of its crudeness and the swathe of lies in which it was wrapped . . . [Washington] began a direct assault on the concept of non-intervention, the rhetorical foundation stone of Latin-American policy enshrined in numerous treaties, declarations, and Pan-American Day speeches . . . Under Secretary Thomas Mann told newspaper correspondents that the OAS and UN charters were drawn up in '19th-century terms' . . . Averell Harriman remarked in Montevideo that the principle of non-intervention was becoming 'obsolete'. By a vote of 315 to 52 the House of Representatives passed a resolution . . . justifying the unilateral use of force on foreign territory by any nation which considers itself threatened by 'international communism, directly or indirectly.' . . . the President [declared in a speech]: 'The first reality is that old concepts and old labels are largely obsolete. In today's world, with enemies of freedom talking about "Wars of national liberation," the old distinction between "Civil War" and "International War" has already lost much of its meaning . . . The moment of decision must become the moment of action.'
>
> This is the essence of the Johnson Doctrine — a virtually unlimited claim of legitimacy for armed intervention in civil strife.[45]

The last American troops did not leave the Dominican Republic until September 1966. The interim period witnessed a succession of ceasefires, broken truces, and protracted negotiations under provisional governments.

In June 1966, elections were held in which Joaquin Balaguer defeated Juan Bosch by a surprisingly large margin. Yet, it was not all that surprising. For five long years the people of the Dominican Republic had lived under a cloud of chaos and violence. The experience had instilled in them a deep longing for a return to "normalcy", to order, without foreign intervention, without soldiers patrolling their streets, without curfews, tear gas and bloodshed. With the US Army still very much in evidence and the American distaste for Bosch well known . . . with the ubiquitous American propaganda hammering home fear of The Red Menace and associating the constitutionalists, and thus Bosch, with communism . . . with the Dominican military still largely Trujillista in personnel and ideology . . . a victory for Bosch would be seen by many voters as a danger that all the horrors would rain down upon their heads once more. Bosch, who had returned several months prior to the election, was himself so fearful for his personal safety that he never left his home during the campaign.

Joachim Balaguer remained in office for 12 years, ruling his people in the grand Latin American style: the rich became richer and the poor had babies, hungry babies; democracy remained an alien concept; the police and military regularly kidnapped, tortured and murdered opponents of the government and terrorized union organizers.[46]

But the man was not, personally, the monster that Trujillo was. There was relative calm and peace. No "communist threat" hovered over the land. The pot was sweetened for foreign investors, and American corporations moved in with big bucks. There was stability and order. And the men who ran the United States looked and were satisfied. Perhaps some of them had come to the realization that the anti-communist liberal government was an impossible ideal; for any movement seeking genuine democracy and social reform would invariably attract individuals whom the United States would invariably categorize as "communist"; the United States would then feel driven to discredit, subvert and eventually overturn the movement. A Catch 22.

30. Cuba 1959 to 1980s
The unforgivable revolution

The existence of a revolutionary socialist government with growing ties to the Soviet Union only 90 miles away, insisted the United States Government, was a situation which no self-respecting superpower should tolerate, and in 1961 it undertook an invasion of Cuba.

But less than 50 miles from the Soviet Union sat Pakistan, a close ally of the United States, a member since 1955 of the South-East Asia Treaty Organization (SEATO), the US-created anti-communist alliance. On the very border of the Soviet Union was Iran, an even closer ally of the United States, with its relentless electronic listening posts, aerial surveillance, and infiltration into Russian territory by American agents. And alongside Iran, also bordering the Soviet Union, was Turkey, a member of the Russians' mortal enemy, NATO, since 1951.

In 1962 during the "Cuban Missile Crisis", Washington, seemingly in a state of near-panic, informed the world that the Russians were installing "offensive" missiles in Cuba — a "quarantine" of the island was instituted: a powerful show of naval and marine forces in the Caribbean would stop and search all vessels heading towards Cuba; any found to contain military cargo would be forced to turn back.

But the United States had missiles and bomber bases already in place in Turkey and other missiles in Western Europe pointed toward the Soviet Union. Russian leader Nikita Khrushchev later wrote that . . .

> The Americans had surrounded our country with military bases and threatened us with nuclear weapons, and now they would learn just what it feels like to have enemy missiles pointing at you; we'd be doing nothing more than giving them a little of their own medicine . . . After all, the United States had no moral or legal quarrel with us. We hadn't given the Cubans anything more than the Americans were giving to their allies. We had the same rights and opportunities as the Americans. Our conduct in the international arena was governed by the same rules and limits as the Americans.[1]

At one point during the confrontation, Khrushchev offered to remove the missiles and jet bombers from Cuba if the United States would do the same in Turkey. President Kennedy categorically refused, insisting that the Soviets must first dismantle their missiles in Cuba as a condition for negotiations on "wider" questions. The Soviets complied. The American missiles in Turkey are still there.

Lest anyone misunderstand, as Khrushchev apparently did, the standards under which Washington was operating, *Time* magazine was quick to explain. "On the part of the Communists," the magazine declared, "this equating [of U.S. and Soviet missiles and bases] had obvious tactical motives. On the part of neutralists and pacifists [who welcomed the offer of mutual dismantling] it betrayed intellectual and moral confusion." The confusion lay, it seems, in not seeing clearly who were the good guys and who were the bad guys, for "The purpose of the U.S. bases [in Turkey] was not to blackmail Russia but to strengthen the defense system of NATO, which had been created as a safeguard against Russian aggression. As a member of NATO, Turkey welcomed the bases as a contribution to her own defense." Cuba, which had been invaded only the year before, could have, it seems, no such concern. *Time* continued its sermon:

> Beyond these differences between the two cases, there is an enormous moral difference between U.S. and Russian objectives . . . To equate U.S. and Russian bases is in effect to equate U.S. and Russian purposes . . . The U.S. bases, such as those in Turkey, have helped keep the peace since World War II, while the Russian bases in Cuba threatened to upset the peace. The Russian bases were intended to further conquest and domination, while U.S. bases were erected to preserve freedom. The difference should have been obvious to all.[2]

Equally obvious was the right of the United States to maintain a military base on Cuban soil – Guantanamo Naval Base by name, a vestige of colonialism staring down the throats of the Cuban people which the United States, to this day, refuses to vacate despite the vehement protest of the Castro government. By way of contrast — apart from the (obvious) American reaction to a Soviet or Cuban base in the United States — Washington has been insisting for over a decade that Cuban military forces leave Angola, though they are there at the express request of the Angolan government to defend the country against attacks by South Africa.

In the American lexicon, in addition to good and bad bases and missiles, there are good and bad revolutions. The American and French Revolutions were good. The Cuban Revolution is bad. It must be bad because so many people have left Cuba as a result of it.

But at least 100,000 people left the British colonies in America during and after the American Revolution. These Tories could not abide by the political and social change, both actual and feared, particularly that which attends all revolutions worthy of the name: those looked down upon as inferiors no longer know their place. (Or as the US Secretary of State put it after the Russian Revolution: the Bolsheviks sought "to make the ignorant and incapable mass of humanity dominant in the earth.")[3]

The Tories fled to Nova Scotia and Britain carrying tales of the godless, dissolute, barbaric American revolutionaries. Those who remained and refused to take an oath of allegiance to the new state governments were denied virtually all civil liberties. Many were jailed, murdered, or forced into exile. After the American Civil War, thousands more fled to South America and other points, again disturbed by the social upheaval. How much more is such an exodus to be expected following the Cuban Revolution? — a true social revolution, giving rise to changes much more profound than anything in the American experience. How many more would have left the United States if 90 miles away lay the world's wealthiest nation welcoming their residence and promising all manner of benefits and rewards?

After the Cuban Revolution in January 1959, we learned that there are also good and bad hijackings. On several occasions Cuban planes and boats were hijacked to the United States but they were not returned to Cuba, nor were the hijackers punished. Instead, some of the planes and boats were seized by US authorities for non-payment of debts claimed by American firms against the Cuban government.[4] But then there were the bad hijackings — planes forced to fly from the United States to Cuba. When there began to be more of these than flights in the opposite direction, Washington was obliged to reconsider its policy.

It appears that there are as well good and bad terrorists. When the Israelis bombed PLO headquarters in Tunis in 1985, Ronald Reagan expressed his approval. The president asserted that nations have the right to retaliate against terrorist attacks "as long as you pick out the people responsible".[5]

But if Cuba were to bomb any of the headquarters of the anti-Castro exiles in Miami or New Jersey, Ronald Reagan would likely go to war, though for 25 years the Castro government has been on the receiving end of an extraordinary series of terrorist attacks carried out in Cuba, in the United States, and in many other countries by the exiles and their CIA mentors. (We shall not discuss the consequences of Cuba bombing CIA headquarters.)

Bombing and strafing attacks of Cuba by planes based in the United States began in October 1959, if not before.[6] In early 1960, there were several fire-bomb air raids on Cuban cane fields and sugar mills, in which American pilots also took part — at least three died in crashes and two others were captured. The State Department acknowledged that one plane which crashed, killing two Americans, had taken off from Florida, but insisted that it was against the wishes of the US government.[7]

In March a French freighter unloading munitions from Belgium exploded in Havana taking 75 lives and injuring 200, some of whom subsequently died. The United States denied Cuba's accusation of sabotage but admitted that it had sought to prevent the shipment.[8]

And so it went . . . reaching a high point in April of the following year in the infamous CIA-organized invasion of Cuba at the Bay of Pigs. Over 100 exiles died in the attack as well as four Americans flying for the CIA. Close to 1,200 other exiles were taken prisoner by the Cubans.*

The Bay of Pigs assault had relied heavily on the Cuban people rising up to join the invaders,[10] but this was not to be the case. As it was, the leadership and ranks of the exile forces were riddled with former supporters and henchmen of Fulgencio Batista, the dictator overthrown by Castro, and would not have been welcomed back by the Cubans under any circumstances.

Despite the fact that the Kennedy administration was acutely embarrassed by the unmitigated defeat — indeed, *because* of it — a campaign of smaller-scale attacks upon Cuba was initiated almost immediately. Throughout the 1960s, the Caribbean island was subjected to countless sea and air commando raids by exiles, at times accompanied by their CIA supervisors, inflicting damage upon oil refineries, chemical plants and railroad bridges, cane fields, sugar mills and sugar warehouses; infiltrating spies, saboteurs and assassins . . . anything to damage the Cuban economy and promote disaffection, taking the lives of Cuban militia members and others in the process . . . pirate attacks on Cuban fishing boats and merchant ships, bombardments of Soviet vessels docked in Cuba, an assault upon a Soviet army camp with twelve Russian soldiers reported wounded . . . a hotel and a theatre shelled from offshore because Russians and East Europeans were supposed to be present there . . .[11]

---

* After the invasion, Castro appeared on a TV show in which he questioned, argued, and sometimes good-naturedly took abuse from about a thousand of the prisoners. "Now be honest," he said to one of them. "You must surely realize that you are the first prisoner in history who has the privilege of arguing in front of the whole population of Cuba and the entire world with the head of a government which you came to overthrow." The prisoners were returned to the United States in exchange for some $62 million worth of medical supplies.[9]

These actions were not always carried out on the direct order of the CIA or with its foreknowledge, but the Agency could hardly plead "rogue elephant". It had created an operations headquarters in Miami that was truly a state within a city — over, above, and outside the laws of the United States, not to mention international law, with a permanent staff in excess of 300 Americans directing a few thousand Cuban agents in just such types of actions, with a budget of more than $50 million a year.[12]

Title 18 of the US Code declares it to be a crime to launch a "military expedition or enterprise" from the United States against a country with which the United States is not (officially) at war. Although US authorities now and then aborted an exile plot or impounded a boat — employing a selectiveness, the criteria of which is unclear — no Cubans were prosecuted under this act. This was no more than to be expected inasmuch as Attorney-General Robert Kennedy had determined after the Bay of Pigs that the invasion did not constitute a military expedition.[13]

The commando raids were combined with a total US trade and credit embargo which continues to this day and which has genuinely hurt the Cuban economy and chipped away at the society's standard of living. So unyielding was the embargo that when Cuba was hard hit by a hurricane in October 1963, and Casa Cuba, a New York social club, raised a large quantity of clothing for relief, the United States refused to grant it an export license on the grounds that such shipment was "contrary to the national interest".[14] Moreover, pressure was brought to bear upon other countries to conform to the embargo, and goods destined for Cuba were sabotaged: machinery damaged, chemicals added to lubricating fluids to cause rapid wear on diesel engines, a manufacturer in West Germany paid to produce ball-bearings off-centre, another to do the same with balanced wheel gears — "You're talking about big money," said a CIA officer involved in the sabotage efforts, "when you ask a manufacturer to go along with you on that kind of project because he has to reset his whole mold. And he is probably going to worry about the effect on future business. You might have to pay him several hundred thousand dollars or more."[15]

One manufacturer who defied the embargo was the British Leyland Company which sold a large number of buses to Cuba in 1964. Repeated expressions of criticism and protest by Washington officials and Congressmen failed to stem deliveries of some of the buses. Then, in October, an East German cargo ship carrying another 42 buses to Cuba collided in thick fog with a Japanese vessel in the Thames. The Japanese ship was able to continue on, but the cargo ship was beached on its side; the buses would have to be "written off" said the Leyland company. In the leading British newspapers it was just an accident story.[16] In the *New York Times* it was not even reported. A decade was to pass before the American columnist Jack Anderson disclosed that his CIA and National Security Agency sources had confirmed that the collision had been arranged by the CIA with the co-operation of British intelligence.[17] Subsequently, another CIA officer stated that he was sceptical about the collision story, although admitting that "it is true that we were sabotaging the Leyland buses going to Cuba from England, and that was pretty sensitive business."[18]

What undoubtedly was a yet more sensitive undertaking was the use of chemical and biological weapons against Cuba by the United States. It is a remarkable record.

In August 1962, a British freighter under Soviet lease, having damaged its propellor on a reef, crept into San Juan harbour (Puerto Rico) for repairs. It was bound for a Soviet port with 80,000 bags of Cuban sugar. The ship was put into dry dock and 14,135 sacks of sugar were unloaded to a warehouse to facilitate the repairs. While in the warehouse, the sugar was contaminated by CIA agents with a harmless but unpalatable substance. When President Kennedy learned of the operation he was furious because it had taken place in US territory and if discovered could provide the Soviet Union with a propaganda field-day and could set a terrible precedent for chemical sabotage in the cold war. He directed that the sugar not be returned to the Russians, although what explanation was given to them is not publicly known.[19] Similar undertakings were apparently not cancelled. The CIA official who helped direct worldwide sabotage efforts, referred to above, later revealed that "There was lots of sugar being sent out from Cuba, and we were putting a lot of contaminants in it."[20]

The same year, a Canadian agricultural technician working as an adviser to the Cuban Government was paid $5,000 by "an American military intelligence agent" to infect Cuban turkeys with a virus which would produce the fatal Newcastle disease. Subsequently, 8,000 turkeys died. The technician later claimed that although he had been to the farm where the turkeys had died, he had not actually administered the virus, but had instead pocketed the money, and that the turkeys had died from neglect and other causes unrelated to the virus. This may have been a self-serving statement. The *Washington Post* reported that "According to U.S. intelligence reports, the Cubans — and some Americans — believe the turkeys died as the result of espionage."[21]

Authors Warren Hinckle and William Turner, citing a participant in the project, have reported in their book on Cuba that:

> During 1969 and 1970, the CIA deployed futuristic weather modification technology to ravage Cuba's sugar crop and undermine the economy. Planes from the China Lake Naval Weapons Center in the California desert, where hi tech was developed, overflew the island, seeding rain clouds with crystals that precipitated torrential rains over non-agricultural areas and left the cane fields arid (the downpours caused killer flash floods in some areas).[22]

In 1971, also according to participants, the CIA turned over to Cuban exiles a virus which causes African swine fever. Six weeks later, an outbreak of the disease in Cuba forced the slaughter of 500,000 pigs to prevent a nationwide animal epidemic. The outbreak, the first ever in the Western hemisphere, was called the "most alarming event" of the year by the United Nations Food and Agricultural Organization.[23]

Ten years later, the target may well have been human beings, as an epidemic of dengue fever swept the Cuban island. Transmitted by blood-eating insects, usually mosquitos, the disease produces severe flu symptoms and incapacitating bone pain. Between May and October 1981, over 300,000 cases were reported in Cuba with 158 fatalities, 101 of which were children under 15.[24] In 1956 and 1958, declassified documents have revealed, the US Army loosed swarms of specially bred mosquitos in Georgia and Florida to see whether disease-carrying insects could be weapons in a biological war. The mosquitos bred for the tests were of the *Aedes Aegypti* type, the precise carrier of dengue fever as well as other diseases.[25] In 1967 it was reported by *Science* magazine that at the US government centre in Fort Detrick, Maryland, dengue fever was amongst those "diseases that are at least the objects of considerable research and that appear to be among those regarded as potential BW [biological warfare] agents."[26] Then, in 1984, a Cuban exile on trial in New York testified that in the latter part of 1980 a ship travelled from Florida to Cuba with

> a mission to carry some germs to introduce them in Cuba to be used against the Soviets and against the Cuban economy, to begin what was called chemical war, which later on produced results that were not what we had expected, because we thought that it was going to be used against the Soviet forces, and it was used against our own people, and with that we did not agree.[27]

How it was expected that the germs would confine their actions to only Russians was not explained.

The full extent of American chemical and biological warfare against Cuba will never be known. Over the years, the Castro government has blamed the United States for a number of other plagues which afflicted various animals and crops.[28] It may be significant that CIA documents released in 1977, as reported by the *Washington Post*, disclosed that the Agency "maintained a clandestine 'anti-crop warfare' research program targeted during the 1960s at a number of countries throughout the world."[29] There was no indication in the documents of any actual attack against crops, but if such did take place it is reasonable to assume that one of the targets was Cuba.*

The ingenuity which went into the chemical and biological warfare was apparent in some of the dozens of plans to assassinate or humiliate Fidel Castro. Devised by the CIA or Cuban exiles, with the co-operation of American mafiosi, the plans ranged from poisoning Castro's cigars and food to a chemical designed to make his hair and beard fall off and LSD to be

---

* It came to pass that the United States felt the need to put some of its chemical and biological warfare (CBW) expertise into the hands of other nations. As of 1969, some 550 students, from 36 countries, had completed courses at the US Army's Chemical School at Fort McClellan, Alabama. The students from at least one country, Egypt, reportedly put their education to use. In 1967 they helped plan poison gas attacks upon Yemen. According to the International Red Cross, some 150 villagers gagged, coughed and bled to death.

The CBW instruction was provided to the students under the guise of "defence" against such weapons, just as in Vietnam, as we have seen, torture was taught. As will be described in the chapter on Uruguay, the manufacture and use of bombs was taught under the cover of combating terrorist bombings.[30]

administered just before a public speech. There were also of course the more traditional approaches of gun and bomb, one being an attempt to drop bombs on a baseball stadium while Castro was speaking; the B-26 bomber was driven away by anti-aircraft fire before it could reach the stadium.[31] It is a combination of such Cuban security measures, informers, incompetence, and luck which has served to keep the bearded one alive to the present day.

Attempts were also made on the lives of Castro's brother Raul and Che Guevara. The latter was the target of a bazooka fired at the United Nations building in New York in December 1964.[32] Various Cuban exile groups have engaged in violence on a regular basis in the United States with relative impunity during a quarter of a century. One of them, going by the name of Omega 7 and headquartered in Union City, New Jersey, was characterized by the FBI in 1980 as "the most dangerous terrorist organization in the United States".[33] Attacks against Cuba itself began to lessen around the end of the 1960s, due probably to a lack of conclusive results combined with ageing warriors, and exile groups turned to targets in the United States and around the world.

During the next decade, while the CIA continued to pour money into the exile community, more than 100 serious "incidents" took place for which Omega 7 and other groups claimed responsibility. (Within the community, the distinction between a terrorist and a non-terrorist group is not especially precise; there is much overlapping identity and frequent creation of new names.) There occurred repeated bombings of the Soviet UN Mission, its Washington Embassy, its automobiles, a Soviet ship docked in New Jersey, the offices of the Soviet airline Aeroflot, with a number of Russians injured from these attacks; several bombings of the Cuban UN Mission and its Interests Section in Washington, many attacks upon Cuban diplomats, including at least one murder; a bomb discovered at New York's Academy of Music in 1976 shortly before a celebration of the Cuban Revolution was to begin; a bombing two years later of the Lincoln Center after the Cuban ballet had performed; a bomb explosion in luggage at JFK Airport about to be loaded on a flight to Los Angeles . . .[34] The single most violent act of this period was the blowing up of a Cuban Airlines plane shortly after it took off from Barbados on 6 October 1976, which took the lives of 73 people including the entire Cuban championship fencing team.[35]

Cuban exiles themselves have often come in for harsh treatment. Those who have visited Cuba for any reason whatever, or publicly suggested, however timidly, a rapprochement with the homeland, they too have been the victims of bombings and shootings in Florida and New Jersey. American groups advocating a resumption of diplomatic relations or an end to the embargo have been similarly attacked, as have travel agencies handling trips to Cuba and a pharmaceutical company in New Jersey which shipped medicines to the island. Dissent in Miami has been effectively silenced, while the police, city officials, and the media look the other way, when not actually demonstrating support for the exiles' campaign of intimidation.[36] In Miami and elsewhere, the CIA has long been employing exiles to spy on their countrymen, to keep files on them as well as on Americans who associate with them. Ostensibly carried out to uncover Castro agents, the tactic has had other obvious uses.[37]

Although there has always been the extreme lunatic fringe in the Cuban exile community (as opposed to the normal lunatic fringe) insisting that Washington has sold out their cause, over the years there has been only the occasional arrest and conviction of an exile for a terrorist attack in the United States, so occasional that the exiles can only assume that Washington's heart is not wholly in it. The exile groups and their key members are well known to the authorities, for the anti-Castroites have not excessively shied away from publicity. They continue to train openly in southern Florida and southern California; pictures of them flaunting their weapons appear in the press.[38] The CIA, with its countless contacts-cum-informers amongst the exiles, can fill in many of the missing pieces for the FBI and the police, if it wished to. In 1980, in a detailed report on Cuban-exile terrorism, *The Village Voice* of New York stated:

> Two stories were squeezed out of New York police officials . . . 'You know, it's funny,' said one cautiously, 'there have been one or two things . . . but let's put it this way. You get just so far on a case and suddenly the dust is blown away. Case closed. You ask the CIA to help, and they say they aren't really interested. You get the message.'
>
> Another investigator said he was working on a narcotics case involving Cuban exiles a couple of years ago, and telephone records he obtained showed a frequently dialed number in Miami. He said he traced the number to a company called Zodiac, 'which turned out to be a CIA front.' He dropped his investigation.[39]

In 1961, amid much fanfare, the Kennedy administration unveiled its showpiece programme, the Alliance for Progress. Conceived as a direct response to Castro's Cuba, it was meant to prove that genuine social change could take place in Latin America without resort to revolution or socialism. "If the only alternatives for the people of Latin America are the status quo and communism," said John F. Kennedy, "then they will inevitably choose communism."[40]

The multi-billion dollar Alliance programme established for itself an ambitious set of goals which it hoped to achieve by the end of the decade. These had to do with economic growth, more equitable distribution of national income, reduced unemployment, agrarian reform, education, housing, health, etc. In 1970, the Twentieth Century Fund of New York — whose list of officers reads like a Who's Who in the government/industry revolving-door world — undertook a study to evaluate how close the Alliance had come to realizing its objectives. One of the study's conclusions was that Cuba, which was not one of the recipient countries, had

> come closer to some of the Alliance objectives than most Alliance members. In education and public health, no country in Latin America has carried out such ambitious and nationally comprehensive programs. Cuba's centrally planned

economy has done more to integrate the rural and urban sectors (through a national income distribution policy) than the market economies of the other Latin American countries.[41]

Cuba's agrarian reform programme as well was recognized as having been more widesweeping than that of any other Latin American country, although the study took a wait-and-see attitude towards its results.*[42]

These and other economic and social gains — achieved despite the US embargo and the inordinate amount of resources and labour Cuba was obliged to devote to defence and security — served finally to still announcements of the collapse of the Cuban economy and the imminent downfall of Fidel Castro which were a regular feature of *Time* and other American publications throughout the 1960s.

This was but one aspect of what has been a relentless effort to disparage the Cuban government. The CIA and the State Department have counted that day lost in which one or the other did not add to the folklore, from the 1963 scheme to affix a Cuban connection to Lee Harvey Oswald, to the 1980s campaign to link the Cuban government to drug smuggling, mafia criminality, and international terrorism. Many other examples appear elsewhere in this book. In addition to its vast overseas journalistic empire, the Agency has maintained anti-Castro news-article factories in the United States for over two decades. The CIA has reportedly subsidized in Miami such publications as *Avance, El Mundo, El Prensa Libre, Bohemia* and *El Diario de Las Americas*, as well as AIP, a radio news agency that produced programmes sent free of charge to more than 100 small stations in Latin America. Two Agency fronts in New York, Foreign Publications, Inc. and Editors Press Service, also served as part of the propaganda system.[43]

Was it inevitable that the United States would attempt to topple the Cuban government? Could relations between the two neighbouring countries have taken a different path? Based on the American record of invariable hostility towards revolutionary governments, the answer would appear to be simply that there is no reason to believe that Cuba might have been an exception. Washington officials, however, were not immediately ill-disposed towards the Cuban Revolution; there were those who even expressed their tentative approval or optimism. This was evidently based on the belief that what had taken place in Cuba was little more than another Latin American change in government, the kind which had occurred with monotonous regularity for over a century, where the names and faces change but subservience to the United States remains fixed. (The fact that John Foster Dulles was dying of cancer at

---

* Though not amongst the stated objectives of the Alliance, there is another area of importance in which Cuba has stood apart from many of its Latin neighbours: there has been no torture, no legions of *desaparecidos*, no death squads.

this time did contribute to the atmosphere of tolerance. (Dulles left the State Department early in February 1959, a month after the revolution. One of his last acts was to withdraw the US military mission from Cuba.)

Then Castro revealed himself to be cut from a wholly different cloth. It was not to be business as usual in the Caribbean. He soon became outspoken in his criticism of the United States. He referred acrimoniously to the 60 years of American control of Cuba; how, at the end of those 60 years, the masses of Cubans found themselves impoverished; how the United States used the sugar quota as a threat. He spoke of the unacceptable presence of the Guantanamo base; and he made it clear enough to Washington that Cuba would pursue a policy of independence and neutralism in the cold war. It was for just such reasons that Castro and Che Guevara had forsaken the prosperous bourgeois careers awaiting them in law and medicine to lead the revolution in the first place. Compromise was not on their agenda; nor on Washington's, which was not prepared to live with such men and such a government; inevitably, "communist" became the description of choice when referring to Castro or his regime.

In April 1959, after meeting with Castro in Washington, Vice President Richard Nixon wrote a memo in which he stated that he was convinced that Castro was "either incredibly naive about Communism or under Communist discipline" and that the Cuban leader would have to be treated and dealt with accordingly. Nixon says that his opinion at this time was a minority one within the Eisenhower administration.[44] But before the year was over, CIA Director Allen Dulles had decided that an invasion of Cuba was necessary. In March of 1960, it was approved by President Eisenhower.[45] Then came the embargo, leaving Castro no alternative but to turn more and more to the Soviet Union, thus confirming in the minds of Washington officials that Castro was indeed a communist. Some speculated that he had been a covert Red all along.

If Castro had toned down his early rhetoric and observed the usual diplomatic niceties, but still pursued the policies of self-determination and socialism which he felt were best for Cuba (or inescapable if certain changes were to be realized), he could only have postponed the day of reckoning, and that not for long. Arbenz of Guatemala, Mossadegh of Iran, and many other leaders have gone out of their way to avoid stepping on Washington's toes unnecessarily, and have been much less radical in their programmes and in their stance toward the United States than Cuba; yet, nonetheless, all of them fell under the CIA axe.

In 1974, by way of marking 15 years of American hostility towards Cuba, Castro observed that "Cuba is the only country in the world where John Foster Dulles is still Secretary of State."[46]

31. Indonesia 1965
Liquidating President Sukarno . . . and 500,000 others

Armed with wide-bladed knives called *parangs*, Moslem bands crept at night into the homes of communists, killing entire families . . . Travellers . . . tell of small rivers and streams that have been literally clogged with bodies. River transportation has at places been seriously impeded.
Time, December 1965[1]

Nearly 100 Communists, or suspected Communists, were herded into the town's botanical garden and mowed down with a machine gun . . . the head that had belonged to the school principal, a P.K.I. [Communist Party] member, was stuck on a pole and paraded among his former pupils, convened in special assembly.
New York Times, May 1966[2]

Estimates of the total number of Indonesians murdered over a period of several years following an aborted coup range from 500,000 to one million.[3]

In the early morning hours of 1 October 1965, a small force of junior military officers abducted and killed six generals and seized several key points in the capital city of Jakarta. They then went on the air to announce that their action was being taken to forestall a *putsch* by a "Generals' Council" scheduled for Army Day, the fifth of October. The *putsch*, they said, had been sponsored by the CIA and was aimed at capturing power from President Sukarno. By the end of the day, however, the rebel officers in Jakarta has been crushed by the army under the direction of General Suharto, although some dissident army groups in other cities, engaged in supporting actions, held out for a day or two longer.[4]

Suharto — a man who has served both the Dutch colonialists and the Japanese invaders[5] — and his colleagues charged that the large and influential PKI was behind the coup* attempt, and that behind the party stood Communist China. The triumphant armed forces moved in to grab the reins of government, curb Sukarno's authority (before long he was reduced to little more than a

---

* The word "coup" is used for want of a better word to describe the venture of the junior military officers; it was not a coup attempt in the traditional sense of the word.

figurehead), and carry out a bloodbath to eliminate once and for all the PKI with whom Sukarno had obliged them to share national power for many years. Here at last was the situation which could legitimatize these long-desired actions.

Anti-Communist organizations and individuals, particularly Muslims, were encouraged to join in the slaying of anyone suspected of being a PKI sympathizer. Indonesians of Chinese descent as well fell victim to crazed zealots. The Indonesian people were stirred up in part by the display of photographs on television and in the press of badly decomposed bodies of the slain generals. The men, the public was told, had been castrated and their eyes gouged out by Communist women. The autopsies, however, revealed no such mutilations.[6]

What ensued was called by the *New York Times* "one of the most savage mass slaughters of modern political history"[7] . . . violence, wrote *Life* magazine, "tinged not only with fanaticism but with blood-lust and something like witchcraft."[8]

Though the massacre put an end to the well-organized PKI national organization, it did not put to rest the basic questions underlying the events of 1965, to wit:

Was there in actual fact a Generals' Council aiming to take over the government within a matter of days? A semi-official account of the whole affair published in Indonesia in 1968 denied the existence of the Council.[9] However, a study written and published by the CIA the same year confirmed that there was indeed a Generals' Council but that its purpose was only to plan how to protect itself from a purported plan of Sukarno to crush the army.[10]

What was the nature and extent, if any, of PKI involvement in the aborted coup? Did some members of the party know of the junior officers' plans in advance and simply lend moral support, or did they take a more active role? The semi-official account stated that the PKI's aim was not to seize political power for itself but to "prevent the army from eliminating the Party after Sukarno's death."[11] (Sukarno had suffered a kidney attack in August, although he quickly recovered. His part in the affair also remains largely a mystery.) The CIA study comes to a similar conclusion: "it now seems clear that the Indonesian coup was not a move to overthrow Sukarno and/or the established government of Indonesia. Essentially, it was a purge of the Army leadership . . ."[12]

What was the role, if any, of the CIA? Was the coup attempt instigated by an agent provocateur who spread the story of the Generals' Council and its imminent *putsch*? (The killing, or even the abduction, of the six generals probably could not have been foreseen — three of them were actually slain resisting abduction.)[13] Was PKI participation induced to provide the excuse for its destruction? There are, in fact, indications of an agent provocateur in the unfolding drama, one Kamarusaman bin Ahmed Mubaidah, known as "Sjam". According to the later testimony of some of the arrested officers, it was Sjam who pushed the idea of the hostile Generals' Council and for the need to counteract it. At the trials and in the CIA study, the attempt is made to establish that, in so doing, Sjam was acting on behalf of PKI leader Aidit — the obvious purpose behind the Agency taking the unique step of publishing such a book was clearly to assign responsibility for the coup attempt to the PKI so as to "justify" the horror which followed.

But Sjam could just as easily have been acting for the CIA and/or the generals in the same manner. He apparently was a trusted aide of Aidit and could have induced the PKI leader into the plot instead of the other way around. Sjam had a politically checkered and mysterious background, and his testimony at one of the trials, in which he appeared as a defendant, was aimed at establishing Aidit as the sole director of the coup attempt.[14]

The CIA, in its intimate involvement in Indonesian political affairs since at least the mid-1950s (cf. Indonesia, 1957-58 chapter), had undoubtedly infiltrated the PKI at various levels, and the military even more so, and was in a good position to disseminate disinformation and plant the ideas for certain actions, whether through Sjam or others.

The desire of the US government to be rid of Sukarno — a leader of the non-aligned and anti-imperialist movements of the Third World, and a protector of the PKI — did not diminish with the failure of the 1958 military uprising. Amongst the various reports of the early 1960s indicating a continuing interest in this end, a CIA memorandum of June 1962 is strikingly to the point. The author of the memo, whose name is deleted, was reporting on the impressions he had received from conversations with "western diplomats" concerning a recent meeting between President Kennedy and British Prime Minister Macmillan. The two leaders agreed, said the memo, to attempt to isolate Sukarno in Asia and Africa. Further, "They agreed to liquidate President Sukarno, depending upon the situation and available opportunities. (It is not clear to me [the CIA officer] whether *murder* or *overthrow* is intended by the word liquidate.)"[15]

Whatever was intended, Sukarno was now, for all practical purposes, eliminated as an international thorn in the flesh. Of even greater significance, the PKI, which had been the largest Communist Party in the world outside the Soviet bloc, had been decimated, its tattered remnants driven underground. It could not have worked out better for the United States and the new military junta if it had been planned.

If the generals had been planning their own coup as alleged, the evidence is compelling that the United States was intimately involved before, during and after the events of 1 October. One aspect of this evidence is the closeness of the relationship between the American and Indonesian military establishments which the United States had been cultivating for some years. President Kennedy, his former aide Arthur Schlesinger has written, was "anxious to strengthen the anti-communist forces, especially the army, in order to make sure that, if anything happened to Sukarno, the powerful Indonesian Communist Party would not inherit the country."[16]

Roger Hilsman, whose career spanned the CIA and the State Department, has noted that by 1963 . . .

one-third of the Indonesian general staff had had some sort of training from Americans and almost half of the officer corps. As a result of both the civic action project and the training program, the American and Indonesian military had come to know each other rather well. Bonds of personal respect and even affection existed . . .[17]

This observation is reinforced by reports of the House Committee on Foreign Affairs:

At the time of the attempted Communist coup and military counter-coup of October 1965, more than 1,200 Indonesian officers including senior military figures, had been trained in the United States. As a result of this experience, numerous friendships and contacts existed between the Indonesian and American military establishments, particularly between members of the two armies. In the post-coup period, when the political situation was still unsettled, the United States, using these existing channels of communication, was able to provide the anti-Communist forces with moral and token material support.[18]

When the average MAP [Military Assistance Program] trainee returns home he may well have some American acquaintances and a fair appreciation of the United States. This impact may provide some valuable future opportunity for communication as occurred in Indonesia during and immediately after the attempted Communist-backed coup of October 1965.[19]

The CIA, wrote the *New York Times*, was said "to have been so successful at infiltrating the top of the Indonesian government and army that the United States was reluctant to disrupt CIA covering operations by withdrawing aid and information programs in 1964 and 1965. What was presented officially in Washington as toleration of President Sukarno's insults and provocations was in much larger measure a desire to keep the CIA fronts in business as long as possible."[20]

Finally, we have the testimony of Secretary of Defense Robert McNamara before a Senate Committee in 1966:

Senator Sparkman: At a time when Indonesia was kicking up pretty badly — when we were getting a lot of criticism for continuing military aid — at that time we could not say what that military aid was for. Is it secret any more?

McNamara: I think in retrospect, that the aid was well justified.

Sparkman: You think it paid dividends?

McNamara: I do, sir.[21]

There are other statements which may be pertinent to the question of American involvement. Marshall Green, the US Ambassador to Indonesia at the time of the coup attempt, speaking in Australia in 1973 where he was then Ambassador, is reported as saying: "In 1965 I remember, Indonesia was poised at the razor's edge. I remember people arguing from here that Indonesia wouldn't go communist. But when Sukarno announced in his August 17 speech that Indonesia would have a communist government within a year [?], then I was almost certain . . . what we did we had to do, and you'd better be glad we did because if we hadn't Asia would be a different place today."[22]

James Reston. writing in the *New York Times* in 1966:

Washington is being careful not to claim any credit for this change [from Sukarno to Suharto] . . . but this does not mean that Washington had nothing to do with it. There was a great deal more contact between the anti-Communist forces in that country and at least one very high official in Washington before and during the Indonesian massacre than is generally realized. General Suharto's forces, at times severely short of food and munitions, have been getting aid from here through various third countries, and it is doubtful if the [Suharto] coup would ever have been attempted without the American show of strength in Vietnam or been sustained without the clandestine aid it has received indirectly from here.[23]

Neville Maxwell, Senior Research Officer, Institute of Commonwealth Studies, Oxford University:

A few years ago I was researching in Pakistan into the diplomatic background of the 1965 Indo-Pakistan conflict, and in foreign ministry papers to which I had been given access came across a letter to the then foreign minister, Mr Bhutto, from one of his ambassadors in Europe (I believe Mr J.A. Rahim, in Paris) reporting a conversation with a Dutch intelligence officer with NATO. According to my note of that letter, the officer had remarked to the Pakistani diplomat that Indonesia was 'ready to fall into the Western lap like a rotten apple'. Western intelligence agencies, he said, would organize a 'premature communist coup . . . [which would be] foredoomed to fail, providing a legitimate and welcome opportunity to the army to crush the communists and make Soekarno a prisoner of the army's goodwill'. The ambassador's report was dated December 1964.[24]

It should be remembered that Indonesia had been a colony of the Netherlands, and the Dutch still had some special links to the country.

Twenty years after General Suharto imposed his "New Order" upon Indonesia, the slaughter continues. Death squads roam at will, killing not only "subversives" but "suspected criminals" by the thousands.[25] The government administers the nation on the level of Chicago gangsters of the 1930s running a protection racket. Political prisoners overflow the jails. Torture is routine.[26]

The wiping out of the PKI became an inspiration to anti-communists the world over. Military leaders in Turkey, Thailand and elsewhere have spoken of following Indonesia's example. In Chile, before the coup which ousted Salvador Allende, "Jakarta, Jakarta" could be seen chalked on walls.[27]

And 100,000 more

In 1975 Indonesia invaded the former Portuguese colony of East Timor which lies at the eastern end of the Indonesian archipelago and which had proclaimed its independence after Portugal relinquished its control. Since that time, with the aim of forcibly annexing East Timor, Indonesian troops have killed well over

100,000 Timorese out of a population of between six and seven hundred thousand, with a level of atrocity equal to that carried out against the PKI in Indonesia itself. The invasion of 7 December 1975 — of which, said the *New York Times*: "By any definition, Indonesia is guilty of naked aggression"[28] — was launched the day after US President Gerald Ford and Secretary of State Henry Kissinger left Indonesia following a meeting with President Suharto. Columnist Jack Anderson later reported:

> By December 3, 1975, an intelligence dispatch to Washington reported that 'Ranking Indonesian civilian government leaders have decided that the only solution in the Portuguese Timor situation is for Indonesia to launch an open offensive against Fretilin [the leading East Timorese political/guerrilla movement].'
>
> But it was essential to neutralize the United States. For the Indonesian army relied heavily on U.S. arms which, under our laws, could not be used for aggression.
>
> As it happened, President Gerald Ford was on his way to Indonesia for a state visit. An intelligence report forewarned that Suharto would bring up the Timor issue and would 'try and elicit a sympathetic attitude.'
>
> That Suharto succeeded is confirmed by Ford himself. The United States had suffered a devastating setback in Vietnam, leaving Indonesia as the most important American ally in the area. The U.S. national interest, Ford concluded, 'had to be on the side of Indonesia.'
>
> Ford gave his tacit approval on December 6, 1975 . . . Five days after the invasion, the United Nations voted to condemn the attack as an arrant act of international aggression. The United States abstained. Thereafter, the U.S. delegate maneuvered behind the scenes to resist U.N. moves aimed at forcing Indonesia to give up its conquest.[29]

Since the invasion, US State Department officials, in statements to the press and in testimony before Congress, have consistently supported Indonesia's claim to East Timor and have downplayed the slaughter to a remarkable extent. Meanwhile, the omnipresent American military advisers, the training, the weapons, the helicopter gunships, and all the other instruments indispensable to efficient, modern counter-insurgency warfare, have been kept flowing into the hands of the Indonesian military. This may not be all, for Fretilin has reported on a number of occasions that American advisers have been directing and even participating in the combat.[30]

32. Ghana 1966
Kwame Nkrumah steps out of line

In October of the year 1965, Kwame Nkrumah, the President of Ghana, published his now-famous book, *Neo-Colonialism — The Last Stage of Imperialism*, dedicated to "the Freedom Fighters of Africa, living and dead". In the book, Nkrumah accused the CIA of being behind numerous setbacks and crises in the Third World and Eastern Europe. Nkrumah later wrote that "the American Government sent me a note of protest, and promptly refused Ghana $35 million of 'aid'."[1] Four months later he was overthrown in a CIA-backed military coup.

To be sure, the coup-makers — members of the Ghanaian army and police — had their own motivations. They were fearful of having their powers stripped from them by a suspicious Nkrumah who was building up his own private army, and they were intent upon furthering their individual professional careers and status. Within days, even hours, of the successful coup in February 1966, majors had become colonels and colonels had become generals. There was more than a touch of the Keystone Kops to the whole episode.

Kwame Nkrumah was a man who, during the Great Depression, had roamed Harlem, slept in the subway and lined up at Father Divine's soup kitchens. Later he was to be hailed as "Africa's brightest star", a leader in the call for an anti-imperialist, pan-African organization and an international non-aligned movement. But from all accounts, Nkrumah engaged in idiosyncratic, one-man rule and thought that socialism could be promoted by edict from above. And though he spoke out boldly against neo-colonialism, he was unable, ultimately, to keep Ghana from falling under the sway of the multinationals. When Nkrumah attempted to lessen Ghana's dependence on the West by strengthening economic and military ties to the Soviet Union, China and East Germany, he effectively sealed his fate.

The United States wanted him out. Great Britain, the former colonial power in Ghana when it was known as the Gold Coast, wanted him out. France and West Germany wanted him out. Those Ghanaians who carried out the coup suffered from no doubts that a move against Nkrumah would be supported by the Western powers.

At the time of the coup, the Soviet press charged that the CIA had been involved, and in 1972 *The Daily Telegraph*, the conservative London newspaper, reported that "By 1965 the Accra [capital of Ghana] CIA Station had two-score active operators, distributing largesse among President

223

Nkrumah's secret adversaries." By February 1966, the report continued, the CIA had its plans ready to end Nkrumah's regime: "The patient and assiduous work of the Accra CIA station was fully rewarded."[2]

It wasn't until 1978, however, that the story "broke" in the United States. Former CIA officer John Stockwell, who had spent most of his career in Africa, published a book in which he revealed the Agency's complicity. Shortly afterwards, the *New York Times*, quoting "first-hand intelligence sources", corroborated that the CIA had advised and supported the dissident Ghanaian army officers.

Stockwell disclosed that the CIA station in Accra "was given a generous budget, and maintained intimate contact with the plotters as a coup was hatched. So close was the station's involvement that it was able to coordinate the recovery of some classified Soviet military equipment by the United States as the coup took place."[3]

The CIA station had also proposed to headquarters in Washington that a small squad of paramilitary experts, members of the agency's Special Operations Group, be on hand at the moment of the coup, with their faces blacked, storm the Chinese Embassy, kill everyone inside, steal their secret records, and blow up the building to cover the fact.[4]

"This proposal was squashed," Stockwell wrote, "but inside CIA headquarters the Accra station was given full, if unofficial credit for the eventual coup, in which eight Soviet advisers were killed."[5] (The Soviet Union categorically denied that any of its advisers had been killed.)

Other intelligence sources who were in Ghana at the time of the coup have taken issue with Stockwell's view that the CIA deserved full credit for Nkrumah's downfall. But they considered the Agency's role to have been pivotal, and at least some officials in Washington apparently agreed, for the CIA station chief in Accra, Howard T. Bane, was quickly promoted to a senior position in the agency.[6]

"When he was successful," one of the *New York Times* sources said of Bane, "everyone in the African division knew it. If it had failed, he would have been transferred and no CIA involvement revealed."

Bane, nevertheless, was enraged by the CIA's high-level decision not to permit the raid on the Chinese Embassy, at the time the Peking government's only embassy in Africa. "They didn't have the guts to do it," he subsequently told an associate.[7]

After the coup, the CIA made a payment of "at least $100,000" to the new Ghanaian regime for the confiscated Soviet material, one item of which was a cigarette lighter that also functioned as a camera.[8]

The Ghanaian leaders soon expelled large numbers of Russians as well as Chinese and East Germans. Virtually all state-owned industries were allowed to pass into private hands. In short order the channels of aid, previously clogged, opened wide, and credit, food and development projects flowed in from the United States, the European powers, and the International Monetary Fund. Washington, for example, three weeks after the coup, approved substantial emergency food assistance in response to an urgent request from Ghana. (A food request from Nkrumah four months earlier had been turned down.)[9] One month later, the international price of cocoa — Ghana's economic lifeblood — had risen 14%.[10]

The CIA's reluctance to approve the action at the Chinese Embassy may have stemmed from the fact that the National Security Council had specifically refused to authorize the Agency's involvement in the coup at all. This was, as we have seen, not the first instance of the CIA taking American foreign policy into its own hands. On such occasions, the *modus operandi* calls for putting as little into writing as feasible, or keeping records out of official CIA files, thus making them immune to Freedom of Information disclosures or congressional investigations; technically the records do not exist, legally they can be destroyed at any time. This was the case with the Ghanian coup and may explain why more details of the CIA role have never been revealed.

33. Uruguay 1964 to 1970
Torture — as American as apple pie

"The precise pain, in the precise place, in the precise amount, for the desired effect."[1]

The words of an instructor in the art of torture. The words of Dan Mitrione, the head of the Office of Public Safety (OPS) mission in Montevideo.

Officially, OPS was a division of the Agency for International Development, but the director of OPS in Washington, Byron Engle, was an old CIA hand. His organization maintained a close working relationship with the CIA, and Agency officers often operated abroad under OPS cover, although Mitrione was not one of them.[2]

OPS had been operating formally in Uruguay since 1965, supplying the police with the equipment, the arms, and the training it was created to do. Four years later, when Mitrione arrived, the Uruguayans had a special need for OPS services. The country was in the midst of a long-running economic decline, its once-heralded prosperity and democracy sinking fast toward the level of its South American neighbours. Labour strikes, student demonstrations, and militant street violence had become normal events during the past year; and, most worrisome to the Uruguayan authorities, there were the revolutionaries who called themselves Tupamaros. Perhaps the cleverest, most resourceful and most sophisticated urban guerrillas the world has ever seen, the Tupamaros had a deft touch for capturing the public's imagination with outrageous actions, and winning sympathizers with their Robin Hood philosophy. Their members and secret partisans held key positions in the government, banks, universities, and the professions, as well as in the military and police.

225

"Unlike other Latin-American guerrilla groups," the *New York Times* stated in 1970, "the Tupamaros normally avoid bloodshed when possible. They try instead to create embarrassment for the Government and general disorder."[3] A favourite tactic was to raid the files of a private corporation to expose corruption and deceit in high places, or kidnap a prominent figure and try him before a "People's Court". It was heady stuff to choose a public villain whose acts went uncensored by the legislature, the courts and the press, subject him to an informed and uncompromising interrogation, and then publicize the results of the intriguing dialogue . . . *O Bailan Todos O No Baila Nadie*, went one of their slogans . . . Either everyone dances or no one dances.

Dan Mitrione did not introduce the practice of torturing political prisoners to Uruguay. It had been perpetrated intermittently from at least the early 1960s by the police. However, in a surprising interview given to a leading Brazilian newspaper in 1970, the former Uruguayan Chief of Police Intelligence, Alejandro Otero, declared that US advisers, and in particular Mitrione, had instituted torture as a more routine measure; to the means of inflicting pain, they had added scientific refinement; and to that a psychology to create despair, such as playing a tape in the next room of women and children screaming and telling the prisoner that it was his family being tortured.[4]

"The violent methods which were beginning to be employed," said Otero, "caused an escalation in Tupamaro activity. Before then their attitude showed that they would use violence only as a last resort."[5]

The newspaper story greatly upset American officials in South America and Washington. Byron Engle later tried to explain it all away by asserting: "The three Brazilian reporters in Montevideo all denied filing that story. We found out later that it was slipped into the paper by someone in the composing room at the *Jornal do Brasil*."[6]

Otero had been a willing agent of the CIA, a student at their International Police Services school in Washington, a recipient of their cash over the years, but he was not a torturer. What finally drove him to speak out was perhaps the torture of a woman who, while a Tupamaro sympathizer, was also a friend of his. When she told him that Mitrione had watched and assisted in her torture, Otero complained to him, about this particular incident as well as his general methods of extracting information. The only outcome of the encounter was Otero's demotion.[7]

Willian Cantrell was a CIA operations officer stationed in Montevideo, ostensibly as a member of the OPS team. In the mid-1960s he was instrumental in setting up a Department of Information and Intelligence (DII), and providing it with funds and equipment.[8] Some of the equipment, innovated by the CIA's Technical Services Division, was for the purpose of torture, for this was one of the functions carried out by the DII.[9]

"One of the pieces of equipment that was found useful," former *New York*

Times correspondent A.J. Langguth has written, "was a wire so very thin that it could be fitted into the mouth between the teeth and by pressing against the gum increase the electrical charge. And it was through the diplomatic pouch that Mitrione got some of the equipment he needed for interrogations, including these fine wires."[10]

Things got so bad in Mitrione's time that the Uruguayan Senate was compelled to undertake an investigation. After a five-month study, the commission concluded unanimously that torture in Uruguay had become a "normal, frequent and habitual occurrence", inflicted upon Tupamaros as well as others. Among the types of torture the commission's report made reference to were electric shocks to the genitals, electric needles under the fingernails, burning with cigarettes, the slow compression of the testicles, daily use of psychological torture . . . "pregnant women were subjected to various brutalities and inhuman treatment" . . . "certain women were imprisoned with their very young infants and subjected to the same treatment" . . .[11]

Eventually the DII came to serve as a cover for the *Escuadrón de la Muerte* (Death Squad), composed, as elsewhere in Latin America, primarily of police officers, who bombed and strafed the homes of suspected Tupamaro sympathizers and engaged in assassination and kidnapping. The Death Squad received some of its special explosive material from the Technical Services Division and, in all likelihood, some of the skills employed by its members were acquired from instruction in the United States.[12] Between 1969 and 1973, at least 16 Uruguayan police officers went through an eight-week course at CIA/OPS schools in Washington and Los Fresnos, Texas in the design, manufacture and employment of bombs and incendiary devices.[13] The official OPS explanation for these courses was that policemen needed such training in order to deal with bombs placed by terrorists. There was, however, no instruction in destroying bombs, only in making them; moreover, on at least one reported occasion, the students were not policemen, but members of a private right-wing organization in Chile (cf. chapter on Chile). Another part of the curriculum which might also have proved to be of value to the Death Squad was the class on Assassination Weapons — "A discussion of various weapons which may be used by the assassin" is how OPS put it.[14]

Equipment and training of this kind was in addition to that normally provided by OPS: riot helmets, transparent shields, tear gas, gas masks, communication gear, vehicles, police batons, and other devices for restraining crowds. The supply of these tools of the trade was increased in 1968 when public disturbances reached the spark-point, and by 1970 American training in riot control techniques had been given to some 1,000 Uruguayan policemen.[15]

Dan Mitrione had built a soundproofed room in the cellar of his house in Montevideo. In this room he assembled selected Uruguayan police officers for a demonstration of torture techniques. Another observer was Manuel Hevia Cosculluela, a Cuban who was with the CIA and worked with Mitrione. Hevia was later to write that the course began with a description of the human anatomy and nervous system . . .

> Soon things turned unpleasant. As subjects for the first testing they took beggars, known in Uruguay as *bichicomes*, from the outskirts of Montevideo, as well as a woman apparently from the frontier area with Brazil. There was no interrogation, only a demonstration of the effects of different voltages on the different parts of the human body, as well as demonstrating the use of a drug which induces vomiting — I don't know why or what for — and another chemical substance.
> The four of them died.[16]

In his book Hevia does not say specifically what Mitrione's direct part in all this was, but he later publicly stated that the OPS chief "personally tortured four beggars to death with electric shocks".[17]

On another occasion, Hevia sat with Mitrione in the latter's house, and over a few drinks the American explained to the Cuban his philosophy of interrogation. Mitrione considered it to be an art. First there should be a softening-up period, with the usual beatings and insults. The object is to humiliate the prisoner, to make him realize his helplessness, to cut him off from reality. No questions, only blows and insults. Then, only blows in silence.

Only after this, said Mitrione, is the interrogation. Here no pain should be produced other than that caused by the instrument which is being used. "The precise pain, in the precise place, in the precise amount, for the desired effect," was his motto.

During the session you have to keep the subject from losing all hope of life, because this can lead to stubborn resistance. "You must always leave him some hope . . . a distant light."

"When you get what you want, and I always get it," Mitrione continued, "it may be good to prolong the session a little to apply another softening-up. Not to extract information now, but only as a political measure, to create a healthy fear of meddling in subversive activities."

The American pointed out that upon receiving a subject the first thing is to determine his physical state, his degree of resistance, by means of a medical examination. "A premature death means a failure by the technician . . . It's important to know in advance if we can permit ourselves the luxury of the subject's death."[18]

Not long after this conversation, Manual Hevia disappeared from Montevideo and turned up in Havana. He had been a Cuban agent — a double agent — all along.

About half a year later, 31 July 1970 to be exact, Dan Mitrione was kidnapped by the Tupamaros. They did not torture him; they demanded the release of some 150 prisoners in exchange for him. With the determined backing of the Nixon administration, the Uruguayan government refused. On 10 August, Mitrione's dead body was found on the back seat of a stolen car. He had turned 50 on his fifth day as a prisoner.

Back in Mitrione's home town of Richmond, Indiana, Secretary of State William Rogers and President Nixon's son-in-law David Eisenhower attended the funeral of the city's former police chief. Frank Sinatra and Jerry Lewis came to town to stage a benefit show for Mitrione's family.

And White House spokesman, Ron Ziegler, solemnly stated that "Mr. Mitrione's devoted service to the cause of peaceful progress in an orderly world will remain as an example for free men everywhere."[19]

"A perfect man," his widow said.

"A great humanitarian," said his daughter Linda.[20]

The military's entry into the escalating conflict signalled the beginning of the end for the Tupamaros. By the end of 1972, the curtain was descending on their guerrilla theatre. Six months later, the military was in charge, Congress was dissolved, and everything not prohibited was compulsory. For the next eleven years, Uruguay competed strongly for the honour of being South America's most repressive dictatorship. It had, at one point, the largest number of political prisoners per capita in the world. And, as every human rights organization and former prisoner could testify, each one of them was tortured. "Torture," said an activist priest, "was routine and automatic."[21]

No one was dancing in Uruguay.

The film "State of Siege" appeared in 1972. It centred around Mitrione and the Tupamaros and depicted a Uruguayan police officer receiving training at a secret bomb school in the United States, though the film strove more to provide a composite picture of the role played by the US in repression throughout Latin America. A scheduled premier showing of the film at the federally-funded John F. Kennedy Arts Center in Washington was cancelled. There was already growing public and congressional criticism of this dark side of American foreign policy without adding to it. During the mid-1970s, however, Congress enacted several pieces of legislation which abolished the entire Public Safety Program. In its time, OPS had provided training for more than one million policemen in the Third World. Ten thousand of them had received advance training in the United States. An estimated $150 million worth of equipment had been shipped to police forces abroad.[22] Now, the "export of repression" was to cease.

That was on paper. The reality appears to be somewhat different.

To a large extent, the Drug Enforcement Administration (DEA) simply picked up where OPS had left off. The drug agency was ideally suited for the task, for its agents were already deployed all over Latin America and elsewhere overseas in routine liaison with foreign police forces. The DEA acknowledged in 1975 that 53 "former" employees of the CIA were now on its staff and that there was a close working relationship between the two organizations. The following year, the General Accounting Office reported that DEA agents were engaging in many of the same activities the OPS had been carrying out.

In addition, some training of foreign policemen was transferred to FBI schools in Washington and Quantico, Virginia; the Defense Department continued to supply police-type equipment to military units engaged in internal security operations; and American arms manufacturers were doing a booming business furnishing arms and training to Third World governments. In some countries, contact between these companies and foreign law enforcement officials was facilitated by the US Embassy or military mission. The largest of the arms manufacturers, Smith and Wesson, ran its own Academy in Springfield, Massachusetts, which provided American and foreign "public and industrial security forces with expert training in riot control".[23]

Said Argentine Minister Jose Lopez Rega at the signing of a US-Argentina anti-drug treaty: "We hope to wipe out drug traffic in Argentina. The guerrillas are the main drug users in Argentina. Therefore, this anti-drug campaign will automatically be an anti-guerrilla campaign as well."[24]

And in 1981, a former Uruguayan intelligence officer charged that US manuals were being used to teach techniques of torture to his country's military. He said that most of the officers who trained him had attended classes run by the United States in Panama. Among other niceties, the manuals listed 35 nerve points where electrodes could be applied.[25]

*   *   *   *   *   *

Philip Agee, after he left Ecuador, was stationed in Uruguay from March 1964 to August 1966. His account of CIA activities in Montevideo is further testimony to the amount of international mischief money can buy. Amongst the multifarious dirty tricks pulled off with impunity by Agee and his cohorts, the following constitute an interesting sample:[26]

A Latin American students conference with a leftist leaning, held in Montevideo, was undermined by promoting the falsehood that it was nothing more than a creature of the Soviet Union — originated, financed and directed by Moscow. Editorials on this theme authored by the CIA appeared in leading newspapers to which the Agency had daily access. This was followed by publication of a forged letter of a student leader thanking the Soviet cultural attaché for his assistance. A banner headline in one paper proclaimed: "Documents for the Break with Russia", which was indeed the primary purpose of the operation.

An inordinate amount of time, energy and creativity was devoted, with moderate success, to schemes aimed at encouraging the expulsion of an assortment of Russians, East Germans, North Koreans, Czechs, and Cubans from Uruguayan soil, if not the breaking of relations with these countries. In addition to planting disparaging media propaganda, the CIA tried to obtain incriminating information by reading the mail and diplomatic cables to and from these countries, tapping embassy phones, and engaging in sundry bugging and surreptitious entry. The Agency would then prepare "Intelligence" reports, containing enough factual information to be plausible, which then made their way innocently into the hands of officials of influence, up to and including the president of the republic.

Anti-communist indoctrination of secondary-level students was promoted by financing particular school organizations and publications.

A Congress of the People, bringing together a host of community groups, labour organizations, students, government workers, etc., Communist and non-Communist, disturbed the CIA because of the potential for a united front being formed for electoral purposes. Accordingly, newspaper editorials and articles were generated attacking the Congress as a classic Communist takeover/duping tactic and calling upon non-Communists to refrain from participating; and a phoney handbill was circulated in which the Congress called upon the Uruguayan people to launch an insurrectional strike with immediate occupation of their places of work. Thousands of the handbills were handed out, provoking angry denials from the Congress organizers, but, as is usual in such cases, the damage was already done.

The Uruguayan Communist Party planned to host an international conference to express solidarity with Cuba. The CIA merely had to turn to their (paid) friend, the Minister of the Interior, and the conference was banned. When it was shifted to Chile, the CIA station in Santiago performed the same magic.

Uruguay at this time was a haven for political exiles from repressive regimes such as in Brazil, Argentina, Bolivia and Paraguay. The CIA, through surveillance and infiltration of the exile community, regularly collected information on exiles' activities, associates, etc., to be sent to CIA stations in the exiles' homelands with likely transmission to their governments which wanted to know what these troublemakers were up to and which did not hesitate to harass them across frontiers.

"Other operations," wrote Agee, "were designed to take control of the streets away from communists and other leftists, and our squads, often with the participation of off-duty policemen, would break up their meetings and generally terrorize them. Torture of communists and other extreme leftists was used in interrogation by our liaison agents in the police."

The monitoring and harassment of Communist diplomatic missions by the CIA, as described above, is standard Agency practice throughout the Western world. This rarely stems from anything more than a juvenile cold-war reflex: making life hard for the commies. Looked at from any angle, it is politically and morally pointless. Richard Gott, the Latin America specialist of *The Guardian* of London, relates an anecdote which is relevant:

> In January 1967 a group of Brazilians and a Uruguayan asked for political asylum in the Czech embassy in Montevideo, stating that they wished to go to a Socialist country to pursue their revolutionary activities. They were, they said, under constant surveillance and harassment from the Uruguayan police. The Czech ambassador was horrified by their request and threw them out, saying that there was no police persecution in Uruguay. When the revolutionaries camped in his garden the ambassador called the police.[27]

34. Chile 1964 to 1973
A hammer and sickle stamped on your child's forehead

When Salvador Allende, a committed Marxist, came within 3% of winning the Chilean presidency in 1958, the United States decided that the next election, in 1964, could not be left in the hands of providence, or democracy.

Washington took it all very gravely. At the outset of the Kennedy administration in 1961, an electoral committee was established, composed of top-level men from the State Department, the CIA and the White House. In Santiago, a parallel committee of embassy and CIA people was set up.[1]

"U.S. government intervention in Chile in 1964 was blatant and almost obscene," said one intelligence officer strategically placed at the time. "We were shipping people off right and left, mainly State Dept. but also CIA, with all sorts of covers." All in all, as many as 100 American operatives were dedicated to the operation.[2]

They began laying the groundwork for the election years ahead, a Senate investigating committee has disclosed, "by establishing operational relationships with key political parties and by creating propaganda and organizational mechanisms capable of influencing key sectors of the population." Projects were undertaken "to help train and organize 'anti-communists'" among peasants, slum dwellers, organized labour, students, the media, etc.[3]

After channelling funds to several non-leftist parties, the electoral team eventually settled on a man of the centre, Eduardo Frei, the candidate of the Christian Democratic Party, as the one most likely to block Allende's rise to power. The CIA underwrote more than half the party's total campaign costs,[4] one of the reasons that the Agency's overall electoral operation reduced the American Treasury by an estimated $20 million,[5] much more per voter than that spent by the Johnson and Goldwater campaigns combined in the same year in the United States. The bulk of the expenditures went toward propaganda. As the Senate committee described it:

> In addition to support for political parties, the CIA mounted a massive anti-communist propaganda campaign. Extensive use was made of the press, radio, films, pamphlets, posters, leaflets, direct mailings, paper streamers, and wall painting. It was a 'scare campaign', which relied heavily on images of Soviet tanks and Cuban firing squads and was directed especially to women. Hundreds

of thousands of copies of the anti-communist pastoral letter of Pope Pius XI were distributed by Christian Democratic organizations. They carried the designation, 'printed privately by citizens without political affiliation, in order more broadly to disseminate its content.' 'Disinformation' and 'black propaganda' — material which purported to originate from another source, such as the Chilean Communist Party — were used as well.[6]

The scare campaign played up to the fact that women in Chile, as elsewhere in Latin America, are traditionally more religious than men, more susceptible to being alarmed by the spectre of "godless-atheist communism". One radio spot featured the sound of a machine gun, followed by a woman's cry: "They have killed my child — the communists." The announcer then added in impassioned tones: "Communism offers only blood and pain. For this not to happen in Chile, we must elect Eduardo Frei president."[7]

Other scare tactics centred around warnings of Russian control, and that the left would confiscate everything near, dear and holy.

The committee report continued:

The propaganda campaign was enormous. During the first week of intensive propaganda activity (the third week of June 1964), a CIA-funded propaganda group produced twenty radio spots per day in Santiago and on 44 provincial stations; twelve-minute news broadcasts five times daily on three Santiago stations and 24 provincial outlets; thousands of cartoons, and much paid press advertising. By the end of June, the group produced 24 daily newscasts in Santiago and the provinces, 26 weekly 'commentary' programs, and distributed 3,000 posters daily.[8]

One poster which appeared in the thousands showed children with a hammer and sickle stamped on their foreheads.[9]

Newspaper articles from elsewhere in Latin America which supported the political lines of the CIA campaign were collected and reprinted in Chile. Undoubtedly, many of these articles had been written in the first place by CIA stations in the particular countries. There were also endorsements of Frei solicited from famous personages abroad, advertisements such as a "messsage from the women of Venezuela",[10] and a vitriolic anti-communist radio broadcast by Juanita Castro, sister of Fidel, who was on a CIA-organized speaking tour of South America: "If the Reds win in Chile," she said, "no type of religious activity will be possible . . . Chilean mother, I know you will not allow your children to be taken from you and sent to the Communist bloc, as in the case of Cuba."[11]

The Senate committee revealed also that:

In addition to buying propaganda piecemeal, the [CIA] Station often purchased it wholesale by subsidizing Chilean media organizations friendly to the United States. Doing so was propaganda writ large. Instead of placing individual items, the CIA supported — or even founded — friendly media outlets which might not have existed in the absence of Agency support.

From 1953 through 1970 in Chile, the Station subsidized wire services, magazines written for intellectual circles, and a right-wing weekly newspaper.[12]

233

Of one subsidized newspaper, a State Department veteran of the campaign recalls that "The layout was magnificent. The photographs were superb. It was a Madison Avenue product far above the standards of Chilean publications."[13]

The same could be said about the electioneering itself. Besides running political action projects on its own in a number of important voting blocks, the CIA directed the Christian Democrats' campaign along American-style lines, with voter registration, get-out-the-vote drives, and professional management firms to carry out public opinion surveys.[14] To top it all off, they sent for a ringer — an election specialist from the staff of that eminent connoisseur and guardian of free elections, Mayor Richard Daley of Chicago. What the function of Daley's man in Chile was, can only be guessed at.[15]

Several of the grassroots programmes funded by the CIA were those run by Roger Vekemans, a Belgian Jesuit priest who arrived in Chile in 1957 and founded a network of social-action organizations, one of which grew to have 100 employees and a $30 million annual budget. By his own declaration in 1963, Vekemans received $5 million from the CIA as well as a like amount from AID to guide his organizations' resources in support of the Christian Democrats and Eduardo Frei, with whom Vekemans had close relations.[16] The Jesuit's programmes served the classic function of channelling revolutionary zeal along safe reformist paths. An extreme anti-communist, Vekemans was a front-line soldier in the struggle of the Christian Democrats and the Catholic Church against the "liberation theology" then gaining momentum amongst the more liberal clergy in Latin America and which would lead to the historic dialogue between Christianity and Marxism.[17]

The operation worked; it worked beyond expectations. Frei received 56% of the vote to Allende's 39%. The CIA regarded "the anti-communist scare campaign as the most effective activity undertaken", noted the Senate committee.[18] This was the tactic directed toward Chilean women in particular. As things turned out, Allende won the men's vote by a comfortable margin over Frei (in Chile men and women vote separately), but the women came out for Frei by a landslide[19] . . . testimony, once again, to the remarkable ease with which the minds of the masses of people can be manipulated, in any and all societies.

What was there about Salvador Allende that warranted all this feverish activity? What threat did he represent, this man against whom the great technical and economic resources of the world's most powerful nation were brought to bear? Allende was a man whose political programme, as described by the committee report, was to "redistribute income [two percent of the population received 46 percent of the income] and reshape the Chilean economy, beginning with the nationalization of major industries, especially the copper companies; greatly expanded agrarian reform; and expanded relations with socialist and communist countries."[20]

A man committed to such a programme, a man whose 27 years in public life were marked by principle and integrity, was a man, American policy-makers knew, who would lead his country along a path independent of the priorities of

US foreign policy and the multinationals. (As his later term as president confirmed, independent of any other country as well.)

The CIA is an ongoing organization. Its covert activities are ongoing, each day, in each country. Between the 1964 and 1970 presidential elections many of the programmes designed to foster an anti-Marxist mentality in different sections of the population continued; much of the propaganda and electioneering mechanisms remained in place to support candidates of the 1965 and 1969 Congressional elections; in the latter election, financial support was given to a splinter socialist party in order to attract votes away from Allende; this reportedly deprived Allende's Socialist Party of a minimum of seven Congressional seats.[21]

The Senate committee described some of the other individual covert projects undertaken by the CIA during this period:

> Wresting control of Chilean university student organizations from the communists;
>
> Supporting a women's group active in Chilean political and intellectual life;
>
> Combatting the communist-dominated *Central Unica de Trabajadores Chilenos* (CUTCh) and supporting democratic [i.e., anti-communist] labor groups;* and,
>
> Exploiting a civic action front group to combat communist influence within cultural and intellectual circles.[22]

"I don't see why we need to stand by and watch a country go communist because of the irresponsibility of its own people."[23]

Thus spoke Henry Kissinger, principal adviser to the President of the United States on matters of national security. The date was 27 June 1970, a meeting of the National Security Council's Forty Committee, and the people Kissinger suspected of imminent irresponsibility were the Chileans whom he feared might finally elect Salvador Allende as their president.

The United States did not stand by idly. At this meeting approval was given to a $300,000 increase in the anti-Allende "spoiling" operation which was already underway. The CIA trained its disinformation heavy artillery on the Chilean electorate, firing shells marked: "An Allende victory means violence and Stalinist repression."[24] Black propaganda was employed to undermine Allende's coalition and support by sowing dissent between the Communist Party and the Socialist Party, the main members of the coalition, and between the Communist Party and the CUTCh.[25]

---

* At the same time, a US Senate committee staff was concluding that the Latin American labour movement had largely abandoned its revolutionary outlook: "Even the Communist-dominated unions, especially those which follow the Moscow line, now generally accept the peaceful road as a viable alternative."

Nonetheless, on 4 September Allende won a plurality of the votes. On 24 October, the Chilean Congress would meet to choose between him and the runnerup, Jorge Alessandri of the conservative National Party. By tradition, Allende was certain of becoming president.

The United States had seven weeks to prevent him from taking office. On 15 September, President Nixon met with Kissinger, CIA Director Richard Helms, and Attorney-General John Mitchell. Helms' handwritten notes of the meeting have become famous: "One in 10 chance perhaps, but save Chile! . . . not concerned with risks involved . . . $10,000,000 available, more if necessary . . . make the economy scream . . ."[26]

Funds were authorized by the Forty Committee to bribe Chilean Congressmen to vote for Alessandri,[27] but this was soon abandoned as infeasible, and under intense pressure from Richard Nixon, American efforts were concentrated on inducing the Chilean military to stage a coup and then cancel the Congressional vote altogether.[28] At the same time, Nixon and Kissinger made it clear to the CIA that an assassination of Allende would not be unwelcome. One White House options paper discussed various ways this could be carried out.[29]

A fresh propaganda campaign was initiated in Chile to impress upon the military, amongst others, the catastrophe which would befall the nation with Allende as president. In addition to the standard communist horror stories, it was made known that there would be a cutoff of American and other foreign assistance; this was accompanied by predictions/rumours of the nationalization of everything down to small shops, and of economic collapse. The campaign did indeed adversely affect the Chilean economy and a major financial panic ensued.[30]

In private, Chilean military officers were warned that American military aid would come to a halt if Allende were seated.[31]

During this interim period, according to the CIA, over 700 articles, broadcasts, editorials and similar items were generated in the Latin American and European media as a direct result of Agency activity. This is apart from the "real" media stories inspired by the planted ones. Moreover, journalists in the pay of the CIA arrived in Chile from at least ten different countries to enhance their material with on-the-spot credibility.[32]

The following portion of an Agency cable of 25 September 1970 offers some indication of the scope of such media operations:

> São Paulo, Tegucigalpa, Buenos Aires, Lima, Montevideo, Bogota, Mexico City report continued replay of Chile theme materials. Items also carried in *New York Times* and *Washington Post*. Propaganda activities continue to generate good coverage of Chile developments along our theme guidance.[33]

The CIA also gave "inside" briefings to American journalists about the situation in Chile. One such briefing provided to *Time* enlightened the magazine as to Allende's intention to support violence and destroy Chile's free press. This, observed the Senate report, "resulted in a change in the basic thrust" of the *Time* story.[34]

When Allende criticized the leading conservative newspaper *El Mercurio* (heavily funded by the CIA), the Agency "orchestrated cables of support and protest from foreign newspapers, a protest statement from an international press association, and world press coverage of the association's protest."[35]

A cable sent from CIA headquarters to Santiago on 19 October expressed concern that the coup still had

> no pretext or justification that it can offer to make it acceptable in Chile or Latin America. It therefore would seem necessary to create one to bolster what will probably be [the military's] claim to a coup to save Chile from communism . . .

One of headquarters' suggestions was the fabrication of:

> Firm intel[ligence] that Cubans planned to reorganize all intelligence services along Soviet/Cuban mold thus creating structure for police state . . . With appropriate military contact can determine how to 'discover' intel[ligence] report which could even be planted during raids planned by Carabineros [the police].[36]

Meanwhile, the Agency was in active consultation with several Chilean military officers who were receptive to the suggestion of a coup. (The difficulty in finding such officers was described by the CIA as a problem in overcoming "the apolitical, constitutional-oriented inertia of the Chilean military.")[37] They were assured that the United States would give them full support short of direct military involvement. The immediate obstacle faced by the officers was the determined opposition of the Commander-in-Chief of the Army, Rene Schneider, who insisted that the constitutional process be followed. He would have to be "removed".

In the early morn of 22 October the CIA passed "sterilized" machine guns and ammunition to some of the conspirators. (Earlier they had passed tear gas.) That same day, Schneider was mortally wounded in an attempted kidnap ("kidnap") on his way to work. The CIA station in Santiago cabled its headquarters that the general had been shot with the same kind of weapons it had delivered to the military plotters, although the Agency later claimed to the Senate that the actual assassins were not the same ones it had passed the weapons to.[38]

The assassination did not avail the conspirators' purpose. It only served to rally the army around the flag of constitutionalism; and time was running out. Two days later, Salvador Allende was confirmed by the Chilean Congress.

The stage was set for a clash of two experiments. One was Allende's "socialist" experiment aimed at lifting Chile from the mire of underdevelopment and dependency and the poor from deprivation. The other was, as CIA Director William Colby later put it, a "prototype or laboratory experiment to test the techniques of heavy financial investment in an effort to discredit and bring down a government."[39]

Although there were few individual features of the latter which were unique for the CIA, in sum total it was perhaps the most multifarious intervention ever undertaken by the United States. In the process it brought a new word into the language: destabilization.

"Not a nut or bolt [will] be allowed to reach Chile under Allende", warned the then-American Ambassador Edward Korry before the confirmation.[40] The Chilean economy, so extraordinarily dependent upon the United States, was the country's soft underbelly, easy to pound. Over the next three years, new US Government assistance programmes for Chile plummeted almost to the vanishing point; similarly with loans from the US Export-Import Bank and the Inter-American Development Bank, in which the United States held what amounted to a veto; the World Bank made no new loans at all to Chile during 1971-73; US government financial assistance or guarantees to American private investment in Chile were cut back sharply and American businesses were given the word to tighten the economic noose.[41]

What this boycott translated into were things like the many buses out of commission in Chile due to a lack of replacement parts; the same with taxis; and similar difficulties in the copper, steel, electricity and petroleum industries. American suppliers refused to sell needed parts despite Chile's offer to pay cash in advance.[42]

ITT, which didn't need to be told what to do, stated in a 1970 memorandum: "A more realistic hope among those who want to block Allende is that a swiftly-deteriorating economy will touch off a wave of violence leading to a military coup."[43]

In the midst of the near disappearance of economic aid, and contrary to its warning, the United States increased its military assistance to Chile during 1972 and 1973 as well as training Chilean military personnel in the United States and Panama.[44] The Allende government, caught between the devil and the deep blue sea, was reluctant to refuse this "assistance" for fear of antagonizing its military leaders.

Perhaps nothing produced more discontent in the population than the shortages, the little daily annoyances when one can't get a favourite food, or flour or cooking oil, or toilet paper, bed sheets or soap, or the one part needed to make the TV set or the car run; or, worst of all, when a nicotine addict can't get a cigarette. Some of the scarcity resulted from Chile being a society in transition: various changeovers to state ownership, experiments in workers' control, etc. But this was minor compared to the effect of the aid squeeze and the practices of the omnipresent American corporations. Equally telling were the extended strikes in Chile which relied heavily on CIA financial support for their prolongation.[45] In October 1972, for example, an association of private truck owners instituted a work-stoppage aimed at disrupting the flow of food and other important commodities, including in their embargo even newspapers which supported the government (subtlety was not the order of the day in this ultra-polarized country); on the heels of this came store closures, countless petit-bourgeois doing their bit to turn the screws of public inconvenience — when they were open, many held back on certain goods to sell them on the black market to those who could afford the higher prices; then most private bus companies stopped running; on top of this, various professional and white-collar workers, largely unsympathetic to the government, walked out, with or without CIA help.

Much of this campaign was aimed at wearing down the patience of the public, convincing them that "socialism can't work in Chile". Yet there had been worse shortages for most of the people before the Allende government, shortages of food, housing, health care, and education, for example. At least half the population had suffered from malnutrition. Allende, who was a medical doctor, explained his free milk programme by pointing out that "Today in Chile there are over 600,000 children mentally retarded because they were not adequately nourished during the first eight months of their lives, because they did not receive the necessary proteins."[46]

Financial aid was not the CIA's only input into the strike scene. More than 100 members of Chilean professional associations and employers' guilds were graduates of the school run by the American Institute for Free Labor Development in Front Royal, Virginia — "The Little Anti-Red Schoolhouse". AIFLD, the CIA's principal Latin America labour organization, also assisted in the formation of a new professional association in May 1971: the Confederation of Chilean Professionals. The labour specialists of AIFLD had more than a decade's experience in the art of fomenting economic turmoil (or keeping workers quiescent when the occasion called for it).[47]

CIA propaganda merchants had a field day with the disorder and the shortages, exacerbating both by instigating panic buying. All the techniques, the whole of the media saturation, the handy organization created for each and every purpose, so efficiently employed in 1964 and 1970, were facilitated by the virtually unlimited license granted the press: headlines and stories which spread rumours about everything from nationalizations to bad meat and undrinkable water . . . "Economic Chaos! Chile on Brink of Doom!" in the largest type one could ever expect to see in a newspaper . . . raising the spectre of civil war, when not actually *calling* for it . . . alarmist stories which anywhere else in the world would have been branded seditious . . . the worst of London's daily tabloids or the *National Enquirer* of the United States appear as staid as a journal of dentistry by comparison.[48] In response, the severest measure taken by the government, on a few scattered occasions, was to close down a newspaper for two or three days.

The Agency's routine support of the political opposition was extended to include the extreme rightist organization *Patria y Libertad*, which the CIA reportedly helped to form, and whose members it trained in guerrilla warfare and bombing techniques at schools in Bolivia and Los Fresnos, Texas. *Patria y Libertad* marched in rallies in full riot gear, engaged repeatedly in acts of violence and provocation, and its publications openly called for a military coup.[49]

The CIA was engaged in courting the military for the same end. Providing military equipment meant the normal presence of US advisers and the opportunity for Americans to work closely with the Chileans. Since 1969, the

Agency had been establishing "intelligence assets" in the Chilean armed services. These assets could be found in all three branches of the military and included "command-level officers, field- and company-grade officers, retired general staff officers and enlisted men."[50] Employing its usual blend of real and fabricated information along with forged documents, the CIA endeavoured to keep the officers "on the alert". One approach was to convince them that, with Allende's approval, the police investigations unit was acting in concert with Cuban intelligence to gather information prejudicial to the army high command.[51]

Newspapers in Santiago supported by the CIA, particularly *El Mercurio*, often concentrated on influencing the military. They alleged communist plots to disband or destroy the armed services, Soviet plans to establish a submarine base in Chile, North Korea setting up a training base, and so forth. The papers stirred up hatred against the government in the ranks, and in some cases entire columns were published which were calculated to change the opinion of a single officer, in one case an officer's wife.[52]

The Agency also subsidized a number of books and other kinds of publications in Chile. One was a short-lived anti-government newsletter directed at the military.[53] Later the CIA made use of a weekly humour and political magazine, *SEPA*, aimed at the same audience. The cover of the 20 March 1973 issue featured the headline: "Robert Moss. An English Recipe for Chile — Military Control." Moss was identified by the magazine as a British sociologist. A more relevant description would have been that he was a "news" specialist associated with known CIA publication fronts. One of these, Forum World Features of London, published Moss's forgettable book *Chile's Marxist Experiment* in 1973 which was widely circulated by the junta to justify its coup.[54]

Moss was associated with a CIA-funded think-tank in Santiago which went by the supremely innocuous name of the Institute of General Studies. The IGS, amongst other activities, conducted seminars for Chilean military officers in which it was explained, in technical, apolitical terms, why Allende was a disaster for the economy and why a laissez-faire system offered a solution to Chile's ills. There is no way of measuring to what extent such lectures influenced future actions of the military, although after the coup the junta did appoint several IGS people to top government posts.[55]

The CIA's Santiago station was meanwhile collecting the operational intelligence necessary in the event of a coup: "arrest lists, key civilian installations and personnel that needed protection, key government installations which need to be taken over, and government contingency plans which would be used in case of a military uprising."[56] The CIA later asserted that this information was never passed to the Chilean military, a claim that does not give one the feeling of having been united with the probable. It should be noted in this context that in the days immediately following the coup the Chilean military went directly to the residences of many Americans living in Santiago who had been sympathetic to the Allende government.[57]

The government contingency plans were presumably obtained by the Agency through its infiltrations of the various parties which made up Allende's

Unidad Popular (UP) coalition. CIA agents in the upper echelons of Allende's own Socialist Party, *Time* magazine reported, were "paid to make mistakes in their jobs".[58] In Washington, burglary was the Agency's tactic of choice for obtaining documents. Papers were taken from the homes of several employees of the Chilean Embassy; and the embassy itself, which had been bugged for some time, was burgled in May 1972 by some of the same men who the next month staged the Watergate break-in.[59]

In March 1973, the UP won about 44% of the vote in Congressional elections, compared to some 36% in 1970. It was said to be the largest increase an incumbent party had ever received in Chile after being in power more than two years. The opposition parties had publicly expressed their optimism about capturing two-thirds of the Congressional seats and thus being able to impeach Allende. Now they faced three more years under him, with the prospect of being unable, despite their best and most underhanded efforts, to prevent his popularity from increasing even further.

During the spring and summer the destabilization process reached frantic levels: a whole series of demonstrations and strikes, with an even longer one by the truckers*, daily sabotage and violence, including assassination; in June, an abortive attack upon the Presidential Palace carried out by the military and *Patria y Libertad*.

In September the military prevailed. "It is clear," said the Senate committee, "the CIA received intelligence reports on the coup planning of the group which carried out the successful September 11 coup throughout the months of July, August, and September 1973."[61]

The American role on that fateful day was one of substance and shadow. The coup began in the Pacific coast port of Valparaiso with the dispatch of Chilean naval troops to Santiago. On this day ships of the US Navy were present offshore, ostensibly to participate in joint manoeuvres with the Chilean Navy. The American ships stayed out of Chilean waters, but remained on the alert. A US WB-575 plane — an airborne communications control system — piloted by US Air Force officers, cruised in the Chilean sky. At the same time, 32 American observation and fighter planes landed at the US air base in Mendoza, Argentina, not far from the Chilean border.[62]

In Valparaiso, US military officers were meeting with their Chilean counterparts. A young American, Charles Horman, who lived in Santiago and was stranded near Valparaiso by the coup, happened to engage in conversation with several Americans, civilian and military. A retired naval engineer told him: "We came down to do a job and it's done." One or two American military

---

* *Time* reported: "While most of the country survived on short rations, the truckers seemed unusually well equipped for a lengthy holdout." A reporter asked a group of truckers who were camping and dining on "a lavish communal meal of steak, vegetables, wine and empanadas" where the money for it came from. "From the CIA," they answered laughingly.[60]

men also gave away clues. A few days later, Horman was arrested in his Santiago residence. They knew where to find him. He was never seen again.[63]

Thus it was that they closed the country to the outside world for a week, while the tanks rolled and the soldiers broke down doors; while the stadiums rang with the sounds of execution and the bodies piled up along the streets and floated in the river; the torture centres opened for business; the subversive books were thrown to the bonfires; soldiers slit the trouser legs of women, shouting that "In Chile women wear dresses!"; the poor returned to their natural state; and the men of the world in Washington and in the halls of international finance opened up their cheque-books.

One year later, President Gerald Ford was moved to declare that what the United States had done in Chile was "in the best interest of the people in Chile and certainly in our own best interest."[64] The remark could have been punctuated with a pinch of snuff.

What the United States had done in Chile, thought Gerald Ford, or so he said, "was to help and assist the preservation of opposition newspapers and electronic media and to preserve opposition political parties."[65] The reporters present were kind, or obsequious, enough not to ask Ford what he thought of the junta's Chile where all opposition, of any kind, in any form, was forbidden.

It was of course *de rigueur* for some other officials and congressmen to assert that what the United States had really done in Chile was repel the Soviet threat to the Western hemisphere. But Soviet behaviour toward the Allende government simply did not tally with any such hypothesis; the language of US intelligence reports confirms that: "Soviet overtures to Allende . . . characterized by caution and restraint"; "Soviet desire to avoid" another Cuba-type commitment; Russians "advising Allende to put his relations with the United States in order . . . to ease the strain between the two countries."[66]

Much has been made of the corporate angle, particularly the nationalization of the US copper-mining companies without compensation (the *Unidad Popular* calculated that due to "excess profits" over many years the companies actually owed Chile money). But that decision was not announced until September 1971, a full year after the White House had decided to overthrow and/or assassinate Allende. The extent of Washington's true interest in the issue was revealed after the coup: in November 1973, the *Reuter* news agency reported that Orlando Saenz, one of the junta's main economic advisers, had said: "Now the Government of the US considers this is a problem for the American mining companies."[67] Moreover, before the coup, the CIA and other US government agencies were "counselling the White House to rebuff Allende's attempts to work out a settlement on the compensations to be paid for nationalized American property."[68]

A Washington official who followed Kissinger throughout the Chile policy put it succinctly: Kissinger, he said, "never gave a shit about the business community. What really underlay it was ideology."[69]

A CIA study of 7 September 1970, three days after Allende's electoral victory, concluded in part:

> The U.S. has no vital national interests within Chile.
> The world military balance of power would not be significantly altered by an Allende government.
> An Allende victory would represent a definite psychological set-back to the U.S. and a definite psychological advantage for the Marxist idea.[70]

Washington knows no heresy but independence. In the case of Salvador Allende independence came clothed in an especially provocative costume — a Marxist constitutionally elected who continued to honour the constitution. This would not do. It shook the very foundation stones upon which the anti-communist tower is built: the doctrine, painstakingly cultivated for decades, that "communists" can take power only through force and deception, that they can retain that power only through terrorizing and brainwashing the population. There could be only one thing worse than an elected Marxist — a *successful* elected Marxist.

35. Greece 1964 to 1974
"Fuck your Parliament and your Constitution," said the President of the United States

"It's the best damn Government since Pericles," the American two-star General declared.[1] (The news report did not mention whether he was chewing on a big fat cigar.)

The government, about which the good General was so ebullient, was that of the Colonel's junta which came to power in a military coup in April 1967, followed immediately by the traditional martial law, censorship, arrests, beatings and killings; the victims totalling some 8,000 in the first month. This was accompanied by the equally traditional declaration that the junta was acting to save the nation from a "communist takeover". Corrupting and subversive influences in Greek life were to be removed. Among these were miniskirts, long hair, and foreign newspapers; church attendance for the young would be compulsory.[2]

Then the torture began in earnest. So brutal and swift was the repression, that by September, Denmark, Norway, Sweden and the Netherlands were before the European Commission of Human Rights to accuse Greece of violating most of the Commission's conventions. Before the year was over, Amnesty International had sent representatives to Greece to investigate the situation. From this came a report which asserted that "Torture as a deliberate practice is carried out by the Security Police and the Military Police."[3]

The coup had taken place two days before the campaign for national elections was to begin, elections which appeared certain to bring the veteran liberal leader George Papandreou back as prime minister. Papandreou had been elected in February 1964 with the only outright majority in the history of modern Greek elections. The successful machinations to unseat him had begun immediately, a joint effort of the Royal Court, the Greek military, and the American military and CIA stationed in Greece.

Philip Deane (the pen name of Gerassimos Gigantes) is a Greek, a former UN official, who worked during this period both for King Constantine and as an envoy to Washington for the Papandreou government. He has written an intimate account of the subtleties and the grossness of this conspiracy to undermine the government and enhance the position of the military plotters, and of the raw power exercised by the CIA in his country.[4] We saw earlier how Greece was looked upon much as a piece of property to be developed according to Washington's needs. A story related by Deane illustrates how this attitude was little changed, and thus the precariousness of Papandreou's position: during one of the perennial disputes between Greece and Turkey over Cyprus, which was now spilling over on to NATO, President Johnson summoned the Greek Ambassador to tell him of Washington's "solution". The Ambassador protested that it would be unacceptable to the Greek parliament and contrary to the Greek constitution. "Then listen to me, Mr Ambassador," said the President of the United States, "fuck your Parliament and your Constitution. America is an elephant. Cyprus is a flea. Greece is a flea. If these two fleas continue itching the elephant, they may just get whacked by the elephant's trunk, whacked good . . . We pay a lot of good American dollars to the Greeks, Mr. Ambassador. If your Prime Minister gives me talk about Democracy, Parliament and Constitutions, he, his Parliament and his Constitution may not last very long."[5]

In July 1965, George Papandreou was finally manoeuvred out of office by royal prerogative. The king had a coalition of breakaway Centre Union Deputies (Papandreou's party) and rightists waiting in the wings to form a new government. It was later revealed by a State Department official that CIA Chief-of-Station in Athens, John Maury, had "worked in behalf of the palace in 1965. He helped King Constantine buy Center Union Deputies so that the George Papandreou Government was toppled."[6]

For nearly two years thereafter, various short-lived cabinets ruled until it was no longer possible to avoid holding the elections prescribed by the constitution.

What concerned the opponents of George Papandreou most about him was his son. Andreas Papandreou, who had been head of the economics department at the University of California at Berkeley and a minister in his father's cabinet, was destined for a leading role in the new government. He was by no means the wild-eyed radical. In the United States, Andreas had been an active supporter of such quintessential liberals as Adlai Stevenson and Hubert Humphrey.[7] His economic views, wrote *Washington Post* columnist Marquis Childs, were "those of the American New Deal".[8]

But Andreas Papandreou did not disguise his wish to take Greece out of the cold war. He publicly questioned the wisdom of the country remaining in NATO, or at least remaining in it as a satellite of the United States. He leaned toward opening relations with the Soviet Union and other Communist countries on Greece's border. He argued that the swollen American military and intelligence teams in Greece compromised the nation's freedom of action. And he viewed the Greek Army as a threat to democracy, wishing to purge it of its most dictatorial- and royalist-minded senior officers.[9]

Andreas Papandreou's notions were worse than his bite, as his later presidency was to amply demonstrate. (He did not, for example, pull Greece out of NATO.) But in Lyndon Johnson's Washington, if you were not totally and unquestioningly with us, you were agin' us. Johnson felt that Andreas, who had become a naturalized US citizen, had "betrayed America". Said LBJ:

> We gave the son of a bitch American citizenship, didn't we? He was an American, with all the rights and privileges. And he had sworn allegiance to the flag. And then he gave up his American citizenship. He went back to just being a Greek. You can't trust a man who breaks his oath of allegiance to the flag of these United States.[10]

What, then, are we to make of the fact that Andreas Papandreou was later reported to have worked with the CIA in the early 1960s? (He criticized publication of the report, but did not deny the charge.)[11] If true, it would not have been incompatible with being a liberal, particularly at that time. It was incompatible, as he subsequently learned, only with his commitment to a Greece independent from US foreign policy.

As for the elder Papandreou, his anti-communist credentials were impeccable, dating back to his role as a British-installed prime minister during the civil war against the left in 1944-45. But he, too, showed stirrings of independence from the Western superpower. He refused to buckle under Johnson's pressure to compromise with Turkey over Cyprus. He accepted an invitation to visit Moscow, and when his government said that it would accept Soviet aid in preparation for a possible war with Turkey, the US Embassy *demanded* an explanation. Moreover, in an attempt to heal the old wounds of the civil war, Papandreou began to reintroduce certain civil liberties and to readmit into Greece some of those who had fought against the government in the civil war period.[12]

When Andreas Papandreou assumed his ministerial duties in 1964 he was shocked to discover what is now a fact of life for every techno-industrial state in the world: an intelligence service gone wild, a shadow government with powers beyond the control of the nation's nominal leaders. This, thought Papandreou, accounted for many of the obstacles the government was encountering in trying to carry out its policies.[13]

The Greek intelligence service, KYP, as we have seen, was created by the OSS/CIA in the course of the civil war, with hundreds of its officers receiving training in the United States. One of these men, George Papadopoulos, was the leader of the junta that seized power in 1967. Andreas Papandreou found that the KYP routinely bugged ministerial conversations and turned the data over to the CIA.* Accordingly, he dismissed the two top KYP men and replaced them with reliable officers. The new director was ordered to protect the cabinet from surveillance. "He came back apologetically," recalls Papandreou, "to say he couldn't do it. All the equipment was American, controlled by the CIA or Greeks under CIA supervision. There was no kind of distinction between the two services. They duplicated functions in a counterpart relationship. In effect, they were a single agency."[14]

The Greek minister's order to abolish the bugging of the cabinet inspired the Deputy Chief of Mission of the US Embassy, Norbert Anshutz (or Anschuetz), to visit him. Anshutz demanded that Papandreou rescind the order. Andreas demanded that the American leave his office, which he did, but not before warning that "there would be consequences".[15]

Papandreou then requested that a thorough search be made of his home and office for electronic devices by the new KYP deputy director. "It wasn't until much later," says Andreas, "that we discovered he'd simply planted a lot of new bugs. Lo and behold, we'd brought in another American-paid operative as our No. 2."[16]

An endeavour by the younger Papandreou to end the practice of KYP's funds coming directly from the CIA without passing through any Greek ministry also met with failure, but he did succeed in transferring the man who had been liaison between the two agencies for several years. This was George Papadopoulos. The change in his position, however, appears to have amounted to little more than a formality, for the organization still took orders from him; even afterwards, Greek "opposition politicians who sought the ear (or the purse) of James Potts, CIA [deputy] chief in Athens before the coup, were often told: 'See George — he's my boy'."[17]

In mid-February 1967, a meeting took place in the White House, reported Marquis Childs, to discuss CIA reports which "left no doubt that a military coup was in the making . . . It could hardly have been a secret. Since 1947 the Greek army and the American military aid group in Athens, numbering several hundred, have worked as part of the same team . . . The solemn question was whether by some subtle political intervention the coup could be prevented" and thus preserve parliamentary government. It was decided that "no course of

---

* Many Western intelligence agencies have long provided the CIA with information about their own government and citizens, and the CIA has reciprocated on occasion. The nature of much of this information has been such that if a private citizen were to pass it to a foreign power he could be charged with treason.

action was feasible. As one of the senior civilians present recalls it, Walt Rostow, the President's adviser on national security affairs, closed the meeting with these words: I hope you understand, gentlemen, that what we have concluded here, or rather have failed to conclude, makes the future course of events in Greece inevitable."

A CIA report dated 23 January 1967 had specifically named the Papadopoulos group as one plotting a coup, and was apparently one of the reports discussed at the February meeting.[18]

Of the cabal of five officers which took power in April, four, reportedly, were intimately connected to the American military or to the CIA in Greece. The fifth man had been brought in because of the armoured units he commanded.[19] George Papadopoulos emerged as the *de facto* leader, taking the title of prime minister later in the year.

The catchword amongst old hands of the US military mission in Greece was that Papadopoulos was "the first CIA agent to become Premier of a European country". "Many Greeks consider this to be the simple truth," reported Charles Foley in *The Observer* of London.[20]

At the time of the coup, Papadopoulos had been on the CIA payroll for some 15 years.[21] Another reason for the success of their marriage may have been the colonel's World War II record. When the Germans invaded Greece, Papadopoulos served as a captain in the Nazi's Security Battalions whose main task was to track down Greek resistance fighters.[22] He was, it is said, a great believer in Hitler's "new order", and his later record in power did little to cast doubt upon that claim. Foley writes that when he mentioned the junta leader's pro-German background to an American military adviser he met at a party in Athens, the American hinted that it was related to Papadopoulos' subservience to US wishes: "George gives good value," he smiled, "because there are documents in Washington he wouldn't like let out."[23]

Foley relates that under Papadopoulos:

> intense official propaganda portrayed Communism as the only enemy Greece had ever had and minimised the German occupation until even Nazi atrocities were seen as provoked by the Communists. This rewriting of history clearly reflects the dictator's concern at the danger that the gap in his official biography may some day be filled in.[24]

As part of the rewriting, members of the Security Battalions became "heroes of the resistance".[25]

It was torture, however, which most indelibly marked the seven-year Greek nightmare. James Becket, an American attorney sent to Greece by Amnesty International, wrote in December 1969 that "a conservative estimate would place at not less than two thousand" the number of people tortured.[26] It was an odious task for Becket to talk to some of the victims:

> People had been mercilessly tortured simply for being in possession of a leaflet criticizing the regime. Brutality and cruelty on one side, frustration and helplessness on the other. They were being tortured and there was nothing to be done. It was like listening to a friend who has cancer. What comfort, what wise

reflection can someone who is comfortable give? Torture might last a short time, but the person will never be the same.[27]

Becket reported that some torturers had told prisoners that some of their equipment had come as US military aid: a special "thick white double cable" whip was one item; another was the headscrew, known as an "iron wreath", which was progressively tightened around the head or ears.[28]

The Amnesty delegation described a number of the other torture methods commonly employed. Among these were:[29]

a) Beating the soles of the feet with a stick or pipe. After four months of this, the soles of one prisoner were covered with thick scar tissue. Another was crippled by broken bones.

b) Numerous incidents of sexually-oriented torture: shoving fingers or an object into the vagina and twisting and tearing brutally; also done with the anus; or a tube was inserted into the anus and water driven in under very high pressure.

c) Techniques of gagging: the throat is grasped in such a way that the windpipe is cut off, or a filthy rag, often soaked in urine, is shoved down the throat; gags dipped in excrement were also used.

d) Tearing out the hair from the head and the pubic region.

e) Jumping on the stomach.

f) Pulling out toe nails and finger nails.

These were not the worst. The worst is what one reads in the many individual testimonies. But these are simply too lengthy to be repeated here.[30]

The junta's response to the first Amnesty report was to declare that it was comprised of charges emanating from "International Communism" and to hire public relations firms in New York and London to improve its image.[31]

In 1969, the European Commission of Human Rights found Greece guilty of torture, murder and other violations. The Council of Europe, a consultative body of 18 European states, under which the Commission falls, was preparing to expel Greece for these reasons and particularly for its abolition of parliamentary democracy. The Council rejected categorically Greece's claim that it had been in danger of a communist takeover. Amnesty International has reported that the United States, though not a member of the Council, actively applied diplomatic pressure on member states not to vote for the expulsion.* The European members, said Amnesty, believed that only the United States had the power to bring about changes in Greece, yet it chose only to defend the junta.[32] On the specific issue of torture, Amnesty's report concluded that:

* While the Council was deliberating, the *New York Times* (11 December 1969) reported that "The State Department said today that the United States had deliberately avoided taking any position on the question of continued Greek membership in the Council of Europe."

American policy on the torture question as expressed in official statements and official testimony has been to deny it where possible and minimize it where denial was not possible. This policy flowed naturally from general support for the military regime.[33]

As matters transpired, Greece walked out before the Council could formalize the expulsion.

In a world grown increasingly hostile, the support of the world's most powerful nation was *sine qua non* for the Greek junta. The two governments thrived upon each other. Said the American Ambassador to Greece, Henry Tosca, "This is the most anti-communist group you'll find anywhere. There is just no place like Greece to offer these facilities with the back up of the kind of Government you have got here." ("You", not "we", noted the reporter, was the only pretense.)[34]

The facilities the ambassador was referring to were dozens of US military installations, from nuclear missile bases to major communication sites, housing tens of thousands of American servicemen. The United States, in turn, provided the junta with ample military hardware despite an official Congressional embargo, as well as the police equipment required by the Greek authorities to maintain their rigid control.

In an attempt to formally end the embargo, the Nixon administration asked Papadopoulos to make some gesture towards constitutional government which the White House could then point to. The Greek prime minister was to be assured, said a secret White House document, that the administration would take "at face value and accept without reservation" any such gesture.[35]

US Vice-President Spiro Agnew, on a visit to the land of his ancestors, was moved to exalt the "achievements" of the Greek Government and its "constant co-operation with US needs and wishes".[36] One of the satisfied needs Agnew may have had in mind was the contribution made by the junta to the 1968 Nixon-Agnew election campaign. Apart from any other consideration, it was suspected that this was money given to the junta by the CIA finding its way back to Washington. A Senate investigation of this question was abruptly cancelled at the direct request of Henry Kissinger.[37]

Perhaps nothing better captures the mystique of the bond felt by the Greeks to their American guardians than the story related about Chief Inspector Basil Lambrou, one of Athens' well-known torturers:

Hundreds of prisoners have listened to the little speech given by Inspector Basil Lambrou, who sits behind his desk which displays the red, white, and blue clasped-hand symbol of American aid. He tries to show the prisoner the absolute futility of resistance: 'You make yourself ridiculous by thinking you can do anything. The world is divided in two. There are the communists on that side and on this side the free world. The Russians and the Americans, no one else. What are we? Americans. Behind me there is the government, behind the government is NATO, behind NATO is the U.S. You can't fight us, we are Americans.'[38]

Amnesty International adds that some torturers would tell their victims things like: "The Human Rights Commission can't help you now . . . The Red Cross can do nothing for you . . . Tell them all, it will do no good, you are helpless." "The torturers from the start," said Amnesty, "had said that the United States supported them and that was what counted."[39]

In November 1973, a falling-out within the Greek inner circle culminated in the ousting of Papadopoulos and his replacement by Col. Demetrios Ioannidis, Commander of the Military Police, torturer, graduate of American training in anti-subversive techniques, confidant of the CIA.[40] Ioannidis named as prime minister a Greek-American, A. Androutsopoulos, who came to Greece after the Second World War as an official employee of the CIA, a fact of which Mr Androutsopoulos had often boasted.[41]

Eight months later, the Ioannidis regime overthrew the government of Cyprus. It was a fatal miscalculation. Turkey invaded Cyprus and the reverberations in Athens resulted in the military giving way to a civilian government. The Greek nightmare had come to an end.

Much of the story of American complicity in the 1967 coup and its aftermath may never be known. At the trials held in 1975 of junta members and torturers, many witnesses made reference to the American role. This may have been the reason a separate investigation of this aspect was scheduled to be undertaken by the Greek Court of Appeals.[42] But it appears that no information resulting from this inquiry, if it actually took place, was ever announced. Philip Deane, upon returning to Greece several months after the civilian government took over, was told by leading politicians that "for the sake of preserving good relations with the US, the evidence of US complicity will not be made fully public".[43]

Andreas Papandreou had been arrested at the time of the coup and held in prison for eight months. Shortly after his release, he and his wife Margaret visited the American Ambassador Phillips Talbot in Athens. Papandreou related the following:

> I asked Talbot whether America could have intervened the night of the coup, to prevent the death of democracy in Greece. He denied that they could have done anything about it. Then Margaret asked a critical question: What if the coup had been a Communist or a Leftist coup? Talbot answered without hesitation. Then, of course, they would have intervened, and they would have crushed the coup.[44]

36. Bolivia 1964 to 1975
Tracking down Che Guevara in the land of *coup d'état*

Victor Paz Estenssoro was given a choice when he was overthrown by yet another Bolivian military coup. He could be taken — one of the officers told him — "either to the cemetery, or to the airport". The president opted to fly to Lima and exile.[1]

The man who led the coup in November 1964 and replaced Paz was none other than his vice-president, General René Barrientos Ortuño. It marked something like the 185th change of government (no one seems certain of the precise number) in Bolivia's 139 years of independence from Spanish rule, very few by elections.

Paz was unseated despite support from the American Ambassador Douglas Henderson, for it happened that both the CIA and the Pentagon wanted the president out. Barrientos, the former commander of the air force, had formed a close relationship with both institutions, primarily through the person of Col. Edward Fox, his "flying instructor and drinking companion"[2] dating back to the Bolivian's military-training days in the United States. The year 1964 found Fox in the Bolivian capital of La Paz working with the CIA, though listed officially as a military attaché.

Not surprisingly, Cuba was one of the sore points between the American colonel and the Bolivian president. Paz had directly opposed American policy by voting against Cuba's expulsion from the Organization of American States in 1962, by declining to join in on the OAS sanctions against the Castro government two years later, and by refusing to break diplomatic relations with Cuba. It was not until August 1964, when Bolivian-American relations were "just short of an open quarrel",[3] that Paz finally broke with the United States' *bête noire*. "It was a case of conforming or of facing a severe cut in United States aid", observed a *New York Times* editorial.[4]

The Bolivian government's attempts to attract economic aid and investment from countries other than the United States, such as the Soviet Union, Czechoslovakia and Yugoslavia were a further source of friction between the two countries. Here, too, the Bolivians eventually yielded.[5]

Although Fox and Ambassador Henderson were divided — deeply it has been said — on the question of Paz remaining in office,[6] both were uneasy about the political and economic power wielded by the tin miners and their leader Juan Lechín, the former vice-president who was an open candidate for Paz's job. The miners controlled their own area of the country; they had their own radio station and their own armed militia; they were intensely opposed to the military; and they were seen as a force potentially more radical than the president. A volatile four-month strike in the mines in mid-1963 which reached crisis proportion could only have served to ring the alarm bells louder in the American Embassy. The Minister of Mines under Paz, René Zavaleta Mercado, later wrote that "For over a year and a half, the American Embassy, in the form of Mr. Henderson, urged with almost weekly regularity that the army be sent to the mining zones, and threatened that otherwise [an American financial programme for the mines] would be suspended."[7]

Although Paz recognized the challenge to his own rule posed by the miners and Lechín, the likely political damage ensuing from an armed intervention was more than he was willing to risk.

The very existence of an army to send in owed more than a little to American efforts to rebuild the shattered Bolivian armed forces. In 1952 that rarity had occurred — an armed popular revolt had defeated the military, displaced the oligarchy, nationalized the tin mines, instituted land reform, and set up a new government under the *Movimiento Nacionalista Revolucionario*. The MNR reduced the military to a small, impotent and discredited force, at the same time fostering "people's militias". Decades of coups and other abuses had cut a wide swathe of anti-military sentiment across the Bolivian population. Despite the entreaties of certain segments of the left, however, the traditional armed forces were not completely dismantled. It proved to be a fatal error for the MNR and the country's fledgling democratic institutions.

Primarily to serve as a counterweight to the strength of the militias, and because of American pressure, both Paz and his predecessor had permitted, however reluctantly, the slow but certain rejuvenation of the military. Under US guidance, the Bolivian army became the first in Latin America to launch a "civic action" programme — building roads, schools, etc. — designed to improve its image amongst the population. The United States employed its potent economic leverage to spur a distinctly more favourable government policy towards the military,* one which allowed the US to "professionalize" the armed forces. More money followed, more recruits, new equipment . . . selected officers were sent to the United States for training . . . political indoctrination courses for officers given by MNR adherents and academics were allowed to lapse, and were replaced by indoctrination at the US School of the Americas in the Panama Canal Zone . . . by 1964, some 1,200 Bolivian officers and men had received training either in the United States or Panama, including 20 of the

---

* American manipulation and control of the Bolivian economy was too extensive and intricate to detail here. Suffice it to note the analysis of the *New York Times* written shortly after the coup: "No country in the Western hemisphere is more dependent on Washington's aid and nowhere has the United States Embassy played a more obtrusive role in establishing that fact."[8]

23 senior Army officers . . . the military had come a long way towards recouping its former size and efficiency, its prestige and its independence.[9]

The School of the Americas, observed the *Washington Post* in 1968, "counts so many important Latin officers as alumni . . . that it is known throughout Latin America as the 'escuela de golpes' or coup school".[10]

Whether the American motivation for reviving the military derived from a desire for an eventual military takeover is impossible to say. At a minimum, it evidenced a basic distrust of the Bolivian revolution with its potential for genuine independence from the United States; and, given the country's history, the culmination of the military process would appear to have been plainly inevitable. The Pentagon has long seen the military of Latin America as its natural partners, the proper "nation builders". This conviction was spelled out by Col. Truman F. Cook of the American military assistance mission in Bolivia in the foreword to a pamphlet on the use of the army in civic action programmes. In the pamphlet, published in Bolivia in 1964 and authored by Bolivian Lt. Col. Julio Sanjinés, a confidant of Pentagon and CIA officers, Cook wrote:

> the military organization is perhaps the only institution endowed with the organization, order, discipline, and self-sacrificing attitude towards objectives for the common good . . . Should political and economic institutions fail . . . then there is a real possibility that the military would move in against graft and corruption in government . . . [It is] naive to assume that they might not move to power in a classic sense.[11]

Another unknown is, at what point Barrientos and his co-conspirators actually decided to oust Paz. What is certain is: 1) the general's ascendancy to the office of vice-president was a crucial part of the process; 2) the role played by the CIA and the Pentagon in obtaining that office for Barrientos was *sine qua non.*

At the MNR's convention in January 1964, Paz sidestepped Barrientos, who had made his candidacy known, and chose a civilian, Frederico Fortún, to be his running mate. Barrientos proved to be a bad loser. He declared publicly that the nomination was a mistake and continued politicking, finally compelling the president to ask for his resignation as air force chief. The general was given one week in which to submit it.[12] A few days later, however, a scenario began to unfold which grabbed Barrientos from the edge of the abyss.

On the evening of 25 February, there supposedly took place a shooting attempt on Barrientos' life. Some accounts have the general near death, others "only wounded". In either event, it does appear rather incongruous that he was moved by military vehicle (twice according to one report) to the airport and then flown in a US Air Force plane to an American hospital in the Panama Canal Zone — 2000 miles away! No Bolivian doctor ever examined Barrientos.[13]

In the days following, while Barrientos was still in the hospital following a "lengthy operation", he was extolled as a national hero by the press in Bolivia. This was particularly the case with *El Diario*, an influential, conservative and strongly anti-Paz newspaper. According to the later testimony of a member of Barrientos' new cabinet, some of the newspaper's staff worked with the CIA.

Equally significant is the fact that one of *El Diario*'s board members was the aforementioned Lt. Col. Sanjinés. Sanjinés, a graduate of West Point, was an employee of the US Embassy, working on Alliance for Progress programmes. After the coup he was appointed minister of economics, later ambassador to Washington.[14]

The press coverage included the story that Barrientos' life was spared only because the bullet had struck the US Air Force silver wings which he wore on his uniform (against regulations). This became the "silver bullet" affair and great sympathy was generated for the courageous general. On top of this, notes one historian of Bolivia, the commander of the army and the political opposition "hinted publicly that Paz's police had been responsible for the alleged attack. Strong pressures from other high officers as well were exerted upon Paz to vindicate both himself and Barrientos by belatedly including the general on the ticket, and Paz felt he could not refuse."[15] Ten days after the mysterious incident, the president dumped Fortún, replaced him with Barrientos, and went on to re-election.

Barrientos himself has conceded that without the "silver bullet" (or "magic bullet" as others have dubbed it), he would never have become vice-president.[16] His eight months as candidate and as vice-president in office served, in turn, to tie up all the loose ends required for the military to return from 12 years in the political wilderness and stage their coup with a minimum of opposition; indeed, with a measure of support.

Barrientos' ascendancy furnished a distinct legitimacy to the military, and the general regularly used his platform to champion the armed forces and defend it against the deep-seated anti-militarism. He denounced the militias, called for their dissolution, and took the anomalous step of undermining the government of which he was the vice-president (or to be) by publicly reproaching the president and the MNR — particularly when they were critical of the military — and by throwing his support to anti-government groups. These tactics served to show up the president's weakness and succeeded in rallying to Barrientos' side many of the military officers who had been dubious about the wisdom or safety of re-entering the political arena and unsure of their own political muscle.[17]

It appears that little if anything further was heard of Barrientos' "injury", although during this period he "miraculously" escaped several other reported assassination attempts, including a bomb which blew up his car when no one was in it and another bomb which somehow found its way to under his bed. He used the latter occasion to declare that he "had more enemies within the MNR than in the ranks of the opposition".[18]

Paz Estenssoro had been "re-elected" because the opposition — claiming, amongst other things, unfair electoral procedure — had decided to abstain. Without pausing for breath, the masochistic, tangled mess that is Bolivian politics continued at his throat. Widespread discontent, arising from long-standing grievances and fuelled by a conflux of personal ambitions, erupted in a series of strikes, demonstrations and violent confrontations, with Barrientos lending his weight to the dissident elements, attacking the beleaguered president, and taking upon himself the role of the defender of order. In October, the vice-president withdrew to his home town and declared himself a rebel.

This period of public chaos and government crisis may have hastened the timing of the coup, at the same time convincing some still-reluctant officers who were disgusted by the constant civilian warfare. When the military finally made its move against Paz at the beginning of November it was not unwelcomed by various segments of the population.

Three years later, the *Washington Post*'s veteran Latin America correspondent John Goshko reported that Paz "still insists that Fox was behind his ouster. Among Bolivians with an awareness of politics, it is hard to find anyone who disagrees."[19]

René Barrientos pressed an unrelenting hard line against the miners. He inflicted upon them an extraordinary 50% cut in salary. Miners' boss Juan Lechín and other union and MNR leaders were ordered into exile and a principal labour confederation was banned. All Bolivian unions were directed to reorganize under guidelines designed to produce an apolitical labour movement.

Then the army moved in. Repeated invasions and occupations of the mining camps over a period of time were needed to pacify the ultra-militant miners. The fighting was bloody, 70 miners lost their lives in one raid alone — *La Noche de San Juan* as it came to be known.[20] The Revolution of 1952 had come to an end.

The United States was not a disinterested observer. In February 1966, Secretary of Defense Robert McNamara, presenting his department's regular "Assessment of the International Situation", told a Congressional committee: "Violence in the mining areas and in the cities of Bolivia has continued to occur intermittently, and we are assisting this country to improve the training and equipping of its military forces."[21]

This was all that the Defense Secretary had to report about Bolivia — a routine report, routinely delivered by the quintessential technocrat, as if the American action was the most natural thing in the world.

As natural as American financial contributions to Barrientos. Antonio Arguedas, Minister of the Interior under Barrientos, later disclosed that the CIA contributed $600,000 to the Bolivian leader in 1966 when he decided to hold an election. Other right-wing parties received lesser sums. Arguedas, an admitted agent of the CIA who, in 1968, gave the world Che Guevara's diary, claiming that the Agency had pushed him too hard, also revealed that Gulf Oil Corp. donated $200,000 to Barrientos' campaign as well as a helicopter for his tours around the provinces. (In 1969, Barrientos died in a crash of the same helicopter.) Gulf subsequently admitted that it had paid Bolivian officials, mainly Barrientos, a total of $460,000 in "political contributions" during the period 1966-69 at the CIA's recommendation, although the company may have needed but little prodding, for the Bolivian president had opened up the economy to multinationals to a greater degree than his predecessors, bestowing upon Gulf especially generous concessions.[22]

In the two years following the disappearance of Che Guevara from public view in early 1965, rumours had placed him at different times in the Dominican Republic, Brazil, Venezuela, Colombia, Peru, Chile, Guatemala, the Congo (which was true), China, Vietnam, and even New York, "always plotting revolution with some menacing and inscrutable bunch of desperados".[23] Word also had it that he had gone mad and was confined to an asylum somewhere, or that he had been imprisoned or executed by his erstwhile comrade-in-arms Fidel Castro for challenging Castro's authority. These latter stories or others like them may have been CIA handiwork. The Agency, ever inventive, had begun generating unfavourable press speculation about Guevara's disappearance as early as autumn 1965 in the hope that he would reappear in order to put an end to the tales.[24]

When evidence began to drift back to CIA headquarters in early 1967 that Che was leading a band of guerrillas in the southern mountains of Bolivia, there was understandable scepticism amongst some Agency officials. Nevertheless, obsessed as the CIA was with tracking down the legendary guerrilla, a multi-phased operation was put into motion. In April, American military supplies suitable for combatting guerrilla forces began to arrive in Bolivia: light arms, communication equipment, helicopters, etc. At the end of the month, a unit of 16 Green Berets was dispatched from Fort Gulick in the Panama Canal Zone to Bolivia to provide on-the-spot training in counter-insurgency tactics to a hand-picked battalion of Bolivian Rangers who had little or no experience in the real thing. The Green Berets had at their disposal a team of experts in communications, intelligence and reconnaissance work, and, before long, aerial photographs taken of approximately 23,500 square miles of southern Bolivia. This undertaking made use of an infra-red detection system, sensitive to thermal radiation rather than visible light, and as such could be employed at night and on cloudy days. The infra-red cameras were able to discriminate targets having less than one degree temperature difference with their background, thus picking up campfires, vehicles, even people. The guerrillas, however, rarely built fires or used vehicles.[25]

In La Paz, the CIA station informed Interior Minister Arguedas that it was sending him several "advisors" whose presence was required, it was stated, because of the ineffectiveness of Bolivia's intelligence services. A few days later, according to Arguedas, four Cuban exiles arrived and assumed their "advisory" positions in his ministry. One of them proceeded to set up two houses of interrogation where Bolivians suspected of aiding the guerrillas were brought for questioning. When Arguedas learned of this, and that in some cases the Cubans were resorting to torture, he was furious and demanded that the CIA put a stop to the operation.[26]

Other Cuban CIA agents were attached to the military high command and sent to the area of guerrilla fighting to collect detailed information from prisoners and peasants. This kind of investigation probably contributed more to locating the elusive Guevara than did the CIA's assortment of technological marvels, although the ultimate value of the Agency's role cannot be stated with any precision. What is clear, however, is that it was a case of overkill. Che's guerrilla movement never amounted to much of a threat. Barely more than 50 men and one woman at its peak, reduced to less than half that number at the end, the rebels could show to their credit only a scattering of skirmishes with the army. They had been largely ignored by the left and hardly swam like fish in the peasants' sea. "The inhabitants of this region," wrote Che in his diary, "are as impenetrable as rocks. You speak to them, but in the deepness of their eyes you can see that they do not believe you."

On 8 October 1967, Che Guevara was captured. The next day the Bolivian government ordered his execution in cold blood despite the vociferous objections of CIA men in the country who clung to the hope that Guevara would eventually talk openly about his sundry guerrilla adventures.

Following the death of René Barrientos in April 1969, Bolivia's statesmen soon reverted to their normal Byzantine convolutions. For a start, the vice-president who succeeded Barrientos lasted but five months before being ousted by General Alfredo Ovando Candía.

Ovando's long-held nationalist sentiments came to the fore. In his first month, he nationalized the Gulf Oil Corporation. The prevailing attitude toward the multinational, said Bolivian leaders, was that Gulf "constituted itself as a shadow government of vast powers over a poor land".[27]

The nationalization left Bolivia open, as the *New York Times* expressed it in December, to "the wrath of the United States" .

> Since the seizure, the United States, which has been the mainstay of Bolivia's economy for years, has indicated that further aid will not be forthcoming . . . Washington has not been impressed by Bolivia's offer to compensate Gulf for the property, which is valued at $140 million, about 50 per cent more than Bolivia's annual budget . . . Two Bolivian cabinet ministers interviewed this week said privately that the United States and Argentina were aware, as were most educated people in this capital, that well financed groups were plotting to overthrow the new Bolivian regime.[28]

This was followed by a dispatch from La Paz of Interpress Service (a major Latin American news agency) reporting that the United States was planning to bring down the Ovando government through economic strangulation.[29] Then, two days later, the government alerted the public about a conspiracy "that was being organized by the CIA in close collaboration with Gulf Oil and some Bolivian rightists."[30]

What fire all this smoke pointed to is not known. Ovando, who had walked the corridors of the Bolivian power structure for many years (it was he who had presented Paz with the choice of cemetery or airport), was no stranger to CIA intrigue in his country, and he may have seen the bright spotlight of publicity as the only means of forestalling his overthrow. This would also explain why, in January 1970, the government made it a point to announce the ordinary: that it had uncovered a CIA office in La Paz with radio transmission and bugging equipment.[31] The same month, Ovando also advocated a rapprochement with Cuba, and it looked like he and the CIA were on a collision course.

But then . . . it seems . . . someone got to Ovando with an offer he couldn't refuse. Slowly but surely, the president drifted to the right; amongst other indications: several anti-US student demonstrations were firmly put down by the police, nothing more was heard about Cuba, and Ovando removed General Juan José Torres as commander of the armed forces, a man highly regarded by most of the Bolivian left.[32] By September, matters had progressed to the point that State Department officials were publicly expressing concern that a deepening split between the Ovando government and its former leftist allies was on the brink of open showdown and might result in a communist government.[33]

Washington's information about the internal Bolivian struggle was not without substance. Two weeks later, a military revolt and power struggle erupted.

General Ovando was out. General Torres was in. Ovando had lasted one year.

Juan José Torres' ten months in office produced the archetypical Latin American political drama. In the opening act, Torres did all the things which make Washington officials see Red: he made overtures of friendship to Allende's Chile and Castro's Cuba; increased commercial ties with the Soviet Union; nationalized tin mines owned by American interests (the US responded by threatening to release large amounts of its tin stockpile onto the world market to deflate the international price); expelled the Peace Corps; and closed down the Inter-American Regional Labor Organization (ORIT, an important vehicle for CIA labour operations in Latin America); on top of all this, Torres indulged at times in Marxist rhetoric, talking of workers' and peasants' power and the like.[34]

Act Two brought on stage one Hugo Banzer, a Bolivian colonel with long and close ties to the American military establishment. He too had attended the *escuela de golpes* in Panama. Later there was further military training at Fort Hood in Texas; eventually, a posting to Washington as Bolivian military attaché. Along the way he picked up the Order of Military Merit from the United States government. Banzer was also reported to be one of the beneficiaries of Gulf Oil's largesse when he served in Barrientos' cabinet.

In January 1971, Col. Banzer led a coup attempt which led to nothing except his own exile to Argentina. The CIA in La Paz had known of Banzer's plan at least two weeks earlier, and had advised Washington of it.[35] Over the next six months, as Banzer and his military cohorts diligently plotted their next attempt to oust Torres, Banzer regularly crossed over the Argentine border into Bolivia where he was in close contact with US Major Robert Lundin, an adviser to the Bolivian Air Force School in Santa Cruz.[36]

Act Three, or the coup which succeeded, took place in August, a few days after Torres had announced an agreement with the Soviet Union for a major development of the Bolivian iron industry,[37] a few days before he was to meet with Salvador Allende to re-establish diplomatic relations with Chile.

When the plotters were in military control of Santa Cruz, a breakdown in their radio communications network caused a delay in rallying other Bolivian military units to their side. At this moment, Major Lundin stepped in to fill the breach by placing the US Air Force radio system at the rebels' disposal.[38]

How important this aid was to the success of the coup, which turned out to be very bloody, or what Lundin's role was otherwise, has not been determined.

One week later, the *San Francisco Chronicle* reported that the coup was "part of a far-reaching movement, backed by the U.S. Central Intelligence Agency (CIA) to seize power in a total of six South American republics. Although it has been officially denied, CIA money, training and advice was liberally given to the rebel strategists who masterminded [the] overthrow of Bolivia's leftist President Juan José Torres."[39]

In the finale, we find that the military-political front which took power was so far to the right that one of its parties called itself by the customary fascist designation "Falange", and that Banzer immediately announced that: his government would maintain very close relations with the United States, efforts to restore ties with Cuba and Chile would be abandoned, the trend toward nationalizations would halt, some already-completed nationalizations would be rescinded, the government would welcome private foreign investment, and all schools would be closed for at least four months because they were hotbeds of "political subversive agitation provoked by anarchists opposed to the new institutional order".[40] Before long, the government ordered the entire Soviet Embassy to leave the country, and Banzer eventually raised a foreign loan to pay Gulf Oil greatly increased compensation.

At the same time, the time-honoured scene known popularly as "reign of terror" was performed: within the first two years of the new regime, more than 2,000 persons were arrested for political reasons without being brought to trial, "all the fundamental laws protecting human rights were regularly violated", torture was "commonly used on prisoners during interrogation . . . beaten, raped and forced to undergo simulated executions . . . hung for hours with their hands tied behind their backs".[41]

By 1975, Catholic religious groups and clergy had taken upon themselves the dangerous burden of speaking out in defence of human rights in Bolivia. The Banzer government responded with a calculated and methodical campaign to divide the church, to isolate its progressive members, harass and censor them, and smear them as communists. Foreign priests and nuns, who made up the bulk of the country's clergy, were especially vulnerable to arrest and deportation. One of them, an American missionary from Iowa, Father Raymond Herman, was found murdered.

The CIA, it has been reported, assisted the Bolivian government in this endeavour by "providing full information on certain priests — personal data, studies, friends, addresses, writings, contacts abroad, etc.". The Agency, with its international data network, was particularly valuable concerning the foreign clergy.[42]

"I will observe the constitution," said Banzer, "whenever it does not contradict military decrees."[43]

"Since the formulation of the current Bolivian Government in August 1971," stated a report of the US Comptroller General's Office in 1975, "the objective of U.S. military assistance has been to provide stability and security. To assist in the objective, the United States provides materiel and training to develop adequate counter-insurgent forces."[44]

In 1978, Hugo Banzer was overthrown in yet another Bolivian coup. The new Bolivian strongman, former Air Force General Juan Pereda Asbun, announced, as Banzer had announced, that he was saving the nation from "international communism".[45]

37. Guatemala 1962 to 1980s
A less publicized "final solution"

> Indians tell harrowing stories of village raids in which their homes have been burned, men tortured hideously and killed, women raped, and scarce crops destroyed. It is Guatemala's final solution to insurgency: only mass slaughter of the Indians will prevent them joining a mass uprising.[1]

This newspaper item appeared in 1983. Very similar stories have appeared many times in the world press since 1966, for Guatemala's "final solution" has been going on rather longer than the more publicized one of the Nazis.

It would be difficult to exaggerate the misery of the mainly-Indian peasants and urban poor of Guatemala who make up three-quarters of the population of this beautiful land so favoured by American tourists. The particulars of their existence derived from the literature of this period sketch a caricature of human life. In a climate where everything grows, very few escape the daily ache of hunger or the progressive malnutrition . . . almost half the children die before the age of five . . . the leading cause of death in the country is gastro-enteritis. Highly toxic pesticides sprayed indiscriminately by airplanes, at times directly onto the heads of peasants, leave a trail of poisoning and death . . . public health services in rural areas are virtually non-existent . . . the same for public education . . . near-total illiteracy. A few hundred families possess almost all the arable land . . . thousands of families without land, without work, jammed together in communities of cardboard and tin houses, with no running water or electricity, a sea of mud during the rainy season, sharing their bathing and toilet facilities with the animal kingdom. Men on coffee plantations earning 20, or 50, cents a day, living in situations closely resembling concentration camps . . . looked upon by other Guatemalans more as beasts of burden than human. A large plantation to sell, reads the advertisement, "with 200 hectares and 300 Indians" . . . this, then, was what remained of the ancient Mayas, whom the American archaeologist Silvanus Morley had called the most splendid indigenous people on the planet.[2]

The worst was yet to come.

We have seen how, in 1954, Guatemala's last reform government, the legally-elected regime of Jacobo Arbenz, was overthrown by the United States. And how, in 1960, nationalist elements of the Guatemalan military who were committed to slightly opening the door to change were summarily crushed by the CIA. Before long, the ever-accumulating discontent again issued forth in a desperate lunge towards alleviation — this time in the form of a guerrilla movement — only to be thrown back by a Guatemalan-American operation reminiscent of the Spanish *conquistadores* in its barbarity.

In the early years of the 1960s, the guerrilla movement, with several military officers of the abortive 1960 uprising prominent amongst the leadership, was slowly finding its way: organizing peasant support in the countryside, attacking a military outpost to gather arms, staging a kidnapping or bank robbery to raise money, trying to avoid direct armed clashes with the Guatemalan military.

Recruitment amongst the Indian peasants (bearing in mind that the ethnic boundary between Indian and non-Indian is often blurred) was painfully slow and difficult; people so preoccupied with a daily struggle to stay alive are compelled to devote almost all their energy to that end; people so downtrodden hardly think they even have the right to resist; as fervent Catholics, they tend to believe that their misery is a punishment from God for sinning.

Some of the guerrilla leaders flirted with Communist Party and Trotskyist ideas and groups, falling prey to the usual factional splits and arguments. Eventually, no ideology or sentiment dominated the movement more than a commitment to the desperately-needed programme of land reform aborted by the 1954 coup, a simple desire for a more equitable society, and nationalist pride vis-à-vis the United States. *New York Times* correspondent Alan Howard, after interviewing guerrilla leader Luis Turcios, wrote:

> . . . though he has suddenly found himself in a position of political leadership, Turcios is essentially a soldier fighting for a new code of honor. If he has an alter ego, it would not be Lenin or Mao or even Castro, whose works he has read and admires, but Augusto Sandino, the Nicaraguan general who fought the U.S. Marines sent to Nicaragua during the Coolidge and Hoover Administrations.[3]

In March 1962, thousands of demonstrators took to the streets in protest against the economic policies, the deep-rooted corruption, and the electoral fraud of the government of General Miguel Ydigoras Fuentes. Initiated by students, the demonstrations soon picked up support from worker and peasant groups. Police and military forces eventually broke the back of the protests, but not before a series of violent confrontations and a general strike had taken place.

The American military mission in Guatemala, permanently stationed there, saw and heard in this, as in the burgeoning guerrilla movement, only the omnipresent "communist threat". As US military equipment flowed in, American advisers began to prod a less-alarmed and less-than-aggressive Guatemalan army to take appropriate measures. In May the United States established a base designed specifically for counter-insurgency training. (The Pentagon prefers the term "counter-insurgency" to "counter-revolutionary" because of the latter's awkward implications.) Set up in the north-east province of Izabal, which, together with adjacent Zacapa province, constituted the area of heaviest guerrilla support, the installation was directed by a team of US Special Forces (Green Berets) of Puerto Rican and Mexican descent to make the North American presence less conspicuous. The staff of the base was augmented by 15 Guatemalan officers trained in counter-insurgency at the US military school at Fort Gulick in the Panama Canal Zone.[4]

American counter-insurgency strategy is typically based on a carrot-and-stick philosophy. Accordingly, while the Guatemalan military were being taught techniques of ambush, booby-traps, jungle survival and search-and-destroy warfare, and provided with aircraft and pilot training, a programme of "civil action" was begun in the north-east area: some wells were built, medicines distributed, school lunches provided etc., as well as promises of other benefits made, all aimed at stealing a bit of the guerrillas' thunder and reducing the peasants' motivation for furnishing support to them; and with the added bonus of allowing American personnel to reconnoitre guerrilla territory under a non-military cover. Land reform, overwhelmingly the most pressing need in rural Guatemala, was not on the agenda.

As matters were to materialize, the attempt at "winning the hearts and minds" of the peasants proved to be as futile in Guatemala as it did in south-east Asia. When all the academic papers on "social systems engineering" were in, and all the counter-insurgency studies of the RAND Corporation and the other think-tanks were said and done, the recourse was to terror: unadulterated, dependable terror. Guerrillas, peasants, students, labour leaders, and professional people were jailed or killed by the hundreds to put a halt, albeit temporarily, to the demands for reform.[5]

The worst was yet to come.

In March 1963, Col. Enrique Peralta Azurdia seized power via a coup, ousting General Ydigoras. Peralta was reported at the time to have made discreet soundings as to what the American reaction would be before making his move.

The United States, which can discourage a coup in Latin America with a frown, gave the colonel at least its tacit approval because Ydigoras was planning to step down from the presidency in 1964, thus leaving the door open to an election. At the time, Ydigoras had given permission for the return to Guatemala of Juan José Arévalo who had led a reform government before Arbenz and still had a strong following. Like the Guatemalan army, Washington, including President Kennedy personally, believed that a free election would reinstate Arévalo to power in a government bent upon the same kind of reforms and independent foreign policy that had led the United States to overthrow Arbenz.[6]

The tone of the Peralta administration was characterized by one of its first acts: the murder of eight political and trade union leaders, accomplished by driving over them with rock-laden trucks.[7] Repressive and brutal as Peralta was, during his three years in power US military advisers felt that the government and the Guatemalan army still did not appreciate sufficiently the threat posed by the guerrillas, still were strangers to the world of unconventional warfare and the systematic methods needed to wipe out the guerrillas once and for all; despite American urging, the army rarely made forays into the hills.

Peralta, moreover, turned out to be somewhat of a nationalist who resented the excessive influence of the United States in Guatemala, particularly in his own sphere, the military. He refused insistent American offers of Green Beret troops trained in guerrilla warfare to fight the rebels, preferring to rely on his own men, and he restricted the number of Guatemalan officers permitted to participate in American training programmes abroad.

Thus it was that the United States gave its clear and firm backing to a civilian, one Julio Cesar Mendez Montenegro, in the election held in March 1966. Mendez won the election, that is, what passes for an election in Guatemala, and committed his regime to something approaching the final solution while granting the United States the free hand it had been chafing at the bit for. He served another important function for the United States: as a civilian, and one with genuine liberal credentials, Mendez could be pointed to by the Johnson administration as a response to human-rights critics at home.

However, whatever social conscience Julio Cesar Mendez may have harboured deep within, he was largely a captive of the Guatemalan army, and his administration far exceeded Peralta's in its cruelty. Yet the army did not trust this former law school professor — in the rarefied atmosphere of Guatemala, some military men regarded him as a communist — and on at least two occasions, the United States had to intervene to stifle a coup attempt against him.

Within days after Mendez took office in July, US Col. John D. Webber, Jr. arrived in Guatemala to take command of the American military mission. *Time* magazine later described his role:

> Webber immediately expanded counterinsurgency training within Guatemala's 5,000-man army, brought in U.S. Jeeps, trucks, communications equipment and helicopters to give the army more firepower and mobility, and breathed new life into the army's civic-action program. Towards the end of 1966 the army was able to launch a major drive against the guerrilla strongholds . . . To aid in the drive,

the army also hired and armed local bands of 'civilian collaborators' licensed to kill peasants whom they considered guerrillas or 'potential' guerrillas. There were those who doubted the wisdom of encouraging such measures in violence-prone Guatemala, but Webber was not among them. 'That's the way this country is,' he said. 'The communists are using everything they have including terror. And it must be met.'[8]

The last was for home consumption. There was never any comparison between the two sides as to the quantity and cruelty of their terror, as well as in the choice of targets; with rare exceptions, the left attacked only legitimate political and military enemies, clear and culpable symbols of their foe;* and they did not torture, nor take vengeance against the families of their enemies.

In the period October 1966 to March 1968, Amnesty International estimated, somewhere between 3,000 and 8,000 Guatemalans were killed by the police, the military, right-wing "death squads" (often the police or military in civilian clothes, carrying out atrocities too bloody for the government to claim credit for), and assorted groups of civilian anti-communist vigilantes. By 1972, the number of their victims was estimated at 13,000. Four years later the count exceeded 20,000, murdered or disappeared without a trace.

Anyone attempting to organize a union or other undertaking to improve the lot of the peasants, or simply suspected of being in support of the guerrillas, was subject . . . unknown, armed men broke into their homes and dragged them away to unknown places . . . their tortured or mutilated or burned bodies found buried in a mass grave, or floating in plastic bags in a lake or river, or lying beside the road, hands tied behind the back . . . bodies dropped into the Pacific from airplanes. In the Gualán area, it was said, no one fished any more; too many corpses were caught in the nets . . . decapitated corpses, or castrated, or pins stuck in the eyes . . . a village rounded up, suspected of supplying the guerrillas with men or food or information, all adult males taken away in front of their families, never to be seen again . . . or everyone massacred, the village bulldozed over to cover the traces . . . seldom were the victims actual members of a guerrilla band.

One method of torture consisted of putting a hood filled with insecticide over the head of the victim; there was also electric shock — to the genital area is the most effective; in those days it was administered by using military field telephones hooked up to small generators; the United States supplied the equipment and the instructions for use to several countries, including South Vietnam where the large-scale counter-insurgency operation was producing new methods and devices for extracting information from uncooperative prisoners; some of these techniques were finding their way to Latin America.[10]

---

* Two of whom were John Webber and the US naval attaché, assassinated in January 1968; a bulletin later issued by a guerrilla group stated that the assassination had "brought to justice the Yanqui officers who were teaching tactics to the Guatemalan army for its war against the people".[9]

The Green Berets taught their Guatemalan trainees various methods of "interrogation", but they were not solely classroom warriors. Their presence in the countryside was reported frequently, accompanying Guatemalan soldiers into battle areas; the line separating the advisory role from the combat role is often a matter of public relations.

Thomas and Marjorie Melville, American Catholic missionaries in Guatemala from the mid-1950s until the end of 1967, have written that Col. Webber "made no secret of the fact that it was his idea and at his instigation that the technique of counter-terror had been implemented by the Guatemalan Army in the Zacapa and Izabal areas."[11] The Melvilles wrote also of Major Bernard Westfall of Iowa City who:

> perished in September 1967 in the crash of a Guatemalan Air Force jet that he was piloting alone. The official notices stated that the US airman was 'testing' the aeroplane. That statement may have been true, but it is also true that it was a common and public topic of conversation at Guatemala's La Aurora air base that the Major often 'tested' Guatemalan aircraft in strafing and bombing runs against guerrilla encampments in the Northeastern territory.[12]

F-51(D) fighter planes modified by the United States for use against guerrillas in Guatemala . . . after modification, the planes are capable of patrolling for five hours over a limited area . . . equipped with six .50-calibre machine guns and wing mountings for bombs, napalm and 5-inch air-to-ground rockets.[13] The napalm falls on villages, on scarce crops, on people . . . American pilots take off from Panama, deliver loads of napalm on targets suspected of being guerrilla refuges, and return to Panama[14] . . . the napalm explodes like fireworks and a mass of brilliant red foam spreads over the land, incinerating all that falls in its way, cedars and pines are burned down to the roots, animals grilled, the earth scorched . . . the guerrillas will not have this place for a sanctuary any longer, nor will they or anyone else derive food from it . . . halfway around the world in Vietnam, there is an instant replay.

In Vietnam they were called "free-fire zones"; in Guatemala, "*zona libres*": "Large areas of the country have been declared off limits and then subjected to heavy bombing. Reconnaissance planes using advanced photographic techniques fly over suspected guerrilla country and jet planes, assigned to specific areas, can be called in within minutes to kill anything that moves on the ground."[15]

In Guatemala City, right-wing terrorists machine-gunned people and houses in full light of day . . . journalists, lawyers, students, teachers, trade unionists, members of opposition parties, anyone who helped or expressed sympathy for the rebel cause, anyone with a vaguely-leftist political association or a moderate criticism of government policy . . . relatives of the victims, guilty of kinship . . . common criminals, eliminated to purify the society, taken from jails and shot. "See a Communist, kill a Communist", the slogan of the New Anticommunist Organization . . . an informer with hooded face accompanies the police along a city street or into the countryside, pointing people out, who shall live and who shall die . . . "this one's a son of a bitch" . . . "that one . . ." . . . men found dead with their eyes gouged out, their testicles in their mouth, without hands or tongues, women with breasts cut off . . . there is rarely a witness to a killing, even when people are dragged from their homes at high noon and executed in the street . . . a relative will choose exile rather than take the matter to the authorities . . . the government joins the family in mourning the victim . . .[16]

One of the death squads, *Mano Blanca* (White Hand), sent a death warning to a student leader. American Maryknoll priest Blase Bonpane has written:

I went alone to visit the head of the Mano Blanca and asked him why he was going to kill this lad. At first he denied sending the letter, but after a bit of discussion with him and his first assistant, the assistant said, 'Well, I know he's a Communist and so we're going to kill him.'

'How do you know?' I asked.

He said, 'I know he's a Communist because I heard him say he would give his life for the poor.'[17]

Mano Blanca distributed leaflets in residential areas suggesting that doors of left-wingers be marked with a black cross.[18]

In November 1967, when the American Ambassador, John Gordon Mein, presented the Guatemalan armed forces with new armoured vehicles, grenade launchers, training and radio equipment, and several HU-1B jet powered helicopters, he publicly stated:

These articles, especially the helicopters, are not easy to obtain at this time since they are being utilized by our forces in defense of the cause of liberty in other parts of the world [i.e., southeast Asia]. But liberty must be defended wherever it is threatened and that liberty is now being threatened in Guatemala.[19]

In August 1968, a young French woman, Michele Kirk, shot herself in Guatemala City as the police came to her room to make "inquiries". In her notebook Michele had written:

It is hard to find the words to express the state of putrefaction that exists in Guatemala, and the permanent terror in which the inhabitants live. Every day bodies are pulled out of the Motagua River, riddled with bullets and partially eaten by fish. Every day men are kidnapped right in the street by unidentified people in cars, armed to the teeth, with no intervention by the police patrols.[20]

The US Agency for International Development (AID), its Office of Public Safety (OPS), and the Alliance for Progress were all there to lend a helping hand.*

---

* "At one time, many AID field offices were infiltrated from top to bottom with CIA people . . . The idea was to plant operatives in every kind of activity we had overseas, government, volunteer, religious, every kind." — John Gilligan, Director of AID during the Carter administration.[21]

These organizations with their reassuring names all contributed to a programme to greatly expand the size of Guatemala's national police force and develop it into a professionalized body skilled at counteracting urban disorder. Senior police officers and technicians were sent for training at the International Police Academy in Washington, a Federal School in Los Fresnos, Texas (where they were taught how to construct and use a variety of explosive devices — cf. Uruguay chapter), and other educational establishments, their instructors often being CIA officers operating under OPS cover. This was also the case with OPS officers stationed in Guatemala to advise local police commands and provide in-country training for rank-and-file policemen. At times, these officers participated directly in interrogating political prisoners, took part in polygraph operations, and accompanied the police on anti-drug patrols.

Additionally, the Guatemala City police force was completely supplied with radio patrol cars and a radio communications network, and funds were provided to build a national police academy and pay for salaries, uniforms, weapons, and riot-control equipment.

The glue which held this package together was the standard OPS classroom tutelage, similar to that given the military, which imparted the insight that "communists", primarily of the Cuban variety, were behind all the unrest in Guatemala, and the advice to "stay out of politics", that is, support whatever pro-US regime happens to be in power.

Also standard was the advice to use "minimum force" and to cultivate good community relations. But the behaviour of the police and military students in practice was so far removed from this that continued American involvement with these forces over a period of decades makes this advice appear to be little more than a self-serving statement for the record, the familiar bureaucratic maxim: cover your ass.[22]

By 1970, over 30,000 Guatemalan police personnel had received CIA/OPS training either at the Inter-American Police Academy in Panama, or in Washington at the International Police Academy which replaced the Panama school in 1964.[23]

By the end of 1968, the counter-insurgency campaign had all but wiped out the guerrilla movement by thwarting the rebels' ability to operate openly and casually in rural areas as they had been accustomed to, and, through sheer terrorization of villagers, isolating the guerrillas from their bases of support in the countryside.

It had been an unequal match. By Pentagon standards it had been a "limited" war, due to the absence of a large and overt US combat force. At the same time, this had provided the American people with the illusion of their country's non-involvement. However, as one observer has noted: "In the lexicon of counterrevolutionaries, these wars are 'limited' only in their consequences for the intervening power. For the people and country under assault, they are total."[24]

Over the ensuing few years, some of Guatemala's revolutionaries began the long, slow reorganization of a more effective movement in the countryside. Not until 1976 did another serious guerrilla movement arise, the Guatemalan Army of the Poor by name. Meanwhile, others vented their frustration through urban warfare in the face of government violence which reached a new high during 1970 and 1971 under a "state of siege" imposed by the president, Col. Carlos Arana Osorio. Arana, who had been close to the US military since serving as Guatemalan military attaché in Washington, and then as commander of the counter-insurgency operation in Zacapa (where his commitment to his work earned him the title of "the butcher of Zacapa"), decreed to himself virtually unlimited power to curb opposition of any stripe.[25]

Amnesty International later stated that Guatemalan sources, including the Committee of the Relatives of Disappeared Persons, claimed that over 7,000 persons disappeared or were found dead in these two years. "Foreign diplomats in Guatemala City," reported *Le Monde* in 1971, "believe that for every political assassination by left-wing revolutionaries fifteen murders are committed by right-wing fanatics."[26]

During a curfew so draconian that even ambulances, doctors and fire engines reportedly were forbidden outside . . . as American police cars and paddy wagons patrolled the streets day and night . . . and American helicopters buzzed overhead . . . the United States saw fit to provide further technical assistance and equipment to initiate a reorganization of Arana's police forces to make them yet more efficient.[27]

"In response to a question [from a Congressional investigator in 1971] as to what he conceived his job to be, a member of the US Military Group (MILGP) in Guatemala replied instantly that it was to make the Guatemalan Armed Forces as efficient as possible. The next question as to why this was in the interest of the United States was followed by a long silence while he reflected on a point which had apparently never occurred to him."[28]

As for the wretched of Guatemala's earth . . . in 1976 a major earthquake shook the land, taking over 20,000 lives, largely of the poor whose houses were the first to crumble . . . the story was reported of the American church relief worker who arrived to help the victims; he was shocked at their appearance and their living conditions; then he was informed that he was not in the earthquake area, that what he was seeing was normal.[29]

"The level of pesticide spraying is the highest in the world," reported the *New York Times* in 1977, "and little concern is shown for the people who live near the cotton fields" . . . 30 or 40 people a day are treated for pesticide poisoning in season, death can come within hours, or a longer lasting liver malfunction . . . the amounts of DDT in mothers' milk in Guatemala are the highest in the Western world. "It's very simple," explained a cotton planter, "more insecticide means more cotton, fewer insects mean higher profits." In an attack, guerrillas destroyed 22 crop-duster planes; the planes were quickly replaced thanks to the genius of American industry[30] . . . and all the pesticide you could ever want, from Monsanto Chemical Company of St. Louis and Guatemala City.

During the Carter presidency, in response to human-rights abuses in Guatemala and other countries, several pieces of Congressional legislation were passed which attempted to curtail military and economic aid to those nations. In the years preceding, similar statements of principle regarding aid to Guatemala had been enacted into law. The efficacy of these laws can be measured by their numbers. In any event, the embargo was never meant to be more than partial. Guatemala also received weapons and military equipment from Israel, at least a portion of which was covertly underwritten by the United States.[31]

As further camouflage, some of the training of Guatemala's security forces was reportedly maintained by transferring it to clandestine sites in Chile and Argentina.[32]

Testimony of an Indian woman:

My name is Rigoberta Menchu Tum. I am a representative of the 'Vincente Menchu' [her father] Revolutionary Christians . . .

On 9 December 1979, my 16-year-old brother Patrocino was captured and tortured for several days and then taken with twenty other young men to the square in Chajul . . . An officer of [President] Lucas Garcia's army of murderers ordered the prisoners to be paraded in a line. Then he started to insult and threaten the inhabitants of the village, who were forced to come out of their houses to witness the event. I was with my mother, and we saw Patrocino; he had had his tongue cut out and his toes cut off. The officer jackal made a speech. Every time he paused the soldiers beat the Indian prisoners.

When he finished his ranting, the bodies of my brother and the other prisoners were swollen, bloody, unrecognizable. It was monstrous, but they were still alive.

They were thrown on the ground and drenched with gasoline. The soldiers set fire to the wretched bodies with torches and the captain laughed like a hyena and forced the inhabitants of Chajul to watch. This was his objective — that they should be terrified and witness the punishment given to the 'guerrillas'.[33]

Testimony of Fred Sherwood (former CIA pilot during the overthrow of the Arbenz government in 1954 who settled in Guatemala and became president of the American Chamber of Commerce), speaking in Guatemala, September 1980:

Why should we be worried about the death squads? They're bumping off the commies, our enemies. I'd give them more power. Hell, I'd get some cartridges if I could, and everyone else would too . . . Why should we criticize them? The death squad — I'm for it . . . Shit! There's no question, we can't wait 'til Reagan gets in. We hope Carter falls in the ocean real quick . . . We all feel that he [Reagan] is our saviour.[34]

The Movement for National Liberation (MLN) is a prominent political party. It was the principal party in the Arana regime. An excerpt from a radio broadcast in 1980 by the head of the party, Mario Sandoval Alarcon . . .

I admit that the MLN is the party of organized violence. Organized violence is vigor, just as organized color is scenery and organized sound is harmony. There

269

is nothing wrong with organized violence; it is vigor, and the MLN is a vigorous movement.[35]

Mario Sandoval Alarcon and former president Arana "spent inaugural week mingling with the stars of the Reagan inner circle", reported syndicated columnist Jack Anderson. Sandoval, who had worked closely with the CIA in the overthrow of Arbenz, announced that he had met with Reagan defence and foreign-policy advisers even before the election. Right-wing Guatemalan leaders were elated by Reagan's victory. They looked forward to a resumption of the hand-in-glove relationship between American and Guatemalan security teams and businessmen which had existed before Carter took office.[36]

Before that could take place, however, the Reagan administration first had to soften the attitude of Congress about this thing called human rights. In March 1981, two months after Reagan's inaugural, Secretary of State Alexander Haig told a congressional committee that there was a Soviet "hit list . . . for the ultimate takeover of Central America". It was a "four phased operation" of which the first part had been the "seizure of Nicaragua". "Next," warned Haig, "is El Salvador, to be followed by Honduras and Guatemala."[37]

This was the kind of intelligence information which one would expect to derive from a captured secret document or KGB defector. But neither one of these was produced or mentioned, nor did any of the assembled congressmen presume to raise the matter.

Two months later, General Vernon Walters, former Deputy Director of the CIA, on a visit to Guatemala as Haig's special emissary, was moved to proclaim that the United States hoped to help the Guatemalan government defend "peace and liberty".[38]

During this period, Guatemalan security forces, official and unofficial, massacred at least 2,000 peasants (accompanied by the usual syndrome of torture, mutilation and decapitation), destroyed several villages, assassinated 76 officials of the opposition Christian Democratic Party, scores of trade unionists, and at least six catholic priests.[39]

August 19, 1981 . . . unidentified gunmen occupy the town of San Miguel Acatan, force the Mayor to give them a list of all those who had contributed funds for the building of a school, pick out 15 from the list (including three of the Mayor's children), make them dig their own graves and shoot them.[40]

In December, Ronald Reagan finally spoke out against government repression. He denounced Poland for crushing by "brute force, the stirrings of liberty . . . Our Government and those of our allies, have expressed moral revulsion at the police-state tactics of Poland's oppressors."[41]

Using the loopholes in the congressional legislation, both real and loosely interpreted, the Reagan administration, in its first two years, chipped away at the spirit of the embargo: $3.1 million of jeeps and trucks, $4 million of helicopter spare parts, $6.3 million of other military supplies.*[42] These were

---

* Any administration which wishes to conduct its foreign-aid programme without excessive

amongst the publicly announced aid shipments; what was transpiring covertly can only be guessed at in light of certain disclosures: Jack Anderson revealed in August 1981 that the United States was using Cuban exiles to train security forces in Guatemala; in this operation, Anderson wrote, the CIA had arranged "for secret training in the finer points of assassination".[43] The following year, it was reported that the Green Berets had been instructing Guatemalan Army officers for over two years in the finer points of warfare.[44] And in 1983, we learned that in the previous two years Guatemala's Air Force helicopter fleet had somehow increased from eight to 27, all of them American made, and that Guatemalan officers were once again being trained at the US School of the Americas in Panama.[45]

In March 1982, a coup in Guatemala put General Efrain Rios Montt, a "born-again Christian" in power. A month later, the Reagan administration announced that it perceived signs of an improvement in the state of human rights in Guatemala, and took the occasion to justify a shipment of military aid.[46]

On the first of July, Rios Montt declared a state of siege. It was to last more than eight months. Amnesty International later reported that 2,600 Indians and peasants were massacred in the first six months of the new regime.[47] In December, Ronald Reagan, also a Christian, went to see for himself. After meeting with Rios Montt, Reagan concluded that the Guatemalan Government was misunderstood. "I very frankly think," he said, "that they've been getting a bad deal."[48]

Statement by the Guatemalan Army of the Poor, made in 1981 (by which time the toll of people murdered by the government since 1954 had reached at least the 60,000 mark, and the sons of one-time death-squad members were now killing the sons of the Indians killed by their fathers):

> The Guatemalan revolution is entering its third decade. Ever since the government of Jacobo Arbenz was overthrown in 1954, the majority of the Guatemalan people have been seeking a way to move the country towards solving the same problems which were present then and have only worsened over time.
>
> The counterrevolution, put in motion by the U.S. Government and those domestic sectors committed to retaining every single one of their privileges, dispersed and disorganized the popular and democratic forces. However, it did not resolve any of the problems which had first given rise to demands for economic, social and political change. These demands have been raised again and again in the last quarter century, by any means that seemed appropriate at the time, and have received each time the same repressive response as in 1954.[49]

oversight by Congress usually has the means available to it; so complex is the US foreign-aid machinery — perhaps as many as two dozen separate channels of bilateral programmes and US-supported multilateral agencies — that Congress gets to debate and review only a minor portion of it on a country-by-country basis.

Statement by Father Thomas Melville, 1968:

Having come to the conclusion that the actual state of violence, composed of the malnutrition, ignorance, sickness and hunger of the vast majority of the Guatemalan population, is the direct result of a capitalist system that makes the defenseless Indian compete against the powerful and well-armed landowner, my brother [Father Arthur Melville] and I decided not to be silent accomplices of the mass murder that this system generates.

We began teaching the Indians that no one will defend their rights, if they do not defend themselves. If the government and oligarchy are using arms to maintain them in their position of misery, then they have the obligation to take up arms and defend their God-given right to be men.

We were accused of being communists along with the people who listened to us, and were asked to leave the country by our religious superiors and the U.S. ambassador [John Gordon Mein]. We did so.

But I say here that I am a communist only if Christ was a communist. I did what I did and will continue to do so because of the teachings of Christ and not because of Marx or Lenin. And I say here too, that we are many more than the hierarchy and the U.S. government think.

When the fight breaks out more in the open, let the world know that we do it not for Russia, not for China, nor any other country, but for Guatemala. Our response to the present situation is not because we have read either Marx or Lenin, but because we have read the New Testament.[50]

38. Costa Rica 1970 to 1971
Trying to topple an ally, part II

Jose Figueres, who headed the Costa Rican Government three times, was always a rather improbable target of destabilization by the United States. He was a bona fide (North) Americaphile, fluent in English, educated at MIT, lecturer at Harvard and other American universities, well-connected in US intellectual circles, particularly among Kennedyites, accorded an honorary membership in the Americans for Democratic Action. Figueres was typically referred to as an "outstanding friend" of the United States, and had long been associated with the CIA in a variety of activities and fronts in Latin America. And if that weren't enough, both of Figueres' wives had been American.

Yet, the CIA tried to overthrow him during his term in office in the 1950s (cf. Costa Rica, mid-1950s chapter) and perhaps again in the 1970s.

To liberal American political figures, Figueres was the quintessential "liberal democrat", the kind of statesman they like to think, and like the world to think, is the natural partner of US foreign policy rather than the military dictators who, somehow, keep popping up as allies.

To American conservatives, Figueres was of questionable ilk, the type that, if not actually a communist himself, doesn't sufficiently appreciate the nature and degree of The International Communist Conspiracy and consequently allows communists too much room to manoeuvre.

It was the latter conviction that was fuelled by Figueres soon after becoming president again in May 1970. He began "building bridges" to the Communist bloc, with Costa Rica becoming the first Central American country to establish diplomatic relations with the Soviet Union and Eastern Europe.

"This diplomatic recognition in no way shakes our loyalty to the United States or to the democratic cause," Figueres cautioned. "People everywhere are tired of the cold war. Russia controls half of Europe, and we want to make the Russians drink coffee [Costa Rica's principal export] instead of tea."[1]

In the previous two years the Soviet Union had purchased $10 million worth of coffee from Costa Rica, an "economic offensive" which reportedly "disturbed United States officials", as well as the hardliners in the American Embassy in San Jose.[2]

Earl (Ted) Williamson, officially listed as First Secretary of the Embassy, but actually CIA Chief of Station, was heard to declare at a party that the Figueres government would not last much longer. He spoke openly against the president's bridge-building endeavours.

Williamson's comments got back to Costa Rican officials, as did reports of his close ties with Figueres' conservative political opponents, and indiscreet remarks made by his Cuban wife regarding the country's alleged march toward Communism. Williamson, who had served in Cuba before the Castro takeover and married the niece of a wealthy sugar baron, was also blamed for the seizure and burning of some Marxist literature coming in through the Costa Rican airport. The blame arose through his involvement in a CIA "technical assistance program on security".

By autumn, the Costa Rican government felt compelled to make an informal suggestion through the State Department's Costa Rican desk in Washington that Williamson be removed. The request was ignored.

Then, on 17 December, a fisherman reported sighting a mysterious ship which had unloaded "long wooden boxes" on a remote Costa Rican beach. The ship was identified as the *Waltham* and the Costa Rican government later received information that the vessel was registered to the "commercial section of the State Department". This was never verified. However, the US Commerce Department at that time did own a 455-foot vessel named the *Waltham Victory*.

It was first reported that the boxes contained weapons. Subsequently, a story was circulated that it was contraband whisky that had been put ashore.

The *Miami Herald*, which had first broken this story, commented that: "The contraband story presumably was put out to dispel rumors of a coup against the government." Americaphile that he was, Figueres was probably anxious to downplay the entire controversy which must have been acutely embarrassing to him. Three congressmen of his party, however, unencumbered by such loyalties, released a statement that accused the CIA of being involved in the ship movements and the alleged arms drop.

By early January 1971, the Costa Rican government seriously feared an uprising. It again asked the Nixon administration to recall Williamson. Not long before, Williamson had publicly forecast that the Figueres government would not survive another two weeks.

The Guardia Civil, Costa Rica's only armed force, was alerted and plans were made to remove Figueres from the capital to a hiding place in the mountains. At Figueres' request, the Panama government covertly delivered over 100 semi-automatic rifles to Costa Rica.

During this entire period, the American Embassy in San Jose was reported to be deeply divided between liberals and conservatives. Perhaps the most conservative, along with Williamson, was Ambassador Walter Ploeser, a Nixon political appointee with a long history of ultra-anti-communist activity. Ploeser vehemently defended Williamson and was said to have made no effort to curb the CIA official's public outbursts against Figueres. At the same time, Ploeser fired the director of the US AID program in Costa Rica, Lawrence Harrison, who took a pro-Figueres stand. The two men reportedly clashed over priorities, with Ploeser wanting an increase in military assistance, although Costa Rica had no army, and a reduction in American economic aid to the country.

Official cables reaching Washington from Ploeser's embassy described the situation in Costa Rica as "dangerous". Figueres was accused of abandoning the West and facing East, of having accepted financial assistance from the communists for his campaign, of permitting communists to infiltrate his government.[3]

In February, Williamson was finally recalled by Washington. Costa Rican officials hoped and expected that Ploeser would be replaced as well, as soon as it could be done with the customary diplomatic face-saving. As it was, Ploeser lingered on at his post for a full year before resigning for "personal reasons".

The announcement of Williamson's departure was perhaps hastened by the fact that a few days earlier the House Subcommittee on Inter-American Affairs had held a briefing to look into the matter. But the congressmen were not about to become the authors of an exposé. After hearing the testimony of two State Department officials, the committee announced that it had all been a big misunderstanding due to "personality conflicts" within the embassy which had "repercussions" outside its walls, and "overzealous actions" by some US officials who would remain nameless, as would everything else heard at the closed-door briefing.[4]

The same day, the *Miami Herald* stated in an editorial: "What is abundantly clear . . . is the power and influence of the United States Embassy in a small country such as Costa Rica. An embassy that even quietly passes the word that it opposes the government can stimulate opposition and perhaps inspire efforts to overthrow it. Open antipathy almost asks for it."[5]

39. Iraq 1972 to 1975
Covert action should not be confused with missionary work

Into the land of ancient Mesopotamia reached the long arm of the CIA, and the Kurdish people of the Zagros and Taurus mountains, but a few decades removed from the life of nomads, joined the Agency's list of clients.

In May of 1972, President Richard Nixon and his National Security Affairs adviser, Henry Kissinger, went to the Soviet Union to meet their Russian counterparts. Afterward, Kissinger told a press conference in Moscow that the two nations had agreed to defuse the tensions in the Middle East and "to contribute what they can to bringing about a general settlement . . . such a settlement would also contribute to a relaxation of the armaments race in that area . . . Speaking for our side," he added, "I can say we will attempt to implement these principles in the spirit in which they were promulgated."[1]

Kissinger and Nixon were moved by the spirit for perhaps 24 hours. On their way home, they stopped in Teheran to visit their friend the Shah of Iran. It seems that Iran and Iraq were embroiled once again in their perennial feud — border disputes and the like — and the Shah asked his pal Richard for a little favour. Could he help arm the Kurds in Iraq who were fighting for autonomy? Just generally heat things up so as to sap the Iraqi resources and distract them from Iran?[2]

Anything for a friend and loyal ally said Richard Milhous, two weeks before the Watergate burglary and still on top of the world.

The Shah was quite capable of arming the Kurds himself, and in fact was doing so to some extent, but the Kurds didn't trust him. They trusted the United States and wanted to be armed by them. Several years later, the Congressional committee known as the Pike Committee, which investigated various CIA operations, put it thusly: "The U.S. acted in effect as a guarantor that the Kurds would not be summarily dropped by the Shah."[*][3]

Before long, the CIA was reaching into its warehouses and a range of Soviet and Chinese small arms and rifles and millions of rounds of ammunition were

---

[*] The Pike report refers to the Kurds as "the ethnic group", Iran or the Shah as "our ally", Iraq as "our ally's enemy", Israel as "another government". Here, the proper names are used.

on their way to the Kurdish rebels. The military aid was ultimately to involve some $16 million. The Communist origin of the weapons was a standard means of ensuring the standard "plausible denial".

The Kurds are a distinct ethnic group, Muslim but, unlike most other Iraqis, not Arab. Their people are to be found in Iraq, Iran and Turkey. For decades, the Iraqi Kurds had been engaged in intermittent warfare against the government in pursuance of a goal of "autonomy", a concept not terribly well-defined by them, it being clear only that it fell short of being an independent state, if that.

The political history of the Iraqi Kurds in their recent past was a remarkable piece of patchwork. Ten years earlier, they had been in close alliance with the Iraqi Communist Party. When the ruling Ba'ath party began to persecute the Communists, they took refuge amongst the Kurds. The Kurdish leader, Mustafa al-Barzani, a man in his seventies, had spent a dozen years in the Soviet Union and spoke Russian. Now the Communists were allies of the Ba'aths in an attempt to suppress the "imperialist agent Barzani" and Kurdish propaganda emphasized Soviet military support of the Iraqi government, including claims that Russians were flying bombing missions against the Kurds. At the same time the Kurds painted themselves as "social-democrats" of the European variety, going so far as to apply for membership in the Socialist International.[4] Nonetheless, Barzani stated frequently that "he trusted no other major power" than the United States and asserted that if his cause were successful, the Kurds were "ready to become the 51st state."[5] All this on top of desiring to establish a Muslim society.

In October 1973, when the Yom Kippur surprise attack on Israel took place and Iraq was preoccupied as an ally of Egypt and Syria, the Kurds were willing to launch a major attack, at Israel's suggestion, that might have been very beneficial to their own cause as well as taking some pressure off Israel by tying down the Iraqi army. But Kissinger refused to let the Kurds move. On 16 October he had the CIA send them a cable which read: "We do not repeat not consider it advisable for you to undertake the offensive military actions that Israel has suggested to you." The Kurds obeyed.[6]

The Pike report regarded this incident as an example of the apparent "no win" policy of the United States and Iran. The committee stated:

> The progressively deteriorating position of the Kurds reflected the fact that none of the nations who were aiding them seriously desired that they realize their objective of an autonomous state. A CIA memo of March 22, 1974 states Iran's and the United States' position clearly: 'We would think that Iran would not look with favor on the establishment of a formalized autonomous government. Iran, like ourselves, has seen benefit in a stalemate situation . . . in which Iraq is intrinsically weakened by the Kurd's refusal to relinquish its semi-autonomy. Neither Iran nor ourselves wish to see the matter resolved one way or the other.'[7]

"This policy," said the report, "was not imparted to our clients, who were encouraged to continue fighting. Even in the context of covert action, ours was a cynical enterprise."[8]

The day after the CIA memo referred to above, 23 March 1974, Soviet Defence Minister Andrei Grechko, who had befriended Barzani when the latter lived in the Soviet Union, arrived in Iraq to help the government reach a settlement with the Kurds. On the advice of Iran and the United States, however, Barzani refused to come to any terms.[9] Earlier that month, the Iraqi government had actually passed a law offering a limited amount of autonomy to the Kurds, but they had rejected that as well, whether or not at the request of their "allies" is not publicly known.

The congressional committee discovered that "The CIA had early information which suggested that the Shah would abandon the Kurds the minute he came to an agreement with Iraq over border disputes." The Shah viewed "the Kurds as 'a card to play' in this dispute with Iraq. And a CIA memo . . . characterizes the Kurds as 'a uniquely useful tool for weakening Iraq's potential for international adventurism'."[10]

The last may have been a reference to Iraq signing a pact of Friendship and Cooperation with the Soviet Union in 1972, under which it received military aid and granted the Soviet Navy certain port privileges. The Iraqis at times also sported "leftist rhetoric". By inexorable cold-war logic, Iraq had thus fallen irretrievably into the "enemy camp".

As it was, it was oil that brought Iran and Iraq together. In 1973, the Shah wanted to strengthen Iran's position with the Organization of Petroleum Exporting Countries (OPEC), and a crucial part of the inducement to Iraq and other Arab neighbours was Iran's willingness to double-cross the troublesome Kurds.[11] None of these countries wanted their own minorities to be getting any ideas from a Kurdish success.

It was not until March 1975 that the Shah was ready to make his move. Events moved swiftly then. The Shah met with the vice-president of Iraq, and, by agreement, the Shah cut off all supplies to the Kurds. The next day the Iraqis unleashed their biggest offensive ever. Several days later the stunned Kurds sent a desperate message to the CIA: "There is confusion and dismay among our people and forces. Our people's fate in unprecedented danger. Complete destruction hanging over our head. No explanation for all this. We appeal you and USG [United States government] intervene according to your promises . . ."[12]

The same day, the Kurds appealed to Kissinger as well:

Your Excellency, having always believed in the peaceful solution of disputes including those between Iran and Iraq, we are pleased to see that their two countries have come to some agreement . . . However, our hearts bleed to see that an immediate byproduct of their agreement is the destruction of our defenseless people . . . Our movement and people are being destroyed in an unbelievable way with silence from everyone. We feel your Excellency that the United States has a moral and political responsibility towards our people who have committed themselves to your country's policy.[13]

The hapless Kurds received no response to either plea. By the end of the month their movement was no more. Several hundred Kurdish leaders were executed.

In conclusion, the Pike report noted:

Over 200,000 refugees managed to escape into Iran. Once there, however, neither the United States nor Iran extended adequate humanitarian assistance. In fact, Iran was later to forcibly return over 40,000 of the refugees and the United States government refused to admit even one refugee into the United States by way of political asylum even though they qualified for such admittance.[14]

When Henry Kissinger was interviewed by the staff of the Pike Committee about the United States role in this melodrama, he responded with his now-famous remark: "Covert action should not be confused with missionary work."[15]

40. Australia 1973 to 1975
Another free election bites the dust

When the leader of a Communist country is removed from office by the Politburo, this is confirmation to the Western mind of the totalitarian, or at least the arbitrary, nature of the Communist system.

What then are we to make of the fact that in 1975 Edward Gough Whitlam, the legally-elected prime minister of Australia, was summarily dismissed by a single non-elected individual, one functioning under the title of "Governor-General"?

Whitlam took office in December 1972 as the head of the first Labor Party government in Australia in 23 years. In short order he set about proving to the opposition parties the correctness of their historical prediction that Labor in power would be "irresponsible and dangerous"[1] — to *whom*, of course, had always been the question.

The war in Vietnam was an immediate example. Australian military personnel serving there under the command of the United States were called home, conscription was halted, and young men jailed for refusing military service were released.[2] Moreover, the Whitlam government recognized North Vietnam, several ministers publicly denounced American bombing of Hanoi and called for rallies to oppose it, and protesting dock workers felt inspired to impose a temporary boycott on American shipping, although the last was opposed by Whitlam.[3]

Condemnation of the US president and his administration volunteered by Labor ministers was most undiplomatic: "corrupt" ... "maniacs" ... "mass murderers" ... were some of the epithets hurled at Washington. American officials were reported to be "shocked and angered".[4]

The overseas side of Australian intelligence (ASIS by acronym), it turned out, was working with the CIA in Chile against the Allende government. Whitlam ordered an immediate halt to the operation in early 1973, although at the time of Allende's downfall in September, ASIS was reportedly still working with the Agency.[5]

The Labor government showed itself less than committed to the games security people play at home as well. Whitlam let it be known immediately that he did not wish to have his staff members undergo the usual security checks because he knew and trusted them. The Australian Security and Intelligence Organization (ASIO) was taken aback by such unorthodoxy and informed its CIA colleagues in Australia; cables went to Washington; before long, a political officer at the American Embassy was informing Richard Hall, one of Whitlam's advisers, somewhat cryptically: "Your Prime Minister has just cut off one of his options."[6]

The new administration also put an end to the discrimination against immigrants who were being denied naturalization for having opposed the military juntas in places like Greece and Chile.[7] Most exceptional and alarming to the security professionals was the behaviour of the Attorney-General who showed up unannounced at ASIO headquarters one day in March 1973 with the police and carted away certain files because he suspected that the intelligence agency was withholding information from him. In all likelihood, ASIO *was* deliberately keeping certain information from its own government, as does every other intelligence agency in the world. The difference here, once again, was that the Labor government simply refused to accept such a state of affairs as normal.

A few years later, after Whitlam's ouster, James Angleton, who had been a high CIA officer in 1973 and directly concerned with intelligence relations with Australia, complained to an Australian television interviewer about the "Attorney-General moving in, barging in, we were deeply concerned as to the sanctity of this information which could compromise sources and methods and compromise human life." The CIA, he said, seriously considered breaking intelligence relations with Australia.[8]

As a consequence of Whitlam's unconventional way of running a government, the CIA became rather concerned about the security and continued functioning of its many military and intelligence facilities in Australia. By the Agency's standards, it was a highly important setup, employing thousands of persons: a vital part of the early warning system; a key tracking station in the United States' global spy satellite system of extremely sophisticated photography and monitoring of activities within the Soviet Union; a US naval communications station which dealt with nuclear submarines; a huge electronics control centre set up by the US National Security Agency (NSA) to intercept messages, of voice, telex, etc., coming in and out of Australia and its Pacific region — that is, eavesdropping on everybody and everything.[9]

Most of this had been built in the latter part of the 1960s and run in such secrecy that not even senior members of the Australian Foreign Ministry had been briefed on exactly what went on in those buildings in Australia's wide open spaces, and the CIA connection was never officially acknowledged.

After the Labor Party took power, some of its members voiced strong criticism of the secret facilities. They increasingly demanded an official explanation for their presence and at times even voted for their removal. This was not carried out because the leaders of the Whitlam administration, for all their radical posturing, were not about to leap into political no-man's-land by cutting off ties to the West. They spoke of neutralism and non-alignment on occasion, but they were willing to settle for independence; which is all the Papandreous wanted before they were ousted in Greece, another site of an American electronics state-within-a-state in which the host intelligence and defence establishments typically demonstrate more loyalty to their American counterparts than to their own government; in addition to Chile, Australian intelligence had aided US operations in Vietnam, Cambodia and Indonesia.[10]

The Whitlam government displayed its independence in other ways, however. In 1973, Whitlam disclosed the existence of an Australian Defence Signals Directorate unit in Singapore — another cold-war toy of the CIA and ASIO which monitored military and civilian radio traffic in Asia.[11] (The DSD is comparable to the American NSA and the British GCHQ.) Later, the Australian prime minister closed the unit down, although he re-established part of it in Australia. His administration also expressed its disapproval of US plans to build up the Indian Ocean island of Diego Garcia as another military-intelligence-nuclear outpost.[12] And in February 1975, the Labor Party conference voted to allow the Provisional Revolutionary Government of Vietnam (the Vietcong) to set up an office in Australia. This was before the fall of Saigon.

"By the end of 1974," writes Joan Coxsedge, a Labor Party member of Parliament in the state of Victoria,

> almost every move by the Whitlam Government or by individual Labor parliamentarians, whether it was a departmental decision, a staff appointment, an international cable, a telex, a phone call, or a confidential letter, quickly became the property of the news media. There was an unparalleled campaign of personal vituperation, hinting at incompetence, dissension, corruption and private scandal within the ranks of the government.[13]

Matters reached the spark point in autumn 1975. Whitlam dismissed the heads of both ASIO and ASIS in separate incidents, the latter because his agency had been secretly assisting the CIA in covert activities in nearby East Timor.[14] Then, at the beginning of November, it was revealed in the press that a former CIA officer, Richard Lee Stallings, had been channelling funds to J. Douglas Anthony, leader of the National Country Party, one of the two main opposition parties. It was reported that Stallings was a close friend and former tenant of Anthony's, that the secret facilities in the hinterland were indeed CIA creations, and that Stallings had been the first head of much of the operation.[15]

A year earlier, an Australian political journalist, Ray Aitchison, had published a book called *Looking at the Liberals* (the Liberal Party, the other important opposition party, was actually rather conservative), in which he claimed that the CIA had offered the opposition unlimited funds in their unsuccessful attempt to defeat the Labor Party in the May 1974 parliamentary elections.[16] Subsequently, former CIA officer Victor Marchetti confirmed that the CIA had funded both opposition parties, and a Sydney newspaper stated that the Liberals had been on the receiving end since the late 1960s.[17]

Whitlam publicly repeated the new charges about Stallings and insisted upon an investigation of the facilities, to identify once and for all their true nature and purpose. (Whether any of it was part of a weapons system was one question which seriously concerned the administration.) At the same time he demanded a list of all CIA operatives in Australia.

The Australian military-intelligence complex appears to have been spurred into a flurry of activity. On 6 November, the head of the Defence Department reportedly met with the Governor-General, Sir John Kerr, and afterward declared publicly: "This is the greatest risk to the nation's security there has ever been."[18]

On the eighth, another senior defence official held a meeting with Kerr in which he briefed the Governor-General about allegations from the CIA that Whitlam was jeopardizing the security of the American bases in Australia.[19] The same day, the CIA in Washington informed the ASIO station there that all intelligence links with Australia would be cut off unless a satisfactory explanation was given of Mr Whitlam's behaviour.[20] The Agency had already expressed reservations about releasing intelligence information to certain government ministers.[21]

If this had been a Third World country, the government would likely have already been sent packing.

On 9 November, Kerr was received at the Defence Signals Directorate for yet another briefing.[22] The following day, the ASIO station in Washington, at the request of the CIA, sent a telex to its headquarters in Australia in which it stated that "CIA can not see how this dialogue with continued reference to CIA can do other than blow the lid off these installations . . ."[23] In addition to Stallings, the names of his successors (also senior CIA officers) and the CIA station chief in Canberra had appeared in the press.

Kerr, who was taken with the world of spookery and regularly saw classified material, in all likelihood was aware of the ASIO telex and the CIA ultimatum.[24] On the 11th, he dismissed Whitlam as Prime Minister, dissolved both houses of Parliament, and appointed Malcolm Fraser, the leader of the Liberal Party, to head an interim government until new elections could be held on 13 December. In the hours between the appointment of Fraser and the dissolution of Parliament, the Labor majority in the House of Representatives pushed through a no-confidence motion against Fraser, an act which obliged the Governor-General to dismiss the Liberal leader in turn. Kerr chose to ignore this manoeuvre, which was a legalistic one, but his dismissal of Whitlam was no less a legalistic act.

On 15 October, the opposition-controlled Senate had refused to vote on a new budget appropriation bill (called "Supply" in Australia) in order to force the government to dissolve Parliament and hold new elections, hoping thus to regain power. Though the constitution gave the Senate the technical right to withhold approval of the budget, it was seldom interpreted literally, as it is in the United States. Precedent was of greater importance, and the fact was that in Australia's 75-year history as a Federation the Senate had never exercised this right against the federal government. Only days earlier, eight leading law professors had publicly declared such action to be constitutionally improper. The opposition tactic was thus at least debatable.

When Whitlam refused to dissolve Parliament and tried to govern without the budget, a constitutional and financial crisis steadily built up over the course of several weeks. Then Kerr invoked a power as archaic and as questionable as that employed by the Senate. It was the first time a Governor-General had ever dismissed a federal prime minister; it had occurred but once before on a state level.[25]

The Melbourne newspaper, *The Age* (which, said the *New York Times*, was "generally held to be one of the nation's most responsible papers"), wrote that Kerr's action was "a triumph of narrow legalism over common sense and popular feeling".[26] It added:

> By bringing down the Government because the Senate refused it Supply, Sir John Kerr acted at least against the spirit of the Australian Constitution. Since 1901, it has been a firmly held convention that the Senate should not reject budgets . . . Sir John has created an awesome precedent — that a hostile Senate can bring down a government whenever it denies it Supply. [Kerr] breathed life into a constitutional relic — the right of kings and queens to unilaterally appoint governments.[27]

The office of Governor-General had traditionally been only that of a figurehead representative of the Queen of England. Kerr's decision, however, appears as a calculated political act. He gave Whitlam no warning or ultimatum before dismissing him, no opportunity to request the dissolution of parliament which would have permitted him to remain in office. One must read Kerr's own account of his confrontation with Whitlam to appreciate how he manoeuvred the Prime Minister into stalking out of the Governor-General's office without requesting the dissolution. Kerr claims he refrained from issuing Whitlam an ultimatum because he feared that the prime minister would leave and then ask the Queen for his removal as Governor-General.[28] But he fails to explain why he didn't give Whitlam an ultimatum that had to be responded to on the spot.

Kerr had been appointed, at least in theory, by the Queen. Ironically, she had done so at Whitlam's recommendation, which he had made against the wishes of his party's left-wing. Kerr's action added to Whitlam's reputation as a bad judge of character, a man easily taken in.

Certainly the warning signs were there. John Kerr had been intimately involved with CIA fronts for a number of years. In the 1950s he joined the Australian Association for Cultural Freedom, an organization spawned by the CIA's Congress for Cultural Freedom (cf. Western Europe chapter). Kerr became a member of the organization's executive board in 1957 and also wrote for its magazine *Quadrant*. One article, in 1960, was entitled "The struggle against communism in the trade unions", a programme to which the CIA has of course consistently accorded a high priority throughout the world.

In 1966 Kerr helped to found Lawasia (or Law Asia), an organization of lawyers in the Far East funded by the Asia Foundation. The Foundation was one of the most prominent CIA fronts for over a decade, with offices and representatives in all the major capitals of Asia; one of its prime missions, Victor Marchetti has written, was "to disseminate throughout Asia a negative vision of mainland China, North Vietnam, and North Korea".[29] Kerr became Lawasia's first president, a position he held until 1970. He describes the organization as "a non-communist group of Asian lawyers" which the Asia Foundation supported because "the rule of law is a good thing, a strong legal profession is a good thing, and talk between lawyers is a good thing."[30]

"There was a bit of a celebration" in the CIA when Whitlam was dismissed by Kerr, reported Christopher Boyce. Boyce is an American who was working at the time for TRW Systems, Inc., Los Angeles, in a cryptographic communications centre which linked CIA headquarters in Virginia with the Agency's satellite surveillance system in Australia. In his position, Boyce was privy to telex communications between the two stations. The CIA, he said, referred to Kerr as "our man".[31]

Boyce also revealed that the CIA had infiltrated Australian labour unions, had been "manipulating the leadership", and had "suppressed their strikes", particularly those involving railroads and airports. The last was reportedly because the strikes were holding up deliveries of equipment to the Agency's installations. Some unions as well had been in the forefront of opposition to the installations.[32]

As matters turned out, Whitlam lost the new election.

One other CIA operation in Australia deserves mention. This is the Nugen Hand Merchant Bank of Sydney, truly a CIA bank. Founded in 1973 by Frank Nugen, an Australian, and Michael Hand, an American formerly with the Green Berets in Vietnam and with the CIA airline Air America, the bank exhibited phenomenal growth over the next few years. It opened branch offices in Saudi Arabia, Hamburg, Malaysia, Thailand, Hong Kong, Singapore, the Philippines, Argentina, Chile, Hawaii, Washington and Annapolis, Maryland, run by men with backgrounds in the CIA, OSS, Green Berets, and similar specialty areas of banking. Former CIA Director William Colby was one of the bank's attorneys.

The Nugen Hand Bank succeeded in expanding the scope of normal banking services. Among the activities it was reportedly involved in were: drug trafficking, international arms dealing, links to organized crime, laundering money for President Suharto of Indonesia, unspecified services for President and Mrs Marcos of the Philippines, assisting the Shah of Iran's family to shift money out of Iran, channelling CIA money into pro-American political parties and operations in Europe, attempting to blackmail an Australian state minister who was investigating organized crime (by opening up a Swiss bank account in his name and threatening to leak the information), transferring $2.4 million to the Australian Liberal Party through one of the bank's many associated companies, and a host of other socially useful projects.

In addition, several mysterious deaths have been connected to the bank, including that of a ranking CIA officer in Maryland. And on 27 January 1980, Frank Nugen was himself found shot dead in his car. In June, Michael Hand disappeared without a trace. The Nugen Hand Merchant Bank collapsed, $50 million or so in debt.[33]

41. Angola 1975 to 1976
The Great Powers Poker Game

It is spring 1975. Saigon has just fallen. The last of the Americans are fleeing for their lives. Fallout from Watergate hangs heavy in the air in the US. The morning papers bring fresh revelations about CIA and FBI misdeeds. The House of Representatives is holding hearings on the CIA. On the Senate side, the Church Committee is doing the same. The Rockefeller Commission has set about investigating the Agency's domestic activities.

The CIA and its influential supporters warn that the crescendo of disclosures will inhibit the Agency from carrying out the functions necessary for national security.

At CIA headquarters in Langley, Virginia, they are busy preparing for their next secret adventure: Angola.

To undertake a military operation at such a moment, the reasons, one would imagine, must have been both compelling and urgent. Yet, in the long history of American interventions it would be difficult to find one more pointless or with less to gain for the United States or the foreign people involved.

The origin of our story dates back to the beginning of the 1960s when two political movements in Angola began to oppose by force the Portuguese colonial government: the MPLA, led by Agostinho Neto, and the FNLA, led by Holden Roberto. (The latter group was known by other names in its early years, but for simplicity will be referred to here only as FNLA.)

The United States, not normally in the business of supporting "liberation" organizations, decided that inasmuch as Portugal would probably be unable to hold on to its colony forever, establishing contact with a possible successor regime might prove beneficial. For reasons lost in the mists of history, the United States, or at least someone in the CIA, decided that Roberto was their man and on to the Agency payroll he went.[1]

At the same time, and during the ensuing years, Washington provided their NATO ally, the Salazar dictatorship in Lisbon, with the military aid and counter-insurgency training needed to suppress the rebellion. John Marcum, an American scholar who walked 800 miles through Angola into the FNLA guerrilla camps in the early 1960s, has written:

> By January 1962 outside observers could watch Portuguese planes bomb and strafe African villages, visit the charred remains of towns like Mbanza M'Pangu and M'Pangala, and copy the data from 750-point napalm bomb casings from which the Portuguese had not removed the labels marked 'Property U.S. Air Force'.[2]

The Soviet Union, for reasons best known to the Kremlin, opted at some point for Neto. In the mid-sixties another movement, UNITA by name, entered the picture and China dealt itself into The Great Powers Poker Game, lending support to UNITA and FNLA.

Although MPLA may have been somewhat more genuine in its leftist convictions than FNLA or UNITA, there was little to distinguish any of the three groups from each other ideologically. When the press has made any distinction amongst them it has usually been to refer to MPLA as "Marxist", but this is ill-defined, if defined at all. Each of the groups spoke of socialism and employed Marxist rhetoric when the occasion called for it, and genuflected to other gods when it did not. In the sixties, each of them was perfectly willing to accept support from any country willing to give it without excessive strings attached. Neto, for example, went to Washington in December 1962 to put his case before the American government and press and to emphasize the fallacy of categorizing the MPLA as communist. The following year, Roberto appealed for aid to the Soviet Union, Cuba and China, and later, Jonas Savimbi, the leader of UNITA, accepted military training for his men from North Korea.[3]

Each group was composed predominantly of members of a particular tribe; each tried to discourage aid or recognition being given to the others; they each suffered from serious internal splits and spent as much time fighting each other as they did the Portuguese army. The Vietcong they were not.

That the CIA's choosing of its ally was largely an arbitrary process is further underlined by a State Department cable to its African Embassies in 1963 which stated: "U.S. policy is not, repeat not, to discourage [an] MPLA ... move toward West and not to choose between these two movements."[4]

Even in 1975, when the head of the CIA, William Colby, was asked by a Congressional committee what the differences were between the three contesting factions, he responded:

> They are all independents. They are all for black Africa. They are all for some fuzzy kind of social system, you know, without really much articulation, but some sort of let's not be exploited by the capitalist nations.

And when asked why the Chinese were backing the FNLA or UNITA, he stated: "Because the Soviets are backing the MPLA is the simplest answer."

"It sounds," said Congressman Aspin, "like that is why we are doing it."

"It is," replied Colby.[5]

Nonetheless, the committee, in its later report, asserted that in view of Colby's statement, "The U.S.'s expressed opposition to the MPLA is puzzling".[6]

Finally, it is instructive to note that all three groups were denounced by the Portuguese as communists and terrorists.

Before April 1974, when a coup in Portugal ousted the dictatorship, the aid given to the Angolan resistance movements by their various foreign patrons was sporadic and insignificant, essentially a matter of the patrons keeping their hands in the game. The coup, however, raised the stakes, for the new Portuguese government soon declared its willingness to grant independence to its African colonies.

In an agreement announced on 15 January 1975, the three movements formed a transitional government with elections to be held in October and formal independence to take place the following month. On 22 January, the Forty Committee of the National Security Council in Washington authorized the CIA to pass $300,000 to Roberto and the FNLA.[7] For the previous five years or so, he had been on a $10,000-a-year retainer from the Agency.[8]

In March, the FNLA, historically the most warlike of the groups, attacked MPLA headquarters and later gunned down 51 unarmed, young MPLA recruits.[9] These incidents served to spark what was to be a full-scale civil war, with UNITA aligning itself with FNLA against MPLA. The elections would never take place.

Also in March, according to the CIA, a large shipment of arms arrived from the Soviet Union for the MPLA.[10] The House investigating committee subsequently stated that "Later events have suggested that this infusion of US aid [the $300,000], unprecedented and massive in the underdeveloped colony, may have panicked the Soviets into arming their MPLA clients".[11] The Soviets may have been as much influenced by the fact that China had sent a huge arms package to the FNLA the previous September and had dispatched over one hundred military advisers to neighbouring Zaire to train Roberto's soldiers, only a month after the coup in Portugal.[12]

The CIA made its first major weapons shipment to the FNLA in July 1975. Thus, like the Russians and the Chinese, the United States was giving aid to one side of the Angolan civil war on a level far greater than it had ever provided during the struggle against Portuguese colonialism.

The United States was directly involved in the civil war to a marked degree. In addition to training Angolan combat units, US personnel did considerable flying between Zaire and Angola carrying out reconnaissance and supply missions,[13] and the CIA spent over a million dollars on an ambitious mercenary program.[14] The *Christian Science Monitor* reported in January 1976 that

"Some 300 Americans are already operating within Angola . . . A similar number is ready to go as soon as the CIA can obtain further funds. This latter group includes 15 South Vietnamese as well as American officers and men either on 'indefinite leave' from their special forces units [Green Berets] . . . or recently discharged." Just over 150 of these men, said the newspaper, were undergoing a refresher course at Fort Benning, Georgia.[15]

The CIA also recruited or financed many British mercenaries, plus a scattering of French and Portuguese.[16] (These included the well-known Englishman and psychopath George Cullen who lined up 14 of his fellow soldiers-of-fortune and shot them all dead because they had mistakenly attacked the wrong side.)[17] Later, Secretary of State Henry Kissinger explicitly told the Senate that "the CIA is not involved" in the recruitment of mercenaries for Angola.[18]

There were also well over a hundred CIA officers and American military advisers scurrying about Angola, Zaire, Zambia and South Africa helping to direct the military operations and practicing their propaganda skills.[19] Through recruited journalists representing major news services, the Agency was able to generate international coverage for false reports of Soviet advisers in Angola. One CIA story, announced to the press by UNITA, was that 20 Russians and 35 Cubans had been captured. Another fabrication concerned alleged rapes committed by Cuban soldiers in Angola; this was elaborated to include their capture, trial, and execution, complete with photos of the young women killing the Cubans who had raped them.[20] Both stories were reported widely in the American and British press and elsewhere. The more responsible newspapers amongst them, such as the *New York Times*, *Washington Post*, and *The Guardian* of London were careful to point out that the only source of the information was UNITA and their articles did not attempt to ascribe any special credence to the reports.[21] But, as always in such cases, this could not prevent the placing of seeds of belief in the minds of readers already conditioned to believe the worst about communists.

The disinformation campaign took place within the United States as well. FNLA delegates came to New York in September to lobby for support at the UN and with the New York press, distributing as they went copies of a "white paper" on the Angolan conflict prepared at CIA headquarters but made to look like it was produced in Zaire, French and all.[22] John Stockwell, the head of the CIA's Angola task force, described the paper as sometimes "false to the point of being ludicrous" and other times "simply inaccurate".[23]

Afterward, representatives of UNITA went to Washington and presented to members of Congress, the State Department, the White House and the media, verbal reports about the situation in Angola which were the product of briefings given them by their CIA case officers.[24]

In January 1976, William Colby sat before the Senate investigating committee and solemnly assured the Senators: "We have taken particular caution to ensure that our operations are focused abroad and not at the United States to influence the opinion of the American people about things from the CIA point of view."[25] There was virtually no important aspect of the Angolan intervention which Colby, Kissinger, and other high officials did not misrepresent to Congress and the media.

The odds never favoured a military victory for the US-backed forces in Angola, particularly in the absence of a relatively large-scale American commitment which, given the political atmosphere, was not in the cards. The MPLA was the most organized and best led of the three factions and early on controlled the capital city of Luanda, which housed almost the entire governmental machinery. Yet, for no reason, apparently, other than anti-Soviet spite, the United States was unwilling to allow a negotiated settlement. When Savimbi of UNITA sent out feelers to the MPLA in September 1975 to discuss a peaceful solution he was admonished by the CIA. Similarly, the following month when an MPLA delegation went to Washington to once again express their potential friendliness to the United States, they received a cool reception, being seen only by a low-level State Department official.[26]

In November MPLA representatives came to Washington to plead for the release of two Boeing jet airliners which their government had paid for but which the State Department would not allow to be exported. John Stockwell relates the unusual development that the MPLA men were accompanied by Bob Temmons, who until shortly before had been the head of the CIA station in Luanda, as well as by the president of Boeing. While the two Angolans and the man from Boeing petitioned the State Department, the CIA man made known to Agency headquarters that he had come to share the view of the US Consul General in Luanda "that the MPLA was best qualified to run the country, that it was not demonstrably hostile to the United States, and that the United States should make peace with it as quickly as possible."

The State Department's response to the MPLA representatives was simple: the price for any American co-operation with their government was Soviet influence out, US influence in.[27]

At one time or another almost two dozen countries, East and West, felt the urge to intervene in the conflict. Principal amongst these were the United States, China, South Africa and Zaire on the side of FNLA/UNITA, and the Soviet Union, Cuba, the Congo Republic and Katangese troops (Zairian rebels) supporting MPLA. The presence of South African forces on their side cost the United States and its Angolan allies dearly in support from other countries, particularly in Africa. Yet, South Africa's participation in the war had been directly solicited by the United States.[28] In sharp contrast to stated American policy, the CIA had been collaborating closely with Pretoria's intelligence service for several years and continued to do so in regard to Angola.[29] In 1975 the Agency set up a covert mechanism whereby arms were delivered to the South Africans over the following three years, a portion of which were more than likely put to use in Angola.[30] South Africa in turn helped to ferry American military aid from Zaire into Angola.[31]

In fairness to the CIA, it must be pointed out that its people were not entirely oblivious or insensitive to what South Africa represented. The Agency was very careful about letting its black officers into the Angola programme.[32]

By February 1976, the MPLA, with indispensable help from Cuban troops* and Soviet military equipment plus a cutoff of CIA Angola funds by Congress, had all but routed the FNLA and UNITA. US Congressmen did not yet know the full truth about the American operation, but enough of the public dumbshow had been exposed to make them angry at how Kissinger, Colby, *et al* had lied to their faces. The consequence was one of the rare occasions in modern times that the US Congress has directly and decisively influenced American foreign policy. In the process, it avoided the slippery slope to another Vietnam, on top of which Henry Kissinger and the CIA were already poised with shoes waxed.[34]

Savimbi at this time again considered reaching an understanding with the MPLA. The response from Washington was: keep fighting. During the two weeks that Savimbi waited for his answer, he lost at least 600 men on the battlefield. Kissinger personally promised UNITA continued support if they maintained their resistance, knowing full well that there was no more support to give.[35] Less than two months before, the Secretary of State had stated: "We are not opposed to the MPLA as such . . . We can live with any of the factions in Angola."[36] Be that as it may, the man was wholly obsessed with countering Soviet moves anywhere on the planet — significant or trivial, real or imagined, *fait accompli* or anticipated. He was perhaps particularly driven in this case, for as he later wrote: "Angola represents the first time that the Soviets have moved militarily at long distance to impose a regime of their choice."[37]

If all this seems far removed from how the academics tell us American foreign policy is made, it's still more plausible than the other explanation commonly advanced for the policy in Angola, viz: it was done to please Sese Seko Mobutu, the head of Zaire, characterized as America's most important ally/client in Africa, if not in the Third World.[38] (Zaire was home to the CIA's largest station in Africa.) Mobutu desired an Angolan government he could sway, primarily to prevent Angola being used as a sanctuary by his arch foes, the rebels from Katanga province in Zaire. Holden Roberto was the natural choice to support, for he happened to be Mobutu's brother-in-law, although Roberto and the FNLA had little else going for them. As Professor Gerald Bender, a leading American authority on Angola, testified before Congress in 1978:

Although the United States has supported the FNLA in Angola for 17 years, it is virtually impossible to find an American official, scholar or journalist, who is

---

* The Cuban presence in Angola was, and is, largely attributable to South African attacks against the MPLA. Wayne Smith, director of the State Department's Office of Cuban Affairs from 1977 to 1979, has written that "South African troops invaded Angola with full U.S. knowledge. No Cuban troops were in Angola prior to this intervention."[33]

familiar with that party, who will testify positively about its organization or leadership. After a debate with a senior State Department official at the end of the Angolan civil war, I asked him why the United States ever bet on the FNLA. He replied, 'I'll be damned if I know; I have never seen a single report or memo which suggests that the FNLA has any organization, solid leaders, or an ideology which we could count on.' Even foreign leaders who have supported Holden Roberto, such as General Mobutu, agree with that assessment. When asked by a visiting U.S. Senator if he thought Roberto would make a good leader for Angola, Mobutu replied, 'Hell no!'[39]

Kissinger himself told the House investigating committee that promoting the stability of Mobutu was one of the prime reasons for the American policy in Angola.[40] Yet, even if this could be a valid justification for serious intervention in a foreign civil war, its application here challenges, if it does not defeat, comprehension; for in June 1975, a month before the United States shipped its first major arms package to the FNLA, Mobutu accused the US of plotting his overthrow and assassination, whereupon he expelled the American Ambassador (cf. Zaire chapter).

The American Ambassador to the United Nations, Daniel Moynihan, did not particularly enhance the level of discussion when he declared that if the United States did not step in "the Communists would take over Angola and will thereby considerably control the oil shipping lanes from the Persian Gulf to Europe. They will be next to Brazil. They will have a large chunk of Africa, and the world will be different in the aftermath if they succeed."[41] A truly baroque train of thought.

Kissinger himself, never at a loss for the glib line custom-made for his immediate audience, told Israeli officials that failure to stop the Russians in Angola "could encourage Arab countries such as Syria to run risks that could lead to a new attack on Israel, backed up by the Russians."[42]

And so the silly season went. With only a change in place names, similar geo-political-domino theories have been put forth to give a veneer of rationality to so many American interventions. In this case, as in the others where the "communists" won, nothing of the sort ensued.

The MPLA in power was restricted by the same domestic and international economic realities which the FNLA or UNITA would have faced. Accordingly, it discouraged union militancy, dealt sternly with strikes, exhorted the workers to produce more, entered into commercial contracts with several multinationals, and did not raise the hammer and sickle over the president's palace.[43] The MPLA urged Gulf Oil Co. to continue its exclusive operation in Cabinda province and guaranteed the safety of the American corporation's employees while the fighting was still heavy. Gulf was completely amenable to this offer, but the CIA and the State Department put pressure on the company to discontinue its royalty payments to the MPLA, thus jeopardizing the entire oil venture in a way that the "Marxist" government never did. One aspect of this pressure was a threat by Kissinger to open an investigation of international bribery by the company. Gulf compromised by putting its payments into an escrow bank account until the civil war came to an end of sorts a few months later, at which time payments to the MPLA were resumed.[44]

Contrary to accepted Western belief, Cuba did not enter the Angolan war as a Soviet surrogate. John Stockwell has noted that after the war the CIA "learned that Cuba had not been ordered into action by the Soviet Union" but that "the Cuban leaders felt compelled to intervene for their own ideological reasons."[45] In 1977, the New York magazine *Africa Report* stated that "The Cubans have supported [MPLA leader Neto's] pragmatic approach toward Western investment and his attempts to maintain a foreign policy of nonalignment." Moreover, the magazine reported that on 27 May the Angolan government had announced that, aided by Cuban troops, it had crushed a rebellion by a faction of the MPLA whose leader claimed to have Soviet support.[46]

The fighting in Angola has lingered on intermittently to the present day. In 1980, a CBS special report could still speak of a "propaganda war" being run by the CIA against Cubans in Africa.[47] And in 1984 a confidential memorandum smuggled out of Zaire revealed that the United States and South Africa had met in November 1983 to discuss destabilization of the Angola government. Plans were drawn up to supply more military aid to UNITA and discussions were held on ways to implement a wide range of tactics: unify the anti-government movements, stir up popular feeling against the government, sabotage factories and transport systems, seize strategic points, disrupt joint Angola-Soviet projects, undermine relations between the government and the Soviet Union and Cuba, bring pressure to bear on Cuba to withdraw its troops, sow divisions in the ranks of the MPLA leadership, infiltrate agents into the Angola army, and apply pressure to stem the flow of foreign investments into Angola.

The United States branded the document a forgery, but UNITA's representative in Washington would neither confirm nor deny that the meeting took place. He stated, however, that UNITA had "contacts with US officials at all levels on a regular basis".

The aim of the operation, according to the memorandum, was to force part of the Angolan leadership to negotiate with UNITA, precisely what Washington had successfully discouraged years earlier.[48]

42. Zaire 1975 to 1978
Mobutu and the CIA, a marriage made in heaven

It can reasonably be said that President Mobutu Sese Seko and the CIA deserved each other. By 1975 the Congo strongman, regarded by the Agency as one of its "successes" in Africa, had ruled over his hapless, impoverished subjects for 10 long years. In the process, with a flair for conspicuous corruption that ranks amongst the best this century has had to offer, Mobutu amassed a personal fortune estimated to run into the billions of dollars sitting in the usual Swiss, New York, etc. banks, while most of the population suffered from severe malnutrition.[1]

It can be said as well that his corruption was matched only by his cruelty. Mobutu, one observer of Zaire has written,

> rules by decree with a grotesque impulsiveness that seems to shock even his former [CIA] case officers. One recalled that in June 1971 Mobutu had forcibly enlisted in the armed forces the entire student body of Lovanium University. 'He was put out by some student demonstrations,' remembered the official. Mobutu finally relented, but ten of the students were sentenced to life imprisonment for crimes of 'public insult' to the Chief of State . . . One intelligence source recalls a fervent Mobutu approach, eventually deflected, that either Zaire with CIA help or the Agency alone undertake an invasion against 'those bastards across the river' in the Congo Republic (Brazzaville). He's a 'real wild man,' said one former official, 'and we've had trouble keeping him under rein.'[2]

This may not have been for lack of trying. In June 1975 Mobutu announced that he had uncovered and suppressed a coup attempt aimed at his "physical elimination". He blamed an unnamed "large foreign power" and Zairian citizens "thirsty for money"(!) The charges appeared in a government-controlled newspaper in the form of a letter from Mobutu. The accompanying editorial indicated plainly that the large foreign power was the United States. A few days later, Zairian newspapers asserted that the CIA had organized tribal dissidents and black Americans for a coup against Mobutu planned for 30 September. It is not clear what relation this allegation had to the earlier one.

Mobutu declared that the "imperialists" were displeased with his breaking off relations with Israel, his nationalizations of many foreign-owned businesses, and the "sincere and reciprocal" friendships which were developing between

Zaire and China and North Korea. (Another illustration of the precariousness of categorizing Third World countries and leaders as being either in the American camp or the Soviet camp.) Several high-ranking Zairian military officers as well as other military men and civilians were arrested. Their number reportedly included most of the CIA's indigenous agents in Zaire. The government announced that one of the arrested officers had returned four months ago from a US military school, another had been the Zairian military attaché in Washington until two weeks before, and a third had recently returned from studies at Fort Bragg, North Carolina where, as a class assignment, he had prepared a report on "How to plan and carry out a coup d'état against the government of Zaire". This last is not as ridiculous as it may sound. Such "hypothetical" exercises have been reported before by former students at CIA schools, although without the name of a real country being used and under the cover of learning how to *suppress* a coup attempt (as torture methods were taught in Vietnam under the cover of "countermeasures to hostile interrogation"; similarly, as we have seen, for the teaching of bombing techniques and chemical/biological warfare).

Eventually, seven of those arrested were condemned to death for the alleged plot (including some of the CIA's agents), seven men were acquitted, and 27 others given prison sentences. No Americans were named as conspirators, but the US Ambassador, Deane R. Hinton, was ordered to leave the country and Zaire recalled its Ambassador from Washington.

The State Department denied the allegations and called upon the Zairian government to provide evidence, which the latter failed to do. Secretary of State Kissinger said that the charges were based on "totally wrong information that fell into the hands of Zaire" and "was probably the result of forgery". It is difficult to evaluate Kissinger's assertion inasmuch as the Zairian government had made no public mention of any documents.[3]

Mobutu may indeed have been taken in by forged documents or, scoundrel that he was, he may have built a mountain out of a molehill of truth. It has been suggested that his action was a pretext to get rid of certain Zairian military officers or that he was looking for a scapegoat for domestic problems. On the other hand, it would not have been the first time that the CIA was involved in a plot to eliminate an ostensible ally of the United States — Trujillo, Figueres and Diem are cases in point. Mobutu, at this time, for his own reasons was deeply involved in the civil war in Angola on the side of the CIA-supported forces. Zaire was serving as an indispensable rear base and training and supply point, and Zairian troops were engaged in the fighting. The Agency may have felt very uneasy that the head of this ally in war was a man as erratic, unpredictable and uncontrollable as Mobutu Sese Seko. "Mobutu is screwing up Zaire pretty good, you know," commented a senior CIA officer upon returning to Washington from a meeting with the Zairian leader, shortly after the accusation against the United States. "He simply has no idea of how to run a country."[4]

Although the Chinese and North Korean military advisers in Zaire were training forces fighting on the same side as the United States in the Angolan free-for-all, the simple tenet of cold-war life was that an American ally does not do things like invite Chinese and North Korean military advisers to their country. Further, the Zairian "wild man" had twice broken relations with the Soviet Union and twice re-established them. There was no telling what whimsy he might pursue next.

There is also the matter of the expelled American Ambassador. Deane Roesch Hinton was no ordinary Foreign Service career diplomat. He appears to have joined the CIA some 20 years earlier under State Department cover and was no stranger to extra-diplomatic operations. From 1967 to 1969 in Guatemala and the following two years in Chile (against Allende), Hinton, under the cover of the AID, had played a significant role in the CIA operations. He then served on a subcommittee of the National Security Council until taking up his post in Zaire in 1974.[5]

From this point on, both the CIA and Mobutu acted as if nothing out of the ordinary had happened, although the Agency did make an appeal to the Zairian president for the freedom of their agents sitting on death row[6] (outcome unknown) and did seem to be remarkably submissive to Mobutu's usual obnoxious and impulsive behaviour. In October, Mobutu asked the CIA to help him annex Cabinda, a province of Angola that was separated from the rest of Angola by a narrow strip of Zairian territory. Mobutu had coveted the province since coming to power in 1965. His greed for it was heightened a few years later when oil was discovered off the Cabindan coastline. The CIA, although busily involved in the Angolan civil war at this time, promptly flew in a one-thousand-man arms package for use by Zairian troops who marched into Cabinda. Agency officials helped to co-ordinate this almost casual invasion of a sovereign nation, but the operation proved to be singularly unsuccessful.[7]

The following April, the CIA gave Mobutu close to $1.4 million to distribute to US-backed Angolan forces, thousands of whom were refugees in Zaire, desperate and hungry. Mobutu simply pocketed the money. The Agency had been aware of this possibility when they delivered the money to him but, in the words of CIA Africa specialist John Stockwell, "They rationalized that it would mollify him, bribe him not to retaliate against the CIA." Stockwell added this observation:

> It is an interesting paradox that the Securities and Exchange Commission has since 1971 investigated, and the Justice Department has prosecuted, several large U.S. corporations for using bribery to facilitate their overseas operations. At the same time, the U.S. government, through the CIA, disburses tens of millions of dollars each year in cash bribes. Bribery is a standard operating technique of the U.S. government, via the CIA, but it is a criminal offense for U.S. business.[8]

The same can be said of murder. A few months earlier, in January 1976, the Justice Department had concluded that no grounds existed for Federal prosecution of CIA officials involved in plots to assassinate several heads of state, including Patrice Lumumba of the Congo (Zaire).[9]

In early March 1977, during a pause in the Angola war, members of the Lunda tribal group who had been in exile in Angola and fighting along with their tribal kin on the side of the MPLA, crossed the border and invaded Zaire in a resumption of their own civil war. The invaders, numbering at least 2,000, were composed largely of former residents of Katanga (now Shaba) province who had fled the Congo during the early 1960s following the failure of their secessionist movement.

Mobutu urgently requested help from Zaire's traditional arms suppliers, Belgium, France and the United States, to put down this threat to his control of the mineral-rich province which accounted for about 70% of Zaire's foreign exchange. The United States responded immediately with some $2 million of military supplies, reaching $15 million worth within a month, while Belgium and France provided large amounts of arms and ammunition as well as 14 Mirage jet bombers from the latter.

Jimmy Carter had been in office less than two months when the Zairian conflict broke out, and he was understandably reluctant to involve his administration deeply in a foreign adventure whose ultimate commitment could not be foreseen. The Angolan involvement had only recently wound down under severe congressional criticism. Compared to this and other American interventions, Carter's action in Zaire constituted a fairly mild response, mild enough to enable Washington to pass off its policy as one of "non-intervention" and effectively obscure the fact that it was actively taking sides in a civil war.

The administration pointed out that its aid was all of a "non-lethal" type (that is, a military transport plane, spare parts, fuel, communication equipment, parachutes, etc.); that the aid represented a drawing of credits already authorized by Congress for Zaire — as if the United States government therefore had no other choice in the matter; and that it had refused a Zairian request for further assistance. President Carter asserted on more than one occasion that the Zairian crisis was an African problem, best solved by Africans, yet he apparently saw no contradiction to this thesis in his own policy, nor did he offer any criticism of France or Belgium, or of China which sent Mobutu a substantial amount of military equipment.

Carter denied the suggestion that US aid to Zaire was part of a co-ordinated venture with France, Belgium, Morocco, Egypt and the Sudan; and, at the same time, the State Department characterized American policy as "a neither help-nor-hinder position" towards Zaire; yet, only a few days earlier, the United States had given its tacit approval to Morocco's decision to send 1,500 of its American-armed troops to aid Mobutu's cause, while confirming that "both by law and bilateral agreement, Morocco would have to obtain Washington's permission in advance if its army used American weapons outside Morocco".[10] Whether the Zairian rebels felt put out by the American non-lethal, non-help-nor-hinder, non-intervention policy was not reported.[11]

In mid-April, *Newsday* broke a story that the CIA was secretly supporting efforts to recruit several hundred mercenaries in the United States and Great Britain to serve alongside Zaire's notoriously ineffective army. David Bufkin, a

38-year-old Californian who, reportedly, was an experienced mercenary himself and had recruited other Americans for Angola, said that American "soldiers of fortune" would leave within a week for Zaire to fight against the rebels. Bufkin had advertised for former military men with combat experience for this particular mission.

The New York newspaper stated that the CIA had "strong links" to Bufkin and had told the Justice Department that it would not co-operate in any investigation of the Californian. (It is a criminal offence in the United States to recruit an American citizen for service with foreign armed forces or to enlist for such service.)

"Diplomats in Washington," the *New York Times* reported, "said they understood that President Mobutu Sese Seko had indicated several weeks ago that Zaire might have to recruit mercenaries to repel the invasion." They added that the aid from France, Belgium, Morocco, the United States and others may have led Mobutu to abandon the idea.

Bufkin denied that he was being financed by the CIA. He claimed that his financial aid "is coming from Africa and that's all I can tell you".[12] (This, of course, would not rule out the CIA channelling money to Bufkin via Zaire.) Several months later, the soldier of fortune revealed that he had worked with the CIA, without specifying when or where, as well as with the Korean CIA, going into some detail about his operations with the latter.[13] What role, if any, was actually played by mercenaries in Zaire has not come to light.

The more experienced rebels had the upper hand during the first month of the 80-day war, and the continuance of Mobutu's rule was reported to be uncertain. But the repeated pumping of men and supplies into Zaire by at least eight Western and African nations proved too much for the Lunda tribesmen. By the end of May, their offensive had been crushed and they were forced to retreat into Angola once again.

Although the Lunda's struggle in Zaire was essentially a tribal conflict, of the kind which has erupted in one African country after another following their independence, Mobutu knew that it was the cold-war, anti-communist card he had to play if he was to provoke greater military support, particularly from the United States. Accordingly, Zaire began to issue regular accusations against Cuba, which had a large military contingent still stationed in Angola.

Cuba had trained and armed the rebels, it was charged. This was true to some extent, but it had not been done necessarily to invade Zaire. The rebels called themselves the Front for the National Liberation of the Congo (FNLC), and some quarters of the international left cloaked them in a revolutionary mantle, but the evidence for this had more to do with the FNLC being opposed by the likes of Mobutu, the United States and France than with any demonstrated revolutionary virtues. On the contrary, they were originally trained by white mercenaries and supported by Belgium and other Western interests in their secession attempt in Katanga. After fleeing to Angola, in return for sanctuary they served with the colonial Portuguese army in its campaign to put down the black nationalist guerrillas of the MPLA. Then, during the ensuing civil war in Angola, the FNLC switched over to fighting on the side of the MPLA and the Cubans.[14]

Cuba was leading the rebels . . . Cuban, Russian and Portuguese troops were fighting with them, insisted the Zairian Government.

The invasion "could not have taken place — and it could not continue — without the material support or acquiescence of the Soviet Union — whether or not Cuban troops are present", chipped in (now former) Secretary of State Henry Kissinger, in a choice example of mechanical anti-communism, if not wishful thinking.[15]

And so it went. To the credit of the Carter administration, it resisted the temptation to embrace all the unfounded and sometimes silly charges, stating on several occasions that there was no evidence of Cuban involvement, and that the United States did not view the conflict as a confrontation between the Soviet Union and the West. An increasingly petulant Mobutu was finally moved to declare that if the United States had indeed "capitulated" in the face of communist danger, it should announce this clearly.[16]

Why then, did the United States intervene at all?

The day after the first American shipment of military aid, Washington expressed its concern about the possible "loss" to American mining interests in Zaire. However, there was not necessarily a logical connection between a Lunda capture of Shaba province, or even toppling Mobutu, and a threat to foreign investment and loans, and the Carter administration offered no elaboration of its statement. In the early 1960s, the secession movement of these same Katangese forces had been supported by Belgium which had a vastly larger investment in the province that the United States ever had. And in neighbouring Angola, as we have seen, when the "Marxist" MPLA took over control of oil-rich Cabinda province, it co-operated fully in business-as-usual with Gulf Oil Company.

The expressed concern about US investments may have been no more than one type of "throwaway" remark that has often been put forth by officials to make a particular foreign involvement sound more reasonable to the American public (most ironic in light of traditional Marxist analysis), while giving the administration time to decide what it is they're actually trying to achieve. No further reference to American investments was made.

The American intervention in this case seems to have been little more than a highly-developed, cold-war reflex action triggered by an invasion originating in a country classified as a member of the Soviet camp, and against a country ostensibly in the American camp. Subsequent developments, or lack of them, may have inspired second thoughts in the administration, producing a dilemma which was succinctly summed up by a *New York Times* editorial observation a month into the war: "The instinct for intervention seems great but the case for it is not at all clear."[17]

Earlier, the *Washington Post* had expressed similar doubts. In an editorial entitled "Why Zaire?", the newspaper stated that it was "a highly dubious proposition for the United States to deepen its involvement in the murk of Zaire in the way that it has." President Carter, it added, "has not explained the contingencies or stakes which require such a(n) abrupt American response, nor the risks of delay".[18]

By his second year in the White House, Jimmy Carter had managed to acquire the unfortunate image of an "indecisive" man, a president who was yet to demonstrate the proverbial sterling qualities of leadership. His moderate response to the events in Zaire the previous year had contributed to this reputation, particularly amongst the hardline anti-communists in the United States and amongst some of the European and African nations which had come to Mobutu's aid.

Thus it was, in the middle of May 1978, when the FNLC again invaded their home province in Zaire, that the Carter administration was once again drawn into the conflict, for reasons no more compelling than in the year before . . . "determination this time, particularly with a meeting in 11 days in Washington of heads of NATO Governments, to act decisively", was the way the *New York Times* paraphrased "high administration officials".[19]

Within days the United States had sent several million dollars more of "non-lethal" military aid to Mobutu (whom the State Department had condemned for human-rights violations only three months earlier) while a fleet of 18 American military transport planes began ferrying Belgian and French troops into Zaire in a rescue mission of (white) foreigners trapped by the war. In the process of evacuating the foreigners, the French troops took a markedly active part in the war against the rebels, inflicting a serious military setback upon them.

Subsequently, the American airlift was extended to delivering Moroccan armed forces into Shaba province, then army units from Senegal and Gabon, and transporting French troops out of the region as they were replaced by African forces.[20]

The fighting in Shaba province this time was over in less than a month. At its conclusion, the *New York Times* reported that "Discussions with officials in recent days, have produced no single cohesive explanation" for American policy in Zaire.[21]

The *Times* apparently was not placing too much weight upon the explanations already put forth by the administration. There were several of these in addition to the rescue mission and the need to act decisively. The president, for example, had discovered something which, it seems, he had not realized the year before; namely, that aiding Zaire was "in the national security interests of the United States".[22] As is customary with such crucial declarations, it was not felt necessary to explain what this actually meant in real terms.

Administration officials also professed "concern for the territorial integrity of all countries in Africa and elsewhere".[23] This marvellous platitude not only managed to do away with the previous 80 years of American foreign policy, including the very recent intervention into Angola, but was irrelevant in the context of a civil war . . . more throwaways.

Several African governments which came to the aid of Mobutu during these two years likewise expressed regard for the territorial integrity of African states, but what these states found disquieting was that a victory for the Shaba rebels might encourage tribal dissidents within their own vulnerable borders.[24]

Another reason offered by the administration was the belief that Cuba and the Soviet Union, and even Angola, were, after all, somehow responsible. (Mobutu added Algeria and Libya.) But inasmuch as no more evidence to support these charges was forthcoming from any quarter than had been the case the year before, Carter was obliged to fall back on an accusation of guilt by omission. On 25 May 1978 he declared that Cuba "obviously did nothing" to hold back the invasion. It then came to light that Castro had informed the US government a week earlier that he had learned of the rebel plans to invade Shaba and had tried unsuccessfully to stop it. Administration officials, clearly embarrassed, had no choice but to reply that they had not believed him.

"It is not a half-lie," commented Fidel Castro to charges of Cuban involvement. "It is an absolute, total, complete lie."

Two days later, the president rejoined: "Castro could have done much more had he genuinely wanted to stop the invasion. He could have interceded with the Katangese themselves; he could certainly have imposed Cuban troops near the border . . ."[25]

In the final scene of this light comedy, Mobutu announced that he was holding Cuban prisoners captured in the fighting — the long-awaited proof of Cuban involvement. But when the American Embassy in Zaire checked into the matter it found nothing to substantiate the claim. "Let's call it charitably a mistake," said one official.[26]

43. Jamaica 1976 to 1980
Kissinger's ultimatum

"I can give you my personal word," said Henry Kissinger to Jamaican Prime Minister Michael Manley, "that there is no attempt now underway involving covert action against the Jamaican government."[1]

Manley has written that at this moment "similar assurances given concerning Chile flashed a little ominously across my mind."*[2]

---

* Kissinger had given his personal word about American non-activity to the Chilean Ambassador in Washington at a time when the US government, and Kissinger in particular, (Footnote continued overleaf)

The American Secretary of State had arrived in Jamaica in December 1975 to suggest to Manley that he change his policies or else US-Jamaican relations "would be reviewed".[5] Kissinger raised the subject of Jamaica's request for a $100 million trade credit. "He said they were looking at it," wrote Manley later, "and let the comment hang in the room for a moment. I had the feeling he was sending me a message."[6]

The Jamaican prime minister — a graduate of the London School of Economics and the son of Norman Manley who had led Jamaica to independence from the British in 1962 — had incurred Washington's displeasure since taking office in 1972 by behaviour such as the following:

● Expressing support for the MPLA regime in Angola which the United States was attempting to topple at the very moment of the Kissinger-Manley meeting, an issue raised by the Secretary of State during the talk.

● Establishing diplomatic relations with Cuba and the Soviet Union and maintaining close ties with the Castro government, although "no closer," says Manley, "than . . . with Mexico and Venezuela".[7]

● Advocating democratic socialism, though maintaining a decidedly mixed economy which featured nothing more radical than could be found in many countries of Western Europe in the areas of health, education, minimum wage, and social services. Manley's party belonged to the Socialist International, as have ruling parties in recent years in Austria, Great Britain, West Germany and Sweden.

● Prevailing against the transnational aluminium companies, principally American, which operated on the island because it is rich in bauxite, the raw material of aluminium. The Jamaican government imposed a production levy to obtain a significant — and what was regarded as long-overdue — increase in the payments made to it by the companies, and then persuaded other bauxite-producing countries in the Third World to do the same. The government also bought 51 percent of the bauxite mining operation, although this did not mean that it ran or controlled the operation.[8]

Manley did not toe the line Kissinger had drawn. Five days after the Secretary of State had departed, Manley let him know that "Jamaica had decided to support the Cuban army presence in Angola because we were satisfied that they were there because of the South African invasion . . . I never heard another word about the hundred million dollar trade credit."[9]

were actively plotting the downfall of the Chilean government. When the ambassador mentioned press references to covert American actions against his country, Kissinger responded: "Absolutely absurd and without foundation."[3]

During the 1972 election campaign, the American Ambassador in Jamaica, Vincent de Roulet, promised Manley that the United States would not interfere in the campaign if Manley did not make nationalization of the foreign-owned bauxite industry an election issue. De Roulet feared that if Manley did so, he would oblige the opposition Jamaica Labour Party to vie with Manley's party for popular support on the question. According to de Roulet, Manley agreed and both sides kept their promise.[4]

Manley was pressured by both Washington and the Jamaican left. "Everyone wants me to be either a capitalist or a communist," he said at one point. "Why can't they just let me be? . . . I've always been a democratic socialist and that's what I want in Jamaica".[10]

At the time of Kissinger's visit, certain destabilization operations had already got off the ground, particularly in the area of propaganda, but it was primarily afterward, beginning in the election year of 1976, that covert actions started to escalate. In January, a few weeks after Kissinger had left, the US Embassy in Kingston was increased by seven. Manley has noted: "Yet all aid to Jamaica suddenly slowed to a virtual halt. The pipelines suddenly became clogged. Economic co-operation contracted as the embassy expanded."[11]

Investigative reporters Ernest Volkman and John Cummings, writing in *Penthouse* magazine and citing "several senior American intelligence sources", state that the destabilization programme drawn up by the CIA station chief in Jamaica (Norman Descoteaux) contained the following elements:

"Covert shipments of arms and other equipment to opposition forces": Politics in Jamaica had long been spiced with strong-arm tactics, but this now intensified in both frequency and deadliness, and in the use of arson, bombing and assassination. Thousands of guns found their way into Jamaica. "The CIA quickly sought to organize and expand the violence: shipments of guns and sophisticated communications equipment began to be smuggled into the island. In one shipment alone, which was grabbed by Manley's security forces, there were 500 submachine guns."[12]

Some of the CIA's army of Cuban exiles arrived on the scene, men employed by the Agency all over the world. One was Luis Posada Cariles, a former officer in Cuban dictator Batista's secret police, now a CIA-trained explosives expert. Posada was reportedly spotted at the scene of a number of bombings in Jamaica.[13]

The well-publicized violence was a body-blow to Jamaica's vital tourist business. The foreign tourists stayed away in droves, forcing many hotels to close their doors and throwing thousands of workers out of their jobs.

"Extensive labor unrest": A wave of strikes by transport, electrical and telephone workers hit the island, reportedly provoked in part by graduates of the American Institute for Free Labor Development, the CIA's principal labour organization in Latin America.[14]

"Economic destabilization": In addition to the US credit squeeze and curtailment of aid, and the damage to tourism, the fragile Jamaican economy suffered from the actions of the aluminium companies. As an act of retaliation for the levy, and with the tacit encouragement of Washington, the companies systematically reduced production which hurt Jamaica in more than one way.[15] Moreover, the American firm, Revere Copper and Brass Company, closed its $90 million aluminium refinery in August 1975 after only four years of operation, saying that it was uneconomical.[16]

A cargo of flour, brought to Jamaica on a German ship, the *Heidelberg*, was discovered to have been contaminated with the poison parathion, an insecticide which had been banned from Jamaica for many years. Much of the flour had already been sold and about 17 people died from it in December 1975 and January 1976. Later in the year, in October, a large shipment of rice from Costa Rica, on board the ship *City of Bochum*, arrived to relieve a rice shortage Jamaicans had been suffering through for months. This too was found to be contaminated by parathion and had to be destroyed.[17] The two incidents are reminiscent of the contaminations of sugar carried out by the CIA against Cuba.

"Covert financial support for the opposition": This was principally the conservative Jamaica Labour Party (JLP). In June 1976, Jamaican security forces announced the uncovering of a plot to overthrow the government involving leading members of the JLP; another arrested party member was found to be making Molotov cocktails in a mineral-bottling plant he owned;[18] no evidence of direct CIA involvement in the conspiracy has been revealed.

"Mobilization of the middle class into CIA-created antigovernment organizations to carry out well-publicized demonstrations": Groups with names such as "Silent Majority" and "Christian Women Agitators for Truth" were formed, the latter attacking those who criticized the United States and the CIA; in one instance, the group brought up the example of the famed and honoured American doctor, Tom Dooley, who had founded seven hospitals for the poor in south-east Asia; the Christian Women could not have known then that Dr Dooley had been a witting, active CIA operative in Indochina.[19] There was also an attempt by a newly-formed "National Council of Women" to replay the pots-and-pans scenario which had worked so well in Chile, but this fizzled out.[20] (This featured housewives banging on pots and pans in a street march to demonstrate the government's inability to provide enough food for their families.)

"Infiltration of security services and armed forces to turn them against the government": "With liberal bribes, the CIA turned many security personnel into paid informants for the agency." Several soldiers were part of a plot to assassinate Manley in July, one of at least three such attempts which "the CIA was directly involved in"; another, in September, employed Cuban exiles; the third turned to Jamaican gunmen to do the job; this last was in December, a final act of desperation on election night; all three attempts failed, not even a shot was fired, and Manley easily won re-election.[21]

CIA officer James Holt was accused of contriving a plot to turn the military against Manley's People's National Party. A tape of a PNP youth rally was spliced with a message, purporting to be from Fidel Castro, urging young people to rise up in armed struggle against the police and the army. The tape was supposed to fall into the hands of the military and cause dissension.[22]

Press attacks against the government were carried out at a level of integrity only slightly above that of Holt's alleged tape. This was particularly the case with the *Daily Gleaner* whose campaign was very similar to that of *El Mercurio* in Chile before the fall of Allende, and it is eminently reasonable to assume that it was similarly financed by the CIA. Both newspapers had close links to the Inter-

American Press Association (IAPA) of Miami, the *Gleaner's* Managing Director, Oliver Clarke, being elected to the association's executive in 1976. The IAPA, though not a formal CIA front, has been a reliable and valuable press asset of the Agency since the 1950s.[23]

The *Gleaner* emphasized the omnipresent Cuban menace and how Manley was a prisoner of Castro and the KGB. One recurrent theme, echoed in the American press, was the presence of Cuban troops in Jamaica, a bald lie and something that would be impossible to conceal on the small island.

Propagandists arrived from outside as well. American evangelists and faith healers came down to set up their tents and preach against communism and the government to the highly religious population,[24] à la the American Christian Anti-Communist Crusade in British Guiana during the CIA's campaign against the government of Cheddi Jagan.

With Henry Kissinger removed from formal power, and with the less interventionist Carter administration taking office in January 1977, American policy toward Jamaica was tempered: the economic pipelines were unclogged to some extent, and the CIA, without the urgency of an upcoming election, diminished its activities.

It cannot be said, however, that Washington officialdom had learned to respect Manley's wish to "just let me be". Pulitzer-prize winner Les Payne reported in *Newsday* in February 1980 that "the Carter Administration remains determined to drive the country's Socialist prime minister from office unless he moderates his pro-Cuban policies." In an earlier article, Payne quoted a State Department source: "If within a 6-month testing period, Manley shows some signs of moderating his position, then we will take a softer line. If not, then we will continue to pursue a hard line."[25]

There was no let-up in the *Gleaner's* diatribes against Manley and his government. The newspaper reprinted numerous unattributed articles from all over the world which bore the standard CIA themes and syntax; it openly encouraged disaffection and mutiny in the security forces, and overthrow of the government. The following, from a column by John Hearne in the 1 June 1980 issue, was not very unusual:

> In many other countries, somebody with a disciplined force of men behind him would have long ago taken the Government away from them ... In most Third World countries, our Ministers, Ministers of State, Party commanders, heads of statutory boards, among others, would now be in forced exile or buried in common graves.[26]

Throughout, the *Gleaner* and other anti-Manley newspapers in Jamaica bemoaned the threat to freedom of the press posed by the government — on the premise, apparently, that this is only what one can expect from a "communist" government — and continued to print freely what in other countries would lead to arrest for sedition.

Manley was defeated for re-election in October 1980, due primarily to a continuing deterioration in the standard of living of the masses of people. While recognizing the importance of this factor, the former prime minister has attributed his defeat also to "propaganda and finely calculated violence", the latter having persisted throughout his second term, being particularly heavy during the election year. Manley has written that "Unless there is overwhelming and widely accepted evidence laying the blame for violence at the door of one party, it tends to damage the government in power, since it is the government that people look to for their personal security."[27] He added:

> The Jamaican establishment had mastered the ways of destabilization. It knew how to use fact and create fiction for maximum effect. We do not know what was the part played by the CIA in the last year. By then it may not have mattered because the *Gleaner* and the JLP had clearly reached postgraduate level.[28]

44. Seychelles 1979 to 1981
Yet another area of great strategic importance

Mr Michael Hoare, in 1981, was an elderly accountant leading a relatively sedate life in Durban, South Africa. There was, however, another side to the man that was somewhat different. In this other role he was "Mad Mike" Hoare, veteran mercenary. He had fought for the CIA in various "trouble spots" of the world, including the Congo in the 1960s, and had done the same for the government of South Africa. In 1981, at the age of 62, he led a mercenary invasion of the Seychelles on behalf of both his old employers.

The Seychelles, for those who don't know, is a country made up of a number of small islands in the Indian Ocean, about 800 miles off the coast of Kenya, with a population of some 62,000. The former British Crown Colony is also the site of a US Air Force installation, officially described as a satellite tracking station, and part of an area that the United States regards as being of great strategic importance. (This should be seen in light of the fact that it would be difficult to locate an area of the globe that Washington policy-makers, at one time or another, have not regarded as being of great strategic importance.)

After France-Albert Rene, a socialist, took power in a 1977 coup, he withdrew South African landing rights, and the United States had to use all its formidable powers of economic and political persuasion to retain its base in the country. Moreover, the lease on the installation expired in 1990, and Washington, which worries about long-term "national security" needs as well as current trouble spots, was apprehensive that it might not be renewed. The United States was also worried about what it saw as the growing friendship between the Seychelles and the Soviet Union, a concern seemingly as common in Washington as areas of great strategic importance.

Rene pursued a policy of non-alignment, a concept which did not preclude friendship with either superpower as long as the terms were not unduly exploitive. He was also a strong advocate of turning the Indian Ocean into a nuclear-free zone, without foreign military bases, including, ideally, the one in his own country. The Seychelles president was particularly critical of American efforts to develop the British-owned Indian Ocean island of Diego Garcia into a major air and naval base.[1]

In 1979, a plot to invade the Seychelles and overthrow Rene was aborted when it was discovered by his government before the mercenaries were able to leave Durban. An official investigation into the matter by the Seychelles government concluded that the United States and France had been directly involved with the plotters, that the American Ambassador in Kenya had been in contact with supporters of James Mancham, the man deposed by Rene, and that the US Charge d'Affaires in the Seychelles was the link man in the conspiracy.[2] Several of the 120 Americans employed at the US base were expelled from the country.[3]

Two years later, in November 1981, an invasion force of more than 40 men, pretending to be members of a club, travelled from South Africa to Swaziland whence they flew to the Seychelles aboard a regular commercial flight of the Royal Swazi Airlines. It appears that the attack was not planned for the arrival but for some time later, after the soldiers of fortune had settled in. But some of the arms hidden in their luggage were discovered upon arrival, and a battle broke out at the airport. The would-be invaders were forced to hijack an Air India plane back to Durban. "Mad Mike" Hoare had survived another close call.[4]

A few days after this debacle, the *Sunday Tribune*, published in Durban where the invasion plot was reportedly hatched, cited "reliable local and foreign sources" for the assertion that the CIA had financed the raising and equipping of the invasion force. "Despite a terse, one-sentence denial by the U.S. government yesterday," the conservative newspaper declared, "separate mercenary sources in South Africa are emphatic that funding for the operation originated with the CIA." At the same time, the *Tribune* made clear the complicity of its own government, an act for which several South African editors were duly prosecuted by the authorities.[5]

On 15 December 1981, the UN Security Council decided to send a commission to the Seychelles to investigate the invasion. Although the United States voted for the motion, the American Ambassador, Jeane Kirkpatrick, suggested that to send the commission was to assume that the "Seychelles affair was not purely internal", and was "prejudging the situation".[6] Even by the standards of Kirkpatrick's renowned cold-war-impaired logic, this was a remarkable statement, when it is considered that South Africans made up about half the invasion force, with the others emanating from Great Britain, Rhodesia, the US and elsewhere. The number of Seychellois dissidents amongst them came to zero.

It appears that someone was still determined that the Rene government should not remain in power. In December 1983, South Africa announced that it had arrested five men for attempting to recruit mercenaries in yet another plot to invade the Seychelles.[7]

45. Grenada 1979 to 1983
Lying — one of the few growth industries in Washington

What can be said about an invasion launched by a nation of 240 million people against one of 110 thousand? And when the invader is, militarily and economically, the most powerful in the world, and the target of its attack is an underdeveloped island of small villages 1,500 miles away, 133 sq. miles in size, whose main exports are cocoa, nutmeg and bananas . . .

The United States Government had a lot to say about it. The relation which its pronouncements bore to the truth can be accurately gauged by the fact that three days after the invasion the deputy White House press secretary for foreign affairs resigned, citing "damage to his personal credibility".[1]

One of the fundamental falsehoods concerning the invasion of Tuesday, 25 October 1983 was that the United States had been requested to intervene by an urgent plea on the 21st from the Organization of Eastern Caribbean States (OECS), comprising six countries, joined by Barbados and Jamaica. These countries purportedly feared some form of aggressive act from the new ultra-leftist regime in Grenada which had deposed socialist leader Maurice Bishop. Bishop had been expelled from the ruling party on 12 October, placed under house arrest the next day, and murdered on the 19th.

Even if the fears were valid, it would constitute a principle heretofore unknown under international law, namely that state A could ask state B to invade state C in the absence of any aggressive act toward state A by state C. In Washington, State Department lawyers worked overtime, finally settling on sections of an OECS mutual assistance pact, the Charter of the OAS, and the United Nations Charter as legal justifications for the American action. These documents, however, even with the most generous interpretation, provide for nothing of the sort. Moreover, Article Six of the OECS pact requires *all* members to approve decisions of the organization's Authority (the heads of government). Grenada, a member, certainly did not approve. It was not even at the meeting, although high US officials were present to steer the direction of the discussions.[2]

As matters later transpired, Tom Adams, the Prime Minister of Barbados, stated that the United States had approached him on 15 October concerning a military intervention. (The State Department declined to comment when asked about Adams' statement.)[3] Then, "sources close to Jamaican Prime Minister Edward Seaga" asserted that the plea by the Caribbean nations "was triggered by an offer from the United States" — "Issue an appeal and we'll respond" was the message conveyed by Washington.[4] Furthermore, on 26 October, the US Ambassador to France, Evan Galbraith, stated over French television that the Reagan Administration had been planning the invasion for the previous two weeks;[5] that is, not only well before the putative request from the Caribbean countries, but, if Galbraith is to be taken literally, even before Bishop was overthrown or before this outcome could have been known with any certainty, unless the CIA had been mixed up in the intra-party feud.

At the same time, the United States, as if to cover its bets, endorsed (if not in fact devised) the claim by the OECS that the Governor-General of Grenada, Paul Scoon, had also sent an urgent appeal for military intervention to the organization. Apart from the highly debatable question of whether Scoon — appointed by the British Queen to his largely ceremonial, figurehead position, a vestige of the days of the Empire — had the constitutional right to make such a momentous decision on behalf of an independent Grenada, there was the mystery of how and when he had sent his request, or, indeed, whether he had sent it at all.

On 31 October, the London press reported that the British Foreign Secretary Sir Geoffrey Howe "was emphatic that there had been no request for intervention from Sir Paul Scoon". Prime Minister Thatcher unequivocally confirmed this. Scoon, said Sir Geoffrey, "had been seen by a British diplomat last Monday — the day before the invasion — and had not mentioned any such desire."[6] The same day (another report places it on Sunday) Scoon spoke by phone to the Commonwealth Secretariat in London and to Buckingham Palace, but, again, made no mention of intervention.[7]

Interviewed later by the BBC, Scoon himself said that an invasion was the "last thing" he wanted.[8]

In the end, after the invasion was underway, Scoon signed a piece of paper aboard the USS *Guam* that made the whole operation nice and legal.[9]

Another justification advanced by the United States for its action, what President Reagan termed "of overriding importance", was the need to evacuate many hundreds of Americans from the island, mainly students at St George's

Medical College who were supposedly in a dangerous position because of the new regime and the chaos surrounding its accession to power.

To refute this contention one does not have to dig for evidence, one is immersed in it, as the following tesitifies:

Two members of the US Embassy in Barbados, Ken Kurze and Linda Flohr, reported over the weekend before the invasion that "US students in Grenada were, for the most part, unwilling to leave or be evacuated. They were too intent on their studies."[10] Another report, in the London press, that three US diplomats visited Grenada at the same time and appeared to have agreed on orderly departures for any Americans wishing to leave, may or may not refer to the same thing.[11]

The White House acknowledged that two days before the invasion, Grenada had offered the United States "an opportunity to evacuate American citizens. But officials said the Reagan Administration came to distrust the offer." This was, they said, because the Grenadian government had promised that the airport would be open on Monday for evacuation flights, but it was instead closed.[12] Only later did the White House admit that four charter flights had indeed left the airport on Monday.[13]

Some of those who left on Monday were American medical students. The Chancellor of the medical school, Dr Charles Modica, who was visiting New York, declared on the day of the invasion that he was in touch with amateur radio operators at the college. "I think the President's information is very wrong," he said, "because some of the Americans started to go out yesterday."[14]

The Grenadian government issued instructions that the American students should be treated with utmost consideration by the army; vehicles and escorts were provided for them to shuttle between their two campuses.[15]

The Cuban government released documents which showed that it had notified the United States on 22 October that no American or other foreign citizen was in danger and said it was ready "to cooperate in the solution of problems without violence or intervention"; it received no reply until after the invasion had begun.[16] On the 23rd the Cubans sent a message to the Grenadian leaders suggesting that the area around the medical school be demilitarized to avoid providing the United States with an excuse for invasion: "the pretext of evacuating its citizens".[17]

Asked repeatedly by journalists if there was any concrete information about threats to Americans in Grenada, the White House spokesman responded: "Nothing that I know of."[18]

After subduing the minor resistance of Grenadian soldiers and Cuban construction workers, the US forces discovered several other things to justify their coming: they found, said Ronald Reagan, "a complete base of weapons and communication equipment which makes it clear a Cuban occupation of the island had been planned". One warehouse "contained weapons and ammunition stacked almost to the ceiling, enough to supply thousands of terrorists". Grenada, the President declared, was "a Soviet-Cuban colony being readied as a major military bastion to export terror and undermine democracy, but we got there just in time."[19]

Documents discovered by the American military allegedly showed that "the Cubans were planning to put their own government in Grenada" and there was found what "appeared to have been a terrorist training center".[20] Moreover, missile silos were being built in Grenada . . . there were 1,100 Cubans on the island, it was announced, almost all professional soldiers; soon the number was 1,600 . . .[21]

The US/Grenada/Cuba scenario staged in Washington is comparable to the Soviet Union invading Great Britain and then announcing that it had prevented an American takeover, and Marx-knows what else, because it had discovered 30,000 US servicemen there, over 100 American military bases, a huge arsenal of nuclear weapons, and "enough arms to supply millions of terrorists". The Soviet president could then declare that "We got there just in time."

Comparable, except that the Soviet discoveries would have been real. The American claims turned out to be as phantom as the other components of the media package, or, as in the case of the weapons, a matter of great uncertainty: a correspondent for *The Guardian* of London reported that in the warehouse "that contained most of the weapons, there were only five mortars to be seen, one recoilless rifle, one Soviet-made quadri-barrelled anti-aircraft gun, and two Korean-vintage British bren guns on display".[22] The *New York Times* reported, without further detail, "significant stockpiles of Soviet arms but also a number of antiquated guns, including rifles manufactured in the 1870's".[23]

More to the point, however, is the fact that the Grenadian government had been threatened with destabilization for over four years by the United States. The leaders of the country knew that they had to develop the country's defences. They were people who had read some recent history.

The Cuban government announced that there were 784 of their people in Grenada and specified all their jobs: 636 were construction workers, mostly in their forties and fifties (an observation made by several American and British journalists); the remainder, which included 44 women, were doctors, dentists, nurses, public health workers, teachers, etc., and 43 military personnel; thereafter, the United States went by the Cuban figures.[24]

The world was asked to believe that there was a major Cuban military presence and control of the country. Yet, the Cubans in Grenada were unable even to save Maurice Bishop and his government which Castro had strongly and warmly supported. The Cuban government had expressed its distaste in no uncertain terms to the Military Revolutionary Council (MRC) which had overthrown Bishop. Before the invasion, Castro had blamed Bishop's death on "grave errors" by extremists[25] (whom Havana began to refer to as the "Pol Pot Group"),[26] and had turned down a request from the MRC for more troops when the American action seemed imminent. The MRC was told that its request was "impossible and unthinkable" after what had happened.[27]

The Russians, on the other hand, had indicated their support for the MRC and its coup, although the Soviet interest in Grenada was generally minimal. Cuba was enough of a Caribbean burden and potential spark-point. The Soviet

Union condemned the American invasion, comparing it to "a daring cavalry attack of armed-to-the-teeth white settlers on a village of Redskins".[28] But this was *de rigueur* cold-war fare. The lack of real concern on the part of Soviet leaders about the invasion, and the fate of Grenada, was made evident six months later when they announced that the USSR would not take part in the Olympics in Los Angeles. Grenada was not even mentioned amongst their reasons although the circumstances truly cried out for it — four years earlier, the United States had cited the Soviet invasion of Afghanistan as its sole reason for boycotting the Moscow Olympics.

Finally, there was the question of why Cuba or the Soviet Union would have needed Grenada as a springboard for their dastardly deeds in Latin America when there was already Cuba itself, militarily and politically more secure and stable than Grenada.

After the invasion, after the overthrow of the Grenadian government, after the US forces had killed hundreds of people . . . officials of the Reagan Administration, reported the *New York Times*, "acknowledge that in their effort to rally public support for the invasion of Grenada, they may have damaged the Government's credibility by making sweeping charges about Soviet and Cuban influence on the island without so far providing detailed evidence." The officials simply asked that the public "reserve judgement until all the information is in".[29]

The New Jewel Movement (NJM) under Maurice Bishop had taken power in March 1979 by ousting, to popular acclaim, Eric Gairy, an erratic personality given increasingly to thuggery to maintain his rule. That accomplished, Bishop, a lawyer educated in London, had to deal with the infinitely more formidable task which faces a socialist revolutionary in power: spurring an underdeveloped country to lift itself up by its own bootstraps when it doesn't have any boots.

They had to start with the basics: jobs, new schools, teacher training, adult literacy, social services, clean water . . . the NJM left private business undisturbed, but instituted free health care, free milk for young children, agricultural co-operatives, and the like.

Nicholas Brathwaite, the Chairman of the US-approved Interim Government following the invasion, and his colleagues, reported *The Guardian*, "readily praise the [NJM] for giving Grenadians new awareness, self-confidence and national pride and admit it is a hard act to follow."[30]

The World Bank gave the Grenadian government good grades also. In 1980 the Bank praised the NJM's sound fiscal management and two years later wrote that "Government objectives are centered on the critical development issues and touch on the country's most promising development areas."[31]

The New Jewel Movement did not hold elections. Bishop explained this decision on one occasion in the following way:

> There are those (some of them our friends) who believe that you cannot have a democracy unless there is a situation where every five years, and for five seconds

in those five years, a people are allowed to put an 'X' next to some candidate's name, and for those five seconds in those five years they become democrats, and for the remainder of the time, four years and 364 days, they return to being non-people without the right to say anything to their government, without any right to be involved in running the country.[32]

In lieu of the traditional system, the NJM claimed, democracy in Grenada was manifested through numerous mass organizations and decentralized structures which received and seriously considered input from large numbers of citizens. However well this form of democracy may have worked, or would have if not interrupted, it reportedly produced resentment as well. People were expected to attend meeting after meeting and were subject to various forms of pressure to conform to the exigencies of the revolution.

Before long, the leaders of nearby Caribbean states, particularly Tom Adams of Barbados and Eugenia Charles of Dominica who were prime supporters of the invasion, evidenced hostility towards the Grenadian government. Bishop believed that this derived from fear of their own people's enthusiasm for Grenada's example, an enthusiasm, he said, which was demonstrated at every public appearance by the Grenadian leaders in the region.[33]

The United States adopted its adversarial position almost immediately. Washington recognized instinctively that the new Grenadian leaders would not fall easily into line in regard to the American obsession with quarantining Cuba. Indeed, Grenada itself might turn out to be that long-dreaded beast, another Cuba. Less than a month after Bishop assumed power, the American Ambassador delivered a note to him which read in part:

> Although my government recognizes your concern over allegations of a possible counter-coup, it also believes that it would not be in Grenada's best interests to seek assistance from a country such as Cuba to forestall such an attack. We would view with displeasure any tendency on the part of Grenada to develop closer ties with Cuba.[34]

The counter-coup the ambassador was referring to was Bishop's fear that Eric Gairy, in exile in the United States, would put together a mercenary army to invade the island. The NJM feared a CIA destabilization programme even more but, in either case, who but "a country such as Cuba" could they turn to for help.

Before the year was out, Grenada had discovered hidden transmitters in its UN Mission,[35] and State Department representatives were visiting travel agents in the United States spreading travel-scare rumours to discourage tourism to the island's sunny beaches, a most important source of foreign exchange.[36]

Over the next four years, Washington tried to harass Grenada in some of the other ways in which it was practiced, more so under Ronald Reagan beginning in 1981 than under President Carter. The United States aggressively lobbied the International Monetary Fund and several other international lending organizations in an attempt to block loans to Grenada although, surprisingly, not with marked success. The IMF, for example, approved a loan to **Grenada** "despite vigorous opposition from the Reagan Administration", opposition based ostensibly on "economic grounds".[37]

In the summer of 1981, the CIA developed plans "to cause economic difficulties for Grenada in hopes of undermining the political control of Prime Minister Maurice Bishop." The operation reportedly was scrapped because of objections by the Senate Intelligence Committee. One committee member, however, remarked that "If they were going to do something . . . I'm not sure they would tell us. I think they would wait until it was all over . . ."[38]

The main thrust of the American campaign against Grenada was in the form of propaganda, the theme of which was that Grenada was a fully paid-up member of the Soviet-Cuban-Nicaraguan Terrorist Network which held a dagger at America's throat. Associating Grenada thusly could serve to further discourage tourism as well as justify an invasion.

The propagation of the general theme was punctuated by specific accusations which were simply fraudulent. One early hoax was that a Soviet submarine base was being constructed on the south coast of the island. This report was given wide currency until 1983 when a correspondent for the *Washington Post* visited the supposed site and pointed out that no submarine base could possibly be built in an area where the sea was so shallow.[39]

In February 1983, an official of the US Defense Department announced, apparently with a straight face, that the Soviet Union had shipped to Grenada assault helicopters, hydrofoil torpedo boats, and supersonic MIG fighters which gave Grenada an air force of 200 (sic) modern planes.[40] The whereabouts of this mighty armada have remained a mystery ever since.

The charge which received the greatest media play was the canard that the new airport being built in Grenada was intended as a military facility for the Russians and Cubans. Grenada insisted that it was only to encourage tourism, its one growth industry. In March 1983, President Reagan told an American television audience that the airfield would have a 10,000 foot runway, but that "Grenada doesn't even have an air force [see previous paragraph]. Who is it intended for? . . . The rapid build-up of Grenada's military potential is unrelated to any conceivable threat . . . The Soviet-Cuban militarization of Grenada . . . can only be seen as a power projection into the region."[41] The President displayed aerial photos of the construction site — there were regular American spy flights over the island — as if to imply something hidden and furtive in the operation when, in fact, the site was very much open to the public.

There is a plethora of evidence that puts Reagan's analysis into question: at least five other Caribbean islands, including Barbados, had similar-sized or larger airfields yet did not possess air forces;[42] the building of the airfield was encouraged by the World Bank which also discussed with Grenada the erection of new tourist hotels;[43] the excavation work was being done by the Layne Dredging Co. of Florida and the communications system installed by Plessey, a British multinational, the Cubans donating labour and machinery;[44] Plessey rejected the US claim: "The airport . . . was being built to purely civilian specifications," it said, and listed a number of technical characteristics of a military airport/base which the new airport would not have.[45]

Further, the European Common Market had contributed money toward the construction — "In our view the airport is for tourism," said a spokesman. "We stand by our commitment."[46] The airport was being funded by about a dozen nations as well, including Canada, Mexico and Venezuela; the United States had turned down a request for assistance, and instead exerted pressure to deter international financing.[47]

After the invasion, the airport was completed, by the United States. "The decision has been taken to complete it by the military, for the military," said one of the sub-contractors. "Equipment for that purpose is already being moved on to the site."[48] (As far as is known, the United States has not yet used the airport for military purposes.)

There were several instances of the Grenadian opposition press featuring entirely unfounded stories of the type mentioned above, as well as fostering harmful local economic rumours. In one case in 1979 a Grenadian newspaper reprinted a story from, of all places, the West German magazine *Bunte* which reported that large military and missile bases were being built in Grenada, something which would be impossible to hide on the tiny island, but it was a lie made of whole cloth.[49] The reprinting tactic, as we have seen, is one often employed by the CIA, and to the NJM leaders it was a clear signal that the Agency had arrived in town. It led eventually to the government closing down independent newspapers. The country, they felt, was simply too vulnerable, even more so than Chile and Jamaica.

It was the same with political prisoners, most of them from Gairy's secret police.[50] The government was afraid to release some of them lest they wind up in a Gairy and/or CIA mercenary force or engage in actions like the June 1980 bombing at an outdoor rally which was apparently designed to remove the entire NJM leadership with one blow, but instead took the lives of three young women.

As to the invasion itself . . . code-named "Urgent Fury" . . . 2,000 American marines and paratroopers the first day, by week's end 7,000 on the island, even more waiting offshore . . . planes fitted with murderous multi-barrelled Gatling guns spraying positions of the People's Revolutionary Army . . . "The People's Revolutionary Army — are they on our side or theirs?" asks the young Marine[51] . . . the home of the Cuban Ambassador damaged and looted by American soldiers, on one wall is written "AA", symbol of the 82nd Airborne Division; beside it the message: "Eat shit, commie faggot." . . .[52] captured Cubans used as hostages, ordered to march in front of American jeeps as they advanced on Cuban positions, a violation of the Geneva Convention[53] . . . promises of all kinds were made to Cuban prisoners, said Castro, to get them to go to the United States; none accepted[54] . . . "I want to fuck communism out of this little island," says a marine, "and fuck it right back to Moscow."[55] . . . "Britain announced that it was sending a destroyer to assist in the rescue," said the

American radio station to the Grenadian people the first morning; not a half-truth, but a complete lie . . . Grenadians who heard the broadcasts said they were a powerful encouragement to accept the occupation[56] . . . the fighting was over in a week, 131 Americans killed or wounded, 81 Cubans, 296 Grenadians, more or less . . .

The land conquered, there remained the people's hearts and minds. At the outset, the invasion radio station engaged in fiery attacks against Bishop — he had brought Grenada into captivity said the announcer.[57] But then the Americans evidently learned that this was an error, that Bishop was still enormously popular; thus, for some time afterward, criticism of his regime was usually made more indirectly and without naming him.

Before long the Psychological Operations Battalion of the US Army was cruising over the island in a helicopter offering the Grenadians, via a loudspeaker, a large serving of anti-Cuban fare: the Cubans had supported those who had killed Bishop, Grenada had been a pawn of Cuba, Castro/communism were still a threat, and so forth. Posters were put up showing alleged captured Cuban weapons with the slogan, "Are these the tools that build airports?" Other posters linked the MRC leaders to Moscow.[58]

In March 1984, a visiting London journalist could report:

> The island remains visibly under American occupation. Jeeps patrol constantly. Helicopters fly over the beaches. Armed military police watch the villagers and frequent the cafes. CIA men supervise the security at the courthouse. The island's only newspaper pours out weekly vitriol about the years of the revolutionary government, 'this gruesome period in our history'. The pressures, in a small community, are heavy.[59]

And in June we learned that schools called after "heroes of the revolution" had been given back their old names, though not without pupil protests. And the US Information Service was showing school children a film entitled "Grenada: Return to Freedom".[60]

The invasion was almost universally condemned in Latin America, only the military dictatorships of Chile, Guatemala and Uruguay expressing support. The United Nations voted its disapproval overwhelmingly. To this President Reagan responded: "One-hundred nations in the UN have not agreed with us on just about everything that's come before them where we're involved, and it didn't upset my breakfast at all."[61]

One of the evils of Communist states, we have always been told, is that they are oblivious to world opinion.

There was, however, the supreme irony that most of the people of Grenada welcomed the invasion. In addition to the conservative minority who knew that the "socialist" experiment would now be decisively put to rest, there were the greater number who were overjoyed to see the murderers of their beloved Maurice Bishop receive the punishment due them. Despite all the hostility and lies directed at Bishop by the United States for over four years, it did not seem to occur to the islanders that the invasion had nothing to do with avenging his death and that the United States had merely used the event as a convenient pretext for an action it had desired to carry out for a long time.

If the average Grenadian seems thus rather ingenuous, with a short political memory, we must consider also that the average American lustily cheered the invasion, believed everything which crossed Ronald Reagan's lips (as if this were the first US intervention in history), and to this day would be hard pressed to recite a single falsehood associated with the entire affair. The president himself appears to have completely repressed the incident. In March 1986, when asked about the possibility of an American invasion of Nicaragua, he replied:

> You're looking at an individual that is the last one in the world that would ever want to put American troops into Latin America, because the memory of the great Colossus in the north is so widespread in Latin America. We'd lose all our friends if we did anything of that kind.[62]

On the fourth day of the invasion Reagan made a speech which succeeded in giving jingoism a bad name. The President managed to link the invasion of Grenada with the shooting down of a Korean airliner by the Soviet Union, the killing of US soldiers in Lebanon, and the taking of American hostages in Iran. Clearly, the invasion symbolized an end to this string of humiliations for the United States. Even Vietnam was being avenged. To commemorate the American Renaissance, over ten thousand US servicemen were designated heroes of the republic and decorated with medals. (Many had done no more than sit on ships near the island.) America regained its manhood, by stepping on a flea.

46. Morocco 1983
A video nasty

The government of Morocco, in January 1983, had the sad duty to announce the "grievous death" in a car accident of General Ahmed Dlimi, a confidant of King Hassan for more than 20 years and commander of the Moroccan Army's southern forces.

When the *Le Monde* correspondent had the temerity to suggest that Dlimi's death was perhaps not an accident, he was summarily expelled from the country.[1]

Then, in March, Ahmed Rami, a Moroccan political scientist living in exile in Sweden, stated unequivocally that Dlimi had been murdered by Hassan and his security men and that the CIA was deeply implicated.[2]

Ahmed Rami had been a lieutenant in the Moroccan Army and a leader of *Le Mouvement des Officiers Libres*, the underground movement of army officers dedicated to overthrowing the King, his tyranny, his personal corruption, and his "crimes against human rights". Rami lives abroad under sentence of death in Morocco for his part in a failed attempt to shoot down a plane carrying Hassan in 1972.

The dissident officers supported the establishment of a democratic Islamic Arab Republic of Morocco and a negotiated settlement in the country's ruinous war with the Polisario guerrillas in the Western Sahara, a war in which US military aid and personnel have reportedly enabled Morocco to maintain a deadlock.[3]

Ahmed Dlimi, while serving as the King's right-hand man, had been secretly associated with *Officiers Libres*. When he went abroad he would meet with Rami and during 1982 the two men were discussing plans for a coup attempt in July of the following year.

"Unknown to us, however," said Rami, "the CIA was investigating him [Dlimi]. When the CIA handed over a dossier to King Hassan in January [1983] it contained videofilm of General Dlimi and I meeting in Stockholm last December. That was enough for Dlimi to be eliminated."[4]

Morocco, said the *New York Times*, had become the United States' "closest and most useful ally in the Arab world."[5] Hassan had clearly tied his fortunes to the Reagan administration. In 1981 alone, he was visited by Secretary of Defense Caspar Weinberger and Secretary of State Alexander Haig, as well as the Deputy Director of the CIA, the chairman of the Senate Foreign Relations Committee, and a host of other high-level Washington officials; the Assistant Secretary of Defense for International Security arrived with a team of 23 military advisers and experts; more than 100 Americans were reported to be working with the Moroccan armed forces.[6]

In the years previous, Hassan had co-operated extensively with US policies in Africa. In both 1977 and 1978 he sent Moroccan troops to Zaire in support of the American actions there, and since the mid-1970s he had been aiding the UNITA forces in Angola along with the United States and South Africa in their continuing effort to overthrow the MPLA government. At the same time, King Hassan had allowed the CIA to build up its station in Morocco to where it was probably one of the Agency's key posts in Africa.[7]

In these and other important ways, Hassan had earned the gratitude and protection of the United States. Thus it was that the CIA exposed General Dlimi's double life to the King. Dlimi, moreover, had reportedly advocated that Morocco receive aid from France, the former colonial power, rather than from the United States. The CIA saw this as a threat to the American position in Morocco and insisted that Hassen get rid of his confidants who favoured closer relations with France.[8]

At eleven o'clock on the night of 23 January 1983, says Ahmed Rami, Dlimi was called to the palace in Marrakesh. There, ten security men escorted him to an underground interrogation room. At one a.m., "two American officers" arrived with the King and went into the interrogation room for several hours. Dlimi was tortured, and, at five a.m., he was shot. His body was later placed in his car which was exploded in a suburb of the city. No one, not even his family, was allowed to see the body.[9]

47. Suriname 1982 to 1984
Once again, the Cuban bogeyman

It was unusual, to be sure, that the Director of the CIA would inform Congress in advance of an Agency plan to overthrow a foreign government. President Reagan, said William Casey to the House and Senate intelligence committees in December 1982, had authorized the CIA to try to topple Suriname ruler Col. Desi Bouterse. The Agency's plan reportedly called for the formation of an exile paramilitary force to invade Suriname because Bouterse, who had taken power in a 1980 military coup, was leading the small South American country into "the Cuban orbit".[1]

The Congressional committee members, "while not opposed in principle to the idea of attempting to overthrow a foreign government",[2] did object to the proposal on the grounds that there was no evidence that Cuba was "manipulating the government in Suriname, or gaining a military foothold in the country".[3]

Inasmuch as rational argument of this sort has never made too deep an impression upon the mind of Ronald Reagan or excessively inhibited the CIA, there is no reason to believe that this was the end of the story.

Or even the beginning. Earlier, at the end of October 1982, the Bouterse regime had threatened to expel two US diplomats it accused of encouraging the country's conservative trade unions and of playing a key role in organizing anti-government demonstrations and strikes aimed at bringing the government down.[4] Then, on 8 December 1982, Suriname announced that a coup attempt had been made against the government. A number of alleged plotters were arrested, some of them winding up "shot while trying to escape", evidently a euphemism for their execution. Bouterse claimed that the arrested men had been conspiring with the CIA.[5] The following month, the two US diplomats were actually asked to leave because of their "destabilizing activities".[6]

In July 1983 the plot thickened. The *New York Times* reported that an invasion of Suriname scheduled for the first of the month by Florida-based mercenaries was called off after the plans for it were discovered by the internal security agency of the Netherlands, the former colonial power in Suriname when it was known as Dutch Guiana. The invasion force reportedly would have been composed of some 300 men — half of them US and South American nationals, the others Surinamese — who were to be flown from Florida to the Suriname capital of Paramaribo on the northern tip of South America. The invaders were then to be augmented by Surinamese exiles in the Netherlands. It was this latter group which the Dutch had infiltrated to learn of the plans.[7]

As has become customary concerning American targets in Latin America, stories about the presence of large numbers of Cuban soldiers in Suriname found their way into international circulation. Like their counterparts in Jamaica and Grenada, these warriors remained mythical figures.

In spring 1983, Suriname entered into agreements with the neighbouring right-wing government of Brazil which provided for economic and military aid and military training. By the reasoning of the Reagan administration, Suriname should then have been in "the Brazilian orbit". The simple truth was that Suriname, like other developing nations, was willing to accept help from wherever it could get it. The Brazilians, for their part, openly admitted that their purpose was "saving Suriname from Cuba".[8]

As matters turned out, in October Bouterse expelled almost all Cuban advisers and embassy personnel, most likely under Brazilian and American pressure. The expulsion was announced on the day the United States invaded Grenada and was influenced by Bouterse's belief that Cuba had played a part in the overthrow of Maurice Bishop and that he might suffer a similar fate, if not a similar invasion.[9] This belief about Cuba, as we have seen, bore no relation to the truth, and may have been encouraged by the United States. *Newsweek* magazine later reported that "U.S. diplomats in the capital of Paramaribo made sure to keep Bouterse current on evidence that Cuba had aided the Grenadian coup, and the rest was left to his well-prepped paranoia."[10]

Desi Bouterse, by all accounts, left much to be desired as a leader and as a person. Long before the events of October, Cuba and Grenada were reported to be privately "irritated, even angry, at the harm done to the Left's image in the region by what they see as immature revolutionaries leading a premature revolution."[11] Although Bouterse had learned to parrot socialist and anti-imperialist clichés, his principles appeared to lie elsewhere. In the words of one diplomat in Suriname, "Bouterse is a chameleon. The first thing for him is his own personal survival. The second thing is his survival as the man-in-charge."[12] Bouterse was accused at times of claiming plots against him as a pretext to get rid of some of those opposed to his rule. (Several other coup attempts were alleged in addition to the one mentioned above.)

During the period December 1983-January 1984, Suriname was shaken by thousands of striking workers protesting against tax increases and steep price rises, and calling for the dismissal of Prime Minister Errol Alibux; serious acts of sabotage to power and water supplies were carried out as well. Bouterse gave in, removing Alibux and cancelling the price rises, but he did not accede to the demand that the military hand power back to civilians.[13] Although the scenario was reminiscent of CIA activities in British Guiana, Jamaica, and elsewhere, as well as what the Suriname government had accused the United States of in October 1982, there is no report of the Agency's hand in the disturbances of this period. However, in 1985 it was revealed that two years earlier President Reagan had set up an $18 million fund to covertly channel money to right-wing organizations in various countries. From this fund the AFL-CIO/CIA international labour mafia had dispersed $830,000 to a French anti-communist union. An unspecified amount of money went to organizations in Suriname.[14]

48. El Salvador 1980-
Human Rights, Reagan style

The United States was supporting the government of El Salvador, said Ronald Reagan, because it was trying "to halt the infiltration into the Americas, by terrorists and by outside interference, and those who aren't just aiming at El Salvador but, I think, are aiming at the whole of Central and possibly later South America and, I'm sure, eventually North America."[1]

Psychiatrists have a term for such perceptions of reality. They call it paranoid schizophrenia.

If the insurgents in El Salvador, the smallest country by far in all of Central and South America, were engaged in what Ronald Reagan perceived as a plot to capture the Western Hemisphere, others saw it as the quintessential revolution.

Viewed in the latter context, it cannot be asserted that the Salvadorean people rushed precipitously into revolution at the first painful sting of repression, or turned to the gun because of a proclivity towards violent solutions, or a refusal to "work within the system", or because of "outside agitators", or any of the other explanations of why people revolt so dear to the hearts of Washington opinion-makers. For as long as anyone could remember, the reins of El Salvador's government had resided in the hands of one military dictatorship or another, while the economy had been controlled by the celebrated 14 coffee and industrial families, with only the occasional, short-lived bursting of accumulated discontent to disturb the neat arrangement.

In the decades following the famed peasant rebellion in 1932, which was crushed by an unholy massacre, a reform government had occupied the political stage only twice: for nine months in 1944, then again in 1960. The latter instance was precipitated by several thousand university students who staged a protest against the curtailment of civil liberties. The government responded by sending in the police who systematically smashed offices, classrooms, and laboratories, beat up the school's president, killed a librarian, bayoneted students, and raped dozens of young women. Finally, when the students amassed anew, troops opened fire upon them point-blank. The bloody incident was one of the turning points for a group of junior military officers. They staged a coup in October aimed at major social and political reforms, but the new government lasted only three months before being overthrown in a counter-coup which the United States was reportedly involved in.[2] Dr Fabio Castillo, former president of the National University of El Salvador and a member of the ousted government, testified years later before the US Congress that the United States "openly intervened" in the ousting of the reform government.[3]

Throughout the 1960s, multifarious American experts occupied themselves in El Salvador by enlarging and refining the state's security and counter-insurgency apparatus: the police, the National Guard, the military, the communications and intelligence networks, the co-ordination with their counterparts in other Central American countries . . . in short, all the forces which would soon be brought into action to impose widespread repression and wage war.[4] If, during this decade, the apparatus could not be charged with the level of murder or torture or disappearance of political opponents reached in Guatemala and elsewhere in Latin America, it had more to do with the modest degree of outspoken dissent and violent unrest it faced than with greater respect for human rights; those opposition groups which were not outlawed were those regarded as unthreatening; the bloated stomachs of malnourished peasant children were not regarded as threatening at all.

For apparently no better reason than the fact that even militarists cherish a veneer of legitimacy, during the 1960s certain political organizations of generally urban middle-class membership were allowed to run candidates for municipal and legislative office. They did well, though the government-calculated returns consistently left the opposition as a minority in the legislature; i.e., without real power. In 1967, the government went through the motions of the first contested election for the presidency since 1931. After declaring its party, PCN, the winner, the government promptly banned one of the major contending parties, PAR, on the grounds that it supported principles "contrary to the Constitution". According to a PAR spokesperson, the "principle" involved was support for agrarian reform. Another source reports that the party was declared illegal "allegedly for dispensing Communist ideologies",[5] which, within the government's frame of reference, may well have been one and the same.

Undeterred, a centre-left coalition, UNO by acronym, was formed and put forth Christian Democrat José Napoléon Duarte as its presidential candidate in 1972. Though UNO was confronted by violence against its candidates and campaigners, including the murder of an aide of Duarte, and the sabotaging of the coalition's radio broadcasts, it arrived at election day with high expectations. Two days after the polling, the Central Election Board, after first announcing a victory for PCN, shocked everyone by declaring that a recount had shown UNO to be the winner instead. The government quickly imposed a news blackout and for the next two days nothing was heard concerning the election results. On the third day, the Election Board announced that PCN was indeed the winner after all.

In the 1974 and 1976 legislative elections, and again in the 1977 presidential election, the government employed similar creative counting along with gross physical intimidation of candidates, voters, and poll watchers, to assure its continuance in office.[6] A mass demonstration following the 1977 polling protesting against electoral fraud was surrounded by government security forces who opened fire. The result was nothing less than a bloodbath, the death toll measurable in the hundreds. In the immediate aftermath, top leaders of UNO were exiled and the party's followers became liable to arrest, torture and murder.[7] The president, Col. Arturo Molina, blamed the protests on "foreign Communists". His response to charges of electoral fraud was: "Only God is perfect."[8]

Government political violence of this sort had been sporadic in the 1960s, but became commonplace in the 1970s as more and more Salvadoreans, frustrated by the futility of achieving social change through elections, resorted to other means. While some limited themselves to more militant demonstrations, strikes, and occupations of sites, an increasing number turned to acts of urban guerrilla warfare such as assassination of individuals seen as part of the repressive machinery, bombings, and kidnappings for ransom. The government and its paramilitary right-wing vigilante groups — "death squads" is the self-named modern genre — countered with a campaign centred upon leaders of labour unions, peasant organizations and political parties, as well as priests and lay religious workers. "Be Patriotic — Kill a Priest" was the slogan of one death squad. Church people were accused of teaching subversion to the peasants, what the church people themselves would call the word of God, in this the only country in the world named after Christ. The CIA and the US military had played an essential role in the conception and organization of the security agencies from which the death squads emanated. CIA surveillance programmes routinely supplied these agencies with information on, and the whereabouts of, various individuals who wound up as death squad victims.[9]

In October 1979, a cabal of younger military officers, repelled by the frequent government massacres of groups of protesters and strikers, and wishing to restore the military's "good name", ousted General Carlos Romero from the presidency and took power in a bloodless coup. A number of prominent civilian political figures were given positions in the new administration which proclaimed an impressive programme of reforms. But it was not to be. The young and politically inexperienced officers were easily co-opted by older, conservative officers, and by pressure exerted by the United States, to install certain military men into key positions.[10] The civilian members of the government found themselves unable to exercise any control over the armed forces and were left to function only as reformist camouflage.

Washington had supported the removal of the brutal Romero because only three months earlier the Sandinistas had overthrown the Somoza dictatorship in Nicaragua, and the Carter administration did not wish to risk the loss of a second client state in Central America·in so short a space of time, but brakes had to be applied to keep the process within manageable bounds.

Meanwhile, the security forces did not miss a beat as they continued to fire into crowds: the body count in the first month of the "reformist" government was greater than in the first nine months of the year. By early January 1980, all the civilian members had resigned in disgust over government-as-usual.[11] The experience was the straw which broke the backs of many moderates and liberals, as well as members of the Salvadorean Communist Party, who still clung to hopes of peaceful reforms. The Communist Party had supported the new government, even contributed the Minister of Labour, "because we believe it is going to comply with its promises and open the possibility of democratizing the country." The party was the last group on the left to join the guerrilla forces.[12]

One of the civilians, Minister of Education Salvador Samayoa, simultaneously announced his resignation and his enlistment with a guerrilla group in front of the TV cameras.[13] For those who yet harboured illusions, a steady drumbeat of terrorism soon brought them into the fold. A demonstration march by a coalition of popular organizations on 22 January was first sprayed with DDT by crop-duster planes along the route of the march; then, when the demonstrators reached San Salvador's central plaza, snipers fired at them from surrounding government buildings; at least 21 dead and 120 seriously wounded was the toll, some of which reportedly resulted from the demonstrators' undisciplined return of fire.

On 17 March, a general strike was met by retaliatory violence — 54 people killed in the capital alone.

A week later, the Archbishop of San Salvador, Oscar Romero, an outspoken critic of the government's human-rights violations, who had called upon President Carter, Christian to Christian, to cease providing military aid, was assassinated. In his last sermon, he had addressed the security forces with these words: "I beseech you, I beg you, I order you, in the name of God: *stop the repression*." The next day he became the eleventh priest murdered in El Salvador in three years.

At the funeral of the martyred Archbishop, who had been a nominee for the Nobel Peace Prize the year before, a bomb was thrown amongst the mourners in the plaza, followed by rifle and automatic fire, all emanating from the National Palace and some of the office buildings flanking the plaza, just as in January; at least 40 people were reported killed and hundreds injured.[14]

During this same period, the government's much-heralded programme of agrarian reform, the *sine qua non* of social change in El Salvador, was being "implemented". A measure of the programme's credibility can be derived from the testimony of a technician of the *Instituto Salvadoreño de Transformación Agraria* (ISTA), established to oversee the operation:

> The troops came and told the workers the land was theirs now. They could elect their own leaders and run it themselves. The peasants couldn't believe their ears, but they held elections that very night. The next morning the troops came back and I watched as they shot every one of the elected leaders.[15]

"Force," wrote Karl Marx, "is the midwife of every old society pregnant with a new one." Revolution was now the only item of importance on El Salvador's political agenda, with the opposition united as never before — united more by a common enemy than by a common ideology, but many saw this pluralism as strength rather than weakness. Leftists would now be fighting alongside (former) Christian Democrats whom, only shortly before, they had accused of serving US imperialism.

If Jimmy Carter's trumpeted devotion to human rights was to be taken seriously, his administration clearly had no alternative but to side with the Salvadorean opposition, or at least keep its hands strictly out of the fighting. The Carter administration, however, with only an occasional backward glance at its professed principles, continued its military support of the government. Within days before his term ended in January 1981, Carter ordered a total of $10 million in military aid along with additional American advisers to be sent to El Salvador, an action characterized by one observer as "President Carter's foreign policy establishment's last convulsive effort to evade responsibility for having been 'too soft' in dealing with the Salvadorean rebels." (Two years later, private citizen Carter stated: "I think the government in El Salvador is one of the bloodthirstiest in [the] hemisphere now.")[16]

The Reagan administration, to whom "human rights" was a four-letter word invented by pinkos, had little fear of the too-soft label. Its approach to the conflict was threefold: a) a sharp escalation, both quantitatively and qualitatively in the American military involvement in El Salvador; b) a public relations campaign to put a human face on the military junta; c) a concurrent exercise in news management to convince the American public and the world that the Salvadorean opposition had no legitimate cause for revolution; which was to say that what the Salvadoreans had experienced during the previous two decades, indeed for half a century, (and the above account merely skims the surface), had little or nothing to do with their uprising — this, it turned out, was the inspiration of (unprovoked, mindless) "left-wing terrorists" abetted by the Soviet Union, by Nicaragua, by Cuba. The Red Devils were at it again.

Military Escalation

El Salvador has not turned into another Vietnam quicksand for the United States as many critics of the left and centre have warned. But for the Salvadorean people the war and its horror have dragged on as interminably as it did for the Vietnamese, and for the same reason: American support of a regime — one even more loathsome than in Vietnam — which would have crumbled dismally if left to its own resources. The rebels' later advances, even in the face of the US presence, make that evident.

The amount of American military aid to El Salvador from 1980 to the present, for the hardware alone, approaches, if it does not exceed, two billion dollars.[17] To this must be added the cost of training Salvadorean military personnel by the thousands in the United States, Honduras, and the Panama

Canal Zone, as well as in El Salvador; the further training provided by Argentina, Chile and Uruguay at US behest; the substantial military aid routed through Israel, a manoeuvre employed by the United States in Guatemala and elsewhere;[18] add in "private" contributions from sources in the US and it becomes clear that the true magnitude of American-initiated aid to the El Salvador government will never be known.

One telling result of this massive provision of material and training has been the sizeable expansion of the Salvadorean armed forces and other security services. Between October 1979 and March 1983, the army alone multiplied its strength from some 7,000 men to 22,400 and had not yet reached its peak.[19] The equipment available to these forces has flowed from a veritable horn of plenty. When, in January 1982, the rebels destroyed 16 to 18 aircraft in a raid upon an airport, the United States replaced them in a matter of weeks with 28 new aircraft.[20] Part of the air power available to the government — the guerrillas have nothing of the kind — are US reconnaissance planes fitted with sophisticated surveillance equipment to track rebel movements and designate bombing targets. Predictably, the bombing, as well as strafing and napalming, have taken the lives of many more civilians than of the guerrillas who have better learned how to avoid the attacks; countless homes have been levelled in the process, villages in guerrilla territory destroyed, a nation of refugees created. Civilian deaths, whether from air or ground raids, have not necessarily been accidental, as the many massacre stories make evident. According to Laurence Bailey, a former US Marine employed in El Salvador as a mercenary, "attacking the civilians is the game plan . . . kill the sympathizers and you win the war."[21]

United States pilots have carried out reconnaissance flights — four Americans, all CIA employees, died when one crashed in October 1984[22] — but officially, have not participated in the aerial assaults. However, at least one American adviser has been wounded while flying a helicopter gunship over a combat area,[23] and the programme for training pilots, bombardiers and gunners may serve to conceal the advisers' direct participation in these operations while accompanying their trainees.[24] Moreover, US military personnel, officially, do not take part in the ground fighting either, yet there have been a number of instances of armed Americans spotted in combat areas,[25] a report by CBS news of US advisers "fighting side by side" with government troops,[26] and reports of other Americans, some ostensibly mercenaries, killed in action.[27] The degree of American mercenary involvement in direct combat has not been made public, though the presence of some of them in El Salvador has been confirmed by Laurence Bailey who has stated that he was part of a team of 40 American soldiers of fortune paid by wealthy Salvadorean families living in Miami to protect their plantations from takeover by the rebels.[28]

The overall nature and extent of the American role in the war is perhaps best captured by an excerpt from a frank interview given to *Playboy* magazine in 1984 by the President of El Salvador, José Napoleón Duarte, one of the few Christian Democrat leaders of the earlier days still playing the government game:

Playboy: Do the American military advisors also tell you how to run the war?

Duarte: This is the problem, no? The root of this problem is that the aid is given under such conditions that its use is really decided by the Americans and not by us. Decisions like how many planes or helicopters we buy, how we spend our money, how many trucks we need, how many bullets and of what caliber, how many pairs of boots and where our priorities should be — all of that . . . And all the money is spent over there. We never even see a penny of it, because everything arrives here already paid for.[29]

In Duarte's previous incarnation as a government opponent, his view of the Yanquis was even harsher. US policy in Latin America, he said, was designed to "maintain the Iberoamerican countries in a condition of direct dependence upon the international political decisions most beneficial to the United States, both at the hemisphere and world levels. Thus [the North Americans] preach to us of democracy while everywhere they support dictatorships."[30]

A Human Face

On 28 January 1982, President Reagan certified to Congress that the El Salvador government was "making a concerted and significant effort to comply with internationally recognized human rights" and that it was "achieving substantial control over all elements of its own armed forces, so as to bring to an end the indiscriminate torture and murder of Salvadorean citizens by these forces." The language was that imposed by Congress upon the administration if the flow of arms and American military personnel was to continue.*

Two days earlier, the American and foreign press had carried the story of how government troops had engaged in a massacre of the people in the area of the village of Mozote in December. More than 700 persons were reported killed. The Catholic Church later estimated that the toll exceeded 1,000, mostly the elderly, women and children, many under 14 years of age.[33] The State Department saw fit to question the number of dead and stated that "Civilians did die during the operation, but no evidence could be found to confirm that Government forces systematically massacred civilians."[34] The State Department's later defence of this position before a Congressional committee left the committee members conspicuously underwhelmed.[35]

---

* In March 1984, the Reagan administration tacked on a request for additional military aid to El Salvador to legislation to send US food supplies to starving Africans. Perhaps to demonstrate that it was not prejudiced against Africans, the administration then tacked on a request for support of the Nicaraguan rebels to a bill to provide emergency fuel spending for the poor in parts of the United States which were suffering a severe winter.[31] Earlier, the European Common Market did not implement its plans to have private organizations distribute cereal and powdered milk to the victims of the fighting in El Salvador, apparently because of opposition by Washington which feared that the food would be diverted to the guerrillas.[32]

Two days after the president's certification, the world could read how Salvadorean soldiers had pulled about 20 people out of their beds in the middle of the night, tortured them and then killed them, meanwhile finding the time to rape several teenage girls.[36]

Earlier the same month, the *New York Times* had published an interview with a deserter from the Salvadorean Army who described a class where severe methods of torture were demonstrated on teenage prisoners. He stated that eight US military advisers, apparently Green Berets, were present. Watching "will make you feel more like a man" a Salvadorean officer apprised the recruits, adding that they should "not feel pity of anyone" but only "hate for those who are enemies of our country."[37]

Amnesty International reported in 1984 that it had received

> regular, often daily, reports identifying El Salvador's regular security and military units as responsible for the torture, 'disappearance' and killing of non-combatant civilians from all sectors of Salvadorean society . . . A number of patients have allegedly been removed from their beds or operating theatres and tortured and murdered . . . Types of torture reported . . . by those who have survived arrest and interrogation included beatings, sexual abuse, use of chemicals to disorient, mock executions, and the burning of flesh with sulphuric acid.[38]

And so it went. Each six months the President of the United States ritually swore to Congress, Scout's honour, that America's ally basically meant well. At the same time, the various arms of that ally were carrying out repeated small- and large-scale atrocities, and the Church's monitoring office in El Salvador was reporting on the ally's responsibility for the murder of non-combatant civilians: between October 1979 and mid-1983 the count was in excess of 40,000.[39] This is in addition to the never-to-be-known number of disappeared persons. The make-up on the junta's face was streaking.*

For some time, the United States also lauded the ongoing pretence that was called agrarian reform until the programme finally fell of its own weight. But Washington continued to hold up for the world to see and applaud the staging of elections even more meaningless than those that had gone before – no Salvadorean with any commitment to serious reform would dare appear in public as a candidate unless as an act of suicide; no Salvadorean citizen would dare not have proof of voting unless similarly inclined or part of the guerrilla forces.

On other days, Washington issued warnings to Salvadorean officials to improve their human rights record, told the world how much worse that record would be if not for American influence, and continued to build up each and every component of the military and paramilitary forces actively engaged in the

---

* By contrast, *Newsweek* magazine reported in 1983 that when the guerrillas "capture a town, they treat the civilians well, paying for food and holding destruction to a minimum. And they have begun to free most of the government troops they capture, which helps to persuade other soldiers to surrender rather than fight to the death."[40]

atrocities. In 1984, in an interview with the *New York Times*, Col. Roberto Eulalio Santibáñez, a former Salvadorean military official who had served at the highest level of the security police, confirmed — for those who may still have harboured doubts — that the network of death squads had been shaped by leading Salvadorean officials and was still directed by them.* He also revealed that one of these officials, Col. Nicolas Carranza, the head of the Treasury Police, which "have long been considered the least disciplined and most brutal of the Salvadorean security forces", had been receiving more than $90,000 a year during the previous five or six years from the CIA. Although some members of the Treasury Police have been linked by the Reagan administration itself to death-squad activities, at least as late as 1985 the United States was still training the Treasury forces.[42]

Outside Agitators

"Sometimes I feel like Sisyphus," said a senior Reagan administration official involved in developing US Latin America policy in March 1982. "Every time we head up the hill to explain or justify our policy, the stone comes crashing down on top of us."[43]

Two weeks earlier, Secretary of State Alexander Haig had asserted that the United States had "overwhelming and irrefutable" evidence that the insurgents were controlled from outside by non-Salvadoreans. Haig, however, declined to provide any details of the evidence, saying it would jeopardize intelligence sources. Challenged to prove his charges two days later, the good General insisted that the United States had "unchallengeable" evidence of Nicaraguan and Cuban involvement in the command and control of the operation in El Salvador and, oddly enough, only the day before a Nicaraguan military man had been captured there. As it turned out, according to the Mexican Embassy in San Salvador, the man was a student on his way back to school in Mexico from Nicaragua, travelling overland because he couldn't afford to fly.[44]

The following week, a Nicaraguan was captured fighting with the guerrillas. He told US Embassy and Salvadorean Army officials that he had been trained in Cuba and Ethiopia, then sent to El Salvador by the Nicaraguan government. The State Department was understandably excited. It presented the young man at a press conference in Washington, at which time he declared that he had never been to Cuba or Ethiopia, had joined the guerrillas on his own, and had made his previous statements under torture by his Salvadorean captors. He added that he had never seen another Nicaraguan or Cuban in El Salvador and denied that Nicaragua had provided aid to the guerrillas.[45]

---

* In November 1983, a senior Pentagon official, Frederic Ikley, charged that the guerrillas were protecting some death-squad activists. As well as not offering any reason why this should be so, Ikley admitted that he had no evidence to support his claim.[41]

"Then there were two Nicaraguan air force defectors," reported *Time* magazine during the same period, "who were scheduled to bear witness to their country's involvement in El Salvador but by week's end were judged 'not ready' to face the press." *Time* entitled its story: "A Lot of Show, but No Tell: The U.S. bungles its evidence of foreign subversion in El Salvador."[46]

In January 1981, US diplomats disclosed that five boats had landed in El Salvador containing 100 "well-armed, well-trained guerrillas", allegedly from Nicaragua. They knew the boats had come from Nicaragua because "they were made from wood of trees not native to El Salvador."[47] No sign, dead or alive, of any of the hundred invaders was ever found however.

One hundred seemed to be the number of choice for the Reagan administration. That was the count of Cuban combat troops, said a senior State Department policymaker, who were sent to El Salvador in the fall of 1981 by way of Nicaragua. "They were brought in clandestinely and given operational responsibilities in El Salvador," he asserted.[48] The later whereabouts and actions of the Cubans likewise remains a mystery.

The world is also informed that Soviet and Chinese weapons have been seized from rebels and this is cited as proof of outside Communist aid.[49] These captures may be real — although the CIA has long had warehouses full of Communist weapons of all kinds, suitable for all occasions — but then what are we to make of the US, Israeli, Belgian and German weapons which, by Washington's admission at another time, are also to be found amongst the rebels?[50] The world arms traffic is indeed wide open and fluid. (In neighbouring Honduras, the US-supported contras use Soviet-made missiles to shoot down Soviet-made helicopters of Nicaragua.)[51] Moreover, the rebels capture weapons from government forces and they claim that they also purchase arms from corrupt Salvadorean Army officers, a practice common to many Latin American guerrilla wars. A source cited by the *New York Times* has corroborated the rebels' claim.[52]

The centre-piece of the Reagan administration's campaign to prove the international-conspiracy nature of the conflict in El Salvador was its White Paper issued a month after taking office and based largely on purported "captured guerrilla documents", selected ones of which were attached. Amongst the various analyses of the White Paper which have cast grave doubt upon its claims, is the one in the *Wall Street Journal* by Jonathan Kwitny. This included an interview with a State Department official, Jon D. Glassman, who is given the major credit for the White Paper. Admitted Mr Glassman: parts of the paper are possibly "misleading" and "over-embellished" . . . it contains "mistakes" and "guessing". Said the *Wall Street Journal*: "A close examination . . . indicates that, if anything, Mr. Glassman may be understating the case in his concession that the White Paper contains mistakes and guessing."

Amongst the many specific shortcomings of the paper pointed out in the article is that "Statistics of armament shipments into El Salvador, supposedly drawn directly from the documents, were extrapolated, Mr. Glassman concedes. And in questionable ways, it seems. Much information in the White Paper can't be found in the documents at all." As an example, the White Paper says that the documents indicate nearly 200 tons of arms sent to El Salvador, mainly via Cuba and Nicaragua, but nowhere in the documents is there any mention of the 200 tons.[53]

It is not merely the accuracy of the White Paper that has been questioned, but the authenticity of the documents themselves. Apropos of this, former US Ambassador to El Salvador, Robert White (sacked by Reagan because of excessive commitment to human rights and reforms), has commented: "The only thing that even makes me think that these documents were genuine was that they proved so little."[54]

When pressed to state what proof his government had of Nicaraguan intervention, President Duarte declined to answer on the grounds that the world would not believe him anyway.[55] But President Reagan has had some evidence to offer. He saw the hand of foreign masters pulling strings in the fact that demonstrators in Canada carried "the same signs" as demonstrators in the United States: "U.S. Out of El Salvador."[56]

Revolutions, however, are not exported like so many cartons of soap. We have seen what the origins were in El Salvador. Ambassador White, no champion of the rebels' cause, observed that "The revolution situation came about in El Salvador because you had what was one of the most selfish oligarchies the world has ever seen, combined with a corrupt security force . . . Whether Cuba existed or not, you would still have a revolutionary situation in El Salvador."[57]

Education-minister-turned-guerrilla, Salvador Samayoa, speaking in 1981, asserted that US charges that the Soviet bloc was directing the guerrilla movement "reveals Washington's deep ignorance of our movement". He pointed out that three of the five guerrilla groups that made up the Farabundo Marti National Liberation Front were "strongly anti-Soviet". Samayoa added: "To say we are run by Cuba because we have a relationship with Cuba is like saying we're a Christian movement because we have received enormous help from the church . . . Instead of seeing us as Communist subversives, the U.S. should see us as a people struggling to survive."[58]

Despite American patrol boats in the Gulf of Fonseca (which separates El Salvador from Nicaragua), Awacs surveillance planes in the skies over the Caribbean, and an abundance of aerial photographs, despite a large US radar installation in Honduras manned by 50 American military technicans, the finest electronic monitoring equipment modern technology has to offer, and all the informers that CIA money can buy[59] . . . despite it all, the United States has singularly failed to support its case that the fires of the Salvadorean revolution are stoked by Nicaraguan and Cuban coals; nor by the Soviet Union, Vietnam, the PLO, Ethiopia, or any of the other countries indicted at one time or another as important suppliers of military aid. In any case, whatever support the Salvadorean rebels may have actually received from abroad, other than moral and diplomatic and office space, it plainly does not belong in the same league as the American aid, in all its forms, to the Salvadorean government. If there is an international conspiracy afoot in El Salvador, we must look to the United States aided by Honduras, Israel, Chile, Argentina, Uruguay, Guatemala, Cuban exiles, and former members of Nicaragua's National Guard.[60]

In 1983, Ronald Reagan ordered the invasion of Grenada on the grounds of possible danger to American citizens living there from the government. In El Salvador, US support of the government continues despite the murder of at least eight Americans (including two semi-official US Government employees and three nuns) at the hands of government-controlled forces and the wounding or disappearance of several others.[61]

49. Nicaragua 1981-
Destabilization in slow motion

I have the most conclusive evidence that arms and munitions in large quantities have been on several occasions . . . shipped to the revolutionists in Nicaragua . . . I am sure it is not the desire of the United States to intervene in the internal affairs of Nicaragua or of any other Central American republic. Nevertheless, it must be said, that we have a very definite and special interest in the maintenance of order and good Government in Nicaragua at the present time . . . The United States cannot, therefore, fail to view with deep concern any serious threat to stability and constitutional government in Nicaragua tending toward anarchy and jeopardizing American interests, especially if such state of affairs is contributed to or brought about by outside influence or by any foreign power.[1]

In this manner did President Calvin Coolidge address the Congress of the United States in 1927. The revolutionaries he was voicing alarm about were those supporters of the Liberal Party (one of whom was Augusto Cesar Sandino) who had taken up arms against the Conservative Party government which they claimed was illegally in office. The foreign power accused of arming the Liberals was the Mexican Government which the Coolidge administration viewed as being "impregnated with Bolshevist ideas". The American interests thought to be in jeopardy were the standard ones of the time: US business investments. Thus it came to pass that the Marines landed in Nicaragua for the twelfth time in less than three-quarters of a century. (See Appendix II).

In the 1980s, it is the revolutionary Nicaraguan government of the Sandinistas which is accused by the administration of Ronald Reagan (who describes Coolidge as his political patron saint) of being in the service of Bolshevism, in this case the Soviet Union and Cuba; the counter-revolutionaries known as the contras who are Washington's marines; and American "interests" which have moved from the "rationality" of economic imperialism to a desire for political hegemony bordering on the pathological.

When the American military forces left Nicaragua for the last time, in 1933, they left behind a souvenir by which the Nicaraguan people could remember them: the National Guard, placed under the direction of one Anastasio Somoza (just as in 1924 the United States had left Trujillo behind for the people of the Dominican Republic). Three years later, Somoza took over the presidency and with the indispensable help of the National Guard established a family dynasty which would rule over Nicaragua, much like a private estate, for the next 43 years. While the Guardsmen, consistently maintained by the United States, passed their time on martial law, rape, torture, murder of the opposition, and massacres of peasants, as well as less violent pursuits such as robbery, extortion, contraband, running brothels and other government functions, the Somoza clan laid claim to the lion's share of Nicaragua's land and businesses. When Anastasio Somoza II was overthrown by the Sandinistas in July 1979, he fled into exile leaving behind a country in which two-thirds of the population earned less than $300 a year. Upon his arrival in Miami, Somoza admitted to being worth $100 million. A US intelligence report, however, placed it at $900 million.[2]

It was fortunate for the new Nicaraguan leaders that they came to power while Jimmy Carter sat in the White House. It gave them a year and a half of relative breathing space to take the first steps in the reconstruction of their impoverished society before the relentless hostility of the Reagan administration descended upon them; which is not to say that Carter welcomed the Sandinista victory.

In 1978, with Somoza nearing collapse, Carter authorized covert CIA support for the press and labour unions in Nicaragua in an attempt to create a "moderate" alternative to the Sandinistas.[3] Towards the same end, American diplomats were conferring with non-leftist Nicaraguan opponents of Somoza. Washington's idea of "moderate", according to a group of prominent Nicaraguans who walked out on the discussions, was the inclusion of Somoza's political party in the future government and "leaving practically intact the corrupt structure of the *somocista* apparatus", including the National Guard, albeit in some reorganized form.[4] Indeed, at this same time, the head of the US Southern Command (Latin America), Lt. General Dennis McAuliffe, was telling Somoza that, although he had to abdicate, the United States had "no intention of permitting a settlement which would lead to the destruction of the National Guard".[5] This was a notion remarkably insensitive to the deep loathing for the Guard felt by the great majority of the Nicaraguan people.

The United States, moreover, tried, unsuccessfully, to convince the Organization of American States to send in a "peace-keeping force",[6] a body which could only have stood in the way of the insurgents' military progress; and in neighbouring Costa Rica the American Ambassador saw fit to complain to the government that Cuba had set up a centre to oversee its military support of the Sandinistas, resulting in the Cubans being forced to move their headquarters to their consulate.[7]

After the Sandinistas took power, Washington pressured them to include certain men in the new junta.[8] Although this tactic failed, the Carter administration did not refuse to give aid to Nicaragua. Ronald Reagan was later to point to this and ask: "Can anybody doubt the generosity and good faith of the American people?" What the president failed to explain was that much, if not most, of the aid had gone to non-governmental agencies and to the private sector, including the American Institute for Free Labor Development, the long-time CIA front; that the primary and expressed motivation for the aid was to strengthen the hands of the moderate opposition and undercut the influence of socialist countries in Nicaragua; and that all military aid was withheld despite repeated pleas from the Nicaraguan government about its need and right to such help[9] — the defeated National Guardsmen and other supporters of Somoza had not, after all, disappeared. (They were regrouped as the "contras" and maintain primacy in the leadership of this force to the present day.)

In January 1981, Ronald Reagan took office under a Republican platform which asserted that it "deplores the Marxist Sandinista takeover of Nicaragua". The president moved quickly to cut off virtually all forms of assistance to the Sandinistas, the opening salvo of his war against their revolution. The American whale, yet again, felt threatened by a minnow in the Caribbean.

Other economic warfare followed: amongst the many measures undertaken, Nicaragua was excluded from US government programmes which promote American investment and trade; sugar imports from Nicaragua were slashed by 90 percent; and, without excessive subtlety but with notable success, Washington pressured the IMF, the Inter-American Development Bank (IDB), the World Bank, and the European Common Market to withhold loans to Nicaragua.[10] The director of the IDB, Mr Kevin O'Sullivan, later revealed that in 1983 the US had opposed a loan to aid Nicaraguan fishermen on the grounds that the country did not have adequate fuel for their boats. A week later, O'Sullivan pointed out, "saboteurs blew up a major Nicaraguan fuel depot in the port of Corinto",[11] an action described by an American intelligence source as "totally a CIA operation".[12]

Washington did, however, offer $5.1 million in aid to private organizations and to the Roman Catholic Church in Nicaragua. This offer was rejected by the government because, it said, "United States congressional hearings revealed that the [aid] agreements have political motivations, designed to promote resistance and destabilize the Revolutionary Government."[13] Nicaragua had already charged several of the previous private aid recipients, such as the Moravian Church, with engaging in just such activities.[14]

The repeated attacks on fuel depots were part of a concerted effort to deprive the Nicaraguan economy of oil. Contra/CIA operations emanating in Honduras also blew up oil pipelines, mined the waters of oil-unloading ports, and threatened to blow up any approaching oil tankers; at least seven foreign ships were damaged by the mines, including a Soviet tanker with five crewmen reported to be badly injured. Nicaragua's ports were under siege: mortar shelling from high-speed motor launches, and aerial bombing, rocket and machine-gun attacks were designed to blockade Nicaragua's exports as well as to starve the country of imports by frightening away foreign shipping.[15] In October 1983, Esso announced that its tankers would no longer carry crude oil to Nicaragua from Mexico, the country's leading supplier; at this point Nicaragua had a ten-day supply of oil.[16]

Agriculture has been another prime target. Raids by contras have caused extensive damage to crops, and demolished tobacco-drying barns, grain silos, irrigation projects, farm houses and machinery; roads, bridges and trucks were destroyed to prevent produce from being moved; numerous state farms and co-operatives incapacitated or harvesting prevented; other farms still intact have been abandoned because of the danger.[17] And in October 1982, the Standard Fruit Company announced that it was suspending all its banana operations in Nicaragua and the marketing of the fruit in the United States. The American multinational, after a century of enriching itself in the country, and in violation of a contract with the government which extended to 1985, left behind the uncertainty of employment for some 4,000 workers and approximately six million cases of bananas to harvest with neither transport nor market.[18]

Nicaragua's fishing industry has suffered not only from lack of fuel for its boats. The fishing fleet has been decimated by mines and attacks, its trawlers idled for want of spare parts due to the US credit blockade. The country has lost millions of dollars from reduced shrimp exports.[19]

It is an American war against Nicaragua. The contras have their own various motivations for wanting to topple the Sandinista government. They do not need to be instigated by the United States. But before the US military arrived in Honduras in the thousands and set up Fortress America, the contras were engaged almost exclusively in hit-and-run forays across the border, small-scale raids on Nicaraguan border patrols and farmers, attacks on patrol boats, and the like; killing a few people here, burning a building down there,[20] there was no future for the contras in a war such as this against a much larger force. Then the American big guns began to arrive in 1982, along with the air power, the landing strips, the docks, the radar stations, the communications centres, built under the cover of repeated joint US-Honduran military exercises;[21] thousands of contras were sent for training to Florida and California;[22] in all, what intelligence officials described as "the most ambitious paramilitary and political action operation mounted by the Central Intelligence Agency in nearly a decade".[23]

US and "Honduran" reconnaissance planes, usually piloted by Americans, began regular overflights into Nicaragua to photograph bombing and sabotage targets, track Sandinista military manoeuvres and equipment, spot the planting of mines, eavesdrop on military communications and map the terrain. Electronic surveillance ships off the coast of Nicaragua partook in the bugging of a nation.[24] Said a former CIA analyst: "Our intelligence from Nicaragua is so good . . . we can hear the toilets flush in Managua."[25]

US ships serviced the motor launches; Americans drove them on raids; CIA explosives technicians assembled and armed the mines and the Agency directed the mining operation; the US provided the underwater equipment and explosives to sabotage teams which blew up installations at Puerto Cabezas.[26] American pilots fly combat missions against Nicaraguan troops or carry supplies to contras inside Nicaraguan territory, several have been shot down and killed;[27] some have flown in civilian clothes and been told by the Pentagon that they would be disavowed if captured;[28] some contras told American Congressmen they were ordered to claim responsibility for a bombing raid organized by the CIA and flown by Agency mercenaries[29] . . . and so it goes . . . as in El Salvador, the full extent of direct American involvement in the fighting will never be known.

The contras' brutality has earned them a wide notoriety. They have destroyed large numbers of health centres, schools, and community centres — symbols of the Sandinistas' social programmes in rural areas. People caught in these assaults are tortured and killed in the most gruesome ways. One example, reported by *The Guardian* of London, suffices. In the words of a survivor of a riad in Jinotega province, which borders on Honduras:

> Rosa had her breasts cut off. Then they cut into her chest and took out her heart. The men had their arms broken, their testicles cut off, and their eyes poked out. They were killed by slitting their throats and pulling the tongue out through the slit.[30]

In November 1984, the Nicaraguan Government announced that since 1981 the contras had assassinated 910 state officials and killed 8,000 civilians.[31]

The analogy is inescapable: if Nicaragua were Israel, and the contras the PLO, the Sandinistas would have long ago made a lightning bombing raid on the bases in Honduras and wiped them out completely. The United States would have applauded the action, the Soviet Union would have condemned it but done nothing, the rest of the world would have raised their eyebrows, and that would have been the end of it.

After many contra atrocity stories had been reported in the world press, it was disclosed in October 1984 that the CIA had prepared a manual of instruction for its clients which, amongst other things, encouraged the use of violence against civilians. In the wake of the furore in Congress caused by the exposé, the State Department was obliged to publicly condemn the contras' terrorist activities. Congressional intelligence committees were informed by the CIA, present and former contra leaders, and others that the contras indeed "raped, tortured and killed unarmed civilians, including children" and that "groups of civilians, including women and children, were burned, dismembered, blinded and beheaded".[32] These are the same rebels whom Ronald Reagan, with his strange mirror language, has called "freedom fighters" and the "moral equal of our founding fathers". (The rebels in El Salvador, in the president's studied opinion, are "murderers and terrorists".)[33]

The CIA manual, entitled *Psychological Operations in Guerrilla Warfare*, gave advice on such niceties as political assassination, blackmailing ordinary citizens, mob violence, kidnapping, and blowing up public buildings. Upon entering a town, it said, "establish a public tribunal" where the guerrillas can "shame, ridicule and humiliate" Sandinistas and their sympathizers by "shouting slogans and jeers". "If . . . it should be necessary . . . to fire on a citizen who was trying to leave the town", guerrillas should explain that "he was an enemy of the people" who would have alerted the Sandinistas who would then "carry out acts of reprisals such as rapes, pillage, destruction, captures, etc."

The contras were advised to explain to the people that "our struggle is not against the nationals but rather against Russian imperialists". This "will foster the sympathy of the peasants, and they will immediately become one of us." (Mao himself couldn't have put it better.) Workers were to be told that "the state is putting an end to factories", and doctors informed that "they are being replaced by Cuban paramedics".

When the population sees the light and begins to rise against the government, "professional criminals should be hired to carry out selective jobs" such as "taking the demonstrators to a confrontation with the authorities to bring about uprisings and shootings that will cause the death of one or more people to create a martyr for the cause." Other people will be "armed with clubs, iron rods and placards and, if possible, small firearms, which they will carry hidden." Still other "shock troops", equipped "with knives, razors, chains, clubs and bludgeons", will "march slightly behind the innocent and gullible participants" as the uprising progresses.

Finally, a section called "Selective Use of Violence" informed the contra student that "It is possible to neutralize carefully selected and planned targets, such as court judges, police and state security officials, etc."[34]

Throughout, the manual reads like what the Western world has always been taught is the way communists scheme and indoctrinate. It proved intensely embarrassing to the Reagan administration, not least because it unequivocally punctured the official balloon which had been floating about bearing the message that the United States was not pursuing the overthrow of the Sandinista government; although at this late date, anyone who still believed that was far enough removed from reality to continue believing it.

White House officials and President Reagan twisted their tongues into knots trying to explain away the manual: the manual made public was only a first draft which was not the one distributed, they said falsely . . . the word "neutralize" didn't mean to assassinate, only to remove from office . . . the author of the manual was some low-level, irresponsible "freelancer" . . .[35]

Not long afterward, the manual, with minor changes, could be found in distribution again in Honduras, put out ostensibly by a private American organization, *Soldier of Fortune* magazine.[36]

The CIA may have tried to provide its students with some object lessons in neutralization, of the Mafia kind. In June 1983, the Nicaraguan Government expelled three US Embassy officials — one of whom was reported to be the CIA's Chief of Station in Managua — charging them with being part of an Agency destabilization network which, amongst other things, was attempting to assassinate Foreign Minister Miguel d'Escoto, who is also a Roman Catholic priest. The intended murder weapon was to be a bottle of Benedictine liqueur containing thalium, a poison almost undetectable in the human body. At a press conference, the government presented evidence which included photos and videotapes of American diplomats meeting with the Nicaraguan officials who had pretended to go along with the plot, as well as copies of intercepted CIA messages.[37]

Two months later, another Agency plot to kill d'Escoto as well as two other Sandinista officials was alleged by the Nicaraguan government. A CIA agent named Mike Tock was charged with being behind this particular conspiracy.[38]

The following June, according to one of the participants, the CIA sent a contra hit team from Honduras to Managua to do away with all nine *comandantes* of the Sandinista National Directorate in one fell swoop by blowing up the building they were meeting in. The team made it to Managua, but the explosives failed to arrive and the plot was aborted.[39]

The Lord and the fight for freedom have something in common: they both work in strange ways. If the CIA's manual was not an odd enough tool of liberty, the Agency's comic book surely was. Entitled *Freedom Fighters' Manual*, the 16-page booklet was supplied to contra forces presumably to distribute amongst the Nicaraguan population. Its 40 illustrations showed the reader how s/he could "liberate Nicaragua from oppression and misery" by "a series of useful sabotage techniques". Amongst these were: stop up toilets with sponges . . . pull down power cables . . . put dirt into gas tanks . . . put nails on roads and highways . . . cut and perforate the upholstery of vehicles . . . cut down trees over highways . . . telephone to make false hotel reservations and false alarms of fires and crimes . . . hoard and steal food from the government . . . leave lights and water taps on . . . steal mail from mailboxes . . . go to work late . . . call in sick . . . short circuit electricity . . . break light bulbs . . . rip up books . . . spread rumours . . . threaten supervisors and officials over the phone . . .[40]

The official explanation for American belligerence towards the Sandinista government, at least the explanation most frequently advanced, has been that military supplies were being sent to the Salvadorean rebels from or via Nicaragua. We have seen in the chapter on El Salvador how little substance lay behind this charge. If any more reason to question Washington's line were needed, it was provided in 1984 by David MacMichael who, a year earlier, had left his position with the CIA in which for two years he had analysed military and political developments in Central America. Said MacMichael: "There has not been a successful interdiction, or a verified report, of arms moving from

Nicaragua to El Salvador since April 1981."*[41]

On one occasion, MacMichael attended an inter-agency meeting to discuss CIA plans to support the contras. Of this meeting he noted that "Although the stated objective was to interdict arms going into El Salvador, there was hardly any discussion of the arms traffic . . . I couldn't understand this failure until months later when I realized, like everyone else, that arms interdiction had never been a serious objective."[45]

The former CIA man said that he had had access to the most sensitive intelligence on Nicaragua, including arms shipments to El Salvador, based on which he concluded that "the Administration and the CIA have systematically misrepresented Nicaraguan involvement in the supply of arms to Salvadorean guerrillas to justify [their] efforts to overthrow the Nicaraguan Government."[46]

At the Agency, MacMichael was asked to prepare a paper on political and social conditions in Nicaragua. After reviewing intelligence and State Department reports going back to 1979, he found that he "could not accept the conclusion, held widely within the Administration, that this was a well-established Marxist-Leninist state." Despite "a surprising degree of support" for his position from colleagues, the paper was never published as an official Agency report. "It made them too uncomfortable," he said.[47]

For a man who spent ten years as an officer in the US Marine Corps and four years as a counter-insurgency expert in South-east Asia, in addition to his tour of service at the CIA, David MacMichael's political thinking has landed in strange territory. He believes that control over Latin America is the motivating force behind American policy in the hemisphere.

> We have control and we don't want to lose it. The ideology of anti-communism then provides the rationalization, although this determination to hold on is actually pathology. Then you have an entire generation of people raised in the foreign policy establishment and specializing in this region who for 25 years have gotten up in the morning and said: 'We'll get that bastard Castro today.'[48]

Washington's explanation number two for its policy appears to be that Nicaragua is a military threat to other Central American countries — not simply to the bases in Honduras, which are a daily, calculated provocation — but to Honduras itself and the other nearby states. This is a weak reed to lean on, for Nicaragua has virtually no air force (and it would be suicidal to attack anyone without proper air cover), even less of a navy, and its tanks are demonstrably unsuitable for the terrain of Honduras.[49] Still less have the Sandinistas a sane reason for invasion. It is questionable whether the men of the

---

* What took place at that time, MacMichael did not explain. On 19 January 1981 it was reported that a Salvadorean cabinet minister had stated that Nicaragua was no longer allowing its territory to be used for arms shipments.[42] A few weeks later, the Sandinista government, alarmed by the suspension of US economic aid, pressed the Salvadorean guerrillas to seek a political settlement.[43] Similar requests were made by the Sandinistas during the following years.[44]

State Department believe this story themselves, any more than do the supposed neighbouring targets. At a conference for journalists in Costa Rica in 1985, the Costa Rican Minister of Information, Armando Vargas, said cheerfully: "No one here really expects Nicaragua to invade us." "And nobody in Honduras does either," said Manuel Gamero, the editor-in-chief of *Tiempo*, one of that country's leading newspapers.[50]

On other days, we are told other reasons why the Sandinistas must be restrained. It may be to protect the Panama Canal (sic) or "the free use of the sea lanes in the Caribbean basin and the Gulf of Mexico". (The danger-to-the-sea-lanes bit has been trotted out by Washington for every corner of the globe in the past 40 years; not once has it materialized.) Or it may be the threat of "another Cuba" or a Soviet base/foothold in the region. These come complete with pictures — an exhibition of aerial photos of Nicaragua showing "Cuban-style military barracks", a "Soviet-style physical training area with chin-bars and other types of equipment to exercise the forces, and a running track", and, most damning of all, a Sandinista garrison "having a standard rectangular configuration like we have seen in Cuba".[51] Leave it to those cunning Castroites to devise a rectangular building.

"The strategic issue is a simple one," asserts Patrick Buchanan, Reagan's Director of Communications. "Who wants Central America more — the West or the Warsaw Pact?"[52]

Fidel Castro is not in any doubt. On at least two occasions he has expressed in no uncertain terms his frustration and annoyance with the Soviet Union for not sufficiently aiding Nicaragua and for what he sees as the Russians' weak and indecisive response to American pressure against the Sandinista government, even in the face of a Russian ship being damaged by CIA mines. The Cuban leader failed to attend the funeral of Soviet leader Chernenko in March 1985 and did not sign the book of condolences at the Soviet Embassy in Havana apparently to register his displeasure with Soviet policy. Responded a Soviet diplomat: "We obviously place a priority on improving relations with our adversary. We have to seek a balance with the US so naturally we will say [to the Cubans] calm down, we are not interested in sharpening the situation in Angola and Nicaragua."[53]

"In the . . . think-tanks and the academic institutes in Moscow where Soviet policy towards Central America is discussed and debated . . .", reported *The Guardian*, "the emphasis is on dialogue and negotiation, and if the Soviet Union agrees on one thing with the United States, it is that there should be 'no more Cubas'," a reference to the heavy economic and political burden Cuba has placed upon Moscow over the years.[54]

Throughout most of 1983-84, the so-called Contadora group, composed of Mexico, Panama, Colombia and Venezuela, met periodically in an attempt to still the troubled waters of Central America. Rejecting at the outset the idea that the conflicts of the region could be seen as part of an East-West confrontation, they conferred with all the nations involved, including the United States.[55] The complex and lengthy discussions finally gave birth to a 21-point treaty which dealt with the most contentious issues: civil war, intervention, elections, and human rights. Washington, which was not itself to be a signatory to the treaty, though obviously indispensable to its implementation, pressed Managua to sign.[56]

Then, something which Washington found strange and unexpected happened. In September 1984, Nicaragua announced its intention to sign the treaty, the first nation to do so. Until this moment, the United States had not publicly criticized the treaty's provisions,[57] but immediately Washington began to find things wrong with it and called for changes. The State Department declared that the Contadora group "didn't intend that this [treaty document] be the end of the process", but a high-ranking diplomat from one of the Contadora countries insisted that "Everyone had treated it as a final document from the beginning", as had the US representatives.[58]

What alarmed Washington was that the treaty was actually serious about ending, or at least sharply curtailing, the hostilities in Central America: it called for the removal in each country of all foreign military personnel, advisers, and bases; an end to large-scale arms supplies to the region; a prohibition of all cross-border attacks or support by one country of insurgents in another; and establishment of procedures to verify these agreements.[59] It was enough to put an interventionist power out of business.

The United States refused to give its blessings to the agreement. Commented Rep. Michael Barnes, chairman of the House Foreign Affairs Subcommittee on the Western Hemisphere: "The Administration's objections to the treaty reinforce my belief that it's never had any real interest in a negotiated settlement."[60]

After the Managua announcement, State Department officials told the *New York Times* that they were concerned that it "might undermine the Administration's efforts to portray the Sandinistas as the primary source of tension in Central America". Some officials argued that a trip scheduled by Sandinista leader Daniel Ortega to Los Angeles "should not be approved, in part, to punish Mr. Ortega and the Sandinistas for accepting the Contadora peace proposal."[61] A month later, an internal National Security Council paper noted that the United States had "effectively blocked" the treaty.[62] Meanwhile, Washington labelled Nicaragua's willingness to sign the treaty "a propaganda ploy",[63] an accusation surely unmatched since the first pot called the first kettle black.

The argument seized upon by the Reagan administration to explain its reluctance to accept the Contadora agreement was that Nicaragua was not prepared to hold a truly free election as called for by the treaty. The quality of the election held in November 1984, which the Sandinistas won by a two-to-one margin, was and remains a controversial issue. On the face of it, by the (flawed) standards of Western elections, the Nicaraguan election cannot be much faulted; by the standards of Latin America, it was a veritable paragon of democracy; the fact that there were no deaths reported in connection with the election, by itself made it rather unique in Latin America; the appearance of minor parties on the ballot in every department (state) of the nation distinguished it from the typical presidential election in the United States.*

The election was open to all parties and candidates, no fraud in the polling was reported, or even seriously charged; it was observed by a reported 400 foreigners from 40 different countries — although such observation can usually detect only the more obvious kinds of irregularities — and on election day the *Washington Post* could report that

> even U.S. diplomats here acknowledge that the Sandinistas have allowed expression of a wide range of political views, including some that were harshly critical of the government. The Sandinistas eased censorship of the sole opposition newspaper, *La Prensa*, at the start of the campaign, and the state television and radio channels have given air time — although limited — for the small but vocal opposition parties to make their case.[64]

The criticism of the election centres on the boycott of it by the Democratic Coordinating Alliance (DCA), a significant coalition of opposition groups headed by Arturo José Cruz. On several occasions, Cruz and his followers were physically harassed by crowds when they appeared in public and on at least one occasion it was reported that many of the protestors had been brought to town on government vehicles. Whether the Sandinistas deliberately intended to harass Cruz or discourage him from running is not known, although it is clear that the government had much more to lose than to gain by keeping the DCA off the ballot. In any event, harassment of a serious nature appears to have been short-lived and did not remain as a stumbling block to Cruz running. The DCA's most persistent stated objection was that not enough time had been allowed for campaigning.

The chronology of events is as follows: the 4 November election date was announced on 21 February; in May, registration of parties and candidates was set for 25 July, at which time seven parties registered: the Sandinistas, three parties which could be considered to their left, and three to their right;[65] the DCA declined to register and Cruz announced that he would not run unless the government opened a dialogue with the contras[66] — a rather remarkable request, comparable to demanding of the British Government that it sit down to tea with the IRA. (The DCA dropped this request three weeks later, stating that the contras had told them they would abide by any accord reached between the party and the government, an arrangement the State Department later took credit for.)[67] The failure to register, it should be noted, occurred before any special harassment had taken place.

Cruz also contended at this time that for five years the population had been too indoctrinated by the government for the opposition to stand a chance,[68] a

---

* Because of the absolute agreement between the Republican and Democratic parties on the fundamental premises underlying the issues of capitalism and anti-communism, it has been said that the United States has a one-party system, but, being America, there are two of them.

charge which could be made with considerable validity by any minor party in any nation of the world.

The day of registration, several of Cruz's aides had met with the government and asked that the deadline for registration be extended,[69] a move indicating perhaps a split in the DCA ranks. The Sandinistas at first refused, but on 22 September announced that registration had been extended to 1 October. The DCA again failed to register, stating that the election date had to be moved from November to January.[70] The Sandinistas suspected, and said so openly, that the DCA knew it would lose anyway and was abstaining from the election at the behest of the United States in order to throw a question mark over the whole process. In August, some of Cruz's backers had stated that they hoped to "discredit the election and force the Sandinistas to grant political concessions". "What we really need," they declared, "is Arturo in jail."[71]

One unmistakable sign of the CIA's hand in the election was the full-page advertisements which appeared in August in newspapers in Venezuela, Costa Rica and Panama. Signed by a fictitious organization called "Friends of Tomás Borge", the ads attempted to split the Sandinista leadership by promoting Borge's candidacy over that of Daniel Ortega who had already been chosen as the Sandinista candidate. "Neither Ortega nor Cruz!" proclaimed the ads.[72]

Throughout this period, the DCA made one demand after another concerning electoral procedures as its price for taking part in the election. By any reasonable standard of power relationships, the government showed itself to be flexible. On 21 September, the *New York Times* reported that the opposition had stated that the Sandinistas had made substantial concessions and that the only major proposal left was postponing the election until January.[73] This was important, said the DCA, because the campaign could not have properly begun before certain things had been agreed upon. The government's position was that it would grant the postponement — a major concession and inconvenience — only if the DCA would arrange a ceasefire with the contras. The party replied that it didn't have the power to do so, and negotiations continued through all of October with many confusing and contradictory reports coming out of the talks until, finally, time ran out.

The United States could certainly have arranged a ceasefire if it was interested in testing the Sandinistas' commitment to what Washington would call a free election. That the US had such an interest is questionable in light of what the *New York Times* revealed on 21 October:

The Reagan Administration, while publicly criticizing the Nov. 4 elections in Nicaragua as 'a sham,' has privately argued against the participation of the leading opposition candidate for fear his involvement would legitimize the electoral process, according to some senior Administration officials.

Since May, when American policy toward the election was formed, the Administration has wanted the opposition candidate, Arturo José Cruz, either not to enter the race or, if he did, to withdraw before the election, claiming the conditions were unfair, the officials said.

'The Administration never contemplated letting Cruz stay in the race,' one official said, 'because then the Sandinistas could justifiably claim that the elections were legitimate, making it much harder for the United States to oppose the Nicaraguan Government.' . . .

Several Administration officials who are familiar with the Administration's activities in Nicaragua said the Central Intelligence Agency had worked with some of Mr. Cruz's supporters to insure that they would object to any potential agreement for his participation in the election.[74]

Later in the month, other rightist parties which had registered claimed that US diplomats were pressing them to drop out of the race.[75] One of the three rightist parties already on the ballot, the Independent Liberal Party, had announced on the 21st that it was no longer in the running.

The American Ambassador to Costa Rica likens Nicaragua under the Sandinistas to an "infected piece of meat" that attracts "insects".[76] Ronald Reagan calls the country a "totalitarian dungeon".[77]

Members of the Kissinger Commission on Central America indicate that today's Nicaragua is as bad or worse than Nicaragua under Somoza. Henry Kissinger believes it to be as bad as or worse than Nazi Germany.[78] The president is in accord — he compares the plight of the contras with Britain's stand against Germany in World War II . . .[79]

"Central America," says Wayne Smith, former head of the US Interests Section in Havana, "now exercises the same influence on American foreign policy as the full moon does on werewolves."[80]

So all-consuming, so unrelenting, is the hatred, that Kissinger demands that the American Ambassador to Nicaragua be removed simply because he reports that the Sandinista government is "performing fairly well in such areas as education".[81]

So eager to turn Nicaragua into an international pariah, that the State Department tells the world, without any evidence, that Nicaragua is exporting drugs, that it is anti-semitic, that it is training Brazilian guerrillas.[82] The Secretary of State refers to a photograph of blazing corpses and declares it an example of the "atrocious genocidal actions that are being taken by the Nicaraguan Government" against the Miskito Indians. We then learn that the photo is from 1978, Somoza's time.[83]

Within a rational framework, it would be proper to inquire what the Sandinistas have done that makes it impossible for the United States to share the same planet with them. David MacMichael has observed that there is no *casus belli* between the two countries . . .

There are no examples of US citizens being killed there. No US property has been expropriated without due process or compensation. These people are so backward that they haven't even bothered to kill any American priests or nuns. Now any half-respectable country in the world can do that, but the Sandinistas don't seem to get round to it.[84]

What the United States has done to the Nicaraguan revolution is clearer.

To transform Nicaraguan society, even if left in peace, would have been uphill all the way. The Sandinistas inherited a country of crushing poverty, backward in most respects, and with a foreign debt of $1.6 billion which they decided to honour (with the exception of money owed to Israel and Argentina for arms shipments to Somoza).[85]

Then came the fearsome American body-blows to foreign trade and credit, to industry and agriculture, and a war which forced the government to devote more than 40 percent of its national budget and an inordinate amount of its labour power to warfare and security.

On top of this: the historically-familiar post-revolutionary flight abroad of capital and of middle-class professionals; the equally familiar sabotage by those who remain[86] — facile in a society where most of the businesses and farms are still in private hands — and the Nicaraguan economy went onto a life-support machine . . . a trail of inefficiencies and shortages of all kinds; taxis and buses and machines grinding to a halt for want of an American spare part . . . a failure to meet the great expectations of the population; mitigated only partly by the progress in agrarian reform, health care, literacy, and other social programmes . . . many who were sympathetic to the revolution at first have drifted away, some into protest and opposition.*

Forty years of anti-communist indoctrination under Somoza and American cultural imperialism has also left a mark. A government militant puts it this way:

> Tell a Nicaraguan factory worker . . . that we are building a system in which workers will control the means of production, in which income will be redistributed to benefit the proletariat, and he will say 'yes — that's what we want.' Call it Socialism and he will tell you he doesn't want any part of it. Tell a peasant — in whom the problem of political education is even more acute — that the revolution is all about destroying the power of the big *latifundistas*, that the agrarian reform and the literacy campaign will incorporate the peasantry into political decisions . . . and he will be enthusiastic, he will recognize that this is right and just. Mention the word Communism and he will run a mile.[88]

In the face of dissension, the Sandinistas have frequently shown themselves unable to distinguish honest and valid criticism from intentions to destabilize. Some opponents have been harassed and jailed, civil liberties have been curtailed, although never in a draconian manner, and credentials of loyalty to the revolution have become more than ever a priority in filling positions high and low.

The process could be seen at work early on. The editor of the opposition

---

* Individuals are turned away from, or attracted to, social revolution for a multitude of reasons, ideological and/or personal. All must be approached with great caution. The most prominent defector from the Sandinistas, Edén Pastora, in between (semi-coherent) political statements, declares that "They [the Sandinistas] attack me for my success with women, out of jealousy because they are all queer and I can make love to their women"[87]

newspaper *La Prensa*, Pablo Antonio Cuadra, said in August 1982 that American hostility towards the Sandinistas was inducing the government to crack down on opposition, such as his newspaper, and making it more difficult to preserve a pluralistic society. "President Reagan's policies toward Nicaragua," said Cuadra, "are stupid."[89]

At this point in history, we do not need to look for new or arcane explanations of why the United States seeks to overthrow a leftist or reformist government, particularly in Latin America. We have seen why Guatemala, the Dominican Republic, Brazil and Bolivia fell, followed by British Guiana, Chile, Jamaica and Grenada. Only Cuba has escaped . . . and Nicaragua. Cuba has a guardian angel, Nicaragua does not. And each passing day that the Sandinistas survive infuriates the anti-communist wind-up toys who inhabit the White House.

The Soviet Union allowed Yugoslavia to escape its orbit. The United States appears incapable of granting Nicaragua the same freedom.

Notes

Introduction

1. *Washington Post*, 24 October 1965, article by Stanley Karnow.
2. Winston Churchill, *The Second World War, Vol. IV, The Hinge of Fate* (London, 1951), p. 428.
3. Winston Churchill, *The World Crisis: The Aftermath* (London, 1929), p. 235.
4. D.F. Fleming, 'The Western Intervention in the Soviet Union, 1918–1920', *New World Review* (New York), Fall 1967; see also Fleming, *The Cold War and its Origins, 1917–1960* (New York, 1961), pp. 16–35 for his earlier account of the intervention.
5. Frederick L. Schuman, *American Policy Toward Russia Since 1917* (New York, 1928), p. 125.
6. Ibid., p. 154.
7. *San Francisco Chronicle*, 4 October 1978, p. 4.
8. *Life*, 29 March 1943, p. 29.
9. *New York Times*, 24 June 1941; for an interesting account of how US officials laid the groundwork for the cold war during and immediately after World War II, see the first two chapters of Blanche Wiesen Cook, *The Declassified Eisenhower* (New York, 1981), a study of previously classified papers at the Eisenhower Library.
10. This has been well documented and would be 'common knowledge' if not for its shameful implications. See, e.g., the British Cabinet papers for 1939, summarized in the *Washington Post*, 2 January 1970 (reprinted from the *Manchester Guardian*); also Fleming, *The Cold War*, pp. 48–97.
11. For a highly insightful and readable description of the anti-communist mentality in the United States, see Michael Parenti, *The Anti-Communist Imperative* (New York, 1969).
12. Related by former French Foreign Minister Christian Pineau in a recorded interview for the Dulles Oral History Project, Princeton University Library; cited in Roger Morgan, *The United States and West Germany, 1945–1973: A Study in Alliance Politics* (Oxford University Press, London, 1974), p. 54, my translation from the French.
13. *International Herald Tribune*, 8 November 1982, N.Y. Times Service.
14. Parenti, p. 35.
15. John Stockwell, *In Search of Enemies* (New York, 1978), p. 101.
16. Ibid., p. 238.
17. Kwame Nkrumah, *Dark Days in Ghana* (London, 1968), pp. 71–2.
18. The full quotation is from the *New York Times*, 11 Janaury 1969, p. 1; the inside quotation is that of the National Commission.
19. *Mother Jones* magazine (San Francisco), April 1981, p. 5.

20. *San Francisco Chronicle*, 14 January 1982, p. 2.
21. Richard F. Grimmett, *Reported Foreign and Domestic Covert Activities of the United States Central Intelligence Agency: 1950–1974*, 18 February 1975.
22. *The Pentagon Papers* (N.Y. Times edition, 1971), p. xiii.
23. *Newsweek*, 22 November 1971, p. 37.
24. Speech before the World Affairs Council at the University of Pennsylvania, 13 January 1950, cited in the Republican Congressional Committee Newsletter, 20 September 1965.
25. The last sentence is borrowed from Michael Parenti, p. 7.

1. China 1945 to 1960s

1. David Barrett, *Dixie Mission: The United States Army Observer Group in Yennan, 1944* (Center for Chinese Studies, University of California, Berkeley, 1970), *passim*; R. Harris Smith, *OSS: The Secret History of America's First CIA* (University of California Press, Berkeley, 1972), pp. 262–3; *New York Times*, 9 December 1945, p. 24.
2. Chiang's policies during and after war: Smith, pp. 259–82; *New York Times*, 19 December 1945, p. 2.
3. Harry S. Truman, *Memoirs, Vol. Two: Years of Trial and Hope, 1946–1953* (Great Britain, 1956), p. 66.
4. Smith, p. 282.
5. D.F. Fleming, *The Cold War and its Origins, 1917–1960* (New York 1961), p. 570.
6. *New York Times*, September-December 1945, *passim*; Barbara W. Tuchman, *Stilwell and the American Experience in China 1911–45* (New York, 1972), pp. 666–77.
7. *Congressional Record*, Appendix, Vol. 92, part 9, 24 January 1946, p. A225, letter to Congressman Hugh de Lacy of State of Washington.
8. *New York Times*, 6 November 1945, p. 1; 19 December 1945, p. 2.
9. Ibid., 9 December 1945, p. 24; 26 December 1945, p. 5.
10. Ibid., 26 December 1945, p. 5.
11. Fleming, p. 587.
12. Christopher Robbins, *Air America* (U.S., 1979), pp. 46–57; published in Great Britain the same year as *The Invisible Air Force: The Story of the CIA's Secret Airlines*; Victor Marchetti and John Marks, *The CIA and the Cult of Intelligence* (New York, 1975), p. 149.
13. Hearings held in executive session before the US Senate Foreign Relations Committee during 1949–50: *Economic Assistance to China and Korea 1949–50*, testimony of Dean Acheson, p. 23, made public January 1974 as part of the Historical Series.
14. Tuchman, p. 676.
15. Fleming, p. 578; *Parade* magazine (*Washington Post*), 27 February 1966.
16. Felix Greene, *A Curtain of Ignorance* (New York, 1964).
17. Soviet position in the civil war: Tuchman, p. 676; Fleming, pp. 572–4, 577, 584–5; Milovan Djilas, *Conversations with Stalin* (London, 1962), p. 164; *New York Times*, 7 November 1945, p. 12; 14 November, p. 1; 21 November, p. 2; 28 November, p. 1; 30 November, p. 3; 2 December, p. 34.

18. *New York Times*, 12 January 1947, p. 44.

19. William Manchester, *American Caesar: Douglas MacArthur 1880–1964* (London, 1979), p. 535.

20. *Foreign Relations of the United States, 1949, Vol. VIII, The Far East: China* (U.S. Government Printing Office, Washington, 1978), *passim* betwen pp. 357 and 399; 768, 779–80; publication of this volume in the State Department's series was held up precisely because it contained the reports about Chou En-Lai's request (see *San Francisco Chronicle*, 27 September 1978, p. F–1).

21. *New York Times*, 25 April 1966, p. 20.

22. Burma: Robbins, pp. 84–7; David Wise and Thomas Ross, *The Invisible Government* (New York, 1965, paperback edition), pp. 138–44; Joseph Burkholder Smith, *Portrait of a Cold Warrior* (New York, 1976), pp. 77–8; *New York Times*, 28 July 1951; 28 December 1951; 22 February 1952; 8 April 1952; 30 December 1952.

23. *Washington Post*, 20 August 1958, Joseph Alsop, a columnist who had been a staff officer under General Chennault and was well connected with Taiwan.

24. Quemoy and Matsu: Stewart Alsop (formerly with the OSS), 'The Story Behind Quemoy: How We Drifted Close to War', *Saturday Evening Post*, 13 December 1958, p. 26; Andrew Tulley, *CIA: The Inside Story* (New York, 1962), pp. 162–5; Fleming, pp. 930–1; Wise and Ross, p. 116; *New York Times*, 27 April 1966, p. 28.

25. Wise and Ross, p. 114.

26. Air drops: Wise and Ross, pp. 112–5; Thomas Powers, *The Man Who Kept the Secrets* (New York, 1979), pp. 43–4; *Newsweek*, 26 March 1973.

27. Overflights: Marchetti and Marks, pp. 150, 287; *Washington Post*, 27 May 1966; *New York Times*, 28 March 1969, p. 40.

28. *Foreign Relations of the United States, 1943, China* (U.S. Government Printing Office, Washington, 1957), p. 630.

29. Tibet: David Wise, *The Politics of Lying* (New York, 1973, paperback edition), pp. 239–54; Robbins, pp. 94–101; Marchetti and Marks, pp. 128–31.

30. *People's China*, English-language magazine, Foreign Languages Press, Peking, 17 September 1952, p. 28.

31. Germ Warfare: *People's China*, 1952, *passim*, beginning 16 March. For another detailed account, see Wilfred Burchett, *Passport: An Autobiography* (Melbourne, 1969), chapter 19, 'Germ Warfare'.

32. *New York Times*, 9 August 1970, IV, p. 3.

33. *Washington Post* article reprinted in the *San Francisco Chronicle*, 17 December 1979, p. 5. 'Whooping-cough cases recorded in Florida jumped from 339 and one death in 1954 to 1,080 and 12 deaths in 1955.' The CIA received the bacteria from the Army's biological warfare centre at Fort Detrick, Md. in January of that year.

34. *San Francisco Chronicle*, 4 December 1979, p. 12.

35. *Department of State Bulletin*, 2 May 1966.

2. Italy 1947 to 1948

1. Addressing the Cathedral Club of Brooklyn (New York), 15 January 1948; cited in David Caute, *The Great Fear: The Anti-Communist Purge Under Truman*

and Eisenhower (London, 1978), p. 15.

2. Robert T. Holt and Robert W. van de Velde, *Strategic Psychological Operations and American Foreign Policy* (University of Chicago Press 1960), p. 169.

3. Cabinet changes, Italy: *New York Times*, 21 January 1947, p. 5; 26 January, p. 31; 3 February, p. 1; 5 May, p. 13; 13 May; 14 May; 29 May, p. 3; 2 June, p. 24.
France: 5 May 1947, p. 1; 11 May, IV, p. 5; 14 May, pp 14 and 24; 17 May, p. 8; 18 May, IV, p. 4; 20 May, p. 2; Howard K. Smith, *The State of Europe* (London, 1950), p. 151 (includes Ramadier quote; similar quote in NYT 20 May).

4. *Time*, 22 March 1948, p. 35.

5. William Colby, *Honourable Men: My Life in the CIA* (London, 1978), p. 109.

6. Except where otherwise indicated, the items in the succeeding list are derived from the following sources:
a) *New York Times*, 16 March to 18 April 1948, *passim*;
b) Howard K. Smith, pp. 198–219;
c) William E. Daugherty and Morris Janowitz, *A Psychological Warfare Casebook* (Johns Hopkins Press, Baltimore, 1958), pp. 319–26;
d) Holt and van de Velde, pp. 159–205;
e) E. Edda Martinez and Edward A. Suchman, 'Letters from America and the 1948 Elections in Italy', *The Public Opinion Quarterly* (Princeton University), Spring 1950, pp. 111–25.

7. Cited in Smith, p. 202, no date of issue given.

8. Tom Braden, 'I'm Glad the CIA is "Immoral" ', *Saturday Evening Post*, 20 May 1967; Braden had been a high-ranking CIA officer.

9. Miles Copeland, *Without Cloak and Dagger* (New York, 1974), pp. 235–6; also published as *The Real Spy World*.

10. CIA memorandum to the Forty Committee (National Security Council), presented to the Select Committee on Intelligence, US House of Representatives (The Pike Committee) during closed hearings held in 1975. The bulk of the committee's report which contained this memorandum was leaked to the press in February 1976 and first appeared in book form as *CIA —The Pike Report* (Nottingham, England, 1977). The memorandum appears on pp. 204–5 of this book. (cf. Notes: Iraq.)

11. *Public Papers of the Presidents of the United States: Harry S. Truman, 1947* (U.S. Government Printing Office, Washington, 1963), pp. 178–9.

12. *New York Times*, 8 April 1948.

13. Ibid., 12 April 1948.

14. Smith, p. 200.

15. Ibid., p. 202.

16. *New York Times*, 15 April 1948.

3. Greece, 1947 to early 1950s

1. Jorge Semprun, *What a Beautiful Sunday!* (English translation, London, 1983), pp. 26–7; Semprun wrote the screenplays for 'Z' and 'La Guerre est finie'.

2. There is ample material available about ELAS and EAM. For a summary of

some of the literature, see Todd Gitlin, 'Counter-Insurgency: Myth and Reality in Greece' in David Horowitz, ed., *Containment and Revolution* (Boston, 1967) pp. 142–7; see also D.F. Fleming, *The Cold War and its Origins, 1917–1960* (New York, 1961) pp. 183–5; Howard K Smith, *The State of Europe* (London, 1950) pp. 225–30; William Hardy McNeill, *The Greek Dilemma: War and Aftermath* (US 1947) *passim*.

3. For accounts of the thoroughly unprincipled British policy in Greece and its dealings with collaborators during 1944–46, see Fleming, pp. 174–87; Smith, pp. 227–31; 234; Lawrence S. Wittner, *American Intervention in Greece, 1943–1949* (Columbia University Press, N.Y., 1982) *passim*.

4. *Parliamentary Debates, House of Commons*, 16 October 1946, column 887 (reference is made here to Bevin's statement of 10 August).

5. Gitlin, p. 157; Wittner, p. 25.

6. Winston Churchill, *The Second World War, Vol. VI, Triumph and Tragedy* (London, 1954), p. 198.

7. Ibid., p. 255. For other evidence of Soviet non-intervention, see Wittner, pp. 26–7.

8. Fleming, p. 182; see also Smith, p. 228.

9. See sources listed in notes 2 and 3 above; see also James Becket, *Barbarism in Greece* (New York, 1970) p. 6; Richard Barnet, *Intervention and Revolution* (London, 1970) pp. 99–101; Edgar O'Ballance, *The Greek Civil War, 1944–1949* (London, 1966) pp. 155, 167.

10. Smith, p. 232.

11. Stephen G. Xydis, *Greece and the Great Powers, 1944–1947* (Institute for Balkan Studies, Thessaloniki, Greece, 1963) p. 479, information from the archives of the Greek Embassy in Washington.

12. *Foreign Relations of the United States, 1947, Vol. V* (U.S. Government Printing Office, Washington, 1971) p. 222.

13. *New York Times Magazine*, 12 October 1947, p. 10.

14. *Foreign Relations . . . 1947*, pp. 222–3.

15. Cited in Fleming, p. 444; see note 9 above for other sources on the nature of the Greek Government.

16. Barnet, p. 109.

17. *Public Papers of the Presidents of the United States: Harry S. Truman, 1947* (U.S. Government Printing Office, Washington, 1963) p. 177.

18. Milovan Djilas, *Conversations with Stalin* (London, 1962) p. 164.

19. For details of the American military effort: O'Ballance, *passim*; Wittner, p. 242; CIA Report to the President, March 1948, appendices D and F in *Declassified Documents Reference System* (Arlington, Va.) 1977, document 168A; Department of the Army internal memorandum, 15 June 1954, *DDRS* 1980, document 253C.

20. O'Ballance, p. 156.

21. Ibid., p. 173

22. Christopher M. Woodhouse, *The Struggle for Greece, 1941–1949* (London, 1976) pp. 260–1.

23. *New York Times*, 28 August 1947, p. 1; 5 September 1947, p. 1.

24. *Foreign Relations . . . 1947*, p. 327.

25. John O. Iatrides, 'American Attitudes Toward the Political System of Postwar Greece' in Theodore A. Couloumbis and John O. Iatrides, eds., *Greek-American Relations: A Critical Review* (N.Y., 1980) pp. 64–65; Lawrence Stern,

The Wrong Horse: The Politics of Intervention and the Failure of American Diplomacy (N.Y. Times Books, 1977) pp. 16–17.

26. Philip Deane, *I Should Have Died* (New York, 1977) pp. 102, 103; Andreas Papandreou, *Democracy at Gunpoint* (New York, 1970) pp. 84–5.

27. Papandreou, p. 80.

28. *New York Times*, 13 July 1947, p. 11.

29. *New York Times*, 11 September 1947, p. 19; 17 October 1947, p. 11.

30. Papandreou, p. 5.

31. Sent by Horace Smith of AMAG, U.S. National Archives, Record Group 59, cited in Michael M. Amen, *American Foreign Policy in Greece 1944/1949: Economic, Military and Institutional Aspects* (Peter Lang Ltd., Frankfurt, W. Gemany, 1978), pp. 114–5.

4. The Philippines, 1940s and 1950s

1. Charles S. Olcott, *The Life of William McKinley* (Boston, 1916) vol. 2, pp. 110–11; from a talk given to a visiting group from the Methodist Episcopal Church.

2. US actions against Huks during Second World War:

a) Luis Taruc, *Born of the People* (New York, 1953, although completed in June 1949) pp. 147–62, 186–211, the autobiography of the Huks' commander-in-chief who surrendered to the government in 1954.

b) William J. Pomeroy, *An American Made Tragedy* (New York, 1974), pp. 74–7; Pomeroy is an American who served in the Philippines during the war where he encountered the Huks. After the war, he returned to fight with them until he was captured in 1952.

c) George E. Taylor, *The Philippines and the United States: Problems of Partnership* (New York, 1964) p. 122 (see note 13 below).

d) *New York Times*, 30 October 1945, p. 3; 12 May 1946, p. 22 (US Army Forces in the Far East).

3. Taruc; Pomeroy; and Taylor, pp. 116–20.

4. Taruc and Pomeroy, *passim*.

5. *New York Times*, 19 December 1952, p. 13.

6. Ibid., 5 January 1946, p. 26.

7. Hearings before the House Committee on Foreign Affairs in executive session, 7 June 1946, released in 1977, p. 31; Arnold was the Deputy Assistant Chief of Staff, Operations Division, War Department General Staff.

8. American servicemen's protests: *New York Times*, 8 January 1946, p. 3; 11 January, p. 4; for more information, see Mary-Alice Waters, *G.I.'s and the Fight Against War* (New York, 1967) pamphlet published by *Young Socialist* magazine.

9. *New York Times*, 20 May 1946, p. 8; 2 June, p. 26; 4 June, p. 22 (letter from Tomas Confessor, prominent Philippine political figure, detailing the illegality of not seating the men); 18 September, p. 4; 19 September, p. 18; Pomeroy, p. 20; Taruc, pp. 214–27.

10. *New York Times*, 12 March 1947, p. 15; the words are those of the *Times*.

11. Pomeroy, p. 28, explains how this came about.

12. Taruc, chapters 23 and 24; Pomeroy, p. 78; the Philippine Army reported

that 600 deaths had occurred from their incursions into Huk areas in the month following the election (*New York Times*, 20 May, 1946, p. 8) but no breakdown between government and insurgent casualties was given in the press account.

13. Taylor, pp. 114, 115. The book was published by Frederick A. Praeger, Inc. for the Council on Foreign Relations, the ultra high-level think-tank whose officers and directors at the time included Allen Dulles, David Rockefeller, and John J. McCloy. Praeger, it was later disclosed, published a number of books in the 1960s under CIA sponsorship. This book, though generally reasonable on most matters, descends to the puerile and semi-hysterical when discussing the Huks or 'communism'.

14. Department of State, *Treaties and Other International Agreements of the United States of America, 1776–1949* (Washington, 1974) pp. 84–9; Pomeroy, pp. 21–3; Taylor, p. 129.

15. *New York Times*, 1 July 1946, $50 million furnished; 11 February 1950, p. 6, $163.5 million furnished under the 1947 agreement.

16. Pomeroy, p. 81; Edward G. Lansdale, *In the Midst of Wars* (New York, 1972) *passim*.

17. William Worden, 'Robin Hood of the Islands', *Saturday Evening Post*, 12 January 1952, p. 76.

18. Lansdale, pp. 24–30, 47.

19. Joseph Burkholder Smith, *Portrait of a Cold Warrior* (New York, 1976) p. 95 (see note 28).

20. Lansdale, pp. 72–3.

21. Ibid., pp. 47–59.

22. Ibid., pp. 70–71, 81–3, 92–3; Smith, p. 106; Taruc, pp. 68–9.

23. L. Fletcher Prouty, *The Secret Team: The CIA and its Allies in Control of the World* (New York, 1974), pp. 38–9.

24. Ibid., pp. 102–3.

25. Smith, p. 95, quoting CIA officer Paul Lineberger.

26. *New York Times*, 17 September 1953.

27. Sherman Adams, *Firsthand Report* (New York, 1961), p. 123.

28. CIA manipulation of Philippine political life – overall detailed description and of Magsaysay in particular: Smith, chapters 7, 15, 16, 17. Smith was a CIA officer who, in the early 1950s, worked in the Far East Division, which included the Philippines, concerned with political and psychological-warfare matters.

29. *Reader's Digest*, April 1963, article entitled 'Democracy Triumphs in the Philippines'.

30. Macapagal: Smith, p. 290.

31. Pomeroy, p. 84.

32. Huks' condition: *New York Times*, 3 April 1949, p. 20; 30 June 1950, p. 4.

33. Taylor, p. 192.

5. Korea, 1945–1953

1. For a discussion of this period, see the sources listed in note 19 below; also see Jon Halliday, 'The United Nations and Korea', in Frank Baldwin, ed., *Without Parallel: The American-Korean Relationship Since 1945* (New York, 1974) pp. 109–42.

2. *New York Times*, 1 October 1950, p. 3.

3. *The U.S. Imperialists Started the Korean War* is the subtle title of the book published in Pyongyang, North Korea, 1977, pp. 109–10.

4. Radio address of 13 April 1950, reprinted in *The Department of State Bulletin*, 24 April 1950, p. 627.

5. For a discussion of the war's immediate origin, see:

a) Karunakar Gupta, 'How Did the Korean War Begin?', *The China Quarterly* (London) October/December 1972, No. 52, pp.699–716.

b) 'Comment: The Korean War', *The China Quarterly*, April/June 1973, No. 54, pp. 354–68. This consists of responses to Gupta's article in issue No. 52 and Gupta's counter-response.

c) *New York Times*, 26 June 1950, p. 3: North Korea's announcement about Haeju; p. 1: South Korea's announcement about Haeju.

d) Glenn D. Paige, *The Korean Decision (June 24–30, 1950)* (New York, 1968) *passim*, see particularly, p. 130.

e) I.F. Stone, *The Hidden History of the Korean War* (New York, 1952) chapter 7 and elsewhere.

6. John Gunther, *The Riddle of MacArthur* (London, 1951), pp. 151–2.

7. *New York Times*, 25 July 1950, p. 4; 30 July, p. 2.

8. *Khruschev Remembers* (London, 1971), chapter 11. Study of transcription *vs.* book: John Merrill, Book Reviews, *Journal of Korean Studies* (University of Washington, Seattle) Vol. 3, 1981, pp. 181–91.

9. Joseph C. Goulden, *Korea: The Untold Story of the War* (New York 1982) p. 64.

10. *New York Times*, 26 June 1950.

11. Ibid., 1 October 1950, p. 4.

12. Goulden, pp. 87–8; Stone, pp. 75, 77.

13. For further discussion of the UN's bias at this time see Halliday, 'The United Nations and Korea'.

14. Trygve Lie, *In the Cause of Peace* (New York, 1954) chapters 18 and 19.

15. CIA memorandum, 28 June 1950, *Declassified Documents Reference System* (Arlington, Virginia) Retrospective Volume, Document 33C.

16. Stone, pp. 77–8.

17. The full text of the Security Council Resolution of 7 July 1950 can be found in the *New York Times*, 8 July 1950, p. 4.

18. Dwight Eisenhower, *The White House Years: Mandate for Change, 1953–1956* (New York 1963) p. 340.

19. For a discussion of the post-war period in general and of the KPR in particular see:

a) Bruce Cumings, *The Origins of the Korean War: Liberation and the Emergence of Separate Regimes, 1945–1947* (Princeton University Press, New Jersey, 1981) *passim*.

b) E. Grant Meade, *American Military Government in Korea* (King's Crown Press, Columbia University, New York, 1951) chapters 3–5.

c) George M. McCune, *Korea Today* (Institute of Pacific Relations, New York, 1950) pp. 46–50 (KPR) and *passim*. Professor McCune worked with the US Government on Korean problems during World War II.

d) D.F. Fleming, *The Cold War and its Origins, 1917–1960* (Doubleday & Co., New York, 1961) pp. 589–97.

e)   Alfred Crofts, 'The Case of Korea: Our Falling Ramparts', *The Nation* (New York) 25 June 1960, pp. 544–8. Crofts was a member of the US Military Government in Korea, beginning in 1945.

20. Crofts, p. 545.

21. Gunther, p. 165.

22. Crofts, p. 545.

23. Ibid.

24. Ibid., p. 546.

25. Collaborators: Cumings, pp. 152–6; Meade, p. 61; McCune, p. 51; plus elsewhere in these sources, as well in Fleming and Crofts.

26. McCune, pp. 83–4, 129–39, 201–9.

27. 1946 election: Mark Gayn, *Japan Diary* (New York, 1948) p. 398; 1948 election: Crofts, p. 546; Halliday, pp. 117–22; 1950 election: Fleming, p. 594.

28. Gunther, pp. 166–7; see also p. 171 comments about how 'disturbances were put down with a ferocity'.

29. Gayn, p. 388.

30. Ibid., p. 352.

31. John Kie-Chiang Oh, *Korea: Democracy on Trial* (Cornell University Press, Ithaca, New York, 1968) p. 35.

32. *The Nation*, 13 August 1949, p. 152.

33. Gunther, p. 171.

34. Oh, p. 206, see also *New York Times*, 11 April 1951, p. 4 for an account of a massacre of some 500 to 1,000 people in March in the same place, which appears to refer to the same incident.

35. Jon Halliday, 'The Political Background', in Gavan McCormack and Mark Selden, eds., *Korea, North and South: The Deepening Crisis* (New York, 1978) p. 56.

36. *New York Times*, 11 April 1951, p. 4.

37. René Cutforth, 'On the Korean War', *The Listener* (BBC publication, London) 11 September 1969, p. 343.

38. Gregory Henderson, *Korea: The Politics of the Vortex* (Harvard University Press, Cambridge, Mass., 1968) p. 167.

39. *New York Times*, 9 February 1951, George Barrett.

40. *New York Times*, 27 November 1951, p. 4.

41. Eugene Kinkead, *Why They Collaborated* (London, 1960) p. 17; published in the US in 1959 in slightly different form as *In Every War But One*. The Army study was not contained in any one volume, but was spread out over a number of separate reports. Kinkead's book, written with the full co-operation of the Army, is composed of a summary of some of these reports and interviews with many government and military officials who were directly involved in or knowledgeable about the study or the subject. For the sake of simplicity, I have referred to the book as if it were the actual study.

42. Ibid., pp. 190, 193.

43. *Keesings Contemporary Archives*, 5–12 January 1952, p. 11931, an announcement on 31 December 1951 from General Ridgeway's headquarters.

44. Kinkead, p. 34.

45. Robert J. Lifton, *Thought Reform and the Psychology of Totalism: A Study of 'Brainwashing' in China* (London, 1961), p. 4.

46. Kinkead, p. 31.

47. Ibid., pp. 17, 34.

---

48. Ibid., pp. 105–6.
49. Ibid., p. 197.
50. For a concise description of the 'terror bombing' of 1952–53, see John Gittings, 'Talks, Bombs and Germs: Another Look at the Korean War', *Journal of Contemporary Asia* (London) Vol. 5, No. 2, 1975, pp. 212–6.
51. Air Force Communiqué, 2 February 1951, cited by Stone, p. 259.
52. *Military Situation in the Far East*, Hearings Before the Senate Committees on Armed Services and Foreign Relations, 25 June 1951, p. 3075.
53. Louis Heren, 'The Korean Scene', in Rear-Admiral H.G. Thursfield, ed., *Brassey's Annual: The Armed Forces Year-Book 1951* (London, 1951) p. 110.
54. *San Francisco Chronicle*, 15 December 1977, p. 11, based on documents released under the Freedom of Information Act.
55. *New York Times*, 12 November 1951, p. 3.
56. Ibid., 14 November 1951, p. 1.

6. Albania 1949–1953

1. Douglas Sutherland, *The Fourth Man* (London, 1980) p. 88.
2. Kim Philby, *My Silent War* (London, 1968) p. 117.
3. Nicholas Bethell, *The Great Betrayal: The Untold Story of Kim Philby's Biggest Coup* (London 1984) *passim* for the most detailed discussion of the recruitment, training and fate of the émigrés; also see Bruce Page, David Leitch, and Philip Knightley, *The Philby Conspiracy* (New York, 1968) pp. 196–203.
4. Philby, p. 117.
5. E. Howard Hunt, *Undercover: Memoirs of an American Secret Agent* (London, 1975) p. 93.
6. See note 3 above.
7. Political background of the émigrés: *New York Times*, 20 June 1982, p. 22; Bethell, *passim*.
8. Radio station, unrest: *New York Times*, 31 March 1951, p. 5; 9 April 1951, p. 1; 26 September 1951.
9. Philby, p. 118.
10. *New York Times*, 27 March 1950; 9 April 1951, p. 1.
11. Bethell, p. 183.
12. *New York Times*, 9 April 1951, p. 1.
13. Bethell, p. 200.

7. Eastern Europe, 1948–1956

1. *New York Times*, 29 September 1954.
2. The story of Operation Splinter Factor comes from the book of the same name by Stewart Steven published in London in 1974. Steven, a veteran British journalist and currently Editor of *The Mail on Sunday* (London), provides much greater detail than my short summary. He presents a strong case, and one has to read the entire book to appreciate this, but his central thesis remains undocumented. Steven states that this thesis – Allen Dulles instigating Jozef Swiatlo to use Noel Field in the manner described – comes from personal interviews with former members of the CIA, the SIS (the British Secret Intelligence Service) and other

people involved in the conspiracy who insisted on remaining anonymous. Flora Lewis, the *Washington Post* correspondent who wrote the definitive work on Noel Field, *Red Pawn: The Story of Noel Field* (New York, 1965; published in London the same year as *The Man Who Disappeared: The Strange History of Noel Field*), stated in that book that she ran into an 'official barrier of silence' when she requested information from American, Swiss, French, British and German intelligence centres on even 'plain questions of dates and places'. And she was not enquiring about Operation Splinter Factor *per se*, which she knew nothing about, only about Noel Field a decade after he had been released. Similarly, the US government, without explanation, flatly refused her access to Jozef Swiatlo.

3. *New York Times*, 25 October 1954, p. 1.

4. Ibid., 19 February 1955, p. 1.

5. Ibid., 17 November 1954, p. 1.

6. Blanche W. Cook, *The Declassified Eisenhower* (New York, 1981) p. 129.

7. Ibid.

8. Cord Meyer, *Facing Reality: From World Federalism to the CIA* (New York, 1980) p.120; Steven, pp. 208–9; Lewis, p. 238 (torture).

9. *New York Times*, 23 July 1948, p. 5.

10. Ibid., 9 April 1951 (column by C. Sulzberger).

11. Cook, pp. 130–1; George Clay, 'Balloons for a Captive Audience', *The Reporter* (New York) 18 November 1954; Robert T. Holt and Robert W. van de Velde, *Strategic Psychological Operations and American Foreign Policy* (University of Chicago Press, 1960) ch. VII.

12. *New York Times*, 30 August 1955, p. 1.

13. Ibid., 30 November 1976.

14. Stephen Ambrose, *Ike's Spies* (Doubleday & Co., New York, 1981) pp. 235, 238.

8. Germany 1950s

1. Dean Acheson, *Present at the Creation: My Years in the State Department* (London 1970) p. 260.

2. Ibid.

3. Failure of de-industrialization: for further discussion, see Richard J. Barnet, *Allies: America, Europe and Japan since the War* (London, 1984) pp. 33–9.

4. Dwight Eisenhower, *The White House Years: Mandate for Change, 1953–1956* (New York, 1963) pp. 79–80.

5. Sabotage and subversion campaign:

a) *Democratic German Report*, various issues from 1952 to 1957 (consult its annual indexes under 'Sabotage', 'Espionage', etc.). This was a small English-language news magazine published fortnightly in East Berlin by Britisher John Peet, former chief correspondent for Reuters News Agency in West Berlin.

b) *Nation's Business* (published by the United States Chamber of Commerce) April 1952, pp. 25–7, 68–9, discusses many of the tactics employed.

c) Sanche de Gramont, *The Secret War* (New York, 1963) pp. 479–80.

d) *The New Yorker*, 8 September 1951, article on the Investigating Committee of Freedom-minded Jurists of the Soviet Zone.

e) *The Nation*, New York, 24 June 1961, pp. 551–2.

f)   Andrew Tully, *CIA: The Inside Story* (New York, 1962) pp. 133–4, CIA activity in June 1953 uprising.
g)   *Saturday Evening Post*, 6 November 1954, p. 64 (part of a series on the CIA) refers to CIA-promoted train derailments in East Germany, and blowing up a railway bridge and promoting factory work slowdowns in unspecified East European countries.
h)   *New York Times*, 6 November 1952, p. 3, reported that members of the Fighting Group Against Inhumanity (the most active of the sabotage groups) said that they had received financial support from the Ford Foundation and the West Berlin government. The *Democratic German Report*, 13 February 1953, published a copy of a letter from the Ford Foundation confirming a grant of $150,000 to the National Committee for a Free Europe 'so that it, in turn, could support the humanitarian activities of "The Fighting Group Against Inhumanity".' The National Committee for a Free Europe was a CIA front organization which also ran Radio Free Europe. (See Victor Marchetti and John Marks, *The CIA and the Cult of Intelligence* (New York, 1975 p. 147.)
     6. *Democratic German Report*, 15 March 1957.
     7. Secret army, hit-list, etc.:
a)   *Newsweek*, 20 October 1952, p. 42.
b)   *New York Times*, 9 October 1952, p. 8; 10 October, p. 3 (under the remarkable headline: 'German Saboteurs Betray U.S. Trust'); 12 October, p. 14.
c)   *Der Spiegel* (West German weekly news magazine), 15 October 1952, pp. 6–8.
d)   *Democratic German Report*, 15 and 24 October 1952; 21 November 1952.
     8. *New York Times*, 14 October 1952, p. 13.

9. Iran 1953

A general account and overview of the events in this chapter can be obtained from the following:
a)   Kermit Roosevelt, *Countercoup: The Struggle for the Control of Iran* (New York, 1979) *passim*.
b)   Bahman Nirumand, *Iran, the New Imperialism in Action* (New York, 1969), chapters 3 and 4; particularly the Iranian case for nationalization, British and American reaction, and post-coup developments.
c)   Stephen Ambrose, *Ike's Spies* (Doubleday & Co., New York, 1981) chapters 14 and 15.
d)   Barry Rubin, *Paved With Good Intentions: The American Experience and Iran* (New York, 1980) chapter 3.
e)   David Wise and Thomas B. Ross, *The Invisible Government* (New York, 1965, paperback edition), pp. 116–21.
f)   Andrew Tully, *CIA: The Inside Story* (New York, 1962), pp. 76–84.
g)   Fred J. Cook in *The Nation* (New York) 24 June 1961, pp. 547–51, particularly poverty and corruption in Iran after the coup.
     1. Roosevelt, p. 8.
     2. Ibid., pp. 18–19.
     3. Anthony Eden, *The Memoirs of the Right Honourable Sir Anthony Eden: Full Circle* (London, 1960) p. 194.

4. Dean Acheson, *Present at the Creation: My Years in the State Department* (London, 1970) pp. 679–85; Eden, pp. 201–2; Nirumand, pp. 73–4.

5. Roosevelt, p. 107.

6. Ibid., pp. II, 2, 3, 91–2, 126, 134, 164, 119.

7. Relations between Mossadegh, Tudeh, and the Soviet Union: Manfred Halpern, 'Middle East and North Africa' in C.E. Black and T.P. Thornton, eds., *Communism and Revolution* (U.S., 1964) pp. 316–19; see also Rubin.

8. *The Declassified Documents Reference System* (Arlington, Va.) 1979 volume, p. 79, E.

9. Ibid.

10. Roosevelt interview by Robert Scheer in the *Los Angeles Times*, as reprinted in the *San Francisco Chronicle*, 4 April 1979, p. F–1.

11. *New York Times*, 10 July 1953, p. 4.

12. Roosevelt, p. 168.

13. Fitzroy Maclean, *Eastern Approaches* (London, 1949) pp. 266, 274; Maclean was a British officer in World War II who kidnapped Zahedi (or Zahidi) to keep him from further aiding the Nazis. (Published in Boston, 1950 as *Escape to Adventure*.)

14. Roosevelt, p. 173; the details of the last days of the Mossadegh regime can be found in Roosevelt, chapters 11 and 12 as well as in the other books listed at the beginning of this section.

15. Roosevelt, p. 179.

16. *New York Times*, 19 August 1953.

17. Halpern, p. 318.

18. Henderson meeting with Mossadegh: Ambrose, pp. 208–9, interview with Henderson by the author; Roosevelt, pp. 183–5.

19. *New York Times*, 19 August 1953.

20. CIA bribes: Tully, p. 81; Cook, p. 549.

21. Roosevelt, p. 191.

22. *New York Times*, 20 August 1953, p. 1; *The Times* (London) 20 August 1953.

23. Hearings in 1954 before the House Foreign Affairs Committee on 'The Mutual Security Act of 1954', pp. 503, 569–70. Stewart was the Director of the Office of Military Assistance, Department of Defense.

24. Kenett Love, *The American Role in the Pahlevi Restoration on 19 August 1953* (Pahlevi was the Shah's name), unpublished manuscript residing amongst the Allen Dulles papers, Princeton University; excerpted in *CounterSpy* magazine (Washington, D.C.) September/October 1980, p. 4.

25. *New York Times*, 18 January 1953, IV, p. 8.

26. Arthur L. Richards, Director, Office of Greek, Turkish and Iranian Affairs, testimony 17 July 1953, before House Committee on Foreign Affairs in executive session, released in 1981, p. 148.

27. *New York Times*, 21 July 1953.

28. Ibid., 23 August 1953, IV, p. 1.

29. Scheer interview.

30. *The Guardian* (London), 2 January 1984, British Government papers of 1953, released 1 January 1984.

31. Testimony at Hearings on the Situation in the Middle East, Senate Committee on Foreign Relations, 24 February 1956, p. 23.

32. Nirumand, pp. 100–108.

33. Roosevelt's post-CIA career: Scheer interview; Wise and Ross, pp. 116–7.

34. Robert Engler, *The Politics of Oil: A Study of Private Power and Democratic Directions* (New York, 1961) p. 310.

35. *San Francisco Chronicle*, 26 December 1979.

36. *Platt's Oilgram News Service* (New York) 31 July 1951, cited in Nirumand, p. 50.

37. Roosevelt, p. 145.

38. *New York Times*, 6 August 1954.

39. Allen Dulles, *The Craft of Intelligence* (New York, 1965) p. 216.

40. *Fortune* (New York) June 1975, p. 90.

41. Love, p. 3.

42. Roosevelt, p. 9.

43. Jesse J. Leaf, Chief CIA analyst on Iran for five years before resigning in 1973, interviewed by Seymour Hersh in the *New York Times*, reprinted in the *San Francisco Chronicle*, 8 January 1979.

44. Martin Ennals, Secretary-General of Amnesty International, cited in an article by Reza Baraheni in *Matchbox* (Amnesty publication in New York) Fall, 1976.

45. Tully, p. 76.

46. See, e.g. Michael Klare, *War Without End* (New York, 1972) pp. 375, 379, 382, based on official US Government tables covering the 1950s and 1960s.

47. Cook, p. 550.

48. *San Francisco Chronicle*, 3 March 1980, p. 15.

10. Guatemala, 1953–1954

The details of the events described in this chapter were derived principally from the following sources:
a)   Stephen Schlesinger and Stephen Kinzer, *Bitter Fruit: The Untold Story of the American Coup in Guatemala* (Doubleday & Co., New York, 1982) *passim*, based partly on documents obtained under the Freedom of Information Act from the State Department, the Defense Department, the CIA, the National Archives, the Navy Department, and the FBI, as well as documents at the Eisenhower Library and amongst the John Foster Dulles and Allen Dulles papers at Princeton University, and interviews with individuals who played a role in the events. This is the primary source where another source is not indicated.
b)   Blanche Wiesen Cook, *The Declassified Eisenhower* (Doubleday & Co., New York, 1981) pp. 222–92, based partly on documents at the Eisenhower Library and the Guatemala archives at the Library of Congress. The latter is composed of papers confiscated by the US after the coup, undoubtedly in the hope of uncovering evidence of a grand Communist conspiracy; if this is what was discovered, it has not been made public.
c)   Richard H. Immerman, *The CIA in Guatemala: The Foreign Policy of Intervention* (University of Texas Press, Austin, 1982) pp. 118–22, ch. 6 and 7, based partly on papers at the Truman and Eisenhower Libraries and interviews.
d)   David Wise and Thomas Ross, *The Invisible Government* (New York, 1965, paperback edition) chapter 11.

e) Thomas and Marjorie Melville, *The Politics of Land Ownership* (New York, 1971), ch. 4 to 6; published in Great Britain the same year in slightly different form as *Guatemala – Another Vietnam?*
1. Schlesinger and Kinzer, pp. 143–4.
2. *New York Times*, 16 June 1954.
3. Ibid., 20 May 1954, p. 18.
4. *Time* magazine, 11 January 1954.
5. *Congressional Record*, 8 February 1954, p. 1475.
6. *Time*, 19 July 1954, p. 34, European edition.
7. Cook, p. 274; Schlesinger and Kinzer, p. 148.
8. Cook, p. 234.
9. Ibid., pp. 240–41.
10. Schlesinger and Kinzer, p. 12.
11. Cook, pp. 242–3, quoting former Guatemalan Foreign Minister Raul Oesegueda.
12. Schlesinger and Kinzer, p. 61.
13. *Washington Post*, 15 November 1953, p. 3B.
14. Schlesinger and Kinzer, pp. 58–9.
15. CIA National Intelligence Estimate, 11 March 1952, pp. 1–3, *Declassified Documents Reference System* (Woodbridge, Connecticut) 1982 Volume, Document no. 6.
16. Immerman, pp. 118–22.
17. Thomas P. McCann, *An American Company: The Tragedy of United Fruit* (New York, 1976) p. 49; McCann was an official with United Fruit; almost all sources differ as to the amount offered by the Guatemalan Government, ranging from McCann's figure to almost $1,200,000.
18. Schlesinger and Kinzer, pp. 106–7 and *passim*; McCann, chapter 4.
19. Schlesinger and Kinzer, p. 52.
20. Ibid., pp. 102–3.
21. Derived primarily from Schlesinger and Kinzer, to a lesser extent from the other sources listed at the beginning of this section, as well as those specified below.
22. Dwight Eisenhower, *The White House Years: Mandate for Change, 1953–1956* (New York, 1963) p. 424.
23. Cook, pp. 270–71.
24. Ibid., pp. 249–52.
25. *Time*, 8 February 1954, p. 36, European edition.
26. *New York Times*, 30 January 1954, pp. 1, 6.
27. McCann, p. 60.
28. David Atlee Phillips, *The Night Watch: Twenty-five Years of Peculiar Service* (London, 1978) pp. 34–5.
29. *Life* magazine, 5 July 1954, p. 8.
30. *Newsweek*, 5 July 1954, p. 46.
31. State Department memo, 23 June 1954, cited in Schlesinger and Kinzer, p. 189.
32. *New York Times*, 24 June 1954; Schlesinger and Kinzer, p. 175.
33. Guillermo Toriello, *La Batalla de Guatemala* (Mexico City, 1955) p. 189; the Guatemalan Foreign Minister related what he was told by Col. Diaz; cited in Schlesinger and Kinzer, p. 207.
34. Cook, p. 285, Wise and Ross, p. 192.

35. Paul Kennedy, *The Middle Beat* (Teachers College Press, Columbia University, New York, 1971) p. 142.

36. *Time*, 12 July 1954, p. 39, European edition.

37. John Gerassi, *The Great Fear in Latin America* (New York, 1965, revised edition) p. 183; originally published as *The Great Fear* (New York, 1963); Wise and Ross, p. 194.

38. Melville, p. 93.

39. Gerassi, p. 183; Cook, p. 231; Schlesinger and Kinzer, p. 60.

40. Wise and Ross, p. 187.

41. Hilda Gadea, *Ernesto: A Memoir of Che Guevara* (London, 1973, translated from the Spanish) p. 54.

42. *New York Times*, 1 July 1954.

43. CIA memo, 16 August 1954, *Declassified Documents Reference System* (Woodbridge, Connecticut) 1983 Volume, Document No. 32.

44. Statement before the Subcommittee on Latin America, House Select Committee on Communist Aggression, 8 October 1954, as reprinted in *Department of State Bulletin*, 8 November 1954, p. 690.

45. Eisenhower, pp. 421–7.

46. *New York Times*, 28 October 1955.

11. Costa Rica, Mid-1950s

1. *Los Angeles Times*, 10 March 1975.

2. *Miami Herald*, 10 March 1975.

3. *Christian Science Monitor* (Boston), 11 March 1975. Notes one to three all refer to the same television interview of Figueres in Mexico City, 9 March 1975. Figueres may have admitted to his CIA connections at this time because shortly before, Philip Agee's book had come out, identifying Figueres as 'a long-time Agency collaborator'. (*Inside the Company: CIA Diary*, New York, 1975, p. 244; published in Great Britain in 1974.)

4. David Wise and Thomas Ross, *The Invisible Government* (New York, 1965, paperback edition) p. 127.

5. Ibid., pp. 127–8.

6. Charles D. Ameringer, *Democracy in Costa Rica* (Praeger, New York and Hoover Institution Press, Stanford University, California, 1982) pp. 83–5.

7. John Gerassi, *The Great Fear in Latin America* (New York, 1965, revised edition) p. 208; originally published as *The Great Fear* (New York, 1963).

8. *Miami Herald*, 13 February 1971.

9. Wise and Ross, p. 128.

10. Charles D. Ameringer, *Don Pepe, A Political Biography of Jose Figueres of Costa Rica* (University of New Mexico Press, 1978) pp. 124–5.

11. *Washington Post*, 9 January 1953; Wise and Ross, p. 127.

12. Syria, 1956–1957

1. *Department of State Bulletin* (Washington), 18 June 1956, pp. 999–1000.

2. U.S. Mutual Security Act of 1955, Sections 142(a) (4) and 413.

3. Wilbur Crane Eveland, *Ropes of Sand: America's Failure in the Middle East* (New York, 1980) pp. 123–4, 132–3.
4. Ibid., pp. 120, 127, 128.
5. Ibid., p. 122, the particular formula of the US Ambassador to Syria, James Moose, Jr.
6. British/Iraqi plotting, influence upon the US: Patrick Seale, *The Struggle for Syria: A Study of Post-War Arab Politics, 1945–1958* (London, 1965) pp. 283–306; Eveland, pp. 135, 169–73.
7. Eveland, p. 182.
8. 1956 plot and background: Eveland, chapters 11-20; *New York Times*, 10 April 1956; 17 October 1956.
9. 1957 plot: Eveland, pp. 253–4; *New York Times*, 14 August 1957, pp. 1, 6; 15 August, pp. 1, 4.
10. *New York Times*, 17 August 1957, p. 3.
11. Ibid., p. 14.
12. Dwight D. Eisenhower, *The White House Years: Waging Peace, 1956–1961* (New York, 1965) p. 196.
13. CIA internal report, author's name deleted, 18 June 1962, the result of conversation with 'Western diplomats', in *Declassified Documents Reference System* (Arlington, Va.) 1975 volume, document 240A.

13. The Middle East, 1957–1958

1. Wilbur Crane Eveland, *Ropes of Sand: America's Failure in the Middle East* (New York, 1980) p. 240.
2. Events in Jordan: *New York Times*, 5 April 1957, p. 1; 25 April, p. 13; 26 April, p. 1; the words of the 'intervention' quotation are those of the *Times*, 26 April.
3. Richard Barnet, *Intervention and Revolution*, (London, 1972) p. 149.
4. *Washington Post*, 18 February 1977.
5. Kennett Love, *Suez: The Twice-Fought War* (Great Britain, 1969) p. 655.
6. Dwight D. Eisenhower, *The White House Years: Waging Peace, 1956–1961* (New York, 1965) p. 201.
7. Ibid., p. 198.
8. Emmet John Hughes, *The Ordeal of Power* (London, 1963) pp. 253–4; the remark was made to Hughes 'a few months after Herter took office' on 22 February 1957.
9. Barry Blechman and Stephen Kaplan, *Force Without War: U.S. Armed Forces as a Political Instrument* (The Brookings Institution, Washington, 1978) p. 84; although the study was undertaken at the Pentagon's request and with its full co-operation, the book stipulates that the views expressed are the authors' alone.
10. Patrick Seale, *The Struggle for Syria: A Study of Post-War Arab Politics, 1945–1958* (London, 1965) p. 303.
11. Events concerning Syria: *New York Times*, 6 September 1957, pp. 1, 2; 8 September, p. 3; 10 September, pp. 1, 8, 9; 11 September, p. 10; 12 September, p. 1; 13 September, pp. 1, 3; Barnet, pp. 149–51; Eisenhower, pp. 196–203.
12. The norm is for the CIA to be accused of involvement in a coup which the Agency or its scribes deny. In this case, it appears that the young CIA had a need

to blow its own horn and it encouraged the word to be passed that it had been the motivating force behind the army coup. But this assertion, found often in the literature, has never been accompanied by any clear, convincing evidence, not even an explanation of *why* the CIA preferred Farouk out and the army in. Miles Copeland, one of the Agency's earliest officers and a great admirer of Kim Roosevelt, goes to some length in his 1969 book, *The Game of Nations*, to propagate the story, but his account is pure crypto-mumbo-jumbo. In the same book, Copeland asserts that the CIA, with himself personally involved, directed a coup in Syria in 1949. This tale, too, is written in a manner that does not inspire credibility. It is probably relevant that CIA colleague Wilbur Crane Eveland (p. 148) has written that 'I'd already had evidence that Copeland tended to exaggerate.'

13. Eveland, pp. 243–4.
14. Ibid., pp. 246–8.
15. *New York Times*, 8, 13–15 August 1957; 21 October 1957; 24, 28 December 1957; 14 February 1958; 6–8, 14, 29 March 1958; 8 October 1958; Eveland, p. 273; Eisenhower, pp. 263–4.
16. Eveland, p. 292n.
17. Soviet proposals: *New York Times*, 6 September 1957, p. 2; 11 September, p. 10.
18. Eisenhower, p. 269.
19. David Wise and Thomas Ross, *The Invisible Government* (New York, 1965, paperback edition) p. 337.
20. 1957 election and aftermath: Eveland, pp. 248–53, 256; Eisenhower, p. 265; Barnet, pp. 143–8.
21. Eisenhower quotations: Eisenhower, pp. 266–7.
22. Dulles news conference, 20 May 1958: *Department of State Bulletin*, 9 June 1958, p. 945.
23. Involvement of Egypt and Syria: Barnet, pp. 147–8; Eisenhower, p. 268.
24. Eveland, p. 276.
25. Robert Murphy, *Diplomat Among Warriors* (US, 1964), p. 492.
26. Eisenhower, p. 273.
27. Ibid., p. 275.
28. Eveland, pp. 294–5; Eisenhower refers to similar situations, p. 277.
29. Eveland, pp. 295–6.
30. Wise and Ross, pp. 337–8; news item from the *St. Louis Post Dispatch*, 23 July 1958, cited on p. 338.
31. Blechman and Kaplan, p. 253.
32. Eisenhower, p. 278.
33. See, e.g., Eisenhower, pp. 274–5.
34. Eisenhower, pp. 290–1.

14. Indonesia, 1957–1958

1. Joseph Burkholder Smith, *Portrait of a Cold Warrior* (New York, 1976) p. 205.
2. *New York Times*, 18 May 1956.
3. *Supplementary Detailed Staff Reports on Foreign and Military Intelligence*, Book 4, Final Report of The Select Committee to Study Governmental Operations

with Respect to Intelligence Activities (U.S. Senate), April 1976, p. 133.

4. A chartered Air India plane which took off from Hong Kong crashed in the South China Sea, 11 April 1955. Chou En-lai was scheduled to be on another chartered Air India flight a day or two later. The Chinese Government, citing what it said were press reports from the *Times of India*, charged that the crash was caused by two time bombs apparently placed aboard the plane in Hong Kong. A clockwork mechanism was later recovered from the wrecked airliner and the Hong Kong police called it a case of 'carefully planned mass murder'. Months later, British police in Hong Kong announced that they were seeking a Chinese Nationalist for conspiracy to cause the crash, but that he had fled to Taiwan. (*New York Times*, 12, 30 April 1955; 3, 4 August 1955; 3 September 1955; 22 November 1967).

In 1967 a curious little book appeared in India, entitled *I was a CIA Agent in India*, by John Discoe Smith, an American. Published by the Communist Party of India, it was based on articles written by Smith for *Literaturnaya Gazeta* in Moscow after he had evidently defected to the Soviet Union around 1960. Smith, born in Quincy, Mass. in 1926, wrote that he had been a communications technician and code clerk at the US Embassy in New Delhi in 1955, performing tasks for the CIA as well. One of these tasks was to deliver a package to a Chinese Nationalist which Smith later learned, he claimed, contained the two time bombs used to blow up the Air India plane. The veracity of Smith's account cannot be determined, although his employment at the US Embassy in New Delhi from 1954 to 1959 is confirmed by the *State Department Biographic Register*. (See also *New York Times*, 25 October 1967, p. 17; 22 November, p. 23; 5 December, p. 12.)

5. *Interim Report: Alleged Assassination Plots Involving Foreign Leaders*, The Select Committee to Study Governmental Operations with Respect to Intelligence Activities (U.S. Senate), 20 November 1975, p. 4 note.

6. David Wise and Thomas Ross, *The Invisible Government* (New York, 1965, paperback edition) pp. 149–50.

7. Julie Southwood and Patrick Flanagan, *Indonesia: Law, Propaganda and Terror* (London, 1983) pp. 26–7.

8. Wise and Ross, p. 148.

9. Smith, pp. 210–11.

10. Ibid., pp. 228–9.

11. Ibid., p. 240.

12. Ibid., pp. 229, 246.

13. Ibid., p. 243.

14. Sex-blackmail operations: ibid., pp. 238–40. Smith errs somewhat in his comment about *Round Table*. The article's only (apparent) reference to the Soviet woman is in the comment on p. 133: 'Other and more scandalous reasons have been put forward for the President's leaning towards the Communist Party.'

15. *New York Times*, 26 January 1976.

16. Smith, see note 14.

17. Truman Smith, 'The Infamous Record of Soviet Espionage', *Reader's Digest*, August 1960.

18. Smith, pp. 220–1.

19. Referred to in a memorandum from Allen Dulles to the White House, 7 April 1961; the memo briefly summarizes the main points of the US intervention: *Declassified Documents Reference System* (Arlington, Va.), released 18 December 1974.

20. The military operation and the Pope affair:

1) Wise and Ross, pp. 145–56;
2) Christopher Robbins, *Air America* (US, 1979), pp. 88–94; published in Great Britain the same year as *The Invisible Air Force: The Story of the CIA's Secret Airlines*;
3) Col. L. Fletcher Prouty, US Air Force, Ret., *The Secret Team: The CIA and its Allies in Control of the World* (New York, 1974) pp. 155, 308, 363–6;
4) *New York Times*, 23 March 1958, p. 2; 19 April; 28 May, p. 9;
5) *Sukarno, An Autobiography*, as told to Cindy Adams (Hong Kong, 1966) pp. 267–71; first printed in the US in 1965; although a poor piece of writing, the book is worth reading for Sukarno's views on why it is foolish to call him a Communist; how he, as a Third-Worlder who didn't toe the line, was repeatedly snubbed and humiliated by the Eisenhower administration, apart from the intervention; and how American sex magazines contrived to make him look ridiculous;
6) Smith, pp. 246–7. There appears to be some confusion about the bombing of the church. Smith states that it was Pope who did it on 18 May before being shot down. Either he or other chroniclers have mixed up the events of April 15 and 18 May.
   21. Wise and Ross, p. 145.

15. Western Europe, 1950s and 1960s

1. Richard Fletcher, 'How CIA Money Took the Teeth Out of British Socialism', in Philip Agee and Louis Wolf, eds., *Dirty Work: The CIA in Western Europe* (New Jersey, 1978) p. 200.

2. Ibid., p. 192.

3. Russell Warren Howe, 'Asset Unwitting: Covering the World for the CIA', *MORE* (New York), May 1978, pp. 20–27, a magazine associated with the Columbia University School of Journalism. Disclosures about the Congress for Cultural Freedom, its activities and publications have appeared in many places; see, e.g., *New York Times*, 27 April 1966, p. 28; 8, 9 May 1967, and other issues in 1967; *Commentary* magazine (New York), September 1967; Fletcher, pp. 188–200.

4. Ray Cline, *Secrets, Spies and Soldiers* (US, 1976), p. 129.

5. *San Francisco Chronicle,* 27 December 1977, p. 6.

6. *Washington Post*, 15 May 1967, p. 1.

7. Forum World Features: Howe; Howe is the Forum writer quoted; CIA budget: House Committee report, cited in Howe, p. 27.

8. *The Nation*, 19 June 1982, p. 738. The article reports that some CIA officers have maintained that Springer was rather liberal in the early 1950s and he was financed to counter neo-Nazi and rightist elements in Germany. This should be taken with a grain of salt, for the bottom line of American occupation policy during this period, regardless of the sentiments of any individual American official, was to suppress the influence of persons and views to the left of centre, Communists and social democrats alike; at the same time, the US authorities were employing 'former' Nazis in every area of administration and intelligence (see chapter on Germany).

9. Tom Braden, 'I'm Glad the CIA is "Immoral" ', *Saturday Evening Post*, 20 May 1967.

10. Ibid.
11. Labour Party/CND: Fletcher, pp. 196–7; *The Times* (London), 5 October 1961.
12. Braden, p. 14.
13. Political parties/CIA: *New York Times*, 7 and 9 January 1976; Jack Anderson in the *San Francisco Chronicle*, 11 and 12 November 1981; Chapman Pincher, *Inside Story: A Documentary of the Pursuit of Power* (London, 1979) p. 28.

16. British Guiana, 1953–1964

1. Events of 1953: *The Guardian* (London), 28 December 1984, for a detailed description of the raw cynicism behind the British action, based on government documents released in 1984; see also *The Times* (London) 7 and 10 October 1953; Cheddi Jagan, *The West on Trial* (London, 1966) chapters 7 and 8.
2. *Parliamentary Debates, House of Commons*, 22 October 1953, column 2170, speech by Oliver Lyttleton.
3. Jagan, p. 149.
4. ORIT: Jagan, pp. 296–7; Philip Agee, *Inside the Company, CIA Diary* (New York, 1975) *passim*; *Survey of the Alliance for Progress: Labor Policies and Programs*, Staff Report of the US Senate Foreign Relations Committee, Subcommittee on American Republics Affairs, 15 July 1968, pp. 8–9.
5. Events of 1957–59: *The Sunday Times* (London) 16 and 23 April 1967.
6. *New York Times*, 22 February 1967, pp. 1, 17.
7. *The Sunday Times*, op. cit.
8. Jagan, p. 304.
9. Richard Barnet, *Intervention and Revolution* (London, 1972) p. 244.
10. Arthur Schlesinger, *A Thousand Days* (London, 1965) pp. 664–9.
11. See notes 23, 25 and 26.
12. Jagan, p. 255.
13. 1962 strike: *New York Times*, 22 February 1967, p. 17; Barnet, p. 245; Agee, pp. 293–4; Jagan, pp. 252–69; *The Times* (London) 13 March 1972, p. 10.
14. 1963 strike, general description: Jagan, chapters 13 and 14.
15. *Parliamentary Debates, House of Commons*, 4 May 1966, columns 1765–7; see also 29 April 1966, columns 1133–4.
16. *New York Times*, 22 February 1967, p. 17.
17. Thomas J. Spinner Jr., *A Political and Social History of Guyana, 1945–1983* (London, 1984) pp. 115–6; Agee, p. 406; *New York Times*, 4 January 1964, p. 10.
18. *The Sunday Times*, op. cit.
19. Ibid.
20. *New York Times*, 11 August 1963, p. 28.
21. Ibid., 11 September 1963, p. 1.
22. *The Sunday Times* (London) 25 May 1975, p. 4.
23. *San Francisco Chronicle*, 21 March 1964, p. 27.
24. Jagan, pp. 372–5.
25. *New York Times*, 31 October 1964, p. 7.

26. *The Times* (London) 29 June 1963, p. 8; the words are those of *The Times*.

27. *Parliamentary Debates, House of Commons*, 27 April 1964, column 109.

28. *The Times* (London) 7 December 1964, p. 8.

29. Events of December 1964: *The Times* (London) 4 to 15 December 1964.

17. Soviet Union, late 1940s to 1960s

1. a) James Bamford, *The Puzzle Palace* (Great Britain, 1983) pp. 136–9, 180–5.
b) Col. L. Fletcher Prouty, USAF, ret., *The Secret Team: The CIA and its Allies in Control of the World* (New York, 1974) pp. 167–72, 187–9, 369–79, 419–29.
c) Sanche de Gramont, *The Secret War* (New York, 1963) chapter 9.
d) Harry Rositzke, *The CIA's Secret Operations* (New York, 1977) p. 23.
e) *New York Times*, 6 May 1960, p. 7, a list of air incidents to that date.
2. *The Guardian* (London) 6 December 1982.
3. *New York Times*, 12 May 1960.
4. Emmet John Hughes, *Ordeal of Power* (London, 1963) p. 301.
5. Prouty, pp. 399, 421–4, 427. CIA official Robert Amory, Jr., later stated that the Agency had called to the attention of the 'White House Staff' the diplomatic risks of continuing the U-2 flights so close to the coming summit meeting in Townsend Hoopes, *The Devil and John Foster Dulles* (Great Britain, 1974) p. 500; interview by the author, 1971. If this was so, it may have been to lay the foundation for subsequent 'plausible denial'. In any event, CIA officers in Turkey, perhaps in conjunction with others in Washington, may have been acting on their own.
Powers, in his book *Operation Overflight* (New York, 1970) doesn't discuss the liquid hydrogen at all. He believed his plane was disabled and forced to descend by the shock waves of a Soviet near-miss. But he recounts technical problems with the plane even before the presumed near-miss.
6. Prouty, p. 189.
7. *New York Times*, 8 May 1960, p. 29.
8. Ibid., 10 May 1960.
9. *Caught in the Act: Facts About U.S. Espionage and Subversion Against the U.S.S.R.* (Foreign Languages Publishing House, Moscow, second revised edition, 1963), p. 95.
10. Emigrés, infiltration into the Soviet Union:
a) De Gramont, pp. 185–9, 480–6.
b) Konstantin Cherezov, *NTS, A Spy Ring Unmasked* (Moscow, 1965) *passim*; the author worked closely with NTS in Western Europe for several years before deciding to return to the Soviet Union.
c) Rositzke, pp. 18–50.
d) *Caught in the Act, passim.*
e) Wilbur Crane Eveland, *Ropes of Sand: America's Failure in the Middle East* (N.Y. 1980) p. 263.
f) Kim Philby, *My Silent War* (MacGibbon and Kee, London 1968) pp. 199–202.

g) Victor Marchetti and John Marks, *The CIA and the Cult of Intelligence* (New York, 1975) pp. 204–6.

h) Louis Hagen, *The Secret War for Europe* (London, 1968) pp. 163–4.

i) *New York Times*, 30 August 1955, p. 1, training of Eastern Europeans at Fort Bragg, N.C. in guerrilla warfare.

j) *Nation's Business* (published by the United States Chamber of Commerce), April 1952, pp. 25–7, 68–9, discusses many of the sabotage and other tactics employed in the Soviet Union and Eastern Europe.

11.Cherezov, *passim*: de Gramont, pp. 480–6; Marchetti and Marks, p. 165.

12. *Foreign and Military Intelligence*, Book 1, Final Report of The Select Committee to Study Governmental Operations with Respect to Intelligence Activities (U.S. Senate), April 1976, p. 193.

13. *Book Week (Washington Post)*, 5 February 1967.

14. Alexander Kendrick, *Prime Time: The Life of Edward R. Murrow* (London, 1970) p. 478.

15. *Foreign and Military Intelligence*, op. cit., p. 194.

16. For further discussion of CIA/USIA books and the source of these and other titles, see the references in notes 12 to 14; also *Washington Post* 28 September 1966; Marchetti and Marks, pp. 180–1; E. Howard Hunt, *Undercover: Memoirs of an American Secret Agent* (London, 1975) pp. 70, 132; *New York Times*, 22 March 1967.

17. Marchetti and Marks, pp. 174–8; de Gramont, pp. 486, 488–92.

18. *Caught in the Act*, p. 147; Thomas C. Sorensen, *The Word War: The Story of American Propaganda* (New York, 1968) p. 156.

19. *Washington Post*, 17 and 20 May 1982; 4 November 1982; *San Francisco Chronicle*, 17 May 1982, 6 November 1982. (The name also appears as Stanislaw Stankievich.) See also Blanche W. Cook, *The Declassified Eisenhower* (New York, 1981) pp. 133, 159.

20. See references for note 10.

21. Hearings before The Select Committee to Study Governmental Operations with Respect to Intelligence Activities (U.S. Senate), Volume 4, 1975; *Washington Post*, 16 January 1975, p. 18; Rositzke, p. 62.

22. *Washington Post*, 25 April 1979.

23. Rositzke, pp. 21, 33, 37. He adds that 'The mere existence of radio-equipped agents on Soviet terrain with no early warnings to report had some cautionary value in tempering the war scare among the military estimators at the height of the Cold War.'

24. *San Francisco Chronicle*, 9 October 1978.

25. Rositzke, p. 15.

18. Italy, 1950s to 1970s

1. Unattributed report dated 19 June 1953; copy reproduced in *Declassified Documents Reference System*, (Arlington, Va.), 1977, document 137A.

2. Philip Agee and Louis Wolf, eds., *Dirty Work: The CIA in Western Europe* (New Jersey, 1978) pp. 168–9, English translation of interview with Victor Marchetti in *Panorama* (Milan, Italy), 2 May 1974, entitled 'Le mani sull'Italia'.

3. CIA memorandum to The Forty Committee (National Security Council), presented to the Select Committee on Intelligence, US House of Representatives

(The Pike Committee) during closed hearings held in 1975. The bulk of the committee's report which contained this memorandum was leaked to the press in February 1976 and first appeared in book form as *CIA – The Pike Report* (Nottingham, England, 1977). The memorandum appears on pp. 204–5 of this book. (cf. Notes: Iraq.)

4. Victor Marchetti and John D. Marks, *The CIA and the Cult of Intelligence* (New York, 1975) p. 172; William Colby, *Honourable Men: My Life in the CIA* (London, 1978) p. 119.

5. *CIA – The Pike Report*, p. 193.

6. *New York Times*, 7 January 1976 (from two separate articles).

7. Ibid.

8. Fred Landis, 'Robert Moss, Arnaud de Borchgrave, and Right-Wing Disinformation', *Covert Action Information Bulletin* (Washington), August-September 1980, p. 43.

9. Colby, p. 124.

10. Agee and Wolf, p. 169.

11. Ibid., p. 171.

12. Colby, chapter 4.

13. *The Sunday Times* (London) 21 March 1976, p. 34.

19. Vietnam, 1950–1973

1. *Le Monde*, 13 April 1950, cited in R.E.M. Irving, *The First Indochinese War* (London, 1975) p. 101.

2. Cited in Hans Askenasy, *Are We All Nazis?* (US, 1978) p. 64.

3. *New York Times*, 21 March 1954, p. 3; 11 April 1954, IV, p. 5; according to Bernard Fall, *The Two Vietnams* (New York, 1967) p. 472, only $954 million of the $1.4 billion had been spent at the time of the ceasefire in 1954.

4. *The Pentagon Papers* (N.Y. Times edition, 1971), p. xi.

5. Ibid., pp. 4, 5, 8, 26.

6. *Washington Post*, 14 September 1969, p. A25. Lansing was the uncle of John Foster and Allen Dulles. He appointed them both to the American delegation at the Versailles Peace Conference in 1918–19, where it was that Ho Chi Minh presented his appeal.

7. Ho Chi Minh and Vietminh working with OSS, admirers of the US: Chester Cooper, *The Lost Crusade: The Full Story of US Involvement in Vietnam from Roosevelt to Nixon* (Great Britain, 1971) pp. 22, 25–7, 40. Cooper was a veteran American diplomat in the Far East who served as the Assistant for Asian Affairs in the Johnson White House. He was also a CIA officer, covertly, for all or part of his career.

French collaboration with the Japanese: Fall, pp. 42–9.

Ho Chi Minh not a genuine nationalist: *Department of State Bulletin* (Washington), 13 February 1950, p. 244, Dean Acheson; 10 April 1950, Ambassador Loy Henderson; 22 May 1950, Dean Acheson.

Ho Chi Minh's desk: Blanche W. Cook, *The Declassified Eisenhower* (New York, 1981), p. 184.

Declaration of Independence: Full text can be found in Ho Chi Minh, *Selected Works* (4 volumes: Hanoi, 1960–62) III, pp. 17–21.

8. Fall, pp. 122, 124.

9. *The Pentagon Papers*, p. 5; Fall, p. 473.

10. Fall, p. 473.

11. Christopher Robbins, *Air America* (US, 1979) pp. 59–60; published the same year in Great Britain as *The Invisible Air Force: The Story of the CIA's Secret Airlines*.

12. *New York Times*, 11 April 1954, IV, p. 5.

13. *The Pentagon Papers*, p. 11.

14. Ibid, p. 36.

15. *The Pentagon Papers*, pp. 5, 11; Dwight Eisenhower, *The White House Years: Mandate for Change, 1953–1956* (New York, 1963) pp. 340–41; Cooper, chapter IV; Sherman Adams, *Firsthand Report* (New York, 1961) p. 122; Adams was Eisenhower's White House chief of staff.

16. Adams, p. 124.

17. *The Pentagon Papers*, p. 46.

18. *The Times* (London) 2 June 1954, quoting from an article by Willoughby.

19. Cooper, p. 72.

20. Bernard Fall, *Hell in a Very Small Place: The Siege of Dien Bien Phu* (Great Britain, 1967) p. 307; *Parade* magazine (*Washington Post*) 24 April 1966; Roscoe Drummond and Gaston Coblentz, *Duel at the Brink* (New York, 1960) pp. 121–2.

21. Joseph Burkholder Smith, *Portrait of a Cold Warrior* (New York, 1976) pp. 172–4.

22. Ibid., pp. 173–4.

23. Eisenhower: *Time* magazine, 12 July 1954.

24. US policy toward the Geneva Conference: Cooper, chapter IV; Cooper was a member of the American delegation at the conference.

25. Fall (Two Vietnams), pp. 153–4.

26. All other actions: *The Pentagon Papers*, Document No. 15: 'Lansdale Team's Report on Covert Saigon Mission in '54 and '55', pp. 53–66.

27. C.L. Sulzberger, *New York Times*, 22 January 1955, p. 10.

28. *New York Times*, 17 July 1955.

29. US Department of Defense, *United States – Vietnam Relations, 1945–67* (the government edition of the Pentagon Papers) book 2, IV, A.5, tab 4, p. 66, cited in Noam Chomsky and Edward Herman, *The Washington Connection and Third World Fascism* (Boston, 1979) p. 370.

30. J.B. Smith, p. 199.

31. Eisenhower, p. 372.

32. *The Pentagon Papers*, p. 22.

33. Ibid., p. 25

34. *Life* magazine, 13 May 1957.

35. *The Pentagon Papers*, p. 23.

36. Emmet John Hughes, *The Ordeal of Power* (London, 1963) p. 208; Hughes was a speech writer for President Eisenhower.

37. Michael Klare, *War Without End* (New York, 1972) pp. 261–3; David Wise and Thomas B. Ross, *The Espionage Establishment* (New York, 1967) p. 152.

38. *Time*, 30 June 1975, p. 32 of European edition.

39. David Wise, 'Colby of CIA – CIA of Colby', *New York Times Magazine*, 1 July 1973, p.9.

40. Donald Duncan, *The New Legions* (London, 1967) pp. 156–9.

41. *Newsweek*, 22 March 1976, pp. 28, 31.

42. *Washington Post* article reprinted in *San Francisco Chronicle*, 20 March 1982, p. 9.

43. In numerous places; see, e.g., *I.F. Stone's Weekly*, 4 March 1968; 'The "Phantom Battle" that Led to War', *U.S. News and World Report*, 23 July 1984, pp.56–67; Joseph C. Goulden, *Truth is the First Casualty: The Gulf of Tonkin Affair – Illusion and Reality* (Rand McNally & Co., U.S., 1969).

44. *Covert Action Information Bulletin* (Washington) No. 10, August-September 1980, p. 43.

45. *Washington Post*, 24 March 1967.

46. *Chicago Daily News*, 20 October 1965; *Washington Post*, 21 October 1965.

47. Copy of Oglesby's speech in author's possession.

48. *Washington Post*, 12 February 1967.

49. Ibid., 18 December 1966.

50. *New York Times*, 28 July 1975, p. 19.

51. *New York Herald Tribune*, 25 April 1965, p. 18.

52. *U.S. Assistance Program in Vietnam*, Hearings Before a Subcommittee of the House Committee on Government Operations, 19 July 1971, p. 189.

53. Ibid., p. 183.

54. Victor Marchetti and John Marks, *The CIA and the Cult of Intelligence* (New York, 1975) pp. 236–7.

55. William Colby, *Honourable Men: My Life in the CIA* (London, 1978) pp. 272, 275–6.

56. Marchetti and Marks, p. 237.

57. Wise, p. 33.

58. *New York Times*, 3 August 1971, p. 10.

59. Wise, p. 34.

60. *Congressional Record*, House, 12 May 1966, pp. 9977–78, reprint of article by Morley Safer of CBS News.

61. *Washington Post*, 25 November 1966.

62. *U.S. Aid to North Vietnam*, Hearings Before the Subcommittee on Asian and Pacific Affairs, House Committee on International Relations, 19 July 1977, Appendix 2.

63. *Atlanta Journal*, 25 September 1965.

64. *San Francisco Chronicle*, 9 January 1971 (New York Times Service); also see Telford Taylor, *Nuremberg and Vietnam: An American Tragedy* (New York, 1970).

20. Cambodia 1953–1973

1. Prince Norodom Sihanouk, as related to Wilfred Burchett, *My War With The CIA* (London, 1974, revised edition) pp. 75–6. The SEATO treaty of 1954 actually had a protocol attached which unilaterally placed Cambodia, Laos and South Vietnam under its umbrella. Sihanouk later asserted that he had rejected Cambodia's inclusion, although at the time he was reportedly amenable to his country being a member of some sort of Western security system for south-east Asia. In any event, for various reasons, he soon moved away from this position and toward the policy of neutralism he maintained thereafter. For a fuller discussion of

these matters, see Michael Leifer, *Cambodia: The Search for Security* (London, 1967) particularly chapter 3.

2. Events of 1956: Sihanouk, pp. 82–6.

3. Ibid., p. 94.

4. *Neak Cheat Niyum* (The Nationalist, Phnom Penh) 29 September 1963, cited in Leifer, p. 144.

5. Pentagon Papers, Vol 10, p. 1100, cited by William Shawcross, *Side-Show: Kissinger, Nixon and the Destruction of Cambodia* (N.Y. 1979, paperback edition) p. 53.

6. Sihanouk, pp. 102–3; *New York Times*, 26 June 1958, p. 1 and 25 April 1966, p. 20.

7. Shawcross, p. 54.

8. Ibid.

9. Ibid., p. 122.

10. *Washington Post*, 2 January 1966, p. E4.

11. US involvement with the Khmer Serei and Khmer Krom: Charles Simpson, III, *Inside the Green Berets – The First 30 Years – A History of the U.S. Army Special Forces* (London, 1983) pp. 114–5; Shawcross, *passim*; Sihanouk, *passim*.

12. Plot of 1958–59: Sihanouk, pp. 102–109; *Washington Post*, 7 September 1965, p. 1; Shawcross, pp. 54–5; *The Observer* (London) 22 February 1959, p. 8.

13. Sihanouk, p. 125.

14. Ibid., pp. 124–5.

15. Ibid., p. 113.

16. Ibid., pp. 114, 115, 118–21.

17. Effects of US aid to Cambodia: Sihanouk, *passim*, particularly pp. 93–6, 133–8; Shawcross, pp. 58–60; *Washington Post*, 2 January 1966, p. E4.

18. Sihanouk, pp. 139–40.

19. See, e.g., *Washington Post*, 4 August 1966 and 15 October 1966.

20. Francois Ponchaud, *Cambodia Year Zero*, translated from the French (London, 1978) p. 186.

21. *San Francisco Chronicle*, 23 July 1973.

22. Ibid., 16 July 1973; Shawcross, pp. 287–90.

23. Shawcross, pp. 148–9.

24. Ibid., pp.114–15, based on interviews with Snepp by Shawcross.

25. Ibid., p. 114.

26. Seymour M. Hersh, *Kissinger: The Price of Power* (London, 1983) p. 176. Hersh, in chapter 15, provides further details of the machinations between the US and Lon Nol and others indicating American foreknowledge and encouragement of the coup.

27. Shawcross, p. 119, citing the assertions of 'Snepp and others'.

28. Ibid., p. 122.

29. Ibid., pp. 118–19.

30. Ibid., p. 120.

31. Roger Morris, *Uncertain Greatness: Henry Kissinger and American Foreign Policy* (Great Britain, 1977) p. 173.

32. Shawcross, pp. 119, 121–2; Snepp's remarks based on interviews with him by Shawcross.

33. *New York Times*, 21 March 1970, p. 1.

34. Blood-bath: Shawcross, pp. 132–3.

35. Morris, p. 174.
36. Shawcross, p. 149.
37. *Newsweek*, 22 November 1971, p. 37.
38. Shawcross, p. 400.
39. Testimony before US Senate Foreign Relations Committee, Hearings on Supplemental Assistance to Cambodia, 24 February 1975, p. 64.

21. Laos, 1957–1973

1. Vientiane correspondent, 'The Labyrinthine War', *Far Eastern Economic Review* (Hong Kong conservative weekly), 16 April 1970, p. 73.
2. Testimony before the US Senate Armed Services Committee, Hearings on Fiscal Year 1972 Authorizations, 22 July 1971, p. 4289.
3. Testimony before the House Subcommittee on Foreign Operations and Monetary Affairs, Committee on Government Operations, Hearings on US Aid Operations in Laos, May-June 1959; see also *New York Times*, 20 January 1961, p. 2 and *Washington Post*, 10 April 1966 for statements of Souvanna Phouma re US opposition to a coalition or neutralist government.
4. *New York Times*, 25 April 1957.
5. Ibid., 18 May 1958, IV, p. 7.
6. Ibid., 23 July 1958, p. 2; 25 July, p. 4.
7. Ibid., 20 January 1961, p. 2; *Washington Post*, 10 April 1966.
8. *New York Times*, 15 January 1959, p. 15.
9. Fred Branfman, *Voices from the Plain of Jars: Life Under an Air War* (Harper & Row, New York, 1972) p. 12; *New York Times*, 18 May 1958, IV, p. 7.
10. *New York Times*, 25 April 1966, p. 20.
11. Arthur Schlesinger, *A Thousand Days* (New York, 1965), p. 325.
12. 1958: Ibid., pp. 325–6 (this has to do with the events of 1958 referred to earlier – see notes 6 and 7 above); 1959: Ibid., p. 326; Branfman, p. 12; 1960: Chester Bowles, *Promises to Keep: My Years in Public Life, 1941–1969* (New York 1971) p. 334; Bowles was a prominent American diplomat.
13. Roger Hilsman, *To Move a Nation* (New York, 1967) pp. 111–2.
14. *New York Times*, 25 January 1958, p. 6; 25 February, p. 6.
15. Ibid., 9 August 1960.
16. Norman Cousins, 'Report from Laos', *Saturday Review*, 18 February 1961, p. 12.
17. Secret Army:
a) *New York Times*, 26 October 1969, p. 1.
b) Fred Branfman, 'The President's Secret Army', in Robert Borosage and John Marks, eds., *The CIA File* (New York, 1976) pp. 46–78.
c) Christopher Robbins, *Air America* (US, 1979) chapters 5 and 8; published in Great Britain the same year as *The Invisible Air Force: The Story of the CIA's Secret Airlines*.
d) Col. L. Fletcher Prouty, US Air Force, Ret., *The Secret Team: The CIA and its Allies in Control of the World* (New York, 1974) pp. 190–93, 438.
e) Victor Marchetti and John Marks, *The CIA and the Cult of Intelligence* (New York, 1975) pp. 54, 132.
f) *San Francisco Chronicle*, 25 July 1973 (reporting deaths).

18. *New York Times*, 18 May 1958, IV, p. 7.
19. Robbins, *passim*.
20. Branfman (CIA File), p. 65.
21. Robbins, *passim*.
22. Testimony of Daniel Oleksiw, USIA, before US Senate Committee on Foreign Relations, Hearings on US Security Agreements and Commitments Abroad: Kingdom of Laos, October 1969, pp. 586–7.
23. *New York Times*, 25 April 1966, p. 20.
24. Ibid., 20 January 1961, p. 2.
25. Marchetti and Marks, p. 132; Branfman (Voices), p. 16.
26. Robbins, p. 116.
27. William Lederer & Eugene Burdick, *A Nation of Sheep* (London, 1961) pp. 12–13; see also Bernard Fall, *Anatomy of a Crisis: The Laotian Crisis of 1960–1961* (New York, 1969), chapter 7.
28. Lederer and Burdick, pp. 15–22.
29. Bernard Fall, *Street Without Joy: Insurgency in Indochina, 1946–63* (London, 1963, Third revised edition) p. 329; *New York Times* 3 January 1961, p. 10.
30. Fall (Street), p. 332.
31. Schlesinger, p. 329.
32. Ibid., p. 517; see also Andrew Tully, *The Super Spies* (London, 1970) p. 165.
33. Robbins, p. 115.
34. Prouty, p. 314.
35. *New York Times*, 3 May 1964, p. 1; 7 May, p. 7; 14 May, p. 11.
36. *Congressional Record*, 18 July 1973, pp. 24520–22.
37. Branfman (Voices), p. 5; Branfman was in Laos, 1967–71, first as an educational adviser to International Voluntary Services ('a Bible Belt version of the Peace Corps' – Robbins), then as a writer and researcher.
38. *Refugee and Civilian War Casualty Problems in Indochina*, Staff Report prepared for the US Senate Subcommittee on Refugees, Committee on the Judiciary, 28 September 1970, pp. 19 and v. (the latter from preface by Senator Edward Kennedy, Chairman).
39. Ibid., p. 32.
40. Robbins, p. 132.
41. Branfman (Voices), p. 15.
42. *The Guardian* (London) 14 October 1971, p. 4.
43. *New York Times*, 23 February 1973, p. 1.
44. Ibid., 8 April 1954.

22. Haiti, 1959

1. Robert I. Rotberg with Christopher K. Clague, *Haiti: The Politics of Squalor* (A Twentieth Century Fund Study, Boston, 1971), p. 244.
2. *New York Times*, 15 and 16 August 1959; Robert Debs Heinl, Jr. and Nancy Gordon Heinl, *The Story of the Haitian People, 1492–1971* (Boston, 1978), p. 600.
3. *Hispanic American Report* (Stanford University, California) October 1959, p. 434.

4. *New York Times*, 17 and 18 August 1959.
5. Heinl, p. 600; *New York Times*, 15 August 1959.
6. Heinl, p. 600; Rotbert, p. 219.
7. *New York Times*, 16 August 1959.
8. Heinl, p. 600.
9. *New York Times*, 16 August 1959.
10. Rotberg, p. 219.

23. Guatemala, 1960

The principal sources of this chapter are:
a) Richard Gott, *Rural Guerrillas in Latin America* (Great Britain, 1973, revised edition) pp. 68–77; first published in 1970 as *Guerrilla Movements in Latin America*.
b) David Wise and Thomas Ross, *The Invisible Government* (New York, 1965, paperback edition) pp. 22–4, 33.
c) Col. L. Fletcher Prouty, US Air Force, Ret., *The Secret Team: The CIA and its Allies in Control of the World* (New York, 1974) pp. 45–6.
d) John Gerassi, *The Great Fear in Latin America* (New York, 1965, revised edition) pp. 184–5; first published as *The Great Fear* (New York, 1963); Gerassi was a correspondent in Latin America for the *New York Times* and an editor of *Time* magazine.
e) *New York Times*, 14, 15, 18, 19 November 1960.
1. Gott, p. 70.
2. *New York Times*, 18 November 1960.
3. Ibid., 15, 19 November 1960.
4. Gott, p. 71; Wise and Ross, p. 33; Prouty, p. 46.
5. Gerassi, p. 185.
6. *New York Times*, 19 November 1960.
7. Gott, p. 76; Thomas and Marjorie Melville, *Guatemala: The Politics of Land Ownership* (US, 1971) p. 142; published the same year in Great Britain in a slightly different form as *Guatemala – Another Vietnam?*.
8. Gott, p. 77.

24. France/Algeria 1960s

1. Andrew Tully, *CIA: The Inside Story* (New York, 1962), p. 44.
2. Allen Dulles, *The Craft of Intelligence* (New York, 1965), p. 175.
3. *New York Times*, 4 May 1961, p. 10.
4. Cited in Tully, p. 45, article by Crosby Noyes, no date of *Washington Star* given.
5. Cited in Sanche de Gramont, *The Secret War* (New York, 1963) pp. 29–30; de Gramont is also known as Ted Morgan, or vice versa.
6. Debré: *New York Times*, 24 April 1961.
7. *Washington Post*, 5 May 1961, p. A16.
8. *Time*, 12 May 1961, p. 19.
9. *New York Times*, 29 April 1961, pp, 1, 3.
10. Ibid., 1 May 1961, p. 28.

11. Cited in de Gramont, pp. 30–31.
12. *Newsweek*, 15 May 1961, pp. 50–51.
13. *L'Express*/Claude Krief: As reported in Alexander Werth, 'The CIA in Algeria', *The Nation*, 20 May 1961, pp. 433–5.
14. Challe/NATO/US officers: *Time*, 12 May 1961, p. 19.
15. *New York Times*, 29 April 1961, p. 3.
16. Ibid., 2 May 1961, p. 18.
17. Ibid., 24 June 1975, p. 11.
18. Christian Plume & Pierre Démaret, *Target: De Gaulle* (translation from the French, London, 1974) *passim*.
19. *Chicago Tribune*, 15 June 1975, p. 1.
20. David Wise, *The Politics of Lying* (New York, 1973, paperback edition) p. 431.
21. *Military Assistance Training*, Hearings before the House Committee on Foreign Affairs, Subcommittee on National Security Policy and Scientific Developments, October and December 1970, p. 120.
22. *Chicago Tribune*, 20 June 1975, p. 6.

25. Ecuador, 1960 to 1963

1. Philip Agee, *Inside the Company: CIA Diary* (New York, 1975) pp. 106–316, *passim*. Agee's book made him Public Enemy No. One of the CIA. In a review of the book, however, former Agency official Miles Copeland – while not concealing his distaste for Agee's 'betrayal' – stated that 'The book is interesting as an authentic account of how an ordinary American or British "case officer" operates ... As a spy handler in Quito, Montevideo and Mexico City, he has first-hand information ... All of it, just as his publisher claims, is presented "with deadly accuracy". ' (*The Spectator*, London, 11 January 1975, p. 40.)
2. *New York Times*, 14 July 1963, p. 20.
For an interesting and concise discussion of the political leanings of Velasco and Arosemana, see John Gerassi, *The Great Fear in Latin America* (New York, 1965, revised edition) pp. 141–8; published originally as *The Great Fear* (New York, 1963).

26. The Congo, 1960–1964

1. *Interim Report: Alleged Assassination Plots Involving Foreign Leaders*, The Select Committee to Study Governmental Operations with Respect to Intelligence Activities (US Senate), 20 November 1975, p. 14; hereafter referred to as Assassination Report.
2. Ibid., p. 15.
3. Ibid., p. 16.
4. *New York Times*, 4 September 1960, IV, p. 3.
5. Roger Hilsman (Director of Intelligence and Research at the State Department), *To Move a Nation* (New York, 1967) p. 240.
6. Andrew Tully, *CIA: The Inside Story* (New York, 1962), p. 180.
7. Assassination Report, p. 16.
8. Victor Marchetti (former executive assistant to the Deputy Director of the

CIA) and John Marks, *The CIA and the Cult of Intelligence* (New York, 1975), p. 53.

9. Assassination Report, pp. 17, 18, 63 respectively.

10. Ibid., p. 19 ff.

11. Ibid., p. 13.

12. *New York Times*, 22 February 1976, p. 55.

13. Assassination Report, pp. 18–19.

14. Ibid., p. 48.

15. Tully, p. 178.

16. John Stockwell, *In Search of Enemies* (New York, 1978) p. 105; see also pp. 137, 236–7.

17. Cables: 18 January 1961, from US Ambassador in Leopoldville to American Consulate in Elizabethville, and 20 January 1961, from Elizabethville to Washington, *Declassified Documents Reference System* (Arlington, Va.), cables declassified 23 September 1975. Both these cables were sent after Lumumba's death, indicating that State Department officials were not privy to the CIA's actions.

18. Arthur Schlesinger, *A Thousand Days* (London, 1965) p. 502.

19. Col. L. Fletcher Prouty, US Air Force, Ret., *The Secret Team: The CIA and its Allies in Control of the World* (New York, 1974) pp. 26, 129–30, 438. Burma: *San Francisco Chronicle* 16 October 1970, p. 22.

20. *Newsweek* 22 November 1971, p. 37.

21. State Department memo, 17 November 1961, from L.D. Battle, Executive Secretary to McGeorge Bundy, Special Assistant to the President for National Security Affairs, *Declassified Documents Reference System* (Arlington, Va.), declassified 27 December 1974.

22. 'CBS Reports', 26 April 1962: 'The Hot and Cold Wars of Allen Dulles', pp. 19–20 of transcript obtained by Stephen Weissman and cited by him in 'The CIA and U.S. Policy in Zaire and Angola' in Ellen Ray, *et. al.*, eds., *Dirty Work 2: The CIA in Africa* (New Jersey, 1979).

23. Stockwell, p. 53.

24. William Atwood, *The Reds and the Blacks* (London, 1967) p. 192; Atwood was US Ambassador to Kenya, 1964–65.

25. Ibid., p. 194.

26. Ernest W. Lefever, *Crisis in the Congo: A United Nations Force in Action* (Brookings Institution, Washington, DC, 1965), p. 131.

27. CIA mercenaries: David Wise and Thomas Ross, *The Espionage Establishment* (New York, 1967) p. 167; Stockwell, pp. 187–8; Marchetti and Marks, p. 131; Roger Morris (former staff member of the National Security Council) and Richard Mauzy, 'Zaire (the Congo): An Exercise in Nation Building' in Robert Borosage and John Marks, eds., *The CIA File* (New York, 1976) pp. 35–7.

28. *New York Times*, 26 April 1966, p. 1.

29. Ibid., 17 June 1964, pp. 1, 12; 18 June, p. 1.

30. Letter dated 6 July 1964 from the USSR representative to the Secretary-General, cited in Lefever, p. 131.

31. M. Crawford Young, 'Rebellion and the Congo', in Robert Rotberg, ed., *Rebellion in Black Africa* (Oxford University Press, 1971), p. 230.

32. Young, p. 227, and *passim*; Atwood, p. 192 (witch doctor).

33. Young, p. 209.

34. *New York Times*, 1 November 1964, p. 12; 3 November, p. 14; Atwood, chapter 16.
35. Richard Barnet, *Intervention and Revolution* (London, 1970) p. 250.
36. Atwood, p. 218.
37. *The Times* (London) 25 November 1964.
38. Marchetti and Marks, p. 139.
39. Atwood, p. 194.
40. Dwight Eisenhower, *The White House Years: Waging Peace, 1956–1961* (New York, 1965) p. 270.

27. Brazil, 1961 to 1964

1. Phyllis R. Parker, *Brazil and the Quiet Revolution, 1964* (University of Texas Press, Austin, 1979) p. 64. This book draws heavily upon declassified documents found at the John F. Kennedy and Lyndon B. Johnson presidential libraries. The author augmented this information with interviews of key figures in the events discussed here.
2. Ibid., p. 67.
3. Ibid., p. 65.
4. Ibid., p. 20, reception at the Brazilian Embassy, Washington, April 1962.
5. Ibid., pp. 30–31, 34.
6. Ibid., p. 31, meeting in Brazil 17 December 1962.
7. Ibid., pp. 45, 21, Walters' report to the Pentagon, 6 August 1963.
8. Ibid., pp. 41–2.
9. Ibid., pp. 44 and *passim*.
10. John Gerassi, *The Great Fear in Latin America* (New York, 1965, revised edition) p. 83; originally published as *The Great Fear* (New York, 1963).
11. Ibid., p. 82.
12. *New York Times*, 12 July 1961, p. 13.
13. Peter Bell, 'Brazilian-American Relations' in Riordan Roett, ed., *Brazil in the Sixties* (Vanderbilt University Press, Nashville, 1972) p. 81; Bell interview of Cabot, Washington, DC, 15 January 1970.
14. Gerassi, p. 84.
15. *New York Times*, 16 March 1962, p. 7.
16. Stephen Schlesinger and Stephen Kinzer, *Bitter Fruit: The Untold Story of the American Coup in Guatemala* (Doubleday & Co., New York, 1982) pp. 103–4, 108.
17. *New York Times*, 16 March 1962, p. 7.
18. Gerassi, p. 84–8.
19. Thomas E. Skidmore, *Politics in Brazil, 1930–1964: An Experiment in Democracy* (Oxford University Press, New York, 1967) p. 130; Gerassi, pp. 80–81.
20. Jan Knippers Black, *United States Penetration of Brazil* (University of Pennsylvania Press, Philadelphia, 1977), p.40; the words quoted are Black's, based on her interview with Lt. Col. Edward L. King, a member of the Joint Brazil-US Defense Commission in the second half of the 1960s; also see Bell, p. 83 re US doubts about Goulart from the beginning of his presidency.
21. *New York Times*, 5 April 1962, p. 3.

22. Arthur Schlesinger, *A Thousand Days* (London, 1965) p. 671; *New York Times*, 5 December 1961, p. 11.
23. *Time*, 3 November 1961, p. 29.
24. Gerassi, pp. 83, 88.
25. Ibid., p. 85.
26. Parker, p. 29, interview with Gordon, 19 January 1976.
27. Philip Agee, *Inside the Company: CIA Diary* (New York, 1975) p. 321.
28. Parker, p. 27.
29. A.J. Langguth, *Hidden Terrors* (New York, 1978) p. 92; Langguth was formerly with the *New York Times* and in 1965 served as Saigon Bureau Chief for the newspaper.
30. Parker, p. 26, memo from President Kennedy to AID administrator Fowler Hamilton, 5 February 1962.
31. Ibid., pp. 87–97.
32. Agee, p. 362.
33. Langguth, pp. 77, 89–90, 92, 108.
34. Parker, p. 40.
35. For the most important incident/example of this see the story of the Navy mutiny in Skidmore, pp. 296–7.
36. Philip Siekman, 'When Executives Turned Revolutionaries', *Fortune* (New York), September 1964, p. 214.
37. Parker, p. 63, interview of Walters.
38. Langguth, pp. 61–2, 98; *Washington Post*, 5 February 1968, p. 1.
39. Skidmore, p. 330; also see James Kohl and John Litt, *Urban Guerrilla Warfare in Latin America* (The MIT Press, Cambridge, Mass., 1974) p. 39 for further discussion of the strong pro-US, anti-leftist bias of the college's curriculum.
40. Parker, p. 98, cable to State Department, 4 March 1964; for further discussion of the closeness of US and Brazilian military officers and the consequential moulding of the latter, see: a) Langguth, pp. 94–6, 162–70; b) Black, chapters 9 and 10; c) Michael Klare, *War Without End* (New York, 1972) chapter 10 ('The Latin American Military'); d) Alfred Stepan, *The Military in Politics: Changing Patterns in Brazil* (Princeton University Press, New Jersey, 1971, a RAND Corp. Study) pp. 123–33.
41. Parker, p. 65.
42. Ibid., p. 68.
43. Ibid., pp. 68–9.
44. Ibid., p. 74.
45. Ibid., p. 75, teletype, Washington to US Embassy, Brazil, 31 March 1964.
46. Ibid., p. 68.
47. Ibid., pp. 74, 77.
48. Ibid., pp. 72, 75–6; also see the statement of former Brazilian Army Col. Pedro Paulo de Baruna, exiled by the junta, about the effect of the naval force upon the thinking of Castelo Branco: Warner Poelchau, ed., *White Paper, Whitewash* (New York, 1981) p. 51; Baruna's statement is questionable in parts, but as an indication of the tenor of the plotters' thinking probably has some value.
49. *Survey of the Alliance for Progress: Labor Policies and Programs*, Staff Report of the US Senate Foreign Relations Committee, Subcommittee on American Republics Affairs, 15 July 1968, p. 53; the background of AIFLD can be found in earlier pages; also see Black, chapter 6.

50. US Senate Report cited in note 49, p. 14 quoting from a radio programme in which Doherty took part.

51. Eugene Methvin, 'Labor's New Weapon for Democracy', *Reader's Digest*, October, 1966, p. 28.

52. Poelchau, pp. 47–51.

53. Langguth, p. 110.

54. Ibid., p. 113.

55. Ibid., pp. 112–13.

56. Ibid., p. 113.

57. Gordon's cables: Parker, pp. 81–3.

58. Ibid., p. 83.

59. Hearing on the Nomination of Lincoln Gordon to be Assistant Secretary of State for Inter-American Affairs, US Senate Foreign Relations Committee, 7 February 1966, pp. 44–5.

60. *The Department of State Bulletin*, 20 April 1964, news conference of 3 April 1964.

61. Langguth, p. 116, presumably from Langguth's interview of Gordon.

62. Senate Hearing cited in note 59.

63. *Foreign Assistance Act of 1965*, Hearings before the House Foreign Affairs Committee, 25 February 1965, p. 346.

64. Langguth, p. 113, citing the Brazil *Herald*, 6 March 1964, p. 4.

65. *New York Times*, 11 July 1965, p. 13.

66. Ibid., 25 November 1966, p. 4.

67. Agee, p. 364.

68. Parker, pp. 85–6.

69. Agee, pp. 364–5.

70. *New York Times*, 6 April 1964, p. 1.

71. *Reader's Digest*, op. cit.

72. Parker, p. 59.

73. The repressiveness of the Branco government and the Washington connection:
a) Penny Lernoux, *Cry of the People: The Struggle for Human Rights in Latin America – The Catholic Church in Conflict with U.S. Policy* (Penguin Books, London, 1982) pp. 166–75, 313–32, and elsewhere;
b) Langguth, chapters 4, 5 and 7 and elsewhere;
c) *Torture and Oppression in Brazil*, Hearing before the Subcommittee on International Organizations and Movements of the House Committee on Foreign Affairs, 11 December, 1974; contains testimony by and about torture victims and reprints of articles from the US press;
d) Noam Chomsky and Edward Herman, *The Washington Connection and Third World Fascism* (Boston, 1979) *passim*.

74. Agency for International Development (AID), *Program and Project Data Presentation to the Congress for Fiscal Year 1971*, p. 26.

75. Langguth, p. 94; Poelchau, p. 65, interview of Langguth.

76. Amnesty International, *Report on Allegations of Torture in Brazil* (London, 1974) p. 40.

77. *Jornal do Brazil*, 25 May 1972, cited in Amnesty International, op. cit., p. 49.

78. *Special Study Mission to Latin America on Military Assistance Training*, House Committee on Foreign Affairs Report, 1970.

79. *New York Times*, 27 April 1966, p. 28.

28. Peru, 1960 to 1965

1. *New York Times*, 22 December 1960, p. 3.
2. Philip Agee, *Inside the Company: CIA Diary* (New York, 1975) pp. 145–6.
3. *Wall Street Journal*, 5 January 1961, p. 1.
4. *New York Times*, 28 December 1960, p. 5.
5. Ibid., 6 and 7 January 1961; Agee, p. 146; Agee does not mention Ramos by name but it appears rather clear that he is referring to the same man.
6. John Gerassi, *The Great Fear in Latin America* (New York, 1965, revised edition) pp. 20, 129; originally published as *The Great Fear* (New York, 1963).
7. For the background, ideology, and fate of the various revolutionary movements in Peru during this period, see Richard Gott, *Rural Guerrillas in Latin America* (Great Britain, 1973, revised edition) pp. 363–463; originally published as *Guerrilla Movements in Latin America* (Great Britain, 1970); James Petras and Maurice Zeitlin, eds., *Latin America: Reform or Revolution?* (New York, 1968) pp. 343–50; *New York Times*, 30 August 1966, p. 1.
8. Victor Marchetti and John Marks, *The CIA and the Cult of Intelligence* (New York, 1975) p. 137.
9. Michael Klare, *War Without End* (New York, 1972) pp. 297–8.
10. *New York Times*, 12 September 1965, p. 32.
11. Agee, p. 440; see also pp. 267–9, 427.
12. Gott, *passim*; Petras, p. 349; Norman Gall, 'The Legacy of Che Guevara', *Commentary* magazine (New York) December 1967, p. 39.
13. Petras, p. 349.

29. Dominican Republic, 1960 to 1966

1. Jerome Slater, 'The Dominican Republic, 1961–66' in Barry Blechman and Stephen Kaplan, *Force Without War: U.S. Armed Forces as a Political Instrument* (The Brookings Institution, Washington, 1978) pp. 290–91; (cf. Notes: The Middle East).
2. Bernard Diederich, *Trujillo: The Death of the Goat* (London, 1978) p. 43.
3. Ibid., pp. 48–9.
4. *Interim Report: Alleged Assassination Plots Involving Foreign Leaders*, The Select Committee to Study Governmental Operations with Respect to Intelligence Activities (US Senate), 20 November 1975, p. 192; hereafter referred to as Assassination Report.
5. Ibid.
6. Diederich, p. 44.
7. Assassination Report, 191–215, *passim*; Diederich, *passim*, particularly pp. 40–56.
8. Assassination Report, p. 210.
9. Arthur M. Schlesinger, *A Thousand Days* (London, 1965) p. 660. Kennedy stated that 'There are three possibilities . . . in descending order of preference: a decent democratic regime, a continuation of the Trujillo regime or a Castro regime. We ought to aim at the first but we really can't renounce the second until we are sure we can avoid the third.'

10. Diederich, pp. 170–249, summary on page 265.

11. Schlesinger, p. 661.

12. Events of 1961 following assassination: Slater, pp. 294–7; Diederich, pp. 220–51.

13. Slater, p. 298; *New York Times*, 20 January 1962, p. 4. (State Department threats to Dominican leaders of a large loss of aid reportedly had a 'great deal' to do with preventing a coup.)

14. John Barlow Martin, *Overtaken by Events: The Dominican Crisis From the Fall of Trujillo to the Civil War* (New York, 1966) p. 100.

15. Ibid., p. 122.

16. *New York Times*, 9 June 1962, p. 10.

17. US involvement in elections: Martin, pp. 227–9, 347–8.

18. Martin, pp. 455–6; Richard Barnet, *Intervention and Revolution* (London, 1972) p. 168.

19. Cited in *Newsweek*, 7 October 1963, p. 64.

20. Martin, p. 451.

21. Ibid., pp. 477–8.

22. Sam Halper, 'The Dominican Upheaval', *The New Leader* (New York), 10 May 1965, p. 4.

23. Martin, pp. 481–90; *New York Times*, 17 July 1963, p. 10.

24. Barnet, pp. 170–71; For CONATRAL's CIA connection, see *Survey of the Alliance for Progress: Labor Policies and Programs*, Staff Report of the U.S. Senate Foreign Relations Committee, Subcommittee on American Republics Affairs, 15 July 1968, p. 18.

25. Martin, p. 570.

26. *Newsweek*, 7 October 1963, pp. 64–5.

27. *New York Times*, 14 December 1963, p. 12.

28. *Washington Post*, 27 June 1965, p. E2.

29. *Wall Street Journal*, 25 June 1965, p. 8.

30. Slater, p. 308; Tad Szulc, *Dominican Diary* (New York, 1965) p. 32; Szulc was the *N.Y. Times* correspondent in the Dominican Republic during this period.

31. Slater, p. 307.

32. Martin, pp. 656–7; *New York Times*, 1 May 1965; Slater, p. 309; *Wall Street Journal*, 25 June 1965, p. 8.

33. Martin, p. 658.

34. *Washington Post*, 27 June 1965, p. E5; Slater, pp. 322–3; *New York Times*, 20 May 1965.

35. *New York Times*, 20 May 1965; Slater, p. 325.

36. *New York Times Magazine*, 14 July 1982, p. 20.

37. Ibid.

38. *New York Times*, 25 February 1967.

39. Communists amongst the rebels: *Washington Post*, 27 June 1965, p. E4; CIA cable: *Declassified Documents Reference System* (Arlington, Virginia) 1977 Volume, Document 14G.

40. Philip Agee, *Inside the Company: CIA Diary* (New York, 1975) p. 421.

41. Barnet, pp. 175–6.

42. Ibid.; Szulc, pp. 71–3; *Washington Post*, 27 June 1965, p. E4.

43. Slater, p. 321; *New York Times*, 22 March 1967.

44. David Wise, *The Politics of Lying* (New York, 1973, paperback edition) p. 32.

45. Barnet, pp. 178–9.

46. See, e.g., *Wall Street Journal*, 7 September 1971, 'In Dominican Republic, Political Murders Rise, and So Does Poverty'; also, various Amnesty International *Reports on Torture* and *Annual Reports* during the 1970s.

30. Cuba, 1959 to 1980s

1. *Khruschev Remembers* (London, 1971) pp. 494, 496.

2. *Time*, 2 November 1962.

3. Cited by William Appleman Williams, 'American Intervention in Russia: 1917–20', in David Horowitz, ed., *Containment and Revolution* (Boston, 1967). Written in a letter to President Wilson by Secretary of State Robert Lansing, uncle of John Foster and Allen Dulles.

4. Facts on File, *Cuba, the U.S. & Russia, 1960–63* (New York, 1964) pp. 56–8.

5. *International Herald Tribune* (Paris), 2 October 1985, p. 1.

6. *New York Times*, 23 October 1959, p. 1.

7. Facts on File, op. cit., pp. 7–8; *New York Times*, 19, 20 February 1960; 22 March 1960.

8. *New York Times*, 5, 6 March 1960.

9. Herbert L. Matthews, *Revolution in Cuba* (New York, 1975) p. 205.

10. A report on the post-invasion inquiry ordered by Kennedy disclosed that 'It was never intended, the planners testified, that the invasion itself would topple Castro. The hope was that an initial success would spur an uprising by thousands of anti-Castro Cubans. Ships in the invasion fleet carried 15,000 weapons to be distributed to the expected volunteers.' (*U.S. News & World Report*, 13 August 1979, p. 82.) Some CIA officials, including Allen Dulles, later denied that an uprising was expected, but this may be no more than an attempt to mask their ideological embarrassment that people living under a 'communist tyranny' did not respond at all to the call of 'The Free World'.

11. Attacks on Cuba:
a) Taylor Branch and George Crile III, 'The Kennedy Vendetta', *Harper's* magazine (New York), August 1975, pp. 49–63;
b) Facts on File, op. cit., *passim*;
c) *New York Times*, 26 August 1962, p. 1; 21 March 1963, p. 3; *Washington Post*, 1 June 1966; 30 September 1966; plus many other articles in both newspapers during the 1960s;
d) Warren Hinckle and William W. Turner, *The Fish is Red: The Story of the Secret War Against Castro* (Harper & Row, New York, 1981) *passim*.

12. Branch and Crile, op. cit., pp. 49–63.

13. *New York Times*, 26 August 1962, p. 1.

14. John Gerassi, *The Great Fear in Latin America* (New York, 1965, revised edition) p. 278; published originally as *The Great Fear* (New York, 1963).

15. Sabotage: Branch and Crile, op. cit., p. 52.

16. *The Times* (London), 8, 10 January 1964; 12 May, p. 10; 21 July, p. 10; 28, 29 October; *The Guardian* (London), 28, 29 October 1964.

17. *Washington Post*, 14 February 1975, p. C31; Anderson's story stated that

there were only 24 buses involved and that they were dried and used in England.

18. Branch and Crile, op. cit., p. 52.

19. *New York Times*, 28 April 1966, p. 1.

20. Branch and Crile, op. cit., p. 52

21. *Washington Post*, 21 March 1977, p. A18.

22. Hinckle and Turner, p. 293, based on their interview with the participant in Ridgecrest, California, 27 September 1975.

23. *San Francisco Chronicle*, 10 January 1977, from *Newsday* (Long Island, New York), 9 January 1977.

24. Bill Schaap, 'The 1981 Cuba Dengue Epidemic', *Covert Action Information Bulletin* (Washington), No. 17, Summer 1982, pp. 28–31.

25. *San Francisco Chronicle*, 30 October 1980.

26. *Science* (American Association for the Advancement of Science, Washington), 13 January 1967, p. 176.

27. *Covert Action Information Bulletin* (Washington), No. 22, Fall 1984, p. 35; the trial of Eduardo Victor Arocena Perez, Federal District Court for the Southern District of New York, transcript of 10 September 1984, pp. 2187–89.

28. See, e.g., *San Francisco Chronicle*, 27 July 1981.

29. *Washington Post*, 16 September 1977, p. A2.

30. Ibid., 25 October 1969, column by Jack Anderson.

31. Reports of the assassination attempts have been disclosed in many places; see *Interim Report: Alleged Assassination Plots Involving Foreign Leaders*, The Select Committee to Study Governmental Operations with Respect to Intelligence Activities (US Senate), 20 November 1975, *passim*, for a detailed, although not complete, account. Stadium bombing attempt: *New York Times*, 22 November 1964, p. 26.

32. *New York Times*, 12 December 1964, p. 1.

33. Ibid., 3 March 1980, p. 1.

34. Terrorist attacks within the United States:

a) Jeff Stein, 'Inside Omega 7', *The Village Voice* (New York), 10 March 1980, *passim*.

b) *New York Times*, 13 September 1980, p. 24; 3 March, 1980, p. 1.

c) John Dinges and Saul Landau, *Assassination on Embassy Row* (London, 1981), pp. 251–52, note (also includes attacks on Cuban targets in other countries).

d) *Covert Action Information Bulletin* (Washington), No. 6, October 1979, pp. 8–9.

35. William Schaap, 'New Spate of Terrorism: Key Leaders Unleashed', *Covert Action Information Bulletin* (Washington), No. 11, December 1980, pp. 4–8; Dinges and Landau, pp. 245–6; Speech by Fidel Castro, 15 October 1976, reprinted in *Toward Improved U.S.–Cuba Relations*, House Committee on International Relations, Appendix A, 23 May 1977.

36. 'Terrorism in Miami: Suppressing Free Speech', *CounterSpy* magazine (Washington), Vol. 8, No. 3, March–May 1984, pp. 26–30; *The Village Voice*, op. cit.; *Covert Action Information Bulletin* (Washington), No. 6, October 1979, pp. 8–9.

37. *New York Times*, 4 January 1975, p. 8.

38. See, e.g., *San Francisco Chronicle*, 12 January 1982, p. 14; *Parade* magazine (*Washington Post*), 15 March 1981, p. 5.

39. *The Village Voice*, op. cit.

40. Jerome Levinson and Juan de Onis, *The Alliance That Lost Its Way: A Critical Report on the Alliance for Progress* (A Twentieth Century Fund Study, Chicago, 1970) p. 56.

41. Ibid., p. 309; the list of Alliance goals can be found on pp. 352–5.

42. Ibid., pp. 226–7.

43. *New York Times*, 27 December 1977; Philip Agee, *Inside the Company: CIA Diary* (New York, 1975) p. 380 (Editors Press Service).

44. Richard Nixon, *Six Crises* (New York, 1962, paperback edition) pp. 416–17.

45. Victor Marchetti and John Marks, *The CIA and the Cult of Intelligence* (New York, 1975), p. 289.

46. *Washington Post*, 1 September 1974, p. B7, column by Jack Anderson.

31. Indonesia, 1965

1. *Time*, 17 December 1965.

2. *New York Times Magazine*, 8 May 1966, p. 89.

3. This is the widely-accepted range; see, e.g., various Amnesty International publications on Indonesia published in the 1970s.

4. Rex Mortimer, *Indonesian Communism Under Sukarno: Ideology and Politics, 1959–1965* (Cornell University Press, Ithaca and London, 1974) pp. 413–17; *Indonesia —1965: The Coup that Backfired* (CIA Research Study, Washington, December 1968) p. 21, hereafter referred to as CIA Study.

5. Mark Selden, ed., *Remaking Asia: Essays on the American Uses of Power* (New York, 1974) pp. 47–8.

6. Noam Chomsky and Edward Herman, *The Washington Connection and Third World Fascism* (Boston, 1979) p. 207.

7. *New York Times*, 12 March 1966, p. 6.

8. *Life*, 11 July 1966.

9. Nugroho Notosusanto and Ismail Saleh, *The Coup Attempt of the 'September 30 Movement' in Indonesia* (Djakarta, 1968), cited by Mortimer p. 419, who notes that 'both authors were closely connected with the Indonesian army', p. 418.

10. CIA Study, p. 199.

11. Notosusanto and Saleh, p. 9, cited by Mortimer, p. 419.

12. CIA Study, from the Foreword.

13. Ibid., pp. 3–4; Mortimer, p. 414.

14. Discussion of Sjam's role:
a) CIA Study, pp. 23, 28, 100, 112, 117, and elsewhere;
b) Mortimer, pp. 418–40, *passim*;
c) W.F. Wertheim, 'Suharto and the Untung Coup — The Missing Link', *Journal of Contemporary Asia* (London) Winter 1970, pp. 53–4;
d) Selden, p. 48;
e) Julie Southwood and Patrick Flanagan, *Indonesia: Law, Propaganda and Terror* (London, 1983), p. 9.

15. CIA Memorandum, 18 June 1962, *Declassified Documents Reference System* (Arlington, Virginia) 1975 volume, Document 240A.

16. Arthur Schlesinger, *A Thousand Days* (London, 1965) p. 464.

17. Roger Hilsman, *To Move a Nation* (New York, 1967) p. 377.
18. *Military Assistance Training in East and Southeast Asia*, a Staff Report for the Subcommittee on National Security Policy and Scientific Developments of the House Committee on Foreign Affairs, 16 February 1971, p. 18.
19. *Military Assistance Training*, ibid., 2 April 1971, p. 13.
20. *New York Times*, 27 April 1966, p. 28.
21. Hearings on Foreign Assistance, 1966, before the Senate Committee on Foreign Relations, 11 May 1966, p. 693.
22. Green has been quoted on this theme in a number of books and periodicals with slight variations here and there, due, apparently, to the fact that he touched upon the same point in several different speeches in Australia. Some sources give only 'what we did we had to do . . . ', others provide a fuller quotation. What I have presented here is a combination taken from: a) Denis Freney, *The CIA's Australian Connection* (Australia, 1977), p. 17, citing a talk Green delivered before the Australian Institute for International Affairs in 1973; and b) Peter Britton, 'Indonesia's Neo-colonial Armed Forces', *Bulletin of Concerned Asian Scholars*, July–September 1975.
23. *New York Times*, 19 June 1966, p. 12E.
24. *Journal of Contemporary Asia* (London), Vol. 9, No. 2, 1979, p. 252.
25. *The Guardian* (London), 12 December 1983.
26. Chomsky and Herman, pp. 208–17.
27. Ibid., p. 403, note 5.
28. *New York Times* 13 December 1975, p. 26, editorial.
29. *San Francisco Chronicle*, 9 November 1979, p. 61.
30. For a fuller discussion of these matters, see: Chomsky and Herman, pp. 129–204; Denis Freney,'US–Australian Role in East Timor Genocide', *Counter-Spy* magazine (Washington), Vol. 4, No. 2, Spring 1980, pp. 10–21.

32. Ghana, 1966

1. Kwame Nkrumah, *Dark Days in Ghana* (London, 1968) p. 96.
2. E.H. Cookridge, 'The Africa Dossier', *The Daily Telegraph Magazine*, 21 January 1972, part 2 of a 3-part series on the CIA.
3. John Stockwell, *In Search of Enemies* (New York, 1978) p. 201, note.
4. Ibid., *New York Times*, 9 May 1978.
5. Stockwell, p. 201, note; another account is that 25 Russians who made up Nkrumah's palace guard were all shot and killed when they tried to surrender: Seymour Friedin and George Bailey, *The Experts* (New York, 1968) p. 210.
6. *New York Times*, 9 May 1978.
7. Ibid.
8. Ibid.
9. *Washington Post*, 17 March 1966.
10. Nkrumah, pp. 97–102 (state-owned industries, price of cocoa).

33. Uruguay, 1964 to 1970

1. Manuel Hevia Cosculluela, *Pasaporte 11333: Ocho Años con la CIA* (Havana, 1978), p. 286.

2. A.J. Langguth, *Hidden Terrors* (New York, 1978) pp. 48–9, 51 and *passim*. Langguth was formerly with the *New York Times* and in 1965 served as Saigon Bureau Chief for the newspaper.

3. *New York Times*, 1 August 1970.

4. Langguth, pp. 285–7; *New York Times*, 15 August 1970.

5. Alain Labrousse, *The Tupamaros: Urban Guerrillas in Uruguay* (Penguin Books, London, 1973, translation from French 1970 edition) p. 103.

6. Langguth, p. 289.

7. Langguth, pp. 232–3, 253–4; Philip Agee, *Inside the Company: CIA Diary* (New York, 1975) *passim* (Otero's relationship to the CIA).

8. Major Carlos Wilson, *The Tupamaros: The Unmentionables* (Boston, 1974) pp. 106–7; Langguth, p. 236.

9. Langguth, p. 252.

10. Interview in the film 'On Company Business' (Directed by Allan Francovich), cited in Warner Poelchau, ed., *White Paper, Whitewash* (New York, 1981) p. 66.

11. Extracts from the report of the Senate Commission of Inquiry into Torture, a document accompanying the film script in *State of Siege* (Ballantine Books, New York, 1973) pp. 194–6; also see 'Death of a Policeman: Unanswered Questions About a Tragedy', *Commonweal* (Catholic biweekly magazine, New York), 18 September 1970, p. 457; Langguth, p. 249.

12. Death Squad, TSD: Langguth, pp. 245–6, 253.

13. Michael Klare and Nancy Stein, 'Police Terrorism in Latin America', *NACLA's Latin America and Empire Report* (North American Congress on Latin America), January 1974, pp. 19–23, based on State Department documents obtained by Senator James Abourezk in 1973; also see Jack Anderson, *Washington Post*, 8 October 1973, p. C33; Langguth, pp. 242–3.

14. Klare and Stein, p. 19.

15. *New York Times*, 25 September 1968, 1 August 1970; Langguth, p. 241.

16. Hevia, p. 284, translated from the Spanish and slightly paraphrased by author; a similar treatment of this and other passages from Hevia can be found in Langguth, pp. 311–13.

17. *New York Times*, 5 August 1978, p. 3.

18. Mitrione's philosophy: Hevia, pp. 286–7 (see note 16 above).

19. Poelchau, p. 68.

20. Langguth, p. 305.

21. *The Guardian* (London) 19 October 1984.

22. Nancy Stein and Michael Klare, 'Merchants of Repression', *NACLA's Latin America and Empire Report* (North American Congress on Latin America), July–August 1976, p. 31.

23. DEA, arms manufacturers, etc.: Stein and Klare, pp. 31–2; *New York Times*, 23 January 1975, p. 38; 26 January 1975, p. 42; Langguth, p. 301.

24. Gar Smith, 'U.S. Narcs Backing Latin "Murder Inc." ', *Berkeley Barb* (Berkeley, California weekly newspaper) 10 September 1976.

25. *San Francisco Chronicle*, 2 November 1981.

26. Agee, pp. 325–493, *passim*.

27. Introduction to Labrousse, p. 7.

34. Chile, 1964 to 1973

1. *Covert Action in Chile, 1963–1973*, a Staff Report of The Select Committee to Study Governmental Operations with Respect to Intelligence Activities (US Senate) 18 December 1975, p. 16; hereafter referred to as Senate Report.
2. *Washington Post*, 6 April 1973.
3. Senate Report, pp. 14, 18.
4. Senate Report, p. 9.
5. *Washington Post*, 6 April 1973.
6. Senate Report, p. 15.
7. Paul E. Sigmund, *The Overthrow of Allende and the Politics of Chile, 1964–1976* (University of Pittsburgh Press, 1977) p. 297.
8. Senate Report, pp. 15–16.
9. Sigmund, p. 34.
10. Propaganda from abroad: Senate Report, p. 16.
11. Sigmund, p. 35; Philip Agee, *Inside the Company: CIA Diary* (New York, 1975) p. 387; Miles Wolpin, *Cuban Foreign Policy and Chilean Politics* (Lexington, Mass., 1972) pp. 88, 176.
12. Senate Report, p. 8.
13. *Washington Post*, 6 April 1973.
14. Senate Report, pp. 9, 16; Wolpin, pp. 175, 372.
15. David Wise, *The Politics of Lying* (New York, 1973, paperback edition) pp. 167–8.
16. *Time* magazine, 11 August 1975, European edition, p. 47.
17. Penny Lernoux, *Cry of the People: The Struggle for Human Rights in Latin America — The Catholic Church in Conflict with U.S. Policy* (Penguin Books, London, 1982) pp. 25–9, 289–92.
18. Senate Report, p. 16.
19. Allende polled 67,000 more votes than Frei amongst men; amongst the women, Frei came out ahead by 469,000.
20. Senate Report, p. 5.
21. Ibid., p. 18.
22. Ibid., p. 9; Senate committee staff quotation: *Survey of the Alliance for Progress: Labor Policies and Programs*, Staff Report of the US Senate Foreign Relations Committee, Subcommittee on American Republics Affairs, 15 July 1968, p. 3.
23. *Newsweek*, 23 September 1974, pp. 51–2, amongst many other places.
24. Senate Report, p. 21.
25. Ibid., pp. 21–2.
26. *Interim Report: Alleged Assassination Plots Involving Foreign Leaders*, The Select Committee to Study Governmental Operations with Respect to Intelligence Activities (US Senate) 20 November 1975, p. 227; hereafter referred to as Assassination Report.
27. Senate Report, p. 24.
28. Assassination Report, *passim*; Senate Report, p. 23.
29. Seymour Hersh, *Kissinger: The Price of Power* (London, 1983) pp. 259, 274, 292.
30. Senate Report, pp. 23, 25; Hersh, p. 273.
31. Senate Report, pp. 26, 37.
32. Ibid., pp. 24, 25.

33. *Foreign and Military Intelligence*, Book 1, Final Report of The Select Committee to Study Governmental Operations with Respect to Intelligence Activities (US Senate), April 1976, p. 200.

34. *Washington Post*, 5 January 1978; Senate Report, p. 25.

35. Senate Report, p. 24.

36. Assassination Report, p. 234.

37. Ibid., p. 240.

38. Ibid., 226, 245, 252, and *passim*; for another overall description of the 4 September–24 October 1970 period, see Hersh, Chapters 21 and 22.

39. *The Sunday Times* (London), 27 October 1974, p. 15, referring to William Colby's testimony before a Congressional committee on 22 April 1974.

40. Senate Report, p. 33.

41. Almost all books dealing with Chile under Allende go into the economic boycott in some detail; e.g., Edward Boorstein, *Allende's Chile: An Inside View* (New York, 1977) and James Petras and Morris H. Morley, *How Allende Fell* (Great Britain, 1974).

42. Adam Schesch and Patricia Garrett, 'The Case of Chile' in Howard Frazier, ed., *Uncloaking the CIA* (New York, 1978) p. 38; Senate Report, pp. 32–3.

43. *The Sunday Times* (London), 27 October 1974, p. 16.

44. Schesch and Garrett, p. 48; Senate Report, pp. 37–8.

45. *Time*, 30 September 1974; Senate Report, p. 31; *New York Times*, 21 September 1974, p. 12.

46. John Dinges and Saul Landau, *Assassination on Embassy Row* (London, 1981) p. 43.

47. AIFLD: Fred Hirsch, *An Analysis of Our AFL-CIO Role in Latin America* (San Jose, California, 1974) *passim*, Chile, pp. 30–42; *NACLA's Latin America and Empire Report* (North American Congress on Latin America, New York and Berkeley, California) October 1973, p. 11; *The Sunday Times* (London), 27 October 1974, pp. 15, 16; Hortensia Bussi de Allende (Salvador Allende's widow) 'The Facts About Chile' in Howard Frazier, ed., *Uncloaking the CIA* (New York, 1978) p. 60.

48. The author's own observations while in Chile from August 1972 to April 1973.

49. Senate Report, p. 31; Hortensia Bussi de Allende, pp. 60, 63; the bombing school in Los Fresnos is described in the chapter on Uruguay.

50. Senate Report, p. 36.

51. Ibid., pp. 37–8.

52. Ellen Ray and Bill Schaap, 'Massive Destabilization in Jamaica', *Covert Action Information Bulletin* (Washington, D.C.) August–September 1980, p. 8; Fred Landis, 'Robert Moss, Arnaud de Borchgrave and Right-wing Disinformation' in ibid., p. 42. (Landis was a consultant to the Senate Select Committee to Study Governmental Operations with Respect to Intelligence Activities.)

53. Landis, p. 42; Senate Report, p. 39.

54. *The Guardian* (London), 20 December 1976, p. 9; Landis, pp. 37–44.

55. Landis, pp. 38–9; Senate Report, p. 30 (refers to 'an opposition research organization'); *Daily Mail* (London) 22 December 1976, p. 6.

56. Senate Report, p. 38.

57. Various published accounts plus the author's personal acquaintance with many Americans and other foreigners who were in Santiago at the time of the coup.

58. *Time*, 30 September 1974.
59. Victor Marchetti and John Marks, *The CIA and the Cult of Intelligence* (New York, 1975), p. 43; Dinges and Landau, p. 50; Hersh, p. 333.
60. *Time*, 24 September 1973, p. 46.
61. Senate Report, p. 39.
62. Hortensia Bussi de Allende, p. 64; she adds that the pilots of the WB-575 plane were Majors V. Duenas and T. Schull.
63. Thomas Hauser, *The Execution of Charles Horman* (New York, 1978) Chapters 9 and 10.
64. *New York Times*, 17 September 1974, p. 22.
65. Ibid.
66. Senate Report, p. 47; *Washington Post*, 21 October 1973, p. C1.
67. *The Sunday Times* (London), 27 October 1974, p. 16.
68. *Washington Post*, 21 October, 1973, p. C1.
69. Roger Morris, *Uncertain Greatness: Henry Kissinger and American Foreign Policy* (Great Britain, 1977) p. 241. (Morris formerly served under Kissinger on the staff of the National Security Council although he is not here speaking of himself.)
70. Assassination Report, p. 229.

35. Greece, 1964 to 1974

1. *The Observer* (London), 1 July 1973, article by Charles Foley.
2. Junta's actions: James Becket, *Barbarism in Greece* (New York, 1970) p. 1; Bernard Nossiter, 'Saving Greece from the Greeks', *New Republic*, 20 May 1967, p. 10; editorial, *The Nation*, 22 May 1967, p. 644.
3. Becket, p. 90 (Amnesty International Report, 27 January 1968).
4. Philip Deane, *I Should Have Died* (New York, 1977) pp. 92–124, composed of conversations with Greek and American individuals in or close to the conspiracy, and references to testimony from the 1975 trials of junta members and torturers.
5. Ibid., pp. 113–14.
6. *New York Times*, 2 August 1974, p. 3; see also *Newsweek*, 12 August 1974, p. 36, concerning CIA buying politicians and votes in Greece before the coup.
7. Stephen Rousseas, 'The Deadlock in Greece', *The Nation*, 27 March 1967, p. 392.
8. *Washington Post*, 15 May 1967, p. A18.
9. Andreas Papandreou's political views: Nossiter, p. 9; Deane, p. 116; Lawrence Stern, *The Wrong Horse: The Politics of Intervention and the Failure of American Diplomacy* (N.Y. Times Books, 1977) pp. 20–30.
10. Deane, pp. 116–17.
11. *New York Times*, 2 August 1974, p. 3; 3 August, p. 4.
12. George Papandreou: Rousseas, pp. 390–1; Nossiter, p. 9; Deane, p. 115.
13. *The Observer*, op. cit.
14. Ibid.; see also Deane, p. 96 re bugging ministers.
15. Deane, p. 96, citing Andreas Papandreou as the source.
16. *The Observer*, op. cit.
17. Ibid.; Deane, p. 96; Becket, p. 13.

18. *Washington Post*, 15 May 1967, p. A18 (February meeting); Stern, pp. 42–3 (CIA report).
19. *The Observer*, op. cit.
20. Ibid.
21. *New York Times*, 2 August 1974, p. 1; Deane, p. 96.
22. *The Observer*, op. cit.; Deane, p. 126.
23. *The Observer*, op. cit.
24. Ibid.
25. Becket, p. 8.
26. Ibid., p. 10.
27. Ibid., p. xi.
28. Ibid., p. 15.
29. Ibid., p. 91.
30. See, e.g., Becket, pp. 18–85; Deane, pp. 128–33; Amnesty International, *Torture in Greece: The First Torturers' Trial in 1975* (London, 1977) *passim*.
31. Becket, pp. 4 and 115.
32. Amnesty International, *Report on Torture* (London, 1973), pp. 93–4; also see Deane, p. 119, for evidence of the fraudulent nature of the junta's claims before the coup of a communist threat.
33. *Report on Torture*, op. cit., p. 77; see pages 88, 89, 95, 98 for choice examples of what Amnesty was referring to.
34. *The Observer*, op. cit.
35. Seymour Hersh, *Kissinger: The Price of Power* (London, 1983) p. 140.
36. *The Observer*, op. cit.
37. Hersh, pp. 138 and 648.
38. Becket, p. 16; see also p. 127.
39. *Report on Torture*, op. cit., p. 96.
40. Deane, p. 134; *New York Times*, 2 August 1974, p. 1.
41. Deane, p. 134.
42. *New York Times*, 7 September 1975, p. 6.
43. Deane, p. 125.
44. Andreas Papandreou, *Democracy at Gunpoint: The Greek Front* (New York, 1970) p. 294.

36. Bolivia, 1964 to 1975

The account of the events leading up to the coup of 1964 was derived primarily from the following sources:

anto
a) Cole Blasier, 'The United States and the Revolution' in James M. Malloy and Richard Thorn, eds., *Beyond the Revolution: Bolivia Since 1952* (University of Pittsburgh Press, 1971) pp. 90–105;
b) James Dunkerley, *Rebellion in the Veins: Political Struggle in Bolivia 1952–1982* (London, 1984) pp. 112–9;
c) Lawrence Whitehead, *The United States and Bolivia: A Case of Neo-Colonialism* (London, 1969), pp. 11–25;
d) Christopher Mitchell, *The Legacy of Populism in Bolivia: From the MNR to Military Rule* (New York, 1977), Chapter 5;
e) William H. Brill, *Military Intervention in Bolivia: The Overthrow of Paz Estenssoro and the MNR* (Washington, 1967), pp. 18–47.

1. Cornelius H. Zondag, 'Bolivia's 1952 Revolution in Jerry R. Ladman, ed., *Modern-Day Bolivia* (Arizona State University, 1982) p. 37.
2. *Washington Post*, 5 February 1968.
3. *New York Times*, 9 August 1964, p. 10.
4. Ibid., 24 August 1964, p. 26.
5. Blasier, pp. 89–90; Whitehead, p. 14; Dunkerley, p. 106.
6. Blasier, pp. 97–8; Dunkerley, p. 113; Whitehead, p. 16; *Washington Post*, 5 February 1968.
7. Miners' strength, Zavaleta quote: Whitehead, pp. 24–5. Henderson had actually been ambassador only one year at the time of the coup, so Zavaleta may have been referring to Henderson's predecessor as well.
8. *New York Times*, 22 November 1964, p. 26.
9. US build-up of armed forces: Dunkerley, p. 114; Blasier, pp. 93–5; Whitehead, p. 24; Richard Harris, *Death of a Revolutionary: Che Guevara's Last Mission* (New York, 1970) p. 172.
10. *Washington Post*, 5 February 1968.
11. Blasier, p. 98.
12. Mitchell, p. 94; Dunkerley, pp. 116–17.
13. Shooting incident and aftermath leading to Barrientos replacing Fortún: Dunkerley, p. 117; Mitchell, pp. 94–5.
14. *El Diario* and Sanjinés: Dunkerley, pp. 113–14; Blasier, p. 95; Whitehead, p. 15 (citing cabinet member Antonio Arguedas).
15. Mitchell, p. 95.
16. Brill, p. 28.
17. Ibid., pp. 27–9, 36–8.
18. Ibid., p. 37.
19. *Washington Post*, 5 February 1968.
20. Mitchell, pp. 100–1.
21. Hearings before the Committee on Armed Services and the Subcommittee on Department of Defense of the Committee on Appropriations (US Senate), 23 February 1966, p. 39.
22. *Washington Post*, 17 May 1975; *New York Times*, 17–18 May 1975. Arguedas made numerous other charges about CIA activities in Bolivia. For a discussion of these, and Arguedas' own fascinating tale, see Harris, ch. 14 or *Intercontinental Press* (New York weekly newsmagazine), 23 September 1968.
23. Norman Gall, 'The Legacy of Che Guevara', *Commentary*, December 1967, p. 35.
24. Philip Agee, *Inside the Company: CIA Diary* (New York, 1975) p. 438.
25. Military operation against Guevara: Michael Klare, *War Without End* (New York, 1972) pp. 173–4, 177–9; Victor Marchetti and John Marks, *The CIA and the Cult of Intelligence* (New York, 1975) pp. 138–45; Harris, pp. 172–8.
26. Harris, pp. 185–6. See note 22 above.
27. *New York Times*, 14 December 1969, p. 22.
28. Ibid.
29. Interpress Service dispatch of 18 December 1969, cited in Gregorio Selser, *La CIA en Bolivia* (Buenos Aires, 1970) p. 5.
30. Associated Press dispatch from La Paz, appearing in *La Nación* (Buenos Aires' leading newspaper), 21 December 1969, p. 4.
31. *New York Times*, 24 January 1970, p. 9.

32. Ibid., 20 July 1970, p. 9.
33. Ibid., 23 September 1970, p. 13.
34. Torres' policies: Latin American Bureau, *Bolivia and Coup d'Etat* (London, 1980) pp. 36–8; Dunkerley, pp. 180, 186.
35. *San Francisco Chronicle*, 30 August 1971.
36. *Washington Post*, 29 August 1971.
37. Dunkerley, p. 197.
38. Dunkerley, p. 200; *Washington Post*, 29 August 1971.
39. *San Francisco Chronicle*, 1 September 1971.
40. Banzer's post-coup statements: *Washington Post*, 25 August 1971; *New York Times*, 25 August 1971; *Los Angeles Times*, 24, 25 August 1971.
41. *New York Times*, 30 December 1973.
42. Penny Lernoux, *Cry of the People: The Struggle for Human Rights in Latin America — The Catholic Church in Conflict with U.S. Policy* (Penguin Books, London, 1982) pp. 142–5.
43. *The Guardian* (London), 15 July 1985, p. 6.
44. *Bolivia — An Assessment of U.S. Policies and Programs: Report to the Congress by the Comptroller General of the United States*, 30 January 1975, p. 29.
45. *New York Times*, 28 July 1978, article by Max Holland.

37. Guatemala, 1962 to 1980s

The details of the events and issues touched upon in this chapter through 1968 were derived primarily from the following sources:
a) Thomas and Marjorie Melville, *Guatemala — Another Vietnam?* (Great Britain, 1971) Chapters 9 to 16; particularly for the conditions of the poor, and US activities in Guatemala; published in the United States the same year in a slightly different form as *Guatemala: The Politics of Land Ownership*;
b) Eduardo Galeano, *Guatemala, Occupied Country* (Mexico, 1967; English translation: New York, 1969) *passim*; for the politics of the guerrillas and the nature of the right-wing terror; Galeano was a Uruguayan journalist who spent some time with the guerrillas;
c) Susanne Jonas and David Tobis, editors, *Guatemala* (Berkeley, California, 1974) *passim*; particularly 'The Vietnamization of Guatemala: U.S. Counter-insurgency Programs', pp. 193–203, by Howard Sharckman; published by the North American Congress on Latin America (NACLA);
d) Amnesty International, *Guatemala* (London, 1976) *passim*; for statistics about the victims of the terror. Other AI reports issued in the 1970s about Guatemala contain comparable information;
e) Richard Gott, *Rural Guerrillas in Latin America* (Great Britain, 1973, revised edition) Chapters 2 to 8; for the politics of the guerrillas; first published 1970 as *Guerrilla Movements in Latin America*.
1. *The Guardian* (London), 22 December 1983, p. 5.
2. The plight of the poor: a montage compiled from the sources cited herein.
3. *New York Times Magazine*, 26 June 1966, p. 8.
4. US counter-insurgency base: *El Imparcial* (Guatemala City conservative newspaper) 17 May 1962 and 4 January 1963, cited in Melville, pp. 163–4.

5. Stephen Schlesinger and Stephen Kinzer, *Bitter Fruit: The Untold Story of the American Coup in Guatemala* (New York, 1982), p. 242.

6. *New York Herald Tribune*, 7 April 1963, article by Bert Quint, section 2, p. 1; also see Schlesinger and Kinzer, pp. 243–4. Arévalo was the author of a book called *The Shark and the Sardines* in which he pictured the US as trying to dominate Latin America. But he had also publicly denounced Castro as 'a danger to the continent, a menace'. (Galeano, p. 55.)

7. Galeano, pp. 55–6.

8. *Time*, 26 January 1968, p. 23.

9. Ibid.

10. Atrocities and torture: compiled from the sources cited herein; also see A.J. Langguth, *Hidden Terrors* (New York, 1978) pp. 139, 193 for US involvement with the use of the field telephones for torture in Brazil.

11. Melville, p. 292.

12. Ibid., p. 291.

13. *Washington Post*, 27 January 1968, p. A4, testimony of Revd Blase Bonpane, also an American missionary in Guatemala at the time.

14. Panama: revealed in September 1967 by Guatemalan Vice-President Clemente Marroquín Rojas in an interview with the international news agency Interpress Service (IPS), reported in *Latin America*, 15 September 1967, p. 159, a weekly published in London. Eduardo Galeano, p. 70, reports a personal conversation he had with Marroquín Rojas in which the vice-president related the same story. Marroquín Rojas was strongly anti-communist, but he apparently resented the casual way in which the American planes violated Guatemalan sovereignty.

15. Norman Diamond, 'Why They Shoot Americans', *The Nation* (New York), 5 February 1968.

16. Right-wing terrorism: compiled from the sources cited herein.

17. *Washington Post*, 4 February 1968, p. B1. The historic dialogue in Latin America between Christianity and Marxism, begun in the 1970s, can be traced in large measure to priests and nuns like Bonpane and the Melvilles and their experiences in Guatemala in the 1950s and 60s.

18. Galeano, p. 63.

19. *El Imparcial* (Guatemala City), 10 November 1967, cited in Melville, p. 289.

20. Richard Gott, in the Foreword to the Melvilles' book, p. 8.

21. George Cotter, 'Spies, strings and missionaries', *The Christian Century* (Chicago), 25 March 1981, p. 321.

22. AID, OPS, Alliance for Progress:

a) 'Guatemala and the Dominican Republic', a Staff Memorandum prepared for the US Senate Subcommittee on Western Hemisphere Affairs, Committee on Foreign Relations, 30 December 1971, p. 6;

b) Jonas and Tobis, pp. 199–200;

c) Galeano, pp. 72–3;

d) Michael Klare, *War Without End* (New York, 1972) pp. 241–69, for discussion of the OPS curriculum and philosophy;

e) Langguth, *passim*, for discussion of OPS practices, including its involvement with torture; the author confines his study primarily to Brazil and Uruguay, but it applies to Guatemala as well;

f) *CounterSpy* magazine (Washington), November 1980–January 1981, pp. 54–5, lists the names of almost 300 Guatemalan police officers who received training in the United States from 1963 to 1974;

g)   See also note No. 13, Uruguay chapter.

23.   Reported by AID, cited in Jenny Pearce, *Under the Eagle* (Great Britain, 1982) p. 67.

24.   Eqbal Ahmad, 'The Theory and Fallacies of Counter-insurgency', *The Nation*, 2 August 1972, p. 73.

25.   Relationship of Arana to US military: Joseph Goulden, 'A Real Good Relationship', *The Nation*, 1 June 1970, p. 646; Norman Gall, 'Guatemalan Slaughter', *N.Y. Review of Books*, 20 May 1971, pp. 13–17.

26.   *Le Monde Weekly* (English edition), 17 February 1971, p. 3.

27.   *New York Times*, 27 December 1970, p. 2; *New York Times Magazine*, 13 June 1971, p. 72.

28.   US Senate Staff Memorandum, *op. cit.*

29.   *New York Times*, 18 February 1976.

30.   Ibid., 9 November 1977, p. 2.

31.   *The Guardian* (London), 9 December 1983; *CounterSpy* magazine (Washington), November 1980–January 1981, p. 53, citing Elias Barahona y Barahona, former press secretary at the Guatemalan Ministry of the Interior.

32.   *CounterSpy*, see note 31.

33.   Pearce, p. 278; a book was published later which transcribed the Indian woman's own account of her life, in which she recounts atrocities of the Guatemalan military much worse than this: Elisabeth Burgos-Debray, ed., *I . . . Rigoberta Menchu: An Indian Woman in Guatemala* (London, 1984, English translation).

34.   Pearce, p. 176; Sherwood's role in 1954: Schlesinger and Kinzer, pp. 116, 122, 128.

35.   *Washington Post*, 22 February 1981, p. C7, column by Jack Anderson; Anderson refers only to an 'official spokesman' of the MLN; the identity of the speaker as Sandoval comes from elsewhere — see, e.g., *The Guardian* (London), 2 March 1984.

36.   *Washington Post*, ibid.; for a discussion of the many ties between American conservatives and the Guatemalan power structure, see the report of the Council on Hemispheric Affairs (Washington), by Allan Nairn in 1981.

37.   *New York Times*, 19 March 1981, p. 10.

38.   *Washington Post*, 14 May 1981, p. A16.

39.   Ibid.; *New York Times*, 18 May 1981, p. 18; Report issued by the Washington Office on Latin America (a respected human-rights lobby which has worked in liaison with the State Department's human-rights section), 4 September 1981.

40.   Report cited in note 39; presumably it was the traditional right-wing fear of the poor being educated which lay behind this incident.

41.   *New York Times*, 28 December 1981.

42.   Ibid., 21 June 1981; 25 April 1982; *The Guardian* (London), 10 January 1983.

43.   *San Francisco Chronicle*, 27 August 1981, p. 57.

44.   *Washington Post*, 21 October 1982, p. A1.

45.   *The Guardian* (London), 10 January 1983; 17 May 1983.

46.   *New York Times*, 25 April 1982, p. 1.

47.   Ibid., 12 October 1982, p. 3.

48.   *Contemporary Marxism* (San Francisco), No. 3, Summer 1981.

49. *New York Times*, 6 December 1982, p. 14.
50. *The National Catholic Reporter* (Kansas City, Missouri weekly), 31 January 1968.

38. Costa Rica, 1970 to 1971

1. *New York Times*, 11 February 1971.
2. Ibid.
3. The primary sources for the overall story are the *Miami Herald*, 7 February 1971 and the *Los Angeles Times*, 28 February 1971; see also the *Miami Herald*, 9, 10, 11, 13 February 1971.
4. *New York Times*, 11 February 1971; *Miami Herald*, 11 February 1971.
5. *Miami Herald*, 10 February 1971.

39. Iraq, 1972 to 1975

The primary source of information for this chapter is the Staff Report of the Select Committee on Intelligence, US House of Representatives, based on hearings held during 1975. Publication of the report was suppressed by the full House until the White House could censor it. But portions of the uncensored report, which came to be known as The Pike Report after the committee's chairman Rep. Otis G. Pike, were leaked to the press, in particular *The Village Voice* of New York which published much of it in its issues of 16 and 23 February 1976. This material first appeared in book form in 1977 in England under the title: *CIA — The Pike Report*, published by Spokesman Books for the Bertrand Russell Peace Foundation, Nottingham. It is this book which is referred to in the present chapter, pp. 56, 195–8, 211–17, hereafter referred to as Pike Report.

1. Seymour Hersh, *Kissinger: The Price of Power* (London, 1983) p. 542n.
2. *New York Times*, 5 February 1976, p. 31, column by William Safire.
3. Pike Report, p. 196.
4. Political background of the Kurds: *The Times* (London), 26–28 November 1974.
5. Pike Report, p. 212.
6. Ibid., pp. 197, 214–15.
7. Ibid., p. 214.
8. Ibid., p. 197.
9. *New York Times*, 12 February 1976, p. 31, column by William Safire.
10. Pike Report, p. 214.
11. *New York Times*, 5 February 1976, p. 31, column by William Safire.
12. Pike Report, p. 215.
13. Ibid., pp. 215–16.
14. Ibid., p. 217.
15. *New York Times*, 12 February 1976, p. 31, column by William Safire.

40. Australia, 1973 to 1975

1. Henry S. Albinski, *Australian External Policy Under Labor* (Australia, 1977) p. 126.

2. Joan Coxsedge, Ken Coldicutt, Gerry Harant, *Rooted in Secrecy: The Clandestine Element in Australian Politics* (Australia, 1982) p. 21.

3. Albinski, p. 125.

4. Ibid.

5. Coxsedge, *et al.*, p. 24.

6. Ibid., p. 22, citing Richard Hall, *The Secret State* (Australia, 1979).

7. Coxsedge, *et al.*, pp. 25–6.

8. Denis Freney, *The CIA's Australian Connection* (Sydney, 1977) pp. 75–80, for the text of the interview. This book deals with many of the events discussed in this chapter.

9. Desmond Ball, *A Suitable Piece of Real Estate: American Installations in Australia* (Sydney, 1980) *passim*.

10. Jim Jose, 'The Whitlam Years: Illusion and Reality' in Pat Flanagan, ed., *Big Brother or Democracy?* (Great Britain, 1981) p. 50; Albinski, p. 11; Ball, *passim*.

11. Albinski, pp. 9, 241.

12. Ibid., pp. 254–6.

13. Coxsedge, *et al.*, p. 26.

14. Jose, p. 50.

15. *The Australian Financial Review* (Sydney daily newspaper), 4 November 1975, p. 1; 5 November, p. 4.

16. *New York Times*, 24 September 1974, p. 2.

17. Ibid., 5 May 1977, citing the *Sydney Sun*, 4 May 1977; contains the Marchetti statement as well.

18. Coxsedge, *et al.*, p. 35.

19. *The Australian Financial Review*, 28 April 1977, p. 1; Jose, p. 51, adds that the official, Dr Farrands, denied the allegation but did admit to visiting Kerr in October and refused to discuss the nature of the meeting.

20. *The Australian Financial Review*, 28 April 1977, p. 1.

21. Albinski, p. 169.

22. Coxsedge, *et al.*, p. 96.

23. Freney, pp. 30–31, for the full text of the telex.

24. Coxsedge, *et al.*, p. 35; Freney, p. 33; *The Village Voice* (New York), 1–7 July 1981.

25. Discussion of the political and legal issues surrounding the budget crisis and Kerr's dismissal of Whitlam can be found in Coxsedge, Freney, and Flanagan; see also: Sir John Kerr, *Matters for Judgment: An Autobiography* (New York, 1979) ch.20–22; Russel Ward, *The History of Australia: The Twentieth Century, 1901–1975* (London, 1978) pp. 398–419; *New York Times*, 12, 14 November 1975.

26. *The Age*, 12 November 1975, p. 9.

27. Ibid., p. 3.

28. Kerr, ch. 20–22.

29. Victor Marchetti and John Marks, *The CIA and the Cult of Intelligence* (New York, 1975) p. 178 (see pp. 178–9 for a description of the Asia Foundation).

30. Kerr in the Association for Cultural Freedom and Lawasia: Kerr, pp. 172–

86, and other books mentioned above; the *Quadrant* article was in the Spring, 1960 issue, pp. 27–38.

31. *San Francisco Chronicle*, 24 May 1982. Whitlam himself, at least in the year or so following his ousting, was careful to avoid accusing the CIA of complicity; there was, after all, no 'smoking gun' which he could point to.

32. *New York Times*, 28 April 1977, p. 18; *The Guardian* (London), 29 April 1977, p. 7.

33. Nugen Hand Bank: *Sunday Times* (London), 31 August 1980, p. 2; *New York Times*, 13 November 1982, p. 31; *The Village Voice*, 1–7 July 1981; *CounterSpy* magazine (Washington, D.C.), November 1980–January 1981, pp. 30–33; *Wall Street Journal*, 1 May 1980, p. 31.

41. Angola, 1975 to 1976

1. *New York Times*, 25 September 1975; 19 December 1975.

2. John A. Marcum, *The Angolan Revolution, Vol. I, 1950–1962* (MIT Press, Cambridge, Mass., 1969) pp. 229–30.

3. Comparison of the three groups: Marcum, Vol. II, 1962–1976 (1978) pp. 14–15, 132, 172 and *passim*; Basil Davidson, *In the Eye of the Storm: Angola's People* (London, 1972) *passim*; Ernest Harsch and Tony Thomas, *Angola: The Hidden History of Washington's War* (New York, 1976) *passim*.

4. State Department Circular 92, 16 July 1963, cited in Marcum II, p. 16.

5. Hearings before the House Select Committee on Intelligence (The Pike Committee) published in *CIA — The Pike Report* (Nottingham, England, 1977) p. 218; hereafter referred to as Pike Report. (See Notes: Iraq for further information.)

6. Ibid., p. 201.

7. John Stockwell, *In Search of Enemies* (New York, 1978) p. 67.

8. *New York Times*, 19 December 1975.

9. Stockwell, pp. 67–8; Marcum II, pp. 257–8 (he cites several international press accounts).

10. *New York Times*, 25 September 1975.

11. Pike Report, p. 199.

12. Stockwell, p. 67.

13. *New York Times*, 12 December 1975; Harsch and Thomas, p. 100, citing CBS-TV and Senator John Tunney.

14. *San Francisco Chronicle*, 17 July 1978.

15. *Christian Science Monitor* (Boston), 2 January 1976, p. 1; see also 5 January, p. 1.

16. Mercenaries: Stockwell, pp. 198–9, 220–26; Chapman Pincher, *Inside Story: A Documentary of the Pursuit of Power* (London, 1978) p. 20 (CIA payment for British mercenaries); Harsch and Thomas, pp. 99–100.

17. Stockwell, p. 225.

18. *San Francisco Chronicle*, 17 July 1978, referring to Kissinger statement of 29 January 1976.

19. Stockwell, pp. 162, 177–8 (Stockwell speaks of 83 additional officers dispatched to the field to beef up the CIA stations in the four countries).

20. Stockwell, pp. 194–5, plus Stockwell interviewed in the film 'On Company Business' (Directed by Allan Francovich), cited in Warner Poelchau, ed., *White Paper, Whitewash* (New York, 1981) p. 38.

21. The capture of Russians and Cubans story appeared in the press 22 November 1975; the rape story, 12 March 1976.

22. Stockwell, p. 196.

23. *San Francisco Chronicle*, 9 May 1978.

24. Stockwell, pp. 196–8.

25. *Foreign and Military Intelligence*, Book 1, Final Report of the Select Committee to Study Governmental Operations with Respect to Intelligence Activities (US Senate), 26 April 1976, p. 129.

26. Stockwell, p. 193.

27. Ibid., pp. 205-6; after the war ended, the State Department did release the planes to Angola.

28. *Newsweek* (International Edition), 17 May 1976, p. 23.

29. Stockwell, pp. 208, 218; *San Francisco Chronicle*, 17 July 1978; Stephen Talbot, 'The CIA and Boss: Thick as Thieves' in Ellen Ray, *et al.*, eds., *Dirty Work 2: The CIA in Africa* (New Jersey, 1979) pp. 266–75.

30. *New York Times*, 25 March 1982, p. 7.

31. Stockwell, p. 209.

32. Ibid., p. 75.

33. Cited in Jonathan Steele, 'Soviet Relations with Angola and Mozambique' in Robert Cassen, ed., *Soviet Interests in The Third World* (Published by Sage for the Royal Institute of International Affairs, London, 1985) Chapter 15.

34. Stockwell, pp. 216–17 discusses this situation.

35. Ibid., pp. 234–5.

36. *New York Times*, 24 December 1975, p. 7.

37. Henry Kissinger, *American Foreign Policy* (New York, 1977, third edition), p. 317.

38. See, for example, *New York Times*, 25 September 1975.

39. Hearings before the Subcommittee on Africa of the House Committee on International Relations, 25 May 1978, p. 7.

40. Pike Report, p. 200.

41. *Washington Post*, 18 December 1975, p. A23.

42. *New York Times*, 9 January 1976, p. 3.

43. MPLA in power: Harsch and Thomas, pp. 82–91; *New York Times*, 8 February 1981, IV, p. 5.

44. Stockwell, pp. 203–4, 241; plus television interview of Stockwell: 'Diverse Reports', Channel 4, London, broadcast 30 October 1985.

45. Stockwell, p. 172.

46. Galen Hull, 'Internationalizing the Shaba Conflict', *Africa Report* (New York) July–August 1977, p. 9.

47. CBS special report, June 1980, cited in the *Christian Science Monitor*, 29 September 1980, p. 15.

48. *The Observer* (London), 22 January 1984.

42. Zaire, 1975 to 1978

1. Mobutu's fortune: *New York Times*, 3 June 1978, article by Michael Kaufman; *The Nation* (New York) 26 February 1983, p. 230. Malnutrition: World Bank report, 1975, cited in *Africa Today* (Denver, Colorado), October–December 1978, p. 7.

2. Roger Morris (former staff member of the National Security Council) and Richard Mauzy, 'Zaire (the Congo): An Exercise in Nation Building' in Robert Borosage and John Marks, eds., *The CIA File* (New York, 1976) pp. 36–7.

3. Coup accusation and attendant events: *New York Times*, 18–23 June 1975; 2 September 1975, p. 21; John Stockwell, *In Search of Enemies* (New York, 1978) p. 44.

4. Stockwell, p. 96, quoting CIA officer Bill Avery.

5. For a profile of Hinton, see *Latin America and Empire Report*, October 1973, pp. 14–15, published by North American Congress on Latin America (NACLA), New York.

6. Stockwell, p. 169.

7. Ibid., p. 164.

8. Ibid., p. 246 and note.

9. *New York Times*, 21 January 1976, p. 1.

10. *New York Times*, 9 April 1977; the words are those of the newspaper.

11. The overall events of 1977: *New York Times*, 16 March to 3 May 1977, *passim*; Galen Hull, 'Internationalizing the Shaba Conflict', *Africa Report* (New York), July–August 1977, pp. 4–9.

12. Bufkin/mercenaries: *Newsday* (Long Island, NY), 17 April 1977; *New York Times*, 17, 18, 20 April 1977.

13. *New York Times*, 8 August 1977.

14. Background of FNLC: Hull, op. cit.; Stockwell, p. 151.

15. *New York Times*, 6 April 1977.

16. Mobutu: Ibid., 13 April 1977.

17. Ibid.

18. *Washington Post*, 16 March 1977.

19. *New York Times*, 20 May 1978.

20. 1978 military events: *New York Times*, 15 May to 24 June 1978, *passim*.

21. Ibid., 23 May 1978.

22. Ibid., 19 May 1978.

23. Ibid., 20 May 1978. The words are those of the *Times*, paraphrasing 'high administration officials'.

24. See, for example, *New York Times*, 10 April 1977.

25. Carter–Castro exchange: *New York Times*, 11, 13, 15 June 1978.

26. Ibid., 24 June 1978.

43. Jamaica, 1976 to 1980

1. Ernest Volkman and John Cummings, 'Murder as Usual', *Penthouse* magazine (New York), December 1977, p. 114, quoting a participant in the meeting between the two men.

2. Michael Manley, *Jamaica: Struggle in the Periphery* (London, 1982) p. 116.

3. John Dinges and Saul Landau, *Assassination on Embassy Row* (London, 1981) p. 44.

4. Testimony by de Roulet before the US Senate: *Multinational Corporations and United States Foreign Policy*, Hearings before the Subcommittee on Multinational Corporations of the Committee on Foreign Relations, 19 July 1973,

pp. 117–18. A State Department official who was testifying at the same time was clearly embarrassed by de Roulet's disclosure and quickly tried to play down the story.

5. Volkman and Cummings, p. 114.
6. Manley, p. 116.
7. Ibid., p. 136.
8. Ibid., pp. 98–103.
9. Ibid., pp. 116–17.
10. *New York Times*, 1 October 1979, p. 2.
11. Manley, p. 117.
12. Volkman and Cummings, p. 182.
13. Ibid., p. 183.
14. Ellen Ray, 'CIA and Local Gunmen Plan Jamaican Coup', *CounterSpy* magazine (Washington), Vol. 3, No. 2, December 1976, p. 39; Volkman and Cummings, p. 182.
15. Volkman and Cummings, p. 182; Manley, p. 103.
16. *New York Times*, 17 July 1976, p. 29.
17. Ray, pp. 38, 40; Manley, pp. 229, 236.
18. Ray, p. 37; Volkman and Cummings, pp. 183, 188.
19. Ray, p. 41; *Washington Post*, 5 July 1979.
20. Volkman and Cummings, p. 182; Ray, p. 41.
21. Assassination attempts: Volkman and Cummings, pp. 112, 183, 188, 190.
22. Ray, p. 40.
23. Fred Landis, 'The CIA and the Media: IAPA and the Jamaica Daily Gleaner', *Covert Action Information Bulletin* (Washington) December 1979–January 1980, pp. 10–12; Manley, p. 231; Fred Landis, 'CIA Media Operations in Chile, Jamaica and Nicaragua', *CAIB*, March 1982, pp. 32–43.
24. Ray, p. 41.
25. *Newsday* (Long Island, NY), 28 February 1980, cited in Ellen Ray and Bill Schaap, 'Massive Destabilization in Jamaica', *Covert Action Information Bulletin*, August–September 1980, p. 14; the date of the earlier article is not cited.
26. *Daily Gleaner* (Kingston, Jamaica), 1 June 1980, p. 10; see also Fred Landis, op. cit. 1982.
27. Manley, pp. 193–4.
28. Ibid., pp. 199–200.

44. Seychelles, 1979 to 1981

1. Rene and US–Seychelles relations: *Sunday Tribune* (Durban, South Africa), 29 November 1981, two separate articles, pp. 1 and 52; Ellen Ray, 'Seychelles Beats Back Mercenaries', *Covert Action Information Bulletin* (CAIB) (Washington) No. 16, March 1982, pp. 4–10.
2. *Sunday Tribune*, op. cit., p. 52.
3. *CAIB*, op. cit., p. 5.
4. *Sunday Tribune*, op. cit., p. 1; *CAIB*, op. cit., pp. 4–10.
5. *Sunday Tribune*, op. cit., p. 1; *New York Times*, 6 November 1982, p. 4 (prosecution of editors).
6. *CAIB*, op. cit., p. 10.
7. *The Guardian* (London), 3 December 1983.

45. Grenada, 1979 to 1983

1. *New York Times*, 1 November 1983; Les Janka was the man whose FBI security check failed to disclose a conscience.

2. US presence: Hugh O'Shaughnessy, *Grenada: Revolution, Invasion and Aftermath* (London, 1984) p. 156; see William C. Gilmore, *The Grenada Intervention: Analysis and Documentation* (London, 1984) Part II, 'The Grenada Intervention in International Law' and Appendix 2 for the relevant sections of the OECS treaty.

3. *The Guardian* (London), 28 October 1983.

4. *The Observer* (London), 30 October 1983.

5. O'Shaughnessy, p. 153.

6. *The Guardian*, 31 October 1983.

7. *The Observer*, 30 October 1983.

8. *The Guardian*, 1 November 1983.

9. *The Guardian*, 28, 29 October 1983; *The Observer*, 30 October 1983.

10. O'Shaughnessy, p. 165; this page contains other evidence which refutes Reagan's contention but which is not discussed here.

11. *The Guardian*, 26 October 1983.

12. *New York Times*, 27 October 1983.

13. O'Shaughnessy, p. 205.

14. *The Guardian*, 26 October 1983.

15. O'Shaughnessy, p. 160.

16. *The Guardian*, 27 October 1983.

17. Ibid., 28 October 1983.

18. *New York Times*, 27 October 1983.

19. Ibid., 28 October 1983.

20. *The Guardian*, 29 October 1983.

21. O'Shaughnessy, p. 204.

22. *The Guardian*, 31 October 1983.

23. *New York Times*, 1 November 1983.

24. O'Shaughnessy, pp. 15, 16, 204.

25. *The Observer*, 23 October 1983.

26. From speech by Fidel Castro on 14 November 1983 in Havana; reprinted in *The Guardian*, 19 November 1983, p. 8.

27. *The Guardian*, 27 October 1983.

28. Ibid., 1 November 1983.

29. *New York Times*, 1 November 1983.

30. *The Guardian*, 12 June 1984.

31. O'Shaughnessy, pp. 87, 95.

32. Ibid., p. 85.

33. *The Guardian*, 4 November 1983.

34. Cited by Bishop in his speech of 13 April 1979, in Chris Searle, ed., *In Nobody's Backyard: Maurice Bishop's Speeches 1979–1983* (London, 1984).

35. *New York Times*, 20 August 1979, p. 4.

36. Chris Searle, *Grenada, The Struggle Against Destabilization* (London, 1983), p. 56; this appeared as a news item in the US press as well, and was seen by myself, but I have been unable to locate it again.

37. *New York Times*, 27 August 1983.

38. *Washington Post*, 27 February 1983, p. 1.

39. O'Shaughnessy, p. 192.
40. *Washington Post*, 27 February 1983, p. 1.
41. *New York Times*, 26 March 1983.
42. *The Nation* (NY), 16 April 1983, p. 467 contains a table which compares the various airports.
43. O'Shaughnessy, p. 90.
44. *The Nation* (NY), 16 April 1983, p. 467; O'Shaughnessy, p. 89.
45. *The Guardian*, 31 October, 2 November 1983.
46. Ibid., 2 May 1983.
47. *Wall Street Journal*, 29 April 1981; *The Guardian*, 2 May 1983.
48. *The Guardian*, 11 November 1983.
49. *New York Times*, 20 August 1979, p. 4.
50. Ibid.
51. *The Observer*, 30 October 1983, p. 9.
52. *The Guardian*, 25 November 1983.
53. Ibid., 27 October 1983, according to the Cuban Ambassador in London.
54. From speech by Fidel Castro on 14 November 1983 in Havana; reprinted in *The Guardian*, 19 November 1983, p. 8.
55. *The Observer*, 30 October 1983, p. 9.
56. *The Guardian*, 16 November 1983.
57. *The Observer*, 30 October 1983.
58. O'Shaughnessy, p. 208; *The Guardian*, 16 November, 19 December 1983.
59. *The Guardian*, 5 March 1984.
60. Ibid., 12 June 1984.
61. *New York Times*, 4 November 1983, p. 16.
62. Ibid., 22 March 1986.

46. Morocco, 1983

1. *The Nation* (New York), 26 March 1983, p. 356.
2. Interview in *Africa Now* (London), March 1983, pp. 14–18.
3. Claudia Wright, 'Showdown in the Sahara', *Inquiry* magazine (Washington), 12 April 1982, p. 24; *New York Times*, 1 February 1983, p. 3.
4. *Africa Now*, op. cit., p. 14.
5. *New York Times*, 1 February 1983, p. 3.
6. Wright, p. 24.
7. Ibid., pp. 24–5; also see Zaire chapter herein.
8. *Africa Now*, op. cit., pp. 14–15.
9. Ibid., p. 14.

47. Suriname, 1982 to 1984

1. *Miami Herald*, 1 June 1983.
2. *New York Times*, 1 June 1983, p. 13.
3. *Miami Herald*, 1 June 1983.
4. *The Guardian* (London), 1 November 1982; 7 January 1983; *New York Times*, 7 January 1983, p. 5.

5. *New York Times*, 12 December 1982, p. 4; 30 November 1983.
6. Ibid., 7 January 1983, p. 5.
7. Ibid., 19 July 1983.
8. *Miami Herald*, 2 June 1983.
9. *New York Times*, 27 October 1983, p. 4; 31 October, p. 10; *Miami Herald*, 29 November 1983.
10. *Newsweek*, 7 November 1983, p. 78.
11. *The Guardian* (London), 22 February 1983, p. 7.
12. *Miami Herald*, 29 November 1983.
13. *The Guardian* (London), 11 and 13 January 1984.
14. Ibid., 28 November 1985.

48. El Salvador, 1980–

1. *New York Times*, 7 March 1981, p. 10.
2. Events of 1960–61: John Gerassi, *The Great Fear in Latin America* (New York, 1965, revised edition) p. 178, originally published as *The Great Fear* (New York, 1963); Michael McClintock, *The American Connection: State Terror and Popular Resistance in El Salvador* (London, 1985) p. 149; *New York Herald Tribune*, 7 April 1963, section 2, page 1.
3. *Human Rights in Nicaragua, Guatemala, and El Salvador: Implications for U.S. Policy*, Hearings before the House Subcommittee on International Organizations of the Committee on International Relations, 8 June 1976, p. 34.
4. The US role in this process in the 1960s and 70s: McClintock, chapter 12; American Civil Liberties Union & Americas Watch Committee, *Report on Human Rights in El Salvador* (Vintage Books, New York, 1982) pp. 179–80, 189–97; James Dunkerley, *The Long War: Dictatorship and Revolution in El Salvador* (London, 1982) pp. 74–5; Jenny Pearce, *Under the Eagle* (London, 1982) pp. 214–16.
5. McClintock, pp. 158, 226 (note 44).
6. Elections of 1960s and 70s: Robert Armstrong and Janet Shenk, *El Salvador: The Face of Revolution* (London, 1982) pp. 50–87; McClintock, pp. 158–183, *passim*; Dunkerley, pp. 79–86, 103–6; Gerassi, p. 179; testimony of Fabio Castillo before US Congress, see note 3 above, pp. 42–4.
7. Armstrong and Shenk, pp. 87–8; McClintock, pp. 183–4; Dunkerley, pp. 106–7.
8. *Facts on File* (New York), 12 March 1977, p. 181.
9. Allan Nairn, 'Behind the Death Squads', *The Progressive* (Madison, Wisconsin) May 1984, pp. 1, 20–29, provides a detailed account of the American connection to the death squads.
10. Carolyn Forché, 'The Road to Reaction in El Salvador', *The Nation* (New York) 14 June 1980, p. 712.
11. October 1979 to January 1980: Dunkerley, pp. 132–44; McClintock, pp. 245–60; Armstrong and Shenk, pp. 115–30.
12. Armstrong and Shenk, p. 122; Dunkerley, pp. 87–8.
13. Dunkerley, p. 144.
14. Events of January to March 1980: *The Guardian* (London) 24 January 1980; 20 March 1980; McClintock, pp. 262–4; Dunkerley, pp. 146, 156–7; also see Liisa North, *Bitter Grounds: Roots of Revolt in El Salvador* (Toronto, 1981)

Appendix I, Chronology of Events — February 1977–June 1981, for further details of government/death squad killings; Armstrong and Shenk, p. 149, quote from Romero's last sermon.

President Duarte tried to put the blame for the funeral carnage on the left. His case rested apparently on bald statement and nothing else, for all eyewitness reports stated that the bomb and gunfire came from the National Palace and the other government buildings. A statement issued by eight bishops and 16 other foreign church visitors who had been present denied the government's version — see James R. Brockman, *Oscar Romero, Bishop and Martyr* (Orbis Books, Maryknoll, New York, 1982) pp. 222, 236 (note 28), Dermit Keogh, *Romero, El Salvador's Martyr* (Dominican Publications, Dublin, 1981) p. 113; *New York Times*, 31 March 1980, p. 1.

15. 'El Salvador — A Revolution Brews', *NACLA Report on the Americas* (North American Congress on Latin America, New York), July–August 1980, p. 17, based on an interview with the technician in San Salvador, 2 June 1980. This evidently was not an isolated case. Philip Wheaton, in his book *Agrarian Reform in El Salvador* (Ecumenical Program for Interamerican Communication and Action, Washington, DC, 1980), p. 13, reports that the Assistant Minister of Agriculture, Jorge Alberto Villacorta, in his resignation letter in March 1980, stated that 'During the first days of the reform — to cite one case — 5 directors and 2 presidents of new *campesino* organizations were assassinated and I am informed that this repressive practice continues to increase.'

16. *New York Times*, 18 January 1981, p. 7; 19 January, p. 11; McClintock, p. 286 (the 'observer'); *The Guardian* (London) 20 July 1983 (Carter's statement).

17. *New York Times*, 12 February 1985, p. 1: a bipartisan Congressional group, the Arms Control and Foreign Policy Caucus, accused the Reagan administration of supplying 'insufficient, misleading and in some cases false information' concerning aid to El Salvador. The caucus traced actual expenditures, rather than accepting budget classifications at face value, and found that of the US aid to El Salvador since 1980 of $1.7 billion, 85% was for the military — as opposed to the 25% claimed by the administration — and only 15% for development. This came to $1.445 billion military aid as of approximately the end of 1984. The caucus discovered further that the administration was undervaluing the real cost of the hardware sent to El Salvador even when it was properly categorized as military aid.

18. Training: a) *New York Times*, 2 December 1981 (Argentina); b) 'Dissent Paper on El Salvador and Central America', 6 November 1980, Section B-3, International Context (Argentina, Chile, Uruguay) — this document, apparently the work of members of the foreign policy establishment who disagreed with American policy in Central America, was circulated throughout official circles in Washington in 1980; reprinted in Poelchau, Appendix B (see note 53 below); c) Clarence Lusane, 'Israeli Arms in Central America', *Covert Action Information Bulletin* (Washington, DC) Winter 1984, No. 20, pp. 34–7.

19. McClintock, p. 337; *New York Times*, 12 February 1985, the caucus (see note 17) disclosed that large amounts of US military aid were devoted to expanding the number of Salvadorean troops; *Newsweek*, 14 March 1983, p. 24, international edition, reported that of the Salvadorean Army's 22,400 men, about 4,100 had been trained in the US.

20. McClintock, p. 334; *New York Times*, 2 February 1982, p. 10.

21. McClintock, p. 305.

22. *New York Times*, 20 October 1984; also see 30 March 1984, p. 1.
23. *The Guardian* (London) 5 February 1983.
24. McClintock, p. 348.
25. For example, see: *Washington Post*, 14 February 1982, p. 1; *The Guardian* (London) 26 March 1984, 22 October 1984; *New York Times*, 13 February 1982, 21 October 1984, 12 February 1985; McClintock, pp. 347–8.
26. *San Francisco Chronicle*, 24 June 1982.
27. *Washington Post*, 19 December 1980, p. A26; 1 January 1981, p. A12.
28. McClintock, p. 345.
29. *Playboy* (Chicago), November 1984, p. 73, interview by Marc Cooper and Gregory Goldin.
30. Stephen Webre, *José Napoleón Duarte and the Christian Democratic Party in Salvadoran Politics, 1960–1972* (Louisiana State University Press, Baton Rouge, La., 1979), p. 57. Duarte's remarks were made in a speech in 1969.
31. *The Guardian* (London) 9 March 1984; 11 March 1984.
32. *New York Times*, 18 February 1981, p. 3.
33. Ibid., 27 January 1982, p. 1; *The Guardian* (London) 29 January 1982; McClintock, pp. 308–9.
34. *New York Times*, 2 February 1982, p. 1.
35. *U.S. Intelligence Performance on Central America: Achievements and Selected Instances of Concern*, Staff Report, House Subcommittee on Oversight and Evaluation, Permanent Select Committee on Intelligence, 22 September 1982, pp. 18–19.
36. *The Guardian* (London) 2 February 1982, p. 7 (from *Los Angeles Times*).
37. *New York Times*, 11 January 1982, p. 2.
38. Amnesty International, *Torture in the Eighties* (London, 1984) pp. 155, 156.
39. Calculation of *Socorro Juridico* and *Tutela Legal*, the legal aid offices of the Archbishopric of San Salvador, cited in McClintock, p. 304; see ibid., pp. 306–12 for further accounts of government massacres; also see *Washington Post*, 14 February 1982, p. C1, for a particularly graphic first-hand account of the indiscriminate barbarity of the Salvadorean armed forces towards the population, a story Washington officials tried hard to discredit before a Congressional committee (see note 35), but the committee saw through the administration's rhetoric.
40. *Newsweek*, 14 March 1983, p. 24, international edition.
41. *The Guardian* (London) 10 November 1983.
42. *New York Times*, 3 March 1984, p. 1; 22 March 1984, p. 1; *Newsweek*, 2 April 1984, identified the official as Santibáñez; *The Guardian* (London) 22 and 29 March 1985.
43. *New York Times*, 17 March 1982, p. 1.
44. Ibid., 3, 5 and 6 March 1982, each p. 1.
45. Ibid., 13 March 1982, p. 1.
46. *Time*, 22 March 1982, p. 5, international edition.
47. *New York Times*, 19 January 1981, p. 11.
48. *San Francisco Examiner*, 20 December 1981.
49. *New York Times*, 19 January 1981, p. 11.
50. US State Department, *Communist Interference in El Salvador*, 23

February 1981, Special Report No. 80 (known as the White Paper), Section II., Communist Military Intervention: A Chronology.

51. *The Guardian* (London) 7 December 1985.

52. Dunkerley, p. 182; *New York Times*, 31 July 1983.

53. *Wall Street Journal*, 8 June 1981, pp. 1 and 10; for other analyses of the White Paper, see: Philip Agee in Warner Poelchau, ed., *White Paper, Whitewash* (New York, 1981), and Ralph McGehee, 'The CIA and the White Paper on El Salvador', *The Nation*, 11 April 1981.

54. *Wall Street Journal*, 8 June 1981, p. 10.

55. *Playboy*, op. cit., p. 74.

56. *Covert Action Information Bulletin* (Washington, DC), March 1982, No. 16, p. 27; this was also reported in the daily press.

57. *U.S. News and World Report*, 26 January 1981, p. 37, interview with White.

58. *San Francisco Chronicle*, 24 February 1981.

59. *New York Times*, 30 July 1982 (equipment); 16 April 1983, p. 1 (Awacs); 31 July 1983, p. 1 (radar); *Time*, 22 March 1982 (aerial photos).

60. See note 18 above; also, McClintock, pp. 343–4; *San Francisco Chronicle*, 28 June 1982; *The Guardian* (London) 28 May 1983; *New York Times*, 3 March 1984.

61. New Congressional legislation added to the certification which the president had to make that the El Salvador government was trying to solve the murder of the eight US citizens (*New York Times*, 16 July 1983, p. 11). The dead included three nuns and a woman lay worker in December 1980, and two employees of the American Institute for Free Labor Development (ironically, a long-time CIA front) working in agrarian reform in January 1981. In mid-1984, four National Guardsmen were convicted of the murders of the churchwomen (it could have happened immediately), but those higher up who were certainly involved are still free.

49. Nicaragua, 1981–

1. *New York Times*, 11 January 1927, p. 2.

2. Ibid., 22 July 1979, III, p. 1.

3. *Newsweek*, 8 November 1982, p. 10, international edition.

4. Shirley Christian, *Nicaragua: Revolution in the Family* (Random House, New York, 1985) pp. 73–4; for a description of the discussion process, see chapter 5; also, Bernard Diederich, *Somoza* (London, 1982) chapter 14.

5. Christian, p. 82.

6. George Black, *Triumph of the People: The Sandinista Revolution in Nicaragua* (London, 1981) p. 176.

7. Christian, p. 81.

8. Black, p. 177.

9. Carter administration aid: Christian, pp. 143–4; Jeff McConnell, 'Counter-revolution in Nicaragua: The U.S. Connection', *CounterSpy* magazine (Washington, DC), Vol. 6, No. 3, May–June 1982, pp. 11–23, particularly concerning aid to private organizations.

10. Economic warfare: *The Times* (London) 1 October 1984; *The Guardian* (London) 1 July 1983, 30 May 1984, 8 March 1985, 1 May 1985; *New York Times*, 11 October 1984.

11. *The Guardian* (London) 24 May 1985, 14 June 1985.

12. *International Herald Tribune*, 18 April 1984.

13. *San Francisco Chronicle*, 4 August 1982.

14. McConnell, pp. 15 and 21.

15. *The Guardian* (London) 8, 13 October 1983; 9, 22 March 1984; 9 April 1984.

16. Ibid., 17 October 1983.

17. Ibid., 18 May 1983, 6 June 1983, 30 May 1984.

18. *Barricada International* (English-language weekly newspaper of the Sandinista National Liberation Front, Managua) 8 November 1982, p. 12.

19. *The Guardian* (London) 30 May 1984.

20. *Bitter Witness: Nicaraguans and the 'Covert War', a Chronology and Several Narratives* (Witness for Peace Documentation Project, Santa Cruz, California, 1984) pp. 7–16, 18–22 (chronology of events, January 1981–June 1982).

21. *The Guardian* (London) 12 May 1984; *Covert Action Information Bulletin* (Washington, DC) No. 22, Fall 1984, pp. 25–9 — a summary of the military exercises appears on p. 26.

22. Eddie Adams, 'How Latin Guerrillas Train on Our Soil', *Parade Magazine (Washington Post)* 15 March 1981, p. 5 ff.; *New York Times*, 17 March 1981.

23. *New York Times*, 4 December 1982, p. 1.

24. *San Francisco Chronicle*, 8 June 1982; *The Guardian* (London) 4, 9 April 1983, 27 April 1984.

25. David MacMichael, in television documentary shown on 'Diverse Reports', Channel 4, London, 30 October 1985, p. 2 of transcript.

26. *The Guardian* (London) 9 April 1984; *International Herald Tribune*, 18 April 1984; *New York Times*, 3 April 1983; *Covert Action Information Bulletin* (Washington, DC) No. 20, Winter 1984, p. 26, citing CBS that US military personnel took part in some of the raids, driving the speedboats used to attack the petroleum depot at Puerto Corinto in October 1983.

27. *New York Times*, 29 August 1984, p. 10; 4 September 1984, p. 1; *Washington Post*, 19–22 January 1984 (US helicopter piloted by Americans shot down in Nicaragua and attempt at cover-up); *International Herald Tribune*, 14 December 1984; *The Guardian* (London) 6, 7 October 1983, 7 September 1984.

28. *New York Times*, 17 December 1984; *The Guardian* (London) 18 December 1984, both based on a story in the *Detroit Free Press* of 16 December 1984.

29. *The Guardian* (London) 4 May 1984.

30. Ibid., 15 November 1984. Accounts of contra atrocities are numerous. See, e.g., *Bitter Witness*, op. cit., *passim*; also, legal brief filed by the Center for Constitutional Rights and the National Lawyers Guild against the US government, excerpts in Peter Rosset and John Vandermeer, editors, *The Nicaragua Reader: Documents of a Revolution under Fire* (New York, 1983), pp. 228–36.

31. *The Guardian* (London) 15 November 1984.

32. *New York Times*, 27 December 1984, p. 1.

33. *The Guardian* (London) 3 June 1983.

34. *New York Times*, 17 October 1984, pp. 1 and 12.

35. Ibid., 20, 24 October 1984.

The CIA: A Forgotten History

36. *The Guardian* (London) 25 January 1985.
37. Ibid., 7 June 1983; *New York Times*, 7 June 1983.
38. *Covert Action Information Bulletin* (Washington, DC) No. 20, Winter 1984, p. 39.
39. 'World in Action' television programme, ITV London, 24 March 1986, documentary on Nicaragua showing an interview with a member of the hit team, part 2, pp. 12–13 of transcript.
40. *New York Times*, 19 October 1984, p. 8; *Covert Action Information Bulletin* (Washington, DC) No. 22, Fall 1984, p. 28.
41. *New York Times*, 11 June 1984, p. B6; also see *The Guardian* (London) 12 June 1984.
42. *New York Times*, 19 January 1981, p. 11.
43. Ibid., 12 February 1981, p. 11.
44. *The Guardian* (London) 23 July 1983.
45. *New York Times*, 11 June 1984, p. B6.
46. Ibid.
47. Ibid.
48. *The Guardian* (London) 9 January 1985.
49. Statement of Lt. Col. John H. Buchanan, USMC, retired, before the House Subcommittee on Inter-American Affairs, Committee on Foreign Affairs, 21 September 1982, reprinted in Rosset and Vandermeer, pp. 48–57.
50. *The Guardian* (London) 30 March 1985.
51. *New York Times*, 10 March 1982, p. 16.
52. *The Guardian* (London) 12 March 1986.
53. Ibid., 25 March 1985, 24 February 1986 (quotation).
54. Ibid., 28 April 1983.
55. Ibid., 17 January 1983.
56. Ibid., 27 September 1984.
57. *Washington Post*, 6 November 1984, p. A1.
58. Ibid., 3 October 1984, p. A24.
59. The exact wording of the treaty had not been made public at this time (and perhaps never has been), but its major provisions were widely and uniformly reported in the press.
60. *New York Times*, 3 October 1984, p. 3.
61. Ibid., 24 September 1984, p. 12.
62. *Washington Post*, 6 November 1984, p. A1.
63. Ibid., 2 October 1984, p. A12.
64. Ibid., 4 November 1984, p. A1; also see *New York Times*, 4 November 1984, p. 20 for a similar report about freedom of speech for the opposition.
65. *New York Times*, 5 November 1984.
66. Ibid., 26 July 1984, p. 5.
67. Ibid., 16 August 1984; 21 October 1984, p. 12.
68. Ibid., 29 July 1984, IV, p. 2.
69. Ibid., 26 July 1984, p. 5.
70. Ibid., 24 September 1984.
71. Ibid., 23 August 1984, p. 10.
72. *Covert Action Information Bulletin* (Washington, DC) No. 22, Fall 1984, p. 27 — a copy of the advertisement is reproduced.
73. *New York Times*, 21 September 1984, p. 3.
74. Ibid., 21 October 1984, p. 12.

75. Ibid., 31 October 1984, p. 1.

76. Ibid., 5 October 1984, p. 3.

77. Ibid., 19 July 1984, p. 6.

78. *International Herald Tribune*, 22 January 1984; both attributions are from a letter of Eugene Stockwell who testified before the commission following a visit to Nicaragua with the World Council of Churches.

79. *The Guardian* (London) 15 March 1986.

80. *Covert Action Information Bulletin* (Washington, DC) No. 20, Winter 1984, p. 25.

81. *New York Times*, 31 December 1983, p. 9; the American Ambassador, Anthony Quainton, was replaced in May 1984.

82. *The Guardian* (London) 21 March 1986.

83. *New York Times*, 3 March 1982, p. 5; remark by Alexander Haig; the photograph was first printed in the right-wing French newspaper *Le Figaro* which then admitted its 'mistake' after being exposed by other French publications; it appears that Haig did not make any public retraction.

84. *The Guardian* (London) 9 January 1985.

85. Black, p. 218.

86. Ibid., pp. 215, 332, 356 give a number of examples of the economic sabotage.

87. *The Guardian* (London) 13 July 1985, p. 7.

88. Black, p. 306.

89. *New York Times*, 29 August 1982, p. 10.

Appendix I

This is How the Money Goes Round

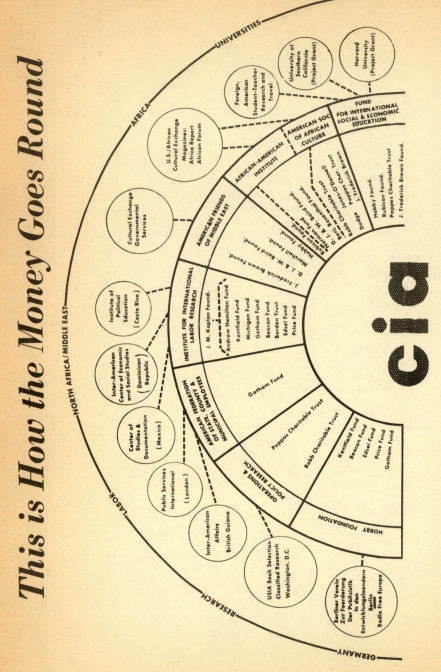

UNIVERSITIES

AFRICA

NORTH AFRICA / MIDDLE EAST

LABOR

RESEARCH

GERMANY

Foreign, American Student-Teacher Research and Travel.

University of Southern California (Project Grant)

Harvard University (Project Grant)

FUND FOR INTERNATIONAL SOCIAL & ECONOMIC EDUCATION

U.S./African Cultural Exchange Magazines: Africa Report African Forum

Cultural Exchange Governmental Services

Institute of Political Education (Costa Rica)

Inter-American Center of Economic and Social Studies (Dominican Republic)

Center of Studies & Documentation (Mexico)

Public Services International (London)

Inter-American Affairs British Guiana

USIA Book Selection Classified Research Washington, D.C.

Berliner Verein Zur Foerderung Der Publizistik in den Entwicklungslaendern Berlin Radio Free Europe

AFRICAN-AMERICAN INSTITUTE

AMERICAN SOC OF AFRICAN CULTURE

AMERICAN FRIENDS OF MIDDLE EAST

INSTITUTE FOR INTERNATIONAL LABOR RESEARCH

AMERICAN FEDERATION OF STATE, COUNTY & MUNICIPAL EMPLOYEES

OPERATIONS & POLICY RESEARCH

HOBBY FOUNDATION

cia

Beacon Charitable Trust
Jones-O'Donnell Fund
Rabb Charitable Trust
Poppas Char. Trust
Dodge J. Frederick Brown

Hobby Found.
Rubicon Found.
Poppas Charitable Trust
J. Frederick Brown Found.

Rubicon Found.
J. & W. Baird Found.
Norman Fund
J. A. Rosenthal Found.

Hobby Found.
D. J. & W. Baird Found.
Marshall Found.

J. Frederick Brown Found.

J. M. Kaplan Found.
Andrew Hamilton Fund
Kentfield Fund
Michigan Fund
Gotham Fund
Beacon Fund
Borden Trust
Edsel Fund
Price Fund

Gotham Fund

Poppas Charitable Trust

Rabb Charitable Trust

Kentfield Fund
Beacon Fund
Edsel Fund
Price Fund
Gotham Fund

410

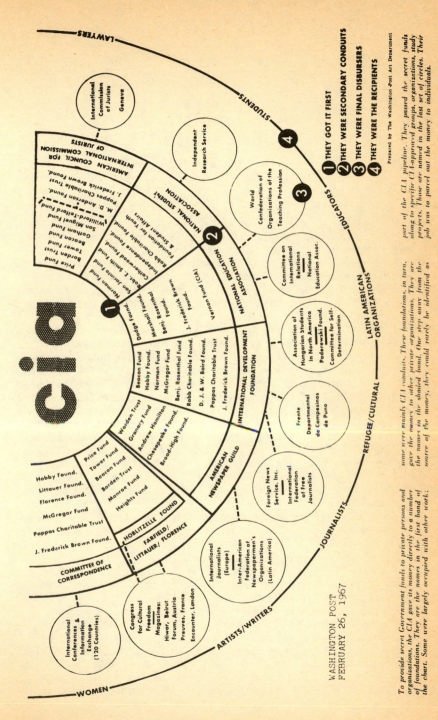

cia

1 THEY GOT IT FIRST
2 THEY WERE SECONDARY CONDUITS
3 THEY WERE FINAL DISBURSERS
4 THEY WERE THE RECIPIENTS

Prepared by The Washington Post Art Department

LAWYERS

STUDENTS

EDUCATORS

LATIN AMERICAN ORGANIZATIONS

REFUGEE/CULTURAL

JOURNALISTS

ARTISTS/WRITERS

WOMEN

International Commission of Jurists, Geneva

AMERICAN COUNCIL FOR INTERNATIONAL COMMISSION OF JURISTS

Price Fund, Borden Trust, Robt. E. Smith Fund, San Jacinto Fund, Norman Fund, Beacon Fund, Gotham Fund, Tower Fund, Williford-Telford Fund, M. D. Anderson Found., Pappas Charitable Trust, J. Frederick Brown Found.

Catherwood Found., Independence Found., Robb Charitable Found., Foundation for Youth & Student Affairs

Independent Research Service

NATIONAL STUDENT ASSOCIATION

World Confederation of Organizations of the Teaching Profession

NATIONAL EDUCATION ASSOCIATION

Dodge Found., Marshall Found., Beni. Rosenthal Found., J. Frederick Brown Found., Vernon Fund (CIA)

Committee on International Relations, National Education Assoc.

INTERNATIONAL DEVELOPMENT FOUNDATION

Beacon Fund, Hobby Found., Norman Fund, McGregor Fund, Beni. Rosenthal Found., Rabb Charitable Found., D. J. & W. Baird Found., Pappas Charitable Trust, J. Frederick Brown Found.

Association of Hungarian Students in North America, Paderewski Found., Committee for Self-Determination

Frente Departmental de Campesinos de Puno

AMERICAN NEWSPAPER GUILD

Warden Trust, Granary Fund, Andrew Hamilton, Chesapeake Found., Broad-High Found.

Foreign News Service, Inc., International Federation of Free Journalists

HOBLITZELLE FOUND.

Price Fund, Tower Fund, Beacon Fund, Borden Trust, Monroe Fund, Heights Fund

FARFIELD/ LITTAUER/ FLORENCE

International Journalists (Europe), Inter-American Federation of Newspapermen's Organizations (Latin America)

Hobby Found., Littauer Found., Florence Found., McGregor Fund, Pappas Charitable Trust, J. Frederick Brown Found.

COMMITTEE OF CORRESPONDENCE

International Conferences & Information Exchange (120 Countries)

Congress for Cultural Freedom, Magazines: Hiwar, Beirut; Forum, Austria; Preuves, France; Encounter, London

WASHINGTON POST
FEBRUARY 26, 1967

To provide secret Government funds to private persons and organizations, the CIA gave its money directly to a number of foundations. They are the names in the first band of the chart. Some were largely occupied with other work; some were mainly CIA conduits. These foundations, in turn, gave the money to other private organizations. They are the names in the shaded band. One step away from the source of the money, they could rarely be identified as part of the CIA pipeline. They passed the secret funds along to specific CIA-approved groups, organizations, study projects. Those are named in the last set of circles. Their job was to parcel out the money to individuals.

411

Appendix II
Instances of Use of United States Armed Forces Abroad, 1798–1945

1798–1800 — Undeclared naval war with France: This contest included land actions, such as that in the Dominican Republic, city of Puerto Plata, where marines captured a French privateer under the guns of the forts.

1801–05 — Tripoli: The First Barbary War, including the *George Washington* and *Philadelphia* affairs and the Eaton expedition, during which a few marines landed with United States agent William Eaton to raise a force against Tripoli in an effort to free the crew of the *Philadelphia*. Tripoli declared war but not the United States.

1806 — Mexico (Spanish territory): Capt. Z.M. Pike, with a platoon of troops, invaded Spanish territory at the headwaters of the Rio Grande deliberately and on orders from Gen. James Wilkinson. He was made prisoner without resistance at a fort he constructed in present day Colorado, taken to Mexico, later released after seizure of his papers. There was a political purpose, still a mystery.

1806–10 — Gulf of Mexico: American gunboats operated from New Orleans against Spanish and French privateers, such as *La Fitte*, off the Mississippi Delta, chiefly under Capt. John Shaw and Master Commandant David Porter.

1810 — West Florida (Spanish territory): Gov. Claiborne of Louisiana, on orders of the President, occupied with troops territory in dispute east of Mississippi as far as the Pearl River, later the eastern boundary of Louisiana. He was authorized to seize as far east as the Perdido River. No armed clash.

1812 — Amelia Island and other parts of east Florida, then under Spain: Temporary possession was authorized by President Madison and by Congress, to prevent occupation by any other power; but possession was obtained by Gen. George Matthews in so irregular a manner that his measures were disavowed by the President.

1812–15 — Great Britain: War of 1812. Formally declared.

1813 — West Florida (Spanish territory): On authority given by Congress, General Wilkinson seized Mobile Bay in April with 600 soldiers. A small Spanish garrison gave way. Thus U.S. advanced into disputed territory to the Perdido River, as projected in 1810. No fighting.

1813–14 — Marquesas Islands: Built a fort on island of Nukahiva to protect three prize ships which had been captured from the British.

1814 — Spanish Florida: Gen. Andrew Jackson took Pensacola and drove out the British with whom the United States was at war.

1814–25 — Caribbean: Engagements between pirates and American ships or squadrons took place repeatedly especially ashore and offshore about Cuba,

Puerto Rico, Santo Domingo, and Yucatan. Three thousand pirate attacks on merchantmen were reported between 1815 and 1823. In 1822 Commodore James Biddle employed a squadron of two frigates, four sloops of war, two brigs, four schooners, and two gunboats in the West Indies.

1815 — Algiers: The second Barbary War, declared by the opponents but not by the United States. Congress authorized an expedition. A large fleet under Decatur attacked Algiers and obtained indemnities.

1815 — Tripoli: After securing an agreement from Algiers, Decatur demonstrated with his squadron at Tunis and Tripoli, where he secured indemnities for offenses during the War of 1812.

1816 — Spanish Florida: United States forces destroyed Nicholls Fort, called also Negro Fort, which harbored raiders into United States territory.

1816–18 — Spanish Florida — First Seminole War: The Seminole Indians, whose area was a resort for escaped slaves and border ruffians, were attacked by troops under Generals Jackson and Gaines and pursued into northern Florida. Spanish posts were attacked and occupied, British citizens executed. There was no declaration or congressional authorization but the Executive was sustained.

1817 — Amelia Island (Spanish territory off Florida): Under orders of President Monroe, United States forces landed and expelled a group of smugglers, adventurers, and freebooters.

1818 — Oregon: The U.S.S. *Ontario*, dispatched from Washington, landed at the Columbia River and in August took possession. Britain had conceded sovereignty but Russia and Spain asserted claims to the area.

1820–23 — Africa: Naval units raided the slave traffic pursuant to the 1819 act of Congress.

1822 — Cuba: United States naval forces suppressing piracy landed on the northwest coast of Cuba and burned a pirate station.

1823 — Cuba: Brief landings in pursuit of pirates occurred April 8 near Escondido; April 16 near Cayo Blanco; July 11 at Siquapa Bay; July 21 at Cape Cruz; and October 23 at Camrioca.

1824 — Cuba: In October the U.S.S. *Porpoise* landed bluejackets near Matanzas in pursuit of pirates. This was during the cruise authorized in 1822.

1824 — Puerto Rico (Spanish territory): Commodore David Porter with a landing party attacked the town of Fajardo which had sheltered pirates and insulted American naval officers. He landed with 200 men in November and forced an apology.

1825 — Cuba: In March cooperating American and British forces landed at Sagua La Grande to capture pirates.

1827 — Greece: In October and November landing parties hunted pirates on the islands of Argenteire, Miconi, and Andross.

1831–32 — Falkland Islands: To investigate the capture of three American sealing vessels and to protect American interests.

1832 — Sumatra — February 6 to 9: To punish natives of the town of Quallah Battoo for depredations on American shipping.

1833 — Argentina — October 31 to November 15: A force was sent ashore at Buenos Aires to protect the interests of the United States and other countries during an insurrection.

1835–36 — Peru — December 10, 1835 to January 24, 1836 and August 31 to December 7, 1836: Marines protected American interests in Callao and Lima during an attempted revolution.

1836 — Mexico: General Gaines occupied Nacogdoches (Tex.), disputed territory from July to December during the Texan war for independence, under orders to cross the "imaginary boundary line" if an Indian outbreak threatened.

1838–39 — Sumatra — December 24, 1838 to January 4, 1839: To punish natives of the towns of Quallah Battoo and Muckie (Mukki) for depredations on American shipping.

1840 — Fiji Islands — July: To punish natives for attacking American exploring and surveying parties.

1841 — Drummond Island, Kingsmill Group: To avenge the murder of a seaman by the natives.

1841 — Samoa — February 24: To avenge the murder of an American seaman on Upolu Island.

1842 — Mexico: Commodore T.A.C. Jones, in command of a squadron long cruising off California, occupied Monterey, Calif., on October 19, believing war had come. He discovered peace, withdrew, and saluted. A similar incident occurred a week later at San Diego.

1843 — China: Sailors and marines from the *St. Louis* were landed after a clash between Americans and Chinese at the trading post of Canton.

1843 — Africa — November 29 to December 16: Four United States vessels demonstrated and landed various parties (one of 200 marines and sailors) to discourage piracy and the slave trade along the Ivory coast, etc., and to punish attacks by the natives on American seamen and shipping.

1844 — Mexico: President Tyler deployed U.S. forces to protect Texas against Mexico, pending Senate approval of a treaty of annexation. (Later rejected.) He defended his action against a Senate resolution of inquiry.

1846–48 — Mexico, the Mexican War: President Polk's occupation of disputed territory precipitated it. War formally declared.

1849 — Smyrna: In July a naval force gained release of an American seized by Austrian officials.

1851 — Turkey: After a massacre of foreigners (including Americans) at Jaffa in January, a demonstration by the Mediterranean Squadron was ordered along the Turkish (Levant) coast. Apparently no shots fired.

1851 — Johanna Island (east of Africa), August: To exact redress for the unlawful imprisonment of the captain of an American whaling brig.

1852–53 — Argentina — February 3 to 12, 1852; September 17, 1852 to April 1853: Marines were landed and maintained in Buenos Aires to protect American interests during a revolution.

1853 — Nicaragua — March 11 to 13: To protect American lives and interests during political disturbances.

1853–54 — Japan: The "opening of Japan" and the Perry Expedition.

1853–54 — Ryukyu and Bonin Islands: Commodore Perry on three visits before going to Japan and while waiting for a reply from Japan made a naval demonstration, landing marines twice, and secured a coaling concession from the ruler of Naha on Okinawa. He also demonstrated in the Bonin Islands. All to secure facilities for commerce.

1854 — China — April 4 to June 15 or 17: To protect American interests in and near Shanghai during Chinese civil strife.

1854 — Nicaragua — July 9 to 15: San Juan del Norte (Greytown) was destroyed to avenge an insult to the American Minister to Nicaragua.

1855 — China — May 19 to 21 (?): To protect American interests in Shanghai.

August 3 to 5 to fight pirates near Hong Kong.

1855 — Fiji Islands — September 12 to November 4: To seek reparations for depredations on Americans.

1855 — Uruguay — November 25 to 29 or 30: United States and European naval forces landed to protect American interests during an attempted revolution in Montevideo.

1856 — Panama, Republic of New Grenada — September 19 to 22: To protect American interests during an insurrection.

1856 — China — October 22 to December 6: To protect American interests at Canton during hostilities between the British and the Chinese; and to avenge an unprovoked assault upon an unarmed boat displaying the United States flag.

1857 — Nicaragua — April to May, November to December: To oppose William Walker's attempt to get control of the country. In May Commander C.H. Davis of the United States Navy, with some marines, received Walker's surrender and protected his men from the retaliation of native allies who had been fighting Walker. In November and December of the same year United States vessels *Saratoga, Wabash*, and *Fulton* opposed another attempt of William Walker on Nicaragua, Commodore Hiram Paulding's act of landing marines and compelling the removal of Walker to the United States, was tacitly disavowed by Secretary of State Lewis Cass, and Paulding was forced into retirement.

1858 — Uruguay — January 2 to 27: Forces from two United States warships landed to protect American property during a revolution in Montevideo.

1858 — Fiji Islands — October 6 to 16: To chastise the natives for the murder of two American citizens.

1858–59 — Turkey: Display of naval force along the Levant at the request of the Secretary of State after massacre of Americans at Jaffa and mistreatment elsewhere "to remind the authorities (of Turkey) . . . of the power of the United States."

1859 — Paraguay: Congress authorized a naval squadron to seek redress for an attack on a naval vessel in the Parana River during 1855. Apologies were made after a large display of force.

1859 — Mexico: Two hundred United States soldiers crossed the Rio Grande in pursuit of the Mexican bandit Cortina.

1859 — China — July 31 to August 2: For the protection of American interests in Shanghai.

1860 — Angola, Portuguese West Africa — March 1: To protect American lives and property at Kissembo when the natives became troublesome.

1860 — Colombia, Bay of Panama — September 27 to October 8: To protect American interests during a revolution.

1863 — Japan — July 16: To redress an insult to the American flag — firing on an American vessel — at Shimonoseki.

1864 — Japan — July 14 to August 3, approximately: To protect the United States Minister to Japan when he visited Yedo to negotiate concerning some American claims against Japan, and to make his negotiations easier by impressing the Japanese with American power.

1864 — Japan — September 4 to 14 — Straits of Shimonoseki: To compel Japan and the Prince of Nagato in particular to permit the Straits to be used by foreign shipping in accordance with treaties already signed.

1865 — Panama — March 9 and 10: To protect the lives and property of American residents during a revolution.

1866 — Mexico: To protect American residents, General Sedgwick and 100 men in November obtained surrender of Matamoras. After 3 days he was ordered by U.S. Government to withdraw. His act was repudiated by the President.

1866 — China — June 20 to July 7: To punish an assault on the American consul at Newchwang; July 14, for consultation with authorities on shore; August 9, at Shanghai, to help extinguish a serious fire in the city.

1867 — Nicaragua: Marines occupied Managua and Leon.

1867 — Island of Formosa — June 13: To punish a horde of savages who were supposed to have murdered the crew of a wrecked American vessel.

1868 — Japan (Osaka, Hiogo, Nagasaki, Yokohama, and Negata) — Mainly, February 4 to 8, April 4 to May 12, June 12 and 13: To protect American interests during the civil war in Japan over the abolition of the Shogunate and the restoration of the Mikado.

1868 — Uruguay — February 7 and 8, 19 to 26: To protect foreign residents and the customhouse during an insurrection at Montevideo.

1868 — Colombia — April 7 — at Aspinwall: To protect passengers and treasure in transit during the absence of local police or troops on the occasion of the death of the President of Colombia.

1870 — Mexico, June 17 and 18: To destroy the pirate ship *Forward*, which had been run aground about 40 miles up the Rio Tecapan.

1870 — Hawaiian Islands — September 21: To place the American flag at half mast upon the death of Queen Kalama, when the American consul at Honolulu would not assume responsibility for so doing.

1871 — Korea — June 10 to 12: To punish natives for depredations on Americans, particularly for murdering the crew of the *General Sherman* and burning the schooner, and for later firing on other American small boats taking soundings up the Salee River.

1873 — Colombia (Bay of Panama) — May 7 to 22, September 23 to October 9: To protect American interests during hostilities over possession of the government of the State of Panama.

1873 — Mexico: United States troops crossed the Mexican border repeatedly in pursuit of cattle and other thieves. There were some reciprocal pursuits by Mexican troops into border territory. The cases were only technically invasions, if that, although Mexico protested constantly. Notable cases were at Remolina in May 1873 and at Las Cuevas in 1875. Washington orders often supported these excursions. Agreements between Mexico and the United States, the first in 1882, finally legitimized such raids. They continued intermittently, with minor disputes, until 1896.

1874 — Hawaiian Islands — February 12 to 20: To preserve order and protect American lives and interests during the coronation of a new king.

1876 — Mexico — May 18: To police the town of Matamoras temporarily while it was without other government.

1882 — Egypt — July 14 to 18: To protect American interests during warfare between British and Egyptians and looting of the city of Alexandria by Arabs.

1885 — Panama (Colon) — January 18 and 19: To guard the valuables in transit over the Panama Railroad, and the safes and vaults of the company during revolutionary activity. In March, April, and May in the cities of Colon and Panama, to re-establish freedom of transit during revolutionary activity.

1888 — Korea — June: To protect American residents in Seoul during unsettled political conditions, when an outbreak of the populace was expected.

1888 — Haiti — December 20: To persuade the Haitian Government to give up an American steamer which had been seized on the charge of breach of blockade.

1888–89 — Samoa — November 14, 1888, to March 20, 1889: To protect American citizens and the consulate during a native civil war.

1889 — Hawaiian Islands — July 30 and 31: To protect American interests at Honolulu during a revolution.

1890 — Argentina: A naval party landed to protect U.S. consulate and legation in Buenos Aires.

1891 — Haiti: To protect American lives and property on Navassa Island.

1891 — Bering Sea — July 2 to October 5: To stop seal poaching.

1891 — Chile — August 28 to 30: To protect the American consulate and the women and children who had taken refuge in it during a revolution in Valparaiso.

1893 — Hawaii — January 16 to April 1: Ostensibly to protect American lives and property; actually to promote a provisional government under Sanford B. Dole. This action was disavowed by the United States.

1894 — Brazil — January: To protect American commerce and shipping at Rio de Janeiro during a Brazilian civil war. No landing was attempted but there was a display of naval force.

1894 — Nicaragua — July 6 to August 7: To protect American interests at Bluefields following a revolution.

1894–95 — China: Marines were stationed at Tientsin and penetrated to Peking for protection purposes during the Sino-Japanese War.

1894–95 — China: Naval vessel beached and used as a fort at Newchwang for protection of American nationals.

1894–96 — Korea — July 24, 1894 to April 3, 1896: To protect American lives and interests at Seoul during and following the Sino-Japanese War. A guard of marines was kept at the American legation most of the time until April 1896.

1895 — Colombia — March 8 to 9: To protect American interests during an attack on the town of Bocas del Toro by a bandit chieftain.

1896 — Nicaragua — May 2 to 4: To protect American interests in Corinto during political unrest.

1898 — Nicaragua — February 7 and 8: To protect American lives and property at Suan Juan del Sur.

1898 — Spain: The Spanish-American War. Fully declared.

1898–99 — China — November 5, 1898, to March 15, 1899: To provide a guard for the legation at Peking and the consulate at Tientsin during contest between the Dowager Empress and her son.

1899 — Nicaragua: To protect American interests at San Juan del Norte, February 22 to March 5, and at Bluefields a few weeks later in connection with the insurrection of Gen. Juan P. Reyes.

1899 — Samoa — March 13, to May 15: To protect American interests and to take part in a bloody contention over the succession to the throne.

1899–1901 — Philippine Islands: To protect American interests following the war with Spain, and to conquer the islands by defeating the Filipinos in their was for independence.

1900 — China — May 24 to September 28: To protect foreign lives during the Boxer rising, particularly at Peking. For many years after this experience a permanent legation guard was maintained in Peking, and was strengthened at times as trouble threatened. It was still there in 1934.

1901 — Colombia (State of Panama) — November 20 to December 4: To protect American property on the Isthmus and to keep transit lines open during serious revolutionary disturbances.

1902 — Columbia — April 16 to 23: To protect American lives and property at Bocas del Toro during a civil war.

1902 — Columbia (State of Panama) — September 17 to November 18: To place armed guards on all trains crossing the Isthmus and to keep the railroad line open.

1903 — Honduras — March 23 to 30 or 31: To protect the American consulate and the steamship wharf at Puerto Cortez during a period of revolutionary activity.

1903 — Dominican Republic — March 30 to April 21: To protect American interests in the city of Santo Domingo during a revolutionary outbreak.

1903 — Syria — September 7 to 12: To protect the American consulate in Beirut when a local Moslem uprising was feared.

1903–04 — Abyssinia: Twenty-five marines were sent to Abyssinia to protect the U.S. Consul General while he negotiated a treaty.

1903–14 — Panama: To protect American interests and lives during and following the revolution for independence from Colombia over the construction of the Isthmian Canal. With brief intermissions, Marines were stationed on the Isthmus from November 4, 1903, to January 21, 1914, to guard American interests.

1904 — Dominican Republic — January 2 to February 11: To protect American interests in Puerto Plata and Sosua and Santo Domingo City during revolutionary fighting.

1904 — Tangier, Morocco: "We want either Perdicaris alive of Raisula dead." Demonstration by a squadron to force release of a kidnapped American Marine guard landed to protect consul general.

1904 — Panama – November 17 to 24: To protect American lives and property at Ancon at the time of a threatened insurrection.

1904–05 — Korea — January 5, 1904, to November 11, 1905: To guard the American Legation in Seoul.

1904–05 — Korea: Marine guard sent to Seoul for protection during Russo-Japanese War.

1906–09 — Cuba — September 1906 to January 23, 1909: Intervention to restore order, protect foreigners, and establish a stable government after serious revolutionary activity.

1907 — Honduras — March 18 to June 8: To protect American interests during a war between Honduras and Nicaragua; troops were stationed for a few days or weeks in Trujillo, Ceiba, Puerto Cortez, San Pedro, Laguna and Choloma.

1910 — Nicaragua — February 22: During a civil war, to get information of conditions at Corinto; May 19 to September 4, to protect American interests at Bluefields.

1911 — Honduras — January 26 and some weeks thereafter: To protect American lives and interests during a civil war in Honduras.

1911 — China: Approaching stages of the nationalist revolution. An ensign and 10 men in October tried to enter Wuchang to rescue missionaries but retired on being warned away.

A small landing force guarded American private property and consulate at Hankow in October.

A marine guard was established in November over the cable stations at Shanghai.

Landing forces were sent for protection in Nanking, Chinkiang, Taku and elsewhere.

1912 — Honduras: Small force landed to prevent seizure by the Government of an American-owned railroad at Puerto Cortez. Forces withdrawn after the United States disapproved of the action.

1912 — Panama: Troops, on request of both political parties, supervised elections outside the Canal Zone.

1912 — Cuba — June 5 to August 5: To protect American interests on the Province of Oriente, and in Habana.

1912 — China — August 24 to 26, on Kentucky Island, and August 26 to 30 at Camp Nicholson: To protect Americans and American interests during revolution activity.

1912 — Turkey — November 18 to December 3: To guard the American legation at Constantinople during a Balkan War.

1912–25 — Nicaragua — August to November 1912: To protect American interests during an attempted revolution. A small force serving as a legation guard and as a promoter of peace and governmental stability, remained until August 5, 1925.

1912–41 — China: The disorders which began with the Kuomintang rebellion in 1912, which were redirected by the invasion of China by Japan and finally ended by war between Japan and the United States in 1941, led to demonstrations and landing parties for the protection of U.S. interests in China continuously and at many points from 1912 to 1941. The guard at Peking and along the route to the sea was maintained until 1941. In 1927, the United States had 5,670 troops ashore in China and 44 naval vessels in its waters. In 1933 U.S. had 3,027 armed men ashore. All this protective action was in general terms based on treaties with China ranging from 1858 to 1901.

1913 — Mexico — September 5 to 7: A few marines landed at Ciaris Estero to aid in evacuating American citizens and others from the Yaqui Valley, made dangerous for foreigners by civil strife.

1914 — Haiti — January 29 to February 9, February 20 to 21, October 19: To protect American nationals in a time of dangerous unrest.

1914 — Dominican Republic — June and July: During a revolutionary movement, United States naval forces by gunfire stopped the bombardment of Puerto Plata, and by threat of force maintained Santo Domingo City as a neutral zone.

1914–17 — Mexico: The undeclared Mexican-American hostilities following the *Dolphin* affair and Villa's raids included capture of Vera Cruz and later Pershing's expedition into northern Mexico.

1915–34 — Haiti — July 28, 1915, to August 15, 1934: To maintain order during a period of chronic and threatened insurrection.

1916 — China: American forces landed to quell a riot taking place on American property in Nanking.

1916–24 — Dominican Republic — May 1916 to September 1924: To maintain order during a period of chronic and threatened insurrection.

1917 — China: American troops were landed at Chungking to protect American lives during a political crisis.

The CIA: A Forgotten History

1917–18: World War I. Fully declared.

1917–22 — Cuba: To protect American interests during an insurrection and subsequent unsettled conditions. Most of the United States armed forces left Cuba by August 1919, but two companies remained at Camaguey until February 1922.

1918–19 — Mexico: After withdrawal of the Pershing expedition, our troops entered Mexico in pursuit of bandits at least three times in 1918 and six in 1919. In August 1918 American and Mexican troops fought at Nogales.

1918–20 — Panama: For police duty according to treaty stipulations, at Chiriqui, during election disturbances and subsequent unrest.

1918–20 — Soviet Russia: Marines were landed at and near Vladivostok in June and July to protect the American consulate and other points in the fighting between the Bolsheviki troops and the Czech Army which had traversed Siberia from the western front. A joint proclamation of emergency government and neutrality was issued by the American, Japanese, British, French, and Czech commanders in July and our party remained until late August.

In August the project expanded. Then 7,000 men were landed in Vladivostok and remained until January 1920, as part of an allied occupation force.

In September 1918, 5,000 American troops joined the allied intervention force at Archangel, suffered 500 casualties and remained until June 1919.

A handful of marines took part earlier in a British landing on the Murman coast (near Norway) but only incidentally.

All these operations were to offset effects of the Bolsheviki revolution in Russia and were partly supported by Czarist or Kerensky elements. No war was declared. Bolsheviki elements participated at times with us but Soviet Russia still claims damages.

1919 — Dalmatia: U.S. Forces were landed at Trau at the request of Italian authorities to police order between the Italians and Serbs.

1919 — Turkey: Marines from the U.S.S. *Arizona* were landed to guard the U.S. Consulate during the Greek occupation of Constantinople.

1919 — Honduras — September 8 to 12: A landing force was sent ashore to maintain order in a neutral zone during an attempted revolution.

1920 — China — March 14: A landing force was sent ashore for a few hours to protect lives during a disturbance at Kiukiang.

1920 — Guatemala — April 9 to 27: To protect the American Legation and other American interests, such as the cable station, during a period of fighting between Unionists and the Government of Guatemala.

1920–22 — Russia (Siberia) — February 16, 1920, to November 19, 1922: A marine guard to protect the United States radio station and property on Russian Island, Bay of Vladivostok.

1921 — Panama-Costa Rica: American naval squadrons demonstrated in April on both sides of the Isthmus to prevent war between the two countries over a boundary dispute.

1922 — Turkey — September and October: A landing force was sent ashore with consent of both Greek and Turkish authorities, to protect American lives and property when the Turkish Nationalists entered Smyrna.

1922–23 — China: Between April 1922 and November 1923 Marines were landed five times to protect Americans during periods of unrest.

1924 — Honduras — February 28 to March 31, September 10 to 15: To protect American lives and interests during election hostilities.

1924 — China — September: Marines were landed to protect Americans and other foreigners in Shanghai during Chinese factional hostilities.

1925 — China — January 15 to August 29: Fighting of Chinese factions accompanied by riots and demonstrations in Shanghai necessitated landing American forces to protect lives and property in the International Settlement.

1925 — Honduras — April 19 to 21: To protect foreigners at La Ceiba during a political upheaval.

1925 — Panama — October 12 to 23: Strikes and rent riots led to the landing of about 600 American troops to keep order and protect American interests.

1926 — China — August and September: The Nationalist attack on Hankow necessitated the landing of American naval forces to protect American citizens. A small guard was maintained at the consulate general even after September 16, when the rest of the forces were withdrawn. Likewise, when Nationalist forces captured Kiukiang, naval forces were landed for the protection of foreigners November 4 to 6.

1926–33 — Nicaragua — May 7 to June 5, 1926; August 27, 1926, to January 3, 1933: The coup d'état of General Chamorro aroused revolutionary activities leading to the landing of American marines to protect the interests of the United States. United States forces came and went, but seem not to have left the country entirely until January 3, 1933. Their work included activity against the outlaw leader Sandino in 1928.

1927 — China — February: Fighting at Shanghai caused American naval forces and marines to be increased there. In March a naval guard was stationed at the American consulate at Nanking after Nationalist forces captured the city. American and British destroyers later used shell fire to protect Americans and other foreigners. "Following this incident additional forces of marines and naval vessels were ordered to China and stationed in the vicinity of Shanghai and Tientsin."

1932 — China: American forces were landed to protect American interests during the Japanese occupation of Shanghai.

1933 — Cuba: During a revolution against President Gerardo Machado naval forces demonstrated but no landing was made.

1934 — China: Marines landed at Foochow to protect the American Consulate.

1940 — Newfoundland, Bermuda, St. Lucia, Bahamas, Jamaica, Antigua, Trinidad, and British Guiana: Troops were sent to guard air and naval bases obtained by negotiation with Great Britain. These were sometimes called lend-lease bases.

1941 — Greenland: Taken under protection of the United States in April.

1941 — Netherlands (Dutch Guiana): In November the President ordered American troops to occupy Dutch Guiana but by agreement with the Netherlands government in exile, Brazil cooperated to protect aluminium ore supply from the bauxite mines in Suriname.

1941 — Iceland: Taken under the protection of the United States, with consent of its Government, for strategic reasons.

1941 — Germany: Sometime in the spring the President ordered the Navy to patrol ship lanes to Europe. By July U.S. warships were convoying and by September were attacking German submarines. There was no authorization of Congress or declaration of war. In November, the Neutrality Act was partly repealed to protect military aid to Britain, Russia, etc.

1941–45 — Germany, Italy, Japan, etc: World War II. Fully declared.

Source for Appendix II — Foreign Affairs Division, Congressional Research Service, Library of Congress (US Government Printing Office, Washington, D.C. 1975).

Index